THE SOUTH

a history

I. A. NEWBY
*Department of History
University of Hawaii*

Holt, Rinehart and Winston

Copyright © 1978 by Holt, Rinehart and Winston

All Rights Reserved

Library of Congress Cataloging in Publication Data
Newby, Idus A
   The South.

   Includes bibliographical references.
   1. Southern States—History. I. Title.
F209.N48   975   78-2417
ISBN 0-03-048461-8
ISBN 0-03-085345-1

Printed in the United States of America

89012   038   987654321

THE SOUTH

a history

To:

Angeline, Virginia, and Ouida
and Ben Hill

Contents

	Preface	xiii
1	**The Search for a Central Theme**	1

Problems of Studying the South ... The Phillips Thesis ... Historians and the Phillips Thesis ... The Phillips Thesis: An Evaluation ... Wilbur J. Cash and the Southern Character ... Climate and History ... C. Vann Woodward and the Influence of History ... The Southern Identity

One The Developing South, 1607–1820 33

2 The Proto-South 37

Roots of Southern Distinctiveness ... The Social Ethic ... The Plantation System ... The Social Structure ... Origins of Racial Patterns ... Emergence of Slavery ... Afro-southerners ... The Indians ... Rise of the Upcountry

3 The Emerging South 69

The American Revolution and Southern Consciousness ... The Impact of Antislavery ... Slavery and the Jeffersonian South ... To Form a More Perfect Union ... The Crystallizing of Racial Fear ... Economic Change and Emergent Sectionalism ... The Social Structure ... A Southern Religion ... The First South

Two The Old South, 1800–1861 — 101

4 The Triumph of Sectionalism — 103

The Missouri Controversy . . . Evolving Sectionalism . . . The Racial Dimension . . . The Nullification Crisis . . . States' Rights . . . John C. Calhoun and Southern Rights . . . The South and the Concurrent Majority

5 The Plantation Regime — 125

The Plantation Economy . . . The Profitability of Slavery . . . Regional Income . . . A Healthy Economy? . . . The Peculiar Institution

6 Society and Thought — 151

Planter Hegemony . . . The Plain Folk . . . *Herrenvolk* Democracy . . . Education . . . Industry and Social Class . . . The Southern Lady . . . The Mind of the Old South . . . The Proslavery Argument

Three The Fighting South, 1846–1877 — 183

7 Causes of the War for Southern Independence — 185

Slavery and Westward Expansion . . . The Compromise of 1850 . . . Failure of the Compromise . . . The Economics of Sectionalism . . . Underlying Issues . . . The Final Crisis

8 The War for Southern Independence — 205

The War Comes . . . The Confederacy . . . Preparing for War . . . Strategic Failures . . . Robert E. Lee . . . Jefferson Davis . . . The Civilian War Effort . . . The Military Verdict . . . Why the War Was Lost . . . Why the Confederacy Failed

9 Reunion and Reconstruction — 235

The War as a Watershed ... Issues of Reconstruction ... Race and Reconstruction ... The Situation at War's End ... Blacks and Reconstruction ... Wartime Policy ... Presidential Reconstruction ... Congressional Counterattack ... Radical Reconstruction ... Radical Race Policy ... Carpetbaggers and Scalawags ... Conservative Race Policy ... The Campaign for Redemption ... The Compromise of 1877 ... The Significance of Reconstruction

Four The New South, 1870–1917 — 277

10 The Economics of Adjustment — 279

Problems of Agricultural Adjustment ... Sharecroppers and Tenants ... The Rise of Farmer Protest ... Industrial Development ... The New South Movement ... The Southernization of Industry ... The Limits of Economic Development

11 The Conservative Regimes — 301

The Conservatives ... The Politics of Conservative Rule ... The Significance of Fraud ... The Potential for Moderation ... The Violent South ... The Mind of the New South ... The Status of Women ... Conservative Religion ... The Traditionalists ... Traditionalism in Literature ... The Conservative Era in Retrospect

12 Race and Reform — 333

Farmer Protest ... Southern Populism ... The Declining Status of Blacks ... Disfranchisement, White and Black ... The Triumph of Segregation ... The Age of Booker T. Washington ... The Progressive South ... Progress in Education and Welfare ... The Limits of Progressive Reform

Five   The Changing South, 1917–1945 — 371

13   The Advancing South — 375

The Return to National Politics ... World War I ... The Economics of Transition ... The Politics of Traditionalism ... The South in National Politics ... Politics at Home ... Change and Tradition in Race Relations

14   The Benighted South — 401

The Benighted Image ... The Culture of Poverty ... Social Fundamentalism ... Fundamental Religion ... Education in the Benighted South ... The Savage Ideal ... Depression and a New Deal ... Currents of Racial Change

15   The Uncertain South — 439

The Flowering of Southern Studies ... Emergence of Southern Liberalism ... The Agrarian Alternative ... Howard W. Odum and Regionalism ... Literary Renaissance ... The Limits of Change

Six   The Present South, Since 1945 — 465

16   The American South — 467

Postwar Alternatives ... The Economic Miracle ... Racial Transformation ... Civil Rights: Action and Reaction ... Civil Rights: Black Liberation ... Civil Rights: Ambiguous Outcome ... Political Transition ... The Politics of White Supremacy

17 The Enduring South?   503

Notes   509

Index   549

Preface

This work is a history of the American South. It is addressed to students who already have some basic knowledge of the subject and are interested in pursuing it more systematically. In the body of the work I have sought to integrate narrative and analysis and to give some indication of the richness of the literature of southern history. Chapter I is a brief introduction to the basic problems of studying the South and finding a central theme in its history.

The purpose is modest. It is not to interpret or reinterpret the section's history or to resolve the disputes that concern historians today, but to overview the South's history and introduce the student to some of the issues that illuminate its study. Toward that end, the views of major historians are often noted and some of the major works and interpretive controversies that concern them are remarked upon. I have chosen to use footnotes rather than separate bibliographical essays to point to major works on major topics. The hope is that these notes together with the content of the text will provide students with guidelines that will help them formulate their own understanding of the South or, more modestly, give them an idea of what such a formulation involves. My understanding is that a textbook should incorporate the findings of recent scholarship, and toward that end I have appropriated the findings of scholars in wholesale fashion. In doing so, I have sought always to acknowledge the source of these findings, especially where the appropriation is of major interpretive ideas. However, many important ideas have been so generally accepted as to have entered the public domain, and their formulators have sometimes been forgotten. I trust that I have slighted no major contributor to the interpretations I have incorporated in the text. I also hope that I have not misused by misstating the ideas of anyone. The reader should keep in mind, however, that no one is responsible for the uses others make of his or her scholarship, and that the interpretations stated herein are my own reading of things.

Southern history, like the South itself, is a large and amorphous thing, and not easily reduced to a brief summary. In deciding what to include and what to omit, I have been guided by pragmatic considerations. I wanted to keep the volume as small as possible and yet provide enough factual information to make the analysis enlightening. The basis for my judgments is the concept of sectional as opposed to regional history discussed on pages 4–5. I have tried to avoid the commonest pitfall of survey texts, the tendency for knowledge (understanding) to get lost in a mass of information (facts). I have therefore focused on forces rather than events and on the meaning of those forces in molding the southern experience. I have also emphasized the distinctive, the peculiarly southern, aspects of the section's past, for those seem to me the most instructive facets of its history and the ones most likely to offer insight into southern character and identity.

The advantages of this approach are numerous. The South is an active and exciting subject of historical study. All the contemporary developments in American historiography are being fruitfully applied to its history—the use of belles lettres, popular literature, and the social sciences to supplement traditional historical sources as well as the emphasis on comparative history, econometrics, and other forms of quantification. The remarkable outpouring of scholarship on Afro-American history also helps inform the study of the South, as do the revisionist study of Reconstruction and the growing stress on race and racialism in the American past.

Over the years the South and its history have attracted a generous amount of scholarly, literary, and journalistic talent. The names of William Faulkner, Wilbur J. Cash, Howard W. Odum, C. Vann Woodward, Gunnar Myrdal, Robert Penn Warren, Ulrich B. Phillips, W. E. B. Du Bois, David Potter, Lewis C. Gray, Donald Davidson, Rupert B. Vance, Jay B. Hubbell, and V. O. Key reflect the quality and diversity of talent devoted to southern studies in the last half century. The long list of historians who have dealt perceptively with the section includes, besides Woodward, Phillips, and Potter, Frank L. Owsley, Charles S. Sydnor, Herman C. Nixon, Francis B. Simkins, E. Merton Coulter, Avery O. Craven, Clement Eaton, John Hope Franklin, David Donald, George B. Tindall, Eugene D. Genovese, T. Harry Williams, Kenneth M. Stampp, Carl N. Degler, and others too numerous to list.

The scholarship of such men makes, or can make, the study of southern history intellectually challenging, esthetically rewarding, even emotionally satisfying. The South's history thus offers a considerable range for the exercise of talent and imaginativeness as well as the indulgence of curiosity. To study the South is to become acquainted with what is certainly the most fascinating segment of the American people. It is also to master a literature of imposing quality, and to seek answers to one of the nation's great riddles: What is it that makes, has always made, the South distinctive? To answer this question, one needs an organizing principle around which to weave the threads of the past and give coherence to the search for understanding. Historians have long sought such a principle, which they call the central theme of southern history, and their failure to find it should spur rather than discourage the student today. The quest, which is simply a search for meaning, has so absorbed historians that it has itself been called the central theme of southern historiography. Perhaps it is better seen as evidence that historians tend to take on the character of the people they study. Students of the South, like southerners themselves, have a veritable compulsion for explanation. "The South," as George Core put it, "is obsessed with itself."

Southern history properly studied will also cast light on American history. In studying the section or the nation, the one is an instructive reference point for the other. American nationality and southern consciousness have always been dual aspects of the same thing, for the nation and the section have always interacted on issues of vital concern to each. Without American nationality, southern consciousness would never have emerged, at least not in the form it took, and without a self-conscious South the nation and its history would have been radically different. Many things central to the South's experience have been equally central to the nation's, but many have not, and it is as instruments of contrast that the two histories best illuminate each other. "The fundamental justification for the study of Southern history," Carl N. Degler has written, "is that the South's history often diverges from and therefore illuminates the history of the United States." The things that distinguish the southern experience from the nation's—the obsessive concern with racial matters, the defeat and poverty and frustration that came after the Civil War, the pervasive sense of grievance, the distinctive history of black southerners—all lend substance to this view.

They suggest, for example, that some of the basic approaches to American history are of limited validity. The recent emphasis on consensus in the American past, for example, is belied by the long record of conflict between the South and the nation and by perennial conflicts within the South. The experience of southerners, whether whites, "poor whites," or blacks, is troublesome for historians who regard Americans as a people of plenty, an affluent society, or heirs to a liberal tradition; or who describe Americans as pragmatists without ideology or a people to whom westward expansion brought democracy, equality, and opportunity; or who try to encompass American history within the economic divisions Charles A. Beard set forth in *The Rise of American Civilization* (1927).

The importance of southern history is underscored by the fact that southerners have been especially conscious of the past. Among the important realities of sectional consciousness have been an enduring sense of history, an awareness of the past and its continuance in the present, a consciousness of tradition, a feeling for time and place and for what has gone before. The most persuasive interpreters of the southern experience have all stressed this, the presentness of the past, and some of them have erased all distinction between past and present.

Historians have recognized this factor too, and made it a part of what they call "the burden of southern history," a phrase suggesting that the weight of the past has been especially heavy for southerners. Every generation since the Revolution has been beset by the burden of the past, every one, that is, until today's. For the present younger generation the weight of the past has been significantly lightened, and as a result southerners are today less sensitive about their history than ever before. What this and related phenomena portend for the future is one of the concerns of this study.

I. A. Newby

The Search for a Central Theme

The South is "an enigma challenging comprehension," a riddle defying "location or analysis." Its geography is "imprecise at best, and the characteristics of its population resist valid generalization." Therefore, any effort to formulate a central theme of its history is "an exercise in faith" which has more in common with theological speculation than historical scholarship.

So writes David Smiley, whose "Quest for the Central Theme of Southern History" (1972)[1] is the latest but by no means most despairing study of the basic problem facing southern historians. More than a decade before Smiley wrote, another historian, David M. Potter, described the section as "a kind of spinx on the American land," "a great insensate monolith, a vast artifact of the past" that presents to those who would understand it "a somewhat metaphysical problem" not unlike that of the Christian trinity. And despite every effort of scholar and poet, it remains, said Potter, "as challenging as it is baffling."

The bafflement, however, is an incentive as well as an obstacle, and sooner or later, it sometimes seems, everyone tries to resolve it. The worst of the resulting efforts are properly relegated to the scrap heaps of historiography, but the best deserve and enjoy a better fate. If collectively these efforts seem at first to constitute a confusion of voices, the discriminating student will find them remarkably illuminating.

In this literature the South is called everything from an emotion to a battle cry—a fascinating nightmare, an organizing principle, an untapped market for shoes, Uncle Sam's other province, a land of sowbelly and segregation. In one of the great slurs of American literature, H. L. Mencken called it "the bunghole of the United States, a cesspool of Baptists, a miasma of Methodists, snake charmers, phoney real estate operators, and syphilitic evangelists." Still others have defined it according to the frequency distribution of mules, Protestants,

Ph.D.s, tenant farmers, Negroes, or mockingbirds, or the nature of its plumbing arrangements, speech patterns, or parasitic diseases.

Labeling the section has been a great game, and everyone has played. Among published works alone, the labels range from "The Solid South" and *The Other South* to *The Southern South* and *The American South,* and that kind of balance—or is it contradiction?—runs throughout a long list of titles. "The Benighted South," "The Provincial South," "The Problem South," "The Horrible South," and "The Squalid South" coexist with "The Growing South," *The Advancing South, The Changing South, The Emerging South,* and "The Arisen South." Similarly, "The Vanishing South" and "The Passing South" counterpose *The Lasting South, The Everlasting South,* and *The Enduring South,* while *The Fighting South, The Militant South,* and "The Battling South" exist alongside "The Hesitant South" and *The Uncertain South.* Finally, *The Silent South* parallels "The Singing South," and for good measure we have "The Elusive South," *The Lazy South,* and even "The Erotic South."

A more serious endeavor has been the effort to define the section. To Smiley the South is "not a place or a thing" nor "a collection of folkways or cultural distinctiveness," but "a controlling idea or belief upon which men [have] acted, risked, and died." To Louis D. Rubin and James J. Kilpatrick it is "not merely a geographical grouping [of states or people] but a way of life and a state of mind." To Francis B. Simkins it was "an attitude of mind and a way of behavior" and only then a geographical area. To Lerone Bennett it is a land "defined not by magnolias but oppression." To sociologist Edgar T. Thompson it is simply "that part of the nation where people who regard themselves as Southerners live in numbers exceeding those who do not regard themselves as Southerners."

A parallel endeavor has been to describe the southern character. That effort too has floundered on the shoals of diversity. Sympathetic observers have stressed such traits as biracialism, paternalism, agrarianism, conservatism, traditionalism, Protestantism, localism, personalism, social graciousness, a strong sense of family, and more interest in being than becoming. Critics, on the other hand, have focused on racism, bigotry, violence, materialism, backwardness, arrogance, and hypocrisy. The irreconcilability of these lists has led historians to forgo the effort to characterize southerners in objective terms and to retreat into a kind of spiritualism. "Those of whatever persuasion or tradition who believe themselves to be Southern are indeed Southern," wrote Smiley, "and the South exists wherever Southerners form the predominant portion of the population." Richard Weaver put it still better: "Being a Southerner is definitely a spiritual condition, like being a

Catholic or a Jew," he wrote some years ago, "and members of the group can recognize one another by signs which are eloquent to them, though too small to be noticed by an outsider."

Problems of Studying the South

Behind all this lies the task of ordering the facts of southern history around a convincing interpretive theme. Such a theme cannot be fixed unalterably. The quest for a central theme must remain just that, a quest, for it must permit continual interaction between interpretation and accumulating data. The study of southern history begins, then, with a recognition of the fact that the South has always resisted definitive analysis. Indeed, Charles S. Sydnor once suggested that if all the books interpreting the section's history were placed side by side, the results would "resemble the contents of a small boy's pockets—a collection of all kinds of things that bear no apparent relationship to each other." In an important sense Sydnor was correct, but it does not follow that the effort to understand the South has been futile.

Every society has an ethos that is difficult, perhaps impossible, for outsiders to comprehend fully, or insiders to view objectively. "Some things can be known, experienced, practiced, but simply cannot be explained," Donald Davidson once said in defending the section against criticism by outsiders; and others have agreed with him. "Southernism is a reality too elusive to be explained in objective terms," declared Francis B. Simkins, who spent a lifetime trying to do just that. "It is something like a song or an emotion, more easily felt than recorded." Poets and novelists have given this idea more credence than historians. "Tell about the South," urged Quentin Compson's Harvard roommate in William Faulkner's *Absalom, Absalom!* "What do they do there? Why do they live there? Why do they live at all?"

"You can't understand it," Quentin replied. "You would have to be born there."

There is a large truth and some danger in the reply. The poet's imagination is often more effective than the historian's research. It was a historian, James G. Randall, who noted that "poets have done better in expressing the oneness of the South than historians in explaining it." Yet the historians' contributions have been significant despite the fact that the most elemental problems in their study of the South have never been resolved.[2]

The first of these problems involves a deceptively simple question: What is the proper focus of southern history? If, to illustrate, the South is a geographical area, its history should encompass everything that happened in a given territory. If, on the other hand, it is an idea, a state of mind, or a set of values, the content of its history must be shifted accordingly. The distinction here is basic, for it points to two different though overlapping Souths. In this discussion, the term "regional South" will be used to specify the South as a geographical area, and "sectional South" to designate the South as an idea or a distinct cultural entity. The failure to distinguish between these two Souths is the source of much of the disputation in the search for a central theme of southern history.

The distinction between region and section was first made by Frederick Jackson Turner. A region, Turner said in effect, is a geographical area, whereas a section is "any one part of a national domain which is geographically and socially sufficiently unified to have a true consciousness of its own ideals and customs and to possess a sense of its distinctiveness from other parts of the country." Therefore, to understand a section one must take cognizance of its "ideals and psychology" and "inherited intellectual habits" as well as its economic interests and geography.

The relevance of this for students of southern history is clear. "[Is] anything which happens anywhere south of the Mason-Dixon line . . . within the province of Southern history?" David M. Potter once asked. "Are Southern historians entirely at the mercy of a geography which makes them responsible for all that occurs within an arbitrarily defined area?" Potter, who inclined toward a sectional definition of the South, thought not. Things that are "purely local" can be excluded from the purview of southern history, he suggested, as can things that are "merely manifestations within the region of national phenomena." Other scholars have agreed with this view. "I think we do not get at the nature or essence of the South by adding up the geographies and the histories of the political divisions which authorities have called the 'southern states,'" declared Edgar T. Thompson. "The South is not a state, nor any one of the states, nor any combination of states. The history of North Carolina is not a chapter in the history of the South." What, then, is the South? Thompson asked. "When we have stripped away that which is common to all humanity, to the people of the Western World, to rural and agricultural people everywhere, to people who live in interracial situations, and to the people of the United States generally, what we have left, or some part of what we have left is the South."

Within limits, the sectional definition of the proper focus of southern history is adhered to in this text. Yet exclusive attention to the purely southern aspects of the South is impossible as well as undesirable, for both regional and sectional approaches to its history are important and defensible, and both have produced significant insights.

Historians inclined toward the sectional approach have been more interested than regionalists in central themes, and all such themes have in fact had sectional purposes. Not everyone, however, has appreciated that fact. It is not uncommon for a critic to define the South as an idea or state of mind or set of values, and then criticize a given interpretation of southern history for not encompassing everything and everybody in a certain geographical area. Yet if the sectional approach is valid, the interpretation should be judged by how well it explains the contents of the idea or state of mind or set of values that is said to be the South. To define the section as an idea is to say that ideology, not geography, is the controlling factor, though there is of course considerable overlap between those two things. It is also to say that generalizations about southerners should be made not according to where people live, but according to the ideology they share. To insist that an interpretation encompass both sectional and regional Souths is to insist that it incorporate two dissimilar entities. *That,* it would seem, is the impossible task historians complain about in trying to interpret the South's history, and it should not inhibit the search for a central theme.

The very idea of southern history would seem to suggest a sectionalist approach, but the danger in that approach must be recognized. The South is both region and section, both American and southern, and the many-sidedness of its nature relates to that fact, its various natures interacting, influencing, delimiting, and tending to offset each other. In an important sense the South was always a product of the interaction between forces pulling it into the American orbit and others drawing it toward a universe of its own. Thus, as George B. Tindall suggests, an emphasis on the distinctive (sectionalist) elements of the South "may be acceptable as a general rule of thumb," but historians "should guard against it as an absolute. It poses a danger of distortion. The Southerners have not only been distinctive in certain respects; they have been Americans as well," products of "the interplay among regional and national and universal factors."

A second major difficulty in studying southern history grows out of this fact. How different is the South from the rest of America? That is, is its southernness more important than its Americanness? In an extreme statement of one side of this issue, Carl Carmer suggested some years ago that Alabama was as different from Massachusetts as the Congo was. C. Vann Woodward, on the other hand, has noted that "the South was American a long time before it was Southern in any self-conscious or distinctive way," and "it remains more American by far than anything else, and has all along."

This is the point at which southern history and American history converge and separate. The history of the South, as already noted, is not a mere corner of American history. It has its own dimensions and concerns, its own purposes to serve, just as does, say, Afro-American history or the history of Arkansas or Miami Beach. Nevertheless, the interaction of section and nation has been close and continuous, and the section's history makes no sense without reference to the nation's. By the same token, it makes no sense unless one of its important purposes is to delineate the distinctive identity of the southern people. It is not necessary to insist that the qualities that distinguish southerners from other Americans be unique to the South, but only to suggest that the specific combination in which they have existed in the section has been unique. A good part of the troublesomeness on this point stems from the fact that there has never been any agreement on what it is that southerners and other Americans have in common and in contrast. Thus the contributors to an informative symposium, *The Southerner as American* (1960), insisted that scholars have overstressed southern distinctiveness but could not themselves agree on what it was that southerners and other Americans have in common. The editor, Charles G. Sellers, described both peoples as "fundamentally liberals, Christians, and Americans." Behind the southerners' obvious qualities of racism and illiberalism he found their truer character in a humane concern for the victims of their own oppression. In contrast another contributor, Grady McWhiney, suggested that the common bond between southerners and Americans was not so much their virtues as their vices, especially material greed and racism. In a different kind of volume, *The Southern Mystique* (1964), Howard Zinn suggested that the South was "really the *essence* of the nation" because it possessed in concentrated form the nation's most characteristic flaws —racism, sexism, violence, hypocrisy, zenophobia, and chauvinism.

The issue here is obviously a basic one, and like most such issues resolvable only through interpretation based on an individual reading of the evidence. It will recur often in the course of this text, but here it might be noted that one of the underlying questions involved is this: Does the essence of the South revolve around the worst or the best qualities of the southern people, or consist in some combination of both?

A third difficulty in studying southern history grows in turn from the complexity that that question implies. This is the phenomenon of contradiction or, to use one of the historians' favorite words, paradox. "At the heart of the riddle of the South is a union of opposites," insists one scholar. "The most notable feature of... Southern life... is a series of apparent contradictions," adds another. Among the obvious contradictions are the southerners' simultaneous urges toward individualism and conformity, toward law and order and populistic activism, toward radical means and conservative purposes, toward Calhounian conservatism and Jeffersonian liberalism, toward hospitality and violence, personalism and racial insensitivity, seigneurial paternalism and bourgeois materialism, agrarianism and commercialism, sectional loyalty and American patriotism. The result is an ostensibly solid South wracked by internal divisions between races, classes, and geographical areas, a fact that plagues every effort to make sense of the section.

For the student it is more important to recognize this element of paradox than to try to resolve it. "It is a commonplace to state that whatever one may come to consider a truly American trait can be shown to have its equally characteristic opposite," Erik H. Erikson wrote in a passage in *Childhood and Society* (1950) that has special meaning for the South. "This, one suspects, is true of all 'national characters,' or (as I would prefer to call them) national identities—so true, in fact, that one may begin rather than end with the proposition that a nation's identity is derived from the ways in which history has, as it were, counterpointed certain opposite potentialities; the ways in which it lifts this counterpoint to a unique style of civilization, or lets it disintegrate into mere contradiction." It is just this—the way in which southerners have lifted their own seeming paradoxes and contradictions into a unique style of civilization—that the history of the South should be concerned with.

A fourth and less troubling difficulty facing the student of southern history is that of locating the South geographically. Sectionalists no less than regionalists face this problem, which stems from the fact that differing definitions of the section imply different geographical boundaries. But however the section is defined, its geography has shifted over the years. Most definitions begin with the area included in the Confederate states, which is the area of chief concern in this text, and go from there. Some add all or parts of the other states where slavery was legal in 1860, that is, Delaware, Maryland, West Virginia, Kentucky, and Missouri, plus the District of Columbia. Others include Oklahoma. The Census Bureau includes all these except Missouri in the Census South. None of these combinations is altogether satisfactory, however, for the South has been a region of fluctuating borders, and distinctively southern influences are sometimes apparent in nonsouthern parts of the country.

Physical geography further complicates this problem. Wherever its boundaries are set, the South is not a geographical unit. It is not set apart from the rest of the country by distinct physical barriers; in fact geography, in the form of the Appalachian mountain chain, divides rather than unifies the section. Its natural geographical components are lowcountry, piedmont, and mountains, plus the lower Mississippi Valley and however much of the Southwest one cares to include; yet culturally its most important divisions have been the deep South (or the black belt) and the peripheral South. Other geographical factors such as soil types, rainfall, growing season, and river systems also encourage diversity and reinforce the idea that the South is a cultural rather than a geographical phenomenon. History, too, has had much the same effect. Colonial Maryland, for example, was culturally a part of the South, but exposure to northern influences after 1800 coupled with changes in the deep South occasioned by the rise of the cotton kingdom pulled that state away from the section, and by 1861 its sectional loyalties were too weak to accomplish secession. Perhaps Maryland belonged in the antebellum South but not in the postbellum. The same is probably true of Kentucky, a state that still had slavery and plantation agriculture in 1860 but escaped the molding impact of Civil War defeat and Reconstruction. As for Delaware, Oklahoma, western Texas, and most of Missouri, they are probably best viewed not as parts of the South, but as border areas in which many southerners lived.

Historically, the geography of the South underwent two important shifts. The first shift produced a major expansion into the cotton kingdom and the Southwest which led in turn to a parallel though less significant diminution of southern influence in the border states. This, in fact, is what the border is: states in the uppermost reaches of the South—Delaware, Maryland, Kentucky, Missouri, and West Virginia —that were differentiated from the rest of the South by the rise of the cotton kingdom and the economic and political changes consequent thereto. This shift was confirmed by secession and its aftermath, which froze the South geographically until after World War I. Then a second major shift commenced. The migration of vast numbers of southerners to other areas of the country spread southern influences into the North and West while changes within the section commenced a slow contraction of the South itself. Yankee immigrants claimed the southern half of Florida, and made that state a part of the peripheral South, as did the influx of nonsouthern peoples into the central part of Texas. More recently, Virginia has begun a similar process. Under the impact of demographic and economic changes since World War II, the Old Dominion, which was always a border state geographically, is now becoming one politically and economically and is thus in the process of following Maryland and Kentucky out of the southern constellation. If the South today is disappearing into the American mainstream, as many people suggest, it is doing so piece by piece rather than all at once.

A fifth problem for the student of southern history is the question of continuity and discontinuity. The New South was "merely a continuation of the Old South," declared Robert S. Cotterill in his 1948 presidential address to the Southern Historical Association. "The War Between the States cannot be considered as a mighty cataclysm engulfing the Old South or as a chasm dividing the Old South from the New.... In no essential way did the war alter or deflect the course of southern development. It was an interruption but not a cleavage.... It marked no end and no beginning; it neither buried the Old South nor brought the New to birth. There is, in fact, no Old South and no New. There is only The South." Other scholars are less sure of this, and point to the disrupting effects of such things as the Civil War, Reconstruction, the Populist uprising, rapid industrialization, and the recent advent of racial desegregation. "The history of the South has always seemed to me characterized by discontinuity, and I have suggested this as one trait that helps account for the distinctiveness of the South and its history," writes Woodward. "Southerners, unlike other Americans, [have] repeatedly felt the solid ground of continuity give way under their feet."

The differences between these two points of view are at least partially reconciled by taking proper cognizance of the element of change over time. One need not regard this as an either/or issue to see that southern history has, as Woodward suggests, had more of discontinuity than American history. That fact, moreover, has important implications for the search for a central theme. "A region's history like a nation's foreign policy," as Earl E. Thorpe notes in *Eros and Freedom* (1967), "may over a long period of time, have different central themes, each valid for only a few decades or generations." It is this idea, perhaps, and thus a tacit acceptance of discontinuity, that explains why so few writers have offered central themes encompassing the whole of southern history. In general, historians of the Old South have been much more interested in central themes than have those of the New South, and those of the twentieth century have dispensed with them altogether and given far more attention to sectional character or identity.

A sixth and final problem that complicates the student's task is how to incorporate blacks, especially the positive dimensions of their history, into the story of the South. Are they southerners too? And whether they are or not, how do they fit into central themes? These questions are more complicated than they appear to be. If being a southerner is simply a condition of geography, the matter is readily resolved, and any interpretation that excludes blacks is unsatisfactory. If, on the other hand, a southerner is someone who possesses a certain set of values, the matter is more complicated, and its resolution depends upon the extent to which blacks share values defined as southern. "The Southernness of the South is a psychological thing," wrote Avery O. Craven in 1930, and "the foundations upon which it rests are certain broad characteristics which give likeness of interest within a wide range of variation." It is certainly possible to incorporate blacks within this definition, though Craven was speaking of whites alone. The tradition of regarding whites alone as southerners originated with whites themselves, but historians have continued it, for they too have traditionally thought of southernness in racial terms and looked at the South through the eyes of whites. Recently, however, they have given new attention to this issue, and have discovered that blacks and whites have shared not only a common residence in the section but a broad range of cultural traits and values as well. In fact David M. Potter went so far as to state that blacks may "have embodied the distinctive qualities of the Southern character even more than the whites," while Francis B. Simkins "regarded [blacks] as genuine Southerners, as much in love with the land of their ancestors as any Southern white."

Woodward, who has addressed this subject more pointedly than Potter or Simkins, has emphasized the molding influence of white-black interaction upon southern history and character. "The ironic thing," he wrote in *American Counterpoint* (1971), "is the degree to which they have shaped each other's destiny, determined each other's isolation [from the American majority], shared and molded a common culture. It is, in fact, impossible to imagine the one without the other and quite futile to try." No one, he concludes, is "more quintessentially Southern than the Southern Negro."

The most systematic discussion of this subject is by Lawrence D. Reddick, himself both southerner and black. "The Negro in the South is a study in attachment and alienation," Reddick writes in *The Southerner as American,* and the attachment is as important as the alienation. "For him identification has always been a problem. Inescapably he has found himself to be a 'Southerner.' He may not have preferred the term, but the objective fact could not be denied." He shares a "remarkable" array of qualities with white southerners, and only the nagging realities of racial discrimination keep the races apart. Even "in revolt or far away from the land of his birth," the Negro cannot escape his southernness, Reddick continues, for he has an "attachment for the South and will own up to it, whenever he can avoid or forget about bad race relations." His life in the South was more than a matter of repression, however large that sometimes loomed. "It is not that I love Maryland less, but freedom more," wrote Frederick Douglass after he fled from slavery in Maryland to comparative freedom in Massachusetts. "There are few [blacks] here who would not return to the South in the event of emancipation," he declared. "We want to live in the land of our birth, and to lay our bones by the side of our fathers'; and nothing short of an intense love of personal freedom keeps us from the South." More than a century later, an illiterate but worldly-wise Alabama sharecropper, Ted Cobb (Nate Shaw), repeated much the same sentiment. "I don't love its ways, but Alabama is as good a state as there is in the world," Cobb told Theodore Rosengarten in Cobb's oral autobiography, *All God's Dangers* (1975). "The land will respond to your labor if you are given a chance to work it and a chance to learn *how* to work it. It's the people here is what my trouble is."

For Douglass who fled as well as for Cobb who remained, the South was always a special place, and that holds true for black southerners generally. "Because the South for so long has denied the Negro his essential manhood, he has become, in a sense, a sort of anti-Southerner," Reddick observed. "The conflict between embracing and rejecting the South has set up a war within the persons of Negro Southerners as well as in the social order. Some of them hate the South; others, despite everything, love it. Most, however, alternate their love and hate, while a few seem to be capable of loving and hating it at the same time."

All, however, have been influenced by it, for they too have been southerners. Yet they were also southerners with a difference, for they were a minority who had little voice in defining sectional values and even less in asserting sectional prerogatives. Moreover, as a large and distinctive ethnic group which itself has had something of the character of a nation within the nation, Afro-Americans have a distinct history of their own. The southern historian is not, therefore, concerned with their history as such, but with the point at which their history intermeshes with the South's. This is of course the point at which white and black southerners interact, but since this interaction has been one of the vital elements of sectional life, blacks and especially race relations and racial policy must have a central role in any history of the South.

The Phillips Thesis

The modern effort to interpret the South's past began in 1928 with the publication of Ulrich B. Phillips's "The Central Theme of Southern History,"[3] the most enduring statement of sectional identity as well as the most important interpretation of southern history ever offered. These are ironic truths, for historians have never been enthusiastic about Phillips's essay. Yet it refuses to die, and as the cycles of historical interpretation are now turning, it is enjoying a new round of attention and appreciation.

In the terminology used above, Phillips's purpose was sectional, not regional. He sought not to explain the whole of southern history, but to pinpoint the essence of southernness, the most characteristic fact of sectional identity. Traditional explanations he found unsatisfactory. "Southernism did not arise from any selectiveness of migration," he began. "It does not lie in religion or language. It was not created by one-crop tillage, nor agriculture." Nor was it destroyed by industrialization or any of the other changes wrought in the New South. Its essence was not states' rights, nor free trade, nor slavery, nor one-party politics, nor one-crop agriculture, nor the plantation system. Those things were important, but not the causal force in southern history. The South, Phillips wrote, "is a land with a unity despite its diversity, with a people having common joys and common sorrows, and, above all, as to the white folk a people with a common resolve indomitably maintained—that it shall be and remain a white man's country. The consciousness of a function in these premises, whether expressed with the frenzy of a demagogue or maintained with a patrician's quietude, is the cardinal test of a Southerner and the central theme of Southern history."

White supremacy, and the white man's determination to maintain it—this was the key, the unifying fact that ran through the section's history. "It arose," said Phillips, "as soon as the negroes became numerous enough to create a problem of race control in the interest of orderly government and the maintenance of Caucasian civilization," and remained thereafter the vital principle of southern life. It was the cause of slavery, an institution whites created "not merely to provide control of labor but also as a system of race adjustment and social order" and which they maintained "not only as a vested interest, but ... as a guarantee of white supremacy and civilization." It was the cause of secession, which came when whites had to choose between "a separate nationality" and "the Africanization of the South"; and its influence was not diminished by defeat and Reconstruction. "Until an issue shall arise predominant over the lingering one of race," Phillips wrote, "political solidarity at the price of provincial status is maintained to keep assurance doubly, trebly sure that the South shall remain 'a white man's country.'"

In Phillips's analysis, the basic fact was not the presence of blacks. It was instead the presence of large numbers of two distinct races in close, personalized contact, and the effects this had on the white majority. Not race alone but race and racism together—the idea of race in the minds of whites and their willingness to act upon it—was controlling.

The distinction here between race and racism is important, not only for Phillips's theme but for southern history as well. A race is "a group that is *socially defined* but on the basis of physical criteria," says sociologist Pierre van den Berghe in *Race and Racism* (1967), a valuable work for students of southern history. And "racism is any set of beliefs that organic, genetically transmitted deficiencies (whether real or imagined) between human groups are intrinsically associated with the presence or the absence of certain socially relevant abilities or characteristics, hence that such differences are a legitimate basis of invidious distinctions between groups socially defined as races." It is "not the presence of objective physical differences between groups that creates races," van den Berghe continues, "but the social recognition of such differences as socially significant or relevant." The relevance of this for southern history is great. Like white southerners before them, historians have tended to make the presence of blacks the key racial factor in the South, a tendency that diverts attention away from white racism. If van den Berghe is correct, the emphasis should be reversed. Racism, not the presence of blacks per se, has been the controlling factor. "Race," says van den Berghe, "has no intrinsic significance, except to a racist."

Though Phillips would hardly have agreed with this, he did focus attention on racism as well as race, and this is the basic contribution of his essay. He provided a clearer basis than anyone ever had for defining the South both geographically and ideologically: the South was that part of the United States where historically large numbers of blacks and whites had lived together in intimate contact, and where as a consequence whites felt threatened and thus preoccupied themselves with racial supremacy. Numbers, then, were a controlling influence, the numbers of blacks in relation to the number of whites. This to Phillips was more important than class or other relationships between the races, for the presence of so many blacks blurred class distinctions among whites and gave them an abiding sense of racial solidarity which expressed itself in their sectional identity and loyalty. By 1860, he said, " 'Southern rights' had come to mean racial security, self-determination by the whites."

Phillips was not the first to suggest the centrality of racial factors in southern history and identity. Indeed, the idea was as old as southern consciousness itself.[4] In the debates over slavery in the Virginia legislature in 1830–31, delegate W. H. Roane had used language strikingly similar to Phillips's in urging the state to encourage the colonization of blacks "till the ratio of the Population between [the blacks] and the whites, attains, at least, that equilibrium, which, in all future time, will give to every white man in the state, that certain assurance that this is his country." A generation later, William Gilmore Simms suggested that the basic difference between North and South was that the North's population "consists of a white Caucasian race, sparsely intermingled, here and there, with an insignificant portion of the descendants of some of the black African tribes," while in the South "the same two races co-exist, but their proportion is materially changed, there being, in point of number, about an equality between them." This difference, Simms declared, has "exercised a controlling influence upon the character and pursuits of the governing population, and the resources and conditions of the country."

Post-Civil War writers reiterated these ideas. "The greatest social problem before the American people to-day," wrote George W. Cable in 1885, "is, as it has been for a hundred years, the presence among us of the negro." When the history of the South is finally written, declared Senator John Sharpe Williams of Mississippi in 1903, "the philosophy of our sectional history—the purpose, conscious or unconscious, of our sectional strivings,—will be shown to have been always consistent." That purpose, Williams said, was "racial integrity—the supremacy in our midst of the white man's peculiar code of ethics and of the civilization growing out of it."

When professional scholars took over the writing of southern history around the turn of the twentieth century, they too often stressed racial factors. William Garrott Brown's "The South in National Politics" (1910) was perhaps the most pointed example. "Because of the African," wrote Brown, "the South fought a fearfully exhausting civil war, and had to endure the natural consequences of defeat." Because of the African the South's "institutions and habits and characteristics" are unlike those of the rest of the country, and because of his continued presence the difference "will persist for a long, long time to come." Because the South has so many Negroes, its "economic and industrial standards" are depressed and it "has been until quite recently, the poorest of the sections." For the same reason, it is educationally backward, intolerant of free speech on some subjects, and willing to subject itself to an "extraordinary political solidarity."

The impact of Phillips's essay is difficult to assess. It seems to have made historians more aware of race, if not racism, in the southern past, and of central themes as well. In time, they developed an unacknowledged consensus that racial factors of one sort or another were the paramount influence in southern history.[5] "The presence of the negro was the most important single factor in the shaping of the history of the section itself, and its relations with the rest of the country," wrote

Frederick Jackson Turner of the crucial years between 1830 and 1850. The presence of blacks, Avery O. Craven declared of the Old South generally, "created a race problem and made the determination to keep this region a white man's country the central theme of Southern history." "The Negro has been the 'central theme of Southern history' and constitutes the chief basis for [regional distinctiveness]," stated Herman C. Nixon of the whole of the section's past. White supremacy "is what makes the South different from the rest of the world," added Francis B. Simkins; "to kill the doctrine of white supremacy would destroy the essence of Southernism [and] reduce the region to a mere geographical segment of the United States." Howard W. Odum put it more pointedly. "No South, no Negro," he wrote, "no Negro, no South."

Recent writers have continued this emphasis. "In the South [the Negro] is a perpetual and immutable part of history itself, a piece of the fabric so integral and necessary that without him the fabric dissolves," novelist William Styron has suggested. "The central theme of Southern history [is] the enduring presence of the Negro," adds historian Bruce Clayton; "the Negro has been the South's one great absolute, through slavery, secession, war, defeat, Reconstruction, and all that has happened since. Dismiss him and the very idea of the South becomes meaningless." "Wherever the South exists as a specifiable culture," adds sociologist Samuel S. Hill, "the pattern of white supremacy, whether aggressive or residual, stands as its primary component."

The agreement in these statements should not obscure the differences between the men who made them. Not all of these men accepted Phillips's views, nor did they endorse a common interpretation of southern history. They did not even agree on which aspects of race were most important in the South's past. Still, their agreement on the centrality of racial factors is important, for on no other subject was there ever such a consensus.

Historians and the Phillips Thesis

On this much, then, there has been agreement; but no more. One of the anomalies of southern historical writing is that many of the historians who agree on the supremacy of racial factors in southern history have disputed the most systematic statement of that supremacy. With few exceptions, they have resisted Phillips's formulation of the role of race in southern history and identity.[6] The reasons for this seem to relate not chiefly to the limitations of Phillips's formulation—which are real enough, as will be noted below—for in spite of its limitations Phillips's essay contains, in David M. Potter's words, a "realistic recognition of the potency of racism as a factor in Southern life." Rather, the reasons seem to stem chiefly from other things: a reluctance to make white supremacy the basic component of southernness, an unwillingness to accept the pessimistic implications of Phillips's theme for the future of the South, and a disapproval of Phillips's implicit endorsement of white supremacy. "If we were not so preoccupied with rejecting the implications of the 'Central Theme' for the future, we might be more impressed by what it reveals concerning Southern white attitudes throughout American history," declared Potter in 1967. "The grim truth is that the evidence in support of the 'Central Theme' is now a great deal stronger than when Phillips formulated it, and it is ironical that liberals, concerned as they are with the 'Sick South,' tend so decisively to reject what is really a fundamental diagnosis of the sickness." They do this, Potter suggested, because Phillips did not consider white supremacy undesirable. Many of his critics have rejected Phillips's interpretation when their real purpose was to deny its ethical acceptability.

After World War II, the racism implicit in Phillips's writings produced an eclipse in his reputation as a scholar, but the growing emphasis on race and racism in American historical scholarship in recent years has led to renewed interest in all of his work. Reviewing several items of this recent scholarship, James M. McPherson has suggested that historians should "dust off" Phillips's thesis and reexamine it in the light of new research. "Without sharing all the assumptions behind Phillips' argument," he wrote, disassociating himself from Phillips's racialism, "one must concede that white supremacy has been not only *the* central theme of Southern history, but *a* major theme of American history and wherever whites and nonwhites have lived in large numbers."

Most historians seem unwilling to go this far. They seem more inclined to agree with the judgments of George B. Tindall, who has written the most systematic and informed critique of Phillips's theme. "It cannot be denied," wrote Tindall in Charles G. Sellers's symposium *The Southerner as American*, "that a preoccupation with the issue of race, its mythology and its symbolism has been one of the major themes of southern history, with innumerable ramifications into every aspect of southern life." Nevertheless, he added, it is distorting to make this *the* central theme of the section's history and support for white supremacy *the* test of southernness. Such a test not only excludes blacks but fails to take account of the variety of racial attitudes among whites, which has ranged from the virulent Negrophobia of Hinton Rowan Helper to the urgent humanitarianism of George W. Cable. In correcting what he regarded as Phillips's overemphasis on white supremacy, Tindall stressed the significance of racial liberalism in southern thought and practice. This better side of the South's racial history, he suggested, drew its strength from New Testament Christianity and Jeffersonian democracy, both of which were always major influences in the southern value system, and from paternalism and that "easy-going 'personalness' in human relations" which characterizes the southern way of life. Among the significant manifestations of this side of things in the twentieth century have been the rise of interracial movements, the decline of racial extremism, and the intellectual and economic progress of Negroes.

To give substance to these criticisms, Tindall applied Phillips's theme to southern history since the Civil War, the period Phillips had neglected. Though conceding its relevance to the Old South, Tindall found the theme increasingly invalid as he approached the present. "The southern way of life has involved infinitely more than a system of segregation and proscription," he wrote, and in view of recent racial changes, white supremacy "can no longer be regarded as the indispensible key to southern distinctiveness."

The Phillips Thesis: An Evaluation

Tindall's criticisms are important, and any evaluation of Phillips's thesis must take due account of them. Phillips did oversimplify the South's racial history, and he did ignore the New South in formulating his theme. Moreover, southern reactions to racial phenomena have varied widely, and blacks are southerners too. Any serious interpretation of southern history must incorporate blacks and moderate whites as well as white supremacists. To formulate such an interpretation, however, it is unnecessary to abandon Phillips's thesis; it is necessary only to enlarge it.

Such an enlargement should begin by recognizing that the South's history—that is, its distinctively southern elements—has revolved around the presence of two distinct races living together in large numbers in intimate personal relationships. It should emphasize the peculiarly southern nature of this relationship and of its impact upon everyone, white and black, racist and moderate. It should not insist that white supremacists alone are southerners. It should instead define a southerner as anyone who is significantly influenced by this relationship, anyone, that is, who finds himself more or less preoccupied with it, his life more or less defined by it. This would encompass everyone from Phillips's frenzied demagogue to his quiet patrician, both of whom were bent upon maintaining white supremacy, and everyone from Hinton Rowan Helper to George W. Cable, each of whom was influenced in an especially southern way by racial phenomena. It would also include white liberals, guilty and otherwise, and blacks too, whether

Uncle Tom, Nat Turner, or the more ordinary individual trying to make a go of life. All these groups, white and black, were southerners, because all reacted to a common fact—intimate interracial contact—and to a common condition—the peculiarly southern context of that contact. The reactions of all of them were thus distinctively southern—personal and passionate and based on close acquaintance with individuals of the other race within the southern structure of white supremacy and racial paternalism.

Such a formulation allows for the unity stressed by Phillips as well as the diversity described by Tindall, both of which are important in understanding the South. The diversity was a factor of time and place and other variables: the strength and self-assurance of blacks in given situations, the extent of outside concern with southern racial policy, the shifting role of the federal government, the changing percentage of blacks in the population, the fluctuating confidence and fears of whites. These variables help explain the different racial histories of the upper and lower South as well as the tidewater, upcountry, and Appalachia, and why from one period to another (say in the 1850s and 1890s and 1960s) racial pressures produced markedly dissimilar responses from blacks as well as whites.

This formulation also permits a better understanding of the unity, the controlling element of southernness, that underlay the diversity Tindall stressed. The liberalism, Christianity, humanitarianism, and democracy which Tindall found in the South have been real enough, but all of them have had a distinctively southern nature. None of them has been incompatible, at least not historically, with white supremacy. Before the present generation only a random white southerner was a racial equalitarian in any real sense of the term. Moderates and paternalists were always white supremacists; or put another way, white supremacy has degrees. Lynchers, outspoken Negrophobes, and other extremists were white supremacists, but not all white supremacists have been lynchers, Negrophobes, or other such extremists. Most in fact were not. Most were, and still are, moderates and paternalists of one degree or another, and most have always thought of themselves as democrats, "good people," New Testament Christians, and even advocates of Negro advancement. Some in fact have joined organizations of interracial cooperation.

This should not be misunderstood, and the significant differences between moderates and extremists must not be understated. Moderates have performed a laudable and highly important role in the South's history. They have undermined the appeal of extremists, helped neutralize the harsher abuses of white supremacy, aided in multiple ways the cause of Negro advancement. But until recently, they have rarely been racial equalitarians, and even more rarely have they challenged, or even questioned, the fundamental structure of white supremacy. They never worked against such obvious aspects of white supremacy as segregated public schools, for example, and never sought to organize themselves and blacks for a frontal assault on white supremacy itself. Instead, they worked to improve the condition of blacks within the framework of white supremacy. What they did was important, and given the context in which they worked, it may have been all they could do. But they were still, almost all of them, white supremacists as Phillips used the term, individuals committed to the idea that whites should retain basic control of politics, economics, and society in the South. Southern liberals have been southern as well as liberal, and the "southern" in their label has traditionally had a specifically racial connotation.

The broadening of Phillips's central theme also helps reconcile some of the contradictions that have plagued the effort to interpret southern history.[7] Interpretations stressing mythology, folk society, agriculture, ruralism, romanticism, climate, history, the English heritage, or some combination of these and other things are all reconcilable with an emphasis on race. That emphasis helps explain the distinctiveness of the South's frontier experience and why westward expansion produced dissimilar results in the South and non-South. It clarifies the dispute over continuity and discontinuity, and the question of whether the South today is or is not disappearing into the American mainstream. The southern preoccupation with race survived the creation and abolition of slavery, the ups and downs of Reconstruction and Redemption (by which Reconstruction was ended), the rise and fall of legalized segregation, the appearance and disappearance of the Solid South, the growth and relative decline of agriculture, the rise and triumph of industry and urbanization, and even the emergence and spread of desegregation. All of these things brought important changes with them, but none of them ended the concern over race and racial policy. That remained, and still remains, the central concern of people who think of themselves as southern, especially in those times when they think and act consciously as southerners.

This fact is especially important in understanding the South in the present era of change, when it seems quite likely that the section is disappearing as a distinctive cultural entity. Over the years the South has demonstrated a remarkable capacity to survive widespread change of the sorts just noted. What it has not demonstrated is an ability to survive change in its fundamental racial realities. If a preoccupation with race has been its characteristic feature, then the South's survival depends on the continuation of that preoccupation and thus of the things that produced it. Historically, those things have sprung from a single taproot, the racial fears of whites, which in turn derived from racial demography, the number and proportion of blacks in the population. For several decades now, the proportion of blacks has been steadily shrinking and talk of the South's disappearance steadily rising. In 1890 the black population of the deep South (Louisiana, Mississippi, Alabama, Georgia, and South Carolina) was 52.6 percent of the total; in 1970 it was 29.1 percent. In the rest of the Confederate South, the black portion of the population has dropped from 29.4 percent to 16.2 percent. This basic fact, which is discussed in detail in a later chapter, has notably reduced the racial fears of whites and made it possible for the present generation to accept changes in racial policy that earlier generations would have resisted with violence. Today, white supremacy of the most fundamental sort—basic white control of politics, society, and the economy—seems secure everywhere except in a few scattered areas, and that is the key fact in questions about the future of southern distinctiveness. Southerners of both races are still concerned with factors of race, but the concern is far less acute than it has been since sectional consciousness first emerged.

Wilbur J. Cash and the Southern Character

Not long after Phillips's essay appeared, Wilbur J. Cash, a North Carolina journalist, began work on another basic interpretation of the section's history. Eventually published in 1941 as *The Mind of the South,* Cash's book soon became the most widely read and influential item in the literature of southern history. A reviewer called it a "literary and moral miracle," and that phrase aptly summarized its reputation for a generation. "Its influence and prestige have mounted cumulatively until it occupies a virtually unchallenged popularity," wrote C. Vann Woodward in 1967. "It is cited, quoted, paraphrased, and plagiarized so regularly as to have practically entered the public domain."[8] No other book ever enjoyed such sustained prestige among southern historians.

Its influence was due to several factors. It is eminently readable, at times almost entrancing, bold in its characterizations, iconoclastic in its treatment of sectional pieties, provocative in its presentation of ideas and insights. Its viewpoint was liberal enough to satisfy critics of the section without seeming (or being) negative or irresponsible. Its sympathy for the white masses, for organized labor and New Deal reform, and its brilliantly executed exposés of racial bigotry, sectional pretense, and class exploitation struck responsive chords among liberals and reformers, in and out of the section. Outsiders who suspected the South of benightedness found their suspicions confirmed, but in assuring language. Southerners who hoped to remake the section in a liberal, American image found optimism enough to kindle their faith. Only conservatives were unimpressed. A piece of Menckenesque journalism, scoffed Donald Davidson. A "reckless" and "uneven book which casts much light but also a great deal of heat," and the "ratio of light to heat is not ... very efficient," added Louis D. Rubin.

Given the nature of Cash's book, its reputation is surprising. It is not the kind of work historians ordinarily take to. It is too personal, too impressionistic, too selective in its choice of subjects. It is not about the southern mind at all, as that term is usually understood. It is not an intellectual history or a study of popular thought or mass culture. It is instead a delineation of the southern temperament, character, and ethos, and despite its title is, in Woodward's phrase, "based on the hypothesis that the South had no mind." The southerner, Cash wrote at one point, "did not (typically speaking) think; he felt."

Because of its nature, the book is impossible to summarize effectively. It commences in the 1830s, when in Cash's reckoning southern consciousness first appeared, and it traces the evolution of southern character into the depression years of the 1930s. Less concerned with the history than the present state of the South, Cash made no effort to balance his treatment of the major periods of the southern past. Of the two centuries and more between Jamestown and John C. Calhoun he said nothing, and well over half the book is devoted to the twentieth century. Cash's interest was in the essence, not in the origins, of southern distinctiveness. In fact, he began by assuming the distinctiveness and proceeded from there. "The peculiar history of the South," he wrote at the outset, "has so greatly modified it from the general American norm that, when viewed as a whole, it decisively justifies the notion that it is—not a nation within a nation, but the next thing to it."

On this assumption Cash rested the two basic themes of his book: that there is a unity in the southern mind (he meant of whites only) and that there is a continuity in southern history. The unity he described as "a fairly definite mental pattern, associated with a fairly definite social pattern—a complex of established relationships and habits of thought, sentiments, prejudices, standards and values, and associations of ideals, which, if not common strictly to every group of white people in the South, is still common in one appreciable measure or another, and is in some part or another, to all but relatively negligible ones." The continuity he stated more succinctly. "The extent of the change and of the break between the Old South that was and the South of our time has been vastly exaggerated," he wrote. The mind of the South today is "continuous with the past."

These themes of unity and continuity run through Cash's depiction of the South. The fundamental character of the southern people emerged in the antebellum generation, he suggested, and never basically changed. True, the Civil War had "smashed the Southern world," but it "left the essential Southern mind and will ... entirely unshaken." And Reconstruction, "so far from having reconstructed the Southern mind in the large and in its essential character," simply "strengthened it almost beyond reckoning." Even the "turn to Progress" in the New South, "so far from representing a deliberate break with the past," had "clearly flowed straight out of that past and constituted in a real sense an emanation from the will to maintain the South in its essential integrity." Like other outside forces that seemed to promise so much in the way of reform, "Progress" had been enveloped in a sectional encasement that walled out the liberalizing changes that were presumed to inhere in it. The South did change, outwardly, as a result of progress and other things the Yankees forced upon it, but "as regards the Southern mind" the changes were "essentially superficial and unrevolutionary," for they occurred "within the ancient framework, and even sometimes contribute[d] to the positive strengthening of the ancient pattern." The cotton mills, for example, the very symbols of progress, brought, not liberal capitalism and progressive unionism, but altered forms of paternalism and exploitation.

Within the parameters of unity and continuity, a series of recurring frontiers had molded southern character. Before the Old South had passed much beyond the state of a physical frontier, the Civil War and Reconstruction thrust southerners into new frontiers, psychological, racial, and economic. And before these were conquered, the industrial revolution created still others. Each frontier brought its own challenges, but in dealing with all of them, southerners relied on the methods and values of the first one. As a result, the devices of the physical frontier endured in the South long after they dissipated elsewhere and, in combination with the presence of blacks and the physical environment, molded the mind of the South.

To embody this mind, Cash created a "basic Southerner." Originally a denizen of the Old South, this "man at the center" survived into Cash's own day, his character emended and modified by history but essentially unchanged. He was, as Woodward has noted, not a composite southerner at all, but an epitome of one group of southerners, the group Cash himself spring from and knew best. This was the upcountrymen, or more familiarly, the hillbillies and "millbillies," the latter a designation Cash applied to cotton mill workers in his first depiction of "The Mind of the South" (1929). The basic southerner was, in Cash's lexicon, "rustic" and "exceedingly simple," "a direct product of the soil," "a hot, stout fellow, full of blood and reared to outdoor activity," a man whose basic character centered around an "intense individualism," a lack of class consciousness, and a tendency toward hedonism.

These traits in turn generated a host of others. Intense individualism produced that "bald, immediate, unsupported assertion of the ego," that "chip-on-the-shoulder swagger" so characteristic of southern demeanor. It also retarded the development of community by discouraging respect for institutions, not only law and government and properly constituted authority but also educational and religious forms and other expressions of social organization. Encouraging reliance on the self, it abetted a tendency toward violence and other forms of direct action.

The absence of class consciousness was equally important. (This refers to its absence among the white masses, for Cash found a well-developed awareness of class interest among planters, mill owners, and their professional apologists, and he omitted blacks from his account.) A central fact about the southern social order, this lack of class consciousness went far toward explaining the resistance to social change. It grew out of several factors. Kinship ties often extended across class lines; the presence of blacks encouraged racial rather than class solidarity; frontier individualism led to the perception of social issues in personal rather than class terms; and the ability of poor whites to earn a subsistence promoted a sense of psychological independence among them. In addition, the "proto-Dorian convention" enabled the upper classes to flatter the masses in order to exploit them. The result was paternalism and an easygoing familiarity between individuals that transcended class lines. Its effect was to guarantee racial supremacy to common whites in return for their acquiescence in economic inequality.

A tendency toward hedonism and romanticism was the third feature of southern character Cash emphasized. This encouraged leisure and undirected social activity as well as escapism, and made impossible the skepticism necessary for realistic social analysis. As a consequence, southerners were forever pursuing chimeras—white supremacy, racial purism, "cardboard medievalism," "downright gyneolotry"—forever blaming their problems on outsiders and ever willing to invoke "the savage ideal" to insure internal conformity.

As Cash saw it, then, the southern mind was a product of conflicting impulses that grew out of culture and environment: Calvinism and hedonism, hospitality and violence, individualism and conformity, the work ethic and a love of leisure, racial repression and a commitment to Jeffersonian democracy and New Testament Christianity. The result was "a sort of social schizophrenia," a "cleft in the Southern psyche" which rent the sectional character. Unable to resolve the resulting contradictions and increasingly aware of the gap between its ideals and actions, the South became "a society beset by the specters of defeat, of shame, of guilt, a society driven by the need to bolster its morale, to nerve its arms against waxing odds, to justify itself in its own eyes and in those of the world."

The Mind of the South was unchallenged by historians for a generation, and so lofty was its reputation that its recent eclipse is a noteworthy historiographical event. In 1964 Dewey W. Grantham, an able historian of the twentieth-century South, described Cash's book as "perhaps the most brilliant essay ever written on the southern character," a "powerful assault on the region's illusions about itself." Eight years later, another able scholar, Sheldon Hackney, dismissed Cash as "the South's foremost mythmaker." Hackney's comment is hyperbolic, but the difference between his and Grantham's evaluations indicates something of the declining stature of Cash's work. The reasons for the decline are not difficult to see. Recent historiographical changes, especially the growing emphasis on race and racism and the advances in economic history, have pointed up weaknesses in many older analyses of the South. In addition, the "postliberal" views of many historians—their recognition of the limitations of traditional liberalism—have led to a reassessment of liberal scholarship, of which Cash's work was a major monument. The same forces which are directing attention back toward Phillips's central theme have raised questions about the value of Cash's.

The reassessment began, ironically, with the publication of Joseph L. Morrison's largely uncritical biography *W. J. Cash: Southern Prophet* (1967), the reviews of which provided an occasion for a reexamination of Cash's work. The chief reassessor has been C. Vann Woodward, who in several articles made a series of telling criticisms from which *The Mind of the South* is unlikely to recover. Though he acknowledges the significance of the work and the value of its many insights, Woodward nevertheless concludes that it is an incomplete and distorting analysis of the South. Its choice of subjects, he notes, is too selective, its treatment of southern history unbalanced. Not only did Cash ignore blacks, but he also neglected the tidewater, the black belt, the deep South, the Southwest, and poor whites, and treated the planting classes largely as objects of criticism. He thus ignored too much and made too many unproved and unprovable generalizations.

Woodward's criticisms seem valid, yet they should be read in light of the nature and purpose of *The Mind of the South*. It was not a conventional work of history or social science, and its purpose was not to survey the history or present state of the region. It was a sectional rather than a regional study, an analysis of the South as a state of mind rather than a geographical area. It was a highly personal and therefore impressionistic search for the essence of southern character, and impressions cannot always be substantiated by conventional scholarship. Nor need they be. Joseph K. Davis, whose field of scholarship is literature rather than history, has pointed toward what seems likely to be the final evaluation of the work. *The Mind of the South,* wrote Davis, "should be counted among those imaginative works of poetry and prose which afford pleasure and give us moments of insight." A book of "metaphorical construction, imaginative suppositions, and brilliant insights," it should not be read literally or as an ordinary history book. It "makes too many leaps by metaphor to meaning, it takes too many risks with facts, and it is finally too multiple, too symbolic in its construction and suggestiveness to be empirically verifiable."

The Mind of the South, it seems, is making the transition from history to literature. In either form, it remains a work of brilliance and significance.

Climate and History

One of the basic disputes in the interpretive literature of southern history concerns the relative influence of environment and culture. Those who stress environment attribute formative powers of one sort or another to geography, including topography, river systems, soil patterns, climate, weather, and latitude. Those who stress culture emphasize the English and British inheritance, racial factors, especially the presence of blacks, cultural isolation, ideology, and history. The disagreement between the two groups is usually a matter of emphasis, for the two approaches are not mutually exclusive. The issues involved may be illustrated by noting the influence attributed to an environmental factor, climate, and to a cultural force, history.

From the outset, climate—that is, weather, rainfall, temperature, storms, sunshine, humidity, and the physical atmosphere these things are said to induce—was considered a controlling influence in the South. The weather in Virginia and Carolina was unlike that of Britain, and Englishmen assumed, apparently, that it *must* be an important reason for the dissimilarities that developed between the southern colonies and England. Since England was the norm, the South must be deviant, and the South's weather came to be considered a warping influence, conducive to peculiarities and exoticisms and eventually degeneration.

This idea is not unique to the South. North Europeans applied it to other warm and humid places; but it became one of the most enduring ideas about the section. Even a questioning man like Henry Adams accepted it uncritically. Visiting the slave states on the eve of the Civil War, Adams found them "dirty, unkempt, poverty-stricken, ignorant, [and] vicious." Yet he was enthralled by "the May sunshine and shadow," "the thickness of foliage and the heavy smells," "the sense of atmosphere," and "the brooding indolence of a warm climate and a negro population." These things, he wrote in *The Education of Henry Adams* (1907), helped explain "the want of barriers, of pavements, of forms; the looseness, the laziness; the indolent Southern drawl; the pigs in the streets; the negro babies and their mothers with bandanas; the freedom, openness, [and] swagger, of nature and man."

Such thinking was based upon two distortions: that the South's climate is tropical or subtropical, and that it is uniform. Neither is even partially true. The South lies entirely within the temperate zone and encompasses, in the words of William A. Foran, every type of North American climate, "from pleasantly tempered Virginia and magnolia-scented Charleston to the arctic blizzards of Texas."[9] Yet writers of many persuasions have used climate to explain the South's history and character. Succumbing for a moment to the romanticism he deplored in others, Cash described the southern physical world as "a cosmic conspiracy against reality in favor of romance." A year after Cash wrote, a more orthodox historian, William O. Lynch, declared that "climate, with emphasis on temperature rather than rainfall, has done more, perhaps, than any other factor to mold the South." Phillips, Avery O. Craven, Francis B. Simkins, John R. Alden, and countless other historians have also stressed the molding influence of climate, and Clarence Cason made it the theme of his characterization of the section, *90° in the Shade* (1935).

Climate has been used by one writer or another to account for everything from the plantation system and Negro slavery to the emotionalism, volatility, and proneness to violence commonly attributed to southerners. Malnutrition, sociability, parasitic diseases, speech patterns, love of outdoors, architectural styles, culinary preferences, the pace of living, the dearth of immigrants, the absence of social protest, and even reading habits have been similarly explained. "Books cannot be read beside a cape jassamine bush in the moonlight," wrote Clarence Cason. Warm climate, he also wrote, encouraged the southerner to relax and thus gave him "an immunity from the everlasting inner demand that he improve his earthly position."

In recent years, the interest in climate has declined markedly. This is a result of several factors. Most of the uses made of climate as a historical influence were insubstantial or deterministic, and most of them derived from an interest in exoticisms, a subject historians are little interested in today. More importantly, most of the things climate was once used to explain have disappeared or diminished in significance. It is difficult to believe that climate once dictated plantation agriculture or slavery or socioeconomic backwardness or slow-paced living after those things have disappeared and the climate remains unchanged. Moreover, southerners themselves have radically altered the uses they make of climate. In the Old South they insisted that climate dictated an economy of cotton and slavery; today they and their chambers of commerce use it to attract industry as well as tourists and thus to diversify the economy. As Foran suggested, climate has been less important than the climate of opinion in molding southern history.

C. Vann Woodward and the Influence of History

While climate is no longer important as an explanation of southern distinctiveness, cultural factors, including history, are receiving increasing attention. Today historians regard the cumulative impact of history, the weight of the past upon the present, as a basic influence upon southern experience. This is due in part at least to the influence of Woodward's illuminating essay "The Search for Southern Identity" (1958), which rivals in significance the works of Cash and Phillips as an interpretation of the southern past.[10] Written in the midst of rapid changes wrought by the "bulldozer" and civil rights revolutions, this essay was concerned with the possible disappearance of the South as a distinctive section. Is the South, Woodward asked, merging into the American mainstream, another victim of the standardizing forces of modern society? All about him he saw suggestive signs. The section's social and economic indicators were approaching national levels; its traditional racial barriers were falling; its white population was less and less attracted to racial extremism; its physical and ideological and economic isolation was rapidly diminishing. In view of changes so profound, was anything left that was identifiably southern?

Acknowledging the magnitude of the changes, Woodward nevertheless concluded that the South was still enduring. The changes were eliminating or neutralizing many of the worst features of southern life and some of the best too, but in Woodward's estimate the essence of the South had never consisted of its faults. Amid all the changes he found one thing untouched, one thing that continued to set the South apart and might therefore preserve its separate identity in the future. This was history, the collective historical experience of the southern people. "It is just in this respect," he wrote, "that the South remains the most distinctive region of the country," and in this that southerners can "find the basis for continuity of their heritage." A distinctive past would preserve a distinctive identity in the future.

Several things set the South apart historically. The first was "a long and quite un-American experience with poverty." In 1880, in the aftermath of the Civil War, the section's per capita wealth was only 27 percent of that of the rest of the country, and decades later, on the eve of World War II, the South was still the nation's number one economic problem. These "generations of scarcity and want constitute one of the distinctive historical experiences of the Southern people," the significance of which is heightened by the contrast with American affluence. A second element of distinctiveness was the large component of frustration, failure, and defeat in the section's past, including "not only an overwhelming military defeat but long decades of defeat in the provinces of economic, social, and political life." A third was the inability of southerners to share in the American legend of innocence, a consequence not only of poverty and defeat but of an intimate and enduring experience with social evil. Despite the fact that "Southerners have repeated the American rhetoric of self-admiration and sung the perfections of American institutions," wrote Woodward, they never shared the "singular moral complacency" of other Americans. The Old South had "writhed in the torments of its own conscience" over slavery, and the New South was just as troubled by segregation and other forms of repression. The southerner's "preoccupation was with guilt, not with innocence, with the reality of evil, not with the dream of perfection," and in this too he differed from other Americans.

Woodward's essay was persuasive. History has in fact set the South apart from the rest of the country. Yet the influence of such things as poverty, frustration, and guilt is far from clear. One of the striking deficiencies of southern historical literature is that the influences of none of these factors have ever been studied systematically over the sweep of the section's history. (A partial exception might be made for some of the immediate consequences of defeat in the Civil War.) What, for example, has been the nature and extent of southern poverty? What precise influence has poverty exerted upon the section and its people? What were its psychological as well as its physical consequences, and how did these affect politics, social thought, and race relations? Did they influence class perceptions? How did the influence vary from time to time, place to place, class to class, white to black?

The list of such questions could be extended indefinitely for each of the subjects stressed by Woodward, and until more definite answers are available, the historical influence of those subjects must remain an open issue. A few scholars have suggested that their influence is less than Woodward claimed. "The South as a whole does not exhibit a style of politics or social behavior which in any way reflects [the] elements of differences [stressed by Woodward]," David Bertelson observes in

The Lazy South (1967). "Quite the contrary, poverty and failure have never discouraged Southerners from pursuing opportunity and success, and protestations of purity are more common than affirmations of guilt."

There is another and much more disturbing issue raised by Woodward's essay—its implications for the future of southern identity. If it is largely in their distinctive historical experience that southerners differ from other Americans and chiefly in this that their hope for preserving a separate identity lies, then the future of the South as a distinctive section is bleak indeed. For the factors Woodward used to account for southern distinctiveness are dissipating rapidly. Those factors were of course the special concern of Woodward's own generation and that of his parents, but they are not the concern of the younger generation today. For southerners who came of age in, say, the Vietnam War, the influences Woodward stressed have little significance. If southern poverty is not disappearing today, it is at least assuming the character of national poverty. The "generations of scarcity and want" have ended for most southerners, as have the "long decades of defeat in the provinces of economic, social, and political life." Memories of the Civil War and Reconstruction constitute no recognizable influence on young Southerners today. The reappearance of the two-party system is only one measure of the abatement of the white South's political isolation and frustration, and ever since the World War II economic boom has focused the attention of southerners on opportunity and success and the assurances that come with those things. As concerns the more abstract matters of guilt and innocence, the situation today is less clear, though insofar as their cause is racial, they too must be changing. Certainly the South's racial problems are less acute than they once were, and less distinct from those of the rest of the nation. The black revolution has made northerners aware of racial difficulties of their own, and their reactions are sometimes strikingly "southern." The Vietnam War shook the "singular moral complacency" of the American people as nothing has since the Civil War, and the moral bankruptcy of the Nixon leadership added further shocks. In these things too perhaps northerners and southerners are becoming more alike, and the future of the South is therefore highly problematical.

The Southern Identity

Despite the insightfulness of the literature discussed above, the southern identity and the central theme of southern history are still elusive things. This is in part a consequence of the most singular fact of southern historical studies: none of the central themes or basic interpretations has been systematically tested against southern experience over an extended period of time. Despite this, the basic features of southern identity now seem apparent even though the specific combination of those features remains a matter of debate.

The most obvious feature is complexity. Southernness consists not of a single quality, but of the specifically southern mix of qualities and of the cultural and physical milieu in which those qualities exist and interact. A second feature is distinctiveness, or rather the southerners' perception of themselves as distinct from other Americans. Such a perception is essential to group identity, and from it derives a third feature, attachment to the South, not as a geographical area, though that is important, but as an idea and a set of principles, and thus a way of life.

What are the elements of the idea that is the South? The most important, as already noted, is race in its many ramifications. By the middle of the colonial period racial factors had combined with other cultural and physical influences to produce a social and economic order, and thus a political structure, that differentiated the South from other American societies. Once this occurred, the differentiation fed on itself, and long before the American Revolution it produced a society characterized by white supremacy, class hierarchy, plantation economy, and a political system that functioned in the interest of the planter class specifically and white people generally. The preservation of planter and white hegemony in an expansive society encouraged certain personal qualities and intellectual and cultural tendencies, among them exaggerated individualism and love of personal freedom (among those who already possessed those things), a tradition of personalism and direct action in dealing with others, a disdain for institutional arrangements that interfered with freedom of action by members of the dominant groups, a certain satisfaction among those groups with things as they were and a certain fatalism among subordinate classes, a kind of traditionalism that perpetuated folk society and provincialism and encouraged romanticism and anti-intellectualism, an attachment to locality and family, and a tendency toward escapism that discouraged skepticism and liberal change. Those too, as they emerged, commenced to feed upon themselves, and thus history, the presence of the past in the present, became a dominating force, holding the section in traditional molds.

The most important of the accumulating influences of history was a sense of grievance, which did not appear until sectional consciousness emerged at the end of the eighteenth century. The process by which this occurred is discussed at length in a later chapter, but here it may be said that the sense of grievance was not a cause but a consequence of sectional consciousness, for it derived from fear attendant upon the change of circumstances produced by the creation of the nation, and in turn from the southerner's matured world view, a world view which, in Sheldon Hackney's words, "defines the social, political, and physical environment [of the nation and world] as hostile and casts the white southerner in the role of the passive victim of malevolent forces." This was the "sense of grievance that is at the heart of the southern identity."[11]

If racial factors are the key to southern history, this sense of grievance seems the essential quality of sectional identity, the characteristic trait of the southern temperament. "Southern self-consciousness was created by the need to protect a peculiar institution from threats originating outside the region," Hackney has explained. "Consequently, the southern identity has been linked from the first to a siege mentality. Though southerners have many other identities, they are likely to be most conscious of being southerners when they are defending their region against attack from outside forces: abolitionists, the Union Army, carpetbaggers, Wall Street and Pittsburgh, civil rights agitators, the federal government, feminism, socialism, trade unionism, Darwinism, Communism, atheism, daylight saving time, and other by-products of modernity. This has produced an extreme sensitivity to criticism from outsiders and a tendency to excuse local faults as the product of forces beyond human or local control. If the South was poor it was because the Yankees stole all the family silver and devastated the region in other ways after the Civil War. If industrialization seemed inordinately slow in the South, it was because of a conspiracy of northern capitalists to maintain the region as an economic colony. Added to this experience with perceived threats has been the fact that almost every significant change in the life of the South has been initiated by external powers." To think of oneself as a southerner, then, "inevitably involves a feeling of persecution at times and a sense of being a passive, insignificant object of alien or impersonal forces. Such a historical experience has fostered a world view that supports the denial of responsibility and locates threats to the region outside the region and threats to the person outside the self."

ONE

THE DEVELOPING SOUTH 1607-1820

"To write about the South when there was no South is a task not without difficulties," wrote Wesley Frank Craven in *The Southern Colonies in the Seventeenth Century* (1949); and his statement embodies the most characteristic fact about the history of the colonial South. If the South is something more than a geographical area, as suggested in the previous chapter, it did not begin when that group of 104 Englishmen and boys arrived in the New World in 1607 at a place they named Jamestown in a land already known as Virginia. Nor had it begun when another group of Englishmen established themselves across Chesapeake Bay in Maryland in 1634, nor in 1653 when a few of the Virginians moved to the Albemarle region of what is now North Carolina. When other newcomers from England and Barbados settled at Charleston in South Carolina in 1670 there was still no South, nor even in 1733 when a small group of English philanthropists, refugees, and imperial planners cooperated to establish the last southern colony, at Savannah in Georgia.

Throughout the long period these colonies remained in the British empire, which for Virginia was equivalent to the time between the inaugurations of Thomas Jefferson and Richard M. Nixon, their inhabitants developed no common awareness, no sense of being a people apart. To themselves as to others, they—the dominant white majority—were Englishmen or Britons and then Virginians or Carolinians, and toward the end of the colonial era perhaps Americans also. But southerners—not yet. To be sure, they came to share many things later generations would consider "southern," but through the colonial era they never had an embracing sense of commonality.

This fact makes it difficult to come to terms with the history of the colonial South. The "baffling diversity and complexity" of the colonies below Pennsylvania and the absence of a specifically southern consciousness explain the general neglect of the *southern* aspects of the history of those colonies.[1] The neglect is thus understandable and to a degree justified, but the usual practice of treating the history of each colony separately has diverted attention from the basic thrust of their common experience, the developing community of interest. It has likewise produced a rather sharp division between the colonial and revolutionary eras of southern history on the one hand and later periods on the other. As Clarence L. Ver Steeg put it recently, "A certain alienation exists between the southern colonies and 'the South' "; and the colonial roots of the South have therefore been insufficiently studied. One result is that historians of the colonial South have given no attention to central themes, or in Ver Steeg's words, they "have not been successful in providing a systematic structure to analyze the southern colonies as a whole." One reason for this is that the central themes used to understand later periods have only limited application to the colonial era. The characteristic features of the Old South—slavery, white supremacy, the plantation system, the country gentleman ideal, or whatever—were less dominating in the earlier period, and things said to characterize the modern South—poverty, defeat, frustration, and guilt, for example—are of no use at all in understanding the colonial period. History was not yet a burden; southerners were not yet a people with a "common resolve indomitably maintained."

Yet in crucial matters of values and institutions there were no sharp breaks between the colonial, revolutionary, and early national periods, nor between the South of those periods and of the pre-Civil War era. Through all these years, the changes that occurred were evolutionary and built upon previous developments, and whatever "alienation" existed between the colonial South and later Souths is thus easily overstated. In the colonial era the section was a kind of proto-South, a South in the process of forming, but the taproot of sectional identity was firmly implanted during that time. That fact provides the most useful device for organizing the history of the colonial South. The most significant developments in the period were those that drew the southern colonies together and at the same time set them apart from the rest of British America. The history of the colonial South should focus on those developments that illuminate the origins and nature of sectional distinctiveness.

The Proto-South

During the colonial era the colonies to the south of Pennsylvania underwent a process of development that differentiated them from those to the north. The process, however, is difficult to trace, especially in its early and murkiest phases. It was long and slow and unconscious, not the result of policy or strategy, and only its details were perceptible to contemporaries. Winthrop D. Jordan has recently remarked that slavery in this country was the result of a series of "unthinking decisions," and his phrase is an apt one for the South as well. When southern consciousness eventually appeared, it was a consequence of differences that had already developed between the South and the rest of the country. Southerners began thinking of themselves as a people apart only after they became so, though the distinction between cause and effect was less clear than that statement suggests.

Roots of Southern Distinctiveness

The process of sectional differentiation began as soon as settlement began, for it originated in the forces that produced colonization. The cultural baggage early colonists brought with them from England, including their motives for coming to the New World and their vision of the good life they hoped to create, was not the same for the northern and southern colonists. Nor was the physical environment in which they settled. For both of these reasons the early colonists made certain social, economic, and other choices that eventually had far-reaching consequences in setting them apart from each other. All of these factors combined to create a specific mixture of cultural elements that formed the root of southern distinctiveness. The latter point is especially important. It was the specific combination of forces rather than any one force that set in motion the process of sectional differentiation and determined its eventual directions. Over the years, the distinction between original causes and effects often broke down, and institutions and ways that grew out of original causes were themselves sometimes transformed by events into determining causes. In this way the combination of controlling forces was always changing.

The South evolved from two focal points, Virginia and South Carolina, of which Virginia was far more important. It was there, in the Old Dominion, that southern institutions and attitudes evolved, there the plantation system and slavery were worked out, there the southern way of life began and achieved its best and most characteristic expressions. The other colonies borrowed generously from Virginia, adapting the borrowings to suit their own circumstances but never changing them fundamentally.

The first Virginians were mostly Englishmen from the middle and lower classes. Among them "were no titled English gentlemen, not an earl, rarely a knight, or even the younger son of a knight,"· Thomas Jefferson Wertenbaker once wrote. "By far the larger part were humble people—ill-paid, ragged farm workers; villeins who had deserted the manor; day-laborers from London or Bristol—carpenters, masons, coopers, blacksmiths, tailors, brickmakers; with now and then a sturdy yeoman crowded off his land by the insatiable maw of the enclosure; or a youthful tradesman or merchant tempted by the fertility of the Chesapeake soil and the reports of huge profits to be had from the culture of tobacco; occasionally an unwary youth who had fallen asleep over his grog in a London tavern and awakened to find himself aboard a tobacco ship with four years of servitude awaiting him in America."

Despite this diversity, which was made even greater by later additions of non-English, chiefly Scots and Scotch-Irish, settlers, these earliest white "southerners"[1] had an important trait that helped set them apart from nonsoutherners: their reasons for coming to the New World tended to be positive and economic rather than negative and socioreligious. They came for the opportunities they hoped to realize, not for the religious or political persecutions they sought to escape. They were neither rebels nor radicals. They sought not a new England, not a society built according to a purist's dream, but a wider England in which they could participate freely and from which they could derive a full share of benefit. The purpose and hope—at least of the articulate among them—was to create a society incorporating the elements of English life that most appealed to them. There were exceptions of course. In the first years, some came chiefly for adventure; later economic or social necessity was a primary cause. Many early Virginians, including the substantial number who came as indentured servants, redemptioners, transported convicts, or slaves, came because they had little or no choice, driven by social and economic forces over which they had no control. For others, religion was the motivating factor, the desire to spread the gospel, to convert the Indians, to claim America for Christianity.

On the surface, the motives that led settlers to Virginia seem very like those which led others to New England. Both areas were peopled by Englishmen for a combination of reasons that centered around economics and religion. The combinations were different, however, and that is the significant point. The religious and economic visions of early Virginians and New Englanders were quite unalike. The Virginians sought to build no city on a hill, but instead to erect a society of maximum opportunity for themselves and others of their kind. Of course these two things were not necessarily incompatible, as the New England experience demonstrated, but the social and economic orientation of the Virginians produced a society unlike that of New England or Pennsylvania.

This orientation derived from several cultural factors which were of primary influence in the early development of Virginia and subsequent colonies. These included a type of Protestant Christianity that was Anglican in form but strongly influenced by Calvinism and congregational control; a social vision that looked to the manor house and the country gentleman rather than the meeting house or counting house; an economic impulse that derived its dynamic from capitalism and individualism; a set of social attitudes that eventuated in a hierarchical class structure but permitted and produced considerable social mobility for whites; a set of ethnic and racial attitudes that eventually produced and then sustained an exploitive caste system for nonwhites; and a political tradition that used racial caste to contain social protest and in the process maximize the consciousness of freedom among what amounted to a white *Herrenvolk*. To these things must be added a heterogeneity of population that made it necessary to modify English social models to accommodate non-English but largely British groups.

Protestant Christianity determined the social and moral values of colonial southerners as well as their cosmology and theology, and in all these things Virginians and New Englanders had much in common and contrast. "However much Virginia and New England differed in ecclesiastical politics," Perry Miller has written, "they were both recruited from the same type of Englishman, pious, hard-working, middle-class, accepting literally and solemnly the tenets of Puritanism—original sin, predestination, and election—who could conceive of the society they were erecting in America only within a religious framework." Puritanism and even Calvinism were compatible with Anglican forms, and the influence of both was always large in the South, and increased with the influx of Scots, Scotch-Irish, and French Huguenots which began in the latter part of the seventeenth century.

Yet however much Virginians and New Englanders drew their religion from common sources, there were important differences between them which helped along the process of sectional differentiation. Virginians kept the Anglican connection until the Revolution, though geography and the desire for congregational control in religious matters produced a system of church governance that was actually independent of the English episcopacy. Church as well as secular government came to be oligarchic and based upon maximum assertion of local prerogative. Actual control was in the hands of a self-perpetuating vestry of prominent laymen who kept the clergy dependent by paying them poorly and keeping them untenured and in these ways compromising their authority and social position.

Anglicanism was the established religion in all the southern colonies. However, the southern brand of Anglicanism was not tied to a religious or social idealism, and because of the desire to attract settlers it was relatively tolerant of dissenters and nonconformists. Virginians were never as intense as New Englanders about religion and piety, and among them secular influences were always stronger. Not even the Great Awakening of the 1740s or the coming of the Baptists and Methodists in the last decades of the colonial era altered this basic secularism, and on the eve of the Revolution theirs was a relatively secular society. To the Virginian, religion was not chiefly an instrument of social sanctification or individual self-improvement, but a vehicle of affirmation, a device that helped the individual define and accept his place in the established order. "Having come away from England not fundamentally dissatisfied with life there, not religiously dissatisfied," as James McBride Dabbs has noted, the southerner "was disposed to be satisfied with life here." He made his religion more pliant and unstrenuous than the New Englander, adapting it to his perceived interests, rationalizing it to fit the social order of which he was a part. Thus when the conversion of slaves raised the question of whether one Christian could own another, he and his church had little difficulty working out an accommodating answer. Here as elsewhere his church affirmed rather than challenged the social order, a characteristic later adopted by Baptists and Methodists.

The Social Ethic

The role of religion in the evolution of sectional distinctiveness was most important in the development of the southern social ethic. This vital aspect of the origin of the South revolves around several basic questions. To what extent did colonial southerners adhere to the values of the work ethic? To what extent did they develop a distinctive version of that ethic? And how did they define the social purposes of work?

These questions have never been resolved definitively.[2] Their significance stems from the connection between attitudes toward work in a given society and larger assumptions concerning the nature and purpose of society itself. The meaning of work in the South during the formative years of the seventeenth and eighteenth centuries is therefore one of the keys to the origin of sectional identity, a fact that is underscored by the differences between southerners and New Englanders on this point. The root of those differences lay in the social and cultural values the early settlers brought from England, which in turn were further differentiated by dissimilar physical environments in the New World. The Puritans who settled New England brought with them what David Bertelson has called the "doctrine of coercion" and a belief in the inner necessity of work. Accordingly, work to them was an obligation imposed upon everyone by God, a responsibility inherent in the social state. It was also its own reward: a source of personal discipline and self-improvement, of moral uplift and material advancement, of social progress and community betterment.

In contrast, the Englishmen who settled the South accepted the "doctrine of allurement," to borrow another of Bertelson's terms, according to which the chief purpose of work was personal rather than social, the material reward it brought the individual rather than the improvement or cohesion it brought the community. Thus southerners displayed little of that purposeful busyness that characterized New Englanders and made their farms and towns so neat and their communities so well integrated. Work in the South lacked the social meaning it had in New England, and was therefore less important in measuring the individual's worth or defining his relationship to society. The result —and this is the important point—was social fragmentation, the exaltation of the individual above the group, and consequently an imperfectly developed sense of community. The differences were relative rather than absolute, but still important. Social cohesion was weaker in the South than in New England, institutional development laggard, towns and civic organizations and a sense of civic responsibility less pronounced. The southerners placed greater stress on individual gain and gave far less attention to the social consequences of economic activity. The latter was not as restrained as it was in New England by ideas of calling and stewardship or by public policies defining the responsibility of the individual to society. Southerners, it seemed, expected social unity and wellbeing to result from the pursuit of individual opportunity, and their social and economic systems reflected that expectation. They stressed leisure and hospitality and gracious living not as recompense for work and self-discipline, but as rewards for those who could live by exploiting the labor of others. Among them social status was a measure not of one's work, but of one's success in having others work for him.

Thus southerners did not reject work or deny its social efficacy; rather, they reformulated the work ethic to fit the circumstances in which they found themselves. Slavery, which was a cause as well as an effect of this evolving process, made labor a punishment rather than a calling. Moreover, most work in the South was long and arduous and not immediately rewarding, and toil amid heat, humidity, and insects was difficult to exalt for its own sake or overlay with divine sanction. The agrarian myth that soon developed to extol the plantation system celebrated agriculture not as a form of work but as a way of life, and the amount and kind of work it assigned to various roles—planter, mistress, overseer, slave, and yeoman—differed markedly. Work itself was not stigmatized but only certain forms of work, especially tasks performed in a context suggesting loss of social standing or racial caste.

The same kind of distinction applied to community and institutional development. The sense of community did develop imperfectly in the South by New England standards, but it also developed unevenly, for only some forms of institutional development were retarded. Institutions dependent upon a sense of social responsibility, such as schools and other expressions of formal culture, were always weak in the South, as were those representing social and personal restraint, like law and respect for legal forms. Institutions of racial or class control, however, such as the plantation and slavery and the laws that upheld them, were not weak; and the same kind of distinction applied to southern individualism. Individualism for white, adult, and relatively successful men *was* exaggerated, but other members of society—nonwhites, apprentices, servants, slaves, and women—were expected to remain in clearly defined and subordinate places that notably restricted their freedom as individuals.

The Plantation System

Economic institutions in the southern colonies were rooted in capitalism and attendant features of private property, individual enterprise, and personal profit. From the beginning, Virginians placed great emphasis on the rights of property and the individual, at least the individual who belonged to the economic and social elite. Yet here too they developed their own version of things, and capitalism in the South developed along lines that were somewhat different from those in New

England and the middle colonies. The southern economy was more concerned with agriculture and less with commercial pursuits, and with large-scale agriculture devoted to staple production. It therefore encouraged plantations and slavery and a way of life built around those things.

The plantation system was begun and maintained for economic reasons, but it was vastly more than an economic institution. From the beginning it exhibited significant components of paternalism and seigneurialism, though its basic purposes were always the exploitation of natural and human resources and the generation of high levels of income necessary to sustain the planters' way of life. It was a product of several factors. Availability of land was the primary economic fact in the southern colonies, and land policy facilitated the engrossment of large holdings. The shortage of labor was also important, and most easily overcome by forms of coercion that grew out of plantation organization. Then too the suitability of soil and climate for staple crops, plus the encouragements of British mercantilism, made plantation agriculture seem the natural economic system for the southern colonies.

The need to coerce labor made the plantation a political as well as an economic institution. As Edgar T. Thompson put it, a plantation is "an organization designed primarily to advance, express, and defend the interests of a planter or a planter class through the formal or political control of a subordinate class." Southern plantations fit that definition precisely, and that fact is basic to understanding them. As exploitive institutions they rested ultimately on authority—the planters' ability to command power to protect their position as well as their willingness to do so. This of course was the major reason for the planters' interest in politics: politics supplied the instruments by which they protected their property and social prerogatives. This was necessarily the case. In exploitive societies dominant classes must preoccupy themselves with politics, though one of their concerns in doing so is to legitimize an ideology that makes the use of naked force unnecessary. In both of these concerns southern planters proved extraordinarily adept.

The plantation system emerged early. In 1612 John Rolfe, best known for his marriage to the Indian "princess" Pocahontas, introduced a sweet-scented West Indian tobacco that suited the soil and climate of Virginia and the tastes of English gentlemen, and taught Virginia farmers how to cultivate and cure it. This soon gave the struggling colony a sound economic base and the plantation system a footing and, fatefully, provided an economic impetus for the forces that eventuated in African slavery. (In South Carolina, rice, first introduced from Madagascar in 1694, played a similar role, though slavery had existed in that colony from the outset.) As early as 1625, 118 Virginians owned one or more servants, the largest holding being forty. Soon prototypes of the southern planter of later generations appeared. In 1648 Captain Samuel Matthews, "an old planter of above thirty years stand," was described by a contemporary in terms that suggested the appearance of a social type. "He hath a fine house and all things answerable to it," wrote the observer; "he sows yearly store of hemp and flax, and causes it to be spun; he keeps weavers, and hath a tanhouse, causes leather to be dressed, hath eight shoemakers employed in this trade, hath forty negro servants, brings them up to trades in his house; he yearly sows abundance of wheat, barley, etc. The wheat he selleth at four shillings a bushel; kills stores of beeves, and sells them to victual the ships when they come thither; hath abundance of kine, a brave dairy, swine great store, and poultry. He married the daughter of Sir Tho. Hinton, and in a word, keeps a good house, lives bravely, and [is] a true lover of Virginia. He is worthy of much honor."

The plantation system and staple agriculture grew up together, and in their wake came African slavery. In 1619 the tiny Virginia colony, still in the dying time, exported 20,000 pounds of tobacco, but by 1627 the total had grown to 500,000 pounds. In 1639 the two Chesapeake colonies, Virginia and Maryland, were producing a total of 1.5 million pounds, and by the end of the century, 40 million pounds. In South Carolina rice production totaled 4,100 tons in 1724, and 55,000 tons on the eve of the Revolution. The development of slavery is discussed below, but here it may be said that the accumulation of slaves and land followed a similar pattern. In 1670 the population of Virginia included 6,000 servants and 2,000 slaves, but by 1715 the slaves alone numbered 23,000, and at the time of the Revolution the black population of Virginia and Maryland was 206,000 out of a total of 469,000. In 1708 the population of South Carolina included 3,500 whites, only 120 of them indentured servants, 4,100 African slaves, and 1,400 Indian slaves. By 1765 this colony contained about 40,000 whites and 90,000 blacks. The growing numbers of blacks made possible the exploitation of large land holdings. At the end of the 1670s, when one man could cultivate only a few acres of land, more than a dozen estates in Virginia exceeded 10,000 acres, and almost 200 contained more than 2,000 acres. Before the seventeenth century ended, the plantation system complete with grandee owners and African slavery had developed in Virginia and assumed the general form it retained until the Civil War. By the second quarter of the eighteenth century a similar process had been completed in South Carolina.

In both areas the plantation system exerted a dominating influence over life, affecting social as well as economic development. Planter and plantation significantly influenced the pattern of westward expansion and population dispersal, dictating a rural pattern of sparse settlement. Thus southerners lived in relative isolation from each other, in contrast to New Englanders, who favored a town pattern of settlement. This too had important consequences. The aim of every plantation was self-sufficiency, a fact that discouraged economic diversification and labor specialization. Skilled artisans and economic middlemen had difficulty competing in a plantation system, and this also inhibited urban development and further differentiated southern society from that of the non-South. Economically as well as culturally, the planters looked to London and often dealt directly with London merchants or their factors, bypassing local middlemen, whether retailers, wholesalers, bankers, insurers, or shippers. The development of these classes was stunted by this and by the proclivity of men with money to invest in land and slaves, which brought social prestige as well as handsome financial returns.

These things fastened agrarian ideals and rural life styles on the South. Isolation and the sparse distribution of population encouraged individualism and self-reliance and helped determine the pattern of institutional development. Long before the image of the benighted South appeared, the section's cultural institutions were developing along distinctive lines. Governor William Berkeley of Virginia exaggerated in 1671 when he thanked God that there was neither printing press nor free schools in Virginia, but the tenor of his remarks reflected some important facts about the direction of social development. The commitment of Virginia to public education, for example, came much later than that of Massachusetts, which always had at least a partial commitment. The Virginians did establish a college, William and Mary, in 1693, more than half a century after the Puritans in Massachusetts had established Harvard, but theirs was the only college founded in the colonial South compared to a total of eight colleges founded in the northern and middle colonies.

It was not that southerners were uninterested in education. Rather, their interest was "English" rather than "American"; that is, it centered around the idea that education was a responsibility of the individual rather than society. The result was education for those who could afford it. Philip Alexander Bruce once examined the names of more than 18,000 persons in the public records of seventeenth-century Virginia and concluded that nearly half the adult white males and three-fourths of the adult white females in the colony could not sign their names. If these estimates were only approximately correct and the factor of marginal literacy is considered as well as the large slave population, the magnitude of this fact becomes obvious: the literate population of the colonial South was small indeed. This makes the scarcity of schools, libraries, books, and newspapers significant as well as intelligible, and helps explain why there was no permanent printing press in the colony before 1730. It also helps explain the derivative nature of southern culture.

The Social Structure

As the plantation system emerged, the social structure crystallized. At the top were the whites, divided unequally into three rather distinct but overlapping categories—a small class of large planters, a much more numerous class of independent property owners, and a large class of poor folk in varying states of dependence. Beneath the whites were the blacks, almost all of them slaves, who in many tidewater areas constituted the largest segment of the population. Outside this structure were the Indians, few of whom interacted socially with whites or blacks.

At the apex of the social pyramid in wealth and prestige were the large planters. For several decades following the settlement of each colony, this class was busy establishing itself, accumulating wealth, and asserting its power and prerogative. But once these things were accomplished, the wealthier and more successful families transformed themselves into a landed gentry, their acquisitive impulses muted by a sense of security and accomplishment and a close relationship with those dependent upon them. At the same time they acquired attributes of high culture and genteel living that set them apart from other classes and provided them with a source of social prestige and, ultimately, with a basis for idealizing and then romanticizing their entire class.

But that was in the future. The origins of the planter families were unpretentiously bourgeois. Myths about their cavalier or genteel ancestors were exploded so long ago that they no longer merit attention. Few men of rank or social standing migrated to the colonies, and those who succeeded in the New World, as the planters did, were ambitious, hardworking, and lucky men, and a bit ruthless too, and they never lost the acquisitive instinct. Based in the first analysis on wealth and success, their class even in its upper ranks was never closed. By the time of its golden age, however, about the second quarter of the eighteenth century in Virginia and a generation later in South Carolina, it was increasingly difficult to enter. Established families had by then monopolized opportunity, and the economy of the tidewater was becoming stagnant. The great planters were materially successful men in a society that honored material success, and as such they imposed themselves and their interests on the South. So great was their success in doing this that their concerns came to be considered the concerns of the South itself.

They were a fascinating and accomplished group of people—the Harrisons, Blands, Carys, Ludwells, Byrds, Randolphs, Carters, Burwells, Pages, Wormleys, Beverleys, Tayloes, Lees, Masons, Fitzhughs, and many others in Virginia, and in South Carolina the Rutledges, Pinckneys, Draytons, Hugers, Pringles, and others. They have captivated historians as well as southerners, and as a result have escaped the kind of critical analysis usually applied to social elites. In fact historians have indulged them to the extent of generally accepting their estimates of themselves and viewing the South and its history through their eyes. On the whole, therefore, the planters are known as an attractive, responsible aristocracy whose social and economic hegemony rested lightly on the lower classes and the South itself. Dazzled by symbols of wealth and culture, accounts of the planters are typically filled with fond description rather than systematic analysis —pictures of the splendid architecture of their spacious Georgian homes, inventories of the fine furniture they imported from Europe and the silverware and crystal and china they used to set their bounteous tables. There are also catalogues of the contents of their libraries and wine cellars, accounts of their tours of Europe and of the education they afforded their eldest sons at the Inns of Court, anecdotes of their fondness for oratory and classical allusions and fox hunting and gracious living.[3]

These things there were, of course, at least among the upper reaches of the class, evidence of a conscious effort to emulate the life style of English country gentlemen and display the qualities such gentlemen were thought to possess. Those qualities included ownership of large estates, residence at a fine country seat, and acceptance of aristocratic social ideas, including class and racial inequalities and the right and duty of gentlemen to direct public affairs. At its best, the result was a sense of class responsibility, even noblesse oblige, that moderated the exploitive impulses from which it derived and was the redeeming quality of the finest segment of this class. Just as important, it produced an enlarged concern for personal honor and prerogative and a preoccupation with the gentlemanly arts and social graces.

Of more intrinsic significance than these things were the planters' wealth and power. As a dominant, exploiting class the planters were necessarily concerned with property, power, and position. This fact determined the parameters within which their paternalism and noblesse oblige were exercised. This does not mean the paternalism was unreal, that it did not mitigate the conditions of dependent groups or ease class relationships in the South. Helped along by racial factors that are described below, it did do these things. But the other side of paternalism is acquiescence or deference, and deference among the lower classes was a major fact in the southern social system. It affected in varying degrees middle- and lower-class whites, including women and indentured servants, and also Afro-southerners, slave and free. This does not mean that social harmony always prevailed, for there was a considerable amount of disharmony. It means instead that once the number of blacks was large in any of the colonies, white social protest was ameliorative rather than radical in thrust, for slavery and the economic opportunities it offered to whites committed the vast majority of them to the social and economic system that had developed in the section.

This deference and its moderating effects upon social protest were partly features of the age and thus existed apart from racial considerations. Modern concepts of democracy and individual rights for dependent classes were absent from colonial America, and the instances of class grievance that developed, the most notable being Bacon's Rebellion in Virginia in 1676, were sporadic and poorly focused. No one regarded a hierarchical society in which power and material goods were unequally distributed as anything other than natural. Middle- and lower-class whites wanted to succeed within the established order, not change the order itself. They identified not with the mass of people who bore the brunt of the economic system, but with those who succeeded on a grand scale. Their social protest was thus concerned with opening the system for themselves, with expanding their own opportunities to do what the planters had done so grandly. They protested not against slavery, indentured servitude, the concentration of wealth, or the public policies that made those things possible, but against too little legislative representation for the western counties, monopolies in the Indian trade, "soft" Indian policies, or, sometimes, the arrogance of slaveowners or established churches. "It would be a misunderstanding of the whole course of southern history to assume that the dissatisfaction of the hinterland was caused by a desire to revolt against the social values of the coastal regime," Francis B. Simkins once wrote. "The men of the back country were not opposed to slavery, plantation leisure, hedonistic living, and other aristocratic practices. They wished to be rid of the tidewater oligarchs so that they too might move forward in keeping with Southern standards already established on the eastern seaboard." This was one of the major forces for social stability in the southern colonies.

That stability, and thus the position of the planter class, was preserved through a sociopolitical system that was relatively open in form but conservative and oligarchic in operation. There was a "firm attachment to the government of the rich, the well-born, and the able," as Charles S. Sydnor observed in *Gentleman Freeholders* (1952), a revealing study of Virginia politics between the 1750s and 1780s; and that was more or less true of Maryland and South Carolina, though less so of North Carolina. That attachment molded the impulse toward self-government which became important in the final decades before the Revolution. The growth of self-government on the local level was the most important political development of those decades, but its effect was to increase the power of the landed, slaveholding classes and thus their ability to protect their interests; for it was those classes that took the lead in asserting local rights and defining local interests. Restrictions on the right to vote served the same ends. Slaves, free blacks, Indians, women, youths, indentured servants, and even propertyless white males, groups that together constituted a vast majority of the population, could not vote. Those were also the groups with the greatest cause for social grievance.

Disfranchisement thus reinforced deference in sustaining the oligarchic nature of politics. Nearly a third of the men who served on the governor's council in Virginia between 1680 and the Revolution came from nine families, and almost another third came from fourteen other families. Of approximately 1,600 men who served as justices of the peace in Virginia in the twenty years preceding the Revolution, a fourth of them belonged to fifty-five families and three-fourths came from less than 400 families. "Birth into one of the ruling families," as Charles S. Sydnor has written, "was almost essential to the making of a political career in eighteenth century Virginia." A study of the House of Burgesses, the lower branch of the Virginia legislature, found that of the 630 men who served in that body between 1720 and 1776, 110 dominated its affairs and thus the internal governance of the colony. Of these, ninety-two were planters or part-time planters, and half were connected by marriage. Until the 1730s the center of political power in the colony remained in the tidewater; then it began shifting westward and northward. By the time of the Revolution, the Burgesses in Virginia and their counterparts in other colonies had usurped considerable power from crown officials, and self-government in local matters was well developed. But factors of race, sex, and property kept politics undemocratic.[4]

None of these limitations, however, excluded the substantial middle class of landowners, who were not only whites but males as well. (Everywhere there were restrictions on property ownership by women, especially married women.) Next below the planters in property, prestige, and power, this class overlapped the planters in all those things. It was from this class that the planters came, and the two groups were interrelated by blood and marriage as well as economic and political interest. The middle class was a heterogeneous grouping of small planters, substantial farmers, independent artisans, professional men, and merchants. It was this diversity, perhaps, that gave the class its lack of focus and caused its interests to be less well articulated than those of the planters. Its members tended to identify with the planters, on whom they were often dependent, and to conform generally to Francis B. Simkins's characterization of the mass of southern white folk. "They admire the good life of big houses, fine dress and pliant Negroes," Simkins wrote, "and on the whole they are ... willing ... to speculate in land and use the toils of others as means of attaining the life of the privileged."

The middle class had a secure status in the South and a high degree of social and economic mobility. Its members were generally able to take advantage of economic opportunity and as a group were a succeeding class of men on the make, of men who had already achieved or were in the process of achieving or could realistically hope to achieve a meaningful degree of economic substance. The values of materialism and individualism, which they accepted, seemed to be confirmed by their own prospects, and they had no developed sense of grievance. Ethnocentric in their social attitudes and white supremacists even when they owned no slaves and found themselves competing with slavery, they entertained no antislavery views, though they did sometimes question the extension of slavery because of the racial threat posed by heavy concentrations of blacks.

In important respects this class was the economic and social backbone of the South, the most dynamic element in its population, and, after the tidewater stagnated and national independence was achieved, the class from which much of the section's leadership sprang. Its success was due chiefly to the fact that the class was so well adapted to the requirements of the economic system. Like the planters, middle-class southerners had an independence of spirit, a disrespect for forms that inhibited expressions of the ego, and a willingness to disregard institutions and conventions that interfered with the pursuit of self-interest; and also like the planters they had a readiness for direct action in public and private affairs that sometimes encouraged, or at least tolerated, illegal or extralegal violence. These qualities, like many others that eventually came to be associated with the South, grew out of the competitiveness that characterized economic and social life in the rapidly expanding society.

Below the middle class was another large and amorphous social class that included not only whites who were poor—landless farmers, agricultural workers, unskilled laborers, dependent artisans, and indentured servants—but a distinctive group already known as "poor whites." While much is known about the planters and the middle classes and their histories are relatively easy to reconstruct, the story of this class is shrouded in obscurity and prejudice. This is unfortunate, for poor white people were always a large segment of the southern population and fuller knowledge of their story would no doubt cast unexpected light on the nature of southern life, especially its pathologies, and thus on the South itself.

The obscurity is due to several factors. Like other inarticulate peoples with low incidence of literacy, the white poor left few written records. Like the slaves, they appear in historical sources through someone else's observations, and thus generally in an unfavorable light. Unlike the slaves, however, they were never the object of discerning scholarly or literary attention, and there is no parallel in their written history to the breakthroughs recently achieved in the study of slaves and blacks. No Kenneth M. Stampp or Eugene D. Genovese has rescued their history from an unsympathetic Ulrich B. Phillips; indeed, they never had a Phillips to recount their story systematically even if distortedly. No Stanley M. Elkins has suggested that the devices of social science and comparative history might uncover the psychological and sociological consequences of the class discrimination that kept them enthralled. No John W. Blassingame has sought out the interior history of their community—their family organization, folk beliefs, Elizabethan cultural survivals, or distinctive religious forms—to understand the positive forces at work among them. No one has chronicled their aspirations and fears, or their perception of the world or the society of which they were a part. Only their foibles and pathologies are recorded. For accounts of them in the colonial period, one must depend on the derisions William Byrd II included in his *History of the Dividing Line* or the contumelies Charles Woodmason, a haughty Anglican clergyman, recorded in *The Carolina Backcountry on the Eve of Revolution.* Works of this kind are today considered unsatisfactory as sources for the history of slaves or blacks, but they are still widely cited in depicting poor whites. There are no "poor white narratives" that do for poor whites what the slave narratives do for slaves—record the positive dimension of their history—yet like the slaves the lowliest whites were outcasts in their own society. And like free blacks in plantation areas they were a third element in a social structure designed for two.

Within the class there were recognizable divisions between "poor whites" and whites who were merely poor. The distinction between these groups, which appeared early in the colonial period and runs throughout southern history, is an important one. It derives from differences in social attitudes and life styles. The whites who were merely poor consisted of those who were impoverished in material goods and opportunities but who accepted, more or less, middle-class values and definitions of success and would if they could have lived according to middle-class standards of conduct. Unlike "poor whites," they seemed not to have been a psychologically defeated or dispirited people, nor resigned to a fate they comprehended only as an edict of the gods. As a group they seem to have enjoyed limited mobility, though modest expectations and class disabilities left most of them where they began, on the lower but not lowest rungs of the social and economic ladder. Preoccupied with getting a meager living, they had scant time for politics and none at all for informed social protest. Uneducated, hardworking, as lacking in social grace as material comfort, they were withal independent-minded but without a politically useful sense of class grievance. Yet they were a dependent folk victimized by the plantation system and the inequities it fostered. Despite a general willingness to work, they had little success in an inequalitarian society, and the reason seems to have been both social and personal. Perhaps many of them aspired and failed, and many hardly aspired at all. Life was hard in either case and full of drudgery and modest prospects.

On the surface at least, "poor whites" did not aspire at all, though their inner longings remain largely a matter of conjecture. They were the ultimate white victims of the southern system, a defeated, hopeless people by middle-class standards, and largely helpless too. Dispirited and dispossessed, living wretched lives in isolation and ignorance, they suffered poverty and powerlessness and failure in a society organized around property and power and success. It might well be that the psychological scars inflicted upon them by the larger society were as great as those inflicted upon blacks by slavery. Certainly the sociological deprivations were almost as large.

Their origins are obscure, though some of them were descended from indentured servants and transported convicts. Certainly social and economic mobility among those groups was low. The categories of unfree white labor, which like African slavery were devised to solve the problem of labor shortage, consisted of individuals who bound themselves to servitude for a number of years, typically four to seven, in return for passage to the colonies. Perhaps a third or a half of all Europeans who came to the southern colonies came under some form of indenture, yet because the period of indenture was short, white servants were not a very high percentage of the population. In 1625, 487 of the 1,227 people in Virginia were indentured servants, though the proportion in later years was far lower than that. Perhaps one person in ten in the southern colonies in 1670 was indentured, and thereafter the influx of Africans reduced that figure.

The status of indentured servants was low, in some respects like that of the slaves. Servants were subject to special codes of laws which spelled out their obligations and disabilities but also their rights, which slaves did not have. They could be bought and sold and whipped, could not vote or engage in trade or marry without consent, and were often barred from the militia. However, their marriages were recognized by law, they could own property of their own, and the master's property was in their labor, not their person. As whites and Christians, they were protected against arbitrary and unnatural cruelties as well as inadequate maintenance, and entitled to specified freedom dues at the end of their service. They also had the important right of appeal to the courts.

Their degraded status gave rise to an unflattering reputation. Indentured servants were "for the most part men and women of low grade," wrote Abbott E. Smith, whose *Colonists in Bondage* (1947) is still the only general study of them, "lazy, unambitious, ignorant, prone to small crimes and petty evasions, an unsavory and sometimes a dangerous class." Perhaps those qualities manifested discontentment among servants as they did among slaves. Certainly the signs of discontent were strong. Criticism of their work was chronic; they ran away in numbers that were relatively much larger than for the slaves; and perhaps half of those who ran away were never apprehended.

What happened to the indentured servants after they became free is not always clear. The vast majority remained poor and anonymous, though a minority became substantial citizens and an occasional one like Daniel Dulany achieved distinction. From a study of land records before 1666, Thomas Jefferson Wertenbaker estimated that 30 percent to 40 percent of the landowners in Virginia had entered the colony under indenture. Of every ten servants who entered Virginia, Abbott E. Smith estimated that one became a prosperous landowner, one more became a useful but not a landowning citizen, and the other eight died while still servants, returned to Europe, or remained poor, landless, and declassed.

Origins of Racial Patterns

At the bottom of the social scale were the Afro-southerners, slave and free, who were separated from whites by lines of caste that were rigid and insurmountable. From the outset, the history of black southerners centered around factors of race and slavery, and their history is therefore a vital part of the story of sectional differentiation. The progression from racial distinction to racial discrimination and on to racist thinking and institutionalized racism began as soon as Europeans and Indians and Africans came together in Virginia, and its results were fateful for all. The Indians were virtually exterminated and the Africans degraded and reduced to slavery, while the whites developed a fierce pride of race and nationality that turned into the doctrine of white supremacy—"the belief," as Francis B. Simkins once put it, "that the excellences of Southern society are dependent upon the maintenance of Anglo-Saxon power and racial continuity."

Just how this came to be is not completely clear. In recent years, however, several impressive studies of race and related factors have thrown much light on the subject, even though none of the studies is specifically concerned with the evolution of southern distinctiveness.[5] As a result of these studies it is now possible to see how an array of disparate racial, ideological, environmental, economic, and institutional factors combined to create some of the most characteristic elements of southern life and identity. Perhaps the most important fact to emerge from these studies is that race and racism and the commitment to white supremacy were far more important in the early history of the South and the nation than was previously believed. It is now apparent that racial factors were a basic aspect of the social, economic, and political history of the colonial era, and that the differences that developed between the South and the North, as well as between the North American mainland and other parts of the New World, grew out of factors that were partly circumstantial and partly cultural.

The cultural factors that most influenced the racial history of Virginia and the South stemmed from the English heritage, and included not only the general forces that encouraged capitalism, the plantation system, and social hierarchy, but a syndrome of specific factors relating to race. These included a pronounced ethnocentrism that was intensified by contact with Africa, which in the minds of Englishmen underscored the cultural and physical differences between themselves and Africans and encouraged the former to regard the latter as backward, savage, and even animalistic. The resulting attitudes were reinforced by feelings of religious superiority and the connotations of black in the English language, and they preconditioned early Virginians to look upon Africans as an inferior people fit only to be exploited and "helped." This made the importation of African laborers acceptable to them, and as the number of Africans in the colony grew, gave rise to an increasing emphasis on racial distinctions in the society and in time produced slavery and hardened racial prejudice.

But these were not the only factors. In Virginia, and later in South Carolina and elsewhere, the position of the planter class was unchallenged by other economic groups and its power was thus unchecked by political or institutional rivals. The crown's power inside the colonies was compromised by the distance from London, and the Protestant church was fragmented and dependent. As a result the planter-capitalist class was relatively unrestrained, and could develop an institution like slavery to fit its own imperatives. The nature of the racial arrangements that eventually emerged in Virginia and the South thus derived in part from what Stanley M. Elkins has called "the liberal, Protestant, secularized, capitalist culture" inherited from England as contrasted to "the conservative, paternalist, Catholic, quasi-medieval culture" that influenced slavery and racial development in Spanish and Portuguese America. One of the things that seems to have grown out of these differences between the two areas was the greater rigidity of racial thought and practice in British America, including the South.

At least part of this rigidity, however, was the result of circumstances, for these too differed greatly between the South and Iberio-America. Among these circumstances, demographic factors, especially the relative numbers and sex ratios among whites and blacks, were most important in influencing the nature of slavery and racial attitudes in the South. In both of these, the southern colonies were notably different from all other areas in which African slavery became significant in the New World. In the South, the proportion of blacks was never overwhelming except in coastal South Carolina, a fact that helps explain the differences between that colony and the rest of the South. Whites were a majority in all the colonies except South Carolina, almost everywhere a substantial majority, and within their own society enjoyed a fully developed social and sexual life. In contrast to the situation in early Brazil, sexual ratios were always balanced in the South, and normal family life was everywhere the rule. The practice of plantation owners' or overseers' taking Negro concubines or wives never developed, and even illicit liaisons were not socially acceptable. As a result, racial intermixture was discouraged, acknowledgment of mulatto offspring frowned upon among whites, and racially and socially mulattoes were lumped together with blacks. There were thus only two racial groups in the South (and the United States), white and black, the latter including everyone with any known or recognizable nonwhite ancestry. The multiple social gradations based on degrees of racial intermixture that had social significance in Iberio-America never developed in North America, nor did what Carl N. Degler calls the "mulatto escape hatch," whereby individuals of mixed ancestry were assigned an intermediate social status that permitted those of talent and accomplishment to achieve places of distinction and responsibility. By blurring racial distinctions, this practice tended to moderate the social meaning of race in Iberio-America, and its absence from the South further encouraged the racial rigidity previously mentioned.

Emergence of Slavery

But this was in the future, a future no one foresaw when a Dutch frigate brought "twenty negars" to Jamestown in the summer of 1619. Not much is known of these earliest Afro-southerners; not even their status in the colony is clear. Some historians have assumed that they were slaves, others that they were indentured servants; some have pictured them as objects of racial prejudice from the outset, others as largely unaffected by prejudice. The most exhaustive investigation of the subject, Winthrop D. Jordan's *White Over Black* (1968), concludes that the surviving evidence is too scant to make definitive generalizations about the status of black Virginians for a generation after 1619. From the beginning, however, blacks were set apart in Virginia in ways that had invidious implications. None of the twenty-two counted in the 1624 census was given a last name, for example, and several were given no name at all but listed as "one negar," "A Negors Woman," or "negors." Only an occasional white was listed so impersonally. This pattern was repeated in later censuses and other public records. In land records blacks were sometimes listed as "Ape" or "Monkey" as well as "Caesar" or "Pedro."[6]

After a generation the evidence becomes clearer, and points to two conclusions: that the status of some blacks was lower than that of white servants, and that racial patterns were evolving toward slavery. That institution did not exist in Britain, and white Virginians did not at once see it as the solution to their labor problem. Not for two generations did it achieve mature form. There is clear evidence that some blacks were slaves by the 1640s; that is, they were being held in lifetime servitude and their status was passed on to their offspring. Others, however, were serving limited indentures, and some were free men and property owners and perhaps voters as well. The trend, however, was away from these things. As early as 1639 Maryland passed a law invidiously distinguishing "slaves" from servants and free people, and in 1640 an instance of lifetime servitude appears in the records of Virginia. The latter involved three runaway servants, two whites and one black, who had been apprehended. As punishment, the court sentenced the whites to four years additional servitude, but directed that "the third being a negro named John Punch shall serve his said master or his assigns for the time of his natural life here or elsewhere."

Thereafter the evidence of slavery becomes more and more plentiful, and in the 1660s the institution was recognized and protected by law in both the Chesapeake colonies. The degradation of the Negro was thenceforth a matter of public policy. "In the last quarter of the seventeenth century," Winthrop D. Jordan has written, "the trend was to treat Negroes more like property and less like men, to send them to the fields at younger ages, to deny them automatic existence as inherent members of the community, to tighten the bonds of their personal and civil freedom, and correspondingly to loosen the traditional restraints on the master's freedom to deal with his human property as he saw fit." By the end of the seventeenth century slavery had achieved its modern form in the Chesapeake colonies and would soon do so in Carolina. In 1705 Virginia codified its laws relating to slavery, and in 1723 prohibited manumission and denied blacks the right to vote. Interracial marriage had been proscribed in 1691.

These developments reflected the emergence of a new racial factor: the number of blacks and their proportion of the population had become large enough to arouse fear among whites. In Virginia blacks were only 3.5 percent of the population in 1660 and 7 percent in 1680, but by 1700 they were 27 percent and thirty years later 40 percent. In South Carolina they were perhaps 65 percent of the population as early as 1720, and they remained about that proportion throughout the colonial period. By 1730 more than a third of the non-Indian population of the southern colonies were blacks.

These figures are of transcendant importance. Long before the antislavery movement began, white southerners came to look upon slavery not just as a device for controlling labor or making money but as a necessary means of controlling an alien and fearsome race. The number of blacks in their midst was far greater than in the northern colonies and far less than in the Caribbean or Brazil. It was large enough to alarm them and make white supremacy seem necessary for their own protection and large enough to tie their economic life to racial exploitation, but it was not so large that they had to make the kind of accommodations to Africans the Portuguese made in Brazil. This simultaneous fear and ability to dominate determined the pattern of racial policy and racial thought that eventually came to be regarded as distinctively southern. "Every aspect of life bore the impress of the slave," as Carl Bridenbaugh observed in *Myths and Realities: Societies of the Colonial South* (1952), "from the introduction of Africanism in the language to the crystallization of social needs and customs in provincial legal codes. Without freedom, articulateness, leadership, property, status or power, the blacks were nevertheless one of the determining factors in Chesapeake society."

Why, then, did African slavery develop and prosper in the southern colonies? Because of the significance of this question, it might be well to recapitulate the answers to it. Racial and ethnocentric attitudes brought from England made it easy for early Virginians to rationalize the exploitation of nonwhite and non-Christian peoples, especially Africans, whom they regarded as barbarous, heathen, libidinous, and cursed. The Virginians' social vision did not encourage the exclusion of people regarded as unassimilable, as did that of early New Englanders. Geography encouraged staple agriculture, land policy facilitated the acquisition of large estates, and both of those things necessitated a large unskilled labor force. The abundance of land and scarcity of labor made regimentation and exploitation of the work force necessary for the accumulation of wealth. Africa proved to be the only available source of a large and exploitable labor supply. Enslaving the Indians produced special difficulties, including problems of security, while indentured servants were whites and Christians, which circumscribed the masters' prerogatives, and the system of brief indentures was economically undesirable. The experience of the Spanish colonies, where African slavery first appeared in the New World, was an inviting example. Finally, the planters who wanted slavery were in a position to get what they wanted.

These things account for the origins of African slavery; other factors explain its growth. Once the institution matured, it proved extraordinarily profitable and took on an economic life of its own. This in turn encouraged the rapid importation of Africans, which then gave the institution a racial life of its own. It *was* a peculiar institution, one that produced both racial fears and high profits while also holding out a promise of racial and class control. Its spread was therefore a contest between fear and avarice, to borrow a phrase from David Brion Davis. Eventually, its racial aspects came to loom larger than its economic features, though both were important and always intertwined. Whether slavery was originally a cause or consequence of racial prejudice among whites, it became a major perpetuator of prejudice. It degraded blacks, inflated the self-perception of whites, poisoned race relations by destroying the basis for interracial trust, and dictated the context in which every consideration of race policy took place.

Afro-southerners

In all this, the interior history of Afro-southerners is largely unknown. All the difficulties of studying their past are multiplied severalfold for the colonial period. The kinds of sources that become available in the pre-Civil War generation—slave narratives and autobiographies, for example, and the writings of free blacks and abolitionists—are almost completely lacking for the long period before the American Revolution. The result is a dearth of studies and relatively little knowledge of the first two centuries of Afro-southern history.[7] Significantly, this was the time of arrival for almost all the Africans who ever came to America and the South, and thus the period of their Americanization.

The pattern of their arrival was strikingly unlike that of Africans brought to other areas of the New World. According to the authoritative estimates in Philip D. Curtin's *The Atlantic Slave Trade: A Census* (1969), only about 427,000 Africans were ever imported into what became the United States, and of these, 54,000 were brought in illegally after 1808. These figures contrast markedly with the estimated 3,647,000 Africans carried to Brazil and the 4,040,000 brought to the Caribbean islands. They also suggest an important difference between the history of Afro-southerners and that of other African populations in the New World. Afro-southerners, who constituted about nine-tenths of all Afro-Americans at the end of the colonial period, not only reproduced themselves but grew rapidly from natural increase. This was not the case in the Caribbean or Brazil, and the reason seems to stem from the demographic factors mentioned earlier. Southern planters lived with their families among their slaves, and encouraged family life and thus balanced sexual ratios among the slaves. This, plus the additional fact that the average slave holding was much smaller in the South than the Caribbean or Brazil, prevented the ills of absentee ownership from emerging in the South, and enhanced the paternal aspects of slavery there. The normal sexual and family life which thus developed among Afro-Americans was unique among the large African populations in the New World.

The vast majority of Africans brought to the South arrived in the eighteenth century, especially in the three decades after 1730 and in the 1790s. The slave trade continued throughout the colonial period but was halted altogether during the revolution and resumed thereafter only for short times by the southernmost states. This means that most of the Africans who came to the South arrived early. By the Revolution, the proportion of native Africans in the population must have begun to diminish, and its rapid fall thereafter weakened African cultural forms. This, coupled with the fact that blacks were always a minority in the South, meant that African culture left relatively a much smaller imprint in the South than in the Caribbean or parts of Brazil.

The Americanization—southernization?—of the Africans must certainly be the most unknown major subject in the South's history. That it was a difficult process can be inferred from many sources, as can the resistance of Africans and Afro-southerners to the various forms of discrimination they encountered. Slaveowners were plagued by recalcitrant and runaway slaves, by conspiracies and suspected conspiracies, by individual acts of sabotage and sometimes of violence, and occasionally by organized unrest and revolt. In the midst of the influx of Africans in the 1740s, a white observer described a problem that must have been widespread. "To be sure," he wrote, "a *new Negro,* if he must be broke, either from Obstinacy, or, which I am more apt to suppose, from Greatness of Soul, will require more hard Discipline than a young Spaniel; You must really be surprised by their Perseverance; let an hundred Men shew him how to hoe, or drive a Wheelbarrow, he'll still take the one by the bottom, and the other by the Wheel; and they often die before they can be conquered."

This was difficult enough, but problems relating to racial security were occasionally a more acute concern. As early as the 1670s white Virginians began to speak of slave conspiracies, and in time the anxiousness that underlay their remarks became a generalized fear throughout the South. "In many areas it was a gnawing, gut-wringing fear, intermittently heightened by undeniable instances of servile discontent," Winthrop D. Jordan has written. "Every planter knew that *the* fundamental purpose of the slave laws was prevention and deterrence of slave insurrection." The fear was strongest in coastal South Carolina, where the concentration of blacks was greatest and where the most sustained wave of slave unrest occurred. In 1711 a contemporary described whites there as filled with "great fear and terror," and for three decades thereafter episodes of unrest and violence flared periodically. In 1720 near Charleston several slaves were burned alive and others transported out of the colony for their involvement in a plot, and a decade later in the same area another major conspiracy was uncovered. The most serious wave of slave unrest in the colonial South occurred in the environs of Charleston in 1739. In the most significant incident, a group of slaves led by Cato captured a storehouse of arms near Stono and after attacking whites in the area sought to escape to Spanish Florida. Thirty whites and forty-four blacks were killed in the attendant fighting. The next year another plot involving a reported 200 blacks was uncovered, and ruthlessly put down. Fifty slaves were hanged, ten a day for five days, as an example to blacks. Later in the same year fire swept the city of Charleston and blacks were suspected of arson. Two of their number were executed.

And thus it went. Racial slavery, an institution that developed unthinkingly, came in time to absorb an inordinate amount of the time and energies of the southern people.

The Indians

The history of the colonial South, especially its racial dimension, is illuminated by the story of the Indians who originally inhabited the area and whose displacement was an integral aspect of the process of the section's growth. The story, however, has never been integrated into the section's history. General histories of the South treat Indians only in passing, if at all, and those of Indians, even southern Indians, ignore the South altogether. Yet from the settlement of Jamestown in 1607 until the last Cherokee was forcibly removed from Georgia in 1838, the fortunes of Indians and the South were closely related. Throughout this long period, Indian policy was a vital concern of white southerners, and relations with the white man dominated the history of southern Indians.[8]

At the time of English settlement, the South was sparsely populated by several Indian groupings. In tidewater Virginia the Powhatans, a confederacy of several small tribes of the Algonquin family, lived in perhaps 200 villages lightly ruled by an "emperor" the English called Powhatan. To the south of them, in North Carolina, were the Tuscaroras, of the Iroquoian family, and below them, in what is now South Carolina, Georgia, Florida, and Alabama, a much larger grouping of several major tribes, whom whites called the Creeks. To the west in present-day Mississippi were the Choctaws and Chickasaws, and to the north, in southern Appalachia, the Cherokees. Like the Tuscaroras, the Cherokees were Iroquoian, while the Creeks, Choctaws, and Chickasaws were Muskhogeans.

Despite differences in language, ancestry, and environment, the southern Indians had much in common. They were sedentary village peoples, subsisting on agriculture, hunting, and fishing, and practiced a degree of social and economic communalism. They were not warlike, though they were less placid than some of the Caribbean tribes, and their lives were generally tranquil and unstrenuous. They had a high regard for human life, and before the whites came engaged in little intertribal warfare. The individual lived in a society that weighed lightly upon him, that minimized intratribal distinctions, and promoted cooperation and solidarity. His life was slow-paced, his living gregarious.

The coming of white men changed things dramatically. The first whites came as traders, bringing new weapons and tools that altered life styles, improved creature comforts, and upset traditional inter- as well as intratribal relationships. Traditional skills fell into disuse, and a dependence on the white man's goods was created. Intertribal rivalries were generated by efforts to secure trade goods, chiefly animal hides and slaves. The slaves were captured in warfare and most of them were sold to white traders who sold them to the West Indies. In 1708 the slave population of South Carolina included 1,400 Indians as well as 4,100 Africans, and in 1716 export duties were paid on 308 Indian slaves shipped from Charleston to the Indies. Indian slavery, however, never became widespread, and other factors were more responsible for the eventual disappearance of the Indians. Competition for hunting grounds intensified as game stocks thinned out. The exploitation of traditional resources, facilitated by firearms, spread at an accelerating pace, and the resulting ecological crisis helped seal the Indians' fate. Between 1699 and 1715, for example, England imported an annual average of almost 54,000 deer skins from Carolina, and in 1748 alone almost 160,000 deer skins were shipped from Charleston.

Human resources were similarly depleted, by European diseases to which Indians had no immunity and by the warfare that often resulted from the white man's insatiable lust for land. Warfare between whites and Indians, as well as Indians and Indians, began in early Virginia and lasted until the Jacksonian era. When Jamestown was first settled, the Powhatan confederacy, in whose territory the settlement occurred, had a population of eight or nine thousand in tidewater Virginia, five thousand of them, according to John Smith's estimate, within sixty miles of Jamestown. In the early years the colony's survival was due in part to supplies from the Indians, though relations between the settlers and Indians were characterized by mistrust and often punctuated by violence. The stereotypes that later distorted white thinking had not yet crystallized, however. "Although the country people be very barbarous," John Smith wrote of the Powhatans, "yet have they amongst them such government, as that their Magistrates for good commanding, and their people for due subjection, and obeying, excel many places that would be counted very civil." "They are of body lusty, strong, and very nimble," wrote an English minister in the early years. "They are a very understanding generation, quick of apprehension, sudden in their dispatches, subtle in their dealings, exquisite in their inventions, and industrious in their labour."

Yet the settlers could deal with the Indians only in ways based on their European experience. Accordingly, they cultivated the chief of the Powhatans, Wahunsonacock, crowned him "emperor," and renamed him Powhatan. Cajoled and pressured and then flattered by the attention he received, Wahunsonacock made concessions to the Virginians, but this combined with instances of insolent treatment and growing pressure for land to rouse the ire of some Powhatans. In 1622, four years after Wahunsonacock was succeeded by Opechancanough, "a Man of large stature, noble Presence, and extraordinary Parts," they attacked the white colony with the aim of destroying it. They almost succeeded, killing 347 colonists before being repelled. In the aftermath the colonists changed their Indian policy from guile and strategy to calculated hostility. "Our hands which before were tied with gentleness and fair usage," wrote one of them, "are now set at liberty by the treacherous violence of the Savages." Officials of the Virginia Company, under whose auspices the colony had been founded, ordered a war against the Indians and dispossession of those in the vicinity of Jamestown.

The Powhatans were pushed out of the environs of the settlement, but their power was not broken. In 1644, still led by Openchancanough, they staged another major attack, this time killing about 500 colonists. In this assault, however, Openchancanough himself was captured and shot, and the white counterattack was more successful. When it was over, the Powhatans were totally defeated, the survivors made tributaries and forced to concede that even their land was held by suffrance of the white man's king. Under threat of death, all of them were excluded from territory below the falls of the James and York Rivers. By 1669 the number of Powhatans was no more than 2,000 and the governor of Virginia exercised final authority over their government, including even the selection of chiefs.

The story of the Carolina Indians was longer and more involved, but the outcome was much the same. By the turn of the eighteenth century intertribal rivalries and the spread of white settlement were causing difficulties for these Indians, as were long-standing disputes between the British in Carolina, the Spanish in Florida, and the French along the lower Mississippi River. The latter factor was a perennial source of difficulty, for the various Indian confederacies often allied themselves with one or another of the European nations, and were inevitably drawn into their fights. In these alliances the Indians often supplied warriors for fights that were essentially contests between European empires. Thus in 1702 the Creeks furnished South Carolina 500 warriors to fight the Spanish, and two years later another 1,000. In this manner Indian often fought Indian, always to their own injury and frequently to the white man's advantage. Between 1690 and 1702 the Chickasaws and Choctaws waged intermittent war upon each other during which 2,600 warriors were killed and another 500 captured and sold to the Carolinians as slaves. In the Yamassee War, which began in 1715, the South Carolinians used Cherokee warriors to help them defeat the Yamassees, of the Creek nation, and the aftermath was a prolonged fight between Creeks and Cherokees in which "the British [i.e., the Carolinians] were clandestinely encouraging the Cherokees and Creeks in a policy of mutual self-destruction."

This successful use of the principle of divide and conquer illustrates the fatal weakness of the Indians, their inability to unite against a common threat. Indeed, they seem not to have comprehended the nature of the threat until it was too late. Whites, on the other hand, always showed a clear sense of purpose. Their dealings with Indians were calculated to achieve specific objectives, the most important of which was economic, the desire for land and trade, but since this sometimes created difficulties, economic considerations were often superseded by the need for security. In pursuing these goals, they operated on two assumptions commonly accepted by Europeans—first, that nonwhite and non-Christian people were somehow inferior to Europeans, and second, that the claims of such people to the land they occupied were not binding on Europeans. "Pocahontas is of a different and despised color," Governor Thomas Dale told John Rolfe when Rolfe proposed to marry her, "of different manners and uneducated; of a hated race, not one of whom has ever looked above the meanest of the colonists." The attitude toward Indian land rights was just as plainly put. According to the European doctrine of discovery, all territory not claimed by a Christian monarch could be so claimed by the monarch whose agents "discovered" it. As Thomas More put it in *Utopia,* taking land in such a manner was justified "when any people holdeth a piece of ground void and vacant to no good or profitable use: keeping others from the use and possession of it, which, not-withstanding, by the law of nature ought thereof to be nourished and relieved."

Another principle that guided Indian policy was the perceived need to keep Indians and blacks apart. These groups had common grievances against whites, and their separation was a matter of necessity wherever their numbers were large. In 1742 in South Carolina a special Committee on Indian Affairs warned against permitting Indians to visit the colony and "particularly in regard to their talking and having too great Intercourse with our Slaves, at the out-plantations, where they camp." There was equal concern to keep slaves out of the Indian territory. "To prevent the Indian country becoming an Asylum for Negroes is a Matter of the Utmost consequence to the prosperity of the provinces," wrote the superintendent of Indian affairs in 1767. The best policy for whites was one that kept Indians and blacks aroused against each other, which was accomplished by circulating stories of Indian atrocities among blacks and rewarding Indians for capturing runaway slaves. Treaties with Indians routinely required the return of runaways. "We make use of a Wile for our pres[en]t Security," wrote a South Carolina minister in 1725, "to make Indians & Negro's a checque upon each other least by their Vastly Superior Numbers we should be crushed by the one or the other."

The antagonism between Indians and whites was thus basic. Indians were neither imitative nor submissive, and generally resisted all effort to "civilize" them. As a result, whites undertook little missionary activity among the tribes, and that little was unsuccessful. Because of the underlying antagonism between the two peoples, Indians suffered almost as much from whites who sought to befriend them as from those who worked to destroy them. Missionaries and philanthropists undermined tribal culture in order to "civilize" them; Indian traders corrupted tribal ways and made them dependent on whites; land speculators and settlers wanted their land and were generally willing to eliminate them to get it. In every case Indians were losers. Yet apart from coastal areas, they remained in control of their lands at the time of the Revolution. Wholesale dispossession began only after white Americans had achieved their own nationhood.

Rise of the Upcountry

By 1770 society in the southern colonies had achieved maturity and stability. An air of permanence, even tradition, had settled over older areas. Social unrest was limited and meliorative in nature, and largely confined to the upcountry. It was important, however, for the upcountry—the piedmont, the vast land between tidewater and Appalachia— was rapidly becoming the most dynamic area of the South. By the middle of the colonial period, settlers had begun filtering into the area, though the pace of settlement was slow by later standards. By 1750 Carolinians had moved inland for 150 miles or more, and Indian traders had long since crossed the Mississippi. The expansion of Virginia had occurred even earlier than this. Back in 1714 Governor Alexander Spottswood had established a settlement on the Rapidan, and by 1770 Scotch-Irish and German settlers were streaming down the western valleys from Pennsylvania. By the time of the Revolution, permanent settlements had been established in present-day Kentucky and Tennessee, and control of the West was an increasing problem for colonial and royal officials.

At the end of the colonial period the South was thus an area of rapid growth. Inevitably, expansion into the wilderness brought changes in the tenor of life as well as in institutional structures. Social and economic forms brought from elsewhere loosened on the frontier and re-formed in new and somewhat different ways. Class divisions were less precise, the influence of great planters was less pervasive, and opportunity for ambitious, risk-taking men greater than in the tidewater. Perhaps also the crasser aspects of life were intensified; certainly, as Arthur K. Moore has shown in *The Frontier Mind* (1957), they became more apparent.

The spread of settlement into the piedmont thus represented an important step in the evolution of the South and southern identity. It was in this area that Wilbur J. Cash located his "man at the center," and here he found the quintessence of the South. To whatever degree Cash's observations have merit, they suggest that the key to sectional identity was not in the tidewater, where aristocratic pretensions were too great, but in the upcountry. They also suggest that sectional identity was a product of backcountry environment acting upon tidewater institutions, and of the modified social and economic order that emerged from the interaction. This process, it should be noted, continued until the cotton kingdom was settled in the first generation of the nineteenth century, and in Cash's view of it, frontier influences tended to prevail over those of the tidewater.

This is obviously an important viewpoint, and not to be rejected out of hand. That a modification of tidewater forms took place is indisputable, and that it intensified the qualities Cash found in his typical southerner is also apparent. Yet the significance of the frontier influence is easily overstated, for no tidewater institution that formed an essential element of southern distinctiveness was shattered by the frontier. In this sense the frontier influence was more apparent than real, and in this sense too it was not the frontier that imposed itself on the tidewater, but the tidewater that set perimeters around the frontier influence. The frontier weakened the tidewater respect for formal culture, encouraged atomistic individualism, materialism, and direct action, and intensified the hold of ruralism and isolation on southern life. But it altered neither institutions nor ideas in a fundamental way. The plantation prospered in the backcountry, especially in the lower South, even though its influence was never as complete as in the tidewater. With the plantation came slavery, which fastened itself on the piedmont, especially in the lower South, and united piedmont and tidewater in a common concern over racial matters. The only tidewater institution that failed to move westward was the Anglican church. Unable to adapt its structure, theology, or ritual to the new environment, that church never had much appeal to upcountrymen. They turned instead to Presbyterianism, which many of them brought with them, or to Baptism or Methodism, whose individualized theology, emotionalized services, and casual forms of church governance better fitted backcountry society. The change, however, meant no break in sectional values. For all the apparent differences between Anglicanism and the newer churches, none of the churches offered a religion incompatible with what came to be known as the southern way of life. The roots of the South would therefore seem to be more deeply embedded in tidewater than piedmont. The piedmont's contribution was substantial, but more in the nature of modification than origination.

In spite of all this and the other developments discussed in this chapter, the South was not yet a social and cultural reality in 1770. Three things were still lacking: an American nationalism against which to contrast a conscious sectionalism; an antislavery movement strong enough to be perceived as a threat to the lynchpin of the section's social, economic, and racial structure; and a feeling of besiegement and grievance strong enough to make group consciousness an overriding concern of public life. The white people south of Pennsylvania did not yet think of themselves as an embattled "us" against a powerful and threatening "them." That feeling would come soon, however, and with it would come the South.

The Emerging South

The question of when the South became a distinctive, self-conscious section is obviously central to an understanding of southern history and identity. Yet it has never received much systematic attention, and is in fact one of the most confused subjects in the historical literature. No one has ever traced the history of sectional consciousness in detail over the crucial years from 1774 to 1833, and there is no agreement even on the criteria for defining sectionalism or the South. There is thus no interpretive framework for gauging the evolution of either of those subjects. The perspectives of most historians have been molded by research in less encompassing subjects, and as a result the emergence of the South has been variously dated from the Constitutional Convention of 1787 to the nullification crisis of 1833, and occasionally even later than that. Its immediate cause has been just as disparately explained as an outgrowth of the political controversies attendant upon nation-making, especially the debates over the Constitution or the financial policies of Alexander Hamilton; or of any one of various racial incidents between the Santo Domingan uprising of 1791 and Nat Turner's rebellion in 1831; or of the panic of 1819 or the controversy over admitting Missouri to the Union in 1819–21; or of any one of a number of subsequent sectional crises.

The confusion on this subject is strikingly illustrated in the nine-volume *History of the South* (1948–1967) edited by Wendell Holmes Stephenson and E. Merton Coulter for the Louisiana State University Press, the volumes of which constitute the most detailed and impressive history of the South ever written. Four of the volumes, which together cover the years from 1763 to 1861, deal in one degree or another with the rise of sectional consciousness, but in each of them the author begins by pointing out that sectional consciousness did not exist when his volume commenced but ends by claiming that it was in full flower when his volume terminated. "The South had emerged as a section and the Southerners as a people different from Northerners," John R. Alden wrote of the year 1789 in *The South in the Revolution, 1763–1789* (1957). "There could be no sectionalism until there was a spirit of nationalism," Thomas P. Abernethy wrote of the same year in *The South and the New Nation, 1789–1819* (1961), and nationalism, he insisted, did not exist until after 1790. Once that began to develop, however, sectional consciousness did too.

The next two volumes follow the same pattern. "There was no Southern political party, no slave-state bloc in Congress, and no sentiment of Southern nationalism," Charles S. Sydnor wrote of the year 1819 in *The Development of Southern Sectionalism, 1819–1848* (1948), and the southern people were "comparatively unaware of and almost totally undisturbed by" the differences between themselves and northerners. But by 1848, Sydnor believed, they had developed a pronounced minority psychology and sectional feelings among them were bitter and pervasive. In *The Growth of Southern Nationalism, 1848–1861* (1953), however, Avery O. Craven found "only a superficial unity" among southerners in 1848, and noted that "much of fear and hatred had yet to be added" before sectionalism became the primary fact of southern life.

Obviously this subject needs attention. To some extent the disagreement among the authors just cited reflects a more fundamental disagreement over what the South is and how it got to be that way. Viewed in the light of recent scholarship,[1] these and other older accounts give too little attention to racial factors in dating and explaining the origins of southern consciousness. It now seems clear that the controlling forces behind this development grew out of demography and other racial circumstances, including the fear those circumstances generated among whites, which in turn led to a preoccupation with racial matters in public policy. To put it in more traditional terms, it was the racial implications of sectional differences that were controlling, whether slavery, the plantation economy, political rivalries, life styles, or social values. This is not to say that the other dimensions of those things were unimportant. But without the acuteness of feeling derived from racial concerns, southern consciousness and the sectionalism it inspired are reduced to little more than the kind of political and economic rivalries that run throughout American history and involve many other groups of people besides southerners. Without the racial dimension, the emotionalism and the staying power of the southerners' concerns are robbed of substance and made explicable only in terms of personal or group derangement.

A recognition of the importance of racial factors has another positive result. It focuses the attention of those who would understand sectional consciousness on the internal history of the South, on what southerners were saying and doing to each other, rather than on their "foreign policy," their dealings with outsiders. This makes sectional consciousness explicable in southern terms, and shows it to have been a product of the most basic developments of southern life. These developments rather than congressional debates or the South's role in national politics are the best gauge of sectional consciousness.

All of this is preliminary to these basic conclusions, which will be demonstrated in the remainder of this chapter: In the last quarter of the eighteenth century, there transpired a series of developments, distinct in origin and unrelated in purpose, that together gave birth to the sectional South. During that period, the American nation was established and the American people developed pronounced feelings of nationality and self-confidence. Southerners shared these feelings no less than northerners, but they came to share something else that northerners did not, a sense of foreboding about the future and their place in the nation. White people from Maryland to Georgia had long sensed that they had common interests and concerns that set them apart from the blacks in their midst. Now, as the nation took shape, they came to see that certain interests and concerns also set them apart from other Americans. A mounting awareness of that fact began to overlay the diversities that had previously divided them, and by the end of the 1790s their sense of foreboding had become sufficiently infused with feelings of grievance and besiegement to engender the characteristic features of sectional consciousness and identity.

Once the ingredients essential to this development were present, the development itself depended upon certain steps that would link the ingredients together and thereby give sectional consciousness a life of its own. The first of these steps was the achievement of nationhood, for nationalism was a necessary precondition of sectionalism. This was completed between 1789 and 1797, as President George Washington fashioned a functioning government under the new Constitution. The second step was the occurrence of a series of events, which are discussed below, that dramatized the South's racial distinctiveness and joined the sectional and racial perceptions of white southerners into a single identity. This was the crucial step, and was completed between the Constitutional Convention of 1787 and the slave rebellion led by Gabriel Prosser near Richmond, Virginia, in 1800. What this did was tie southern identity to an acutely felt and widely recognized peculiar interest. The next step was the intrusion of national politics and economic rivalry upon that interest, which sharpened awareness of the interest by dramatizing the extent to which the interest was synonymous with the southern way of life. One further step was necessary, the development of a feeling among southerners that their peculiar interest and thus their way of life, indeed their very safety, was threatened by outsiders, whether the federal government, antislavery forces, or even impersonal historical forces. This too occurred between the Revolution and the turn of the nineteenth century, and coupled with the conviction that the threat was undeserved, it generated that special sense of grievance that was at the heart of southern identity. When that occurred, the South had become a conscious section.

Having said all this, several reservations must be entered before examining this process in depth. Sectional consciousness was not only an expression of perceived interests but a matter of symbols and subtleties that sometimes defy positivist description. It was the product of a long evolution, and no single incident can be said to pinpoint its appearance. If one needs a single episode from which to date it, Gabriel Prosser's slave conspiracy is perhaps as good as any, but even that represented no sharp break in the course of southern history. On the contrary, the intensity of sectional feelings continued to ebb and flow at least until the early 1830s as perceptions of the degree of immediate danger to southern interests rose and fell. This is but to say that the rise of southern consciousness did not mean the end of American nationalism in the South. In fact nationalist feelings remained quite strong. National and sectional loyalties are only potentially contradictory, and only once in their history, in 1860–61, were southerners forced to choose absolutely between them.

The American Revolution and Southern Consciousness

The first Continental Congress, which met in 1774, was the initial act of cooperation by the American colonies, and the war for independence, which began the following year, was the first national undertaking by the American people. Both in and out of Congress, white southerners played a major role in these undertakings, and did so with a genuine commitment to national interests. Like northerners, they recognized the necessity of national cooperation and the value of things that encouraged national unity. "The distinctions between Virginians, Pennsylvanians, New Yorkers, and New Englanders, are no more," said Patrick Henry at the time of the first Continental Congress. "I am not a Virginian, but an American."

National unity, however, was more easily exhorted than achieved, and as if to recognize that fact, Henry omitted the South Carolinians, who were perhaps more conscious of their own special interests than any other group in the country. Leaders of the revolution had remarkable success in creating and sustaining a national cause, but throughout the revolutionary era Americans remained a people with strong local attachments. Clearly, each area of the country had "sectional" interests, for every national policy tended to benefit one or another area more than the others. Thus "sectional" divisions appeared in the first Continental Congress over such things as slavery, economic policy, and the powers of the national government, and reappeared in all subsequent Congresses. The agreements of association adopted by the first Congress to bind the colonies in a political union provided that the overseas slave trade would be halted and the shipment of goods to England embargoed, both of which actions affected the South and non-South in different degrees. The embargo created special hardships for the rice planters of Carolina and Georgia, and they sought to have their product exempted from its provisions.

Their effort was symbolic of the kinds of issues raised by the prospects of a war for independence. Would slaves be counted in apportioning taxes among the states? It made a great deal of difference, to southerners and nonsoutherners alike; the one would gain and the other lose, however the question was settled. Did slavery violate the principles of the Revolution and undercut the effort to achieve independence? More importantly for southerners, did the principles of the Revolution threaten slavery? Or did each threaten the other? How could slaves be utilized in the war without threatening slavery or white supremacy? Would blacks, slave or free, be permitted in the Continental army? Above all, did national union threaten any of the vital interests of white southerners? Such questions were never far from the surface.

Something important was happening. The encounter with outsiders and the prospects of national union heightened everyone's awareness of national interests, but that in turn meant defining local and thus sectional interests as well. For the first time in their history, southerners were forced to articulate their public interests, and the articulation made them more conscious of the interests and of their common concerns as southerners. (At the same time, a parallel process was enlarging their awareness of things that made them Americans.) In effect the rise of nationalism was generating a countercurrent of sectionalism. The South Carolinians saw it most clearly. One of them, William Henry Drayton, a delegate to the Continental Congress, voiced their doubts in debate over the Articles of Confederation, under which voting in Congress would be by states with the assent of only nine of the thirteen necessary for approving legislation. "When I reflect, that from the nature of the climate, soil and produce of the several states, a northern and southern interest in many particulars naturally and unavoidably rise," Drayton said, "I cannot but be displeased with the prospect, that the most important transactions in Congress, may be done contrary to the united opposition of Virginia, the two Carolinas and Georgia; states possessing more than one half of the whole territory of the confederacy; and forming, as I may say, the body of the southern interest." Under this arrangement, "the honor, interest and sovereignty of the south, are in effect delivered up to the care of the north," he warned his fellow southerners. "Do we intend to make such a surrender?"

The unease reflected in this query surfaced again and again in congressional debates between 1774 and 1787. Like most statements of the issue, this one cast sectional differences in economic and political rather than racial terms and explained the differences by environmental rather than social factors. This construction, however, cannot explain the alarm often expressed by southerners, for northerners were disinclined to interfere with vital southern interests and the central government was unable to do so. It is this fact that makes the more deeply felt but less pointedly spoken concerns over racial matters so important. The ideology of the Revolution, so compellingly stated in the Declaration of Independence and other state papers, underscored the emerging contradictions in southern society and forced southerners to confront them. The southerners came at once to see that the enlightened, democratic ideals that so appealed to them as revolutionaries were contradicted by slavery and racial attitudes they had always accepted without question. The rise of antislavery sentiment, first among Quakers and then among the evangelical churches, had a similar effect, exposing the contradictions between slavery and New Testament humanism, a basic source of moral values for most southerners. The abolition of slavery in the northern states, which was well underway before the war for independence was formally ended by the Treaty of Paris in 1783, underscored the meaning of that concentration. The criticism of slavery which accompanied these developments forced southerners to do something they had never done before, think systematically about race and slavery, and some of them were troubled by their thoughts.

This is not to suggest that they suddenly realized that slavery was "wrong," but to note that they came to see that it posed a dilemma for them. They could not easily reconcile ideal and reality. "It is evident, that the bondage we have imposed on the African, is absolutely repugnant to justice," said Arthur Lee of Virginia as early as 1764. "It is highly inconsistent with civil policy" for "it tends to suppress all improvements in arts and sciences," to "deprave the minds of the freemen," and to expose the community to "the destructive effects of civil commotion." Besides, "it is shocking to humanity, violative of every generous sentiment, [and] abhorrent utterly to the Christian religion."

Such condemnation was rare. Much more typical was a statement by Patrick Henry, a man more widely known for his preference for liberty above everything else. "Would anyone believe that I am master of slaves of my own purchase?" Henry asked in 1773; and his exculpation was one of the most poignant ever made by a southerner. "I am drawn along," he said, "by the general inconvenience of living here without them. I will not, I cannot justify it." This was not mere hypocrisy. Henry's dilemma was not unlike that of today's environmentalists who find it impossible to get rid of their air-polluting automobiles. They too are "drawn along by the general inconvenience of living here without them."

The spread of revolutionary ideology increased awareness of the gap between ideal and reality in the South, and the gap became a source of anxiety. In the convention that met to adopt a constitution for the new state of Virginia, someone objected that George Mason's language declaring "all men are by nature equally free and independent" seemed to apply to blacks and thus to threaten slavery. It had to be explained that the passage concerned only "constituent members" of society and thus excluded blacks. The objection was withdrawn.

Anxiety, however, was not so easily dealt with, for slavery was a practical as well as a theoretical problem, and one that repeatedly intruded into the war effort. In the fall of 1775, not long after the war began, Edward Rutledge of South Carolina asked Congress to instruct General Washington to discharge all blacks from the Continental army. The request, in the words of the Congressional clerk, was "strongly supported by many of the Southern delegates but so powerfully opposed that he lost the Point." Shortly thereafter, on his own initiative, Washington instructed recruiters to enlist no more Negroes. Though Congress approved the policy, the issue persisted. As Washington and Congress were excluding blacks from the patriot cause, Lord Dunmore, the royal governor of Virginia, issued a proclamation promising freedom to all slaves who joined the British effort to put down the rebellious Americans. Fearful of the consequences of this appeal—some 800 slaves responded to the short-lived offer—Congress removed the prohibition against free blacks enlisting in the army, and perhaps 5,000 eventually served. Nothing could better dramatize the potential threat the war posed to slavery, and thus to white supremacy, than this series of events. The potential, however, was never realized. The British refused to exploit the threat, for they were not racial revolutionaries either, and slavery remained intact. Nevertheless, the Virginia slaveholders lost perhaps 30,000 slaves during the war and those in South Carolina about 25,000.

These matters illustrate not only the nature of the American Revolution in the South but also the vastly different meaning the Revolution had for slaves and masters. For masters, and whites generally, the Revolution was a struggle for self-government; for slaves and blacks it was an uprising of reactionary classes that had the effect of strengthening slavery and the power of slaveholders by removing the restraints of imperial authority. The remarkable thing is thus not that slaveholders sought to keep their slave property, but that any blacks took the American side against the British. The Treaty of Paris not only acknowledged the independence of the United States but also guaranteed the return of runaway slaves to their owners. For black southerners the advent of nationhood thus meant not freedom or self-government, but reenslavement for some thousands who had run away to join the British cause.

The Impact of Antislavery

These things determined the context in which white southerners responded to the rise of antislavery during the revolutionary era. Antislavery was much more important outside than inside the region, but it was sufficiently widespread in the upper South to force southerners to confront the issues it raised. The sources of antislavery were at work in the South as well as the North. These included enlightenment environmentalism, which suggested that human nature was environmentally determined and thus malleable and improvable; the theory of natural rights, which assigned to "all men" certain unalienable rights, among which were life, liberty, property, and the pursuit of happiness; and Christian humanism, which included a belief in the equality of all believers before God. "By the 1760s broad changes in cultural values had undermined traditional religious and philosophical justifications for slavery," David Brion Davis has written. These changes had already produced the Great Awakening and the rise of evangelicalism, both of which emphasized individual salvation and the doctrine of immediatism. Now, acknowledging the "continuing tension between slavery and Christian ideals," they operated to weaken Biblical and historical justifications for the peculiar institution. The result was a growing conviction among northerners, and some southerners too, that slavery violated Christian doctrine.

This was an important factor in the emergence of southern consciousness. Rather suddenly, southerners came to realize that their way of life differed from that of the rest of the country in ways that other Americans considered undesirable if not reprehensible. The institution upon which their very safety depended, as they saw it, was scorned by the outside world.

Southerners and northerners thus responded in different ways to the rise of antislavery, but the difference was due to different circumstances rather than different moral standards. Both groups accepted racial inequality with no bother, but southern whites lived among large numbers of blacks and depended upon slave labor for their economic wellbeing. About 90 percent of all Afro-Americans lived in the South in 1790, where they constituted more than a third (36.4 percent) of the population. In New England, in contrast, blacks were but 1.7 percent of the population, and in the middle Atlantic states 5.3 percent. As southerners saw it, they confronted a condition, not a theory, and were in no position to give free rein to certain ideals of the enlightenment and evangelical Christianity. Yet they took those ideals seriously, and the gap between their beliefs and their institutions made them defensive and sometimes guilt-ridden as well. They felt compelled by circumstances to defend an institution and a set of social ideals that affronted the sensibilities of many outsiders and about which they themselves had ambivalent feelings. In later years their defensiveness turned to adamancy, and they were accused of hypocrisy and even schizophrenia. But the root of their problem was the set of circumstances that led them to act differently from northerners.

Pennsylvania Quakers were the first group of Americans to criticize slavery, and their initial criticisms were aimed not at southerners, but at Quaker slaveholders. As early as the 1740s Anthony Benezet of the Philadelphia Meeting had begun to speak against slavery, and soon the fervent John Woolman joined him. Their preachments were compelling, and other Friends were soon witnessing against slavery. In 1758 the Philadelphia Meeting condemned slavery, and in 1773 New England Quakers did likewise. Three years later, in 1776, the Philadelphia Meeting took the decisive step and voted to expel members who refused to manumit their bondsmen. With that action by the most important group of Friends in the country, American Quakers began formally dissociating themselves from slavery.

The meaning of this action was not lost upon southern slaveholders, even though Quaker antislavery had little direct impact in the South. Few southerners were Quakers and those few largely in Virginia and North Carolina, and fewer still were both Quakers and slaveholders. The Quaker example, however, soon spread to evangelical churches, and some of these were influential in the section. The principal denominations were Methodists, Baptists, and Presbyterians, and their transformation to antislavery and then back to proslavery in the last quarter of the eighteenth century is an important incident in the emergence of sectional consciousness.

The key role was that of the Methodists, who for two decades after 1774 exerted an influence against slavery in the upper South. In doing so they helped bring about the initial confrontation with slavery, only to capitulate themselves to slaveholders around the turn of the century and thereby bring peace between religion and slavery in the South. In 1774, not long after Methodism first appeared in the section, John Wesley, founder of the church in England, published *Thoughts upon Slavery*. His forthright condemnation of the institution influenced Bishops Francis Asbury and Thomas Coke to take a similar stand. In 1780 a conference of ministers of the church denounced the institution as "contrary to God, man, and nature, and hurtful to society," and four years later the General Conference in Baltimore that organized the Methodist Episcopal Church in this country voted to require all Methodists to manumit their slaves under threat of expulsion. The reaction to this was immediate, especially in Virginia and North Carolina, both centers of Methodist strength, and the next year the policy was suspended. The decision was fateful, for Methodists, slaveholders, and the South. The antislavery pronouncement had threatened to end the rapid growth of the church and doom Methodists to the fate of Quakers in the section, inconsequence. To avoid this, church leaders retreated. Methodists would not have to manumit their slaves after all; the denomination would remain open to slaveholders. More than that, the church soon abandoned antislavery altogether and by the turn of the century had begun to defend the institution. "Let our preachers," urged the General Conference of 1804, "from time to time as occasion serves, admonish and exhort all slaves to render due respect and obedience to the commands and interest of their respective masters."

Baptists and Presbyterians, two other rapidly growing denominations, followed a similar path. In 1785 the Baptist General Committee of Virginia, the largest organization of Baptists in the country, denounced slavery as "contrary to the word of God," and five years later repeated the judgment and urged that the institution be extirpated. By 1793, however, opposition to this position had developed and the Committee removed slavery from its deliberations on the grounds that it was a political rather than a religious subject. Presbyterians varied this pattern only by making their initial condemnation of slavery less emphatic.

By the turn of the nineteenth century, then, the largest and most dynamic churches in the South had made peace with slaveholders. The transformation was important, for with it the slaveholders had turned a challenge into a prop. Evangelicalism, like the enlightenment, proved to have an ambivalent meaning for blacks. "The canons of religious evangelicalism," as one historian has noted, "provided logical and emotional justification for the defense of slavery as well as for the assault upon the institution."[2] The explanation for this paradox is revealing. Evangelicalism encouraged an intense awareness of personal sin and a consequent compulsion to bring one's fellow man, black as well as white, to salvation. The saving of souls was thus more important than social policy. Evangelicals overcame their initial opposition to slavery by cultivating a greater concern for the souls of slaves—and slaveholders too—a concern they could act on only if they had the good will of slaveholders.

While this was happening, antislavery led to emancipation in the northern states, and that too was a major factor in the emergence of sectional consciousness. Before 1790 Pennsylvania and all the New England states had abolished slavery or made provision for its gradual elimination, and in 1799 and 1804 New Jersey and New York did likewise. By the latter year the Mason-Dixon line had come to mark the boundary between the slave and nonslave states as well as between those with large and small black populations. The division on both accounts was portentous.

Slavery and the Jeffersonian South

The significance assigned to slavery and racial factors in this discussion is much greater than that traditionally assigned those things in the Jeffersonian South—a term used here to encompass the section during the period of Jefferson's career in public office, 1775 to 1809. According to traditional interpretations of this period,[3] slavery was one of several things that distinguished the Jeffersonian South but not an especially important one. Southerners of Jefferson's day, this view runs, were apologetic but not sensitive about slavery, and without pronounced fears on racial matters. Antislavery was still unimportant, the slaves were quiescent, even satisfied with their lot, and, in the upper South at least, slavery was uneconomic and widely regarded as an undesirable and decaying institution. The planter class is pictured as having a deep aversion to slavery on pragmatic as well as philosophical grounds, but as not having emancipated its slaves because of a sincere belief that blacks could not function as responsible citizens and emancipation would therefore create more problems than it solved, including a decline in the physical wellbeing of slaves.

In broader terms, the Jeffersonian South is presented in traditional histories as a liberal, humane society committed to equalitarianism for whites and paternalism in the best sense for blacks. "The

Southerners of this period shared in the European movement of the Enlightenment," wrote Clement Eaton, whose many informative works on the pre-Civil War South suggest that sometime after 1820 the section fell from the high state of Jeffersonian liberalism to the much more benighted condition of Calhounian reaction. Men of the Jeffersonian South were "enthusiastic disciples" of Locke, Eaton wrote, devotees of a "liberalism" in which an "appeal to reason" was "the centralizing principle," progressives committed to "the natural rights theory that supported democracy and freedom of thought." They were also deists, freethinkers whose views of the world and their fellow man were uncluttered by obscurantism and obeisance to irrational authority.

There were of course all of these things in the Jeffersonian South, but there were other and less admirable things too. The rhetoric of the Jeffersonians is so appealing and their political performance so impressive that it is tempting to take them and their liberal professions at face value, and therefore downplay their illiberal actions and the force of the racial factors with which they had to deal. But when these factors are considered and rhetoric measured against action, a quite different picture of Jefferson's South emerges.[4] Slavery, it is now clear, was always profitable under proper management, and the peculiar institution was not dying, even in Jeffersonian Virginia. Antislavery sentiment among the Jeffersonians was weak, and far less significant than their proslavery actions. The Jeffersonians were caught in a dilemma. Their philosophical objections to slavery were compromised by the much stronger commitment to a life style that depended upon that institution, and whenever those two things conflicted, theoretical antislavery invariably lost out to self-interest.

But this was not the whole story. Southerners of Jefferson's day were preoccupied with race and racial fear and determined to maintain white supremacy. Thus the protection of slavery was a primary concern to them in national politics, and they reacted sharply whenever northerners criticized the institution or threatened action against it. Slavery, it is now apparent, was not about to disappear even from the upper South, any more than was the race problem, and the Founding Fathers from both sides of the Mason-Dixon line recognized that fact. Their decision "to try to ignore the challenge posed by slavery and racial prejudice" by sweeping it under the rug, so to speak, was, as Donald L. Robinson has remarked, "based not on confidence that the institution was vanishing, but on the conviction that slavery was ungovernable." The peculiar institution was so firmly entrenched as to be beyond the reach of the law.

This fact was manifested in the evolution of racial thought. Antislavery begot proslavery. In the Jeffersonian South proslavery was chiefly a matter of negative apologetics, but as William S. Jenkins noted in his *Pro-Slavery Thought in the Old South* (1935), all the positive defenses used after 1830 had been put forth between 1790 and 1820. This early version of the proslavery argument was a significant feature of the intellectual history of Jefferson's South, a product of racial and economic circumstances but notably influenced by Christian humanism and enlightenment liberalism.

The latter was especially important. Slavery is "contracy to the light of nature, to every principle of Justice and Humanity, and even good policy," declared Thomas Paine in 1775; and that statement seems a logical application of the revolutionary theory of natural rights. Negroes, Paine said, have "a natural, perfect right" to freedom, and their government "should, in justice, set them free, and punish those who hold them in slavery." The crux of the southerners' problem was to neutralize this idea, which Anthony Benezet, the Quaker, put more pointedly than anyone else. "If those solemn *truths,* uttered at such an awful crisis, are *self-evident,*" Benezet wrote in 1783, they must apply equally to white and black, "unless we can show that the African race are not *men.*" Yet "the very people who make these pompous declarations are slave holders, and, by their legislation, tell us, that these blessings were only meant to be the *rights of white men,* not of all *men.*"

The process by which southerners resolved this contradiction is not entirely clear. Pierre van den Berghe has observed that wherever whites and blacks have come together in significant numbers, whites have tended "to dichotomize humanity between men and submen (or the 'civilized' and the 'savages')" and apply their ideas of liberty and natural rights to "civilized" folk alone, whom they designate "the people." This idea helps explain what happened in the Jeffersonian South when whites completed the intellectual rationalization of slavery. As rationalizations often do, this one seemed to reconcile incompatible things and thereby enabled slaveholders to fight a revolutionary war in the cause of human freedom. It had important social results also. It encouraged racial paternalism by muting some of the harshness implicit in the exclusion of blacks from "the people," while making it possible to extend "the blessings of liberty" to whites of all social and economic classes. In this way the justification of slavery for blacks enabled white men of conservative instinct to accept democracy for the mass of whites. The existence of slavery, moreover, made all whites more jealous of their own liberties. Where slavery exists, as Edmund Burke put it, "those who are free are, by far, the most proud and jealous of their freedom. Freedom to them is not only an enjoyment, but a kind of rank and privilege."

The defense of slavery was thus an integral part of the liberal ideology of the Jeffersonian South, an intrinsic aspect of the defense of individual and property rights and of the white man's sense of his own wellbeing. Grounded in the philosophy of John Locke, the southerners' liberal ideology emphasized individual rights and drew a sharp distinction between slavery and freedom. "According to the liberal creed," Carl N. Degler has written, "all men are created equal; the thrust of the ideology is in the direction of freedom and equality. It follows therefore that slaves ought to be either free or declared to be something less than men—as women were."

But the defense of slavery rested upon pragmatic grounds as well. The slaves represented too large an investment to be given up voluntarily. At an average price of $200 each, the value of those in Virginia alone was more than $60 million in 1790, and the value rose rapidly after the middle of the decade. In Richmond the price of a prime field hand was $300 in 1797 and more than $500 in 1805. Emancipation would therefore have produced severe economic dislocations.

A final factor to be noted in the role of slavery in the Jeffersonian South was the nature of the antislavery sentiment that appeared there. That sentiment rarely grew out of a concern for the slaves, and did not tap the wellsprings of moral concern that might have provided a counterweight to economic interest and racial fear. Instead, it originated in a concern for the welfare of whites, especially nonslaveholding whites, and for the adverse effects slavery and the presence of so many blacks was thought to have upon them and the South. Many southerners felt that slavery limited economic opportunity for whites, forced them to migrate to the West, stunted the South's economic diversification and cultural progress, and encouraged arrogance among slaveholders.

The lack of concern for slaves among critics of slavery reflected what Jefferson himself called the "deep rooted prejudices" of whites toward blacks. So widespread were these prejudices that their recognition may be said to be one of the things that inhibited emancipation. Throughout the Jeffersonian era, as George Frederickson notes in *The Black Image in the White Mind* (1971), there was "a growing awareness, even among those most strongly opposed to slavery as an institution, of the power of white 'prejudice' and the likelihood that freed blacks would run up against barriers of equality which would inevitably make them a dangerous and degraded class."

This prejudice rested on a belief in black inferiority, a belief reflected in Jefferson's *Notes on Virginia* (1782), which among other things is the best statement of racial thought published in the Jeffersonian South. Though presented in tentative language and notably influenced by environmentalism, Jefferson's discussion of blacks showed the disdain that even enlightened whites had for the race. While crediting blacks with a "moral sense," Jefferson nevertheless suggested that they were inferior to whites in capacity to reason and faculties of forethought and imagination, that they were crasser and more ardent in their sexual desires and more animalistic in some of their other impulses. All in all, he felt, they were equal to whites in qualities "of the heart" but not those "of the head," and he advanced it "as a suspicion only" that they "are inferior to the whites in the endowments both of body and mind." For anyone who accepts these limitations, emancipation becomes objectionable for social as well as racial reasons. Not only did those limitations imply that blacks were incapable of exercising the responsibilities of citizenship but they also suggested that the race needed the restraints of slavery to keep its baser impulses controlled.

The most remarkable thing about these views is that they were Jefferson's. One of the most imaginative and liberated thinkers of his day, Jefferson was singularly myopic on racial matters. On these he reflected rather than led. As a slaveholder he was paternal and his actions were unexceptional. He did not manumit his slaves as Washington did, but only seven of them, including the family of Sally Hemmings, who was apparently his wife's half-sister and whose children have been rumored to be his own. Like other masters, he advertised for runaway slaves and sometimes hired slavecatchers to apprehend them. On occasion he had slaves flogged, and when necessary he sold one or more to pay off debts, sometimes breaking up families to do so. Moreover, he never took part in any antislavery endeavor, and later criticized the effort of northerners to exclude slavery from Missouri. These things were part of belonging to a slaveholding class, and that Jefferson had a part in them is a measure of how enmeshed in slavery the South had become.

To Form a More Perfect Union

These things—the rise of antislavery in the North and upper South, the emergence of proslavery and anti-Negro thought, the conflicting influences of evangelicalism and enlightenment liberalism, the realities of racial demography and economic self-interest—formed the context in which southerners participated in the effort to create a national union of the American states. When their representatives joined others from the North at the Constitutional Convention in Philadelphia in 1787 to fashion a new organic law for the Union, southern elites had a much clearer perception of sectional concerns than they had had in 1774. They were therefore surer of themselves in dealing with northerners, more insistent in guarding their interests, and more successful in what they accomplished. The Constitution that emerged from the deliberations at Philadelphia was something of a sectional compromise, the first of a series of such compromises that included settlement of the Missouri dispute in 1820 and of the nullification controversy in 1833, and the compromises of 1850 and 1877. In fashioning the Constitution, however, southerners gave up nothing they considered vital but gained a great deal, and only the most sensitive among them found anything in the finished document to criticize on sectional grounds. Had this not been the case, it is entirely possible they would have rejected the Constitution and with it the Union.

Most of the major controversies in the Constitutional Convention had a sectional dimension. There were disagreements over the powers to be assigned the federal government and reserved to the states; over economic policy, including tariffs, taxation, public finance, and the differing interests of agriculture and commerce; over foreign policy and westward expansion; and over slavery and racial policy. The compromisability of these issues varied considerably, but collectively they represented a major stumbling block to national unity. Pierce Butler, a delegate from South Carolina, exaggerated when he told the convention that the interests of eastern and southern states were "as different as the interests of Russia and Turkey," but his statement reflected the apprehension of sectionally conscious southerners.

Their apprehension was deep-seated, and only written assurances would relieve it. "There is a striking difference and great contrariety of interests between the [northern and southern] states," Patrick Henry told members of the Virginia ratifying convention. "They are naturally divided into carrying and productive states." This too was overstatement, but Henry's perception of the Union in those terms was important. Once a strong nationalist, Henry now opposed the new Constitution because he thought it threatened the interests of agricultural states. The government it created, he warned, "is not a Virginian but an American government."

This was correct in an important sense, for policies the new government was to undertake, especially in economics, public finance, and westward expansion, would facilitate the growth of the North and West at the expense of the South and thus erode the South's position within the Union. That was in the future, but the prospect was foreseen from the beginning. The potential danger to the South from actions by the central government had in fact only recently been illustrated by the

Jay-Gardoqui treaty of 1785. In that treaty the American negotiator, John Jay of New York, agreed to give up to the Spanish, who controlled Louisiana and Florida, the right to navigate the mouth of the Mississippi River for twenty-five years. This would have deprived southerners of access to the Gulf of Mexico and effectively halted development of the Southwest. The southerners concluded, not without justification, that the treaty had been negotiated at their expense, and they succeeded in having it rejected. The incident, however, increased their suspicion of northerners and a strong national government, and was still rankling when the Constitutional Convention met. "The great danger to our general government *is the great southern and northern interests of the continent, being opposed to each other,*" wrote James Madison during the convention. "*Look to the votes of Congress* [under the Articles of Confederation], *and most of them stand divided by the geography of the country.*"

The fundamental difference was slavery and the racial currents underlying it. Pierce Butler put the matter bluntly. "The security the Southern states want," he said, "is that their Negroes may not be taken from them." Specifically, they wanted slavery put beyond the reach of federal power. James Madison's perspectives were broader than Butler's and his role in working out the sectional compromises was more important, but the Virginian was hardly less concerned than the Carolinian about the slavery issue. "It seems now to be pretty well understood that the real difference of interest lay not between the large and small but between the Northern and Southern states," he said later. "The institution of slavery and its consequences formed the line of discrimination."

The reason for this was the peculiar nature of slavery. It was an exploitive and anachronistic institution that aroused moral and racial sensibilities, and as such it required special protections in law that other forms of property and social organization did not. The protection must be absolute, and since state law already safeguarded the institution, a strong federal government, in which the slaveholders' control would be far less secure than in the slave states, could only be viewed as a potential threat. The Constitution must therefore recognize the special nature of slavery and the federal government must be denied power to tamper with it. The first of these requirements was met in Article I, Section 2, the famous "three-fifths clause," which provided that three-fifths of the slave population would be counted in apportioning representation in the lower house of Congress and thus in electoral voting for the presidency. This made slavery unique, a form of property represented in Congress and the electoral college. In addition the Constitution provided for the return of slaves who escaped to the free states, and bestowed upon slavery the explicit protections provided all forms of property.

In return for these guarantees, southerners agreed that Congress could abolish the overseas slave trade after twenty years and, indirectly, that it could regulate slavery in the territories. In view of the fact that most whites thought the South already had too many blacks and that cutting off the supply from overseas would raise the price of the slaves they already had, these provisions hardly represented a hardship. As for slavery in the territories, southerners seem to have believed that new states carved out of the West, including the Midwest, would be agricultural and thus allied to the South economically. Moreover, the Northwest Ordinance, which prohibited slavery in the territory beyond the Ohio River and which was passed by Congress while the Constitutional Convention was in session, was taken as an implicit guarantee that slavery would be permitted in the territory south of the Ohio.[5]

So when southerners read the finished Constitution, they were satisfied "that their Negroes may not be taken from them." "We have made the best terms for the security of this species of property it was in our power to make," Charles Cotesworth Pinckney told his fellow South Carolinians. "On the whole I do not think them bad." Ironically, northerners of antislavery persuasion also found assurances in the Constitution. The implicit power to regulate slavery in the territories, they assumed, would be exercised to prohibit its spread beyond the states where it already existed. But this assumption tended to obscure a more important fact. In the Constitutional Convention northerners showed themselves ready to accommodate the vital interests of southerners. Their disagreements with the southerners involved perceived interests, not moral convictions. The northerners were neither abolitionists nor even antislavery as that term was later defined, and they shared the general belief in black inferiority and white supremacy. Years later, the Chief Justice of the United States, Roger B. Taney, looked back upon the Constitutional Convention and insisted that its members represented a population that regarded blacks as "beings of an inferior order, and altogether unfit to associate with the white race, either socially or politically, and so far inferior that they had no rights which the white man was bound to respect." Whatever the constitutional merits of the *Dred Scott* decision in which Taney made this observation, the observation itself was not without historical validity.

The Crystallizing of Racial Fear

In view of the large areas of agreement between northerners and southerners in the 1780s and 1790s, it seems apparent that the southerners' apprehension over northern intentions was exaggerated. The apprehension, however, was fed by other sources, and no sooner had the new government been launched than those other sources began to have a dramatic impact. The most obvious of these was the slave uprising in Santo Domingo that began in 1791 and continued until, a dozen years later, all whites in the country had been driven out and the nation of Haiti was proclaimed an independent republic. This was a blood-curdling example of the worst fate that could befall white southerners, and one they could not ignore. Some of the whites who fled the island nation settled in the South, and their graphic accounts of the horrors experienced there added immediacy to the sense of danger. The house slaves some of them brought with them were widely believed to be spreading tales of the uprising among southern blacks. For a decade the South was swept by rumors of slave unrest and violence.

The actual danger that existed is difficult to measure. But according to Winthrop D. Jordan, who has made the most systematic study of the subject, "even the most cursory reading in the newspapers suggests persuasively that there was enough [danger] to give contemporaries cause for alarm." In Virginia alone, Jordan reports, the state compensated owners of 434 slaves executed for crimes between 1783 and 1814, a substantial figure in view of the fact that slaves were executed only for the most serious crimes. In a different time span, 1786 to 1810, at least thirty-one Virginia slaves were executed for murdering their masters, and there were enough instances of poisonings and arson to keep whites tense and fearful. Complete evidence on the number of slaves executed or otherwise sentenced for serious crimes in all the southern states, or killed by their masters, overseers, or patrols as known or suspected criminals, would no doubt underscore the seriousness of the concern.

In 1800, near the end of this period of alarm, there occurred near Richmond, Virginia, the largest rebellion of slaves in American history. Led by Gabriel Prosser, at least a thousand blacks and perhaps twice that number, some of them free, staged an abortive uprising that was foiled by treachery and a sudden torrential rain. It was a close call, and the example was not lost upon whites. Prosser's rebellion helped crystallize thinking on several things, and is thus something of a milestone in southern history. It dramatized the need for slavery as a means of race control, and in its aftermath antislavery disappeared in the upper South. (It had never existed in the lower South.) "I have long since given up the expectation of any early provision for the extinguishment of slavery among us," Jefferson wrote in 1805; and as if to ratify his sentiment, the Virginia legislature the following year passed a law forbidding manumission unless the persons manumitted left the state. Out of felt necessity, a new attitude toward slavery crystallized. "A large majority of the people of the Southern States do not consider slavery as a crime," Congressman Peter Early of Georgia declared in 1806. "They do not consider it immoral to hold human flesh in bondage. Many deprecate slavery as an evil; as a political evil; but not as a crime," and "a large majority" of them do not consider it an evil.

The articulation of this hardened position first came in Congress, where slavery was an object of sporadic contention in the two decades around 1800. Quakers and other groups sent antislavery petitions, and northern congressmen tried from time to time to abolish the overseas slave trade. Disputes erupted periodically over the domestic slave trade, the treatment of fugitive slaves or free blacks, and the extension of slavery into the territories. Northerners were especially resentful of the advantages the South derived from the three-fifths clause, which in the 1790s amounted to a dozen additional seats in Congress and that many extra votes in the electoral college. At the same time, southerners regarded the clause as an essential defense for their vital interests. Without it, Jefferson would not have won the presidency in 1800 and Missouri might not have been admitted to the Union as a slave state twenty years later.

Demographic and other changes underscored the southerners' need for the three-fifths clause. No sooner was the Union achieved than it became clear that the South was growing less rapidly than the rest of the country and was thus an ever smaller part of the nation. The congressional redistricting that followed the census of 1810 assigned 56 percent of the seats in the House of Representatives to nonslave states. At the same time, the westward movement of whites from the seaboard slave states was steadily increasing the proportion of blacks in those states, from 36.4 percent in 1790 to 41.6 percent in 1820.

Economic Change and Emergent Sectionalism

As sectional consciousness grew, the South underwent a physical and economic transformation brought on by the rise of cotton and sugar, and this transformation in turn increased sectional distinctiveness. In 1775 the southern colonies had consisted of the narrow strip of territory between the Atlantic Ocean and the Appalachian Mountains, and even there large areas were still "sprawling wilderness inhabited by elusive Indians and hard-bitten pioneers." By the time George Washington became President of the new nation in 1789, the Indians had been driven out of almost all the land east of Appalachia, but were still in possession of the western three-quarters of Georgia, all of Alabama and Mississippi, and a lion's share of Tennessee. They also occupied most of Florida and Louisiana, both of which were Spanish territories.

In the census of 1790, the non-Indian population of the southern states was approximately 1.8 million, a little more than a third of it black and most of it confined to the eastern half of the states from Maryland through Georgia. During the next thirty years, settlement surged across Appalachia into the Mississippi Valley and through the Southwest into Louisiana. Before the turn of the century, Kentucky (1792) and Tennessee (1796) had been admitted to the Union, and by the time of the Missouri controversy, Louisiana (1812), Mississippi (1817), and Alabama (1819) had too, and in 1819 Florida was added to the national domain. By this time, also, the Indians had lost most of what they had in 1789, and their remaining territories—large chunks of Georgia, Alabama, and Mississippi and smaller portions of Florida and Tennessee—were already coveted by land-hungry whites. The non-Indian population of the slave states (not including Delaware and the District of Columbia) had grown to 4.3 million in 1820, of which three-eighths was black. This population was overwhelmingly rural; 90 percent of all southerners, compared to 77 percent of other Americans, derived their livelihood directly from agriculture. Baltimore, New Orleans, and Charleston were the only southern cities of any size, and the economies of Baltimore and New Orleans were partly national in orientation.

In view of the dislocations caused by the war for independence and the difficulties of transportation and communication, this was a remarkable record of growth. A great deal of agricultural property, including thousands of slaves, had been lost during the war, and independence meant exclusion from British markets and loss of the benefits of mercantilism, including crop subsidies, guaranteed markets, and traditional sources of credit. The overseas slave trade, also interrupted by the war, was never resumed on a general basis.

Independence thus brought a new economic era. After the war, southern agriculturalists turned toward general farming and away from staple crops, which in turn encouraged settlement of the backcountry and increased internal trade. This stimulated economic development and rapid population growth as well as physical expansion. By improving economic opportunity for other groups, these changes tended to undermine the position of the planter class, some of whose members suffered severe losses from the depredations of war and inflation. The southern economy, it seemed, was moving toward balance and diversification.

This trend was halted in the 1790s by three factors that produced a major change in the course of southern economic history. These were invention of the cotton gin in 1793, introduction of sugar in Louisiana in 1794–95, and feverish speculation in western lands.[6] When these things began to have an impact, the section's economy was at a crossroads. The world market for traditional staples—tobacco, rice, and indigo—had not been expanding sufficiently, yet the South's capital investment was in land and slaves and the social structure was geared to plantation agriculture. This is the reason it seemed to many that slavery was becoming unprofitable and that the Jeffersonian South would have to undergo a major economic reorientation. Cotton and sugar changed all this. The turn to these new crops was marked by enormous profits for a fortunate few, and the result was a rapid movement of men and money into the Southwest, that is, into the deep South, the cotton kingdom, and the black belt, a movement facilitated by the purchases of Louisiana in 1803 and Florida in 1819. A major shift in the economic and political center of the South commenced. The South of Jefferson began giving way to the South of Calhoun. In 1809 Jefferson retired from the presidency and political office; a year later Calhoun was elected to his first political office, a seat in the House of Representatives.

The change was more than symbolic. The new South of Calhoun differed from that of Jefferson in important respects. Younger and more dynamic economically and crasser in its material values and aspirations, it was more exploitive of its human and natural resources. Without traditions and institutions of its own, it lacked the restraint and self-assurance of established society. Its values were those of the booster, the speculator, the man on the make. In its domain the cotton snob held sway, and the paternalism of the tidewater gave way to the prerogatives of economic individualism. The contrast between the two areas was far from absolute, but it was nevertheless important, especially for a generation or two. Searching self-consciously for roots and moorings, the new South sought to recreate the institutions and life style of the old, and in this and other ways to assert its southern identity. The results were not entirely satisfactory. In significant respects the newer South was more illiberal and provincial than the older, less exposed to outside intellectual currents, more preoccupied with concerns of its own. The South was changing, ideologically as well as geographically. The locus of the southern mind was shifting.

The character of this newer South derived not only from the rawness of frontier life and a greater concern with acquisitiveness, but from racial factors too. The rapid growth of the cotton kingdom was made possible only by the labor of slaves, who were brought into the region in rapidly increasing numbers. The average size of plantations and slave holdings was larger than in the upper South. Within a few years, the statistical center of the nation's black population shifted from the Chesapeake to southwest Georgia. In 1790, 56 percent of all slaves in the South were in Virginia and Maryland; by 1820 this figure was down to 35 percent. By the latter year, 47.6 percent of the non-Indian population was black in the tier of states that runs from South Carolina and Georgia westward through Louisiana, and in South Carolina and Louisiana the percentage surpassed 50. In the black belt in these states, which was also the plantation belt, the proportion of blacks was often much larger than that. Significantly, it was the white population of that belt that dominated politics and economics in the deep South and eventually in the South itself. This too was fateful. The rise of the cotton and sugar kingdoms increased the economic dependence of whites on slavery at the same time that the growing numbers of blacks was increasing their dependence on that institution as a means of race control. This had the effect of enlarging the economic dimension of the slavery issue and of the growing sense of sectional insecurity as well.

Cotton, the chief cause of all this, was not a new crop. It had been introduced before the Revolution, but only the long-staple variety was profitable and it was a delicate plant that could be successfully cultivated only on the sea islands of South Carolina and Georgia. The hardy short-staple variety, which thrived everywhere from southeastern Virginia to central Texas, was unprofitable because of the difficulty in separating the fiber from the seed. One worker could separate only about a pound a day. It was this problem that Eli Whitney's cotton gin solved. Operated by a hand crank, Whitney's invention consisted of a roller equipped with wire teeth which tore the fiber from the seed as the teeth revolved between the slats of a hopper. Using the original model, one worker could separate fifty pounds of fiber a day, and improvements soon increased this manyfold.

Cotton was ideally suited to the South's economic needs. Demand for the crop was high and land to grow it cheap; an exploitable labor force was available and on virgin land production costs were low and profitability was high. In addition the labor required was unskilled and almost year-round, and readily adapted to existing forms of plantation organization. In 1799 in central South Carolina, Wade Hampton produced 600 small bales which at prices then current were worth about $90,000. Cultivation spread rapidly through the Carolinas and Georgia, on into Alabama, Mississippi, and western Tennessee, across the Mississippi to Louisiana, and then to Arkansas and Texas. Production rose from 3,135 bales in 1790 to 73,145 in 1800, to 177,638 in 1810, and 334,378 in 1820. The South had committed itself to cotton.

The economic effects of doing so were important. The trend toward diversified agriculture stopped; the reliance on staple production increased. Total income grew rapidly but failed to have the same multiplier effect a similar rise in income from commerce and manufacturing was having in the North. There, rising income from those sources encouraged economic diversification, including a variety of middleman activities, and investment in education and other forms of social overhead. The nature of cotton and sugar production was such that it stunted those things by failing to encourage them. The chief reason was income structure. Slaves and poor whites lived so near the subsistence level that they could not properly be said to be a part of the market economy, and with so large a part of the population relegated to that level, the South failed to develop an expanding market for manufactured goods and services. The planters saw little need for investment in the social overhead necessary for economic diversification, for they saw little need for economic diversification. The growing of agricultural staples was highly profitable for them, more profitable than anything else they might have done, and their social and racial interests discouraged alternative investment. Thus the section's economy remained centered around staple agriculture while that of the North and West was diversifying. An important result of this was that much of the income from cotton and other staples flowed out of the section to purchase transportation and marketing services, manufactured goods, and some foodstuffs as well.

In effect the South, or at least its dominant economic groups, opted for economic specialization, and they and the section reaped the advantages and disadvantages of that. The advantages went disproportionately to the planters, who realized a generally high level of return on investments in land and slaves, and the disadvantages, which were akin to those of a colonial economy, were felt chiefly by other groups. Because southerners failed to develop marketing and transport facilities of their own, including banking, credit, and insurance resources, shipping companies, marketing connections, and other middleman activities, they turned perforce to the North for those services, and by 1815 New York City was already the financial center of the cotton trade. This arrangement developed and continued not because the South's was a colonial economy, for it was not. Southerners owned their own resources, made their own economic decisions, and had a primary voice in national politics and government. Instead, it developed and continued because it was economic for planters and the middlemen with whom they dealt. But it fastened onto the South the distinctive economy that became the object of so much controversy in the pre-Civil War era.

The Social Structure

Except in the area of religion, which is discussed below, the social and political history of the Jeffersonian South witnessed no transformations as significant as those in economics. In those areas the impact of the Revolution was limited. The social structure was largely undisturbed, though the thrust of the changes that did occur was toward democracy and expanded opportunity for whites and a temporary relaxation of the rigidities of slavery in the upper South. Imperial authority was eliminated, and with it went entail, primogeniture, titles of privilege, state-supported religion, and other vestiges of European prerogative. These changes were more symbolic than profound, but together they helped turn southern society away from English models. More important were the legal and political reforms adopted by the new state governments, many of which were written into new state constitutions. State laws were codified and generally made more humane; government was made more democratic for whites. State legislatures became more representative, which meant that western areas were given a larger voice in government, while executive branches were weakened to prevent the abuse of power. The right to vote was broadened, and democratic bills of rights were incorporated in state constitutions. In the upper South, the appearance of antislavery sentiment produced manumission laws in several states.

These changes were important but also limited. In most instances western areas remained underrepresented, and state governments conceived of the general welfare in negative, Jeffersonian terms. Slavery was retained and after 1790 slave codes were strengthened, the right to vote and hold office was still restricted by property and sometimes religious qualifications, and women, youths, free blacks, slaves, and Indians still suffered legal and other disabilities. The revolutionary impulse toward a more democratic society, so compellingly captured by Jefferson in the Declaration of Independence, subsided before it produced fundamental changes in the South.

This can be seen in two key areas, the right to vote and the social structure. After the Revolution, all the southern states retained significant limitations on the suffrage. A voter not only had to be an adult male but had to own property, and almost everywhere, though this was not always written down, he had to be white. The property qualification varied from state to state. In Maryland and South Carolina, it was fifty acres of land, in Virginia twenty-five acres of improved or 500 acres of unimproved land; in Georgia and North Carolina, the voter simply had to be a taxpayer. These qualifications were sufficiently low to permit widespread political participation by adult white males, and to that extent the southern states were democratic by eighteenth-century standards. However, democracy is more than a matter of form, of who can vote. It is also a matter of substance, of who does vote and for whom he can and does vote, of who runs for office and what influences dominate politics. These are more difficult matters to evaluate, involving as they do such amorphous forces as deference, which remained an important if unmeasurable influence, and the extent to which voters and the governments they elect are committed to the rights of minorities. Fletcher M. Green, one of the first scholars to study these things in depth, thought deference and tradition operated to limit the substance of democracy in the postrevolutionary era and to preserve the position of the planter class. "The training and prejudice of the past, the distinctions between rich and poor, still held sway and helped to maintain a governing class," Green wrote in *Constitutional Development in the South Atlantic States, 1776–1860* (1930). The forms of democracy, he suggested, were more apparent than the substance.

The weight of evidence seems to support this view. Voting was oral and thus subject to pressure from employers, creditors, and public opinion, and it was quite low as well. According to figures compiled by Charles S. Sydnor, of 747,610 people in Virginia in 1790, 442,117 were whites, of whom 227,071 were males. Of these, 90,000 to 100,000 were adults, of whom 35,000 to 40,000 were qualified voters, and of that number about half actually voted in the elections of 1786 and 1789. The actual voters were thus only 2 or 3 percent of the total population. By the standards of the time, this was a democratic system, at least for whites. "Political powers truly rested with the people," wrote Sydnor; "democracy was a real and active force." But "at the same time," he added, "a large measure of political power was vested in the few; aristocracy was also a strong and active force in politics." The thing which reconciled these factors was the continuing deference, the willingness of those who participated in politics to accept the leadership of their "betters." This willingness was due in part to the fact that government rested lightly on the white populace. Taxes were low, officeholders accessible, and opportunity sufficiently open to prevent the accumulation of resentments. Groups who might have used the vote as an instrument of social protest were still disfranchised.

The significance of this may be seen in a look at the social structure of the postrevolutionary South.[7] Property was rather widely distributed among white males throughout the section, but the proportions of the total population that could be called rich or poor were higher in the South than in other parts of the nation and there were other important differences as well. The large slave population meant that a much larger percentage of the southern people were landless, that economic dependence was more widespread and wealth far more concentrated. In none of these things had the Revolution produced much change. Back in 1770, according to the calculations of Alice H. Jones, the wealth per free adult capita had been 147 pounds sterling in the South compared to 47 pounds in the middle colonies and 38 pounds in New England.

The continuing maldistribution of wealth was most pronounced in older areas. In some counties in the Northern Neck of Virginia, for example, no more than 30 percent of the adult white males were freeholders, and in Jackson Turner Main's words, a "very small number of wealthy men—many of them absentees—held as much as 70 per cent of the real property." In the state as a whole, Main noted, "a majority of the adult white males were not landowners," and most of the non-owners "were very poor" indeed. Among landowners, "the vast majority" were small farmers, two-thirds of them having between 100 and 500 acres. Only about 20 percent owned more than 500 acres, but together that group held more than half of all land in the state and a much larger share of the good land. Only 4 percent of the adult white males owned 500 or more acres of land plus twenty or more slaves.

In newer areas, the disparity was less than in the tidewater, but there too the proportions of landless families and large landowners were greater than in the North. Including slaves, who constituted about 8 percent of the population in frontier areas, Main found that "1/3 of southern frontiersmen were landless workers," though the typical frontiersman was a small farmer. In urban centers the contrast with the North was also notable. In Charleston, the most important southern city in the 1780s, the poor white class was smaller than in comparable northern cities, but when slaves were counted the class of urban poor was about 65 percent of the total population. Yet more than a fourth of the adult males in Charleston owned personal property worth 1,000 pounds or more, compared to a fifth of those in Boston. In the South as a whole, Main estimated, the wealthiest 10 percent of the population owned 55 percent of the wealth, including slaves; in the North the comparable group owned 45 percent. Yet the mass of southern whites were relatively affluent by European standards, and the economic and social fluidity this permitted discouraged class protest.

A Southern Religion

Apart from slavery and race, the most important changes in southern social thought around the turn of the nineteenth century concerned religion. The spread of evangelical denominations, the eclipse of Anglicanism, and the decline of deism were followed closely by a wave of revivalism after 1800, and these things combined with certain sectional influences to produce the kind of religion that came to be regarded as characteristically southern. Secularism declined, as did rationalism in religious thought, and in their stead rose a religion dominated by precepts of Protestant fundamentalism. Methodists, Baptists, and Presbyterians made the readiest transition to the emerging South, and thus became the most important denominations in the section. The basic causes of their successes seem obvious. They succeeded where other denominations failed in meeting the challenges of the westward expansion. More than that, the evangelicals found it easier than authoritarian or tradition-directed churches to adapt to the social and intellectual changes that accompanied the rise of sectional consciousness. By circuit riders, lay preachers, itinerant evangelists, and camp meetings, evangelical churches solved the physical and institutional problems presented by the frontier, and by throwing aside theological and ecclesiastical rigidities they overcame the social problems too. Offering a religion of the heart, they won the allegiance of the mass of white people in frontier and rural areas of the South, and by coming to terms with slavery, white supremacy, and other essentials of southern life, they held onto their loyalties after the frontier passed. In the process, orthodoxy and theological niceties gave way to emotional fervor and a concern with saving souls, while denominational distinctions blurred and the institutional aspects of religion were undermined.

Revivalism was not a new thing in the South as the nineteenth century began. It first appeared back in the 1740s when the Great Awakening spread into the section from New England. Until 1801, however, revivals tended to be localized phenomena of only temporary consequence. Developed by dissenting (non-Anglican) churches, revivalism was ideally suited to the needs of the evangelical denominations which arose in the last half of the eighteenth century. By the end of the Revolution, those denominations had a foothold in the South, but their success was not complete until the turn of the century. "Few nations," wrote a French traveler in 1793, "are less addicted to religious practices than the Virginians."

This situation changed with the Great Revival of 1801–05, which began in the frontier settlement of Cane Ridge, Kentucky, and spread rapidly across the frontier states of Kentucky and Tennessee and into the seaboard states as well. Church membership grew rapidly, the number of Baptists doubling within a few years, and church attendance also. From everywhere came reports of large numbers of dramatic conversions, even among hardened sinners, and the effect was lasting. The South became a churched society. Even southern gentlemen became, by their own reckoning, Christian gentlemen. Pious conduct became the standard for all classes. "Formerly, when [people] collected together, drinking, swearing, horseracing, fighting, and such like practices, were common among them," wrote a Virginian after his neighborhood had experienced a revival. "But now ... you will seldom see one pursuing any of those practices. [Even] those who make no pretensions to religion, still appear under great restraint."

Revivalism was in part a product of frontier conditions, especially loneliness, monotony, and hardship. For emotionally and socially starved people it acted as a cathartic. The nearness of death or other catastrophe, the absence of law and order, and the dearth of intellectual activity encouraged a religion of the heart rather than the mind. However, these factors better explain the origin than the total effect of the Great Revival. This seems to have been a product of broader forces, especially the religious mind, including the world view of those people attracted to revivalism, and a vague feeling of crisis that pervaded areas where the revival became strongest. Around the turn of the century, as John Boles has noted in *The Great Revival, 1789–1805* (1972), many southerners had a general sense of foreboding about the future, and not only about matters relating to sectional concerns. They feared that social constraints and regularities were loosening too rapidly in the rapid movement of people to the West, that society was in danger of falling apart. Some worried that changes wrought by the Revolution were producing an excess of democracy, while others were disquieted by racial or economic factors. The total effect was one of disturbing social disruption. It seems plausible, though the matter needs further study, that the anxiety and insecurity thus produced encouraged the turn to fundamental religion. Certainly fundamentalism promised assurance, in public as well as personal concerns, and in the aftermath of the Great Revival religion emerged as a major prop for the southern social order.

It was this that made the revival an important event in the history of the South and the emergence of sectional consciousness. The "southernization" of religion led the mass of southerners to accept a set of religious beliefs and practices that centered around Protestant fundamentalism. The chief tenet was the omnipotence and omniscience of God, who was regarded as a distinctly anthropomorphic being personally concerned with the lives and fortunes of everyone. Man himself was born in sin and subject to eternal damnation unless he availed himself of the grace of God and earned salvation by confessing his sins and professing absolute faith in God and in the sacrifice of His son Jesus Christ. A second tenet was the literal truth of the Bible, which meant belief in the existence of a physical heaven and hell and in the imminent second coming of Jesus Christ, who would create a new millenium for the saved and banish the "lost" to a hell of fire and brimstone.

The social implications of these beliefs were important. The most basic was the intimation that this life is less important than the hereafter and that its chief purpose is to earn salvation. The function of the church is thus to save souls, for personal redemption is far more significant than social issues. The individual believer is therefore the center of concern, not the church as an institution nor theology as a coherent system of thought nor society as a whole. The individual communicates directly with God, interprets the Bible in his own way, makes his own decisions regarding sin and salvation. At the same time, his dependence on God is made absolute and his sense of unworthiness compounded, and because it is impossible to live up to the perfectionist creed of personal conduct he professes, a sense of guilt is created. Out of these things came an increase in piety, the individual's effort to demonstrate his or her redemption by living according to puritanical standards of conduct. Because sin and salvation were personalized, sin came to be viewed as a consequence of succumbing to personal temptations, the weaknesses of the flesh—alcohol, illicit sex, swearing, dancing, profaning the Sabbath. Salvation, in contrast, was demonstrated by success in resisting those temptations and believing in God.

Religiousness grew, but churches remained weak. Revivals were nondenominational and everyone was welcome. Ritual and even theology in its traditional meaning were dispensed with. The individual's right to decide all matters for himself encouraged congregational splits wherever controversial matters, whether theological or political, were brought into religion, and controversy was therefore avoided. As a result the revivalist denominations became more and more alike on matters of social significance, and little inclined to give attention to public issues unrelated to personal sin. Thus churches approved of laws to promote puritanical conduct but rarely took a stand on other public issues. In the milieu of social unease that characterized the South around the turn of the nineteenth century, religious involvement in public life thus tended to encourage conformity and intolerance. For all its democratic implications, evangelicalism became an escapist, otherworldly religion whose influence was profoundly conservative.

The First South

As the above discussion suggests, the distinctive, self-conscious South was a product of circumstances within the section and of the way those circumstances caused southerners to react to certain basic forces at work in the nation and the Western world. Its emergence was an evolutionary process that began about the time of the first Continental Congress and lasted for about three decades. In more specific terms it was due to the fact that racial demography and economic interest led southern elites to try to resist the ideological and social changes then transforming the North Atlantic community. These changes included enlightenment liberalism, the industrial revolution, liberal capitalism, political democracy, individualism, urbanization, and nationalism. The white South could not welcome these things, for the changes they promised were more or less subversive of its social and economic system. The North, in contrast, could and did welcome them and indeed came to equate them with progress. The problem was that once the Union was formed, southern opposition to "progress" inhibited northern efforts to achieve it, and the resulting conflict spilled into national politics. Ordinarily this would have led to the usual give-and-take of political rivalry and compromise, but racial factors dictated otherwise. As white southerners viewed the situation, their political rivalries and economic competition with the North involved vital matters of racial security which took precedence over everything else. In their unease, they exaggerated the immediate danger, but this was not a subject they weighed by the ordinary canons of politics or economics. They were apprehensive, even fearful, and to a degree guilt-ridden because of the gap that separated the realities of their situation with the ideals they professed. The result was defensiveness, which was enlarged by a growing amount of outside criticism they considered undeserved and unfair, and which generated a minority psychology among them and then a feeling of persecution and, finally, a matured sense of grievance and besiegement.

In an important sense, this happened because of the failure of the southern people, especially the more liberally inclined among them, to keep the section attuned to "modern" developments. Had they been able to abolish slavery, or even contain it, to mute their racist impulses, to keep the South abreast of intellectual and social change, the South would have become less and less rather than more and more distinctive. Their failure, if that be what it was, was the failure of Jeffersonian liberalism, and it made sectional consciousness—southernism itself—reactionary in thrust and more negative than positive in nature. The South thus came to be identified more with what its people opposed than what they approved. In the crucial period around 1800, the facts of racial demography and inherited interest became too strong to permit the evolution of a vibrant liberal tradition in the section. The burden of history had become heavy enough to create the South, and once created to give it a cultural life of its own.

Jefferson himself was the representative figure in the transformation. Not only was he one of the most liberal-minded men of his day, but one of the most pronounced racialists as well. In the Declaration of Independence he penned the most exalted sentiments of his generation; but long before modern theories of racism had been worked out, he regarded blacks invidiously and suspected that their manifest social and cultural disabilities were the result of inheritance rather than environment. And his racialist sentiments were more congruent with his actions on matters relevant to sectional identity than were his liberal views, which, in factors affecting race and the interest of the planter class, tended to become intellectual abstractions. In these areas he was like the emerging South: his actions reflected his worst rather than his best impulses. He and the section too were caught in a web, a web in part of their own making, from which neither could escape. That web, or at least an important part of it, was the sum of those things that came to be known as the South. Of course the web—the South—had its attractions. It offered a pleasant life for many people, a sense of place and identity, a friendly refuge from outside hostility. And it looked appealing, as webs do, from outside as well as inside. Its most attractive features—leisure, hospitality, personalism, the plantation setting—seemed as enticing as gossamer, and much more substantial. But it was still a web—home, refuge, cocoon, and prison—and not all those it enmeshed were blacks.

TWO

THE OLD SOUTH 1800-61

The history of the Old South is not easy to understand or distill into a few sections of a textbook. It constitutes one of the singular chapters in the history of the nation as well as the section, yet so brief was the life of the Old South that its temporal limits are difficult to appreciate. An individual who was born at the turn of the nineteenth century and lived the Biblical span of three score and ten years would have experienced the whole of its history as an adult. He would have reached his majority just as the Missouri controversy was settled, have been a young man when South Carolina nullified the tariff of 1832, hardly into middle age when the war with Mexico brought a new and more intense struggle over slavery in the territories, and still of vigorous years when Edmund Ruffin, himself aged sixty-seven, fired the shot at Fort Sumter in 1861 that ignited the conflagration that consumed the Old South itself. Within the next few years he would have experienced the joys of emancipation if he were black or the disappointments of Appomattox if he were white, and before he died, the most important phases of R construction too.

This brief was the history of the Old South! Whether for good or ill, this *ancien regime* never grew old, not even as individuals measure their lives. Yet if the sectional approach to southern history is valid, the brief span of years between 1820 and 1861 is a pivotal period in the story of the South. In those four decades, white southerners were not only acutely conscious of their sectional identity but better able to control their destiny than in any subsequent generation. In that time, the qualities usually thought of as southern blossomed, and the southern way of life achieved its most brilliant and some of its most appalling expressions.

4

The Triumph of Sectionalism

The emergence of sectionalism was a process of ebb and flow. No sooner had sectional consciousness crested, around 1800, than it began to abate. For a generation after Jefferson's election to the presidency in that year, the federal government was in friendly hands and the southern voice in national politics was so great that the government came to be looked upon as a friend rather than a foe. The economic policies of Jefferson and his successors, James Madison and James Monroe, were acceptable, and the rapid growth of the cotton kingdom brought higher slave prices and new economic confidence. At the same time, racial fears subsided. The end of the African slave trade in 1808 removed a source of sectional controversy as well as antislavery activity, while revisions in the slave codes and restrictions on manumission and the rights of free blacks made white supremacy more secure. As these things eased sectional concerns, the long controversy with Great Britain that eventuated in the War of 1812 aroused national loyalties among southerners more than northerners.

The result was a dramatic shift in the locus of sectional grievance from the South to New England. By 1814–15 it was New Englanders whose suspicions of the national government were provoking criticism and fear, New Englanders who were questioning the value of the Union, and New Englanders whose political and economic leaders, at a convention in Hartford, Connecticut, threatened drastic actions to protect their sectional interests. By 1815, when the war with Britain had ended, southern sectionalism was less pronounced than at any time since 1787. Only such purists—or were they clairvoyants?—as John Randolph of Roanoke and John Taylor of Caroline questioned the new mood. A more representative figure, John C. Calhoun, already a prominent spokesman for the lower South in national politics, supported Henry Clay's "American System" of political and economic nationalism, which endorsed a new national bank, a protective tariff, internal improvements at federal expense, and other measures designed to integrate the nation politically and economically. It also endorsed a construction of the Constitution broad enough to enable the federal government to accomplish these things.

The Missouri Controversy

Southern support for such a program was inherently contradictory, however, and at the first sign of that fact it dissipated rapidly. Two developments provided that sign. The panic of 1819 showed that the South would benefit from Clay's economic program only if its economy were altered to fit the northern pattern of development. And before the panic had subsided, the controversy surrounding the admission of Missouri to the Union reminded southerners anew of the distinctive nature of their racial interests and their vulnerability to outside pressure. The latter was especially important. Southern sectionalism was not born of the Missouri controversy; rather, the controversy was a product of deep, preexisting sectional differences. Yet it came after a period of nationalist feelings, and its impact on popular opinion was therefore great. For the first time, as Glover Moore noted in *The Missouri Controversy, 1819–1821* (1953), "all the strands in the fabric of North-South sectionalism were brought together and paraded before the public in magnitudinous proportions."

The stage for the controversy was set in 1819 when the Missouri territory, in which slavery already existed, applied for statehood. The peculiar institution was not very important in the territory, either racially or economically, but its existence there was the immediate cause of a national controversy. The admission of the territory would add a slave state to the Union with no immediate prospect of a new nonslave state to preserve the regional balance in the Senate. Moreover, the geographical position of Missouri in the heart of the Louisiana purchase territory lying athwart the path of westward expansion from the Midwest made the question of slavery there a matter of special importance for the future of the Union. Thus when a bill authorizing its admission to the Union came before Congress, Representative James Tallmadge of New York offered an amendment prohibiting further importation of slaves into Missouri and requiring the gradual emancipation of those already there. The effect of the amendment was to require abolition as a condition of statehood. It thereby asserted the right of Congress to prohibit slavery in a territory and a new state, and would therefore, its supporters hoped, mark the end of the expansion of slavery. The amendment passed the House of Representatives, where the nonslave states had a considerable majority, but failed in the Senate, half of whose members came from areas of slavery. In both houses, the voting was close and decidedly sectional, the debate long and acrimonious.

The basic issue at stake in this controversy was not slavery in Missouri, but the direction of national development, or more specifically the political control necessary to channel national development in one direction or another. The entire range of sectional issues was thus involved: slavery and antislavery and the future of both in the nation, agriculture versus manufacturing and commerce and the influence of each in the federal government, the rights of states and the nature of the federal union, and the pace of westward expansion. Behind these were the more fundamental forces, emotional, moral, and cultural, that set the South apart from the rest of the country. As southerners saw things, they had no choice but to resist the Tallmadge amendment and the principles behind it. Otherwise, they feared, the South would lose the ability to protect its vital economic and racial interests. Northerners, on the other hand, resented the political and economic influence of slavery, which they regarded as a threat to the kind of liberal, capitalist, democratic nation they wanted to develop. At the same time, their liberal, New Testament values encouraged them to view the peculiar institution in moral terms.

For northerners, the Tallmadge amendment was an ideal weapon, and they used it adroitly to focus the Missouri debates on slavery rather than the political issues at stake. Their success in doing this reflected the fact that the peculiar institution was an anachronism in 1820 and for that reason the most conspicuous symbol of the South and of the things that set it apart from the North. Southerners were also disadvantaged by this fact as well as their own ambivalence toward slavery, which stemmed from economic and racial considerations rather than moral or humanitarian concerns. Many of them questioned the desirability of the peculiar institution because of its economic and social influence on the white South and because it was responsible for the presence of so many blacks in the South. They preferred to defend it as a necessary evil rather than a positive good, a difficult position in debate. "We do not vindicate servitude," said one of them opposing the Tallmadge amendment. "We wish no slave had touched our soil"; but "does not every man, unless he be a fanatic, conceive how difficult it is for us to be rid of it, in a manner consistent with our future peace and tranquility?" Slavery was necessary, but for reasons of racial security. The argument that it was a positive good did appear, however, and more frequently than ever before, which suggests that the mounting criticism was having an effect. The debate dramatized the precarious, even deteriorating position of white southerners in the Union. Back in 1787 they had been able to protect their interests. Now, however, factors they could not control and which were likely to grow larger in the future were undermining their ability to do that. The physical growth of the nation was making them an ever smaller minority; economic change was rendering them more and more dependent on the North; and nonsoutherners were increasingly critical of slavery and prepared to act against it. The South was again under assault.

These things were not fully apparent at once. The compromise that resolved the Missouri dispute was widely considered a southern victory. Missouri was admitted as a slave state, and Maine, heretofore a part of Massachusetts, as a nonslave state. Concerning the more important issue of slavery in the territories, a line was drawn across the Louisiana purchase territory at 36°30', north of which slavery was prohibited everywhere except in Missouri. The southerners did not really accept this arrangement, for a majority of them voted against it and in that sense the compromise represented no agreement between the sections. By acquiescing in the line, southerners acquiesced in an assertion by Congress of the power to exclude slavery from the territories. But in return they got what seemed the better of the substantive issue at stake, slavery in Missouri, the object of immediate concern, and presumably also in Arkansas and the Indian territory (Oklahoma) when those areas became states. They could also expect that Florida, only recently acquired from Spain, would in due course become a slave state. These seemed like concrete gains, measured against which the exclusion of slavery from a vast area of the northern great plains, then thought to be virtual desert, seemed like an empty abstraction. This was, however, a serious miscalculation. The area was not desert at all, and before the Civil War several nonslave states and territories would be carved from it. The exclusion of slavery above 36°30' thus eventually worked to the serious disadvantage of the South.

When the Missouri controversy was over, the South was more self-consciously sectional than ever before. Yet a note of caution must accompany the statement of that fact. Out of the ebb and flow of sectional consciousness eventually came secession and the Civil War, and for that reason it is tempting to see the Missouri controversy as a "cause" of the war. It is equally tempting to treat the entire history of the Old South as a preliminary to that war and subsume it under a study of the coming of the conflict. The temptation must be resisted, for the Old South is worthy of study in its own right. Neither the Missouri controversy nor any of the subsequent milestones in the history of sectionalism is best seen as a "cause" of the Civil War or a step in an irrepressible conflict between the South and the rest of the nation. Sectionalism and union were not necessarily incompatible, as the history of the Old South proved. The Civil War was always avoidable, at least until Lincoln's election and South Carolina's secession in 1860, though sectionalism was a major fact of life from 1820 onward. "This monstrous question, like a firebell in the night, awakened and filled me with terror," Jefferson wrote of the slavery issue when the Missouri controversy was compromised. "I considered it at once as the knell of the Union. It is hushed, indeed, for the moment. But this is a reprieve only, not a final sentence."

Evolving Sectionalism

Jefferson was correct. "A geographical line coinciding with a marked principle, moral and political, once conceived and held up to the angry passions of men," he warned, "will never be obliterated; and every new irritation will mark it deeper and deeper." The forebodings which underlay these remarks were most pronounced in the deep South. In Charleston, South Carolina, where they were especially acute, a major slave conspiracy was uncovered in 1822. Organized by Denmark Vesey and Gullah Jack, the plot was thought to involve scores, perhaps hundreds, of slaves and free blacks who collected caches of weapons and hoped to make contact with the black republic of Haiti. Only the timely confession of two conspirators saved the whites, who hastily moved against the plotters. The incident left a residue of fear, which fed upon the continuing controversies over slavery in national politics. In 1824 the Ohio legislature petitioned Congress to enact a program of gradual, compensated emancipation for all slaves, and two years later John Quincy Adams's administration proposed to send representatives to an inter-American congress at Panama where some of the new nations of Latin America would be represented by racially mixed delegations. Both incidents provoked extended debate in Congress and a new round of argument over slavery.

These things, though, were minor compared to a series of developments around 1830 that propelled sectional consciousness into its matured phase. Together those developments placed the slave states in an altered relationship with the nonslave states and with the Union as well. Rapid economic growth continued to differentiate the sections socially as well as economically. In the South this brought high commodity prices and strengthened the plantation-slave regime, while in the North it produced further diversification and the kinds of social change associated with progress in liberal capitalist societies. Those changes included physical improvements, the growth of cities and rising living standards for most people, and changes in social outlook. Compared to southerners, northerners came to have more faith in progress, more tolerance for new ideas and social innovation, greater willingness to support public education and other social services, and more appreciation for the value of political and intellectual dissent. In none of these things were the differences absolute, but they were nevertheless important. In the North the forces promoting liberal change came to be welcomed, and acquired a dynamic of their own. In the South they were viewed much more skeptically, as threats to be contained rather than opportunities to be seized, and as a consequence took on no life of their own. The resulting differences were far more important collectively than individually. Each of them alone could have been readily contained within the American pattern of regional variation, but together they constituted sectional identities that were stronger than the total of their individual parts. Sectional consciousness became a force apart from the things that created it.

The census returns reflected the relentless pressures now working against the South. Swollen by immigration from the slave states as well as Europe, the population of the non-South grew much more rapidly than that of the South. By 1860, 3,582,999 persons of foreign birth were living in the nonslave states compared to 553,176 in the slave states, and 713,421 persons born in the slave states were living in the nonslave states. Only 371,421 persons had moved from the nonslave states into those with slavery, and of these 208,059 were in the border states of Missouri and Kentucky. The older slave states especially were hurt by out-migration. In 1850 census takers counted 155,078 natives of Virginia living in nonslave states, a figure equal to 17 percent of the state's white population. So large was this out-migration that in the 1830s, to cite two examples, the white population of Virginia increased less than 7 percent and that of South Carolina less than half of 1 percent.

The South's proportion of the nation's population shrank steadily; southerners became literally a minority in their own country. Back in 1790 the slave states from Maryland southward contained half (49.9 percent) of the total population in the nation and 40.1 percent of the whites. By 1830 these figures had dropped to 45.3 percent and 34.6 percent respectively, and by 1860 to 39.1 percent and 29.9 percent. For the Confederate South, where sectional concerns were most acute, the figures were even more striking. In 1830 the states that eventually joined the Confederacy contained only a quarter (25.7 percent) of all white Americans, and in 1860 only a fifth (20.2 percent). Representation in Congress declined accordingly. In 1830 the slave states less Delaware had 40.5 percent of the membership of the House of Representatives, and the Confederate South 31.4 percent. Thirty years later the respective proportions were 34.5 percent and 25.1 percent.

To understand the minority psychology these figures helped induce, it is necessary to remember that the differences between the Confederate South and the border South (Delaware, Maryland, Kentucky, Missouri, and the area that eventually became West Virginia) were becoming increasingly obvious. While it is easy to overstress those differences, they were nonetheless important, as the refusal of the border states to leave the Union and join the Confederacy later demonstrated. The border South produced no cotton, sugar, or rice, and was less resistant to economic diversification and liberal social change than the deep South. Economically less dependent on slavery, whites in the border states were also less insecure racially. Inevitably, those states became less and less "southern" as the locus of sectional identity shifted to the lower South. Part of the reason for this was demographic. In 1860 less than 8 percent of the blacks in Delaware were slaves, and only a few more than half of the blacks in Maryland were slaves. In the latter state, the number of slaves actually decreased from 103,036 in 1790 to 87,189 in 1860, during which time the number of free blacks rose more than tenfold, from 8,046 to 83,942. In the four slave states that did not secede from the Union, blacks constituted 27 percent of the population in 1830 but only 17 percent in 1860, and in the first census taken in West Virginia, in 1870, they constituted only 4 percent.

These economic and demographic factors had political repercussions that contributed to the maturing of sectionalism around 1830. There had always been sectional differences over economic issues, but they were never absolute. Sugar planters benefited from high tariffs, for example, while cotton growers did not. Similarly, land speculators and other expansive interests objected to the national bank, while other groups supported the bank and its conservative monetary policies. For the South as a whole, however, the real economic issue was not the tariff or banking policy, but the direction of national development, or, in political terms, what kind of economic development the federal government would encourage. More and more, northern economic groups wanted federal assistance for roads, harbors, railroads, and other internal improvements to facilitate the movement of goods and people and thereby enlarge markets and economic enterprise. They wanted a merchant marine encouraged by subsidies, manufacturing protected by higher tariffs, and a national banking policy that would systematize the issuance of paper money and credit. Southern interests, on the other hand, often found themselves on the other side of these issues.

This was not the only difference. The growth of manufacturing and cities brought new problems relating to urban congestion, factory labor, and economic interdependence, as well as new opportunities for development, which the laissez faire principles of Jeffersonian democracy were ill equipped to deal with. Many northerners saw a growing need for expanding the role of government in social and economic areas, especially in encouraging economic development, at the very time southerners were developing a constitutional philosophy of states' rights and strict construction to contain the political threat to slavery. For northerners, progress and nationalism and an active federal government were coming to be tied together. To them progress depended on an expanding government, a diversified and nationally integrated economy, and liberal social change. Southern interests dictated a different set of priorities. As northerners turned to nationalism and progress, southerners found themselves driven toward sectionalism and tradition. The differences were entirely matters of interest. Northerners could best serve their interests by expanding the national government, appealing to national ideals, and encouraging economic development and other forms of "progress," while southerners could accomplish their purposes only by turning to states' rights, localism, tradition, and economic specialization, all of which to northerners had an increasingly negative cast. Circumstances were thus forcing southerners but not northerners to choose between conflicting loyalties to section and nation. To protect their economic and racial interests, southerners had to become sectionalists; for northerners self-interest and nationalism were complementary.

National politics was the chief arena in which the resulting rivalries were contested, and though southerners held their own until 1860, the course of events worked slowly against them. Their hold on the federal government became less and less secure. The House of Representatives had always had a free state majority; by 1850 the Senate did also. Between 1800 and 1832 residents of the Confederate South won eight of the nine presidential elections, but between 1836 and 1860 only two of seven. Of twenty-nine men appointed to the Supreme Court before 1838, nineteen were from the slave South; of the seven appointed between that year and the outbreak of the Civil War, only two were. The declining strength reflected in these figures had to be offset by political acumen, and until extremists seized the initiative in the deep South in 1860–61, the effort to protect southern interests was remarkably successful. The success inhibited the growth of sectionalism, and as much as any other factor was responsible for postponing the eventual crisis until 1860–61.

The Racial Dimension

The driving force behind sectional consciousness, however, was not political but racial. "Many men of the South," wrote Ulrich B. Phillips of the antebellum generation, "thought of themselves and their neighbors as living above a loaded mine, in which the negro slaves were the powder, the abolitionists the sparks, and the free negroes the fire." Demography, slave restiveness, and the rise of militant abolitionism were the major factors behind this apprehensiveness. As the South became an ever smaller part of the Union, its black population continued to grow. In 1790 blacks had constituted 36.6 percent of the non-Indian population of the Confederate South, but by 1830 they were 40.4 percent and remained at that level throughout the antebellum era.

The significance of these figures was enhanced by internal pressures against slavery. Despite the thoroughness with which Denmark Vesey's conspiracy had been suppressed in 1822, rumors of slave unrest sporadically swept across the South. The actual extent of unrest is impossible to know, but it was certainly sufficient to account for widespread unease. In the state archives of Virginia, one scholar found records of eighty-four slaves sentenced to death for actual or threatened insurrection in the Old Dominion between 1800 and 1830 and more than 200 slaves executed for such violent crimes against whites as murder and arson.[1] The problem of security reflected in these figures was increased by the appearance of radical abolitionism around 1830. Copies of David Walker's *Appeal . . . to the Colored Citizens of the World* (1829) to rise against slavery appeared in various parts of the South, as did other incendiary publications. In 1831 came the greatest shock of all, the most important slave uprising in the South's history. Led by Nat Turner, a visionary and determined preacher, a band of blacks, mostly slaves, rose in Southampton County, Virginia, and before they were suppressed killed sixty whites. The effect was everywhere electric, and in the aftermath slave codes were tightened again and slave patrols increased, the movement of free blacks was restricted, and suspicious activity by blacks and strange whites was carefully watched. The white South became more security-conscious, and the status of blacks declined during the ensuing generation. Turner's rebellion was duly noted by abolitionists, who spread word of it, and was an important episode in the polarization of sectional feelings. It produced "something resembling a mass trauma," Kenneth M. Stampp has written; and in one sense Turner's life "made an impact upon the people of his section as great as that of John C. Calhoun and Jefferson Davis."

These pressures from within the South were reinforced by others from without. The year of Turner's rebellion was a pivotal one in the history of antislavery. After the northern states had abolished slavery, between 1780 and 1804, the antislavery movement became quiescent, its progress in the South stymied by the fear widespread among whites that a large population of free blacks would threaten the public safety and welfare. To overcome this fear, antislavery activists organized the American Colonization Society in 1817 to encourage manumission by aiding in the removal of free blacks to Africa. For a dozen years thereafter, this was the most important antislavery effort in the country. Its endeavors were compromised, however, by its own ambivalence as well as the impossibility of the task it assumed. It won little support from slaveholders and even less from blacks, and abolitionists soon came to regard it as proslavery in disguise. Would getting rid of free blacks encourage manumission and thus bring an end to slavery? Some colonizationists said it would, but others felt that removing free blacks, whom slaveowners considered a threat to slavery, would actually strengthen the institution.

The Society was never a very significant force. At best it diverted attention for a few years away from abolition and gave the appearance without the substance of antislavery. In 1827 Benjamin Lundy, an antislavery editor, counted 106 antislavery societies with 5,150 members in the slave states, compared to 24 societies of 1,475 members in nonslave states (plus a few societies about which he had no information). These figures are sometimes used to suggest that there was a vigorous antislavery movement in the South which was destroyed by the rise of abolitionist extremism after 1830. However, all the societies Lundy reported were in areas of the upper South with almost no slaves, and they were more concerned with colonization than abolition.

Then, suddenly, the antislavery movement changed. Around 1830 new leaders, who rejected colonization and other meliorative approaches, took control of the antislavery movement and directed it toward militancy and immediate abolition. In 1831 William Lloyd Garrison, the chief voice of the new militancy, organized the New England Anti-Slavery Society and began publishing *The Liberator*. Two years later the more moderate American Anti-Slavery Society was formed; and in the same year abolitionists everywhere took heart from the decision to abolish slavery in the British empire. By the time that decision was fully implemented in 1838, slavery had also been abolished in most of Latin America except Brazil and the remnants of the Spanish empire. The South was now one of the last remaining slave societies in the Western world. An appreciation of these developments is necessary for an understanding of the evolution of sectional consciousness, for white southerners were much more conscious of radical abolition than any of the other outside pressures they reacted to.

The new militants shifted the basis of antislavery from expediency to moral principle. "Every person ... has the right to *immediate* freedom," insisted the New England Anti-Slavery Society. "We hold that man cannot, consistent with reason, religion, and the eternal and immutable principles of justice, be the property of man"; and "whoever retains his fellow man in bondage is guilty of grievous wrong." "A mere difference of complexion is no reason why any man should be deprived of any of his natural rights, or subjected to any political disability."

Here was everything white southerners feared: a demand for immediate abolition, a charge that slaveholding was immoral, un-Christian, and unnatural, a suggestion that blacks were entitled to political equality, a hint that the races were physically and morally equal. The reaction was predictable. The southerners began developing an elaborate intellectual defense of slavery, and pronounced anathemas on even the most innocuous criticism of the institution within the South. Southern antislavery died, and the pressure for orthodoxy on controversial subjects became so great that free speech itself became a casualty. With this, the white South closed its mind on its most important social problem, and the result affected all areas of intellectual inquiry. The last public debate on slavery occurred in the Virginia legislature in the aftermath of Nat Turner's rebellion, when legislators from the largely white counties in the western part of the state endeavored to rid the state of slavery. Their effort provoked from Professor Thomas R. Dew of William and Mary College the first major statement of proslavery thought in the Old South, *Review of the Debates in the Virginia Legislature of 1831 and 1832* (1832). Thereafter, public discussion of slavery began with an assumption that the institution was a permanent fixture of southern life.

The Nullification Crisis

The events around 1830 did not affect everyone equally or achieve their full impact at once. Social and economic elites were affected most pointedly and responded most directly, and the lower South was more alarmed than the upper South. Using the advantages of hindsight, it is clear that the most sensitive groups overreacted to the immediate threat, yet the threat was real even if long range. "It is useless and impracticable to disguise the fact that the South is in a permanent minority, and that there is a *sectional* majority against it—a majority of different views and interests and little common sympathy," declared William Harper of South Carolina in the early 1830s. "This is the origin of the evil and the great fountain of the waters of bitterness. We are divided into slave-holding and non-slave-holding states; and this difference creates the necessity for a different mode of labour, different interests and different feelings; ... this is the broad and marked distinction that must separate us at last." If this was exaggeration, it did reflect the concerns of the most sensitive southerners.

The crisis which provoked Harper's remarks was the most portentous episode of those crowded years around 1830. The nullification crisis of 1832–33 was, as events turned out, a premature showdown provoked at the wrong time over the wrong issue and perhaps for the cause of southern unity at the wrong place. It was, in a strict sense, a South Carolina rather than a southern crisis, but its aftereffects were important for the section as a whole. Ostensibly the nullifiers were protecting against high tariff rates, but their protest was "to a crucial extent," as William W. Freehling has shown in *Prelude to the Civil War* (1966), "a revealing expression of South Carolina's morbid sensitivity to the beginnings of the anti-slavery campaign." This sensitivity, Freehling also showed, was due to racial anxieties that had been building in the state since the Vesey conspiracy of 1822 and were brought to a head by the rise of radical abolition and rumors of slave unrest. The attempt to nullify the tariff of 1832, then was an effort not so much to secure lower taxes on imports as a desperate try to limit the power of the federal government in order to prevent its acting against slavery. In the circumstances of 1832, the tariff provided the clearest basis for challenging the federal government, for radical abolitionism was still prepolitical.

In 1828 Congress, for a mixture of political and economic motives, enacted what was then the highest tariff in the nation's history. South Carolinians, who feared the economic consequences of the new tariff, protested on constitutional grounds. The federal government, they argued, had no authority to use the taxing power to encourage manufacturing. Their leader, Vice-President John C. Calhoun, detailed their protest in *The South Carolina Exposition* (1828), and offered the doctrine of states' rights, which is discussed below, to justify their position. Calhoun asserted the right of a state to nullify—veto—an unconstitutional act of the federal government, but urged the Carolinians to take a wait-and-see attitude. He kept his authorship of the *Exposition* secret lest it jeopardize his chances for reelection to the vice-presidency and his hopes of being President Andrew Jackson's political heir, as well as his political efforts to get the tariff reduced. He was reelected as Jackson's running mate but neither of his other hopes was realized, and when Congress finally revised the tariff in 1832, the revisions met none of his objections. The response was immediate. At a convention called especially for the purpose, the Carolinians exercised the right of nullification which they had only asserted before, and declared the 1832 tariff null and void and uncollectable in the ports of South Carolina. This was a direct challenge to federal authority, something Andrew Jackson was unwilling to tolerate unless he agreed with the substance of the challenge. (At the same time these events were taking place, the state of Georgia, with Jackson's assent, was nullifying a decision of the Supreme Court by asserting its authority over tribal lands of the Cherokee Indians and forcing the Cherokees to move to Oklahoma.) A crisis developed. Calhoun resigned the vice-presidency and returned to South Carolina to direct the expected confrontation with the federal government, and at Jackson's urging Congress began considering a measure, which the nullifiers called the Force Act, asserting the supremacy of federal authority over the states and authorizing the use of force against any state that defied federal law.

To avert an impasse and possibly violence, Henry Clay and other moderates worked out a compromise. The Force Act was passed, but the rates of the 1832 tariff were lowered over a period of several years. The Carolinians accepted the gradual reduction of the tariff and repealed their nullification ordinance, but in a show of defiance then declared the Force Act null and void! The declaration was moot, however, for the act was never invoked against them. The nullifiers had won the battle and lost the war. They got tariff rates lowered but did not establish a limit on federal authority. Moreover, no other state had come to their aid or even agreed with them that the principle of nullification was valid. The crisis showed that despite their racial and economic anxieties, southerners were not yet prepared to take extreme action. To most of them the federal government was a problem to be dealt with but not yet an enemy to be confronted.

States' Rights

But the federal government was a problem, and one that loomed larger and larger. To neutralize the problem, southerners turned naturally to politics, which was their first and most effective line of defense throughout the antebellum era, and to political theory, specifically the doctrine of states' rights on which Calhoun based his stance in the nullification crisis. That doctrine had developed over a long period of time and continued to evolve after 1833, but the uses to which the southerners put it in that and subsequent years reveal much about the impact events around 1830 had on southern thinking. As Calhoun and others expounded the doctrine, it was defensive, strained, and absolutist, and their formulation reflected the turning inward of southern thought as well as the growth of the siege mentality. It also reflected a growing penchant for legalism and abstraction, and for defining concrete interests in terms of abstract principles and then confusing the one with the other.

The southerners' attraction to states' rights went all the way back to the Revolution, but not until 1798 had two of their number, Thomas Jefferson and James Madison, made a systematic statement of states' rights ideology, and even then the concern had been civil liberty, not sectional interest. In that year the administration of John Adams had used the occasion of an undeclared naval war with France to enact a series of Alien and Sedition Laws aimed at political critics of the national government. The laws were flagrant violations of the constitutional guarantee of free speech and press, but the Federalist administration used them against some of its Republican critics, whose party leaders were Jefferson and Madison. The dispute involved an issue that often confronted the South in later years: What can be done when the federal government does something that is an abuse of its power and a violation of the Constitution? Or in broader terms, how is the minority to protect itself from tyranny by the majority?

These are the basic problems of American democracy. On an abstract level they involve the rights of all minorities, but as concrete political matters they have until recently been of concern to only some minorities. The Constitution did not, originally, protect all groups equally. Under its provisions, slaves, free blacks, women, Indians, and propertyless whites were in varying degrees deprived of political and legal rights, and since they also had no economic power, they found it difficult or impossible to seek redress through politics. The interests of these groups were not encompassed in the term "minority rights" as it was then understood, and political protest on their part was likely to be regarded as criminal conspiracy. There were other groups, however, who were recognized as legitimate minorities, for they had political and legal rights as well as the economic power to make themselves heard. It was these groups who fought the early battles for minority rights in America. Southerners, that is, the economic and social elites in the section, were one such minority, a segment of the body politic often at odds with the majority. They came to regard themselves as an aggrieved minority and to express their grievances in terms of minority rights. In disputes with the majority, they accordingly raised such issues as the rights of the individual and the numerical minority against society and the numerical majority, and the tendency of government to enlarge and centralize its power at the expense of individual freedom and local rights.

The Founding Fathers had recognized these problems and tried to neutralize them by placing specific limits on the power and function of the federal government. By checks and balances they had sought to disperse power through several branches of government and by the federal principle to divide sovereignty between the nation and the states. They also added a Bill of Rights to the Constitution spelling out certain of the citizen's basic rights and guarding them from action by the government and the political majority. One question they left unanswered: How were violations of the Constitution to be dealt with when the federal government itself was the offender? Who would check and balance the highest authority of all?

In time the Supreme Court asserted that function, but in 1798 it had not done so, and Jefferson and his party would have viewed such an assertion as unacceptable. (Not only would that have involved a Federalist court checking a Federalist administration and Congress, but it would have made the federal government the judge of its own powers.) The Alien and Sedition Laws thus posed a serious problem for the political minority, and Jefferson and Madison expressed their concern through the states. They authored a set of resolutions, adopted by the legislatures of Virginia and Kentucky, in which they put forth ideas that came to be known as the theory of states' rights.

The theory revolved around the idea, widely accepted in the early Republic, that the Constitution was a contract voluntarily agreed to by sovereign states for specific and limited purposes. To serve these purposes, the idea ran, the states had created a general government to which they delegated definite powers and functions while reserving all other powers and functions to themselves or the people. Any violation of this arrangement by the federal government had the character of all contractual violations: it was null and void and not binding on the contracting parties and, if persisted in, released the parties from the terms of the contract. "Whensoever the general government assumes undelegated powers," wrote Jefferson in the Kentucky Resolution of 1798, "its acts are unauthoritative, void, and of no force." The central grovernment "was not made the exclusive or final judge of the extent of the powers delegated to itself"; instead, that function belonged to the states, which also had the right to decide "the mode and measure of redress" against violations including, in the language of the second Kentucky Resolution, the right to "nullify" unconstitutional acts of the federal government. Jefferson asserted this principle only; he made no effort to implement it, and the Alien and Sedition Laws remained on the books until he himself became President.

Jefferson's doctrine was appealing to southerners, who were uneasy about the great power of the central government during the Federalist years, but during the long ensuing period when Jefferson and his party controlled the national government they had little occasion for unease. The "unconstitutional" actions of the Jeffersonians, such as the purchase of Louisiana and the Embargo Act of 1807, helped rather than hurt the South, and it was left to New Englanders to protest those things in the name of states' rights. When they did so, at the Hartford Convention in 1814–15, they transformed states' rights into a device for defending sectional interests by attacking the federal government in the language of civil liberties and individual freedom. In other words, states' rights was simply a means by which any political out-group might seek to limit the prerogatives of an in-group, and it might be used in widely differing causes. When Calhoun revived the doctrine in the nullification crisis, he used it for purposes much closer to those of the New Englanders in 1814–15 than of Jefferson in 1798–99. A doctrine originated to protect civil liberties thus became a major defense of slavery and economic privilege.

John C. Calhoun and Southern Rights

The man most responsible for this transformation was John C. Calhoun, the central figure in southern politics in the second quarter of the nineteenth century.[2] "Whatever road one travels" in studying the Old South, Vernon Louis Parrington once wrote, "one comes at last upon the austere figure of Calhoun commanding every highway of the southern mind." Calhoun was the Old South's most important political leader, its most systematic political philosopher, one of its most cogent social thinkers, and after 1830 the symbol of its consciousness as a sectional minority. No man so well embodied the will of the elites that controlled the Old South, and no man so pointedly illustrated their limitations and frustrations. Born in the South Carolina upcountry in 1782, Calhoun was first elected to Congress in 1810, and thereafter continued to hold national office until his death in 1850. He served in both houses of Congress, in the Cabinets of James Monroe and James K. Polk, and as Vice-President under John Quincy Adams and Andrew Jackson. He was also a perennial presidential candidate whose burning ambition for the presidency was an important factor in sectional and national politics.

Calhoun's place in southern history rests on his leadership in the struggle for sectional rights against the federal government and on the political and constitutional defenses he devised to facilitate that struggle. Given the problems inherent in his task, which was to defend a social order that stood against the most dynamic forces of the nineteenth century, his performance was impressive, even brilliant. Contemporaries outside the South were often unkind to him, especially his political theories, which they viewed as rationalizations for slavery and the destruction of the Union. Historians have on the whole been kinder. Parrington thought Calhoun deserved "a distinguished place among American political thinkers," while Margaret Coit, his most popular biographer, insisted that he was "without doubt this country's most original political thinker." "Judged by later times and his meaning for them," Miss Coit wrote, "Calhoun stands in the first rank of men America has produced," and his writings represent "perhaps the most powerful defense of minority rights in a democracy ever written."

That is high praise indeed for a man who stood outside and far to the right of the American political consensus. Calhoun's political thought, which is the major concern here, was part of a broader social philosophy that drew heavily upon Aristotle, Burke, and especially Thomas Hobbes. It was conservative and elitist, even racist, had little faith in liberal democracy and none at all in human nature, and placed great emphasis on the economic basis of politics. Its major aspects were embodied in Calhoun's two political theories, that of nullification and that of the concurrent majority. The first of these Calhoun developed in *The South Carolina Exposition* (1828) and the second in a *Discourse on the Constitution,* published posthumously, both of which are informed by the most systematic statement of his social thought, *Disquisition on Government,* also published after his death.

Calhoun's nullification theory was basically a restatement of Jefferson's modified to fit the circumstances of 1828–33. Unlike Jefferson, however, Calhoun was not satisfied simply to state the principle of nullification; he also developed a procedure for implementing it, and in 1832–33 led an effort to put his procedure into effect. His procedure worked this way: In a specially elected convention representing the sovereignty of its people, a state could examine any action by the federal government, and if an action was deemed unconstitutional, the convention could, after a formal finding to that effect, declare the action null and void. This declaration, the official act of nullification, would constitute a temporary veto, which would obligate the federal government to suspend the action and submit it to all the states in the form of a constitutional amendment. If three-fourths of the states ratified the action, it would become part of the Constitution, and the nullifying state would acquiesce in it and end the matter. However, since the state was sovereign, it might decide that the offending action, now a constitutional amendment, was of such a nature that it amounted to a change in the constitutional contract; and since the change was unilaterally imposed on the state, the contract itself had been broken. In that case, the state could withdraw from the contract, that is, secede from the Union.

The nullification crisis was compromised before Calhoun and the Carolinians carried this procedure to its logical conclusion, but the problem that concerned them remained after the tariff was lowered. They had gotten one offensive federal action rescinded by provoking a crisis, but they had not removed the threat of future offenses. Furthermore, the crisis had shown that nullification was a long and clumsy procedure that might divide the South and eventuate in the secession of one or more states. Calhoun's purpose was not to destroy the Union or devise a theory justifying peaceful secession. It was to find a formula that would enable the southern states to remain in the Union assured that their racial and economic interests were protected. What Calhoun wanted was not a procedure for getting states out of the Union, but a set of foolproof guarantees to keep the slave states in on their own terms.

Some years after the nullification controversy, Calhoun found these guarantees, and formulated them into his most startling and original contribution to American political theory, the doctrine of the concurrent majority. Societies, Calhoun believed, are made up of interest groups, and government is the science of balancing and restraining those groups. The problem in doing so is that the groups are more or less antagonistic and predatory. They have a tendency to form combinations for self-protection and aggrandizement, out of which come political majorities and minorities. In a system based on majority rule, the majority is able to control government and use it for its own purposes. This is tyranny: one interest or combination of interests using government to its own advantage and the detriment of legitimate interests of other groups. It was also, in Calhoun's formulation, the chief problem of American democracy—the willingness of the nonslaveholding majority to use the federal government against the vital interests of the slaveholding minority. This forced upon the South a Hobson's choice of submission or secession. The South, Calhoun warned bluntly, would not submit.

To forestall the necessity of secession, Calhoun developed his doctrine of the concurrent majority. There were not one but two majorities in the nation, he said, the slaveholding and nonslaveholding interests, and what was needed was "an organism of the government" that would allow each of them "separately, through its own majority," to express itself and that would give each "through its [own] appropriate organ, either a concurrent voice in making and executing the [federal] laws, or a veto of their execution." To give institutional form to this "organism," Calhoun proposed a dual presidency, one president from the South and another from the non-South, each with an absolute veto over all actions by the federal government, which would then be unable to do anything the majority in either section objected to.

Would such a system work? Political groups are interest groups, Calhoun declared, and as such are concerned with power. Yet "power can only be resisted by power." Rulers (majorities) and ruled (minorities) stand in antagonistic relationship to each other, and the ruled must have ways to resist the aggrandizing tendencies of rulers. Government must recognize and respond to interests other than the numerical majority, which is itself no more than one interest. On one level this is not more than the principle of countervailing power which has always operated in American politics, but Calhoun's formulation poses a special difficulty: How are the majorities that are entitled to a concurrent voice in government to be determined? How many majorities are there, and how does one qualify as such? Calhoun was specifically concerned with only two majorities, or rather one majority (non-slaveholding interests) and one minority (slaveholding interests) in formulating his theory of the concurrent majority, but elsewhere he clearly recognized others, especially labor and property. And others come readily to mind—the West and New England, agriculture and manufacturing, even women and blacks. If slaveholders or the South was entitled to be a concurrent majority, why were not these? Within the South, moreover, and even among slaveholders, there were majorities and minorities by Calhoun's own definitions. Breaking down the body politic into interest groups, once begun, might logically end only when every individual was recognized as an interest unto himself.

Thus in the institutional form Calhoun gave it, the concurrent majority was a political absurdity. But was it a useful instrument for protecting minority rights? That it was ever accepted as such says more about American scholarship than about Calhoun's theory itself. Like other political doctrines, states' rights and the concurrent majority grew out of specific circumstances. As such, neither was an objective philosophy of minority rights so much as a defense of the group that originated or used it to defend a political position. "The state rights doctrine," Arthur M. Schlesinger, Sr., wrote long ago, "has never had any real vitality independent of underlying conditions of vast social, economic or political significance." This seems equally true of Calhoun's concurrent majority, which was, as David M. Potter has pointed out, "less a philosophical position than a tactical device."

Calhoun sought to do something quite specific, protect the slaveholding South from unfavorable acts by the federal government. For this purpose a political theory that enlarged the power of the southern states while restraining the federal government was essential, and one couched in the language of minority rights and civil liberty was ideal. The doctrine of states' rights met all these needs. Moreover, it had been widely accepted on both sides of the Mason-Dixon line since the days of the Founding Fathers. It *had* sometimes been used in the interest of minority rights, but that was not Calhoun's purpose, and the fact that his concurrent majority has been read as such is a tribute to his persuasiveness as an advocate. Calhoun wrote in terms of abstract principles rather than the concrete interests he was rationalizing, and as a result historians and political scientists have sometimes taken him at face value when he treated the slaveholding elite as a minority whose relationship to the federal government was the same as that of other minorities. But a theory of minority rights must apply more or less equally to all minorities, and a fair test of Calhoun's stature as an advocate of minority rights is the relevance of his ideas for the problems of other groups such as racial or ideological minorities today. He does not pass that test. "Not in the slightest," as Richard Hofstadter has written, "was [Calhoun] concerned with minority rights as they are chiefly of interest to the modern liberal mind—the rights of dissenters to express unorthodox opinions, of the individual conscience against the State, least of all of ethnic minorities."

Yet this is not the full truth, either. Calhoun was, as Hofstadter noted, interested in one minority, a propertied racial elite, and for that minority his ideas still have the usefulness of rationalization. Hofstadter called Calhoun "the Marx of the master class" and suggested that Calhoun rationalized the hegemony of property owners as frankly as Marx did the dictatorship of the proletariat. The analogy is perhaps overdrawn, but Calhoun did develop a carefully argued defense of the prerogatives of a racial and economic elite. (At one time he tried to form a political alliance between southern slaveholders and northern manufacturers.) This point is underscored by the fact that in recent years the only minorities to make substantial use of states' rights ideas have been racial segregationists and certain conservative business groups opposed to federal activity on behalf of blacks, labor, or the poor. Only segregationists have made specific use of Calhoun's ideas, and they did so in claiming rights for themselves as a minority which they would deny to blacks. In doing so, they made no abuse of the meaning of Calhoun's ideas. In 1831 one of the Calhoun slaves, Aleck by name, ran away and was apprehended. As punishment Calhoun directed that Aleck be "lodged in jail for one week," "fed on bread and water," and given "30 lashes well laid on."

Perhaps, as Richard Hofstadter suggested, these instructions are a fit commentary on Calhoun's concern for minority rights. If so, they make his and the South's use of the doctrine of minority rights all the more remarkable. Given the fact that their purpose was to defend slavery, white supremacy, and economic privilege, the southerners' posture as an oppressed minority was extraordinary, and their success in basing their stand on a political theory ostensibly concerned with personal liberty was a brilliant achievement. This rather than the content of his political theories was the mark of Calhoun's genius. He presented the southerners' case so effectively that their essential interests were not successfully challenged until the southerners themselves made what proved to be serious errors of judgment. When their debacle came, in secession and civil war, it was a consequence of choices they made themselves. Perhaps Calhoun deserves credit—or blame—for this too: so persuasive were his rationalizations that southerners confused them with truth, and only after acting them out did they find them unreal.

The South and the Concurrent Majority

Yet if Calhoun's theories belong in the dustbin of history, the South's use of states' rights does not. The slaveholding South *was* an interest, as Calhoun said, and as such concerned to protect itself. Slavery "is to us a vital question," he stated. "It involves not only our liberty, but, what is greater (if to freemen anything can be), existence itself.... We will not, cannot, permit it to be destroyed.... Come what will, should it cost every drop of blood and every cent of property we must defend ourselves." "The difficulty is the diversity of races," he also said. "So strongly drawn is the line between the two..., and so strengthened by the force of habit and education, that it is impossible for them to exist together in the community, where their numbers are so nearly equal as in the slaveholding States, under any other relation than that which now exists. Social and political equality between them is impossible. No power on earth can overcome the difficulty. The causes lie too deep in the principles of our nature to be surmounted."

The desperate nature of this concern gave southerners a determination and political cohesion northerners rarely achieved. As already noted, dominant classes in an exploitive society are forced to preoccupy themselves with politics, for politics is the device through which they preserve their dominance. Accordingly, southern elites developed a political genius that enabled them to maintain their interests. They never tried to implement Calhoun's finespun theories. Instead, they made adroit use of the nation's political system, for which purpose Calhoun's theories were far too literal and doctrinaire. But the principle behind those theories—that the South should work to prevent undesirable actions by the federal government—was altogether realistic; and in this sense, as David M. Potter pointed out in *The South and the Concurrent Majority* (1972), "the principle of the concurrent majority, far from being a metaphysical abstraction, has been one of the dominant facts of American political life throughout most of our history." Except in the unusual circumstances created by the Civil War and its immediate aftermath, southern whites have always been able to manipulate the institutions of national governance to protect their vital interests. During the years of the Virginia Dynasty (the presidencies of Jefferson, Madison, and James Monroe, 1801–1825) they controlled the executive branch and had parity in the Senate, and benefited greatly from the three-fifths clause. Beginning in the Jacksonian era, they resorted to more informal devices, notably the rules and structure of Congress and their dominance within the Democratic party, through which they either controlled the national government or constituted as it were the official opposition. In 1836 the Democratic party adopted a rule requiring that its nominees for president and vice-president receive not a simple majority but a two-thirds majority in national conventions, and one major effect was to give a united South a veto over nominations. The rule was not abolished until 1936. The seniority system in Congress, which emerged in the 1840s, was another weapon southerners used effectively. As early as 1858 a northern senator was complaining that that system "has operated to give Senators from slave-holding states the chairmanship of every single committee that controls the public business of government. There is not one exception." A century later the same complaint was still being made.

Between the 1830s and 1850s a vigorous two-party system existed in the section, and southerners turned that too to their advantage, forming political alliances on both sides of the national political aisle. When one of the parties, the Whigs, died in the mid-1850s and all politically active southerners became Democrats, they used the one-party system to make the Democratic party virtually an instrument of their will. For about eighty years thereafter (again excepting the 1860s), until Franklin D. Roosevelt and the New Deal effected a political revolution, southerners formed the largest element in the Democratic party. In almost every Congress between 1854 and 1932 (except those in the 1860s), a majority of Democratic congressmen and senators, especially those with seniority, were from the Confederate and border Souths. This gave southerners control of the party's congressional caucus and a large say-so in party affairs between presidential elections. Throughout the long period of Republican supremacy between the Civil War and the Great Depression, southerners were thus a kind of concurrent majority at least on issues they considered vital. As a result, between Reconstruction and the New Deal, the federal government did nothing important in the field of racial policy that white southerners objected to, and not much for a generation after the New Deal. *This* was the meaning of states' rights and the concurrent majority, and the mark of southern political genius. It was also a legacy of the sectional consciousness that matured around 1830.

5

The Plantation Regime

The Old South was a land of variety as well as unity. Race sometimes pitted itself against race, class against class, area against area. The force of tradition contended with pressure for change, the lures of paternalism contested the promises of the market place, American loyalties competed with sectional imperatives. These points of conflict themselves vied with even stronger forces of unity and coherence, and from the resulting interplay came the sectional character, an elusive combination of qualities that made the Old South a land apart.

Its people had much in common with other Americans. Their history and culture were American in fundamental respects, and so were their values and impulses. Even their commitment to white supremacy had a national counterpart. Yet in the antebellum generation they and their section were far more distinguishable from the rest of the nation than they had been a century earlier or would be a century later. This element of difference is the key to their history. The things they shared with the rest of America were important, but the substance of sectional identity, the motive force in the Old South's history, was the sum of those things that set them apart. The industrial revolution, to illustrate, brought manufacturing to the South as well as the North, even if on a smaller scale, but there was a difference between northern and southern manufacturing that was not merely, or even chiefly, a matter of scale. Graniteville, South Carolina, where William Gregg established his famous textile factory and mill village in 1846, was as unlike Lowell, Massachusetts, a northern center of textile manufacturing, as the deep South was unlike New England. Similarly, New Orleans and Richmond were prosperous urban centers, yet prosperity did not make them like New York or Pittsburgh.

The same was true of social movements. The South as well as the North felt the impact of Jacksonian democracy between 1815 and 1860, but the substance of politics and the extent of democracy were never the same in the two sections. Even on matters of race, the common acceptance of white supremacy did not prevent major sectional differences over racial policy.

What this means is that the social order of the Old South was strong enough to impose itself on outside forces that impinged upon it. Urbanization and democracy were potentially subversive forces, but southerners molded them to their own purposes, and neither had the same results in the South as in the North. Cities sprang up in the South and a few of them prospered, but they were appendages of the plantation regime, not independent centers of social and economic innovation. The Jacksonian movement democratized southern politics, but the new democracy buttressed the old order rather than forged a new one.

The sum of such distinctions, some of them gross and others too subtle to express, constituted the special character of the Old South. The symbol as well as the focus of that character was the plantation, and the major elements of the plantation regime—the economic and racial components that defined it, the social structure that comprised it, the ideology that justified and sustained it—are the key elements in the history of the Old South.

The Plantation Economy

The plantation regime was an agricultural economy. In 1860 more than three-quarters of all southerners earned their livelihood directly from agriculture, and most of the others did so indirectly, by processing, transporting, or otherwise handling agricultural products. The largest industries were flour and corn milling and lumbering, and in certain localities, the production of naval stores, cotton textiles, or tobacco products. In spite of a considerable growth in nonagricultural enterprise in the 1850s, agriculture always controlled the economy, rural ideals dominated social thought, the concerns of agriculture were the chief business of politics, and social prestige was determined by one's relationship to plantation elites. Commerce and transportation were adjuncts to agriculture rather than independent economic activities.

Statistically, the typical agricultural unit was a family farm, owned and worked by a white man for subsistence. Most farms were quite small, containing well under 100 acres of improved land, and the annual value of their marketed crops and consumer purchases was so low that it hardly affected the market economy. In modern terminology they were an underdeveloped sector of the economy, and their economic significance was chiefly negative. Their cash income and expenditures were so small they retarded the growth of consumer demand and economic diversification.

The plantation was the important unit of production. Fewer in number than family farms but much larger in size, the plantations were devoted chiefly to growing staple crops for the market. Virtually all of them were owned by whites and worked by black slaves. They and their work forces and the products they produced constituted the largest economic resource of the South. In the crop year covered by the census of 1860, the slave states produced virtually all the cotton, sugar, and rice in the country, about seven-eighths of the tobacco and hemp, more than half the corn, about three-eighths of the wheat, one-fifth of the oats and rye, and varying but substantial portions of other cereal and food crops. In addition, they contained about half the cattle and more than half the swine in the country, and vast numbers of other livestock and work animals. Contrary to the view once widely held, the Old South was self-sufficient in basic food- and feedstuffs,[1] and its agriculture was quite diverse.

Cotton was the basic crop, and more than anything else its fortunes controlled the section's economy. It was extensively cultivated everywhere from southeastern Virginia to central Texas. In only a few areas was it unimportant—in the tobacco- and hemp-growing districts of the upper South, the rice districts of coastal South Carolina and Georgia, the sugar counties of southern Louisiana, and the mountain districts of Appalachia—and even in the upper South the sale of surplus slaves to the cotton and sugar kingdoms was an important source of plantation income. Between 1830 and 1860 Virginia exported an annual average of 9,000 slaves to the deep South, and Kentucky 3,000.

Cotton was also the most dynamic sector of the economy. Total production, which was 731,000 bales in 1830, surpassed 2 million bales in 1842, 3 million in 1852, and 4.5 million in 1859, the largest crop year before the Civil War. Prices fluctuated notably. In the mid-1830s, they rose above 15 cents a pound in New Orleans, and the result was general prosperity. In 1842, 1844, and 1848, however, they were below 6 cents, and times were hard everywhere. The economic optimism of the late 1850s, which stimulated a vast increase in cotton production, was sustained by the long period of good prices, which averaged more than 11 cents between 1856 and 1860. On the basis of New Orleans prices, the value of the total crop rose from $28 million in 1830 to $69 million in 1835, and to $135 million in 1849 and $249 million in 1860, to cite peak years.

Cotton was also the principal item of export, and thus the chief source of outside earnings and the inflow of income into the section. The consequences of this fact were important in molding the nature of the plantation economy. The generation after 1815 was especially significant in the economic history of the United States. Both North and South confronted the forces generated by the industrial revolution, but reactions in the two sections were quite different. As a result, the two economies became increasingly divergent, that of the North becoming "dynamic" and "progressive" while that of the South remained "static" or even "backward." How did this occur, and why?

The questions should be rephrased. To describe the North's economy as progressive and the Old South's as backward is to oversimplify and even misrepresent the situation. Those terms are too value-laden, and with northern values. The Old South's economy was backward by standards which equated progress with industrialization, urbanization, and diversification, but by other criteria it was quite dynamic. Between 1815 and 1860 it grew rapidly, but its growth was channeled into staple agriculture and related services rather than manufacturing and commerce. Why and how this occurred are best explained by a look at the manner in which southerners used the money they earned from exports.[2]

The exports, almost all of them agricultural staples destined for the North or Europe, were enormous. Between 1816 and 1820, for example, cotton alone constituted 39 percent of the value of all exports from the United States, and twenty years later the figure was 63 percent. Throughout the antebellum generation, the products of southern plantations and forests represented the lion's share of the nation's exports, and since these resources were owned by southerners, a great deal of income flowed into the section. To understand how this income was spent, it must first be understood how it was earned. Southern staple agriculture was characterized by labor intensity and significant economies of scale. Cotton, sugar, and rice were most profitably produced on large plantations by gangs of unskilled laborers. The tendency was toward concentration of income and wealth. Thus while all the slaves and many whites were only marginally involved in the market economy, a small class of wealthy planters received large incomes from exports. They were the only group in the South with substantial amounts of capital for investment, and the group that determined the course of economic development.

As the chief beneficiaries of an established system, they had few reasons for encouraging change and many for not. The social and racial order they dominated was organized around the plantation, and economic innovation might produce change in other areas. Thus class and racial factors, as well as personal inclination and rational economic factors, encouraged them to invest in enterprises that could be accommodated within the existing system, and that basically is what they did. Unlike their economic counterparts in the North, they used their income to increase agricultural production and reinforce the plantation regime rather than foster economic diversification.

The results were fateful, and may be seen in what the planters did and did not do. Economic diversification would have necessitated a certain liberalizing of the social order and a substantial investment in education and public services. This in turn would have required taxation beyond levels the planters were willing to tolerate. So taxes remained low, education and public services lagged, and the pool of technical and entrepreneurial talent necessary for economic diversification never developed. As late as 1860, only 10 percent of the industrial workers in the nation were in the South, and half of those were concerned with processing agricultural products. The section's transportation system, chiefly railroads and waterways, was financed almost exclusively by southern capital, but it was not so much a system as a series of uncoordinated enterprises that served the needs of the plantations while doing little to generate new enterprise or integrate and balance the section's economy. Here too the contrast with the North was revealing. One of the principal results of building the railroad system there was to tie the economy of the Midwest to that of the Northeast by creating a new set of dependencies. In 1835 as the railroad age began, less than a quarter of the commodity trade of the Midwest went eastward, chiefly through the Erie Canal, the rest going southward through the Mississippi River system. By 1853 five-eighths of a much-expanded trade was going eastward, most of it over railroads to Atlantic ports.

Even more important in illustrating how southerners disposed of export earnings was the cotton trade itself. That trade involved not only cotton but a long list of middleman services as well. Cotton had to be financed, shipped, insured, bought, and sold before it reached the factories of Europe or New England, and each step involved costs and potential profits. By 1815 these services were already monopolized by northerners, and New York City had become the financial center of the cotton trade. The significance of this was twofold. Utilizing the services of northern middlemen drained away from the South a large share of the income from cotton, which in turn retarded the development of commercial and credit resources within the section and funneled most of the financial advantages of the cotton trade into the North. As a result, as Harold D. Woodman observed in *King Cotton and His Retainers* (1968), "the financial center of the South was in the North." In 1860 the seven cotton states of South Carolina, Georgia, Alabama, Mississippi, Louisiana, Tennessee, and Arkansas had a total of 104 banks, including branches, with capital resources of $69.1 million and loans and discounts outstanding of $105.3 million. In contrast the three northern states of New York, Pennsylvania, and Massachusetts had 567 banks with capital resources of $201.5 million and loans and discounts of $358 million.

These factors also contributed to the lag in manufacturing. Consumer markets in the South were too small to encourage manufacturing on a significant scale. A majority of the population was almost outside the market economy, as already noted, and the planter class purchased its luxuries and many of its other manufactured goods from the North or Europe. Ships carrying southern cotton to Europe returned with manufactured goods to northern ports, and the small portion of their cargoes destined for southern markets was reshipped. Only about one-tenth of the nation's imports came directly to southern ports. Even retailing remained underdeveloped in the South, as did urbanization, an important generator of economic growth in the North. In 1860 only 7 percent of the population of the lower South was urban, compared to 37 percent of New England's.

The net result was that the export earnings of southerners had less multiplier-accelerator effect on the section's economy than might have been expected. But this was, to repeat, a result of choice, not outside dictation. The Old South's economy was not colonial despite the frequent complaints that it was. Southerners traded with the North and Europe on equitable terms, and after the nullification crisis federal economic policy was quite satisfactory to planter interests. Specialization in staple production persisted for the same reason that it began: it was socially and racially desirable for the planters and economically rational as well. "The comparative advantage of cotton over alternative forms of production was so great that this was the rational investment for the southerner to make," Douglass C. North has observed. "The southerner felt—and rightly so—that his income was higher by remaining in cotton than it would have been had he devoted his slaves, his land, and his other resources to any other type of economic activity."

The Profitability of Slavery

North's statement reflects a major reinterpretation of traditional views concerning the economic history of the Old South. The new interpretation suggests that despite the social and racial influences intruding upon them, the planters behaved in economically rational ways, making economic decisions on economic grounds with a view toward maximizing profits. It suggests, in other words, that southerners opted for staple agriculture, plantation organization, slave labor, economic specialization, and dependence on outsiders for manufactured goods and commercial services not because the planters were poor or helpless or impractical romantics, but because it made economic sense to do so. Stated in this form, the new interpretation, which is almost exclusively a product of the work of economic and econometric historians, almost certainly overstates the economic influence at work on the planters. But if the economic influence, which the reinterpretation has greatly clarified, is joined with others of ideology and race and the planters' commitment to the good life the plantation provided them, the nature of planter hegemony and thus of the plantation regime is made much clearer.

This may be illustrated by a look at one of the most important subjects in the economic history of the plantation regime, the profitability of slavery and the economic impact of the peculiar institution on the Old South. "Slave labor proved to be a type of labor peculiarly unprofitable to its employers in a multitude of cases," wrote Ulrich B. Phillips some years ago, "and peculiarly burdensome in the long run to nearly all the communities which maintained [it]." This view, which contradicts the interpretation of the Old South's economy just noted, was accepted for so long by so many historians that it may be used to approach the general subject of the economics of slavery.[3]

According to this older view, slavery had by 1860 become both unprofitable and uneconomic, unprofitable because planters made less money from it than they might have made from other investments, and uneconomic because its effects upon the southern economy were generally harmful. The two factors were interrelated. Slavery, this view ran, had originated because it was profitable for planters and necessary for white supremacy, and had remained profitable until sometime after the turn of the nineteenth century. Not long after the turn of the century, however, the rise of the cotton kingdom increased the demand for slaves just as the overseas slave trade was abolished, and the result was a long-term rise in slave prices that was not offset by equal increases in productivity. As a result plantation work forces became overcapitalized to such an extent that by 1860 only the best-managed plantations on the richest lands in the Southwest were still profitable. Slavery had therefore passed the point of economic viability, and the forces that kept it alive were not economic but racial and political. Abolitionist agitation, which aroused racial fears and resentments, made white southerners unwilling to consider alternative forms of labor.

Slavery, this traditional view continued, was also uneconomic and became more so as the nation developed a modern capitalist economy. Slave labor, it was said, was less flexible than free labor and impeded economic change in the era of the industrial revolution. Thus the Old South's economy had become increasingly rigid. The basic problem was said to be the capitalization of labor, the necessity of buying a labor force, which placed planters at a competitive disadvantage with employers of free labor. This not only required a much larger outlay of capital but drained capital from plantation districts and tied up so much capital that little was left for investment in other things. The total effect was to inhibit diversification, concentrate wealth, restrict opportunity for small investors, and otherwise foster economic imbalance.

Another weakness of slavery, according to this view, stemmed from the inherent inefficiency of slave labor and the innate inferiority of black labor. Black slaves, it was suggested, could not compete economically with free whites. As slaves they had none of the normal incentives of free laborers—higher prospects of promotions or enhanced prestige, or pride of craftsmanship—and as blacks they were naturally lazy, incompetent, and unimaginative. Slavery made it difficult for intelligent and industrious blacks to get specialized training, and those few who did get such training could not transfer their services from one employer to another. This too impeded economic growth, and by 1860 the South suffered from a hardening of its economic arteries. Important areas of the economy had become stagnant and others remained underdeveloped, and the section fell steadily behind other parts of the country.

If these problems were not enough, this view continued, there were other difficulties relating to westward expansion and dependence on world markets. The economic viability of slavery after 1800, it was said, depended upon two factors that were coming to an end by 1860. These were continued expansion of cotton production into new lands, which kept productivity high, and sustained growth in the world demand for the white staple, which kept prices high. In central Texas cotton had reached the natural limits of its westward expansion, but there was still so much unused land in the South that production was likely to continue increasing for some time. The rise in world demand, however, was slackening, and in 1860 the South faced an immediate prospect of overproduction, glutted markets, and sagging prices. When these things transpired, the price of slaves would fall below the cost of rearing them, and the expense of keeping them would exceed their earning capacity. Slavery would then be unprofitable, and economic forces would generate irresistible pressures for abolishing it. Even without the Civil War, then, slavery would have disappeared soon after 1860. "It seems evident that slavery had about reached its zenith by 1860 and must shortly have begun to decline," Charles W. Ramsdell wrote, "for the economic forces which had carried it into the region west of the Mississippi had about reached their maximum effectiveness."

This view with its corollaries—that the Old South was poor and its economy governed by irrational factors—always had its critics,[4] but only in recent years have sufficient data been amassed to refute it. The first major step in the refutation was the demonstration that slavery had indeed been a profitable institution,[5] a step that was accomplished by transforming the issue from a matter of accounting principles, in which partisans on each side of the question cited examples of individual planters who did or did not make satisfactory returns of their capital investment, into one of economic principles, in which the techniques and data of econometrics could be brought to bear. What had heretofore been viewed as a question of individual profit thus became a matter of capital investment. The important question was no longer whether an individual planter had or had not made money—individual examples might always be unrepresentative—but whether an individual who invested in land and slavery between 1830 and 1860 could reasonably expect through prudent management to earn a satisfactory return on his capital. To answer this question necessitated a general study of the economics of slavery, but the results provided a much clearer understanding of the economic nature of the peculiar institution and thus of the plantation economy.

The relevant data included quantitative information on such things as birth rates and life expectancy among slaves, productivity of field hands, the capital costs of slaveholding, fluctuations in commodity prices, and potential income from alternative investments. Allowing for variations in land quality, commodity prices, and yield per hand, Alfred H. Conrad and John R. Meyer, who made the basic study on the subject, calculated that the annual rate of return on capital invested in plantation slavery ranged from 2 percent to 13 percent and averaged 5 percent to 8 percent. Their data have been rechecked by a host of other scholars and, despite some emendations that tend to suggest a somewhat higher level of return, have stood up well. Investment in slavery was therefore economically rational, and the institution was economically viable in 1860. The price of slaves in that year was not uneconomic; on the contrary, the crop value per slave was seven times greater in 1860 than it had been in 1802, while the price of slaves was only three times as high. Earnings per slave were thus more than twice as large as they had been; plantation work forces were not overcapitalized; profits were large and growing. In fact, capitalizing the labor supply was a source of profit rather than of the rigidities once ascribed to it. The purchase of slaves did not drain capital from the South, but merely transferred it from one southerner to another. The Old South's economy had remained undiversified not because of a shortage of capital, but because slavery was more profitable than anything else.

Regional Income

This suggests that the Old South's economy was far more sophisticated than heretofore suspected, more dynamic, adaptable, and viable. Parallel studies of regional income, commodity output, and gross national product support this view.[6] Using econometric data and methodologies, Robert E. Gallman has calculated that per capita commodity output in agriculture and manufacturing in the South ($77) was equal to that of the Northeast ($78) in 1860, and considerably higher than that of the North Central states ($64). In the same way, Richard A. Easterlin has reconstructed income trends in the section between 1840 and 1860. Expressed as a percentage of the national average (which equals 100 percent), Easterlin's estimates of the relative position of each census subdivision are indicated in Table 5-1.[7]

Table 5-1 Per Capita Income by Regions as Percent of U.S. Average

	1840	1860
Northeast (New England and Mid-Atlantic states, including Maryland and Delaware)	135	139
North Central states (Midwest)	68	68
South	76	72
South Atlantic states (Virginia through Florida)	70	65
East South Central states (Kentucky, Tennessee, Alabama, Mississippi)	73	68
West South Central states (Arkansas, Louisiana, Oklahoma, Texas)	144	115

Stanley L. Engerman combined Easterlin's data with estimates of national income developed by Gallman, and arrived at the levels of per capita regional income shown in Table 5-2.[8]

These figures may be variously interpreted. Assuming their general accuracy, the basic fact seems to be that average income was significantly higher in the North than the South, but the North's advantage was due entirely to the Northeast. The South as a whole was better off than the Midwest, which seems important, but the contrast between the income of northeasterners and southeasterners in 1860 is especially striking. In regional comparisons, older parts of the North

Table 5-2   Average Per Capita Income by Regions

	TOTAL POPULATION		FREE POPULATION ONLY*	
	1840	1860	1840	1860
United States	$96	$128	$109	$144
North	109	141	110	142
Northeast	129	181	130	183
North Central	65	89	66	90
South	74	103	105	150
South Atlantic	66	84	96	124
East South Central	69	89	92	124
West South Central	151	184	238	274

*Calculating slaves as intermediate goods rather than consumers.

and newer parts of the South fare best, a fact that illustrates the economic significance of the expansion of the cotton kingdom in the South and the growth of manufacturing and commerce in the North.

At first glance the figures seem to suggest that the Old South was in fact economically backward. Yet this is probably not the best and certainly not the only meaning of the data. Engerman's calculations based on free population reveal that the South's showing was notably influenced by its large slave population. When the data are expressed in terms of growth rates, they show the South, with an annual rate of 1.7 percent by Engerman's calculations, in an especially favorable light, for the national rate was 1.4 percent. Both figures are impressive evidence of the dynamism of the American economy, but that for the South is especially so. Few modern economies have ever matched that rate of real growth over so long a period of time. The Old South's economy was not stagnant or at the point of collapse on the eve of the Civil War.

Still, there were significant North-South differences, most of them to the South's disadvantage. To appreciate the meaning of these differences, it should be remembered that backwardness and affluence are relative terms. If the South failed to match the overall performance of the Northeast, that does not necessarily mean its economy was stagnant or the section itself was poor. The South's performance was better than that of the Midwest, an area never thought of as backward or poor. It was also superior to that of most of the affluent nations of the world, as Robert W. Fogel and Stanley L. Engerman have shown in *Time on the Cross* (1974). In 1860 average per capita income in the South, even with its huge slave population, was higher than that of

Canada, Germany, or France. It was in fact higher than that of every nation in the world except Australia, Great Britain—and the North. It is therefore distorting to describe the Old South as poverty-ridden or economically stagnant. In overall terms at least its economy was characterized by high levels of income and dynamic growth, and in purely economic terms by a high level of efficiency. Slavery was highly profitable because of economies of scale, good plantation management, and effective use of labor. Slaves had fewer holidays than free workers, and the total plantation setting made possible wider use of women, children, and elderly members of the work force. The use of incentives, rewards, and other paternal measures, reinforced by the whip and close supervision, induced more work from slaves than employers were able to get from free workers.

Thus the plantation regime was not plagued by rigidity and economic contradictions. On the contrary, it was entirely compatible with modern capitalism. Slaves were employed in industry and other nonagricultural activities on a large scale and with profitable results, as Robert S. Starobin has shown in *Industrial Slavery in the Old South* (1970). By 1860, 5 percent of all slaves were employed in industry, and their employers generally earned a higher return on investment than those of free laborers. The ability to buy, sell, and rent laborers made slave work forces more flexible than free labor, and facilitated specialization in training and work assignments. In purely economic terms, then, slavery had not reached its economic limits in 1860. Not only could slave labor have been diverted to nonagricultural pursuits, but there was still plenty of unused land available for cotton cultivation. The future therefore depended to a considerable degree on continued rising world demand for cotton.

A Healthy Economy?

This positive view of the Old South's economy rests largely upon a body of data accumulated by econometric historians. Many of the data are synthetic statistics constructed by computer-assisted inferential analysis of quantitative information gathered from nineteenth-century sources, and questions naturally arise concerning their validity. Consider one example, Richard A. Easterlin's estimates of regional income trends between 1840 and 1860. Easterlin himself has warned that his estimates for 1840 required a great deal of extrapolating from incomplete data and that those for 1860 were derived in part by extrapolating the 1840 estimates. They are, therefore, as Marvin Fischbaum and Julius Rubin have noted, "subject to errors of uncertain magnitude,"[9] and to accept them literally requires an act of some faith. But even if they are accepted, there is still the question of what they measure. Were 1840 and 1860 representative years for the Southern economy? They were selected as reference points because the census returns provide more data for them than other years. In addition 1840 is the earliest year for which meaningful estimates are possible, and 1860 came at the end of the antebellum era. Yet neither was an altogether typical year. In 1840 the economy was in a downturn, while 1860 was a time of general prosperity. The progress reflected in Easterlin's figures might therefore be partly deceptive.

There is a further possibility. Even if the progress was real, it might have been due to factors outside the South rather than the strength of the southern economy itself. One, if not the, cause of general prosperity after 1855 was the rapid rise in world demand for cotton, and if and when the demand slackened, the highly specialized southern economy would suffer accordingly. Between 1830 and 1860 the world demand grew approximately 5 percent a year, but from 1866 to 1895 annual growth averaged less than 1.5 percent. These figures suggest that the chief dynamic force in the antebellum economy was external, the extraordinary expansion in the world demand for cotton. This in turn suggests that the primary fact about the Old South's economy was not its relative prosperity or backwardness, but its dependence on an outside force over which southerners had no control. The consequences of this dependence were evidenced after the Civil War when the South suffered the ill effects of overspecialization in cotton —overproduction, low prices, and general agricultural depression. The Old South's was one of those economies, in Gavin Wright's words, that exhibit "rapid growth during a period of high external demand for a resource-intensive export, but which do not develop the institutions or acquire the skills needed for sustained growth once this era has passed."[10] This does not mean that slavery would have died for economic reasons soon after 1860 had the Civil War not occurred, but that prosperity would not have continued for long and the resulting dislocations would have necessitated certain changes.

In assessing the Old South's economy, it is imperative to remember the noneconomic factors that impinged upon it. One can accept recent findings that in a strictly economic sense an investor could make money out of slavery, that per capita income, overall growth rates, and productivity on the plantations were high by world standards, and that in 1860 the plantation-slave economy was viable in the sense that there was no economic reason why it could not have continued to function. But the southern economy was especially susceptible to noneconomic influences. This was necessarily the case, for it functioned in a liberal capitalist nation and therefore had to be justified, protected, worried over, and legislated about in ways that the northern factory system, for example, did not.

The economic importance of these noneconomic factors may be illustrated by a brief look at the future prospects of the southern economy in 1860. Those prospects were not as dire as Ulrich B. Phillips and others once believed, but neither were they as bright as a purely economic analysis might suggest. Despite the profitability of slavery and high levels of average per capita income, there were important indications that in 1860 the southern economy faced an uncertain future. The diminished growth in world demand for cotton after the Civil War, which has already been noted, was perhaps the basic factor, but there were others, more apparent at the time, that tended to inhibit orderly economic change.[11] The basic fact was that any significant change might threaten the established social order, but without change there was an increasing likelihood of economic dislocation and a resulting rise in class and racial tension. There is little in the history of the Old South, or indeed of the New South after the Civil War, to suggest that the necessary changes could or would have been made voluntarily.

One factor inhibiting orderly change was the pattern of wealth and income distribution. This pattern is discussed in detail in the next chapter, but here it may be noted that in the cotton South in 1860, by the calculations of Gavin Wright, the richest 5 percent of farm operators owned 36.2 percent of the agricultural wealth while the poorest 50 percent owned 5.9 percent. These figures do not count slaves and other agricultural laborers who were not farm operators. If it be remembered that over two-fifths of the population of the cotton South were slaves and a minority of whites were agricultural laborers or more marginal workers and thus not farm operators, the inequities in this distribution become apparent. Another scholar, Robert E. Gallman, has estimated that the wealthiest 2 percent of white families, counting slaves as property, owned 25.4 percent of the gross wealth in the cotton South, 37.3 percent of the gross wealth in Louisiana outside New Orleans, and 59.6 percent in New Orleans.[12] It is obvious from these figures that the numerically typical southerner, including the slaves, received far less than the statistically average income reported in Stanley L. Engerman's estimates above. Slavery meant widespread poverty as well as great wealth, and both are important in considering the viability of the plantation regime. Poverty as well as profitability was an economic force, and the appearance of farmer protest movements in the South after 1870 suggests that its significance would intensify when westward expansion of cotton cultivation ended. Southern agricultural poverty was not relieved to the same degree as that of the North by expanding opportunities in other economic sectors. Southern cities were not the economic safety valves that northern and midwestern cities proved to be.

Still other forces threatened the viability of the plantation economy in 1860. Abolitionism was a relatively minor influence on northern opinion, but free soilism—the doctrine that slavery should be barred from all western territories and thus from further expansion—was widely accepted, as Lincoln's election to the presidency showed. Moreover, northern economic interests were pressuring the federal government for policies favoring business over agriculture, and Lincoln's election showed that this too was a triumphant force. Lincoln's victory meant that southern domination of the federal government was coming to an end. Could the plantation-slave regime remain prosperous in a nation whose economic policy was dictated by business and manufacturing and free soil? Could the regime even survive in such a circumstance? Perhaps, but major changes would be needed. The economic consequences of free soilism and Republican domination of the federal government were not certain and therefore to be feared. Of course the planters might have turned to manufacturing and economic diversification, but the racial and social consequences of doing that were uncertain too. If slavery was economically viable in manufacturing, was it socially viable? Many southerners thought not.

Nothing better illustrated the Old South's economic dilemma. Economically, diversification was becoming more and more desirable. It would open new areas of investment, relieve some of the pressures generated by the exclusion of slavery from the territories, and eliminate the potentially embarrassing dependence on the North for manufactured goods and marketing services. Yet it might subvert the social order, including white supremacy, and had to be approached warily. In the lower South, capital invested in manufacturing increased from $17.5 million in 1840 to $23.1 million in 1850 and $43.7 million in 1860, but the whole South's share of national investment in manufacturing dropped from 13.6 percent in 1840 to 9.5 percent in 1860. In the latter year only 3.7 percent of the section's work force was in manufacturing compared to the 77.6 percent in agriculture. The imbalance in the southern economy became increasingly large.

One need not regard these factors as absolutes to appreciate their cumulative significance. The failure to diversify made economic sense for individual southerners, but it rendered the section's economy vulnerable to outside manipulation. The full extent of the vulnerability became apparent only after the Civil War, when large segments of the southern economy came under outside ownership. If this was partly due to economic losses suffered in the Civil War, it was also partly due to the prewar economic system which left the South unable to compete with the North.

The economic backwardness that became so widespread after the war was also due in part to social attitudes which the plantation regime encouraged. Those attitudes were designed to inhibit social and racial change in the antebellum era, and they had the same effect in the postbellum era. They were among the major reasons for the South's inability to deal evenhandedly with political defeat in 1860 and military defeat in 1865. Capacity to change is essential to the viability of modern capitalist societies. The South in 1860 lacked that capacity. The plantation regime had idealized itself to such an extent that its people became extraordinarily resistant to changes that could not be incorporated into existing structures. In the long run this may have been the most important legacy of the plantation regime. Certainly it took the South much longer to recover from the Civil War than other societies have taken to get over far more crushing defeats.

Why this was so will be examined more closely in a later chapter. Here it may be said that part of the reason involved the social, racial, and intellectual rigidities built into the plantation regime. That regime encouraged southerners to blind themselves to social and economic realities and to mistake the nature of their own institutions. By crushing freedom of thought on social issues, perpetuating racial and class exploitation, discouraging agricultural reform and economic diversification, and restricting economic opportunity for large segments of the population, the regime inhibited self-examination and reform and dimmed the prospects for orderly change after 1860. These were intrinsic aspects of the plantation regime, as relevant to its economic survival as the profitability of slavery and the high levels of per capita income. In fact the latter features derived in part from the former. The plantation regime was much more than an economy; as Ulrich B. Phillips once said, it was chiefly a way of life. Its elites were not primarily economic men who responded rationally to economic stimuli. They were plantation patriarchs and southern whites, and as such were more concerned about social status and racial security than profits and losses. Of course these things were not unrelated, and the planters' purpose was not to choose between them, but to develop an economic system that made such choices unnecessary.

The important thing about the Old South's economy, then, was not profit and loss, but the peculiarly southern relationship between the competing economic, social, and racial factors that determined its direction. When these factors clashed, white elites invariably showed most concern about race, and in this sense the racial dimension of the plantation regime overshadowed the economic dimension. But in fact the separate aspects of the regime rarely clashed, at least in the minds of planters, who thought of the plantation system as an exclusively economic order. For that reason the regime cannot today be understood in economic terms alone.

The Peculiar Institution

The plantation regime was also a system of race relations, and a look into the interior history of slavery will shed further light on it and on the Old South itself. "You cannot speak, you cannot think of the South without slavery," William Gilmore Simms wrote before the Civil War. "*It is included in her idea.*" Simms had the white South in mind, but slavery was a far more important part of the lives of blacks than whites. For black southerners the most elemental aspects of living were determined by slavery and its social concomitant, racial discrimination. The peculiar institution set parameters around their lives, even the small minority who were not enslaved, and gave slaves a perspective on slavery and the Old South that whites never had.

The census of 1860 counted 3,950,513 slaves divided into 383,635 holdings. Most holdings were small, half of them consisting of fewer than five slaves—less than the size of an average family—and seven-eighths containing fewer than twenty slaves. Because some holdings were quite large, however, the typical slave was part of a holding of more than twenty. The slaves and their owners were concentrated on plantations and large farms in a belt of counties that ran from eastern Virginia and North Carolina through South Carolina, across south central Georgia and Alabama into Mississippi, then along both sides of the Mississippi River from Memphis, Tennessee, to the Gulf of Mexico, and across southern Louisiana to the easternmost counties of Texas. This was the black belt, originally so called for the color of its soil but in the antebellum generation for the color of its population, which was everywhere more than 50 percent black and in a few counties over 90 percent black. This concentration was significant for blacks as well as whites. The slaves were not a scattered minority population living apart from others of their kind, but denizens of communities of their own which were sometimes quite large. This fact notably influenced their lives, providing them with some assurance in facing the pressures of slavery. Their numbers combined with their economic importance to make their condition less oppressive than it might otherwise have been. Together the slave and slaveholding populations constituted most of the people of the South, 64.5 percent of those in the lower South and 38.5 percent of those in the upper South. In 1860, 31 percent of all white families in the Confederate South owned at least one slave, and in South Carolina and Mississippi the figure was 48 percent. Both figures far exceed any similar indicator of economic status in the section today. Whatever affected slaves therefore affected vast numbers of whites and thus the South as well.

The two populations coexisted in a close relationship that bound them together in mutual dependence while separating them into unbridgeable castes. This relationship—the point at which white and black, slave and master came together and remained apart—was a crucial one in the lives of all, but especially in the slaves' lives. For masters, slavery was an institution to be used and defended for racial and economic advantage. For slaves, it was life itself. One of the tragedies of the Old South was that its white people, so intimately associated with slavery, never saw that institution as the slaves saw it.

What kind of institution was it? The slaves knew better than anyone else, and their knowledge and the experience that informed it must be the focal point of any realistic effort to understand the nature and meaning of slavery, whether as an episode in the history of black southerners or in that of the South itself. Fortunately, historians of slavery have in recent years directed their attention away from its institutional aspects and onto the slaves and its racial dimensions, and as a result slavery is today perhaps the most imaginatively studied subject in American history.[13] The historians have, figuratively, shifted their point of vision from the big house to the slave quarters. The old debate over whether slavery was benign or brutal, moral or immoral ended some time ago, and has been superseded by less emotionally charged but vastly more informative study of other questions. What were the origin and nature of slavery in America, and what was its relationship to racism? How did slavery affect the slaves and the nation? What were its psychological and sociological effects on the slaves? How did the slaves withstand, absorb, or adjust to its pressures?

Obviously such questions cannot be answered to the agreement of everyone, in part because slavery was a complex, dynamic social institution that varied from time to time and place to place and affected different people in widely differing ways. This is necessarily the case with human institutions. The difficulties of generalizing about slavery are the same as those involved in generalizing about, say, American capitalism or American agriculture. One would therefore expect to find many gradations in slavery, in the slaves' conditions of life, and in their responses to their conditions.

At its worst slavery was a powerful, oppressive institution that victimized the slaves by destroying their African culture, stunting their community and institutional development, denying them a sense of individuality, and warping their personality growth. The results in these cases were broken families, social disorganization, antisocial or asocial conduct, and disrespect among the slaves for themselves and each other. Most important of all, at its worst, slavery infantilized the slave, making him into a Sambo, a being who in Stanley M. Elkins's words "was docile but irresponsible, loyal but lazy, humble but chronically given to lying and stealing," an adult whose "behavior [was] full of infantile silliness," whose "talk [was] inflated with childish exaggeration," and whose relationship with his master "was one of utter dependence and childlike attachment." Sambo was, in short, a dependent individual who had accepted the values and interests of his master, and was thus loyal, obedient, and unassertive—in a word, a "good slave."

If Sambo was the typical or even a numerous result of slavery, then slavery was perforce a closed, almost totalitarian institution that denied the slaves any meaningful autonomy as individuals and any significant opportunity for self-expression. Instead of permitting the kind of individual and group awareness and self-assertiveness normal to human development, such an institution would have forced the slaves, like children, to identify with their master, absorb his view of themselves and internalize his values and perspectives. It would have been a system of irresistible psychological and physical pressures designed to produce "good slaves" as masters defined that term by making it impossible for slaves to achieve psychological adulthood. Such an institution might have accomplished its purposes by socialization, brainwashing, or physical force, or all of these together.

Was slavery such an institution? On the surface there is much to suggest that it was. The slave codes as written down were frighteningly harsh, and the law was a sometimes brutal instrument for keeping slaves subjugated. Moreover, the law and its enforcement were supplemented by slave patrols and other devices that gave the South something of the nature of a police state for slaves. The purpose behind those things was security for whites, which was to be accomplished in part by overawing the slaves and inducing in them feelings of helplessness and hopelessness and absolute dependence. This purpose was reinforced by other devices that had the effect of brainwashing the slave. Every institution of the larger society—the church, the clergy, newspapers, educators, political leaders, and others—told the slave he was despised, racially inferior to whites, destined by God and nature only for slavery, descended from a people who never contributed anything to civilization or human advancement. In addition, his master often developed a system of favoritism and incentives that rewarded "good slaves" and punished the troublesome or recalcitrant. The slave's position was thus always difficult, and the easiest way to accommodate to it was resignation and nonresistance.

Yet it is one thing to recognize these aspects of slavery and quite another to make them the controlling factors in slave life. Even the most cursory study of the peculiar institution suggests that Sambo was only one of many different slave types, and that like all dynamic social institutions, slavery was far different in the reality from what it seemed to be on paper and in law. It is apparent that the personalities of slaves varied widely, that they in fact encompassed a full range of human types, and that whatever their intent, the physical and institutional pressures of slavery did not operate to produce a completely closed social system. There was, in other words, a considerable gap between the letter of the slave codes and the actualities of plantation life. The variety within the institution suggests that in spite of the oppressiveness of their situation, the slaves had resources of their own that enabled them to preserve a significant degree of psychological autonomy and thus an appreciation of their individuality as human beings and African-Americans. Most of them, it seems, resisted the very real pressures intended to make them Samboes.

The implications of these statements are far-reaching. They suggest that the study of slavery should not focus on what was done to the slaves, but on what the slaves did for themselves. The generality of slaves, it is now apparent, were neither inert bystanders along the sidelines of history nor absolute victims of a totalitarian institution, but active participants in the society of which they were a part. They had vastly more influence over their lives than the Sambo model allows for, far more room to exercise initiative, think for themselves, and cooperate for their own purposes. Their history, like that of all peoples, has positive dimensions that must be appreciated if the full story of their past is to be understood. The meaning of slavery for the history of black southerners is thus not to be found in victimization alone, though there was victimization aplenty, not only in heroics or quiet resistance, though there was plenty of those things too, but in the specific combination of oppression, resistance, and achievement that determined the context of daily life and the impact of slavery upon Afro-southerners. The proportion and relationship of these things are what were controlling. Insofar as slaves withstood the pressures intended to victimize them, the significant thing in their history is not oppression, but the victory over it. When slavery ended, black southerners were not a demoralized people demeaned in their own eyes, but one who had confidence in themselves, understood what freedom was, and avidly sought to avail themselves of the opportunities and responsibilities of American life.

The slaves' achievement grew out of the dynamics of slavery, which like all social arrangements was an evolving process as well as a continuous institution. It contained elements of flux as well as stability. The stability derived from the masters' power and the things that gave it substance. The flux came from the give-and-take that characterized the relationship between master and slave and the resources the slaves had to influence that relationship.

The master-slave relationship was not one between an all-powerful master and his completely helpless slaves, but one of ebbing and flowing tension between human beings caught in a web of mutual antagonisms and dependencies. The master had powers to exercise and favors to dispense, and his supremacy was reinforced by legal and other arrangements that on the surface seemed absolute. But in the workaday world of plantation life, the slaves had means of influencing the master's exercise of his prerogatives and of resisting what custom defined as their abuse. These means varied of course, but they boiled down to an ability to get back at an overbearing master and thereby compromise the purpose of his overbearance. The result was an uneasy and a hardly recognized modus vivendi between the two that devolved into a special kind of paternalism and had the effect of meliorating the harshness inherent in slavery for both master and slave. But this arrangement demanded from the slaves a certain accommodation to slavery and the system of white supremacy that underlay it. This accommodation, which was basically no more than a recognition that they were unable to force their own emancipation and that they must acquiesce in a system they could not destroy, enabled the slaves to induce from the master class certain concessions that eased the potential brutality of the institution and incidentally enabled them to preserve a meaningful degree of autonomy in their personal and group lives. In effect, by forgoing the effort to challenge slavery itself, they made it possible for their masters to tolerate certain limited activities that enabled them to influence their own conditions for the better. This had the effect of channeling their activities in directions that were "pre-political," to borrow a term from Eugene D. Genovese's *Roll, Jordan, Roll* (1974). It also permitted the masters to accommodate their patriarchal and paternal impulses to what was really an exploitive institution. The result in both cases was to enhance awareness of the mutual relationship that was both intimate and antagonistic, and conducive to degradation on the one hand and arrogance on the other.

On the lowest and most obvious level, the slaves influenced this relationship by being troublesome or not. When they considered work demands or punishments or general living conditions unreasonable, they might retaliate by slovenly work, feigned illness, abusing tools or livestock, pilferage, or other nuisance activities that helped their master understand the advantages of a certain tolerance for accustomed ways. For more serious grievances they had more desperate remedies. They might run away during crucial periods of harvest or planting, and though punishment was sure to follow, the result was a sabotage of work schedules. On extreme occasions they might resort to permanent flight, to arson or other forms of property destruction, or to violence, conspiracy, or even rebellion.

These things hardly threatened the existence of slavery or white supremacy, but they did notably influence the actualities of day-to-day life for the slaves. Each plantation had its own arrangements, the result of its own combination of personalities and countervailing forces. As concerned the slaves, the key factor was the strength of their individual and collective will, which in turn depended upon more fundamental things, especially the quality of their leadership and the strength of the community life they had apart from whites. Especially on large plantations, as Kenneth M. Stampp noted in *The Peculiar Institution* (1956), the slaves had "their own substantial communities" in which they could escape the presence of whites, "be at ease, express their thoughts and feelings with less restraint, and find their diversions amid a wide circle of friends." Within these communities, they "showed remarkable loyalty to each other," "formed enduring friendships," and strove to preserve individual and racial self-respect.

The most important insights developed in the recent scholarship on slavery derive from the discovery of this slave community and the positive functions it performed in slave life. The discovery is in part a result of effective use of sources which earlier scholars had tended to neglect or discount. These sources include the slave narratives, a substantial collection of autobiographies and reminiscences of slaves and ex-slaves published during the middle decades of the nineteenth century. These narratives are uneven in value, but together they constitute the best single source of information concerning the interior history of slavery. The best and most important of them, such as *The Narrative of the Life of Frederick Douglass* (1845), convey the meaning of slavery to sensitive, intelligent beings and provide an unsurpassed look into the tensions and complexities of master-slave relationships. A second set of sources, almost as valuable as the narratives, is the collection of interviews with ex-slaves conducted by researchers from Fisk University in the 1920s and the Works Progress Administration (WPA) in the 1930s. In these interviews, published recently by Greenwood Publishing Company as *The American Slave: A Composite Autobiography* (19 vols., 1972), a large number of quite elderly men and women were asked to reminisce about their experiences as slaves. The results are one of the important resources of American history and folklore, at once invaluable and dangerous for historians, but now an indispensable source for students of slave life.[14]

These and other sources reveal the existence and operation of the slave community. They show that the slaves clearly understood their condition both as blacks and slaves, and that they engaged in a wide range of cooperative endeavors to make their condition more tolerable. Slavery and racism gave them a common bond, and dealing with those things gave their communities the strength that comes from common purpose. Cooperative resistance to oppression promoted individual and group respect and gave coherence to public life. It also increased opportunities for self-expression and leadership and for the confidence that comes from belonging.

An important source of community strength and identity was African cultural survivals, which, though weakened by the manifold pressures of Americanization and the early end of the African slave trade, remained an important determinant of cultural forms among slaves. By the antebellum generation, African survivals had melded with New World and European influences into a distinctive slave culture that was neither African nor European, nor white American either, but had much of all three as well as the special contributions of Afro-Americans themselves, which grew out of their own needs and gave expression to their own hopes. The slave culture was best manifested in the slaves' religion, a syncretic mixture of African and Christian elements which acted as an important source of solace and inspiration, but it was also expressed in various forms of folk culture such as folklore, music, songs, and dance, all of which were notably influenced by the African heritage as well as the slave experience, and in the social role of community leaders—slave-drivers, preachers, individuals believed to have special spiritual powers, or others assigned special respect. "African culture was much more resistant to the bludgeon of slavery than historians have hitherto suspected," John W. Blassingame has written in *The Slave Community* (1972); "many African cultural forms" survived in the antebellum era. The slave culture, in other words, met the test of viability, for it served the elemental needs of the people who shared it. It identified them, articulated their sense of purpose, rationalized their existence as a people, and gave them strength to endure and hope for the future.

Much of its strength derived from the slave family, an institution unprotected by law and thus always precarious, but which was nevertheless a functioning entity that performed most of the responsibilities commonly expected of American families.[15] It was typically nuclear, consisting of parents and children, and in it roles were defined and responsibilities assigned according to patriarchal notions. The father, not the mother, was usually its strongest and most important figure, and through his leadership the family played its important social role. It was the primary agency for socializing youths and teaching them how to survive in slave society. It imparted moral and social values, and gave its members identity and self-esteem as well as "companionship, love, sexual gratification, sympathetic understanding," and the kinds of assurances that made life livable.

Above all, it helped slaves withstand the Sambo-izing pressures of slavery and develop a full range of personality types. If some slaves succumbed to those pressures and developed according to the Uncle Tom stereotype, most did not. If chronic troublemakers and active resisters were few among the slaves, they are also few in other societies, though slave society had a full share of violence directed sometimes against other slaves as well as whites and masters. The social and racial tensions within the Old South belie assertions that the generality of slaves absorbed the values of the master class and suggest instead that in important particulars at least they consciously rejected them. If their public demeanor often displayed some of the bowing and scraping that characterized the Sambo image, that was not typically the case. On the contrary, the generality of slaves seem to have been "sullenly obedient and hostilely submissive," to quote John W. Blassingame again, a people who by their own devices "escaped from total dependency, infantilism, and abject docility." The individual often displayed humbleness before whites, but this might be role playing, "a sham, a mask to hide his true feelings," part of a complex survival strategy. Recognizing his situation and the dimensions (as well as the limits) of his master's power, he knew that rebellion was foolhardy. Guile, however, was not, and he used his wits to manipulate whites and ease the onerous burdens of life. Under normal circumstances he gave no trouble, but he resisted all efforts to drive him beyond the pace he considered proper. Typically, he seems to have disliked contact with whites, and his relationship with them was usually uneasy and sometimes tense. The slaves thus paid a price for the accommodation that made their position tolerable, even though it seems that the choice they made was unavoidable. Some of the conditions under which they lived can be explained in class terms—they were after all an agricultural work force, and work forces in the nineteenth century, in America as elsewhere, generally lived and worked under unenviable conditions. In fact, comparisons of the slaves with other work forces of the time are not altogether unfavorable to the slaves on purely material things. Both economic and paternal motives encouraged masters to supply their slaves with adequate, even if coarse, food, housing, clothing, and medical attention. Moreover, the tasks they assigned and hours of labor were not unusual for the time, and the force of public opinion as well as the humane instincts of most masters served to meliorate the physical abuse of slaves. If the lash was the ubiquitous symbol of slavery and if the most revolting kinds of physical cruelties are easy to find, the most important brutality of slavery was probably psychological rather than physical. To be a slave in a society that placed great value on individual freedom was to be subject to deprivations of a psychological and sociological nature that transcended physical and material considerations. It was to be denied the things most esteemed by the larger society—personal liberty, economic opportunity, the freedom to take care of oneself, the opportunity to develop one's talents—all the things that made one a "good American" as that term was then defined.

Instead of these things, the slaves were forced into a series of social relationships that were fundamentally compromising despite their own success in withstanding the worst of the pressures. The positive relationships they developed with each other were always fragile because they might be suddenly broken by the exigencies of slavery, and whatever personal attachments they developed with whites were compromising in the most basic sense of the term, for they existed only by the master's sufferance and the slave's subservience. This was perhaps the most tragic aspect of slavery as an episode in the history of the South. It permitted no genuine respect between white and black or master and slave, for respect exists only between equals. It thus corrupted race relations while degrading blacks and bloating the self-esteem of whites. Its characteristic features were racism and resentment. Power corrupts and absolute power corrupts absolutely as the adage has it, and the same is true of dependence. To conceal their corruption, the masters practiced a smothering paternalism; to avoid theirs, the slaves resorted to accommodation and role playing—"puttin' Ole Massa on." Maybe Ole Massa was deceived; but it seems more likely that he as well as his slaves understood the ugly truth about slavery. Certainly he, as well as they, was a long time in overcoming its legacy, and so too was the South.

6

Society and Thought

The social structure of the plantation regime changed little between the Revolution and the Civil War. The small class of wealthy slaveholding planters remained at the top and, in tandem with the large middle class just below it in social prestige and economic power, owned the Old South, controlled its politics, and dominated its social life. Beneath these classes, which together constituted a majority of the white population, was the large mass of dependent people, most of them landless, who constituted a majority of the total population. These included the various groups of poor whites as well as all blacks, whether slave or free, and the Indians who remained in large parts of the southwestern half of the Confederate South until the 1830s.

The social history of the plantation regime is best seen in the relationships between these classes, especially the relationship of the lesser classes to the planters. The regime was an organic society that revolved around plantation elites, and both its unity and its stresses are best seen in group interaction. Perhaps the most revealing nonracial fact about the society was that only the planters had a developed sense of class consciousness. This facilitated their social tasks and helps explain their dominance of the Old South. Group consciousness among other whites remained racial rather than economic, a fact that gave the plantation regime a social quality not always easy to understand.

The planter class was extraordinarily successful in maintaining its social hegemony. No significant threat to its position ever emerged from within the section, but because of pressures from outside and the fear of disruption from inside, it was not a relaxed elite. As a group the planters exhibited attributes of the siege mentality and tended to overreact to threats, whether from abolitionists, the federal government, slave rebelliousness, or individual critics like Hinton Rowan Helper. Yet the potential for class unrest was always great. The slave regime was easier to attack and more difficult to defend than the liberal capitalism of the North, and the planters had to give more time than northern elites to warding off threats to their position. For these reasons social class provides a useful perspective for viewing the history of the plantation regime. That is not to suggest, however, that class was more important than race in the Old South. "Habitat [i.e. racial] grouping," as Ulrich B. Phillips observed of the Old South, "had a cementing force great enough to overcome the cleaving tendencies of economic stratification."

Planter Hegemony

The hegemony of the planter class derived in the first instance from its wealth. In his remarkable study *The Large Slaveholders of Louisiana, 1860* (1964), Joseph K. Menn amassed an astonishing amount of information from manuscript census reports on the 1,640 individuals who owned fifty or more slaves in that state on the eve of the Civil War, and the results suggest something of the dimensions of planter wealth. Six of the owners were blacks, about 200 were white women, and all but eleven employed their slaves in agriculture. The 1,640 holdings equaled about 10 percent of the agricultural units in Louisiana, but together they accounted for 48 percent of all slaves in the state (a total of 160,500 bondsmen), 42.7 percent of all improved agricultural acreage, and, by value, 60.4 percent of all agricultural wealth, 67.4 percent of all farm machinery, and 45 percent of all livestock. They also produced 48.7 percent of the state's cotton crop, 76.2 percent of the sugar crop, 77.7 percent of the molasses, 43 percent of the corn, and 43 percent of the peas and beans. They likewise contained a disproportionate share of the good agricultural land in the state, and their productivity per acre was greater than that of smaller plantations. The high concentration of wealth this represents was more characteristic of the black belt than other parts of the South and more characteristic of Louisiana and South Carolina than other states, but the significance of the picture described by Menn is underscored by the fact that political power was also concentrated in the black belt.

The slaveholding elite consisted of "aristocratic" and "bourgeois" elements. The former comprised families whose wealth had been inherited for three generations or more and whose "breeding" and tradition of leadership gave them standing as "true" aristocrats. The latter, a much larger group, were "cotton snobs," to borrow the phrase of Daniel R. Hundley, whose *Social Relations in Our Southern States* (1860) was the most systematic contemporary effort to describe the social structure of the Old South. These were self-made men who by their own or their fathers' effort and luck and sometimes larceny had wrestled fortunes from the uncertain opportunities of the cotton kingdom. Though they lacked the prestige and gentility of more "aristocratic" families, their numbers, wealth, and assertiveness enabled them to dominate the cotton kingdom.

The division between these two elements was not clearcut, but it was sufficiently so to give the planter class a dual character that complicates the problem of understanding it. Is the class best described as paternal, seigneurial, premodern, and precapitalist, as Eugene D. Genovese suggests in *The Political Economy of Slavery* (1965)? Or was it basically bourgeois, materialist, capitalist, and modern, as others have insisted? The evidence seems contradictory, and the issue itself of secondary importance if the purpose of the debate is to try to categorize the planters as one or the other. The planters functioned in a capitalist system that rewarded the virtues and vices of the market place, but their social role included a patriarchal and premodern dimension. They responded to both circumstances, and that fact underscores the dual nature of the class.

As a functioning elite the planters were no more and no less selfless or moral than other American elites. They were born into a system they considered natural and basically decent. They were concerned with their own material and moral wellbeing and that of their dependents, and they saw no conflict between those concerns. Their understanding of what constituted the welfare of their dependents did not conform to modern equalitarian ideals, but this does not mean they were hypocritical or mean-spirited. It means instead that their world view consisted of moral, racial, and social values unlike those of modern equalitarians.

In their society as in others, there was a gap between ideals and actualities. No society ever lived up to the ideals its best elements profess—that is after all what distinguishes ideals from realities. But historians and others have assigned a special significance to the Old South's failure in this regard and have made that failure a major factor in their analysis of the planter class. Is this special treatment justified?

The gap had a personal as well as a social dimension. In personal terms it involved the planters' simultaneous concern for and exploitation of those dependent upon them, especially their slaves. In social terms it grew out of the difference between the public obeisances paid the tenets of democracy and New Testament Christianity on the one hand and the practice of slavery and other forms of social inequality on the other. The resulting disparities, and the difficulties southerners sometimes went to in trying to reconcile them, have led many historians to suggest that white southerners and especially the planters had substantial feelings of guilt. They were, after all, a people influenced by Calvinism who benefited handsomely from the exploitiveness of a social system that seemed on the surface irreconcilable with certain of their basic values. Because of this, Wilbur J. Cash made guilt a basic component of the white southern mentality, and scholars such as Charles G. Sellers, Kenneth M. Stampp, and William H. Freehling have agreed.[1]

The evidence on this too is contradictory, but the issue involved is important. In autobiographies, diaries, letters, and elsewhere, individual southerners often expressed feelings of ambivalence, anxiety, and/or guilt about slavery and the moral contradictions in their society. Many others, however, did not. Social actions showed a similar contradictory pattern. Some southerners were so troubled over slavery that they manumitted their slaves. A few actually left the South and became active abolitionists, and a larger number, less acutely troubled, remained to speak or work quietly against the institution. The vast majority, however, did none of these things, and in fact actively defended the institution with no apparent ambivalence. There is no reason to disregard any of this evidence in trying to resolve the matter. The disparities might be evidence of the dual nature of the planter class and the Old South itself, but the best explanation seems simpler than that. Individuals of whatever class or station in life respond in different ways to social stimuli. This has already been seen in the matter of slave personality, and it is shown here in the case of the master class. Some whites felt guilty and others did not. If, as some recent critics of the guilt hypothesis have maintained, the hypothesis itself grows out of the guilt feelings of modern-day liberals, the same might be true of antebellum southerners. Perhaps those of liberal bent were prone to feel guilty while others were not.

Perhaps, also, guilt is not the best term to describe the inner conflict southerners sometimes expressed over social matters. Their doubts may have been expressions of concern not over slavery itself but over specific abuses within slavery, in the same manner that liberal social critics today are often critical of aspects of American capitalism but not capitalism itself. Hypocrisy and even racism might also have been sources of some of the apparent ambivalence. On occasion it was good social form to discuss slavery as a necessary evil rather than a positive good. Similarly, much of the concern over slavery stemmed from the fact that the slaves were blacks, and to some degree the desire to be rid of slavery was a desire to be rid of blacks. At the same time, many whites were convinced that though slavery was beneficial to blacks, it was burdensome for whites, especially poor whites, and the South would be better off without it for that reason.

The matter of guilt can be further illuminated by comparative history. Presumably, there is some guilt among some people in every society, and also, presumably, some basis for the guilt. The relevant question, therefore, is not whether some southerners felt guilty, but whether they as a whole felt more guilty than other people. Were white southerners who exploited blacks more guilt-ridden than, say, white westerners who expropriated Indians? Or easterners who discriminated against immigrant groups? Or, indeed, Europeans who for centuries ran roughshod over non-Europeans? Was the disparity between ideal and reality in the Old South so much greater than elsewhere in the nation or the Western world that southerners but not other peoples were guilt-ridden? While historians often make guilt a major theme of southern history, they almost never do so for the rest of America or western Europe.

Is this justified? Perhaps the Old South *was* unlike the rest of the country in this as in many other things. Perhaps its exploitiveness was grosser; certainly it was more obvious to its elites, whose direct involvement on a continuing basis was required to sustain it and who could not therefore deny or ignore it. For this reason if no other, the burden of racism was greater in the Old South than most other societies. Once the Indians were killed off or placed on reservations, white westerners could and did forget about them, for it was no longer necessary to center social policy around "keeping the Indian in his place." The same was true of the East. There immigrants were subjected to varying degrees of discrimination until they became Americanized, but when that happened they entered the majority population and were no longer the object of calculated social policy. But in the South blacks were enslaved and kept in the midst of whites, and could not be forgotten. They and their containment had to be the center of perpetual concern lest white supremacy be threatened.

This suggests that guilt feelings were more important in the Old South than elsewhere, but it also suggests that guilt was not the basic fact of life there. However much some southerners felt guilty about their social system, the fact was that as a people they accepted the system, including slavery, as natural and permanent. Then too the whole question of guilt rests on the erroneous assumption that white southerners understood democracy and New Testament Christianity as modern liberals understand those things. This was not the case at all. To southerners democracy and Christianity were functioning entities, not theoretical constructs, and when they spoke of them, they had in mind not lofty ideals of equality and brotherhood, but the actualities of politics and religion in the Old South. Democracy and Christianity were thus thoroughly compatible with slavery and socioeconomic inequality, for those things had always existed in the democratic and

Christian South. Guilt was therefore far less important to southerners than fear, and its importance consists largely of the fact that it exacerbated tendencies which grew out of fear.

The Plain Folk

Back in the 1930s historian Frank L. Owsley and several of his students at Vanderbilt University undertook a major effort "to make a case study of the plain people of the Old South as Phillips and his followers [had] done for the larger planter class." Making widespread use of hitherto neglected records such as court proceedings, will books, tax lists, and manuscript census reports, they suggested that *The Plain Folk of the Old South* (1949), as Owsley titled his major work on the subject, were not only the largest but most important social and economic class in the antebellum era.[2] The most important of the records used to support this conclusion were the manuscript census reports of 1850 and 1860, the same reports that econometric historians have used so fruitfully in recent years. Before 1850 census takers gathered little information of a social and economic nature, but in that year and again in 1860 they collected detailed data on several important subjects. On a Schedule of Free Inhabitants they recorded the name, age, and sex of every free person, the value of his or her personal estate, and the occupation of everyone over fifteen years of age. On a Schedule of Slave Inhabitants they gathered the same information for each slaveowner, plus the age and sex of each of his or her slaves. A Schedule of Agricultural Production listed the owner, agent, or tenant of each farm, as well as improved acreage, the value of implements and machinery, an inventory of livestock, and the production of basic crops for the preceding year. The value of such information is apparent, but so is the difficulty of using it. Its sheer mass was unassimilable until the advent of computers and cooperative research projects.

Using these records to study selected counties in Louisiana, Tennessee, Alabama, and Mississippi, Owsley and his students demonstrated that land ownership among the white farm population was widespread, ranging from 70 percent to 90 percent in every sample county, and that the typical holding was small, 80 percent of them being less than 200 acres. Owsley concluded that "the great mass" of white southerners were middle class and that the Old South was an open and progressive society, economically and politically democratic. Being the largest and most important social class of whites, the plain folk, he reckoned, controlled politics, set the tone of social life, and molded the economic system to their needs. The mass of white southerners had "a high degree of economic and social security," and "on the whole" their condition was "constantly improving." Good land was plentiful and easily acquired, and "the opportunity for acquiring education—the gateway to the professions and to success—was quite favorable for the ambitious youth, however poor he might be." These things removed the occasion for class animosity, and the result was a society that enjoyed a "sense of unity between all social and economic groups."

Was this rosy picture accurate? Alas, no. The numerical significance of the plain folk may be readily acknowledged, though the above percentages are of white farm operators only and thus exclude urban dwellers and blacks as well as rural nonfarm whites such as woodcutters, turpentine workers, drovers, and hunters, and even agricultural laborers who did not operate their own farms. When these groups are included, a far different picture emerges. In Hancock County in the black belt of Georgia, for example, two-thirds of the people in the 1850s were blacks, and one-third of the whites owned neither land nor slaves.[3] Of almost 300 white farm laborers and textile workers in that county in 1860, more than nine-tenths owned no land at all. The very poor were thus a large minority of the white population, and more than that, their condition was deteriorating in the antebellum decade.

In such a society the economic and political significance of the middle class is not to be determined by counting the number of people who own land. Where land is cheap and labor dear, the ownership of labor (slaves) is a much more important indicator of economic status. Moreover, the significance of an economic class depends not on its numbers, but on its share of the total wealth. The typical land holding and the typical farm were small in the Old South, but the typical acre of land and the typical slave were parts of large holdings. Thus agricultural wealth was quite heavily concentrated. While 63.9 percent of the farms in the cotton South had less than 100 acres of improved land and only 5.3 percent had 500 or more acres, the latter contained more than twice as much improved acreage as the former (37.8 percent of the total compared to 18.8 percent). For other types of agricultural wealth the disparities are even greater. In 1860 the largest 5 percent of agricultural units in the cotton South represented 36.2 percent of the total value of agricultural wealth, while the poorest 50 percent represented only 5.9 percent. As this suggests, slave ownership was more concentrated than land ownership: the wealthiest 5 percent of the plantations in the cotton South contained 38.9 percent of all the slaves, while the poorest 60 percent contained only 4.3 percent. Furthermore, the largest 5 percent of the agricultural units produced 42 percent of the cotton crop, while the smallest 50 percent produced 4 percent. "The social implication of the slave-cotton regime," wrote Gavin Wright summarizing these data, "was a highly unequal distribution of wealth."[4]

Herrenvolk Democracy

The social implications of these data should not, however, be carried too far. The status of middle-class whites was influenced by factors other than their share of the wealth, the most important of which were their economic independence and the planters' desire for white racial solidarity. As a result, their importance was less than their numbers would suggest but more than their share of the wealth might indicate.

This intermediate position reflected the nature and content of democracy in the Old South. The extent of democracy in any society is difficult to measure, for democracy is a state of mind as well as a political condition, and its economic and social realities are more important than its political forms. In all of these areas there were significant developments in the antebellum era, and the thrust of them all was toward greater democracy for whites. Class lines remained important, but their abrasiveness was reduced by paternalism, economic and social opportunity, and the fact that whites of all classes tended to identify with their social betters. Yet the democratic impulse was limited. It never threatened the unequal distribution of property, never concerned itself with the problems of the poor and dispossessed, and never addressed itself to racial, class, or sexual discrimination.

The crucial tests of democracy in any society are the extent to which people are temperamentally democratic and the degree to which political and economic elites are committed to and restrained by the philosophical and institutional underpinnings of democracy. By these tests, the plantation regime was not very democratic. Even if such matters as slavery, racism, sexism, Indian removal, and indifference to the plight of poor whites be dismissed as concerns of twentieth- but not nineteenth-century democracy, there were still significant limitations on democracy in the Old South. On sensitive social issues, there was little commitment to freedom of thought and little insistence on the equality of all people, not even all whites, before the law. The political and legal systems were instruments of class and racial rule, taxation was inequitable, the mails were censored, dissent on certain issues was stifled, and freedom of speech and petition was sometimes denied. On occasion, there was a willingness to disregard the law and tolerate extralegal activity, including vigilantism and violence, to accomplish popular purposes.

Yet the practical impact of these things was limited, too, so that white southerners considered themselves democrats in a democratic society. Their public discourse was in democratic language, which meant that they sometimes said one thing and meant another. "It is always a most delicate and dangerous task for one set of people to legislate for another, without any community of interest," wrote one of them in 1832. "It is sure to destroy the great principle of responsibility, and in the end to lay the weaker interest at the mercy of the stronger. It subverts the very end for which all governments are established" and violates "the fundamental rights of man." No democrat could argue with that passage, but it was written by Thomas R. Dew in defense of the rights of slaveholders. It was prompted by the effort of legislators from counties which had few or no slaves to pass legislation abolishing slavery in Virginia over the objections of legislators from counties which had many slaves.

This simultaneous commitment to democracy and slavery was a basic fact about the Old South which has been difficult to explain. Historians have used such terms as "paradox" and "schizophrenia" to account for it. While those terms are useful, "*Herrenvolk* democracy," first used by Pierre van den Berghe in *Race and Racism* (1967), is a better one. Van den Berghe used the term to characterize "regimes like those of the United States and South Africa that are democratic for the master race but tyrannical for the subordinate group." The distinguishing feature of such regimes, to borrow William L. Barney's equally useful term, is "egalitarian racism," a concept that is especially relevent for the Old South. "*Herrenvolk* egalitarianism," George Fredrickson has written, "was the dominant public ideology of the South."[5]

Evidence for this is abundant. Political discourse in the Old South revolved around the *Herrenvolk* idea that all white men are created equal and have inalienable rights the preservation of which depends in part upon the same rights being withheld from blacks. "Break down slavery," declared Henry A. Wise of Virginia, "and you would with the same blow destroy the great Democratic principle of equality among men." Since "the mass of laborers [i.e., slaves]" are not recognized as citizens in the South, everyone who is a citizen "feels that he belongs to an elevated class," explained Thomas R. R. Cobb of Georgia. "It matters not that he is no slaveholder; he is not of the inferior race; he is a freeborn citizen; he engages in no menial occupation. The poorest meets the richest as an equal; sits at his table with him; salutes him as a neighbor; meets him in every public assembly, and stands on the same social platform. Hence there is no war of classes." In this manner slavery generated a condition "extremely favorable to republican liberty," to quote another Virginian, Abel P. Upshur. "Negro slavery tends to inspire in the white man a strong love of freedom, to give him a high estimate of its value, and to inspire him with those feelings of independence, self-respect and proper pride, which fit him for the enjoyment of free institutions."

These ideas flowered as Jacksonian democracy spread across the

South, and the two phenomena interlocked and influenced each other. What the Jacksonian movement contributed to *Herrenvolk* democracy was not slavery or racial elitism, things that already existed, but the racial ideas of Frank L. Owsley's plain folk, which differed from those of the planter elite by being cruder, less ambiguous, and more literally applied. As the mass of white men secured the right to vote, politics responded to their concerns. "Simply because the ordinary citizen played a growing part in the government in the United States," Carl N. Degler has written of the Jacksonian period, "he was able to have his concern about status and mobility translated into laws as well as practice." Southern politics was emotionalized, and slavery and race were the most emotional issues of all. To what extent, if any, this was encouraged by the planters as a device for diverting the new democracy away from economic protest is not clear. If that was the purpose, it was easily achieved, for the new electorate already had a developed sense of racial concern but little or no articulated sense of class grievance.

In any event, the spread of democracy in the white South was paralleled by a deterioration in the black South. In the years after Nat Turner's rebellion in 1831, as previously noted, slave codes were strengthened again and their police state provisions more systematically enforced. The status of free blacks declined. Between 1829 and 1836 six southern states passed laws requiring newly freed blacks to leave the state forthwith, thereby effectively eliminating the right of manumission. States that had not already done so now disfranchised free blacks. In the same years the defense of slavery as a positive good crystallized, and pressures for intellectual conformity increased. "Democratization of Southern politics gave pro-slavery advocates a stronger hold upon the Southern consciousness," wrote Francis B. Simkins some years ago. He might have added that it also strengthened equalitarian racism.

Jacksonian democracy produced notable political changes all across the South. White manhood suffrage became the general rule, property and religious qualifications for officeholding disappeared, and legislative apportionment became more equitable. The number of offices filled by popular election increased, as did the responsiveness of government to white public opinion. The specifics varied from state to state. South Carolina was affected least of all. There all state officials, even the governor and presidential electors, were still selected by the legislature in 1860. In most states the legislatures continued to be apportioned to the advantage of the black belt and slaveholders. In South Carolina, to illustrate, representation was based on a formula combining population and taxable wealth in a way that insured the lowcountry control of the state senate and the upcountry dominance in the lower house. (Calhoun cited this as an example of the concurrent majority at work.) The same effect was achieved in Louisiana by counting the slaves in apportioning legislative seats, and in North Carolina by counting three-fifths of the slaves.

Yet by 1850 the form of southern politics was relatively democratic for whites. Voter qualifications were about the same as in the North and political participation by qualified voters was about as high. There was rapid turnover of elected officials, at least on the state and congressional levels, widespread election to high office of men of modest social origins, and until the 1850s a vigorous two-party system. But the substance of politics was less democratic. State and local governments gave little attention to economic and social problems. This was due partly to the fact that this was an age of political laissez faire, and partly to the fact that planters were the only constituency with a developed sense of class interest and thus the only one that made significant demands on government. The Whig and Democratic parties represented the same basic interests, and neither wanted social change. Low taxes meant among other things that government remained a bulwark of the status quo. Clement Eaton has cited the example of a Georgia planter whose estate included 210 slaves and more than 5,000 acres of land but who in 1848 paid taxes totaling $65.62. In 1850 Virginians paid an average tax per capita of 77 cents. The reason for this was political, not economic. The South had considerable wealth to tax; public money could and was raised for certain purposes. Of $245 million invested in southern railroads before the Civil War, for example, more than 55 percent came from the same state and local governments that pleaded poverty when asked to finance education or welfare services. "The masses," wrote Roger Shugg in *Origins of the Class Struggle in Louisiana* (1939), "having no real voice in the government, received from it no benefit."

But that was not the whole truth either. The white population did have substantial influence in government, but it was channeled into racial rather than economic concerns. The mass of whites received few economic benefits from government because they made few demands for such benefits, but in racial matters, where they did make demands, they got everything from government they wanted.

Education

The results may be seen in public education, an area in which the Old South lagged notably behind the North. The basic difficulty was not poverty or sparse population, though these were contributing factors, but the absence of a general appreciation of the value of education. The controlling attitude was elitist rather than populist. It incorporated neither the democratic idea that education is necessary for the effective functioning of democracy nor the bourgeois idea that it is essential for economic growth, nor even the Protestant idea that it is vital for religious wellbeing. Instead, it held that education is necessary for those whose position in life requires it. "Whenever a child is to be educated, it should be ascertained what is to be his probable destiny," wrote a contributor to the *Southern Quarterly Review* in 1852. "Men whose lives are spent in humble toil, have little time for reflection," and education exposes them "to the danger of attacks from the demagogue, as well as to the wholesome admonitions of the patriotic." Education, this writer continued, "effects no change in the nature of man. It is but an instrument—to the good, of good, to the bad . . . of evil," and in the wrong hands "is a power quite as dangerous as gunpowder in the hands of an infant, or a revolver in the paws of a monkey."

This was an extreme statement of sentiments that had wide acceptance. The idea that government has an obligation to educate the citizenry spread much more slowly in the South than in the North, and of the states that eventually joined the Confederacy only North Carolina made significant progress in developing a system of public education before the Civil War. Virginia was representative of the upper South. There as elsewhere the immediate problem was financial. To avoid taxation, the legislature established a "literary fund" which was invested in state bonds and the income used to finance "pauper" schools (i.e., schools to which pupils were admitted without tuition if their parents signed a paupers' oath). By 1860 this fund amounted to $1.7 million and the stigma attached to free schools by the necessity of having to sign a paupers' oath had abated to the extent that half the pupils in the state were enrolled in those schools which became the nucleus of the states' public school system. For localities willing to tax themselves for public schools for everyone, there were local option laws, and in 1855 ten counties and three cities had taken advantage of them. For the middle classes who could afford the tuition, there were private academies, which constituted the most important element in the educational system. At the end of the antebellum period, 317 academies in the state employed 547 teachers to instruct 9,000 pupils.

In other states the progress was less substantial. In 1840 the ratio of pupils enrolled in school to white school-age population was only one-third as high in the slave states as in the nonslave states. On the eve of the Civil War, according to one estimate, an average white youth in the North received five times as many days schooling as a typical white youth in the South. In 1854 an Alabama legislative committee estimated that less than 30 percent of white school-age children in the state were receiving any formal schooling. The result in all the states was an unschooled population. The 1850 census reported that illiteracy among native-born white southerners over twenty years of age was 20.3 percent compared to 3 percent in the middle Atlantic states and 0.42 percent in New England. If these figures are even approximately correct, and contemporary estimates suggest they are too low, they indicate that more than half, perhaps substantially more than half, of the total population of the Confederate South was illiterate. Since it is likely that a considerable proportion of the literates were only marginally so, it may be concluded that a substantial majority of the people in the Old South were totally or functionally illiterate. This was in fact one of the section's most distinctive features.

On the college level, the record was comparatively better. When the Civil War began, the Old South had for its white population proportionately more colleges and college students than the North. In Virginia, for example, there were twenty-three institutions calling themselves colleges with a total enrollment of 2,824 students, while in Massachusetts there were only eight such institutions with 1,733 students, a few of whom were Virginians. Numbers, however, are a poor measure of higher education, and the quality of southern colleges, which was never as high as that of New England, suffered a relative decline in the antebellum period as every institution of any significance came under the influence of sectional and religious orthodoxists. Even the University of Virginia, which Jefferson had hoped to make the nation's greatest center of learning when he established it late in his life, succumbed, and not until after World War I did it and other universities recover from the resulting blight. By the 1850s the South's educational system at all levels was more concerned with defending the established order than seeking truth. "Southerners must be educated as Southerners, as slaveholders," wrote an advocate of a central university of the South in 1857. They must "be taught to support and defend the institution of slavery, and all the rights of the South at all times and in all places."

Industry and Social Class

Education, then, like democracy, the press, and other institutions, was harnessed to the established order and functioned to contain social stress. Yet planter elites remained uneasy, and one indication of their unease was the concern raised by the prospects of a large factory working class in the section.

On the whole, the planters regarded industrialization as desirable and possibly subversive. Where they could control it, they welcomed it, for they believed factories could bring significant economic advantages to themselves and the South. Control meant one thing: the ability to tie ownership and labor to the plantation regime. "Slaveholders were determined to industrialize the South under their own auspices exclusively, so that existing class and caste relationships would remain unchanged," Robert Starobin has written. "They therefore opposed the creation not only of a slaveless industrial bourgeoisie independent of planter control, but also of a free industrial labor force. Had either of these two groups come into being, it might have challenged the slaveowners' domination of southern society."[6]

Since planters controlled most of the investment capital in the section, they were able to control industrial development. They financed and owned most industry, so the major problem was labor. An industrial working class had no place in the established social order, and it might therefore lead to a problem that slavery was said to have solved, the conflict between capital and labor. The possibility of such conflict focused the public debate over the growth of industry on the question of whether factories should use slave or free labor.

One round of the debate was touched off by William Gregg of South Carolina, who in the middle of the 1840s became the most prominent advocate of industry in the cotton South. In a series of *Essays on Domestic Industry* (1845), Gregg not only argued the advantages of manufacturing but discussed the relative merits of slave and free labor in the factories. Planter opinion was divided on the question, but those on both sides were concerned about the same thing, the social role of the working class. Gregg himself as well as James H. Hammond, a former governor and later United States senator from South Carolina, and George Fitzhugh of Virginia, a prominent advocate of slavery, championed white labor. On the other hand, Congressman Christopher C. Memminger of Charleston, who was to be Secretary of the Treasury in the Confederacy, and William Harper, another prominent proslavery spokesman, wanted only slaves to be employed. A white urban proletariat, Memminger warned, would constitute a large class with economic motives for opposing slavery. It would consist of "the same men who make the cry in the Northern cities against the tyranny of Capital—and there as here would drive all before them who interfere with them—and would soon raise hue and cry against the Negro, and be hot Abolitionists—and every one of those men would have a vote." "You know that even in our lower Country," Memminger wrote Hammond, "there are many that could be marshalled against the Planters upon the idea that they were fighting against the aristocracy."

Hammond eventually took the other side of the argument. "Whenever a slave is made a mechanic," he believed, "he is more than half freed." Only in a plantation setting could the discipline of slavery be maintained, and thus an urban slave proletariat would be dangerous. On the other hand, the employment of poor whites in textile factories would give that group an economic stake in slavery and thereby solve an existing social problem. At present, Hammond wrote in 1850, this class "languishes for employment; and, as a necessary consequence, is working evil to both our social and political system." A job in a factory processing the products of slave labor would cause even the poorest white to see "that the whole fabric of his own fortune was based on the slave system." That accomplished, he and his class could be "relied on to sustain, as firmly and faithfully as any other, the social institutions of the South."

But what about the possibility of antagonism between capital and white labor? In the South, Gregg wrote, "capital will be able to control labor, even in manufactures with whites, for blacks can always be resorted to in case of need." The threat of slave strikebreakers would keep white labor controlled. This was not an idle observation. In 1847 white workers went on strike against the Tredegar Iron Works in Richmond, one of the South's largest industrial enterprises, in part because slaves were being hired to perform tasks previously assigned to white workers. The action demonstrated the anomalous position of free labor in a slave society. The strikers were in effect contending that employer-slaveholders could not use their slaves wherever they pleased, a contention that, in the words of a Richmond newspaper, "strikes at the root of all the rights and privileges of the masters, and, if acknowledged, or permitted to gain a foothold, will soon wholly destroy the value of slave property." By 1860 half the work force at Tredegar were slaves.

For these and other reasons, industrialization did not develop in the Old South as it did in the North. Where it did occur, as at Tredegar and Richmond, it brought not liberal social change, but new forms of paternalism and exploitation. The law, the courts, the political process, economic leadership, public opinion—all served to mold industry along southern lines, which meant undermining labor unions, neutralizing working-class consciousness, and otherwise preserving the existing social order. In this too the racial issue proved useful. Frederick Douglass was not the only one who noted "the conflict of slavery with the interests of white mechanics and laborers." "Both [white and black workers] were plundered, and by the same plunderers," Douglass wrote. "The impression was cunningly made that slavery was the only power that could prevent the laboring white man from falling to the level of the slave's poverty and degeneration." And so effectively was the impression cultivated that it became a social fact. "Now just suppose you had a family of children," a white Alabama farmer told the peripatetic Yankee traveler Frederick L. Olmsted. "How would you like to hev a niggar steppin' up to your darter?"

Where such a view was widely held, even in less literal form, unity between white and black labor was impossible. The most pointed class appeal to nonslaveholding whites, Hinton Rowan Helper's *The Impending Crisis of the South* (1857), was notable for the lack of response it provoked from them. Slaveholders "have purposely kept you in ignorance," Helper told nonslaveholders, "and have, by moulding your passions and prejudices to suit themselves, induced you to act in direct opposition to your dearest rights and interests." But only slaveholders paid Helper any attention, banning both him and his book from the South.

The Southern Lady

The largest social minority in the Old South was white women, and their story too sheds light on the nature of antebellum society. Their story, however, is still largely unwritten. It has attracted far less study than that of the slaves, and has been the subject of much less imaginative and fruitful inquiry. Sexual equality is a much more radical idea than racial equality in both the southern and American contexts, for to implement it would require social changes so basic that they can only be described as revolutionary. In the Old South the subordinate role of women was more deeply woven into the fabric of life than the subordinate role of blacks. It was, however, far less significant historically because awareness of it was less distinct and reactions to it were less urgent. Its existence produced fewer problems of public policy, for it was generally accepted as a natural form of social inequality.

Because of the radical nature of complete sexual equality, the women's rights movement came to focus on a set of meliorative social reforms: removing legal and political disabilities against women and enlarging their economic opportunities and social horizons, but not affecting the basic social role of each sex. The perspective this program gives to the history of the Old South is that women like slaves were an oppressed minority in need of liberal reform. In her *Diary from Dixie,* a revealing glimpse into the social life of upper-class women during the Civil War, Mary Boykin Chesnut remarked to a friend that her husband, Senator James Chesnut of South Carolina, "hates all forms of slavery, especially African slavery." "Why do you say 'African'?" her friend asked. "Why, to distinguish that from the inevitable slavery of the world," she replied. "All married women, all children and girls who live in their fathers' houses are slaves!"

Whether or not that was indeed the case—and many slaves would no doubt have disputed it—there were some noteworthy parallels between the status of women and that of slaves. Both groups had a clearly defined place, a subordinate social role, which they were expected to know and accept, and which was said to be determined by nature. Slavery was justified by historical, religious, and scientific arguments which "proved" that blacks were physically and mentally inferior to whites; the dependent and subordinate position of women was similarly accounted for. Women too were said to be inferior and for the same reasons. The purpose of this formulation was to preserve a social system in which male supremacy was secure, and to do so by socialization rather than force. Like slaves, women were encouraged to believe in their own inferiority, and to consider themselves dependent creatures predestined by biology, temperament, and ability to a limited role in life. Similarly, they were urged to internalize the social values that justified male dominance, and to view themselves and their social role through the eyes of men.

This process and its results are badly in need of study, but indications are that the process itself was more effective than the parallel one among slaves. Women in the Old South seem to have accepted their "inferiority" to a greater degree than slaves did. "The social role of women was unusually confining," Anne F. Scott has written in *The Southern Lady* (1970), "and the sanctions used to enforce obedience peculiarly effective." There was no substantial resistance to sexual discrimination. "Most Southern women," Mrs. Scott also wrote, "would not have tried, or known how, to free themselves" from their social position.

The status of women in the antebellum generation was not altogether different from what it had been in the colonial period. "Women were without political rights," as Julia C. Spruill observed in *Women's Life and Work in the Southern Colonies* (1938). "Generally wives were legal non-entities" in the colonial era, though single women had some important legal rights, including the right to sue and be sued in the courts and to own property and transact business in their own names. Then and later the legal restrictions on women seem to have been intended to protect patriarchal forms of marriage and the family rather than to suppress women as such. Sexual equality was incompatible with those forms as they existed in the colonial South, and lawmakers were more concerned with protecting the family than with women's rights one way or the other. At the time of marriage, a woman's legal existence was absorbed into her husband's. The law recognized his right in her property and services, and conferred upon him, in the words of Guion Griffis Johnson, "power to use such a degree of force as is necessary to make the wife behave herself and know her place."

The American Revolution changed none of this. The Founding Fathers believed a woman's place was in the home, and they hoped, in Jefferson's words, that women in republican America would be "too wise to wrinkle their foreheads with politics." Such phrases as "the rights of man" and "all men are created equal" were apt: they had little positive meaning for women. Jacksonian democracy, however, did bring some meaningful improvements, especially in the legal status of married women. Their property rights were recognized, and they were given access to the courts and the guarantees of procedural due process. But they still could not vote or effectively organize and work for their own emancipation. Their social position remained anomalous, and their economic opportunities were restricted. Their social status derived from that of their husbands or fathers, for they had no economic or political power of their own. Their relationships with men and not the letter of the law determined their actual position. Like the slave codes, laws governing the status of women were tempered by personalism and paternalism. The devoted wife like the good slave was rewarded for loyalty, obedience, and hard work.

There were, however, important differences between the condition of women and slaves. The social role of women was defined by a social myth that had little to do with reality but does help illuminate the difference between the status of these two groups. The myth was concerned with genteel women alone; nothing in it had anything to do with poor whites, and as far as black and Indian women were concerned it can only be described as bizarre. Yet it was one of the most vital social myths in a society especially given to myth, and better than any other single factor it explains the distinctive position of women in the Old South. It went something like this: As mothers of the race, women have a special mission in life, the chief responsibility for preserving moral values and encouraging the better side of man's nature. They must do this by example: by living a more moral and virtuous life than men, by cultivating the feminine virtues—delicacy, modesty, chastity, love, obedience—and by being happy homemakers, loyal wives, devoted mothers. The social role these things entail was designed by God and ratified by nature, which adapted the female temperament, intellect, and physiology to its demands. Law and social custom acknowledged this cosmic design, and women must do likewise. They must devote themselves to domestic activities and limit their public role to religious and charitable endeavors of the most modest and worthy sort. Above all, they must avoid politics and "causes" lest they disgrace their families, "unsex" themselves, and affront the natural order of things.

Apologists for the Old South spent a surprising amount of time defending this myth. There was a natural order of things, they insisted, that applied to the sexes as well as to races and classes. "Women, like children have but one right and that is the right of protection," wrote George Fitzhugh in *Sociology for the South* (1854). "The right to protection involves the obligation to obey. A husband, a lord and master, whom she should love, honor, and obey, nature designed for every woman." And "if she be obedient she stands little danger of maltreatment." William Gilmore Simms put it less bluntly. "One does not want an equal, but an ally in marriage," Captain Porgy remarked in Simms's novel *Woodcraft* (1854). "A man ought to be wise enough for his wife and himself. To get a woman who shall best comprehend one is the sufficient secret; and no woman can properly comprehend her husband, who is not prepared to recognize his full superiority."

Sectional apologists insisted that the actual role of women in the Old South conformed to this myth. Those of the planter class "are the model women of the age in which we live," wrote Daniel R. Hundley in *Social Relations in Our Southern States* (1860). "Simple and unaffected" in manners, they are as "pure in speech as ... in soul, and ever blessed with an inborn grace of gentleness of spirit lovely to look upon." They live "only to make home happy," and know "literally nothing of 'women's rights,' or of 'free love,' or 'free thinking.' " The reason for this pure and elevated state was at least partly slavery. "The Slave Institution of the South increases the tendency to dignify the family," wrote Christopher C. Memminger in 1851. "Each planter is in fact a Patriarch—his position compels him to be a ruler in his household" and increases his concern with domestic relations. His wife, as well as his slaves, is a beneficiary. "She is now surrounded by her domestics, and the abundance of their labor lightens the toil and hardships of the whole family," wrote Thomas R. Dew. She is no longer a beast of burden, as women once were, but "the cheering and animating center of the family circle." Slavery has freed her "for reflection and the cultivation of all those mild and fascinating virtues, which throw a charm and delight around our homes and firesides, and calm and tranquilize the harsher tempers and more restless propensities of the male." "Clothed with all her charms, mingling with and directing the society of which she belongs, [she is] no longer the slave, but the equal and idol of the man."

The actualities, at least for most women, were different. "[Her] labors are onerous in the extreme," Daniel R. Hundley wrote of the middle-class woman. "Besides the cares of a mother, the anxieties of a housekeeper, and the wants of her husband, she has also to look after the wants of the blacks." Expanded to include the myriad duties of housekeeping and adapted to the conditions of different social classes, Hundley's statement suggests something of the disparity between the myth of the "southern lady" and the reality that governed the lives of most women. Life for women in the Old South was difficult. Marriage involved considerations of property, family, ambition, and necessity, as well as romantic love. It usually meant large numbers of children and thus the risks of pregnancy and the pains of childbirth. Death rates from both were agonizingly high, and perhaps sexual enjoyment was constricted by fear as well as the convention that sex was something only men and abandoned women could enjoy.

The response of women, especially those of the middle and lower classes, to their condition is not always clear. The systematic study of women and the family has thus far produced little insight into their lives. The response of upper-class women is better understood. While they organized no resistance to their subordinate position, there is, as Anne F. Scott has found, "considerable evidence that many of them found the 'sphere' [to which they were restricted] very confining." There was good cause for discontent. They had to contend with a double standard in public conduct as well as sexual matters. Legal and political disabilities, and social prejudice as well, excluded them from most forms of constructive public activity, and homemaking and childrearing were physically confining and intellectually deadening. Slavery placed physical and psychological burdens on them, and there is some evidence of emotional and sexual frustration as well. In addition they had to tolerate a male paternalism that was ubiquitous and sometimes stifling. "Oh! the disadvantages we labor under, in not possessing the agreeable independence of men," one of them confided to her diary; "tis shameful that all the superiority, authority and freedom in all things should by partial Nature be thrown into their scale." "What a drag it is sometimes on a woman," wrote another, "to 'lug about' the ladder upon which man plants his foot and ascends to the intellectual heaven of peace in ignorance of the machinery which feeds his daily life."

Organized protest was impossible. As a social class, women in the Old South were more atomized than the slaves. They had no political or economic power, no activist organizations of their own, and their sense of grievance was less developed even than that of poor whites. The women's rights movement, which by the time of the Seneca Falls Convention of 1848 was well underway in the North, made no headway in the Old South. In fact, in the slave states in 1850 or 1860 there was probably more support for abolishing slavery than enacting women's suffrage.

Activists in women's causes therefore had no choice but to remain silent or leave the section. The two most famous activists, Sarah and Angelina Grimke, chose to leave. Of rebellious spirit and good Charleston family, the sisters Grimke early developed a dislike for certain aspects of southern life. In the 1830s, while other Charlestonians were hardening their sectional feelings, they moved to Philadelphia, joined the Quakers, and enlisted in the antislavery movement. At once they encountered the prejudice against women speaking in public and leading public causes. Like Frederick Douglass, William Lloyd Garrison, and some other male abolitionists, they saw immediately that the oppression of women was not unrelated to that of blacks and slaves, and they saw too the incongruity of working against one while ignoring the other. Angelina Grimke's pamphlet "Appeal to the Christian Women of the South" to speak and act against slavery was thus a logical precursor of Sarah Grimke's *The Equality of the Sexes and the Condition of Women* (1838), which Anne F. Scott has described as "the earliest systematic expression in America of the whole set of ideas constituting the ideology of 'woman's rights.'"

The latter pamphlet, easily the most remarkable document written by an antebellum southern woman, contained an arresting critique of the status of women in America and the ideology that kept them subordinate. Miss Grimke not only criticized the American and southern ideal of womanhood but urged women to develop an alternative ideal of their own. The difficulty, she saw, was that most women accepted an ideal of womanhood that relegated them to a dependent social role. "By flattery, by an appeal to [woman's] passions," she wrote, man "seeks access to her heart; and when he has gained her affections, he uses her as the instrument of his pleasure—the minister of his temporal comfort. He furnishes himself with a housekeeper, whose chief business is in the kitchen, or the nursery. And whilst he goes abroad and enjoys the means of improvement afforded by collision of intellect and cultivated minds, his wife is condemned to draw nearly all her instruction from books ... whilst engaged in those domestic duties, which are necessary for the comfort of her lord and master." Thus were women kept subordinate. "I ask no favors for my sex," she declared. "I surrender not our claim of equality. All I ask of our brethren is that they will take their feet from off our necks, and permit us to stand upright." "God has made no distinction between men and women as moral beings.... Whatever it is morally right for a man to do, it is morally right for a woman to do."

The Mind of the Old South

If the stresses of life in the Old South were reflected in its social history, its basic unity was revealed in its intellectual history. The mind of the Old South embodied a social philosophy accepted in one degree or another by all significant elements of the white population. Essentially a rationalization of the social, economic, and political interests of the powerful and articulate, it was formulated by apologists for the plantation regime, was given currency by publicists of the middle class, and was a major instrument of social conservatism. This does not mean the southern mind was unitary; there were always differences among its representative spokesmen. But the differences were within a range of agreement that preserved consensus, and in retrospect the consensus seems far more important than the differences. The white South had no social radicals, and its few reformers were notable for their conservatism.

The mind of the Old South crystallized as sectional antagonisms increased after 1830. Its chief concerns were sectional in nature, and its best expressions came from a broad array of men who took the lead in defining sectional values and defending sectional causes. John C. Calhoun was the representative political figure, though the speeches of almost any prominent politician are likely to illustrate most of its important elements. William Gilmore Simms, also a South Carolinian, was the representative literary figure and the man whose writings best reflect the intellectual history of the Old South. Simms's essays on political and social subjects, many of which appeared in the *Southern Quarterly Review* and the other magazines he edited, are instructive examples of the matured mind of the Old South.[7] Other examples are *De Bow's Review*, published in New Orleans by an indefatigable champion of southern causes, J. D. B. De Bow, and the *Southern Literary Messenger*, which was published in Richmond and which was the section's most important literary journal. The editorial and news columns of newspapers, ranging from John Hampden Pleasants' moderate Richmond *Whig* to Robert Barnwell Rhett's extremist *Charleston Mercury*, reflected as well as molded sectional thought, as did the works of a host of popular novelists, of whom John Pendleton Kennedy, John Esten Cooke, and Beverley Tucker, as well as Simms, were representative. George Fitzhugh's most systematic work, *Cannibals All!* (1857), and the manuscript *Diary of Edmund Ruffin*, published in 1972, are important examples of the thought of extremists and fire eaters, men who tended to carry sectional causes further than most southerners were willing to go.

Out of the disparate influences on southern thought, these and other men fashioned a social philosophy which, as southerners understood it, was coherent and functional. The qualifying phrase is important. The mind of the Old South makes sense only as southerners comprehended it. Like the society from which it sprang, it was an incongrous mixture of liberal, conservative, and reactionary elements that cannot be understood by ordinary canons of logic or intellectual history. By those canons it is internally contradictory and in a sense fraudulent, as Louis Hartz concluded after a notable analysis in *The Liberal Tradition in America* (1955). But that is not the best judgment on it. Southerners gave words and ideas special meanings of their own. This was true even of basic concepts like slavery, freedom, democracy, and minority rights. Only if these special meanings are understood and accepted for purposes of analysis can southern thought be made comprehensible.

In addition the constituent parts of southern thought must be considered in organic relationship to each other. The cement that held them together was a unique species of social and philosophical conservatism that grew out of southern life. "The conservative philosophy of the planters pervaded nearly every department of southern life," Clement Eaton has written, "creating a political theory, a social ethics, a code of manners, a race theory, a set of economic principles, and a profoundly conservative religion." Its source was racial slavery, which white southerners viewed as vital to their safety. This plus the fact that the South was the smaller part of a liberal democratic nation made southerners especially concerned about matters relating to their own security and thus about guarding the status quo against change. In such a society realistic social analysis is difficult.

The conservative impulse was responsible for not only the elaborate defense of slavery, which was the hallmark of antebellum thought, but for the widespread appeal of hierarchical social ideas. Social and racial hierarchies are natural states of mankind, southerners tended to believe, and property rights the essential basis of stable society. This derived from a Hobbesian view of human nature and government, according to which human beings are selfishly inclined and in need of nothing so much as a strong government to keep their natural inclinations in check. The appeal of this view tended to undermine faith in Jeffersonian democracy and Lockean environmentalism, and to encourage a certain social pessimism. At least some southerners thus looked backward to a golden age in the past, perhaps in medieval Europe, before the corruptions of modern times had worked their way into public life. This tendency nourished some of the quainter traits of sectional character, especially the fondness for romance and archaic social ideals. The works of literary romanticists, especially the novels of Sir Walter Scott, enjoyed an enormous vogue for a time. Believing themselves under siege in a world of rapid change, some southerners sought mental refuge in the medieval world Scott described in *Ivanhoe* (1820) and elsewhere, with its great manor houses, chivalric ideals, gallant knights, martial glory—and social stability.

It is easy to make too much of this, but it was important. In one of his lampoons of the Old South, Mark Twain suggested that antebellum southerners had been afflicted with "the Sir Walter disease," which led them to confuse reality with Scott's "fantastic heroes and their grotesque 'chivalry' doings and romantic juvenilities." Rollin G. Osterweis, a historian whose judgments are more restrained than Twain's, used this fondness for the romantic as a basis for explaining the antebellum mind. Scott and other romancers imbued southerners with a "glorification of the chivalric ideal," Osterweis wrote in *Romanticism and Nationalism in the Old South* (1949), with "the cult of manners, the cult of women, the cult of the gallant knight, [and] the loyalty of caste." A few were afflicted enough to stage jousting tournaments and other medieval entertainments, while many more named their plantations and horses after those in Scott's novels and in other ways sought to identify their way of life with that of the middle ages.[8]

These things were spectacular but not basic. Understood as a tendency to confuse the ideal with the real, romanticism was an important facet of southern thought, but "the Sir Walter disease" was not its most important manifestation. That was the plantation legend, an idealization of the southern way of life built around the plantation.[9] This legend grew out of the same impulse that made Scott's works popular, and was best expressed in the novels of plantation life which came into vogue after 1830. Among these were John Pendleton Kennedy's *Swallow Barn* (1832) and *Horseshoe Robinson* (1835), William A. Caruthers's *The Cavaliers of Virginia* (1834) and *Knights of the Horseshoe* (1841), Beverley Tucker's *George Balcombe* (1836), and John Esten Cooke's *The Virginia Comedians* (1854).

The best of these books, both as an example of the plantation legend and as a work of literature, is Kennedy's *Swallow Barn*. In its first edition this novel was rather detached, at times even satiric, in its description of plantation life, but in a revision published in 1851 Kennedy softened the satire and increased the romance. The result was an appealing depiction of life at Swallow Barn, a Virginia plantation, in the early nineteenth century before "time, and what is called 'the progress'" had destroyed traditional ways. The "early population" of Virginia had "consisted of gentlemen of good name and condition," who had given the state a "singularly brilliant" history. This "old time society," with "its good fellowship, its hearty and constitutional *companionableness*, the thriftless gayety of the people, their dogged but amiable invincibility of opinion, and that overflowing hospitality which knew no ebb," had been "mellow, bland, and [filled with] sunny luxuriance." Even today, Kennedy wrote in 1851, Virginia's "wealth is territorial; her institutions all savour of the soil; her population consists of landholders, of many descents, unmixed with foreign alloy"; and she "has no large towns where men may meet and devise improvements or changes in the arts of life." As a result the state is "less disturbed by popular commotions, less influenced by popular fervors, than other communities," and its "laws and habits ... have a certain fixedness, which even reject many of the valuable improvements of the day."

Life at Swallow Barn and the surrounding community mirrored this image. It was ordered, satisfying, free of social or racial tension. In their large "halls" surrounded by bondsmen and other dependents, planters lived in a manner that "affords a tolerable picture of feudal munificence." High-minded and high-spirited, sagacious and courageous, and generous to a fault, they and their way of life were rooted in the historic past. There was a young neighbor who "reads descriptions of ladies of chivalry, and takes the field in imitation of them," and "almost persuades herself that this is the fourteenth century." There was even an elderly slave who was rewarded with a glass of julep for strumming his banjo while the young ladies and their gallants sat under the rose arbor in the light of a full moon.

Slavery like everything else at Swallow Barn was idyllic. The slave quarters were "exceedingly picturesque," their attractiveness enhanced by "the rudeness of their construction." The slaves themselves exhibited an "air of contentment and good humor," had "no want of what, in all countries, would be considered a reasonable supply of luxuries," and "always hailed with pleasure" the visits of their "kind and considerate" master. "I am quite sure they never could become a happier people than I find them here," observed Kennedy's narrator.

Here, then, was the plantation legend: a magnificent physical setting, the virtues of rural life, an organic social structure, class and racial harmony, material sufficiency without the corruptions of wealth or poverty. Swallow Barn was a community of people dependent on each other, each satisfied in his own secure place. Harmony, modest prosperity, and contentment were its earmarks.

The specifics of the legend varied from writer to writer, but the legend itself was rarely questioned. It came in fact to constitute the vision white southerners had of their way of life. It was the contents of the legend they had in mind when they spoke of the harmony and superiority of life in the South. When they praised the planter regime and southern hospitality or spoke of the virtues of traditionalism and agrarianism, it was this legend that informed their vision. If the vision was removed from actuality, as it was, it was still the vision and not the actuality that to them was the South. The South they sought to preserve was not to them the brutal, exploitive, racist society of abolitionist literature, but the South of the plantation legend.

That southerners idealized their way of life is not surprising; all societies do that to one degree or another. The significant fact was that they chose the plantation legend as their basic social myth. They might have selected another myth, that of the frontier, which celebrated sturdy pioneers and self-made yeoman farmers of more democratic and earthy virtues. Certainly such people were more numerous than the planters, and certainly too the frontier and its aftereffects were important influences in antebellum life. In 1860 the frontier experience was still recent in all the areas west and southwest of the Appalachian Mountains.[10] Not until 1815 or later had most of the cotton kingdom been settled by substantial numbers of whites, and not until much later were Arkansas (1836), Florida (1845), and Texas (1845) admitted to the Union. When he traveled through the South in the 1850s, Frederick L. Olmsted was everywhere impressed by the frontier-like appearance of things—vast stretches of unsettled land, unkempt settlements, the absence of towns, poor or nonexistent roads and bridges, and a general lack of what his fellow New Englanders considered the accouterments of civilization.

Olmsted's impressions were accurate. In 1860 population density in the Confederate South was less than 18 per square mile compared to 158 in Massachusetts and 59 in Ohio. In the same year, only a fifth of the land in the Southeast was improved and little more than a fiftieth of that in the Southwest. Southerners were still remarkably migratory people, driven from place to place by soil exhaustion, wasteful agriculture, and the lures of the cotton kingdom and Texas. Joseph G. Baldwin's depiction of social and moral fluidities in *The Flush Times of Alabama and Mississippi* (1853) was not, for much of the Southwest, overdrawn. Southerners like other Americans were uprooted by the frontier and westward expansion, and their experience with rootlessness and isolation exposed them to influences markedly different from those idealized in the plantation legend.

Yet the influence of the frontier was limited too, and this perhaps explains why southerners, unlike northerners, opted for a plantation-conservative-aristocratic ideal rather than a frontier-liberal-democratic one. The racial dimension of the frontier concerned Indians, not blacks, and the frontier itself hardly affected social and economic structures. The plantation imposed itself on the frontier, and thus social thought looked toward the plantation.

The attractiveness of the plantation legend was due in part to its incorporation of the southerners' concept of natural harmonies. Every category of people, they believed, had a place in the social order that derived from natural abilities and disabilities. This was the basic concept of southern social thought. "Degree, or things in their proper place, is well insisted upon," wrote William Gilmore Simms in 1837. "All harmonies, whether in the moral or physical worlds—arise, entirely, from the inequalities of tones." Democracy is not to be equated with equality; it is instead "the harmony of the moral world." It "insists upon inequalities," upon the principle "that all men should hold the place [in society] to which they are properly entitled." Nor is "true liberty" to be confused with equality; it is rather "the undisturbed possession of that place in society to which our moral and intellectual merits entitle us. *He is a freeman, whatever his condition, who fills his proper place. He is a slave only, who is forced into a position in society below the claims of his intellect. He cannot but be a tyrant who is found in a position for which his mind is unprepared, and to which he is inferior.*"

Political and social rights are thus not absolute or inalienable for all people. They derive not from nature or God or the condition of humanity, but, in Simms's words, they depend *"entirely upon the degree of obedience which we pay to the laws of our creation. All our rights . . . result from the performance of our duties."* The individual derives his rights not from the fact of his humanity, but from the group to which he belongs and from the relationship of his group to society. Society assigns rights on the basis of demonstrated capacity to use them wisely. The demonstration is not a matter of individual effort or theoretical speculation, but of group testing over "long years of preparation, of great trial, hardships, severe labor and perilous enterprise." Rights cannot be forced by an undeserving group nor effectively denied the deserving. The law can and must protect everyone, but only *"in his place."* This was the southerner's concept of community: the interdependence of unequal groups within a social organism that benefited everyone according to his ability to appreciate the benefits. Inequality was an integral part of it.

This concept of individual rights is quite un-American. "All men are created equal," wrote Jefferson, "and are endowed by their creator with certain inalienable rights." "Men are not born physically, morally, or intellectually equal," countered George Fitzhugh, the section's most systematic social thinker, and "their natural inequalities beget inequalities of rights." "It would be far nearer the truth to say that some were born with saddles on their backs, and others booted and spurred to ride them—and the riding does them good." The individual was not, as Jefferson had sometimes suggested, a rational creature who knew his own and society's best interest, but an irrational being controlled by emotion and self-interest and requiring socially imposed restraints.

These things southerners accepted as self-evident truths, and they criticized reformers and "levelers" for ignoring them and working to break down "all barriers of present distinction." "We are losing our veneration of the past," lamented Simms. "We are overthrowing all sacred and hallowing associations and authorities. Marriage is now a bond which we may rend at pleasure. The Sabbath is a wrong and a superstition." Modern society is too willing to experiment, too anxious to pursue a perfectionism that flouts human nature. Where the condition is worst, as in the North and western Europe, irresponsible groups spread subversion without restraint, and the results are alarming. In the North "government—property-rights—everything is subject to the capricious will of a dominant multitude. Agrarianism . . . is rapidly gaining ground . . . and the vagaries of the French communist, Proudhon, have been applauded without shame in . . . public assemblies. . . . Women and grown up men, abandon their own imperative duties of every day life, and devote their time, and even their money, to the wildest schemes of religious and political reform."

In this manner southerners came to a critique of modern capitalist society. Not surprisingly they focused their critique on the ills of industrialism and liberalism, especially the impersonality of factory labor, the "unnatural" conditions of urban life, and the lack of community in modern liberal society. Industrialism eliminated personalism and paternalism in economic relations, they said, turned labor into a commodity to be bought and sold, and turned laborers into automatons. Factory workers were thus tied by the machines they tended to monotonous tasks which destroyed creativity and deadened the senses and for which they were paid hardly enough to keep body and soul together. The results were individual and group degradation and the inevitable consequences of social disorganization: frustration, alienation, and rising class animosity as workers were forced to take desperate measures to redress their grievances.

This analysis was not so much wrong as incomplete, for it mistook the worst of industrial society for the typical. The antebellum North was in the throes of rapid industrialization, and if "mobs, riots, [and] murders" were not "the daily events" southerners made them out to be, they nevertheless did occur. The problem was not that southerners pointed to fanciful ills in the North, but that they ignored real ones in the South. In their eyes the South had escaped the problems they found in the North, and the reason was slavery. In free society, they insisted, employers and employees are forced into an antagonistic relationship. What benefits the one hurts the other. In the conflict this inevitably produces, workers are invariably losers—but so too is society. Only a system like slavery which fused the interests of employers and employees could prevent antagonism between labor and capital and thereby preclude the kinds of problems that plague industrial societies everywhere. Under slavery the interests of masters and slaves were said to be reciprocal. What was good for one was held to be equally good for the other, and neither had any cause for resentment against the other.

The Proslavery Argument

The whole of southern thought was ultimately a defense of slavery. Proslavery thought thus overlapped and partook of the conservative philosophy, the plantation legend, the critique of industrial society, and the doctrine of states' rights.[11] The intellectual defense of slavery matured in the 1830s, and was a phase in the history of white thinking about blacks and racial policy. It was notably influenced by the emergence of scientific racism and reflected the shift in attitude toward slavery that followed the rise of militant abolitionism. "Many in the South once believed that [slavery] was a moral and political evil," wrote Calhoun in 1838. "That folly and delusion are gone. We see it now in its true light, and regard it as the most safe and stable basis for free institutions in the world." "When two races of different origin and distinguished by color, and other physical differences, as well as intellectual [differences] are brought together," Calhoun had said a year earlier, "the relation now existing in the slave-holding states between the two, is instead of an evil, a good—a positive good."

The latter phrase embodied the new attitude toward the peculiar institution, and the purpose of the proslavery argument was to give it substance. By the time Calhoun made the above remarks, Thomas R. Dew's *Review of the Debate in the Virginia Legislature of 1831 and 1832* (1832) had appeared, as had William Gilmore Simms's "The Morals of Slavery" (1837) and William Harper's *Memoir on Slavery* (1837); and from then until the Civil War southern writing was filled with proslavery ideas. Harriet Beecher Stowe's *Uncle Tom's Cabin* (1852), the most influential piece of abolitionist literature, provoked a flood of proslavery responses, among them a collective effort, *The Pro-Slavery Argument* (1852), William J. Grayson's "The Hireling and the Slave" (1856), and Josiah Priest's *Bible Defense of Slavery* (1852). George Fitzhugh's *Sociology for the South* and Henry Hughes's *Treatise on Sociology* appeared in 1854 and reflected the effort to give greater coherence to proslavery thought, as did Josiah C. Nott and George R. Gliddon's *Types of Mankind* (1854), the most important item in the literature of scientific racism. In a huge compendium, *The Industrial Resources, Statistics, etc. of the United States* (3 vols., 1854), J. D. B. De Bow reprinted proslavery items by Calhoun, Harper, and James H. Hammond, as well as Dr. Samuel A. Cartwright, who believed that whites and blacks were so unalike physically that they required different medications and regimens to keep them healthy. Finally, in 1860 E. N. Elliott brought together the most complete anthology on the subject, *Cotton Is King, and Pro-Slavery Arguments.*

Proslavery writers used every literary form and drew upon every authority from the Bible and Aristotle to science and even social science, including physiology, craniology, anthropology, and sociology. History, natural and moral philosophy, Christian apologetics, constitutional theory—all were mined for support of the peculiar institution. It was the largest intellectual enterprise in the Old South and, given the state of scientific and other knowledge at the time, not an unworthy effort. It was an exercise of social necessity rather than a search for truth, but its authority and conclusions were still, in the terms of the day, far from fanciful. If it began with a set of a priori assumptions, it was also able to call on "objective" authority. In antebellum America, scientists and social scientists almost to a man accepted racial inequality and black inferiority as facts requiring no demonstration. They also accepted the "obvious" social implication of those "facts"—that white supremacy was desirable and necessary. Historians, natural scientists, moral philosophers, theologians, and constitutional theorists agreed. The difference between these groups and proslavery apologists was not over the principles of racial inequality and white supremacy, but over the specific matter of slavery. Proslavery writers were thus able to draw upon disinterested authorities in arguing that races are unequal and must have unequal places in society. Only an occasional white abolitionist and the few blacks who made themselves heard disputed these premises.

Still, the defense of slavery was troublesome. White supremacy might exist without slavery, as was already the case in the North, and to enlightened thinkers slavery was a relic of the dark ages. Moreover, southerners were defending the institution in a society whose heritage included a flight from tyranny in the Old World and a revolt against it in the New, and whose commitment was to economic individualism, Jeffersonian democracy, and New Testament Christianity. How could slavery be reconciled with these things?

The answer—race—was obvious to southerners but not always to outsiders, and the proslavery argument thus offers some especially valuable insights into the mind of the Old South. The basic fact about the argument was not logic but perceived need. The argument did not urge southern society toward philosophical, religious, or ethical truth, but tried to reconcile truth with southern society. It was thus an exercise in affirmation and rationalization. Much of it was offered as general social analysis, but was in fact a specific justification for the Old South and thus for social hierarchy, white supremacy, the plantation regime, and conservative, even reactionary, social values. It was redeemed from hypocrisy by paternalism and the plantation legend, which enabled proslavery spokesmen to perceive the society they defended as benevolent rather than exploitive.

The basic contention was simply that slavery for blacks was a good thing for everyone. It was good for whites, and thus for the South, because it kept a necessary but unruly labor force constrained and productive and thereby insured racial order and economic prosperity. It also served as a social stabilizer, keeping whites conservative and unreceptive to those "philosophical reveries" and irresponsible social movements that plagued the North. Blacks benefited too, for slavery provided them a social milieu adapted to their capacities and needs as a race and enabled them to live in a civilized society and profit from close association with a superior people.

Around 1830 these traditional ideas received new authority from the physiological and social sciences then emerging as systematic branches of knowledge. The basic idea of the resulting scientific racism was that blacks as a race were not only different from whites physiologically and mentally but inferior as well, and that the inferiority made them incapable of functioning effectively in a free society. Specifically, blacks were held to be incapable of comprehending the responsibilities of citizenship. They required special laws and social controls to tame their savage instincts, special compulsions to make them work and earn their keep, and special goadings to encourage their moral sense. In developing social policy, race therefore had to be the primary consideration, for it set limits on individual abilities and thus on group development. Because of its biracial population and the large number of blacks, the South had to be especially cognizant of race. The white race is responsible for all "the highest advances in civilization" and "everything that tends to adorn and elevate human nature," wrote a contributor to the *Southern Literary Messenger* in 1839. As for other races, "in precisely the same proportion as their physical organization has varied from, and been inferior to" that of whites, they "have manifested those traits of character which belong to savage life—ignorance debauchery, sensuality, cruelty [and] idolatry."

The importance of these ideas is obvious, but southerners were not a scientific people, and for most of them the Bible was a more important source of proslavery attitudes. Proslavery literature was filled with admonitions to servants to obey their masters and be "subject for the Lord's sake to every human institution," while the Noachian curse on

Canaan was widely offered as proof of black inferiority.[12] The golden rule, indeed the whole of Christian theology was reconciled with slavery. Love, it was said, did not necessitate equality; a master could love his slave as readily as his peer. The New Testament contains "not one single passage at all calculated to disturb the conscience of an honest slaveholder," wrote Thomas R. Dew. "No one can read it without seeing and admiring that the meek and humble savior of the world in no instance meddled with the established institutions of mankind; he came to save a fallen world, and not to excite the black passions of men, and array them in deadly hostility against each other."

That social thought in the Old South reached these conclusions and stopped was a measure of the limitations of the planter regime and of the social order it imposed on the section. If that social order grew in part from circumstance, as it did, it showed little capacity of transcendance or even adaptability. It thus led the South and its people into a cul-de-sac where, eventually, they were overwhelmed.

THREE

THE FIGHTING SOUTH 1846-77

The fruit of antebellum sectionalism was the Civil War, the war for southern independence. By acts of secession and war, white southerners made a desperate bid for nationhood, and when they failed, the Old South came shattering down. The result was a major shift in the course of southern history. "In the South, the war is what A. D. is elsewhere; they date from it," Mark Twain wrote in 1883. "The shock of the Civil War is the paramount historical fact about the South," Louis D. Rubin could still write in 1957. "It is the memory of the Civil War more than anything else that distinguishes the South from other areas of the country."

Certainly the war was, as Walter Hines Page observed, "the intensest experience" of those who lived through it. For the planters it was an unspeakable catastrophe that destroyed their property and much of their prestige, and forced them to stand by as the life they fought for fell victim to the ways of the Yankees. For slaves and blacks it brought emancipation and the promise of better things to come. For the mass of whites its results were more mixed. Like the planters, they suffered materially and spiritually from the debacle, but in its aftermath some of the restrictions of the old regime were loosened. Generally speaking, the transition to the new era was easiest for those who were least committed to the values of the old. But no one escaped the impact of the war and its aftermath, Reconstruction. In later years few whites could look back at the troubled events of the 1860s and 1870s and see anything but disaster—for the South as well as themselves.

7

Causes of the War for Southern Independence

Why did white southerners, a people who had everything to gain from preserving the status quo, risk their all on such uncertain acts as secession and war? That question has never been answered definitively, but the long effort to do so has thrown much light on the nature of the Old South as well as the causes of the Civil War.

"More scholarly man years have probably been devoted to 'the coming of the Civil War' than to any other past event, American or non-American," Lee Benson observed with pardonable exaggeration in 1971; yet "specialists no more agree now on the 'causes of the Civil War' than they did decades ago."[1] Nor did contemporaries. When the war began, there were already three distinct explanations for it, one for partisans of the southern cause, a second for partisans of the northern cause, and a third for those who supported compromise and peace in the final crisis of 1860–61. Most subsequent explanations have drawn in one degree or another from these three. To southerners, the war grew out of a political crisis involving basic issues of self-government and constitutional law. Its roots lay in the fact that northerners, in disregard of the true nature of the Union and the vital interests of the South, attempted to create a centralized nation with a unitary, majoritarian government powerful enough to impose their own interests on the country and thus powerful enough to trample on the rights and wellbeing of the South. Toward this end, northerners were said to have undertaken a series of political and economic aggressions against the South, capped in 1860 by the election of Abraham Lincoln, a purely sectional candidate, to the presidency on a platform that promised eventually to destroy the South. Southerners were thus forced to take desperate measures to protect themselves. The war resulted from "the systematic and persistent struggle to deprive the Southern States of equality in the Union," Jefferson Davis wrote in his apologia *The Rise and Fall of the Confederate Government* (1889). "To whatever extent the question of slavery may have served as an occasion it was far from being the *cause* of the conflict."[2]

The northern explanation was quite different but just as narrow. It grew out of the abolitionist view of prewar disputes and focused on the expansionist impulse of the slave regime. The South, it held, was an "aggressive slavocracy" determined to spread slavery into the territories, the Caribbean and Central America, and even the free states, and prepared to do whatever was necessary to achieve that goal. In resisting this design, northerners were eventually forced to fight to preserve the Union and in doing so, defend democracy and human freedom against the slave power. In a more moderate and complex form, this northern version of the war's coming became the "nationalist" interpretation that dominated historical writing between the 1890s and 1930s.[3]

Both southern and northern explanations of the war stressed the fundamental nature of sectional differences, and tended to make those differences irreconcilable and the war itself unavoidable. A third explanation, however, which followed the thinking of those who favored compromise and peace in 1859–61, disputed those contentions. This view stressed not the things that divided the sections, but the bonds that held them together, and assumed that men of good will could and should have resolved the controversy short of war. If sectional differences were not fundamental, the war had presumably been avoidable, in which case the crisis that produced it had been the work of irresponsible extremists on both sides who emotionalized issues and inflamed public opinion unnecessarily, and seized control of politics in both sections for their own selfish purposes. The war "did not come simply because one section was agricultural and the other industrial; because one exploited free labor and the other slaves; or because a sectional majority refused to respect the constitutional rights of the minority," wrote Avery O. Craven, whose *The Coming of the Civil War* (1942) is the best modern statement of this view. It came because "politicians and pious cranks" emotionalized issues that would otherwise have been compromised, and needlessly aroused the people in the two sections against each other.

Until recently, the long effort by historians to explain the coming of the war was basically an attempt to isolate the factor or factors most responsible for disrupting the Union. In the vast literature this effort produced, every imaginable item of sectional difference was at one point or another offered as *the* cause of the war. But all such explanations were ultimately unsatisfactory, for each of them left too much unexplained. As a result historians in the last two or three decades have turned away from the effort to isolate a specific cause of the war and have focused instead on antebellum society in the two sections and on the forces at work transforming each section. The results have been encouraging. The war, it now seems, grew out of certain elemental forces at work in both societies, the most important of which relate to race in the broadest sense of the term, including not only such obvious factors as slavery, antislavery, and racism, but the deeper issues that underlay those things and tied them together. The basic factor was the dilemma over race, which is now seen as a national rather than a southern problem, that expressed itself in a question of public policy: What is to be the place of the black minority in a nation whose political majority is steadfastly committed to white supremacy and *Herrenvolk* democracy? Despite the common commitment to white supremacy, whites in the North and the South differed widely over the form that supremacy should take. Demography, economics, and life style combined to cause southerners to support slavery as the only adequate form of racial policy. Northerners, on the other hand, came to see slavery as a threat to the wellbeing of the Union—to economic development, social progress, and political democracy for the mass of whites —and they wanted to contain and eventually eliminate the peculiar institution.

These and related topics have been the focal point of recent efforts to explain the coming of the war. "Increasingly in recent years," wrote David M. Potter in 1968, "the period preceding the Civil War has been discussed in terms of racism and the subordination of the Negro." It has also been discussed in terms of the interrelationship of the many factors that contributed to the sectional break. The change may be dated from the appearance of Allan Nevins's masterful *Ordeal of the Union* (2 vols., 1947) and *The Emergence of Lincoln* (2 vols., 1950), the most detailed study of the antebellum years ever to appear. "The main root of the conflict (and there were minor roots) was the problem of slavery *with its complementary problem of race adjustment,*" Nevins wrote. "It was a war over slavery *and* the future position of the Negro race in North America."

A number of recent studies have broadened and deepened Nevins's idea, and together they offer the most persuasive explanation yet made for the South's role in the coming of the war.[4] This explanation does not reject earlier explanations so much as it enlarges them or subsumes them under the broad subject of race. Despite their tendency later to rationalize the war as a constitutional struggle, southerners during the long period of sectional animosity often acknowledged the racial basis of their concern. "The Southern people find [slavery] penetrating their entire social system," wrote one of them in 1847. "Their industrial pursuits, business relations, investments of capital, family arrangements, and political organizations are constituted with reference to its existence. The existing order, is constructed on the durability of that relation," and any effort to undermine it will be resisted.

During the final crisis, southerners were also more candid in stating their racial concerns than they were in later years. After the war was over, Alexander H. Stephens, who was Vice-President of the Confederacy, published a long and exhausting rationalization of the southern cause, *A Constitutional View of the Late War Between the States* (2 vols., 1868–70), in which he argued that the South's concerns had been states' rights, individual liberty, and constitutional government. But in 1861 he offered a quite different explanation. "The proper status of the negro in our form of civilization," he said shortly after being elected to the vice-presidency, "this was the immediate cause of the late rupture and present revolution." "Our new government," he also said, "is founded upon exactly the opposite idea [from racial equality]; its foundations are laid, its corner stone rests upon the great truth, that the Negro is not the equal to the white man; that slavery—the subordination to the superior race—is his natural and normal condition." Early in 1861 William Cabell Rives told the Virginia Peace Convention much the same thing. "It is not a question of slavery at all," he said of the southerners' concern, "it is a question of race."

Historians have often repeated these judgments. "Slavery was undoubtedly a potent cause; but more powerful than slavery was the Negro himself," E. Merton Coulter wrote in *The Confederate States of America, 1861–1865* (1950); "it was fear of what would ultimately happen to the South if the Negro should be freed by the North." "The fear-of-insurrection-abolition syndrome was the core of the secession impulse," wrote Steven A. Channing in *Crisis of Fear* (1970), a work of quite different persuasion from Coulter's. "The multiplicity of fears revolving around the maintenance of race controls for the Negro" was "so very vast and frightening that it literally consumed the mass of lesser 'causes' of secession."

Slavery and Westward Expansion

These ideas must be related to the developments that produced secession. As concerns the South, those developments grew out of many things in addition to racial considerations, especially economic forces and the emotionalization of moral issues. Together these factors intensified minority consciousness and the long-standing sense of racial unease, and the result was a heightened sense of insecurity which encouraged compensatory impulses toward cultural nationalism and political combativeness. In the final analysis, it was the cumulative impact of all these things that produced the decision to leave the Union, but if any one of them was more important than the others it was the insecurity of whites, which was chiefly racial but also economic and political, and the manner in which that insecurity was fed by sustained sectional controversy between 1846 and 1861.

For an overwhelming majority of southerners, those insecurities remained generalized and tolerable until a series of events between late 1859 and early 1861 made them acute and intolerable, at least for most whites in the cotton states. In October 1859 John Brown and a small band of supporters, with the foreknowledge of a handful of prominent abolitionists, raided the United States army arsenal at Harper's Ferry, Virginia, to capture weapons with which to arm the slaves and launch a general insurrection. This raid and the ensuing apotheosis of Brown in the North burst upon a South that in C. Vann Woodward's words "had been living in a crisis atmosphere for a long time." Already "in the grip of an insecurity complex, a tension resulting from both rational and irrational fears," white southerners were frightened and outraged by Brown's action, and their feelings of insecurity entered a new phase. They were thereby conditioned to read the results of the election of 1860 in the most alarmist manner possible. In that election the nonslave states united behind a man and a party southerners regarded as threatening. The vote that elected Abraham Lincoln President of the United States was totally sectional. Most of the southern states had refused to put Lincoln's name on the ballot, and 99 percent of the votes he received were in the nonslave states. Altogether Lincoln received only 40 percent of the total vote cast in that remarkable election, but so concentrated was his support that had the remaining 60 percent gone to only one of the other three candidates, he would still have won.

How did the South become so alienated from the northern majority? The answer lies in the history of politics between the Mexican War (1846–48) and the secession crisis (1860–61), for it was in politics that the growth of sectionalism was dramatized. As a Virginia editor recalled with some hyperbole after the war, southern politics by the 1850s "could have been reduced to the simple question of, How can we save the institution of slavery? That was the substratum of our society, its very life and soul, and it must be saved at all hazards."

Slavery and other sectional issues had been important ever since the Revolution, but with the help of moderates and compromisers on both sides politicians had kept them within the bounds of political give-and-take. The Mexican War, which began and ended in sectional dispute, made that task vastly more difficult. Many northerners of antislavery persuasion believed President James K. Polk, a Tennessee slaveholder and ardent expansionist, had conspired with the "aggressive slavocracy" to provoke war with a weak neighbor to acquire territory for the expansion of slavery (while compromising with a powerful rival, Great Britain, over the disputed part of the Oregon territory). They resolved therefore to exclude slavery from all territory acquired from Mexico and the Oregon settlement. The area involved was the vast expanse of land from Texas to California and from the Mexican border to Canada. The resulting dispute over slavery in the territories opened a new era in sectional relations.

Early in the war with Mexico, Representative David Wilmot of Pennsylvania proposed an amendment to an appropriations bill that would prohibit slavery from all territory acquired as a result of the war. The Wilmot Proviso, as the amendment was known, was never enacted into law, but it was the vehicle through which slavery was injected into national politics as an issue of overriding importance. It also determined the form that issue took. Political antislavery never dealt directly with slavery itself or with the racial issues that underlay it, but with the collateral issue of the extension of slavery into the territories. It thus focused on this relatively narrow question: Should, or could, Congress make the western territories "free soil" by excluding slavery from them? The decision to accept the Missouri Compromise, in which Congress had exercised the right to prohibit slavery in the Louisiana purchase territory above 36°30', now returned to haunt the southerners.

A glance at the map in 1848 will show why. The western half of the nation was unorganized territory. In one large part of that territory, the great plains northward from the Indian reserves in Oklahoma to the Canadian border and westward to the Rocky Mountains, slavery was excluded by the Missouri Compromise. Now in 1848, over strenuous southern objections, Congress voted to extend this exclusion to Oregon. Therefore, if the Wilmot Proviso were applied to the Mexican cession, there would be no territory open to slavery and no new slave states ever, but many new nonslave states (eventually sixteen states were carved out of the territories in question). The handwriting was on the wall, and sooner or later, southerners reasoned, the nonslave states would be able to act through the federal government against slavery even in the states where it already existed.

These political prospects were alarming enough, but there were also racial and economic issues at stake. Excluding slavery from the territories meant also excluding blacks, and if that prospect pleased free soilers (it was one reason many of them supported exclusion), it alarmed white southerners, who felt it would mean a rising proportion of blacks in the South as more and more whites moved westward. It would also mean—if their analysis was correct—that the economic basis of slavery and southern prosperity would be undermined. The planters believed, and there is much evidence to support them, that the slave-plantation regime had to expand to remain prosperous. In that regime agricultural reform and economic diversification were difficult to achieve, and planters were well aware of the correlation between high productivity and profitability on the one hand and the availability of new land on the other. The amount of unused land in the slave states was still great, but much of it was isolated, expensive to bring into production, or of indifferent quality, and continued westward expansion seemed the easiest way to avoid a potential problem. In this sense the slave system was expansionist by nature, and that fact is of primary importance in understanding southern resistance to the free soil movement. The planters concluded that their exclusion from the territories would eventually mean the end of slavery and their way of life, and was therefore intolerable. The conclusion was reasonable, and if one grants them the premise that every social order has the right to protect itself, their reaction against the free soil movement was neither hysterical nor malevolent, but an imperative act of self-preservation.

One result of their reaction was the crisis that gripped the nation for two years after the war with Mexico and led to the Compromise of 1850. The new territory had to be organized, that is, divided into political units under civil governments. This required action by Congress and the President, which meant decisions concerning the issue of slavery in the territories. In 1849 Zachary Taylor, a hero of the war, became President. Although he was a slaveholder from Louisiana, Taylor was unsympathetic to the southern position on free soil, but he was impatient to organize civil governments in the new territories. His efforts, however, were stymied by Congress, where sectional divisions were so deep that action on any issue with sectional overtones was impossible. (The new House of Representatives that convened in December 1849 required 63 ballots to elect a speaker!) In the meantime the population of New Mexico, long an outpost of Spanish and Mexican settlement, petitioned for territorial organization, and discovery of gold in California in 1848 made the situation there acute.

With Congress immobilized, Taylor took the initiative and announced that California, its population suddenly swollen by the gold rush, would be admitted to the Union without going through the territorial stage. This would bypass Congress and the necessity for a direct decision on the slavery question, but it would make California a nonslave state, since most of its people opposed slavery. It would also end the sectional balance in the Senate, and thus posed a major problem for southerners. Those who were most concerned about it got the Mississippi legislature to call for a convention of representatives from all the slave states to meet in Nashville in June 1850 to decide a course of action. Outspoken sectionalists began to talk openly of secession.

The Compromise of 1850

As the crisis built, other controversial aspects of slavery assumed new importance. Antislavery groups had long objected to slavery in the nation's capital and were now in the midst of a vigorous campaign to get Congress to abolish the institution in the District of Columbia. Southerners feared that such an action would undermine slavery in Maryland and Virginia and make the District a haven for runaway slaves. Already in some areas of the North the federal fugitive slave law was openly disregarded, and this too was a source of sectional resentments. Bondsmen who escaped to those areas were difficult to apprehend, and though the numbers involved were negligible, the principle was important to southerners. Then, too, militant abolitionists continued their relentless denunciation of the South.

In the animosity provoked by these issues, the bonds of union seemed to loosen. As that became apparent, centrist groups who cared more for the Union than slavery or abolition set in motion the machinery of compromise. Their first efforts centered around extending the 36°30' line to the Pacific Ocean. This had the advantage of concreteness and simplicity, but it would split California, much of which was below the line, and reserve the lion's share of the Mexican cession for free soil. Another basis for compromise talk was squatter sovereignty, allowing the people who settled in each territory to decide the slavery issue for themselves. This might take a divisive issue out of the hands of Congress and national politics, and to many it seemed a democratic solution to a vexing problem. But its mechanics could not be worked out. When and how would the decision be made? If slavery were prohibited when the territory was first organized, southerners would be deprived of equal access during the territorial stage. If it could not be prohibited until the territory became a state, the institution might by that time be too well established to dislodge.

The leader of the compromise efforts was Henry Clay, still a senator from Kentucky. Alarmed by the threat to the Union, Clay believed that all the major items of sectional discord should be brought together and dealt with in a general compromise that everyone of good will could support as a definitive solution to a problem that was threatening the Union itself. Accordingly, he proposed an omnibus bill to admit California to the Union as a nonslave state in accord with the wishes of its people, organize the rest of the Mexican cession into the territories of New Mexico and Utah with no mention of slavery and in this way bypass the issue for areas that would not be ready for statehood for some time, abolish slave trading but not slavery in the District of Columbia, and enact a strong fugitive slave law that would guarantee the return of runaway bondsmen to their legal owners.

The eventual acceptance of these measures eased the immediate crisis but left the basic problem untouched. The sectional division was too deep to resolve, and the Compromise of 1850, as the settlement was called, thus avoided the basic issues and dealt instead with the most pressing extrusions of those issues, which it treated with an ambiguity that concealed the depths of the breach in the Union. Even the issue that provoked the crisis, slavery in the territories, was deliberately avoided. By organizing New Mexico and Utah without mentioning slavery, that issue was left open for future dispute. More importantly, neither side accepted the compromise. Its passage was engineered not by Clay, but by the more adroit Senator Stephen A. Douglas of Illinois, who took Clay's omnibus proposal and divided it into separate bills so each provision could be voted on separately. This enabled proslavery congressmen to vote for the proslavery provisions and antislavery congressmen to vote for the antislavery provisions, while a small group of compromisers voted for both and thus created majorities for all. The compromise thus rested on no consensus, no meeting of the minds between the disputants.

The crisis that produced the compromise had important consequences for the South. Sectional leaders emerged from it more convinced than ever of the right of secession. During the compromise debates, more of them talked openly of secession than ever before, and many who did not were persuaded that the right existed and could be used if necessary. Sectionalists learned something else too, that the South was governed largely by political moderates and any effort to get the states to act together would result in delay and probably prove futile. The Nashville Convention, which met only after it became apparent that the compromise would pass, was dominated by moderates and was thus a major disappointment to the sectionalists who had called it. In the next great crisis, in 1860–61, sectionalists therefore avoided Southwide conventions in favor of action by individual states.

Failure of the Compromise

Compromise won in 1850 because unionist sentiment was strong and political leaders in both sections hoped and believed a general compromise would remove a cancerous problem from national politics. The hope proved ephemeral. Slavery was never removed from politics, although centrist politicians pretended for a time that it was and Franklin Pierce won the presidency in 1852 on the basis of that pretense. The new fugitive slave law, which required northern citizens and public officials to cooperate actively in the return of runaway slaves, was widely resisted, and the effort to enforce it only intensified antislavery and antisouthern opinion in the North. In a series of spectacular incidents like the Anthony Burns affair in Boston, concerted public efforts were made to prevent the return of fugitives, and in several states "personal liberty laws" and court decisions effectively nullified the statute, exercises in states' rights that southerners did not appreciate. The appearance of *Uncle Tom's Cabin* (1852), Harriet Beecher Stowe's enormously popular antislavery novel, which southerners considered an irresponsible and slanderous misrepresentation of the peculiar institution, provoked another wave of sectional acrimony. As this occurred, southerners continued to nourish hopes that the nation would annex areas in the Caribbean or Central America as potential slave territories. Their actions toward this end, such as the Ostend Manifesto of 1854 and filibustering expeditions to Cuba and Nicaragua, seemed to confirm abolitionist depictions of the South as an aggressive slavocracy.

It was the Kansas-Nebraska Act of 1854 that ended all hope that the Compromise of 1850 had solved the slavery problem. Put forward by the same Senator Douglas who shepherded the compromise through Congress, this measure provided for the political organization of two new territories, Kansas and Nebraska, in the area from which slavery had been excluded by the Missouri Compromise back in 1820. The bill Douglas proposed to Congress, however, in effect repealed that earlier compromise and the 36°30' line by providing that the question of slavery in the two new territories would be settled by the people there according to the principle of squatter sovereignty. This proposal was vigorously supported by southerners, though they had no hand in originating it, for it held out the possibility of one or more new slave states. Most northerners, however, were adamantly opposed to it, and Douglas's bill generated an immediate and sustained controversy that did not end when the bill passed with support from the administration of President Franklin Pierce.

One of the most fateful pieces of legislation in the nation's history, the Kansas-Nebraska Act grew not out of sectional imperatives, but out of Douglas's interest in a transcontinental railroad. Federal assistance was essential for such a road, and Douglas wanted the road to connect with Chicago. To accomplish these purposes he thought it necessary to organize territorial governments in Kansas and Nebraska, through which his railroad would run. But to get the necessary legislation through Congress, he would have to have southern support, for southerners were protesting their unequal treatment in the territories by obstructing legislation organizing all new territorial governments. To get their support, or at least their acquiescence, Douglas had to offer them something they wanted badly, the possibility that slavery might be introduced in one or both of the territories. Douglas himself thought slavery was unsuited to Kansas and Nebraska and would never exist in either, and that the issue was therefore moot, or rather one of symbols and principles only. His strategy worked in that he got his bill enacted into law, but its aftermath was not what he had anticipated. Neither northerners nor southerners were satisfied to leave the matter of slavery in the new territories to work itself out in its own good time. Instead, each set about trying to insure a victory for its side. The result was an intensification of the struggle over slavery in the territories and the first of the series of episodes that led directly to the Civil War.

That episode took place in "Bleeding Kansas." Kansas was the first of the new territories to attract settlers, and in the South and North alike organized efforts were undertaken to send settlers in order to win the territory for the one side or the other. Inevitably the pro- and antislavery settlers clashed, and the result was a heated and sometimes violent struggle for control of the territory. The rival groups of settlers set up rival territorial governments which refused to deal with each other. In Congress tempers flared to such a point that in 1856 Representative Preston Brooks of South Carolina caned Senator Charles Sumner of Massachusetts into insensibility for remarks Sumner made about the South and a kinsman of Brooks, the elderly Senator Andrew P. Butler of South Carolina.

Never before had sectional passions been so aroused, and in the aftermath a major realignment of national political forces commenced. The Whig party died and the Republican party was born and grew so rapidly in the North that by 1856 it had become the political voice of antislavery and northern sectional consciousness. The northern wing of the Democratic party began to fragment over slavery and related sectional issues. This increased southern influence in the Democratic party, and as the party became more and more southern in its stand on sectional issues, ex-Whigs and everyone else in electoral politics in the section were forced to become Democrats. The solid, one-party

South began to emerge. The rapidity with which these developments were occurring was reflected in the presidential election of 1856, in which James Buchanan, the Democratic candidate, carried fourteen of the fifteen slave states and won the election, while the Republican nominee, John C. Fremont, carried eleven of the sixteen nonslave states.

The immediate issue behind this polarization was still slavery in the territories. Senator Douglas had hoped to defuse that issue by the principle of squatter sovereignty, which he thought would remove it from national politics and Congress by letting settlers resolve the matter in the distant territory. Not long after Douglas's failure became apparent, the Supreme Court tried its hand at settling the question, in the case of *Dred Scott v. Sanford* (1857). In one of the most curious decisions in its history, the Court read into the constitutional law of the land the complete southern position on slavery in the territories. Congress, the Court ruled, has no power to exclude slavery from any of the territories. The Missouri Compromise and the 36°30' line were thus unconstitutional, as were other restrictive laws dating all the way back to the Northwest Ordinance of 1787. Slaves like other property could be taken into any of the territories and there slave property was constitutionally entitled to full protection of the law.

Coming fast on the heels of the Kansas-Nebraska Act, the *Dred Scott* ruling alarmed northern opinion in much the same way the Wilmot Proviso and *Uncle Tom's Cabin* had alarmed southerners. The implication of the decision was that slavery was national, not sectional, and that it was entitled to protection not only in hitherto free territories but in the free states as well. Alarm and aggravated emotions now existed on both sides, and formed the context in which each received the news of John Brown's raid in 1859 and each conducted itself in the national elections of 1860.

The Economics of Sectionalism

Political events interacted with economic developments which were themselves a major force behind the drift toward sectional polarization. After the Mexican War the slave-plantation regime, already declining in the upper South, suddenly found itself boxed in in the West. At the same time, the effort to form a political alliance with northern industrialists was destroyed by a basic economic shift. Until the 1840s southern exports had provided the major source of income for commercial and industrial growth in the North, and the complementary nature of the two sectional economies helped neutralize political rivalries. By that time, however, this relationship was changing. "During [that] decade," as Barrington Moore noted in *The Social Origins of Dictatorship and Democracy* (1966), "the pace of industrial growth accelerated to the point where the Northeast became a manufacturing region. This expansion ended the dependence of the American economy on an agricultural staple [cotton]. The Northeast and the West ... became less dependent on the South and more on each other. Cotton remained important to the North but ceased to dominate it." As that happened, differences between the northern and southern economies began to loom larger in public consciousness and politics, and the interdependence of the two economies became less controlling. Southerners grew resentful of their economic relationship with the North, especially northern control of the export trade. In 1837 a few of them held a convention in Baltimore to discuss the situation, and out of their discussion came a series of Southern Commercial Conventions, which from then until the Civil War constituted the most important voice of economic protest in the section. As the years passed, the Conventions gave less and less attention to the economics of southern problems and spent more and more time on politics and sectional rights. During the 1850s they played the leading role in encouraging a sense of economic grievance and popularizing the idea that the South was being exploited economically by the North. *Southern Wealth and Northern Profits* (1860) was the illustrative title of Thomas P. Kettell's book on this subject.

These were trends, not absolute conditions. The northern and southern economies remained interdependent, but more and more their differences were intruding into politics, and this, more than abolitionist or even antislavery sentiment, was responsible for the emergence of the Republican party in the North. By the 1850s more and more northerners wanted from national politics economic policies that southerners and the Democratic party had always been unwilling to support—reestablishment of a national banking system, which the Jacksonians had destroyed back in the 1830s; enactment of higher tariffs, which by the 1850s had fallen almost to free trade levels; federal assistance to business in hard times such as the panic of 1857; encouragement of immigration to insure a large labor supply; and stimulation of western settlement and development by such measures as a federally assisted transcontinental railroad and free homesteads to settlers. Economic shifts made this program increasingly attractive to midwesterners too, but southerners used their control of the Democratic party and the federal government to prevent its enactment. During his administration (1857–61), President James Buchanan, a Democrat and a "doughface" ("a northern man with southern principles"), vetoed a homestead act, a land grant college act, and a tariff act and refused to support other aspects of the northerners' economic program. Resentment against this "obstructionism" coalesced with rising antislavery sentiment and the economic changes just noted to encourage the new alignment of political forces mentioned earlier.

Northerners united politically. As the economies of the Northeast and Midwest became more convergent, so did their politics and ideology. One by one, major economic groups in those areas moved into the Republican party. Industrial workers who favored high tariffs to protect their jobs and midwestern farmers who wanted a homestead law joined with manufacturers and other proponents of economic development as well as a varied assortment of free soilers and antislavery groups in the Republican party, and together they made the party a broadly based organization that reflected northern sentiment on a wide range of sectional and economic issues. By 1860 this process was complete, and the Republican platform that year promised not only free soil and the containment of slavery but a national banking system, a higher tariff, a homestead act, and other incentives for economic development. Enactment of such a program would transform national politics and economics; more than that, it would change the nature of the American union. The loose federal system of the past would begin to give way to a centralized nation-state committed to industrialization and national economic integration, and with it would go the doctrine of states' rights and limited government and all the other things that southerners relied on to protect their interests.

The growth of northern unity paralleled the breakdown of national institutions. In 1844–45 the Baptist and Methodist denominations, the largest religious bodies in the country, split along sectional lines as a result of disputes involving slavery. In both instances southerners withdrew from their affiliation with national bodies and formed their own organizations, the Southern Baptist Convention and the Methodist Episcopal Church, South. In politics only the Democratic party weathered the sectional storm until 1860, when it too broke apart. American institutions proved unable to handle an issue whose emotional and moral dimensions could not be compromised or smothered in a larger consensus.

Underlying Issues

The problem, to repeat, was not any one of these things, but all of them. They came to be tied together in public thinking, and thus in politics. Individuals and groups who would compromise one or another of them would not compromise all of them, and every effort to resolve the sectional division foundered on the shoals of racial and political insecurity made worse by economic interest and the emotionalization of public issues that had a large moral dimension. These things were fundamental; they affected the vital interests of both sections and thus the distribution of political and economic power in the nation. Politicians responded to them as they had to, by defending the interests of the people they represented. In the normal course of events this is a satisfactory response, for divisive issues are usually resolved within the framework of American consensus or, in many cases, losers are compelled to submit to winners.

But by 1860 none of these normal conditions applied. The national consensus among dominant groups had broken down on a cluster of issues of transcendant importance, and the nation had to make fundamental choices on those issues. The country could in fact no longer exist half slave and half free, or more correctly, half southern and half northern. Forces of political centralization and economic integration were forcing it to choose and at the same time dictating the choice. The federal government and the national consensus had always been sympathetic to southern, agrarian, and slavery interests, but in 1860 Lincoln and the Republican party promised to transform the government by tilting it toward northern, manufacturing, and free soil interests. This signaled the emergence of a new political majority in the nation, and its appearance is what made the election of 1860 so important. The South had long been a minority, but not until 1860 were its opponents sufficiently united behind a common purpose to challenge its political supremacy. When this occurred, southerners, that is, those who controlled politics and economics in the section, concluded that the federal government and the Union itself had become threats to their wellbeing, and drastic measures of self-protection were necessary. If one grants them their premises, this conclusion was realistic and perhaps inevitable, even though Lincoln and the Republicans intended to make no immediate moves against slavery or the South. Sooner or later, southerners concluded, slavery—the economic and social order of the Old South—would be submerged in the sea of national integration and centralization.

But in the final analysis, what made the crisis of 1860–61 unique in American history was not the southerners' conclusion that they were an aggrieved minority threatened by an unrestrained majority. There have been many such minorities in the nation's history—slaves, blacks, labor groups, and economic and social radicals, for example—who have found themselves in desperate straits, but none of them was ever able to act effectively against the majority. What made the southerners different was geography, which gave them a unique ability to do so. Unlike all other aggrieved minorities in American history, the southerners enjoyed political and economic hegemony in a large geographical area. This gave them the kind of political and economic base no other minority ever had. It also gave them the psychological assurance that comes from unity and apartness, and encouraged them to look to themselves rather than the American system for redress of their grievances. For the first and only time in the nation's history, a large group of people with important political and economic resources concluded that their best interests would be served by withdrawing from the American system. The lack of such resources has forced other aggrieved minorities to acquiesce in decisions of the majority and work within established structures to redress their grievances—or, occasionally, to resort to desperate acts of violence that had no chance of success and only invited repression from the majority.

But southerners in 1860–61 had another option. Unity and apartness gave them the kind of resolve typically associated with nationalism. They therefore determined not to voice their protest within the American system, but to withdraw and make a system, a nation, of their own.

The Final Crisis

Of course the processes that produced the war were less straightforward than this implies. Neither northerners nor southerners were ever united. Among both were groupings of opinion on all issues and divided counsel as well. In the South moderates of all stripes vied with secessionists and unionists of every hue. To oversimplify, the degree of commitment to sectional rights bore a relationship to latitude, demography, and time. Whites in the deep South were more concerned about slavery and sectional causes than those in the upper South, whose concern was in turn greater than that in the border states. In the same manner, whites in the black belt were more "southern" than those who lived elsewhere, and out-and-out unionists were concentrated in the border states and Appalachia, the whitest areas in the section. And everywhere the trend was toward increased concern over sectional issues. By election time in 1860, whites in the cotton South, indeed throughout the Confederate South, agreed that events were closing in on them and unless something was done to reassure them soon, protective measures of some sort would be necessary. Many in the deep South openly advocated secession if Lincoln were elected. Others, more cautious, wanted to wait until the federal government committed an "aggression." Some, especially in South Carolina, wanted their state to act alone; most, however, favored consultation and joint action by all the slave states, or at least all the cotton states.

In the unusual times of 1860, established political forms broke down. The Democratic party, the only organization with significant strength in all sections, held its national convention in Charleston, South Carolina, a city singularly unsuited to calm deliberations. That, however, was the least of the reasons for what happened at the convention. A majority of the delegates were from nonslave states, and most of them supported Stephen A. Douglas for the presidency and a compromise position on slavery in the territories. Most southern delegates, however, considered Douglas unacceptable and demanded a platform endorsing the *Dred Scott* decision and the protection of slavery in all the territories. The division was deep, and irreconcilable. When the northern majority voted down the southern platform, delegates from the seven deep South states, led by William L. Yancey of Alabama, walked out of the convention. This earliest of all "Dixiecrat" revolts against the Democratic party was a product of mixed motives. Some of those who walked out did so to pressure northern Democrats into accepting the southern platform; others, however, hoped to break up the party as a step toward breaking up the Union. With the southerners gone, it was impossible to nominate a candidate by the necessary two-thirds vote, and the convention adjourned, to meet later in Baltimore. Meanwhile, the breakaway southerners called a convention of their own in Richmond.

Efforts to reconcile the groups failed; the Democrats were hopelessly split for the upcoming election. The northern wing of the party nominated Douglas for the presidency on a platform of squatter sovereignty, while the southerners nominated Vice-President John C. Breckenridge of Kentucky, a strong advocate of southern rights but not of secession. With the Democrats divided and the Union threatened, an assortment of ex-Whigs, ex-Know Nothings, border state unionists, and other moderates began working to paste over the sectional crisis and save the Union once more. They organized the Constitutional Union party and ran John Bell of Tennessee for the presidency. Foregoing the usual political platform, Bell and his party campaigned for the Union, which they believed was more important than slavery or antislavery or the grievances or interests of either section. The Republicans, clearly now a major party, nominated Abraham Lincoln of Illinois, a moderate on sectional issues, who ran on a platform of free soil and economic development.

The results of the election have been variously analyzed. Though there were four candidates, the election really amounted to two two-way contests, between Lincoln and Douglas in the nonslave states, where together they received 86 percent of the popular votes, and between Breckenridge and Bell in the slave states, where together they received 85 percent of the votes. Lincoln won by carrying all eighteen of the nonslave states, fifteen of them by clear majorities. In the slave states, however, the results were less decisive. They showed the unity of the lower South and the divisions in the upper South. In the latter (Delaware, Maryland, Virginia, Kentucky, Missouri, Tennessee, and North Carolina), Bell, the unionist, received 43 percent of the total vote, and carried Virginia, Kentucky, and Tennessee by pluralities. Breckenridge, on the other hand, the southern rights candidate, received 38 percent of the vote there and carried Delaware and Maryland by pluralities and North Carolina by a clear majority. Douglas, the northern Democrat, had 15 percent of the vote in the upper South, including a plurality in Missouri. In the lower South the results were quite different. There Breckenridge received an overwhelming 69 percent of the popular vote, with majorities in Florida, Alabama, Mississippi, Arkansas, and Texas and pluralities in Georgia and Louisiana. He also received the electoral vote of South Carolina, which was cast by the legislature. Altogether, Breckenridge carried every state of the Confederate South by a majority or plurality except Virginia and Tennessee, which voted for Bell. These results are often studied to find the degree of southern support for secession,[5] but that issue was not before the voters and the results are ambiguous. Breckenridge did not advocate secession, though virtually all secessionists seem to have supported him.

For many southerners, Lincoln's victory confirmed the long-standing fear that the North would one day unite against the South. The presidency would now be in hostile hands, and in cooperation with the substantial free state majorities in both houses of Congress Lincoln would be able to act against the South. The process of secession therefore began as soon as Lincoln's election was confirmed. Within a week, the legislature of South Carolina authorized a special convention to consider "the dangers incident to the position of the State in the Federal Union." A substantial majority of the voters in that state regarded Lincoln's election as sufficient cause for leaving the Union, and that fact worked to the advantage of advocates of immediate secession. Their strategy was to get South Carolina, the only state whose political leadership favored immediate secession, out of the Union at once, both as an example to other states and a means of avoiding the delay and indecision that cooperation with other states would entail. Once the process of secession was begun, they believed, it would generate its own dynamic and carry all the slave states out of the Union.

The problem for secessionists, even after Lincoln's election, was the divided mind of the South. The division was not over southern rights or even the right of secession, but over when and how—and whether—to exercise that right. Immediate secessionists, fire eaters mostly, men like Robert Barnwell Rhett in South Carolina, Edmund Ruffin in Virginia, Senator William L. Yancey of Alabama, and Governors Joseph E. Brown of Georgia and John J. Pettus of Mississippi, wanted the states to act individually and withdraw from the Union at once. In November this was a minority position in all the states except South Carolina, but everywhere in the deep South it had substantial support, including that of many well-placed political leaders. A more popular stance at that time was taken by cooperationists, who accepted the right of secession but wanted to delay action for the moment while the slave states consulted together and awaited the actions of the Lincoln administration, which would not enter office until March 1861. Proponents of this view included men like Alexander H. Stephens in Georgia, Jefferson Davis in Mississippi, Jeremiah Clemens in Alabama, and James L. Orr in South Carolina. A third opinion, also shared by a large minority, especially in the upper South, was unionism, which regarded secession as a revolutionary act to be exercised only in the event of intolerable provocation, which had not yet occurred. Such men as Governor Sam Houston of Texas, Herschel V. Johnson of Georgia, who had been Stephen A. Douglas's running mate in the recent election, and John Bell of Tennessee were prominent proponents of this view.

The South Carolina convention met on December 20 and unanimously passed an ordinance dissolving the union with the United States. By that time, six weeks after Lincoln's election but almost two months before his inauguration, secession movements were well under way in other states. In January Mississippi, Florida, Alabama, Georgia, and Louisiana withdrew from the Union, and on February 1, Texas did likewise. On February 4, delegates from the first six of these states, joined presently by those from Texas, met at Montgomery, Alabama, to create the Confederate States of America. They adopted a constitution, copied largely from that of the old Union, and organized a government, also copied from the American model. In less than three weeks, they completed their work by naming Jefferson Davis of Mississippi provisional President of the new nation and Alexander H. Stephens of Georgia provisional Vice-President, and constituting the Montgomery convention as a provisional Congress. Ten days before Lincoln's inauguration, the Confederates presented themselves to the world as a completed nation.

Things had gone well. Between December 20 and February 1 seven states had considered secession and all seven had seceded, and everywhere the transition was smooth. Then came a series of unexpected reverses. On February 4, the very day the Montgomery convention assembled, voters in Virginia elected a unionist majority to a convention to consider that state's future, and ten days later those in Arkansas and Missouri did the same thing. Meanwhile, on February 9, the Tennessee electorate refused even to authorize a convention, and on the last day of the month North Carolina voters did likewise. The Confederacy was confined to the lower South. Eight slave states remained in the Union. The section was split. The secessionists had misjudged the South.

They had also misjudged the North, though that was not yet so obvious. Secession had radically changed the nature of the sectional controversy. Before the southern states left the Union, the object of dispute had been slavery, about which most northerners were indifferent and the others divided and lacking in unity of purpose. But secession transformed the dispute from one involving slavery to one concerned with the future of the Union, and on the latter subject northerners could readily unite. Slavery was one thing, a threat to the Union quite another. A united and determined North would be a formidable adversary, but one to which secessionists had not yet given much thought.

8

The War for Southern Independence

Everywhere, secession evoked enthusiasm. The hesitancy which marked the first reaction to Lincoln's election gave way to the boundless confidence that signaled the birth of a new nation. For the moment, old divisions were forgotten as everyone joined in celebrating the remarkable happenings. Even before the Confederacy was born, an Alabamian was sure the southern nation was "destined to become the proudest and most powerful country that ever flourished in the tide of time." An equally exuberant Louisianan was certain that "no country upon the face of the globe" combined "all the elements of greatness, power and wealth so beautifully" as the South.

The pervasive optimism was fed by a general conviction that the Confederacy would expand to include all the slave states and perhaps many nonslave states too. The final outcome, some suggested, would be a reconstructed union with only abolitionist New England excluded. "The truth is, we shall be much more troubled with the question hereafter—'Who shall we keep out,'—rather than 'How many will come in?'" declared William Gilmore Simms in February 1861. "It is impossible to conceive the extent of spread of this Southern Empire of ours, if we keep ourselves free from entanglements and blunders. We only need to be firm, to be independent, and only need to be independent to be the most prosperous nation on the Earth. . . . Let us not bother our heads to please England and the North on the score of negro slavery and the slave trade. They have already voted us barbarians. But we have them in our power."

Even the less exalted were just as sure of the South's success. When the war was over and the Confederacy had gone with the wind, Sidney Lanier looked back upon its springtime of hope and tried to recall the universal anticipation. Still a teenager back then, the delicate Lanier remembered he had been convinced "not only that he personally could whip five Yankees, but *any* southern boy could do it[.] [O]ur old men said at the street corners, if they were young they could do it, and by the Eternal, they believed they could do it anyhow (whereat great applause and 'Hurrah for ole Harris!')[.] [T]he young men said they'd be blanked if they couldn't do it, and the young ladies said they wouldn't marry a young man who couldn't do it."

Amid this kind of headiness, events unfolded. The Confederacy asserted its sovereignty over American facilities within its borders, and assumed the functions of the federal government. The process was astonishingly smooth. There were no border incidents, no violence even in the transfer of military installations. Southerners withdrew from American service, civil and military, and transferred their allegiance and functions to the Confederacy or the states. The mails continued to run, the courts to operate, the police power to function. Law and order were everywhere preserved. Only in three instances did American commanders refuse to surrender their installations, at Forts Pickens and Taylor in faraway Florida and, fatefully, at Fort Sumter in the harbor of Charleston, South Carolina, the epicenter of Confederate zeal.

As these things transpired, President Davis sent commissioners to Washington to treat with the United States government and insure a peaceful relationship between the two nations. The Lincoln administration, just settling into office and unsure of the best course of action, refused to receive the commissioners, and its unofficial contacts with them, largely through Secretary of State William H. Seward, were, the commissioners eventually concluded, duplicitous. They could hardly have been otherwise. The policy of the Lincoln administration was just beginning to reflect the transformation of northern public opinion away from indecision and acquiescence in secession to a determination to save the Union. By the time he became President, Lincoln was apparently convinced that a confrontation was inevitable and further placation of the southerners unwise. Others on both sides were coming to a similar conclusion, and public thinking gradually became more realistic. By the time the war began, however, both sides had lost precious time.

The War Comes

Almost certainly, secession made war inevitable. That was an age of nationalism and centralization, and the idea that the nation would consent to its own division seems absurd. Even had the initial separation been peaceful, even had there been no Fort Sumter to ignite the spark of war immediately, the problems outstanding between the two countries must surely have defied peaceful solution. Even as the crisis built between December 1860 and April 1861, there had been several major efforts to compromise the dispute and enable the southern states to return to or remain in the Union. In Congress, a Senate committee of thirteen and a House committee of thirty-three worked long and hard to resolve the problem. The most notable effort was that of Senator John L. Crittenden of Kentucky, who proposed an irrevocable constitutional amendment guaranteeing slavery in the states where it already existed and restoring the 36°30' line to all present and future territory. These terms were probably acceptable to enough southerners to neutralize the secessionist impulse for the time being, but Lincoln and the Republicans refused to accept any provision that permitted the spread of slavery, and all compromise efforts collapsed.

The failure of compromise within the Union suggests that the Confederacy and the United States could not have coexisted peacefully. All the old problems remained, and secession created some new ones. The question of the territories was still there, but in a new form. Could the Confederacy claim territories such as Oklahoma and New Mexico where there was considerable prosouthern sentiment? How would the problem of divided loyalties in the upper South and border states be resolved? Were Confederate agents free to urge these areas to secede? Could the United States tolerate such urgings? What about the Mississippi River? And fugitive slaves? And the Monroe Doctrine? Could midwesterners tolerate the closing of the Mississippi by the Confederates? Could Confederates tolerate refusals to return their runaway slaves, or the urgings of abolitionists for a slave revolt? Could the United States permit the Confederacy to make foreign alliances that violated the Monroe Doctrine? What if the Confederacy itself sought to expand into the Caribbean? The list of such questions was endless, each one of which involved an issue that might have sparked war. Because of their differences, the two countries would no doubt have felt compelled to maintain large standing armies in the European manner, and given the sensitivity of both peoples and the rules of international conduct that then prevailed, war would certainly have come later if not sooner.

As things turned out, it came sooner. Against the divided counsel of his Cabinet, Lincoln decided to reprovision the garrison at Fort Sumter rather than permit its surrender when supplies ran out. His message informing the governor of South Carolina of this decision prompted action by the Confederate government, which felt the American presence in one of its principal ports was intolerable. General Pierre G. T. Beauregard, in command of military forces in Charleston, was directed to demand the garrison's surrender. When its commander, Major Robert Anderson, refused, the Confederates, in the predawn hours of April 12, 1861, opened fire. The following day, Anderson and his small force surrendered.

The war had come, and as Confederates saw it, by Yankee perfidy —but as Americans saw it, by Confederate aggression. The effect was electric. Confederates cheered the victory at Sumter as the logical result of determination and decisive action. Americans ended their irresolution. Both the North and deep South were now relatively united and sure of themselves. The great border, however, was still divided. But the times no longer permitted drift and indecision. Despite the deep divisions, choices would have to be made. Immediately after the incident at Fort Sumter, Lincoln called on the states to furnish 75,000 volunteers for military service against the Confederates, and the eight slave states still in the Union were forced to take a stand. Virginia, North Carolina, Arkansas, and Tennessee joined the Confederacy. Delaware, Maryland, Kentucky, and Missouri remained in the Union, and fifty counties in Virgina "seceded" from the Old Dominion and formed the loyal state of West Virginia. Divisions remained deep in all these states, however, even after the decisions were made—the secession vote in Virginia had been 88 to 55—and the first skirmishings in the war were between pro- and antisecession forces in the border region. The acquisition of four new states helped the Confederacy immensely. It brought much in resources, manpower, and territory, and it also brought Virginia, birthplace of the South and to most Confederates a symbol of the best of their heritage. But it also brought large pockets of people who were indifferent or actually opposed to the Confederacy and its cause. The new nation was much more powerful as a result of the addition, but far less united.

The Confederacy

The die was cast. Southerners had made a nation of their own and must defend it in war. As the supreme expression of southern consciousness, the Confederacy provides an instructive view of the sectional South— what it was and what it might have become had it been freed of American influence. Better than anything else in southern history, it reveals what the South meant to its own (white) people. Yet it is difficult to appreciate or express this—to describe the positive dimension of the Confederate experience. Historians as well as novelists, and southerners as well as nonsoutherners, have always had trouble doing so,[1] and no one has ever done it in a completely satisfactory way. Louis D. Rubin has noted that "no single Confederate war novel exists which we can read and then say with satisfaction, *That* was the Lost Cause"; and his observation is equally true of other literary and scholarly genres. The great Confederate apologia was never written, and the Confederacy itself, as Frank E. Vandiver suggests, became nothing more than "a terrible anachronism" even in the history of the South.

Why was this so? In *The Unwritten War* (1973), a perceptive study of Civil War literature, Daniel Aaron suggests that the answer is race. The racial crosscurrents of the war, Aaron believes, created an "emotional resistance" which ever afterwards blurred literary insight into the conflict and its deepest meaning. Aaron said this of the war itself and with the generality of American writers in mind, but the insight seems especially important for the South and southerners. No Tolstoy ever wrote the Confederacy's *War and Peace;* no Jefferson ever ennobled its cause in an inspiring declaration of independence; no Lincoln ever enshrined its concerns in a Gettysburg Address. Every Confederate counterpart to these great works is verbose or sentimental, and notable for its special pleading. The Confederacy never produced a single state paper of universal appeal. The talk of local rights and self-government was too clearly a disguise for white supremacy, the discourse on agrarianism and traditionalism too obviously a cover for special privilege.

This compounds the problem of those who would understand the positive dimension of Confederate history. The Confederacy represented an effort to break up the American union for purposes that were in significant part illiberal. Moreover, its brief history was a genuine tragedy and difficult to depict without caricature or evasion. Thus, notes Clifford Dowdy, whose sympathies for the Confederates sometimes leads him to mute their faults, the Confederacy "is usually studied from the outside for its weaknesses," and "little is learned about the matrix of [its] civilization" or what it represented to its people. Others have noted similar problems. "Historians will give credit to the South's bravery but damn its leaders, its mores, and its un-Americanness," Frank E. Vandiver has written. The Confederacy "is studied, by Southerners usually, to find flaws in an agrarian economy and in Jefferson Davis' executive leadership, to show the greatness of Robert E. Lee and Stonewall Jackson. But even Southern historians have shied away from a positive approach to the Confederate years in Southern history."[2]

Such an approach would seem to dictate an emphasis not on the Americanness of the Confederacy, which is what Vandiver was discussing, but on its un-Americanness, its distinctiveness, its southernness, the very aspects that are most difficult to recover. "The history of the Confederacy, when it shall be fully and fairly written," wrote George

Cary Eggleston in 1874, "will appear the story of a dream to those who shall read it, and there are parts of it at least which already seem a nightmare to those who helped make it." The story of the war is equally difficult to recover. "Future years," wrote Walt Whitman, "will never know the seething hell of the black infernal background of countless minor scenes and interiors (not the official surface courteousness of the generals, not the few great battles) of the Secession War, and it is best they should not. The real war will never get in the books."

If there is truth in these statements, if there remains a dimension of Confederate history that cannot be recaptured on paper, the same is true of all supremely intense experiences.[3] Since the Confederate experience was a war experience, a "Confederate way of life" never crystallized. Within two months of its creation, the Confederacy was plunged into a war it did not survive, and no sooner had the war begun in earnest than the resulting adversities began destroying the political and social consensus on which the southern nation depended and from which its national ideals derived. The Confederacy had no counterpart to that long generation after the Revolution in which the American people defined their national identity and sense of purpose. Moreover, the Confederate revolt was much more negative than the American Revolution, and much more difficult to put into positive terms. The Confederacy was born of a desire to hold onto a traditional way of life that was threatened by change. It promised no brave new world in the revolutionary future, but a preservation of the past. It "was a revolt of conservatism against the modernism of the North," wrote E. Merton Coulter; "the normal reaction of an isolated landed civilization against the world currents of trade and industry."

Thus Confederates usually defined their cause in terms of what they opposed or feared rather than what they supported or hoped for. "We are fighting to prevent ourselves from being transferred from American republicanism to French democracy," said Stephen Elliott, the Episcopal Bishop of Georgia, in a fast-day sermon in the summer of 1861. "We are fighting to protect and preserve a race who form a part of our household, and who stand with us next to our children. We are fighting to drive away from our sanctuaries the infidel and rationalist principles which are sweeping over the land and substituting a gospel of the stars and stripes for the gospel of Jesus Christ." To its citizens the Confederacy represented a conservative anchor in a swirling sea of change, or as one of them put it, "a bulwark against the worst developments of human nature, fanaticism, democracy, license, and atheism."

If this view ignored the exploitive aspects of Confederate society and the poisonous influence of its worst features, it also represented a reminder that not all the changes wrought by the "currents of trade and industry" were improvements. It was a reminder worth heeding, as the postwar history of the nation proved. When the Confederacy collapsed, with it went slavery and many of the ills of the *ancien regime*, but the restraining influence of the South upon the excesses of industrial capitalism was also lost. The real tragedy of the Confederacy was that its positive features—its emphasis on the individual citizen and tradition and locality, on political and economic decentralization, on such elements of community as personalism and the positive aspects of paternalism—were organically tied to its worst faults—slavery, racism, white supremacy, arrogance, exaggerated individualism, and a penchant for the undesirable aspects of paternalism. In getting rid of the latter, the Yankees destroyed much of the former. In the postwar world, the positive qualities of the Confederacy no longer had a basis in social reality, and like everything else in the Confederacy they ended up as parts of the myth of the Lost Cause.

This was probably inevitable, and Confederates as well as Yankees were responsible for it. As Vandiver has noted, the Confederacy was "an old order caught in a fundamental shift of history," and in trying too hard to hold onto the past, its people lost everything. They and their values, and the section itself, were shunted into one of the backwaters of history. Circumstance as well as history had equipped them poorly for change.

The Confederacy was thus founded on a contradiction, and the war made that fact painfully manifest. The Yankees would not let the new nation exist in peace. To endure, the Confederacy would have to prevail in war. But a major war would necessarily be a modern war, and a modern war of any duration would inevitably transform the Confederacy. Wars generate their own dynamic, and one of their first casualties is traditional ways of living. The Confederates were attempting an anomaly, a conservative revolution, a political change to prevent social and economic change. Unlike other modern movements for independence and nationhood, theirs was conservative and counterrevolutionary rather than radical and revolutionary. But that is not the full truth, either. What they were doing was trying to use revolutionary means to achieve conservative ends.

The effort could succeed only if they were let alone. A war of any duration and difficulty would inevitably compromise their purpose. It would force them to change their priorities, to sacrifice the ends that led them to secede for the means necessary to make secession permanent. Such is the fate of traditional societies forced to fight modern wars. The war the Confederates faced could not be fought by traditional methods on or off the battlefield, and had Grant surrendered to Lee at Appomattox, had the Confederacy survived its long and ghastly war for independence, the postwar Confederacy would have been almost as different from the Old South as the New South actually was. Without anyone determining that it should be so, and over the pointed objections of many, the Confederacy was revolutionized by the war it lost. Its political life was centralized and bureaucratized, its racial system was undermined, its economy was revolutionized by the growth of manufacturing and diversified agriculture, its faith in traditional ideals was shaken by hardship and disappointment, its concept of war was changed radically, much of its property was destroyed, many of its people were demoralized, its class relationships were ruffled, and its cities were swollen in size and economic significance. How the Confederate people bore up under these changes is the vital part of their history during the war for independence.

Preparing for War

The Confederates' first task was to assess their situation vis-à-vis the Americans, to weigh their advantages and disadvantages and devise a war plan that promised success. But southerners were never a systematic folk, and there is no evidence that they ever planned their war effort. That was probably their basic error, for a realistic assessment of the situation would certainly have led them to a war plan quite different from the one they followed.

By every material measure the Confederacy was disadvantaged, and this should have been the primary consideration of political and military strategists. Its population was only 9.1 million compared to 23.7 million in the United States, and though substantial numbers of the Americans sympathized with the Confederacy or were in faraway places like California and Oregon, 3.5 million of the Confederates were slaves. Racial and institutional considerations prevented the full utilization of blacks in the war effort, though their use in work details did free a larger proportion of white manpower for war purposes than would otherwise have been the case. In the states that joined the Confederacy, there were in 1860 1.1 million white males between the ages of fifteen and forty, compared to more than 4 million in the rest of the United States. How many of these served in the military is not known exactly. Estimates for the Confederacy usually center around 900,000 to 1,000,000, with those for the Union about twice as large. At its peak strength, in June 1863, the Confederate army had a total of 261,000 men present for duty, whereas the Union army reached its maximum strength of 622,000 in the spring of 1865.

The disparity in physical resources was even greater. "At the outbreak of war," Charles P. Roland has noted, "the North produced annually, according to value, 17 times as much cotton and woolen goods as did the South; 30 times as many boots and shoes; 20 times as much pig iron; 13 times as much bar, sheet, and railroad iron; 24 times as many locomotive engines; more than 500 times as much general hardware; 17 times as much agricultural machinery; 32 times as many firearms; and 11 times as many ships and boats." All of this bore directly on the kind of war the Confederates might hope to win. When the war began, the Confederacy had no munitions industry to speak of, no steel and machine tools industry, and only a limited amount of the technological and organizational expertise necessary to create major industries. The Confederacy did have about 9,000 miles of railroads, compared to 22,000 in the Union, but most of its trackage had been constructed to carry agricultural staples to port cities and was not integrated into a system to provide maximum support for military efforts along the nation's land borders. Much of it was in fact unconnected. Only one road, through Chattanooga, Tennessee, connected Virginia and the Southwest from Alabama and Tennessee westward.

These physical disadvantages were among the decisive factors in the Confederate defeat, but the Confederacy also had other less tangible limitations. It lacked many of the attributes of nationhood, including some of those of established governments. It had no diplomatic recognition, no foreign alliances or trade treaties, no treasury or monetary system and but little specie, virtually no navy to defend its long and exposed coastline and little capacity to build one. Moreover, its land frontiers were not easily defensible; on the contrary, the north-south direction of the valleys in Appalachia invited military invasion. Finally, its government at all levels was beset by personal rivalries and unclear divisions of authority.

These things had significance for Confederate strategists. So too did the character of the Confederate people. Some of the very qualities that led southerners to leave the Union now interfered with the effort to achieve independence. These included an outdated and romantic concept of war, one that stressed commitment, bravery, and individual fighting ability rather than technology, organization, and supply. As Robert Penn Warren has observed, the Confederate was a good fighting man but a poor soldier. Man for man he was certainly as good a warrior as his enemy; in combat he regularly displayed remarkable qualities of daring and endurance. But he learned at great cost to himself and the Confederacy that dedication and fighting ability are only two of the ingredients necessary for victory in modern war, that one may be wholly committed to a cause and fight selflessly and well for it and still lose. His chief weakness was the obverse of his greatest virtue: both he and his civilian counterpart were too individualistic to be entirely effective in modern warfare. Both found it difficult to accept discipline, to subordinate local and state interests to the general cause, and to maintain their morale once the war's exactions became acute. The premodern, preindustrial qualities of the Old South took their toll on the Confederacy.

If these things suggest that the Confederate cause was hopeless, they are only the negative side of the ledger. There was a positive side too. The Confederacy had a number of important advantages which skillfully exploited might well have resulted in victory and independence. At the outset the white population was united, its morale was high, and confidence in the justness of its cause almost universal. The population contained a considerable reservoir of political, diplomatic, and military talent that promised notable achievements in those important fields. The fact that only the military talent even partially fulfilled its promise is one of the mysteries of the Confederacy; the overall performance in politics and diplomacy, areas in which southerners had always excelled, can only be ranked as disappointing. Then, too, the Confederates had the advantages that inhere in wars for independence. Their effort could be largely defensive. They did not have to defeat the enemy militarily; like George Washington in the American Revolution, they had only to endure, to avoid defeat until cost and casualties and general weariness destroyed the enemy's will to continue. The effort to do so would be facilitated by fighting in friendly territory, which relieved them of the need to occupy and hold hostile territory, and by the advantages of interior lines of communication and supply.

There were other advantages. If the Confederates had little industrial capacity, they had an important agricultural resource, cotton, the essential raw material for one of the vital industries of Great Britain. The importance of this resource should not be underestimated. It offered the very real possibility of a diplomatic and economic alliance with Britain, an economic and naval power that not only needed cotton but had reasons of *realpolitik* for wanting to see the United States, a potentially powerful naval and economic rival, broken in two. An alliance with Britain would have had the practical effect of breaking the naval blockade the Americans imposed on the Confederacy, or at least of causing a naval war between the Americans and the British, and might well have been as decisive as the French alliance in the American Revolution. In addition, France and other European powers cast covetous eyes on Latin America, from which they had been lately excluded by the Monroe Doctrine and the British navy. By adroit diplomacy, the Confederates might have gained diplomatic recognition from these countries by agreeing to violations of the Monroe Doctrine. That this was not a fanciful consideration was illustrated by the French effort during the war to make Mexico a French protectorate.

Because of these advantages, most of which were potential rather than actual, the Confederate cause was far from hopeless in 1861. Wars of independence have been won by people with far greater disadvantages. The fact that the Confederates were able to fight four years and inflict so much suffering on the Union forces suggests that had they made optimum use of their potential advantages, they might well have prevailed. But in important respects the history of their war for independence is a story of failure, of their double failure to exploit the possibilities in their own situation and neutralize the advantages of the enemy.

Strategic Failures

The first failure was in conceptualizing the war and devising an overall strategy that maximized the Confederacy's advantages. To put it oversimply, the Confederates chose to fight the wrong kind of war, one that tended to enhance their enemies' advantages while doing little to exploit their own. In formulating a war plan, the Confederates had two basic options. They might fight a conventional war in the manner of established nations and according to the modes of warfare then current, which grew out of the Napoleonic campaigns. Or in modern parlance, they might wage a war of national liberation such as George Washington had fought in the Revolution. A third possibility was to combine in some eclectic fashion features of the first two most suited to their circumstances. To a limited extent they drew upon the second and third options, but basically they followed the first one. They chose in effect to fight a conventional international war rather than a revolutionary war of national liberation.

This was not so much the result of conscious planning as the lack of it. Conventional warfare was just that, conventional, and only that kind of warfare conformed to Confederate ideas about how a nation should conduct itself. Each of the three options just noted had advantages and disadvantages for the Confederacy, but hindsight suggests that the decision to fight a conventional war was a basic error. Conventional war meant massed armies and pitched battles, sacrificing men and materiel for territory, all for the purpose of defeating the enemy militarily. This meant a war in which organization, supply, discipline, technology, and massed manpower were the keys to victory. The problem with such a war was that these were the very things in which the enemy's superiority was greatest, and to win such a war the Confederates would have to beat the Americans at their own game, something they could hope to do only in a short, *blitzkrieg*-type war. The longer a conventional war lasted, the more controlling the Americans' advantages would become and the more the Confederate people would be forced to change themselves as the war dictated.

If a conventional war was ill suited to the Confederates' circumstances, the alternative was uncongenial to their temperament as a people. A war of national liberation would involve not massed armies but a citizen soldiery, guerillas and irregulars organized on local bases across the country, each man fighting in his own locality, each depending on his own resources in the manner of Quantrill's raiders on the western border, Mosby's rangers in northern Virginia, and other groups that effectively harassed hostile populations and invading armies. This type of total warfare, which involved civilian populations and irregular conduct, violated the Confederates' concept of how civilized people conduct themselves. In a war of this kind, the Confederates would have avoided major battles except on advantageous terms, and sacrificed territory in order to preserve men and materiel. This would have meant strategic retreats, permitting large areas of the Confederacy to be occupied by the enemy, whose invading armies and occupying forces would be harassed until Union leaders and the northern people decided that the effort to restore the Union was too costly. It would have aimed not to defeat the enemy, but to wear him down.

Using the advantages of hindsight, some historians have suggested that this kind of warfare offered the best chance of victory. In a strictly military sense they are probably correct, but it was impossible for the Confederates to wage such a war. Not only did that kind of warfare violate their concept of honorable conduct, but it had great potential for arousing the latent social discontent in the South. Its success would have depended not on social and economic elites, but on the mass of the people, small farmers, lesser whites, and slaves. In these groups, however, there was considerable potential for social unrest, and in the case of the slaves, of revolutionary change, which a popular war of national liberation might have unleased. The decision to fight a conventional war was not only understandable, then, but predictable. The Confederates had no other real choice, and their decision confirms an observation by Clausewitz that Confederate historians are fond of quoting, that the nature of a society determines the kind of war its people will fight.

The overall military strategy was "offensive-defensive"; that is, within a basically defensive posture, offensive thrusts, especially for tactical advantage, were employed.[4] This strategy was devised by President Jefferson Davis, who directed military planning himself, and Robert E. Lee, who in the summer of 1862 became commanding general of the Army of Northern Virginia and was thereafter the principal military figure in the Confederacy. The strategy reflected their assessment of political and military factors, including the Confederacy's position vis-à-vis the United States and potential foreign allies, and their evaluation of enemy intentions. The enemy's strategy was simple and ultimately effective: surround the Confederacy and squeeze it to death. Its basic elements were a naval blockade to cut off the Confederacy from outside supplies essential to the war effort and civilian life; capture of strategic coastal areas to facilitate the blockade and tie down Confederate defense forces; bottle up navigable rivers; isolate the Confederacy diplomatically and prevent foreign recognition and assistance; ring the Confederacy's northern frontiers with armies and send those armies into its heartland to search out and destroy its military forces; and through these and other measures break the will of the southern people to continue the war.

The Confederate response to this soundly conceived strategy was piecemeal and ineffectual. The Confederacy had no navy and little capacity to build one, and never gave sufficient attention to naval affairs. To undermine the blockade, which was extremely porous at first, it relied on privateers, blockade runners, and the hope of British intervention. The hope was never realized, and though individual blockade runners performed some spectacular deeds, military and civilian goods were in short supply within a few months of its proclamation, and its most important result, the sapping of civilian morale, had already commenced.

The army necessarily received the most attention. Davis, a West Point graduate who had served in the Mexican War and been Secretary of War in Franklin Pierce's Cabinet, divided the Confederacy into military theaters, each with an independent command under his own control. The most important theaters were northern Virginia, which Davis and Lee always regarded as the focal point of the war, and the West, which centered in Tennessee. After Union forces split the Confederacy down the Mississippi River in 1863, the area beyond the Mississippi, commanded by Kirby Smith, was a virtually autonomous domain, but it had little effect on the course of the war.

The task Davis assigned the principal armies, especially Lee's Army of Northern Virginia and the Army of Tennessee, which had a succession of commanders, was to hold the territory in their theaters by repulsing Union intruders. The decision to defend every inch of territory was dictated in part by political pressure on Davis, but it was a questionable military policy. It had the effect of spreading Confederate troops thinly over a vast area and thus leaving them vulnerable to piecemeal attack by massed American armies. This was especially true in the West, where distances were great and the size of Confederate forces relative to the territory they had to defend was much less than in northern Virginia. For political and strategic as well as personal reasons, Davis and Lee made northern Virginia the focus of their attention, and an unintended result of this was relative neglect of the western theater. There were sound reasons for wanting to hold on to northern Virginia. It was a geographical dagger pointing into the heart of the North from which Confederate forces were able to harass the Union by keeping much of its army tied down defending Washington, D.C., and in other ways plaguing the Union's military effort. Moreover, Richmond was the chief industrial center of the Confederacy as well as its political capital, and Virginia was the symbolic core of the South.

The problem with the Davis-Lee strategy was therefore not that northern Virginia was unimportant, but that the West was just as important for other reasons, and the emphasis on northern Virginia produced a serious imbalance in the overall military effort. As a consequence, while the valiant and costly effort to protect Richmond was successful—the city was abandoned only a week before Lee surrendered—the rest of the Confederacy was systematically destroyed, and when that was accomplished, Richmond too was lost.

This illustrates the difference between the Confederate war plan and that of the Americans in the Revolution, who also faced a superior military foe. In the Revolution, George Washington had avoided set battles and the casualties they would bring, for he knew the Revolution was alive as long as his army was not destroyed. Knowing also that he had little chance to destroy the British army, he sought to keep his own army and the revolutionary cause intact until cost and weariness sapped the will of the British government to continue the fight. The British occupied large areas of the country and every major city, but were never able to extinguish the patriot cause or eliminate the patriot military effort. Indeed, the more successful they were, the more territory they overran, the more costly the war became. It was a contest of endurance, and Washington won by not losing. The Revolution had thus been a long war, far longer than the Civil War, but one with remarkably few battles and casualties. Altogether, the Americans suffered fewer than 5,000 battlefield deaths in the Revolution, an almost negligible figure by Civil War standards. One reason for the difference was the willingness, indeed eagerness, of Confederate armies to engage the enemy in battle. But unable to destroy the Union military force, the southern armies bled themselves into impotence, and when that happened the Confederate cause expired.

Robert E. Lee

The major responsibility for this policy was Lee's.[5] Lee was the Confederacy's finest general and most authentic hero, and after the war the personification of the Lost Cause; and if his strategic planning is a legitimate subject for dispute, his tactical maneuvering and battlefield performance are unsurpassed in the annals of generalship. At these things he was a genius. A member of one of the South's most distinguished families and a graduate of West Point, he had a long and competent career in the United States army, from which he resigned during the secession crisis. Questioning the wisdom of secession and repelled by the chauvinism of sectional extremists, he personally opposed slavery—he freed his own slaves long before the war—but was absolutely devoted to Virginia. A man of unsurpassed personal virtue, he seems nevertheless a baffling personality. He "was one of the small company of great men in whom there is no inconsistency to be explained, no enigma to be solved," wrote Douglas Southall Freeman, his greatest biographer. "What he seemed, he was—a wholly human gentlemam, the essential elements of whose positive character were two and only two, simplicity and spirituality."

This seems an incomplete assessment of so complex and enigmatic a man. Lee was in the best and most limiting senses of the term a principled southern gentleman, and he honored his principles to the extent of paradox if not contradiction. He was a states' rights nationalist who thought secession unwise but followed his state out of the Union unquestioningly, and in the ensuing war showed his loyalty to Virginia by commanding the Confederate army in a strike for independence, and bled the Confederate army to death in defense of his home state. A gentle, Christian gentleman in the finest sense of the term, he alone kept the Army of Northern Virginia alive and bleeding for months after its cause was militarily hopeless. Truly in the last months of the war thousands of his men died for a lost cause. In all of this, Lee avoided the political consequences of his actions. A man of immense stature and prestige, he refused to use his standing to influence politics, leaving Virginia and the Confederacy to face political problems without benefit of his counsel. Certainly he was a singular southerner, a gentleman of public prominence who was utterly devoid of political ambition.

In military affairs, however, Lee was a man of definite ideas and demonstrated ability, and once he assumed command of the Army of Northern Virginia, he was the principle architect of Confederate strategy in the East and, indirectly, in the West. He was not responsible for the original emphasis on northern Virginia, but he supported the emphasis throughout the war, and that policy like his propensity for the military offensive proved to be strategically questionable because of the Confederacy's physical limitations. Lee, however, was convinced that the Confederacy could never win a long war, for in such a war American superiority in materiel and manpower would prevail. The Confederacy's only chance, he reasoned, lay in taking a chance, in trying to achieve a military victory in a short time. Given the decision to fight a conventional war, this was certainly sound reasoning, but by the time Lee was able to act on it, the American advantages had already begun to take effect. The result was that Lee won those notable tactical victories for which he is justly famous, but the enormous casualties they entailed were beyond the capacity of the Confederacy to endure, and the victories were therefore pyrrhic.

Jefferson Davis

As strategic planning evolved, the civilian war effort took shape. It too involved major difficulties, and a fair assessment must conclude that the Confederacy's civilian performance was poorer than the military. Optimists like J. D. B. De Bow might insist in the summer of 1861 that "the war cannot last long—we can beat them on every field when they do not out-number us more than 3 to 1." But more realistic men like President Davis knew better. They knew by the first summer that the war might well be a long one, and that victory or defeat depended on the government's success in marshaling the manpower and material resources of the country. To do this, the Confederacy needed nothing as much as inspired, effective political leadership.

The structure of the government created at Montgomery in February 1861 was about the same as that of the United States government. The major differences were certain provisions written into the Confederate constitution to protect slavery and states' rights, prevent enlargement of the central government, and maintain a conservative, agrarian society. In any government, however, the men who run it are more important than its institutional forms, and here the Confederacy was not fortunate. Why this was so is not entirely clear, but the government never functioned smoothly, and as the manifold problems of war increased, its ineffectuality became a major source of weakness.

The key man was President Davis. Born of yeoman parents in Kentucky in 1808 and educated at West Point, he was in 1861 a man of wide political experience, demonstrated ability, and utter devotion to the Confederate cause. His election to the presidency cast him in a role he did not covet and one in which no one might have succeeded, and given the needs of the office, Davis was not the ideal man to fill it. Neither his personal qualities nor his special abilities were suited to the task he faced, which was to win a revolutionary war of national independence. He was a proud and reserved man, sometimes petty, often difficult to work with. He frequently let personal considerations intrude into matters of state, and had difficulty delegating authority, especially in military affairs. He also had poor health, which sometimes inhibited his work.

More importantly, Davis had little of the charisma and none of the iron will and ruthless determination that make successful revolutionary leaders. He lacked ability to inspire the masses to sacrifices beyond themselves or to sustain their faith when things went badly. He could not even inspire his subordinates in government to work together—he was forced, for example, to make thirteen changes in his Cabinet during the course of the war. He lacked the instincts of a successful revolutionary leader—the willingness to do whatever is necessary to win, or to put it in modern parlance, the will to victory. He never conceived of his role as that of a revolutionary, and he was temperamentally incapable of doing effectively some of the things which, had they been done thoroughly and vigorously, might have brought victory. And when he was forced by circumstances to do some of those things, he did them incompletely and half-heartedly. The result was that he violated principles to which he and the Confederacy were committed and thereby aroused the opposition of his critics, but without accomplishing the necessary results. He never acted effectively against men like Governor Joseph E. Brown of Georgia who used states' rights to sabotage the war effort, or against newspapers like Edward A. Pollard's Richmond *Enquirer,* whose criticisms of Davis and the war effort undermined morale. He undertook no systematic propaganda effort to keep up public morale, and was reluctant to use martial law or interfere with property rights and individual liberty. A leader with the thoroughness of Fidel Castro or Mao Tse-tung, or even Bismarck or Napoleon, might have done such things and made good the Confederate bid for independence. But such men are not southerners in principles or methods, and for the Confederacy to have turned to or followed such a leader would have been to lose its soul—its essential southernness. The Confederates turned naturally to men like Davis and Lee, who gave them not independence but exemplary leadership of the kind their principles and way of life permitted.

As troubles mounted during the war, Davis became an object of great controversy, and historians have variously estimated his performance.[6] Frank E. Vandiver has concluded that the Confederacy was "singularly fortunate" in having Davis as a leader, for "he provided almost exactly the type of man suited to the time and to Confederate circumstance." That, however, is a minority view. "There is a great deal of evidence to justify placing a considerable share of the responsibility for the Confederacy's misfortune directly at the door of Jefferson Davis," David M. Potter wrote in a more typical evaluation. For whatever reason, Davis proved to be a mediocre President, especially in comparison to his rival, Abraham Lincoln. "He could not grasp the vital fact that the Confederacy was not a going, recognized government," T. Harry Williams has observed, "but a revolution, and that in order to win, it would have to act with remorseless revolutionary vigor." "There is no evidence in all the literature," adds Potter, "that Davis ever at any one time gave extended consideration to the basic question of what the South would have to do in order to win the war."

That is a damning indictment. Without effective leadership, the Confederacy could not hope to succeed. No revolution was ever won without aggressive and inspired leadership. Only that could have harnessed the initial enthusiasm of the people and sustained it through adversity, and lacking that, the enthusiasm turned into disillusionment and resentment. Civilian morale collapsed though that of the army never did, and Davis became the object of widespread criticism that seemed only to make him more withdrawn and unbending. The rapid turnover of Cabinet members and other staff personnel reflected the difficulty many had in working with him. As military and diplomatic reverses mounted and the situation on the home front degenerated, bickering within the government worsened, not only within the executive branch but in Congress and between Congress and Davis, and between the central government and some of the states. Not all, maybe not even most, of the responsibility for this was Davis's. The basic cause was the mounting toll of military reverses and the sagging morale this and other problems engendered. The Confederacy in effect came apart at the seams, something that perhaps no one could have prevented. The fact that able men preferred military to civilian service certainly contributed to the overall political ineffectuality.

The Civilian War Effort

Yet the civilian effort accomplished some remarkable, even miraculous things. In spite of the blockade, the shortage of consumer goods, the gradual breakdown of the transportation system, the limited manufacturing capacity, and the incursion of Union armies, Confederate forces never lost a major battle or campaign from a lack of supplies until the very end. Much of the credit for that achievement belongs to Josiah Gorgas, the resourceful chief of the Ordnance Bureau of the War Department. To support the war effort, old factories were converted to war production and new ones established, railroads and other utilities were pressed into public service, plantations were converted to food production and slaves set to work in defense-related tasks, white women assumed volunteer duties of a sort they had never done before, and financial resources were invested in Confederate bonds to support the war effort. Altogether the Confederate people compiled a remarkable record of sacrifice and achievement, one that illustrated not only their great dedication to a popular cause but also remarkable ingenuity and resourcefulness in serving that cause. What compromised the effort were the military misfortunes. After the disastrous summer of 1863 when the Confederacy's prospects plummeted, morale sagged, and as a result of that and the mounting shortage of consumer goods, the civilian effort was less and less effective.

A major problem and one that was never solved was financing the war. The basic problem, the lack of liquid wealth, was complicated by inflation, unrealistically low taxes at first, and an unwillingness to commit the South's entire resources to the war effort. There was not enough specie or circulating paper to finance the war by direct taxation, even had the government been willing to do so. But the taxes that were levied by the central government early in the war were compromised by the states, which issued bonds rather than pass the high rates along to the people. Only about 1 percent of the total expenditure of the Confederate government was covered by income from taxation. To offset the resistance to high taxes, the central government resorted to borrowing. At first southerners responded enthusiastically to the sale of Confederate bonds, but their liquid capital was soon exhausted, and efforts, never very successful, were made to borrow from European sources. As these sources dried up, taxes were increased and a tax in kind imposed on agricultural produce. The latter was an essential war measure, but it immediately became the object of resentment and widespread resistance. To many it seemed like confiscation of property, to others a violation of civil rights. It was both of course, but the basic objection to it was the violence it did to the southerner's sense of individualism. Inevitably, the tax was collected unevenly and violations prosecuted uncertainly, and this increased the resentment. In the end the tax was a failure, for it probably generated more opposition to the Confederate cause than produce for the Confederate army.

When other sources of revenue failed, the government resorted to the printing press, and issued mountains of paper money backed only by the promise of redemption after the war. In 1861, $311 million worth of paper was printed, and before the war was over more than $1.5 billion. The purchasing power of this money depended entirely on confidence in Confederate victory, and in view of that fact it held up remarkably well. In early 1863 four Confederate dollars would still buy as much as a gold dollar, and a year later twenty Confederate dollars would do the same.

One reason so much paper money was printed was inflation, which was another insoluble problem that had a devastating effect on morale. The sources of inflation were obvious: the shortage of consumer goods created by the blockade, the ravenous demands of the military for food and other supplies, and the gradual breakdown of the transportation system, which produced serious problems of distribution. More than any other wartime problem, inflation touched all the population. Its insidious effects robbed rich and poor alike, encouraged hoarding and black marketing, and sapped the spirit of cooperation and the will to sacrifice. The dimensions of the problem are difficult to express in a few sentences, but an index of consumer prices that equaled 100 in April 1861 stood at 279 a year later, 1,168 another year later, and 2,776 still another year later in April 1864. In Richmond and other areas near the war zones the situation was worse, and cannot adequately be reflected in statistics. Many goods, including necessities, were sometimes unavailable, and in several cities, including Richmond, there were food riots by people unable to get enough to eat. J. B. Jones, whose *Rebel War Clerk's Diary* (1866) is an interesting picture of wartime Richmond, reported that in May 1864 flour in the Confederate capital was selling for $275 a barrel, potatoes for $25 a bushel, and bacon for $9 a pound.

Like inflation and taxation in kind, Confederate manpower policies caused hardships that were both great and inequitable. In April 1862 the central government imposed a military draft. All able-bodied white males between eighteen and thirty-five were made subject to three years military service; however, many nonagricultural workers were exempted, as were owners (or their overseers) of twenty or more slaves. The latter exemption was considered necessary to insure racial safety as well as effective direction of agricultural labor, but it and other factors made this law too a source of resentment and disaffection. The effect of the law was to conscript the work force of small farms but not large plantations. It caused great hardship to the families of many small farmers, whose women and children were left without a man to work the farm, but exacted no similar sacrifice from planter families. More than anything else, this encouraged class resentments in the Confederacy and nourished the sentiment embodied in the slogan "a rich man's war and a poor man's fight."

In retrospect the policy of conscripting free but not slave labor seems to have been shortsighted. Even if conscripted slaves could not be used in combat, they could have been put to other uses, including work on the farms of white men who were drafted. Of course slaves were sometimes requisitioned or volunteered by their owners for public work details, but they were not drafted into Confederate service for the duration of the war, and the reason seems to have been that such an action threatened slavery. Only in the final extremity of defeat did the government change this policy, by deciding to conscript blacks into the Confederate army, but then it was too late. As it was, the conscription of whites entailed hardship on many people and affected many who were unwilling to serve, and for both reasons it was a major cause of the antiwar sentiment that grew as Confederate fortunes sank. Draft dodging, desertion, and other forms of slacking were among its important consequences. The number of men who deserted from the Confederate armies has been estimated at 100,000 or more, some of whom joined guerilla bands to prey upon the citizenry in remote areas. It seems likely that the manpower the conscription law procured for the army only partially offset the ill effects it generated.

The Military Verdict

In the final analysis, all the domestic difficulties grew out of the misfortunes of the military. For several months after Fort Sumter, military activity was limited to skirmishings in the border areas that had the effect of defining lines between the opposing forces, but this was chiefly a time of preparation. The first significant battle between major armies did not occur until July 21, 1861, more than three months after Fort Sumter, when a Union force under Irwin McDowell engaged the principal Confederate force in northern Virginia, under General Beauregard, at Bull Run, south of Washington, D.C. McDowell's army was about to carry the day, but an opportune reinforcement gave the Confederates a clear victory. The unseasoned Union troops gave way and fled in rout to the defenses around Washington, but the Confederates were just as unseasoned, and almost as disorganized in victory as the Americans in defeat. They therefore failed to pursue the retreating enemy, and thereby lost the best chance they ever had for a clear military victory before the Union could take advantage of its material superiority. The battle at Bull Run was thus of little military consequence, but its psychological impact was great. It reinforced the Confederates' overconfidence, but made the Americans realize that they were in for a long and difficult struggle.

Not until early 1862 did large-scale fighting occur again. By that time the Americans were ready to implement their plan to surround the Confederacy and squeeze its life away. Toward that end they undertook a series of simultaneous actions, and by the time the Union Army of the Potomac, under George B. McClellan, moved against Richmond in the last of these actions in April 1862, the overall strategy was already bearing fruit. A naval blockade of the Confederate coast was proclaimed soon after the war began, and though it was still not completely effective in the spring of 1862, its impact was already pronounced. Strategic sites along the Atlantic and Gulf coasts had been occupied, including Hatteras and several other points in North Carolina as well as Port Royal and the surrounding sea islands in South Carolina and Fort Pulaski at the mouth of the Savannah River in Georgia. The major port cities of Wilmington, Charleston, and Savannah were thereby neutralized, and McClellan's army soon occupied Norfolk, Virginia, another important port. About the same time, in April 1862, an American force moved up the Mississippi River from the Gulf of Mexico and captured New Orleans, the Confederacy's largest city and principal seaport. Meanwhile, other forces in the West were penetrating deep into the Confederate heartland. In February 1862 a force under Ulysses S. Grant captured Forts Henry and Donelson in southwest Kentucky, and with them access to the Tennessee and Cumberland Rivers. Before that month was out Nashville, on the Cumberland, had been occupied, and most of Tennessee was under American control less than a year after secession. By April the principal army in the West, under Grant, had reached northern Mississippi, where at Shiloh on the 6th and 7th of the month it was nearly defeated by a major Confederate force commanded by Albert Sidney Johnston. However, Grant rallied his army and defeated Johnston, who himself died in the battle.

Everywhere things were going badly for the Confederacy when McClellan began his long-awaited move against Richmond. He came not across country from Washington, however, but transported his army by sea to the peninsula formed by the York and James Rivers, and after extraordinarily slow progress reached the outskirts of Richmond. The Confederacy itself was imperiled, and had McClellan succeeded it might have died an early death.

But then, almost suddenly, things brightened as the fighting forces and the people staged the first of those great rallies that turned adversity into hope and enabled the Confederacy to keep struggling for so long and so well. At the battle of Seven Pines, the first major engagement with McClellan's army in the environs of Richmond, the Confederate commander, Joseph E. Johnston was wounded, and replaced by Lee. A bold and imaginative tactician, Lee believed that Richmond could be saved only if the Confederate army seized the tactical initiative. This would not only give Lee the opportunity to determine the time and place of battle, but it was the best way to counter McClellan, who despite considerable superiority of manpower and materiel was one of the most cautious men ever to command an army. After sending a detachment under Stonewall Jackson toward Washington, a move that forced the Americans to split McClellan's force, Lee began his assault. In a series of battles known as the Seven Days (June 25 to July 1), he broke McClellan's advance and forced his army out of the peninsula. Richmond was saved.

But Lee was not content to save Richmond. He continued his pressure on the enemy army. After besting it in a major engagement, the second battle of Bull Run, in early September he crossed his army into Maryland hoping to end the war by inflicting a major defeat on the Union army on Union soil. Meanwhile, Confederate fortunes were looking up in the west. A force under Braxton Bragg began moving northward through Tennessee into Kentucky, and a series of offensive moves was undertaken to break the threat Union forces were mounting against Vicksburg, Mississippi, by now the only link to the trans-Mississippi Confederacy and its vital supplies.

All three efforts were unsuccessful. In mid-September Lee's army fought a major engagement at Antietam Creek near Sharpsburg, Maryland, and though the result was militarily inconclusive, Lee was forced to return to Virginia. The psychological and diplomatic results of his failure exceeded the military results. The Confederates had expected much from the invasion, and a clear victory at Antietam might have brought diplomatic recognition from the British. But no sooner had Lee met disappointment than Bragg's advance was checked at Perryville, Kentucky, in October, and his army too was forced to return southward, to Tennessee. Nor were the efforts to end the Union threat to Vicksburg successful, though that city, almost impregnable to attacking armies, was not itself immediately threatened.

At the end of 1862, then, the Confederates had nothing to show for their efforts except lengthening casualty lists, growing shortages of consumer goods, sagging civilian morale—and hope. The Confederacy was still alive, most of its territory intact, and its military forces were unvanquished. The British might yet grant recognition; the Union might still quit the fight if only the Confederacy could hold out; and Lee's army, which had captured the imagination of the Confederate people, might still win a conclusive victory. At Fredericksburg in December and again at Chancellorsville the following May, Lee inflicted major defeats on the main American army, achieving in the latter battle perhaps his most spectacular victory. Still, the vise around the Confederacy seemed to clamp harder. The pressure against Vicksburg mounted, and the Army of Tennessee, which had been forced out of Murfreesboro in December 1862, had fallen back to Chattanooga with its vital rail connection between Virginia and the Southwest.

In each of the three areas the war reached a climactic turning point in the summer or early fall of 1863, the decisive period in the military history of the war. Everywhere the results were disastrous, or at best misfortunate. In the East, Lee concluded that the Confederacy's position would soon be desperate unless he achieved a convincing victory over the Army of the Potomac on Union soil, and accordingly he moved his army out of Virginia, across western Maryland, into southern Pennsylvania, and the fateful battle at Gettysburg. There, in the first three days of July, he and his army were defeated with such heavy and irreplaceable losses that for the rest of the war he remained on the strategic defensive. His invasion was the high-water mark of Confederate military effort, and together with the loss of Vicksburg on the following day, its failure was a mortal wound from which the Confederacy never recovered. As the news of Lee's defeat spread across the country, Vicksburg, the last contact with the western Confederacy, collapsed on July 4 after a long and ghastly siege. The Confederacy was now split in two and its ports already bottled up. But this was not the sum of adversity, for presently a second split was threatened. In early September Bragg's army was maneuvered out of Chattanooga, and, despite a near victory at Chickamauga in north Georgia on September 19–20, it was soundly beaten in battles at Lookout Mountain and Missionary Ridge along the Tennessee-Georgia border in late November. Confederate strength in the area was thereby reduced and what was left of Bragg's army was no match for the enemy force opposing it.

The war lasted twenty-one months after Gettysburg and Vicksburg, and almost sixteen after Lookout Mountain and Missionary Ridge, but the military decision had been rendered. It remained only to convince the Confederates, whose hopes rested on British recognition and Union weariness. Toward this end, Sherman went on his destructive march through Georgia, and Ulysses S. Grant, now moved to northern Virginia, undertook a bloody and relentless assault against Lee and Richmond. For Sherman the going was easy, and the physical and psychological damage he inflicted on the reeling Confederacy was devastating. Grant's task was vastly more difficult, for he had to dislodge Lee's army from entrenched defensive positions around Richmond and Petersburg. In one of the bloodiest sustained campaigns in the annals of warfare, Grant ignored his own replaceable losses and simply wore Lee's army out through attrition. As his effort ran its course through the summer and fall of 1864 and into the following spring, the Confederacy disintegrated. Its fate was sealed at Appomattox Courthouse on April 9, 1865. There, in the most compelling and pathetic moment in southern history, Lee surrendered the remnants of his shattered, starving army to a magnanimous Grant.

The South and its people were never the same again.

Why the War Was Lost

Why had they failed? Why did the bid for independence, which began with such enthusism, end in total failure?[7] The most obvious reasons for the military defeat have already been noted, from poor planning to inferior resources. Two other factors must also be noted, the failure of Confederate diplomacy and the excessive rate of military casualties.

Confederate diplomacy was based on two things, the premise embodied in the slogan "Cotton is King" and a belief that the justness of the South's cause and the self-interest of Great Britain would bring diplomatic recognition and with it the assistance necessary to win the war. Neither of these factors was altogether fanciful, but events would soon belie the southerners' expectations in each of them. Much of the error was due to miscalculations born of over-optimism. Confederates vastly overestimated the diplomatic significance of cotton and thus used their most important weapon poorly, and many of their actions suggest that they misunderstood the nature of international relations. The Confederacy needed an alliance with Great Britain almost as much as it needed the support of its own people, for only Britain, whose navy controlled the Atlantic, was in a position to provide the assistance necessary for victory. Almost any sacrifice would have been justified in order to secure a British alliance. The confederacy might have made major diplomatic, economic, or naval concessions, or all of these, including guaranteed supplies of cotton at prices highly favorable to the British.

As soon as the war began, the government embargoed the shipment of cotton, and dispatched a mission to Europe, headed by William L. Yancey, to work for diplomatic recognition from Britain and France and other nations. The purpose of the embargo was to create a shortage of cotton in Britain and thereby generate pressure for diplomatic recognition by dramatizing the dependence of the British economy on southern cotton. The effect, however, was otherwise. The British already had large stockpiles of cotton, and resenting their dependence on the South, they used the occasion of the embargo to encourage production within the empire. In addition cereal crop failures in Britain created an unusual and more immediate demand for foreign grains, which the Union had in large supply. As it turned out, then, Britain was far less dependent on southern cotton than the Confederates believed, and the major premise of their diplomacy was thus proved false.

But probably the most important reason for the failure to win British recognition was the conventional factors that govern diplomacy. Not even the *Trent* affair, in which a United States naval vessel forcibly removed Confederate diplomats James M. Mason and John Slidell from a British steamer on the high seas, could overcome these. The Confederate view of British self-interest was far too simplistic and assigned far too much diplomatic significance to sentiment and abstract principles. Of course the British government saw certain advantages in siding with the Confederacy. And among the upper classes there was considerable sympathy for the Confederate cause, although they also saw certain disadvantages. An alliance with the Confederacy would mean an almost certain war with the United States, for which there was little support in Britain. In addition the British saw in the American declaration of a "paper" blockade—one the navy was unable to enforce completely—a principle that might serve their own purposes in the future. In the final analysis, British recognition depended on the military situation. It would come if and when the Confederates proved on the battlefield that they were likely to endure as a nation. The two best opportunities to do this were Lee's invasions into Maryland in 1862 and Pennsylvania in 1863, and both were unsuccessful. Thus British recognition never came; but it might have, had the Confederacy used its initial advantages more effectively.

Another major cause of defeat was the massive military casualties which, as nothing else, made the tragedy of the war real. Altogether, Confederate casualties represent the greatest relative sacrifice ever endured by any large population of Americans except the Indians. So great were the casualties that the Confederacy may be said almost literally to have bled to death. The 258,000 military deaths, which included 94,000 battlefield deaths, were equivalent to 4.6 percent of the white population of the eleven Confederate states in 1860 and almost a quarter of the number of white males between the ages of fifteen and forty. Union casualties, which totaled 360,000 military dead, were drawn from a much larger population.

What caused such slaughter? One major factor was poor strategic and tactical judgment on the part of field commanders, including a propensity for offense and a tardiness in adapting tactics to new weapons. The romantic concept of war, which placed great emphasis on acts of personal daring, was also important, as was the primitive state of medical care for sick and wounded. It should also be remembered that the Confederates kept fighting for months after the war as a military endeavor had become hopeless.

The propensity for offense was probably the most important reason for the extraordinary number of deaths. The state of weaponry at the time gave defense a certain advantage over offense, and offensive maneuvering was thus costly in manpower. This affected the Confederacy much more than the Union, for its manpower pool was much smaller. In the peninsula campaign against McClellan, to illustrate, Lee determined to hold Richmond at all costs. The series of tactical offensives he staged to achieve that purpose cost his army of 80,000 men about 20,000 casualties, including about 3,300 dead. Shortly afterward, at second Bull Run, his army suffered 9,000 casualties compared to 16,000 inflicted on the enemy, but in this clear victory Lee's casualties were about 19 percent of his army while the enemy's were only 13 percent. The Confederacy could ill afford such victories. At Gettysburg about three of every ten soldiers in Lee's command were casualties. In eight major battles in which the Confederates were the attackers—Shiloh, Fair Oaks, the Seven Days, second Bull Run, Antietam, Perryville, Fredericksburg, Murfreesboro, Chancellorsville, Vicksburg, Gettysburg, and Chickamauga—Confederate casualties totaled 97,000, a figure larger by 20,000 than that for the Americans in those battles.

If many of these casualties were due to the propensity for attack, many were also due to the fact that the attacks were launched against entrenched defenders, whose weapons, especially the rifle, gave them a distinct advantage. Compared to smoothbores, rifled weapons had deadly accuracy and at much greater range, and together with the trench they gave defensive forces a distinct advantage. Cavalry charges with drawn swords and other traditional forms of frontal assault, such as Pickett's famous charge up Cemetery Ridge at Gettysburg, were rendered obsolete, even suicidal. (Pickett lost about 6,000 men in the charge.) A defensive strategy which avoided offensive action was certainly better suited to the Confederacy's manpower resources.

Poor medical care was another major killer. The leaden bullets used in the war tore gaping holes in the flesh, and surgical practices were so primitive and hospital facilities so lacking that penetrating wounds except in the extremities were generally fatal. According to one estimate, mortality in the Union army, which had much better medical care than the Confederacy, averaged 62 percent from gunshot wounds in the chest and 87 percent in the abdomen. Because of the lack of ambulance services and field hospitals, many wounded who might have been saved were abandoned on the battlefield to bleed to death or die from exposure. Occasionally, as at the Wilderness in 1864, hundreds of wounded men burned to death when exploding shells set fire to wooded battlefields. Sanitary practices were also appallingly bad, and most wounds became infected from neglect or failure to appreciate the principles of bacteriology. Finally, mortality from sickness in army camps averaged more than 5 percent annually. Typhoid, dysentery, and diarrhea were common camp infections because of unsanitary water and food supplies.

Why the Confederacy Failed

These things explain the loss of the war but do not account for the failure of the Confederacy, which is a much more important issue for the student of southern history. Why did the Confederacy not endure, even after defeat, as a living ideal or even an organized movement? Why did it immediately become only a memory, a Lost Cause of interest only to escapists, antiquarians, and myth makers? Why did the apparent nationalism that marked its founding die so completely at Appomattox? Unlike the Irish, the Poles, and others, the Confederates were unable to keep their nationalism alive and vital once their political state had been defeated and dismembered. On the contrary, when Lee surrendered southern nationalism died, and southerners returned to the Union not as a frustrated nation but as a disaffected section, the same role they had played before 1861.

The reason for this is one of the most important facts of southern history: southerners never developed a bona fide nationalism. Even as Confederates they remained Americans—peculiar and distinctive, but Americans nonetheless. "The readiness with which the South returned to the Union," David M. Potter has written in an especially perceptive essay, "will defy explanation unless it is recognized that Southern loyalties to the Union were never really obliterated but rather were eclipsed by other loyalties with which, for a time, they conflicted."[8] The South was a section, never a nation, and this is probably the best explanation for the failure of the Confederacy. The Confederacy failed because its people never achieved the psychological and emotional dimensions of nationhood, and were therefore unwilling to do all the things necessary to win independence. The southerners had grievances, not a national identity. "Few Southerners thought much about the whole South," Frank E. Vandiver has written of the prewar era. "Some talked of it, recited the catechism of cotton, chivalry, and courage, but they usually saw the South in terms of their own locality." American nationalism was always strong among them, even when they championed the South or complained of the federal government or outside interference in their affairs. They never really wanted to be anything but southerners and Americans. It was just that circumstances in 1860–61 forced them to choose the one over the other.

It is in this sense that their identity as Confederates was more negative than positive and in this sense too that the Confederate mind was divided against itself. During their brief experience as Confederates, southerners found their dual identities in more pronounced conflict than ever before or since. The necessities of war contested with the desire to hold on to the old order, and the result was the irresolution that ultimately compromised the bid for independence. As Confederates, southerners were forced to violate many of their most cherished principles, but not with the resoluteness necessary to win the war, and in the process they lost some of their principles as well as the war. As the war took its toll, the sacrifice seemed less and less acceptable, and so did independence. The will to nationhood was not there. Disaffection grew, disloyalty spread, the Confederacy lost the support of too many of its own people.

Yet an important question remains. If the racial fears of white Confederates were strong enough to produce secession, why were they not strong enough to create a sense of nationhood and inspire the sacrifices necessary to achieve independence? Certainly in an independent Confederacy whites would have felt more secure in their control of racial policy than they had in the Union, and certainly too the Emancipation Proclamation confirmed their worst fears about Lincoln and the Republicans. If racial factors were as strong as previously suggested in this study, should not the Proclamation have united white Confederates and reinforced their determination to become independent whatever the cost? The Proclamation was in fact greeted with outrage and forebodings of the direst sort, but it did not brake the spiral of disloyalty and disaffection from the Confederate cause.

To understand why this was so, it is necessary to remember that the southerners' cause was not just proslavery. It was the defense of a way of life under siege, the elemental feature of which was white supremacy. The intellectual history of the Confederacy has never been written, and the evolution of Confederate thinking on this and other subjects is not altogether clear. It seems, however, that during the war, as the sufferings and destructions and radical changes came one on top of the other, the conviction spread that the old way of life was being, had already been, irrevocably destroyed. This explains much of the defeatism that pervaded the section at the end of the war. But it also seems that in their despair and desperation, white southerners came to see that slavery and white supremacy were not necessarily synonymous.[9] From the beginning of the war, slavery began slowly but surely to be eroded away, but white supremacy remained intact. The wartime conduct of blacks—the fact that they organized no significant uprisings or revolutionary conspiracies—seems to have reinforced the conviction among whites that they could manage the race if outsiders left them alone. They were well aware that the end of slavery in the North had not affected white supremacy there, and they came to believe, in their hour of necessity, that that could also be the case in the South.

No doubt they also sensed what historians have only recently documented, that the northern war effort, which had the limited purpose of saving the Union, included no commitment to racial equality and was in fact permeated by a hardened racism of its own.[10] It was not unreasonable for them to conclude that what the North sought to impose on the South was reunion and emancipation but not racial equality. As soon as they saw this, it was possible to see that the alternative to slavery was not necessarily freedom, that is, racial equality, for blacks. When that became apparent, they could resign themselves to the prospect of defeat and reunion. When the war was over, they could and did insist in good faith that they accepted its results. As they understood Union war aims, those results were reunion and emancipation and loss of the right of secession and of the property they had invested in the Confederacy. In accepting defeat, they did not understand that they were agreeing to be "reconstructed." Above all, they did not agree to anything that threatened white supremacy.

They miscalculated, but only to a degree. They did not yet understand that when northerners talked of postwar adjustments, they were more concerned with the appearance than the reality of racial equality. Nor did they understand that their erstwhile adversary might push pro-Negro policies for reasons that had nothing to do with the wellbeing of Negroes. So when the war ended and dust began to settle over the battlefields, white southerners were still concerned with the problem that prompted them to secede, and still faced with their old nemesis—outside interference in racial matters. In the summer of 1865 the Confederacy died but the South was still alive and with a whole new set of aggrievements.

9

Reunion and Reconstruction

The war's toll was frightful. Perhaps a million men had served the Confederate cause, of whom 258,000 died, another 150,000 were disabled, and countless others suffered the lingering effects of wounds or disease. Every third white family had someone killed, and across the South unnumbered widows and never-to-be-married spinsters lived only to guard their graves, as Augusta Evans Wilson later put it. The 1870 census counted 36,000 more women than men in Georgia alone, and the number of children orphaned by the war was never totaled.

Material losses were just as great, and almost as painful to bear. The Confederacy expended perhaps four times as much of its wealth on the war as did the Union, and in 1865 much of its economy was in shambles. The war and not slavery or Reconstruction or laziness made the South poor and economically backward. In the 1860s the assessed valuation of real estate in the section dropped an astonishing 48 percent while that in the rest of the country rose 73 percent, and those figures reflect something of the war's total impact. The South's share of the nation's wealth declined from 30 percent in 1860 to 12 percent in 1870.

The damage to agriculture was massive. Livestock, farm implements, seed stocks, orchards, and homes and out-buildings were ravaged or depleted, and the magnitude of the total loss made those things doubly difficult to replace. The number of livestock declined by about a third in the war decade, and the value of farm implements was down 46 percent. Much land fell fallow during the war or was laid waste by military quartermasters or civilian scavengers, and was difficult to reclaim. Cotton production did not surpass the 1859 bumper crop until 1878, and the story was much the same for other crops. Large areas of the section, crossed and sometimes recrossed by armies, lay desolate—northern Virginia, the Shenandoah Valley, vast portions of Tennessee and Mississippi, the wide swath Sherman cut across Georgia and Carolina. Much of the railroad system was destroyed or bankrupt. Towns and cities were sometimes in ruins—Richmond, Atlanta, and Columbia, South Carolina, for example—or partially destroyed or abandoned. Money was worthless, the credit system destroyed, the public debt invalid. The principle item of liquid wealth, a few million bales of cotton, was largely destroyed to prevent its capture by the enemy or stolen by marauders or confiscated by Union agents as contraband.

For most people the result was poverty and want, and for many destitution and hunger. If whites lost more than blacks, it was only because they had more to lose, for at war's end both races were in such straits that getting a living was a pressing concern. Peace came too late in the planting season for 1865 to be a good crop year, and the disorganization produced by defeat and emancipation impeded recovery.

For whites these problems were complicated by a spiritual malaise that came from defeat, and for blacks by the uncertain meaning of freedom. White southerners were a proud, even arrogant people whose faith in their cause had been as complete as public faith can be. That had been the source of their great expectations, and as their expectations evaporated, the despondency was as deep as the hope had been high. Everything, they told themselves, had been lost—save honor.

Their mood was depressed but kaleidoscopic. Edmund Ruffin, who fired the first shot at Fort Sumter, committed suicide upon hearing of Lee's surrender. Jefferson Davis was captured while fleeing Union forces, and he and several other officials were imprisoned for a short time. Secretary of State Judah P. Benjamin fled to England where he took up a successful legal career. A few people expatriated themselves in permanent Confederate colonies in Mexico or Brazil. Robert Toombs became a temporary exile, fleeing the expected wrath of the enemy, but when that failed to materialize he returned home. All of these were a tiny few. From necessity and choice, almost everyone took Robert E. Lee's advice to remain in the South and pick up the pieces of their shattered world.

Many were dismayed by defeat. "Virginia, like Poland, belongs to the past," wept John R. Thompson. "Touch it not—unfold it never," Abram J. Ryan wrote of "The Conquered Banner"; "Let it droop there, furled forever, / For its peoples' hopes are dead." The initial despair was numbing. "I forget my humiliation for a while in sleep," wrote a Richmond minister, "but the memory of every bereavement comes back heavily, like a sullen sea surge, on awakening, flooding and submerging my soul with anguish. The idolized expectation of a separate nationality, of a social life and literature and civilization of our own, together with a gospel guarded against the contamination of New England infidelity, all this has perished, and I feel like seaweed on a desert's shore.... God's dark providence enwraps me like a pall." "I have no country, no flag, no emblems, no public spirit," a young diarist wrote in Savannah. "I live now simply to live, and for my family."

The despair of some was enveloped in consuming bitterness. "We hear that Lincoln is dead," wrote Kate Stone in her diary at "Brokenburn" in Louisiana. "All honor to J. Wilkes Booth, who has rid the world of a tyrant and made himself famous for generations.... It is a terrible tragedy, but what is war but one long tragedy? What torrents of blood Lincoln has caused to flow, and how Seward[1] has aided him in his bloody work. I cannot be sorry for their fate. They deserve it." Such passion soon ebbed for all save the most unbending. "I do not forgive," the Reverend Robert Lewis Dabney could still say in 1870. "I try not to forgive. What! forgive those people, who have invaded our country, burned our cities, destroyed our homes, slain our young men, and spread desolation and ruin over our land! No, I do not forgive them."

The pathos of defeat complicated the problems of adjustment. "The empty sleeve and the crutch made men who had unflinchingly faced death in battle impotent to face the future," one woman confided to her diary. "Sadder still was it to follow to the grave the army of men, of fifty years and over when the war began, whose hearts broke with the loss of a half century's accumulations and ambitions, and with the failure of the cause for which they had risked everything. Communities were accustomed to lean upon these trusted advisers; it was almost like the slaughter of another army—so many sank beneath the shocks of reconstruction." Women, conditioned by war to an expanded social role, were often forced to assume the responsibilities that wearied broken men. Youth, too, had been traumatized by war and had its own special difficulties adapting to the new era of poverty and swirl. "Perhaps you know," wrote Sidney Lanier, who died before his fortieth birthday from consumption contracted in a Union prison, "that with us the young generation in the South, since the war, pretty much the whole of life has been merely not dying."

The War as a Watershed

Southerners paid dearly for the war, and continued to pay long after it ended. A major part of the price was change, mostly for the worse, but in important particulars for the better. The war was a watershed in southern history, the deepest nature of which is still in need of study.[2] One of the mystifying gaps in southern historical writing is the absence of systematic inquiries into the war's impact on the course of sectional history. Its influence has been more widely assumed than researched, though certain aspects have been investigated carefully and there are some insightful impressionistic assessments of its total effect. But there is no integrated study of its whole impact, and thus the most basic questions remain open. To what extent was the war a turning point in the section's history? Is continuity or discontinuity the better perspective for viewing the relationship between the prewar and postwar eras? What were the effects of defeat on the mind and social psychology of the white South? The defeat was one of principles and hopes, even of faith, and its psychological scars seem as deep and abiding as its material costs.

The war brought great change, great discontinuity, in many things vital to sectional life and identity. Slavery was destroyed, as was the old relationship with the Union, and prewar prosperity gave way to abiding poverty. The hegemony of the planters was undermined, and the dominant influence of agriculture and agrarianism lessened. The wartime movement of people probably diminished localism and enhanced state and especially sectional loyalties. Feelings of apartness and grievance were strengthened, as was the sense of racial insecurity among whites. The war "smashed the Southern world," Wilbur J. Cash wrote, but "left the essential Southern mind and will entirely unshaken"; and in its aftermath white southerners were "far more self-conscious than they had been before, far more aware of their differences and of the line which divided what was Southern from what was not."

Southerners learned many things from the war, none of them more important than the meaning of defeat, of knowing it is possible to strive and sacrifice and do one's best and still lose. The lesson was difficult for a people oriented toward success and self-assertion, and it was one of the things that set the postwar South apart from the rest of the country. Southerners had tried and failed, and unlike northerners could not forget the war. They lost control of their destiny and were forced to submit to a superior will, and the experience left them frustrated and outraged. Arnold Toynbee once defined history as something unpleasant that happens to other people, and his definition is especially apt for the defeated southerners. "History" had happened to them; they had been forced to do against their will, and the trauma, as Walter Hines Page put it, "stopped the thought of most of them as an earthquake stops a clock. The fierce blow of battle paralyzed the mind." One need not go that far to recognize the transcendant nature of the war's influence on postwar life, especially its baser features. Violence, cynicism, political scoundrelism, economic exploitiveness, and hardened racism were all encouraged by the experience.

The war and its aftermath also discredited reform, especially racial reform, and made the white southerner more than ever unwilling to confront his section's problems. The war gave him what Robert Penn Warren has called "the Great Alibi" of defeat and oppression by which he "explains, condones, and transmutes everything" and "turns defeat into victory, defects into virtues." His critical faculties were diminished by disuse, and his politics became a vehicle of avoidance. The cleft in his psyche broadened. "Four lines of cleavage within the spirit of the South ... were widened disastrously" by the war and Reconstruction, James McBride Dabbs observed, "the division of the future from the past, of the South from the rest of the world, of Negroes from whites, and of formal religion from life." The South became a backwater. To preserve their racial order, white southerners retreated into their own world of grievance, prejudice, and self-concern. "Our people have failed to perceive the deeper movements underrunning the times," Sidney Lanier lamented after the war. "They lie wholly off, out of the stream of thought, and whirl their poor dead leaves of recollection round and round, in a piteous eddy that has all the wear and tear of motion without the rewards of progress."

Much of this came from social dislocation. As a result of the war, the planter class lost its preeminence to a business and professional elite centered in the towns and cities. This change was rapid, and in its wake the section suffered. It took two generations for the new elite to acquire the assurance necessary to mute its crassest qualities and assert its better nature, generations that spanned the period from Appomattox to World War I and were the crudest, least attractive in the section's history.

The eclipse of the planters was due to obvious things. As a class the planters had been chiefly responsible for secession and war, and thus for the resulting debacle. More importantly, the war destroyed the basis of their ascendancy. The end of slavery meant an end to the patriarchy it sustained, and military defeat meant the loss of wealth and self-confidence and the aura of invincibility that surrounded the planters. Only their land remained, and land alone could not sustain the old order. The plantation survived the war, but not the plantation system. That system had been a social and racial patriarchy as well as an economic order. Gang labor and ownership of the work force had been its essential features, not concentrated land holdings and staple production. Postwar agriculture incorporated the latter features but not the former, and the social and racial relationships it involved were quite different from those of the antebellum era. Under the new arrangement economic interest and racial animosity compromised the sense of mutuality that had sometimes moderated the old system, and the new arrangement never had the efficiency, élan, or discipline of the old. It extruded an economic paternalism of the worst sort, but not a social patriarchy. Economic and political dominance, and then social prestige, slipped from the planters. The postwar elite "drew some recruits from the old planter class," C. Vann Woodward has written, "but in spirit as well as in outer aspects it was essentially new."

Issues of Reconstruction

Defeat necessitated Reconstruction, as the complex of issues, policies, and processes of postwar adjustment was called.[3] Reconstruction was a basal episode in southern history, in some respects more important than the Civil War.[4] Even more than the war, it brought southerners face to face with history, and led them to make decisions that were still affecting the section a century later. Reconstruction involved the most elemental concerns of the southern people, visceral issues of race and power and property, and its failures and excesses left permanent scars.

The issues of Reconstruction raised a series of basic questions. What was the status of the defeated states? Were they in or out of the Union? In either case, they were obviously out of their normal relationship to the federal government and the rest of the country, and an immediate concern was how to restore that relationship. And what about Confederate leaders? Were they "war criminals"? Should they be imprisoned, exiled, deprived of property or civil rights—or left alone? And the freedmen, the 3.5 million slaves made suddenly free by the war—were they now citizens? What would freedom mean for them? What did it imply concerning the right to vote, equality before the law, economic and educational opportunity? More pointedly, did it imply anything concerning positive protection against racial discrimination or public assistance in achieving and maintaining equality?

These questions were complicated by the fact that no one knew who would answer them. Would the Union impose terms of peace in the usual manner or postwar settlements, or would there be negotiations? In either case would the terms be harsh or lenient? There was little support for vengeance in the North even in the first days of victory, but there was wide disagreement over everything else. Who in the federal government would have the final say? The President, Congress, the army, the Freedman's Bureau? If southerners were to be consulted, which southerners? Confederates, unionists, blacks?

None of these questions was ever answered definitively, for no one ever sat down and reasoned through the issues. The actual processes of Reconstruction were products not of design, but of shifting currents of power and interest. The political and racial developments that are the familiar components of Reconstruction took place in a national context that was much changed by the war. The Union that southerners reentered in 1865 was not the same as the one they left in 1860–61. The North's victory in the war ratified the shift from a decentralized confederation to a nation-state, and thereby enlarged the powers and functions of the national government. The doctrine of states' rights lost its logical conclusion, the right of secession, and without that it was no longer a constitutional theory. More than this, the northern victory consolidated the economic promise of Lincoln's election, tilting the national balance of power away from the South, the states, and agriculture and toward the Northeast, the federal government, and assorted interests favoring industry and economic development.

During the war the latter interests had taken advantage of the South's withdrawal from the federal government to turn national economic policy in their favor. They created a system of national banks tied to federal fiscal arrangements and centralized control over the supply of circulating financial paper. By higher tariffs, direct and indirect subsidies, and other devices they encouraged corporate capital and industrial development. In 1865 these policies were still new and their future dependent on continued Republican control of the federal government. Since most white southerners could be expected to oppose these policies, their return to the Union and Congress might have important economic consequences.

The Republican party thus represented a specific economic program in 1865, and many of its leaders were primarily concerned with protecting that program. But the party represented much more than that. To many northerners it was the chief symbol of the Union and the best hope for preserving the fruits of the hard-earned victory over the South. During the war, many northern Democrats had sympathized with the Confederates, and Republicans rightly suspected that the Democratic party was less concerned than they were about preserving the fruits of victory and suppressing the spirit of rebellion in the South.

These things tended to divide northern and southern whites, but there were other things that drew them together. The two peoples had many values in common, and both were weary of sectional animosity. Within limits, both wanted a speedy and painless reconciliation, a hope encouraged by what Thomas B. Alexander has called "persistent Whiggery" in the South and by a common commitment to white supremacy.

For a generation before the Kansas-Nebraska Act was passed back in 1854, the South had had a vigorous two-party system. Democrats and Whigs had vied with each other everywhere in the section and enjoyed equal success. The two parties had differed not so much in social makeup as in economic programs.[5] Democrats had tended to favor agriculture and political decentralization and to oppose federal encouragement of commercial and industrial development. Whigs on the other hand had inclined toward a program not unlike that enacted by Republicans during the war. The division had been important, but as the prewar controversies intensified, it had been transcended by stronger concerns over slavery and other sectional issues. The Whig party had died, and southern Whigs were forced to affiliate with the Democratic party in order to remain politically alive. The affiliation, however, involved party labels only, for ex-Whigs retained their economic principles and, indeed, their personal rivalries with Democrats.

The Democrats had co-opted the issue of sectional rights, and thus overwhelmed the more moderate ex-Whigs in the elections of 1860 and 1861. But as Confederate fortunes declined, those of the ex-Whigs rose, and in 1863 and 1865 large numbers of them were elected to office as nominal Democrats. Since they were not unsympathetic to Republican economic policies, when the war was over they represented the basis for a potential coalition of Republicans and moderate southerners that might resolve sectional issues amicably without threatening Republican economic interests.

This potential was eventually realized in part, but at the end rather than the beginning of Reconstruction and as the result of a self-serving bargain between "Bourbon" Democrats and business Republicans. It thus accomplished the worst rather than the best of the original prospect, and was an instrument not of political and economic moderation but of unfettered white supremacy and economic exploitation.

Race and Reconstruction

That bargain, which is discussed later, suggests that racial policy was the principal concern of southern elites in Reconstruction, whereas economic policy and control of the national government were the chief concerns of Republican leadership. The southerners understood this perhaps better than their adversaries. In the new world created by defeat and emancipation, the race issue was a volatile, even treacherous problem, too deep-seated to be solved in the short run. The long-range danger was that the cancerous problem of slavery, which had eaten away at the vitals of the Old South and almost destroyed the Union, would be replaced by an equally malignant problem of race. The immediate difficulty was the legacy of slavery. For blacks that legacy was poverty, illiteracy, and dependence, and in turn inexperience in leadership and citizenship as well as retarded institutional development and the psychological consequences of prolonged dependence. Together these things were an enormous burden for the race in 1865.

Whites too had been hobbled by slavery, but in altogether different ways. Slavery left them with a superiority complex, a habit of domination, and a profound racism which, in combination with the fear that grew out of demography and centuries of exploitation, blinded them to their own and the South's best interest and froze their sense of decency on racial matters.

The problems of Reconstruction, then, revolved around the racism of whites, the disabilities of blacks, and the sectional and national contexts in which these and other postwar issues had to be faced.[6] The hub of the problem was this: it was impossible to formulate a Reconstruction policy acceptable to both races and just as impossible to implement a policy that addressed itself to basic racial issues. A policy that to whites was lenient, liberal, and conciliatory was to blacks a surrender to white supremacy. Most of what whites regarded as harsh and vengeful in Reconstruction was to blacks no more than necessary devices to protect their freedom.

One way to understand how deep this problem was is to try to imagine what a successful Reconstruction policy might have entailed. Such a policy would have had to neutralize white racism, deal effectively with black need, and promote interracial cooperation. To do those things, it would have had to get at the source of the basic problem, which was the proclivity of whites to practice racial discrimination. But that source was and still is imperfectly understood. Is racism an intrinsic element of European-American culture or a consequence of specific circumstances under which whites and nonwhites came together as Europe expanded? Or is it an extrusion of the American form of capitalism, or of the competitiveness rooted in the Protestant ethic? Perhaps it is simply an inevitable consequence of two races living together in large numbers, a manifestation of some innate "consciousness of kind" that leads human beings to prefer others like themselves and thus to dislike those who are different? Or is it a product of some unique diabolism of the white South?

Whatever its source, it permeated the institutions of southern life —economics, politics, law, education, and social customs—and its elimination would require that those institutions be remade to the extent necessary to cause them to serve blacks on an equal basis with whites. This would necessitate basic reforms imposed from outside by the federal government. It would also necessitate positive assistance to blacks and negative restraints upon whites, both on a scale that violated the laissez faire political and economic faith of nineteenth-century Americans. There was at that time no body of political theory or constitutional law to justify such actions, nor of social or scientific thought either. No body of positivist social science evidence existed to suggest that the degradation of blacks might stem from something other than racial inferiority. Nor of religious thought either. To the extent that white religious spokesmen endorsed racial equality, it was the spiritual equality of men before God and the endorsement implied no support for equalitarian social policies.

Here was the source of failure. The South and the nation were both inequalitarian societies and could not transform themselves. Yet both had always espoused equalitarian ideals, and emancipation and Reconstruction made the anomalies of *Herrenvolk* democracy more apparent than ever. As long as blacks had been slaves their exclusion from the body politic had been rationalized by the peculiar nature of slavery. Now, however, they were free men and citizens, and how could the commitment to democratic ideals be preserved if those ideals were denied a large body of citizens? It was a troublesome question, and its troublesomeness was underscored by the realization that racial equality could be achieved only by massive social changes. Property rights, local self-government, states' rights, majority rule, state control of education and voter qualifications, even the principle of voluntary association for political or social purposes—all of these things operated to maintain white supremacy, and all would have to be violated to achieve racial equality. White racism and black powerlessness gave blacks a special problem whites did not have, and one that architects of the American political system never dealt with: racial discrimination. This special problem demanded special protections for the race, protections whites did not need, and thus special restrictions on whites. In effect, blacks needed something that was alien to the idea upon which American democracy was based: protection from their own local and state governments and from the will of the majority of their fellow citizens. This is to say that what they really needed was protection from American democracy itself.

The Situation at War's End

Neither whites nor blacks thought much in these terms. In the spring of 1865 whites hoped and expected that postwar readjustments would be a matter of restoration, not reconstruction. They based their hopes on the wartime policies of the Lincoln administration and their own view of the nature of the war. The war to them was a constitutional and political crisis and postwar settlement a matter of resolving the constitutional and political issues involved in reunion. They expected to have to do the things explicitly required by Union war aims, but nothing more. Thus they expected to return to the Union, reorganize their state governments, renounce the right of secession, and give up their slaves, but they expected that the process of doing those things would be in their own hands. This view of the situation was too simple, for it gave no attention to nonpolitical factors and to the new power relationship within the Union. The South's place in this relationship was not yet clear in 1865, but it was apparent that the section would not be able to resume its dominant position in national affairs.

When the war ended the situation was extremely fluid, and white southerners had considerable range within which to influence the course of events. Their situation demanded flexibility and moderation more than anything else, qualities southerners were never noted for, and as things turned out their own brittleness would be their undoing. Emancipation necessitated changes in racial policy in which the North and the federal government as well as blacks had legitimate interests. Those groups had an equally legitimate interest in other aspects of postwar policy. The war had raised northern passions and black hopes, and these too must be accommodated. In the spring of 1865 the victorious northerners were within limits prepared to be generous, but the limits as well as the generosity were important in assessing their mood. The northerners would be conciliatory so long as the postwar settlement did not jeopardize what they considered the fruits of victory. Put another way, they wanted assurance that the 360,000 Union dead had not died in vain. This was a matter of emotion and patriotism as well as policy. In policy terms it meant the establishment of loyal governments in the defeated states and assurances that slavery was not being reinstituted under another form. These things required not that the South and Confederate leaders be punished, but that southern unionists be favored, and not racial equality but minimum protection for the freedmen.

The situation also required symbolic concessions from the Confederates that amounted to an indirect confession of error in leading the South into secession and war. The desire for such concessions sprang not from vindictiveness, as many southerners believed, but from the sacrifices northerners had made in the war, and was an expression of the northerners' belief in the rightness of their own cause. Counterparts to this desire have existed after every American war. Following World War II, for example, Americans expected the Germans and Japanese to act contritely in defeat, confess their error, and turn away from the leadership and ideology that led them to war. The fact that both peoples complied with these wishes made "reconstruction" after that war much less "radical" than it might otherwise have been. Southerners in 1865 refused to make similar concessions, and northerners concluded that the virus of rebellion was still alive.

Blacks and Reconstruction

As these things developed, black southerners contemplated strategies of their own. For them the first jubilations of freedom gave way at once to the uncertainties of living without the restraints and securities of slavery. Their place in the new South was far from certain, though in the spring of 1865 the future seemed promising. In the first burst of freedom they demonstrated the reality of emancipation by moving away from the old plantation, seeking lost friends and relatives, or looking for the new opportunities their new status seemed to promise. The physical and social movement this entailed was a conscious assertion of independence and self-possession and began the quest for place and identity in a new world of nonslavery.

The story of blacks in Reconstruction is usually told in terms of politics and civil rights,[7] subjects that are more important for the history of the South than for the history of blacks. For the latter, the most important aspects of Reconstruction were those developments concerned with community organization, institutional development, and the struggle for education and property. It is easy to minimize the progress made in these areas, especially in economics and education, but it was impressive when measured against conditions that existed in 1865 and the obstacles that lay across the path of black advancement. Family life emerged intact from slavery, and around it and the other social forms of slave and free communities developed new and more complete communities. Blacks withdrew from white churches into congregations and denominations of their own, and the church began at once to play its special role in black life. New leadership, tested in Reconstruction, emerged, and the task of getting on in a new social order commenced.

Despite the legacy of slavery, the race was not without resources of its own. Emancipation became a major Union war aim and that plus the important contribution blacks made to the Union victory enabled the race to count on northern support in the postwar era. The Freedman's Bureau and the army offered important forms of assistance, especially protection against white extremists. Moreover, the race had a considerable reservoir of talented leadership, and a resourcefulness that belied the Sambo stereotype. Given the obstacles they and their race met at every turn, black leaders performed quite capably in Reconstruction. The race had another asset too. It was still an essential element in the southern work force, and without its labor the section would never prosper. The mutual dependence of white and black, so evident during slavery, continued after emancipation.

Like whites, blacks were divided on matters of postwar policy. All of them expected emancipation to mean better things, but they disagreed over how to go about achieving those better things. What was the best way to deal with whites in and out of the South? How could the federal government, the Republican party, and northern reformers and philanthropy be used to maximum advantage? It was obvious that the assistance of whites was needed, but the whites must, perforce, be kept at arm's length to discourage paternalism. As much as they needed interracial cooperation, blacks needed community development of their own even more, and as blacks in a white-dominated society they had special needs that few whites appreciated.

They needed so much it was difficult to know where to begin. Historian August Meier has discerned a major division between racial leaders and the mass of freedmen concerning Reconstruction policy.[8] The leaders, relatively educated and experienced, wanted civil rights first of all, including the right to vote and participate in politics, and then attention to education and economic problems. This order of priorities reflected the liberal, integrationist, and bourgeois ideals of most race leaders, and their optimism that American institutions could be opened for blacks in the same way they had been opened for other minorities. The masses had different priorities. They wanted land first, and after that education and political rights. Their orientation was toward their own communities rather than interracialism, toward building black institutions instead of gaining access to those of whites. This reflected the pessimism about the United States implicit in race nationalism, which, recognizing the intensity of white prejudice, encouraged separatist as opposed to integrationist goals. The difference between the two groups reflected the debate over matters of racial strategy that runs through the history of black Americans. Did self-help or interracial cooperation promise greater racial advancement? Was economics or politics more immediately important? Was forty acres of land a matter of greater concern than the right to vote?

The most significant fact about both sides in this debate during Reconstruction was the conventionality of their objectives. Nothing better showed how thoroughly blacks had been Americanized than their rejection of radical approaches to their problems. They supported no policies of vengeance and made no demands for racial separatism. They mounted no assault on the capitalist system, private property, the Constitution, two-party politics, or any other basic institution, unless racial discrimination be counted as such. They asked not that established institutions be overturned, but that blacks be given access to those institutions on the same terms as whites. That, however, was the rub, for in the South in 1865 that was radicalism of the profoundest sort.

Wartime Policy

Reconstruction actually began during the war. As soon as Union armies began occupying Confederate territory, political questions were raised. How were occupied areas to be governed? How was civil authority to be restored and the civilian population treated? The most immediate question concerned slaves who escaped from Confederate masters to invading armies. What was to be done with them? In the early months of war, this question had been especially delicate. Any action against slavery by the Lincoln administration at that time would have encouraged secessionists in the border states, and it was vital to keep those states in the Union. Such action would also have connected the war effort with antislavery and thus with racial policy, something Lincoln and Congress had both wanted to avoid. The war was being waged to preserve the Union, Congress declared in the summer of 1861, and not "for any purpose ... of overthrowing or interfering with the rights of established institutions."

But slavery and racial policy *were* involved in the war, and both sides were soon forced to acknowledge that fact. Early in the fighting, Union commanders in Missouri and South Carolina issued orders declaring the slaves of Confederate sympathizers in their jurisdiction to be proper contraband of war, but Lincoln countermanded the orders and otherwise worked to keep the slavery issue separate from the war.

In this effort to pretend that the war was unrelated to the race issue lay the seeds of the ultimate failure of Reconstruction. During the first years of the war, Lincoln and other leaders laid the grounds for losing the peace. The cause was the racialism that influenced all their dealings with racial matters.[9] Despite the general antipathy for slavery and "the slave power," northerners were not racial equalitarians, and in considering the issues of postwar racial policy they were more concerned with keeping blacks in the South than building an equalitarian society. The North was "a race-conscious, segregated society devoted to the doctrine of white supremacy and Negro inferiority," C. Vann Woodward has written, and it "entered the Civil War as part of a slave republic to defend a constitution that guaranteed slave property, led by a party with a platform pledged to protect slavery where it existed, and headed by a President who declared in his inaugural address that he had 'no lawful right' and 'no inclination' to interfere with slavery in the South."

Yet the North was not the South. Its racial demography was different and its commitment to liberal values greater, and as a result its leaders were less rigid on racial matters and better able to adjust to the changing imperatives of the war. Thus within a year and a half after

Fort Sumter Lincoln's position had moved so far that he issued the preliminary Emancipation Proclamation, and on January 1, 1863, he made that action official. This added emancipation to Union war aims and revolutionized the meaning of the conflict. It was a response to the fortunes of war and reflected no general conviction that emancipation was a good idea, but it was no less important for that fact. From the beginning of the war, blacks and white abolitionists had urged Lincoln to act against slavery and allow blacks to play a larger role in the conflict. They made much of the anomaly of fighting a slave power without moving against slavery. The pressures they generated were enhanced by the propaganda and diplomatic advantages emancipation would have, and when Lee's invasion of Maryland was checked at Antietam Creek in September 1862, Lincoln used the occasion to announce his preliminary Proclamation. (Congress had already acted on the issue; the Confiscation Act of July 1862 provided that the slaves of everyone supporting the rebellion should be freed, but the administration never acted on that provision.)

Lincoln moved conservatively, basing his Proclamation not on the revolutionary grounds of natural rights or racial equality, but on his power as commander-in-chief in a military emergency; and he proclaimed freedom not for all slaves but only for those whose owners were supporting the rebellion. Assuming a Union victory, this would eventually free those in all the Confederacy except the occupied areas. In those areas, chiefly Tennessee and significant parts of Louisiana and northern Virginia, and the four slave states that remained in the Union, the institution was unaffected by the Proclamation. Continued existence of slavery in those areas was made untenable, however, and before the war was over West Virginia, Maryland, Missouri, and Tennessee had acted to end slavery. Elsewhere, emancipation was not legally completed until the Thirteenth Amendment was adopted in December 1865.

Emancipation was an essential first step, but the next logical step of committing the nation to a policy of racial equality was never taken. Lincoln made several motions in that general direction but stopped far short of what was required. After January 1, 1863, blacks were able to serve in the Union army and play a generally expanded role in the war effort, but only with the harassments of segregation and other forms of discrimination. Altogether, about 180,000 blacks served in Union military forces, more than half of them recruited in occupied areas of the Confederacy. But in considering questions of postwar racial policy, Lincoln and his administration were hampered by the hope that the freedmen could be colonized outside the United States, and when that hope proved to be ephemeral they acted to make sure the mass of blacks remained in the South.

These objectives are explained by Lincoln's racial views, which by the standards of the day were moderate. His belief in black inferiority was tempered by a commitment to humane and democratic ideals that made racial extremism unacceptable to him. He believed, however, that black inferiority and white prejudice would prevent the races from ever living together in harmony. He hoped therefore that emancipation would be followed by colonization, and since he had been forced to emancipate the blacks, he felt obliged to find a suitable home for them. Toward that end he encouraged experiments in colonization in Panama and Haiti, both of which were dismal failures. By the end of the war he was reconciled to the impracticality of colonization and had concluded that the race would remain in the country. But for political reasons he "adopted a deliberate policy designed to keep the freedmen in the South."[10] That is, through the protection and assistance provided them in the South, the freedmen would be induced to stay away from the North. There would therefore be federal support for relief programs, minimal protections in law, and perhaps limited suffrage.

Jefferson Davis and the Confederates also faced the issues of slavery and race, but dealt with them with even less flexibility. The institution of slavery began to crumble as soon as the war began. Invading Union armies acted as magnets for runaway slaves, and before the war was over perhaps half a million had fled behind Union lines, but even as this occurred Davis and his government avoided the question of slavery for a much longer time than Lincoln had. Voluntary emancipation would obviously have enhanced the Confederacy's international image and increased the possibility of British recognition, and it might also have undercut northern morale. But it was too drastic a step to take. Almost to a man, white Confederates were outraged by Lincoln's Emancipation Proclamation, and agreed with Davis that it was "the most execrable measure recorded in the history of guilty man."

But as Confederate fortunes declined, southerners were forced to do many drastic things. Some of them began to talk openly of the hindering effects of slavery, and to realize that one day they might have to choose between slavery and independence. "Slavery has become a military weakness," General Patrick R. Cleburne wrote in January 1864, "a source of great strength to the enemy" and of "home and foreign prejudice" against the Confederacy. Wherever a Union army appeared, Cleburne noted, slaveowners muted their Confederate loyalties in an effort to hold on to their slaves, while the slaves either ran away and disrupted labor or remained as spies and disloyalists. By the end of 1864, when the Confederacy's position was desperate, Davis dispatched Duncan F. Kenner to Europe to discuss the possibility of emancipation in return for Anglo-French recognition. The offer was rejected, in part because it came after Union victory was certain. The Confederates had waited too long. That was the same mistake they made in the decision to use blacks in the military service. A month before Lee's surrender, the Confederate Congress authorized the enlistment of blacks, including slaves, in the army, and a handful were actually enlisted, but the action came too late to have any effect one way or the other.

The formal Reconstruction policies of the Lincoln administration dealt only indirectly with racial matters, and concentrated instead on the political process of restoring the seceded states to the Union. The policies embodied several assumptions that boded ill for the freedmen and racial reform—that reunion should be rapid and painless, that punitive measures should be avoided, and that the primary goal should be the revival of voluntary allegiance to the Union. Lincoln announced the basic policy in December 1863 when he outlined procedures for establishing loyal governments in occupied areas and readmitting the states to the Union. The procedures could be begun in any seceded state by a group of citizens eligible to vote under state law and equal to 10 percent of the number who voted in 1860. When such a group took individual oaths of loyalty to the Union and accepted emancipation, its members would be empowered to organize a state government and apply for readmission to the Union. The United States would recognize the new government formed by the group, readmit the state, and pardon all Confederates (except certain classes of high officials) who took a loyalty oath. Property rights except for slaves would also be restored to those who took the oath. The plan required no period of probation for cooperative states and individuals, no military occupation, and the loss of no property except slaves, and Confederates themselves would control its procedures. It excluded blacks from the political process because they were ineligible to vote under state law, but not Confederates, for the required oath was one of future, not past, loyalty to the Union.

This plan was certainly lenient for white southerners but not for blacks, whose welfare it left in the hands of whites. It was immediately challenged by a group of men in the Radical wing of the Republican party, who spoke for northerners of abolitionist persuasion and for those who thought sterner measures were necessary to eradicate the spirit of rebellion. The challenge, however, was on procedural, not racial, grounds, and was contained in the Wade-Davis Act, which Congress passed in the summer of 1864 and which Lincoln vetoed. This act increased the percentage of qualified voters necessary to begin the readmission process from 10 to 50, and required all voters to take an "ironclad" oath of past as well as future loyalty to the Union. It was therefore "harsher" on whites than Lincoln's plan, and since most of them could not take the required oath, it necessitated a lengthy probationary period before loyal governments could be organized. It would also presumably give political control of the seceded states to unionists rather than Confederates. But it had one important feature in common with Lincoln's plan: it too omitted blacks from political participation.

Neither of these plans was implemented during the war, though Lincoln's was partially instituted in occupied areas of several states. In the last year of the war both Lincoln and the Radicals became less and less concerned with leniency for the Confederates and more and more preoccupied with the racial aspects of postwar policy. That is, postwar planning began to reflect the concerns of peace rather than the imperatives of war. The evolution was reflected in Lincoln's suggestion, made a few days before his death, that "very intelligent" blacks and "those who serve our cause as soldiers" might be granted the right to vote. It was also reflected in increasing concern over the freedmen's problems. In March 1865 Congress created the Freedman's Bureau to deal with those problems and help the freedmen make the transition from slavery to freedom. The Bureau proved its worth at once. It functioned as a welfare agency, providing blacks, and some whites too, with such essential services as direct relief, legal aid, employment assistance, and political guidance. It was directed by men of charitable but not equalitarian impulses, however, and the nature of its assistance was meliorative and conservative. The help it gave was vital, but the total effect was to preserve the established racial and economic order. It never challenged the unequal relationship between white landlords and black tenants, but sought to provide the latter certain minimum protections within that relationship.

Presidential Reconstruction

Such was the situation at war's end. Numbed by defeat, southerners awaited peace terms. "They expected nothing; were prepared for the worst; would have been thankful for anything," wrote Whitelaw Reid, who made several trips into the South at the time. "The people wanted civil government and a settlement. They asked no terms, made no conditions. They were defeated and helpless—they submitted." This assessment seems accurate, but only if its real meaning is understood. Southerners did submit; they did accept the results of the war and were not dissembling when they said so. But as Michael Perman has shown in *Reunion Without Compromise* (1973), their submission was conditional upon their own understanding of what defeat entailed. As one of them told a touring delegation of northerners, they were prepared to accept "any terms that could be honorably offered a proud, high-minded people."

Lincoln's plan of December 1863 met that specification, and not unnaturally they expected that it or something like it would form the heart of the peace settlement. The moderate nature of that plan had hastened the collapse of their will to fight (which was no doubt a part of Lincoln's intention in formulating it), for it was essentially a promise of easy peace terms. There is every indication that Lincoln intended to apply the spirit of his plan, though what he would actually have done must remain a matter of speculation. "With malice toward none, with charity toward all," he promised in his second inaugural in March 1865 "to bind up the nation's wounds" and restore national harmony as speedily and easily as possible.

White southerners heard this and took heart, and ignored other, more discordant sounds. They took no note of the Radical Republicans, or of blacks either, both of whom had other thoughts about postwar policy. Nor did they consider that the transition from war to peace might change Reconstruction policy altogether.

As the war ended, Lincoln was assassinated and succeeded in the presidency by a southerner, Andrew Johnson of Tennessee, a states' rights Democrat of Jacksonian proclivities, who had received the Republican vice-presidential nomination in 1864 as part of the party's effort to broaden its support and ensure Lincoln's reelection. Johnson had been a senator from Tennessee when his state seceded, and was the only southerner in Congress who had refused to resign and follow his constituency into the Confederacy. He remained loyal to the Union and critical of the planter class, which he blamed for the war as well as the economic plight of the white masses in the South. When Union armies occupied most of Tennessee early in the war, Lincoln appointed him military governor of the state, and now by historical accident he and not Lincoln would preside over the Reconstruction of the Union.

When Johnson became President in April 1865, Congress was in recess and would not reconvene in regular session until December.[11] His decision not to call a special session meant that he had a free hand in Reconstruction policy for eight months after the war ended. During that time he instituted policies of his own, which remained in effect during the period of Presidential Reconstruction, from April 1865 to March 1867. The policies reflected his desire for a speedy restoration of the Union along the general lines of Lincoln's 10 percent plan. He would require southerners to organize loyal state governments, renounce the right of secession, repudiate Confederate debts, and ratify the Thirteenth Amendment abolishing slavery. These things he coupled with a generous policy of pardons for Confederate leaders for the purpose of achieving an early end of sectional animosities. The total program, Johnson believed, was conservative and thus likely to attract support from the conservative political coalition he wanted to form. It would preserve white supremacy and thereby thwart what he saw as an effort to "Africanize" the South. It was also in his judgment the only Reconstruction program that would be constitutional. A constitutional literalist, Johnson insisted that the defeated states had never been out of the Union, and now that their people had given up the rebellion, the federal government had no authority to assume plenary powers over them. The only constitutional terms of peace were those that derived from explicitly announced war aims.

Johnson did not plan his program to be as one-sided as it proved to be in execution. But as criticism of the program mounted, first from Radical Republicans and then congressional leaders and blacks and finally from moderate northerners, he became adamantly committed to it, and found himself driven into political alliance with those who supported it, conservative northern Democrats and the ex-Confederates. This was an ominous turn of events for white southerners, whose own inflexibilities were partly responsible for it. By 1866 they and Johnson were in open alliance, and each was encouraging the other in a course of action that was alienating the Republican party and the northern majority.

Soon after he became President, Johnson set his plan in motion. He appointed provisional governors in each of the defeated states, empowered them to continue in office lesser officials who took the oath of loyalty and to conduct elections for state constitutional conventions. In the meantime, he issued a proclamation of pardon and amnesty and restored property rights to all those who swore loyalty to the Union except certain categories of Confederate leaders and persons whose property was valued at more than $20,000. These would have to apply individually for presidential pardons; but because pardon carried with it the restoration of property rights, applications began flooding in at once, and Johnson was exceedingly generous in approving them. As these things transpired in the summer and fall of 1865, the state constitutional conventions met and completed their business, and within a few months after Lee's surrender the defeated states had governments functioning according to Johnson's policies.

The entire procedure had an air of unreality about it. The army remained in the South and had the power to disallow acts of the new governments, and the Freedman's Bureau continued to function. Moreover, Johnson's haste and some of the actions of the new state governments deprived the whole arrangement of the national consensus essential to its success. As a result criticism mounted, and the deficiencies of the program loomed larger and larger. Those deficiencies derived from several sources. Johnson's program ignored the constitutional, political, and economic changes wrought by the war, and did nothing to assure northerners that the fruits of victory were being protected. It entailed no punishment for the Confederates, demanded no confessions of error or guilt from them, offered no encouragement to southern unionists, did nothing to protect the Republican party and its economic interests, offered no help to the freedmen, and placed no restraints on the racial extremism of whites.

Deficient in substance, the program was worse in execution. The conduct of the new state governments was, to say the least, impolitic. Johnson left political power in the hands of the same men who had governed the Confederacy and the Old South, few of whom were prepared to act circumspectly. Naturally they wanted to maintain their position within the section. The federal government would get from them only what it demanded, and Johnson was demanding very little and that not very firmly. Thus delegates to the constitutional conventions of 1865 were always independent and sometimes defiant. The Mississippi convention refused to ratify the Thirteenth Amendment, though Johnson had made that a precondition for readmission. The same convention, and that of South Carolina too, refused to repudiate the Confederate debt. Some of the conventions repealed rather than nullified their states' secession ordinances, since nullification implied that the ordinances had been invalid all along. None of them considered the issue of Negro suffrage, though Johnson suggested that token suffrage might defuse the mounting criticism of his program. The conventions in effect challenged Johnson, and Johnson acquiesced in the challenges. He accepted the new governments even though some of them had not fulfilled the requirements of his original plan. The experience was important for the southerners, for they concluded that firmness was the best way to deal with the federal government on Reconstruction policy.

They continued this independent course of action after the new governments were organized. In 1865 and 1866 the legislatures of all the states except North Carolina enacted a series of "black codes" to replace the now defunct slave codes. The action was necessary, they insisted, to clarify the freedmen's legal and economic status. The codes varied from state to state, but had certain common features. They legalized slave marriages and legitimized their offspring, and conferred important legal rights upon freedmen, including the right to trial by jury and to testify in court proceedings involving blacks. They also spelled out conditions under which blacks could make contracts and own real property. But they did much more. They excluded blacks from jury service and from testifying against whites, and placed important restrictions on their employment and ownership of land. They drew racial distinctions in civil and criminal law to the disadvantage of blacks, and imposed special restrictions on economic opportunity and social mobility. In lengthy sections dealing ostensibly with vagrancy, they in effect assured whites a steady supply of dependent labor. The total effect was to make blacks second-class citizens by denying them important political and civil rights, and to institutionalize that status by depriving them of opportunity and rendering them perpetually dependent on whites. The freedmen were no longer slaves, but they were not free either, not if what whites themselves had was freedom.

The inequities in this were obvious even to northerners who had no real interest in racial equality. "All penal and criminal laws now in force ... defining offenses and describing the mode of punishment of crimes and misdemeanors committed by slaves, free negroes, or mulattoes," read the black code of Mississippi, "are hereby re-enacted, and decreed to be in full force and effect, against freedmen, free negroes and mulattoes." This seemed too much like slavery, and it influenced the reaction of northern moderates to the upsurge of violence and other forms of racial extremism that occurred in the South. In the late spring and early summer of 1866 major race riots took place in New Orleans and Memphis in which scores of blacks were killed by rioting whites. The significance of the codes, which were suspended by the army and the Freedman's Bureau before they became effective, lay in what they said about white racial thinking in 1865–66. They indicated that the generality of white southerners was determined that emancipation not threaten white supremacy and was prepared to do whatever was necessary to sustain that determination.

The codes suggested that if whites had their way, then blacks had gained little from emancipation. Other things suggested that the Confederates had lost little from defeat. The elections of 1865 represented no repudiation of Confederate leadership and no turn to unionists. Across the South prominent Confederates were returned to office. Among those elected to Congress that year were Alexander H. Stephens, recently Vice-President of the Confederacy, nine men who had served the Confederacy as generals or colonels, six who had been cabinet officers, and fifty-eight who had served in the Confederate Congress. When the United States Congress adjourned in March 1865 these men had been leading a rebellion, but when it reconvened in December they were seeking admission to the Congress itself as if nothing had happened.

Congressional Counterattack

The Congress demurred, and using the powers to judge their own members, both houses refused to seat the southerners. Instead, they created a Joint Committee on Reconstruction to inquire into the matter of postwar policy, including the conduct of the Johnson state governments and their treatment of the freedmen. In the course of a lengthy investigation sometimes marred by partisanship, the Committee documented the harsh treatment of freedmen, including the fact that most freedmen were being forced into a servile status not far removed from slavery. It also found the spirit of rebelliousness unchecked. The northern victory had seemed to mean nothing but a political restoration of the Union and an end to the traditional form of slavery. One of its chief results, in fact, would be to enlarge southern influence in Congress. The end of slavery meant the end of the three-fifths clause in the Constitution, under which only three-fifths of the slaves had been counted in apportioning congressional representation. Now all blacks would be counted, and to the approximately eighteen seats the southern states already had because of their black population would be added a dozen more, all presumably to be filled by whites with Confederate sympathies.

The building reaction against Johnson's Reconstruction program centered in Congress and produced two pieces of major legislation in early 1866, one extending the life of the Freedman's Bureau and the other counteracting the black codes. The Freedman's Bureau was scheduled to expire in April, a year after the war ended, but most northerners regarded it as a nonpolitical agency performing a useful function and supported the bill to extend its life. Johnson, however, vetoed the bill, and his veto was an important step in the alienation of northern moderates from his policies. Johnson argued in his veto message that since the defeated states had been restored to the Union, a federal welfare agency was both unnecessary and unconstitutional. The effort to override his veto failed to muster the necessary two-thirds majority. Johnson's veto of the second piece of legislation, the Civil Rights Act of 1866, was another and more important step in his growing political isolation. This act was designed to neutralize the black codes by declaring the freedmen to be American citizens and providing them with federal protection against violations of their civil rights by the states. Congress immediately overrode the veto of this act, and reenacted legislation continuing the Freedman's Bureau over Johnson's veto.

The effect of these developments was to convince Johnson's congressional critics that an alternative Reconstruction program was necessary, and that the alternative would have to be written into the Constitution to remove it from presidential tampering.[12] The result was the Fourteenth Amendment, the most important piece of Reconstruction legislation, which was in essence Congress's terms for reunion and Reconstruction; and had the southerners accepted it, the subsequent history of the postwar era would have been markedly different.

The terms were not harsh. The first section of the proposed amendment reenacted the major provisions of the Civil Rights Act of 1866, which some thought might be ruled unconstitutional by the courts. It declared that all persons (except Indians not taxed) who were born or naturalized in the United States were citizens of the United States and of the states in which they reside. This made blacks citizens, and their civil rights were then protected by provisions prohibiting the states from depriving any citizen of life, liberty, or property without due process of law, or denying the citizen equal protection of the laws, or in any other way abridging the privileges and immunities of citizenship.

The second section of the proposed Fourteenth Amendment imposed political disabilities on anyone who had ever held public office and sworn allegiance to the United States, and subsequently participated in rebellion. This included everyone who had held local, state, or federal office, civil or military, before the Civil War and had then served the Confederacy in an official capacity. These people were denied the right to hold office but not the right to vote, and the disability could be removed by a two-thirds vote of Congress.

The third section of the amendment dealt with the crucial issue of black suffrage. It required not that the southern states enfranchise the blacks, but that they enfranchise them or lose the seats in Congress that represented the black population. This bizarre provision was intended not to make sure that blacks were enfranchised, but to protect the Republican party and its economic program whether they were or not. If white southerners were willing to give up about a third of their congressional seats, they could avoid black suffrage. If blacks were enfranchised, they would presumably vote for the party of union and emancipation, in which case a substantial minority of the South's congressional seats would be won by Republicans; but if the race was not permitted to vote, southern Democrats would lose up to a third of their seats in Congress. In either case, the interests of the Republican party would be served.

The fourth section of the proposed amendment voided the Confederate debt and affirmed the federal debt.

Of the defeated states, only Tennessee ratified the amendment, and that state was readmitted to the Union and escaped the subsequent Reconstruction. All the others rejected it by unanimous or nearly unanimous votes between October 1866 and February 1867. They were encouraged in this stance by Johnson, but they also considered the terms of the amendment harsh and believed that northern opinion would not support an effort to impose the amendment on them. Southerners feared the terms would be literally applied, and recalling their successful handling of Johnson's plan of Reconstruction they saw no reason to help their enemies impose objectionable conditions on themselves. In these things too they miscalculated, misreading both the amendment and northern opinion. Actually, each of the amendment's provisions was a compromise between moderates and Radicals, and much less demanding than the southerners assumed. The civil rights guarantees in Section I were couched in vague language that was difficult to enforce; the political disabilities against ex-Confederates applied to only a portion of the leadership class; black voting was not required; and the Confederate debt was already a dead issue.

Radical Reconstruction

By November 1866, when the first postwar congressional elections were held, northern opinion had completed the shift against Johnson and the southerners, and in those elections Johnson's policies were repudiated. Control of Reconstruction thus shifted to his opponents, the Radicals and their allies, who worked through the swollen Republican majority in Congress. The Radical coalition was not concerned to punish the South, as southerners assumed, but to protect the freedmen in minimal ways, restrict the political role of Confederate leaders while enlarging that of southern unionists, and place the southern states under the political control of groups who were tolerant of the Republican party and its economic policy. Because of the opposition of most whites to these objectives, the Radicals (as all those who supported the new policies will be called) decided that blacks would have to be enfranchised to provide a large Republican electorate in the South and some Confederates politically disabled for a while, and the state governments would have to be reorganized once more.

The Radical program was spelled out in a series of Reconstruction Acts in the spring and summer of 1867. These acts dissolved the Johnson state governments, divided the Confederacy (except Tennessee) into five military districts, and established procedures for creating new governments. Military governors, appointed by Johnson, conducted a new voter registration in which blacks as well as whites participated, and supervised the election of new constitutional conventions and the formation of new governments. The new constitutions were submitted to the new electorate for approval, and the new state legislatures were required to ratify the Fourteenth Amendment. Only when that amendment became a part of the federal Constitution could the states be readmitted to the Union.

This program, and the period of Republican control of the southern state governments it initiated, constituted Congressional or Radical Reconstruction. As soon as it began, whites commenced to weave around it one of the most enduring myths of southern history, depicting it variously as a "soul-sickening spectacle," "a time of party abuse, of corruption, of vindictive bigotry," "a riot of Africanism," and a "crusade of hate and social equality."[13] "It was a policy of lawlessness under the forms of law, of disfranchisement, robbery, oppression and fraud," wrote Joel Chandler Harris, who lived through it. "It was a deliberate attempt to humiliate the people who had lost everything by the war, and it aroused passions on both sides that were unknown when the war was in actual progress. It banished for years the hope of reconciliation, delayed the natural progress of the country," and "history will justly charge to this policy all the demoralization at the South and the desperate efforts to resist it." It was, in short, the sum of all villanies.

Since the reality was quite otherwise, a basic purpose of any study of Reconstruction as an episode in southern history must be to understand why there was such a chasm between what actually happened and what white southerners believed happened. Viewed dispassionately, the "harshness" they perceived in Radical Reconstruction consisted chiefly of the fact that political control of the South was temporarily taken from groups that had always been dominant and placed in the hands of new groups whom the old groups feared and despised. The new groups were Carpetbaggers (whites who had moved to the South since 1860), Scalawags (southern whites who supported the Radical governments), and blacks. Except for the extension of political rights to blacks, the "radical" policies these groups initiated amounted to no more than a modest program of liberal reform.

Despite the alarm of Conservatives, as whites who opposed the Radical program called themselves, there were no mass arrests and only one man, Captain Henry Wirz, who had commanded Andersonville prison during the war, was ever tried for war crimes. A handful of political leaders had been imprisoned just after the war for a short time, but all were released without trial. Jefferson Davis was kept in prison for about two years, but Robert E. Lee was untouched. There was no substantial loss of property except slaves, and by the early 1870s everyone who requested it had had his political and civil rights restored. The instances of injustice, thievery, and scoundrelism that became the basis for so many lurid accounts of Reconstruction were due to personal villainy rather than Radical policy. In any case those things cut across ideological and party lines and are best understood as manifestations of the lowered tone of public life that characterized the postwar era in all parts of the country. Most remarkable of all, there was no systematic effort to cultivate a spirit of vengeance among blacks, and the individual acts of vengeance that occurred were not political in nature.

Far from being vindictive or radical, even the "harshest" measures, such as the enfranchisement of blacks, the civil rights laws, and the Enforcement Acts of 1870–71, were thoroughly consistent with the theory if not the practice of American democracy. All of the Reconstruction legislation was the product of compromise, because genuine Radicals were never a very large group. As it affected the South directly, the Radical program consisted primarily of military occupation that lasted from one to three years, new and more liberal state governments, the Fourteenth and Fifteenth Amendments, a series of civil rights laws, and certain efforts to promote interracialism in politics and integration in some public accommodations. Plainly it was not the harshness of these things that outraged Conservatives. It was instead the loss of political control to groups they feared and despised and the insecurity this generated, especially in racial matters. "The whites of the South," E. Merton Coulter wrote in *The South During Reconstruction* (1947), "came to see in Radical Reconstruction more and more a question of the survival of the integrity and dignity of the Caucasian race." Conservatives opposed the Radical program because it threatened white supremacy and their own supremacy among whites.

The military occupation hardly deserved the name. When it began, the United States army had less than 20,000 troops in the ten occupied states including Texas, where the concern was Indians rather than Confederates. In 1870–71, when Congress passed the Enforcement Acts against the Ku Klux Klan and other terrorist groups, the number was only 9,000. In November 1869 the recalcitrant state of Mississippi was being "occupied" by 716 officers and men. Moreover, the army had been in the South all along, and neither before nor during Radical Reconstruction did it oppress the white population. At most its presence was a restraining influence, reminding whites that extreme action on their part might provoke an enlarged federal presence.

Black voting was also no cause for outrage. In the initial registration, an undetermined number of whites refused to register and another undetermined number were disfranchised by the required loyalty oath. Yet registration totals were not far out of line with population totals, especially if it be remembered that a vigorous registration effort was undertaken among blacks but not whites. The final number of registrants was 660,000 whites and 703,000 blacks.[14] There were white majorities in Virginia, North Carolina, Georgia, Arkansas, and Texas, and black majorities in South Carolina, Florida, Alabama, Mississippi, and Louisiana. In the 1870 census, the population of these ten states was 56 percent whites and 44 percent blacks, whereas the registration totals were 48 percent whites and 52 percent blacks, an imbalance of 8 percentage points. Despite the temporary edge they enjoyed in registration, blacks never controlled Reconstruction in any state. Less than a quarter of the delegates to the constitutional conventions of 1867–68 were blacks, and in only one, that of South Carolina, were they a majority. Richard L. Hume, who studied these conventions in depth, identified 884 of the 1,027 delegates, of whom 257 were blacks, 149 Carpetbaggers, and 478 southern whites. Of 447 southern whites who voted in the conventions, Hume determined that 232 generally supported Radical measures and may thus be counted as Scalawags.[15]

In 1868 Radical governments were organized in Arkansas, Alabama, Florida, Louisiana, and the Carolinas, and those states were restored to the Union. However, various acts of resistance or uncooperativeness on the part of Conservatives delayed the process in the other states, and it was not completed until 1870. The constitutions under which these governments functioned were quite liberal by southern standards. Modeled after those of the most liberal northern states, they incorporated the principle of the equality of all men before the law, and thus mandated universal manhood suffrage and equal legislative apportionment. They also increased the number of public offices filled by election, expanded the functions of state and local government in the area of social welfare, authorized statewide systems of public education, improved the civil status of women and blacks, and in various ways encouraged economic growth and diversification. Had these things been vigorously pushed over a long period of time, they would eventually have improved race relations and the status of blacks, enlarged economic and educational opportunity for everyone, and generally bettered the quality of southern life. But they were no blueprint for social revolution.

The thrust of Radical Reconstruction was thus liberal, and only to a small degree did it involve the things Conservatives complained most about—Negro rule, outside interference, excessive taxation, public corruption, and the insecurity of person and property. Negro rule existed in some black belt counties for a while, and black influence was felt in all the states. Carpetbaggers did hold a disproportionate share of high public offices, but political control was always in the hands of citizens of the South. Real property taxes were increased to pay for expanded social services, and the rates were sometimes burdensome for a people impoverished by war, but they remained low by national standards. Public corruption was sometimes spectacular and in places like South Carolina and Louisiana was quite widespread, and the property and person of whites were jeopardized on occasion. But these were not the typical facts of Reconstruction, and their importance in southern history is due to the success Conservatives had in using them to discredit Radical Reconstruction and the things it stood for, including racial reform, social welfare programs, black voting and office-holding, and two-party politics.

Radical Race Policy

The moderate and impermanent nature of Radical Reconstruction is seen most clearly in the racial policies it espoused. Blacks constituted the mass of Republican voters in the South, but they never enjoyed a proportionate share of power or influence in the Republican party or any of the Republican state governments, and those governments were never committed to genuine racial equality. Black influence was greatest in South Carolina, where members of the race constituted about three-fifths of the population. There for six years they were a majority in the lower house of the legislature, but they were never a majority in the senate, and their participation in most of the executive departments hardly exceeded tokenism. No black was ever elected governor of any of the states, though P. B. S. Pinchback was acting governor of Louisiana for six weeks. In South Carolina, Mississippi, and Louisiana blacks were elected lieutenant governor. A handful served in cabinet-level positions and other statewide offices in several states, and a much larger number served in the state legislatures and local offices, especially in the black belt. A dozen served in the national House of Representatives during Radical Reconstruction, and two, Hiram Revels and Blanche K. Bruce of Mississippi, in the United States Senate.

Because they were a minority of the population with little economic power or political experience, blacks were forced to ally themselves with white Republicans. The alliance was ultimately compromising, because few white Republicans were committed to racial equality and most of them were unwilling to support the kind of positive measures necessary to achieve it. They were racial moderates by the standards of the day, which meant they eschewed extremism and sought to help the freedmen advance within the confines of social segregation and white supremacy. Almost none of them supported integrated education or condoned interracial marriage, and the governments they created never addressed themselves to the implications of racial segregation, the familiar forms of which began to crystallize during Reconstruction. Outside politics they did little to promote interracialism, and none of them developed meaningful programs to deal with the economic problems of freedmen.

These were crucial failures. Political participation was vital for blacks, but it was not enough to solve the problems of the race. Land ownership was one key to those problems, and had the head of each household received an economically viable holding and been protected in its use, the other problems might have been easier to solve. The mass of blacks had been agricultural workers as slaves and expected to remain so as freedmen. Farming was what they knew, and they also knew that land ownership was the sine qua non of economic and psychological independence in an agricultural society, perhaps even more important than the right to vote.

Immediately following the war, many, perhaps most, blacks expected to receive land grants from the federal government.[16] The expectation was based on several actions by the government or its representatives during and after the war. When federal forces occupied the South Carolina sea islands in 1861 land-owning whites fled, and possession of the land passed to freedmen, who cultivated it in small farms. They expected to keep their farms when the war ended, and some of them were able to do so. Later in the war, about 40,000 blacks settled on land in coastal South Carolina opened to them by the army, and their titles were seemingly protected when General William T. Sherman in early 1865 ordered a strip of coastal territory thirty miles wide set aside for the exclusive use of freedmen and gave them "possessory title" to tracts of no more than forty acres each. In the Confiscation Act of 1862 Congress authorized the confiscation of the land as well as the slaves of Confederates, an action inspired in part by the desire to distribute land to the freedmen. Lincoln, however, never used this measure.

The most substantial basis for the expectation of land was the act creating the Freedman's Bureau. In that act Congress authorized the Bureau "to set apart, for the use of loyal refugees and freedmen, such tracts of land within the insurrectionary states as shall have been abandoned, or to which the United States shall have acquired title by confiscation or sale." From these tracts each freedman or refugee "shall be assigned not more than forty acres of such land, and the person to whom it was so assigned shall be protected in the use and enjoyment of the land for the term of three years." At that time the assignee could purchase the land "and receive such title thereto as the United States can convey." This seemed a great deal on the surface, but in actuality it was nothing more than a highly tentative promise to sell land to which legal title might be obtained. It resulted in almost no land for freedmen. Nor did the Southern Homestead Act, passed in 1866, which offered public land in the South for sale at $1.25 an acre.

Thus no meaningful program of land distribution was ever undertaken. South Carolina was the only state with even a modest program, and among national Republican leaders only Thaddeus Stevens seriously considered this matter. The reasons for the failure seem obvious. Freedmen were too poor to acquire land on their own, and Congress was unwilling to confiscate that of the planters. As a result the only substantial transfer of land that occurred during Reconstruction was not from planters to freedmen, but from resident planters to northerners and southern merchants. It should also be added that the popular proposal to give forty acres to each freedman was not one that would have solved the freedmen's economic problems. A forty-acre farm was too small to provide anything but subsistence, and in the agricultural depression that plagued the South through the last third of the nineteenth century most freedmen would surely have remained poor in any case and probably have lost their farms as well.

Carpetbaggers and Scalawags

The Carpetbaggers and Scalawags, whites who cooperated with Radical Reconstruction, are difficult to know.[17] Both their numbers and purposes were obscured by the unsavory reputation Conservatives attached to them, and both are still difficult to piece together. Reuben O. Davis of Mississippi summarized their reputation when he defined a Scalawag as "a mean, low, dirty white man, who is capable of selling himself and his honor for the sake of having an opportunity to plunder honest men."

Like Radical Reconstruction itself, these groups are important in southern history chiefly because of the reaction against them. Building upon the black electorate, they controlled the Radical governments, but those governments lasted only about five years on the average and nowhere longer than nine, and the evil as well as the good they could do was limited by that fact. In fact they left nothing of substance that was not erased or emasculated in the reaction that followed the return of political control to the Conservatives. The state constitutions they helped write were rewritten or ignored by the Conservative governments, as were the programs of social service they initiated. Their efforts toward racial moderation were overwhelmed by Conservative extremism, and even their record as spoilsmen and scoundrels was surpassed by their Democratic successors.

Yet as participants in Reconstruction the Carpetbaggers and

Scalawags are reminders of what might have been. Like any sizable political group they were a mixed lot of men. Governors Adelbert Ames of Mississippi and Daniel H. Chamberlain of South Carolina, both Carpetbaggers, were men of probity and honorable purpose, but Governors Henry C. Warmouth of Louisiana, also a Carpetbagger, and Franklin J. Moses of South Carolina, a Scalawag, were not. An appraisal of both groups must begin by recognizing that they were legitimate political factions that offered moderate alternatives to the policies supported by most white southerners. Most Carpetbaggers who achieved high office came to the South before the advent of Radical Reconstruction, as army officers, federal officials, or business investors, and they were not spoilsmen or political adventurers. The Scalawags, on the other hand, were political heirs of the prewar Whigs or Jacksonian democrats, groups that had always opposed many of the things the Conservatives stood for. Many of them had been unionists before and during the war, and they had economic as well as political grounds for opposing the Conservatives. Those of Whiggish bent were generally moderate on sectional issues, and those of the Jacksonian persuasion were concerned about the socioeconomic wellbeing of plain whites. Both differed with Conservatives over how the South could best overcome the effects of defeat and adapt to the postwar world. They were more likely to favor "progress" and federal expenditures to encourage it, and were more concerned to placate northern opinion, encourage racial moderation, and assist the freedmen.

The Scalawags of Mississippi have been studied more thoroughly than any other group of Scalawags or Carpetbaggers. They were a surprisingly large and broadly based group. During the five years of Republican rule in the state, one of three governors, two of the three state supreme court justices, and about a third of the United States congressmen and state legislators were southern-born whites. According to their most recent historian, the Mississippi Scalawags were men who "looked to the future and the quick, complete, and harmonious restoration of the state to the Union under the auspices of the young and energetic Republican party." They viewed Reconstruction as an opportunity to produce "a thorough-going reform" of the state "after years of Democratic mismanagement and blundering." They acquiesced in the racial policies of the Radicals, though they opposed social equality. They accepted the Fourteenth and Fifteenth Amendments, and hoped that moderate racial policies would discourage white extremism. They supported the Republican party because they believed economic development and moderate social reform promised to alleviate their state's pressing problems. "They wanted to bring Mississippi into conformity with [national] trends," William C. Harris has written, "yet purposefully stopping short of revamping the society of the state."

And that, in substance, was what Radical Reconstruction was intended to do.

Conservative Race Policy

Most white southerners, who identified with the Conservatives, had a different vision of the postwar South. They were alarmed by Radical Reconstruction, especially its racial policies and constitutional implications.[18] The one they regarded as a threat to white supremacy and the other as a threat to the white South's ability to protect itself. Their major concerns were to preserve white supremacy, restore the old relationship with the Union, and guard their own interests as a social and economic class. To accomplish these things, the Conservatives felt it imperative to keep whites politically united under their leadership and to resist the intrusions of outsiders, whether blacks, Scalawags, Carpetbaggers, or the federal government.

They were especially concerned over racial matters. The destruction of slavery had begun a new era in the history of white supremacy. Emancipation removed the basis upon which whites and blacks had interacted, eliminating both the paternal and the exploitive aspects of the old relationship. The existence of slavery had served to make racial control a matter chiefly of institutional arrangements, which had the effect of curbing acts of random violence or extralegal extremism. Masters not only disciplined their slaves but protected them from abuse by others. The arrangement had of course been far from perfect, but it had operated to contain racial violence by assuring whites that blacks were under control. Emancipation removed that assurance by eliminating the institutional devices that underlay it, and the result was increased uncertainty. How were blacks to be controlled without the restraints and paternalism of slavery? The conduct of blacks during the final disintegration of slavery, when so many of them, including trusted house servants, ran away and forwent the obeisances of slavery, was especially disillusioning. With slavery gone, whites felt unprotected—one of the things that determined their actions in the first months after the war was the widespread fear that a general black uprising was planned during Christmastime in 1865—and blacks were more exposed to the threat of random violence. The result was a significant upsurge of white violence aimed at keeping blacks "in their place," and various efforts by blacks to protect themselves. This rather than the policies of Radical Reconstruction explains why race relations degenerated after the war. The situation fed on itself. The more violent or intimidating whites became, the more blacks appealed to the army or the federal government or turned to politics; and the more they did these things, the more alarmed whites became.

With the institutional safeguards of white supremacy in disarray after emancipation, whites turned more and more to the idea of race to justify their dominance. Before the war, the defense of white supremacy had been subsumed in the larger defense of slavery and a way of life. Now, however, it shifted to racial thought, and its major premises became the idea that blacks are physically, morally, and mentally inferior to whites and the corollary notion that whites must protect themselves and their civilization from black contamination. In the context created by emancipation, this led to an alternating emphasis on two contradictory views. According to the first of these views, blacks were a race of childlike people who needed help in the long period of tutelage necessary for them to earn the privileges of citizenship. According to the second, the Negro was a beast whose savage, animalistic qualities must be restrained by law and public policy. The import of both views was that the race must be kept in line by superior authority lest it become a burden and a menace to the larger community.

Accepting these lines of reasoning, Conservative leaders sought not to restore slavery, but to create a new racial order based on clearly delineated relationships of superior and inferior which both races accepted and obeyed. In its positive dimension this represented an effort to develop new institutional forms that would serve the restraining functions once performed by slavery. From this standpoint the first requirement of racial peace was to remove the ambiguities in the Negroes' status created by emancipation and Radical Reconstruction and the expectation of equality those things instilled in the Negroes' minds. That expectation was the source of what whites called "uppitiness" in the freedmen, and whites saw no prospect for racial harmony until it was eliminated. Like everyone else Conservative leaders wanted a stable, untroubled racial order, but like the mass of white southerners they were convinced that this was possible only if absolute white supremacy were guaranteed. They were therefore prepared to devote the entire resources of the law and public policy to that task. When blacks were convinced that they had no choice but to acquiesce —to leave politics alone and accept their dependent status—then and only then would racial peace return.

The racial policies of Radical Reconstruction were thus intolerable to Conservatives. There must be no ambiguity on racial matters except the moderation permitted by paternalism within a framework of absolute white supremacy. Paternalism, as they saw it, would offer wide leeway for black improvement, while absolute supremacy would alleviate white fear and enable whites to tolerate, indeed support, black improvement.

The Campaign for Redemption

Like other groups in Reconstruction, the Conservatives had complex motives, and no more than Carpetbaggers and Scalawags can they be understood as creatures of base motives alone. The differences between them and their opponents were ultimately differences of values, of what the South is and was and what it might become. Because these differences were irreconcilable through the normal processes of political give-and-take, Reconstruction became a contest of will, and the only groups that had power and resources sufficient to prevail were southern whites—the Conservatives—and the business wing of the Republican party. The concerns of the two groups, however, were notably different. The southerners were interested in white supremacy and home rule, the Republicans in controlling the national government and protecting their economic policies. As time passed and the nation wearied of Reconstruction, it became clear to more and more people in the two groups that they could settle their differences without sacrificing anything vital to either of them. Those whose interests would be sacrificed—blacks, southern Republicans, racial and economic liberals—were able to generate no effective counterpressure.

The campaign against Radical Reconstruction began as soon as the first Republican government was established in 1868 and continued until the last three of those governments were overthrown in 1877. The task must have seemed impossible at the outset. The Republican party had overwhelming majorities in Congress in 1868, and was about to nominate a national hero, General Ulysses S. Grant, to stand for the presidency. The incumbent President, Andrew Johnson, was being humiliated by impeachment, and the real case against him was that his Reconstruction policies had been too partial to the white South. The army was still in the South, and what seemed like hordes of federal agents, northern do-gooders, unruly blacks, and other undesirables were swarming across the section.

Yet even then the course of events was shifting. Northern weariness over Reconstruction began to bear its first fruit. More and more northerners were coming to blame sectional animosities on Radical policies, and support for those policies was beginning to wane. The Senate failed to convict Johnson on the impeachment charges, and he remained in office, though with little power. In the fall elections Grant's margin of victory was unexpectedly small. Democrats did surprisingly well, a happy omen for white southerners, and Grant himself used his inaugural address to plead for sectional reconciliation. "Let us have peace," he said at a time when peace could only mean the end of federal intervention in behalf of Negro rights. Soon thereafter, a coalition of white Democrats and moderate Republicans won the first elections held in Virginia under the Radical constitution, and that state never had a Radical government. The moderation of this Virginia government on racial matters and the sympathy its leaders showed for Republican economic policies suggested to many northerners that Radical measures of Reconstruction might be unnecessary. In the same year of 1869 Democrats won control of the state government of Tennessee, and in the following year the governments of North Carolina and Georgia as well.

White southerners called this Redemption, this process by which they overthrew the Radical Republican governments and reasserted their own supremacy in the defeated states. The men who directed the process, which combined legitimate political activity with wholesale violence and mayhem, they called Redeemers. The process itself varied greatly from state to state. In Virginia the Republicans were thwarted by astute political maneuvering, but in Mississippi and South Carolina wholesale violence and intimidation were the essential weapons. Altogether, the Redemption campaign involved the largest sustained application of violence and organized lawlessness in the peacetime history of the United States (unless one counts the campaign against the Indians as a peacetime operation). Everywhere the result was the same: governments dominated by Conservative white Democrats replaced those controlled by Radical Republicans. One by one the states were redeemed—North Carolina and Georgia as already noted, Texas, Arkansas, and Alabama in 1874, Mississippi in 1876, and Florida, South Carolina, and Louisiana in 1877.

In all of these states the process was underwritten to greater or lesser degree by violence. The best-known agency of violence was the Ku Klux Klan, organized in Tennessee in 1865 and most active in the first few years of Radical Reconstruction. "Typically the Klan was a reactionary and racist crusade against equal rights which sought to overthrow the most democratic society or government the South had yet known," Allen W. Trelease has written in *White Terror* (1971). During its brief existence in Reconstruction this hooded, secret organization "whipped, shot, hanged, robbed, raped, and otherwise outraged Negroes and Republicans across the South in the name of preserving white civilization." Klansmen were recruited from all levels of society and government, including law enforcement agencies, and used their numbers as well as their positions to disrupt political activities by blacks and Republicans and deprive those groups of the ordinary rights of citizenship. The Klan was an organized conspiracy against the civil rights of a large segment of society, but so considerable were its powers of intimidation in many areas that even officials who opposed it were helpless against it.

According to the Conservative view, the Klan was originally an organization of responsible men reluctantly forced to take extreme measures to protect society against the greater lawlessness of Radical misrule, and because of its effectiveness Radical excesses diminished and person and property were made safe again in the South. At the height of its effectiveness, however, so this view ran, rowdies and charlatans were attracted to the Klan and began to use it for base and selfish purposes. When that occurred General Nathan Bedford Forrest, its leader, disbanded the organization, and the real Klan ceased to exist.

Even if this view of the Klan's origins is accepted (and the evidence for doing so is unconvincing), a secret organization engaged in terrorist activities inevitably becomes a slave to its methods. Thus Klan violence got out of the control of those who wanted to use it for political purposes only, and the organization became an instrument of personal vendetta and racial vengeance. Its example spawned imitators such as the Knights of the White Camellia and the White Brotherhood, and the excesses of all these groups forced the federal government to act. In 1870–71 Congress passed three Enforcement Acts against terrorist groups aimed at protecting the civil rights of their victims. These acts forbade racial discrimination by state and local officials in the conduct of elections and made it a crime for anyone to use force, bribery, threats, or intimidation against voters or to withhold employment in order to influence voting. It was also made a criminal offense to interfere with the civil rights of another person. In areas where terrorist activities had occurred, federal officials were authorized to supervise voter registration, conduct elections, and certify returns.

The problem was not with these laws, but with their enforcement. It is impossible to enforce any law actively opposed by political and economic elites, and that was the case with the Enforcement Acts, though for a while the Grant administration made a meaningful effort to enforce them. Several thousand individuals were prosecuted under those laws, and for a while the government won most of the cases brought into court. Nine counties in South Carolina where terrorism was especially widespread were placed under martial law for a time, and elsewhere the army acted to counteract instances of lawlessness.

The effort began to have positive effects. The secret organizations were disbanded or transformed into open societies. This, however, was only partially the result of federal activity. It was also due to the success terrorists had had in spreading fear and the Democrats had had in winning office. Together these two things dictated a change in tactics. The Enforcement Acts raised the specter of a larger federal intervention, something Conservatives wanted earnestly to avoid. Obviously the best policy under the circumstances was to give federal officials, who were reluctant to use coercive measures anyway, convincing excuses for not doing so. Toward that end hooded organizations and surreptitious violence were counterproductive. They were too easy targets for those who wanted federal intervention. By 1872–73 secret terrorist organizations had disappeared, and in their stead appeared new groups who called themselves rifle companies, Red Shirts, or other such names. The new groups were committed to the same purposes as the old, but did their work more openly. They exhibited their strength in such public activities as parades, target practice, and other demonstrations of white power and determination.

They did other things too. They made public as well as private threats against Republicans and black activists, and forced many in those groups to flee or withdraw from politics. A favorite device was the staged race riot in which black or Republican gatherings were invaded and broken up by violence. Often the result was wholesale murder, but to the new groups overt violence was less important than it had been to the Klan. Intimidation, voting fraud, social ostracism, and the threat of violence were more important. Landowners refused to rent to Republicans or politically active blacks, merchants refused them credit, even doctors refused to treat their ills. Their lives were rendered intolerable, and they had no choice but to submit. Those who remained active found it increasingly difficult to register to vote and, if they voted, to have their votes counted. The period of Redemption and its aftermath was the most fraudulent in the electoral history of the South, and the effect of the fraud was to place Conservatives in office and keep them there, and in that way to preserve white supremacy.

These techniques were perfected in Mississippi, where in 1875–76 they enabled Conservatives to win control of the legislature and force the resignation of Carpetbagger Governor Adelbert Ames. In 1876–77 the "Mississippi plan," as it was called, provided the strategy for unseating the last Republican governments in South Carolina, Louisiana, and Florida, and when the results of this endeavor were ratified in the Compromise of 1877, the formal phase of Reconstruction was over.

The Compromise of 1877

That compromise began a new era in the history of the South and its relationship to the rest of the country. It signaled an end to the half-century-long endeavor of northern liberals to force their ideas about racial policy on the white South. The threat of outside interference in racial matters was thus greatly diminished, and after 1890 it disappeared altogether.

The compromise was occasioned by the disputed presidential election of 1876, the same election in which Conservatives ousted the Radical governments in Louisiana, South Carolina, and Florida. In the presidential contest that year, Democrat Samuel J. Tilden won a majority of the popular vote and 184 of the 185 electoral votes required for victory, Republican Rutherford B. Hayes won 165 electoral votes, and the remaining 20 votes were disputed. One of the disputed votes was in Oregon, which Hayes had won, and involved a legal technicality, but the other 19 were in South Carolina, Louisiana, and Florida, and involved contested results and widespread fraud on both sides. It is impossible to say with certainty who won in any of these three states, though it seems likely that the Republicans would have won an honest and open election in South Carolina and Louisiana. It also seems likely that an honest count of the ballots actually cast would have given the Democrats a victory in Florida, and Tilden was therefore entitled to the presidency.

In each of these states Republican election boards threw out enough Democratic votes to certify the Hayes slate of electors, and in each case Democrats challenged the count and sent in rival certifications of their own. The resulting struggle was unprecedented, and threatened to generate a major political crisis. That struggle provided the occasion for a political deal between southern Democrats—the Conservatives—and national Republicans that not only ended Reconstruction but legitimized the Conservative regimes that had replaced the Radicals.

Republicans wanted the presidency badly in 1876, and they also wanted to organize the House of Representatives, in which they were a minority, and protect the economic interests the party represented. To achieve all this, they were willing to give the Conservatives several things they wanted badly. The northern Republicans were willing to abandon the southern Republicans, who were an anomaly in the party anyway (the party represented big business and economic development in the North, but blacks and liberal reform in the South). This meant abandoning blacks too, or put more diplomatically, it meant surrendering primary control of race policy in the South to whites. The conservatives wanted other things too, that only northern Republicans could give them. They wanted Reconstruction ended, the Democratic governments of Florida, Louisiana, and South Carolina recognized, the army withdrawn, and the end of federal interference in southern racial matters.

But that was not all they wanted. The Conservatives were not merely a group of racial reactionaries, but also political spokesmen for the new economic order emerging in the South. That order is discussed in a later chapter, but here it may be said that it represented economic development and other interests of the urban middle class. Since 1865 the economic groups that controlled the South had undergone something of a metamorphosis. They were no longer planter-oriented, but promoters of industrial and commercial growth and of political policies that encouraged such growth. For these purposes, home rule and the end of racial turbulence were no more important than federal largesse. The Conservatives, in short, had become the economic heirs of Whiggery, and many of them were in fact ex-Whigs. As such they wanted federal assistance of the kind already extended to northern developers —river and harbor improvements, levee construction, railroad subsidies, and other kinds of pork barrel legislation, especially federal aid in constructing a transcontinental railroad between New Orleans and San Diego. These things were much more important to Conservatives than a Democratic victory in the presidential election of 1876, especially since northern Republicans were more likely to support these policies than northern Democrats.

A bargain was struck. The Compromise of 1877 was necessarily more informal than the better-known antebellum compromises, but in many ways it was more important in the subsequent history of the South. Southerners agreed to accept Hayes's election by not joining a congressional challenge to the findings of a special electoral commission that gave the Republicans victory in all three of the disputed states. They also agreed to help Republicans organize the House of Representatives and to mute their opposition to Republican economic policies. In return the Republicans agreed to end Reconstruction, recognize the primacy of whites in racial matters in the South, support federal largesse for the South, and give white Democrats a voice in federal patronage in the South during Hayes's administration. In the aftermath the role of Republicans and blacks in southern politics diminished, and northern interest in racial reform ebbed. Rather rapidly, the measures of Radical Reconstruction were neutralized and after 1890 eliminated altogether.

The Significance of Reconstruction

When Reconstruction was over, white southerners looked back upon it as a harrowing experience, and the memory made it one of the molding influences in southern history. It was in fact a kind of molten experience that melted down the white South and recast it, but the source of the heat was not Radical Reconstruction. During the Redemption campaign, white southerners showed themselves willing to risk racial warfare to have their way. It is difficult to convey the frightfulness of what they did. Vernon Lane Wharton's *The Negro in Mississippi, 1865–1890* (1947) gives a short account of what happened in one of the worst states. Within three pages Wharton describes incidents at Austin in which six blacks were killed; in Vicksburg where "about thirty-five" died in one affray and two in another; at Water Valley in which "an unknown number" perished; at Louisville where two were injured; at Macon where "twelve or thirteen" died; at Yazoo City where "several Negroes were wounded" in one incident and "White militia ... systematically lynched the Negro leaders in each supervisor's district" in another; at Clinton where perhaps ten to thirty blacks died and another ten to fifty were killed in the surrounding countryside; at Satartia where one was killed; in Coahoma County where five died; and at Columbus where the toll was four. He also includes reports of the murder of several whites sympathetic to blacks and the death by violence of several who were not.

This is what left the searing scars of Reconstruction on the southern psyche and produced the moral deformities that plagued the section for generations afterwards. No society can whip itself into such frenzy, can so terrorize itself and flout its own values without suffering profound emotional damage; and that is what happened to the South. The frenzy was basically irrational—the limited reforms of Radical Reconstruction represented no direct challenge to white supremacy—and it thus bespoke the depth of white fear and prejudice. This was the real significance of Reconstruction. By placing whites in a position they considered menacing and ignominious, it brought to the surface a hidden dimension of their deepest nature. It showed just how far they would go to have their way.

"It was the lasting damage to the mind, spirit, and culture of the South that made it so devastating," Henry Savage once wrote of the experience. "Reconstruction broke the South's spirit, planted hampering prejudices and frustrating hates, and paralyzed its will to move forward with the nation and the world." This assessment has been widely endorsed by whites since 1877, but it is difficult to accept as Savage meant it. Certainly there was damage to the section's mind, spirit, and culture by Reconstruction, but the damage came not from Radicalism, but from the extremism of whites themselves. The Radicals did not plant hampering prejudices and frustrating hates in the white mind. Rather, their program brought to the surface prejudices and hates already there. It might of course be said that without Radical Reconstruction the prejudices and hates would have remained dormant, and the Radicals were thus responsible for what happened. But such a view makes the appearance of racial peace more important than the rights of blacks. Before Radical Reconstruction whites had confidently insisted that blacks had no desire for political rights, but were satisfied in their subordinate place. Reconstruction destroyed that illusion and the sense of security it gave. The problem was that Reconstruction did not provide blacks with the strength and resources necessary to withstand the extremism the whites' loss of security provoked. Reconstruction was in effect "radical" enough to arouse whites but not to safeguard blacks. In this important sense it was not radical enough.

Such was the shock of Reconstruction. Their fears aroused, whites decided that the ends they sought justified the means they employed to achieve them; but then the means consumed the ends. The aftermath was not an absence of racial fear but a duller, more diffuse unease, a sense not of security, but of the guilt that comes from violating one set of values to preserve another. The violence and bitterness necessary to preserve the settlement of 1877 thus had direful consequences in later years. The experience arrested the democratic impulse of the southern white people, frustrated their generous instincts and outgoing nature, and forced them to ignore their most pressing problems. The purpose was served, white supremacy prevailed—but in a South whose very soul was scarred.

FOUR

THE NEW SOUTH 1870-1917

"The New South" is an ambiguous term variously used to connote a period of time in southern history, an ideology of boosterism and economic progress, and the South of industry or social reform or even school desegregation. There have thus been many New Souths and will be others in the future as long as the term is used, for the term itself implies not only a changing South but one forever becoming less southern and more American. Here it will be used to designate a period of southern history, the years in which southerners were preoccupied with the adjustments dictated by defeat, Reconstruction, and Redemption. In politics this encompassed the era of Conservative supremacy from Redemption to World War I. In race relations it spanned the years from Reconstruction to about 1910, during which time the policies of Radical Reconstruction were neutralized and then replaced by segregation and disfranchisement. In economics it continued through the first decade of the twentieth century, when the effects of the Civil War began at last to recede.

The study of this phase of southern history has only recently blossomed, and the literature on the period is less rich than that on the antebellum era.[1] In addition, historians of the New South have given little attention to monistic interpretations of the era. The New South seems at once less exotic and thus less in need of "interpreting," and its history less easily subsumed under a single theme. With the advent of the New South, southern history becomes more complex and sectional qualities more diffuse. To the transcendant issue of race must now be added the molding influence of historical trauma. Defeat in the Civil War was followed by impoverishment, Reconstruction, and the desperate measures of Redemption. These things not only reinforced the "common resolve, indomitably maintained" to preserve white supremacy but also nurtured feelings of grievance and apartness and of living in the midst of evil. As never before or again in their history, southerners felt frustrated and victimized, and the chip on their shoulder seemed now to assume the nature of a monkey on their back.

10

The Economics of Adjustment

The overriding fact of economic life in the New South was poverty. The dispirit that enveloped the section after Appomattox was not long indulged. The problems of getting a living were immediate, and the processes of revival began at once. Union armies had commandeered many of the railroads and restored them to use, and after the war returned them to their owners on generous terms. The multiple tasks of rebuilding were soon underway. In 1865–66 the Georgia legislature incorporated seventeen new manufacturing companies. Within two years after Lee's surrender, the cotton mills of Columbus, Georgia, and elsewhere were being rebuilt, and those in Greenville, South Carolina, and other localities had already reopened. The cotton crop in 1865 was almost 2.3 million bales, and the high prices it brought helped desperate farmers through difficult times. Gross farm income in 1866 was 85 percent of the prewar level and in 1870 actually exceeded that level.

These were hopeful signs, but the larger facts were poverty and need.[1] As previously seen, the war was economically disastrous for the South, and its retarding effects on growth rates between 1865 and 1885, especially in agriculture, enveloped the section in enduring poverty. According to Stanley L. Engerman's calculations, the per capita value of commodity output in agriculture and manufacturing dropped from $77 in 1860 to $50 in 1870, and was still only $62 in 1880 (compared to $105 in the rest of the country in the latter year). Per capita income followed a similar pattern, dropping, in Richard A. Easterlin's estimate, from 72 percent of the national average in 1860 to 51 percent in 1880, where it remained in 1900. In the South Atlantic states, the figure was only 45 percent of the national average in 1880 and 1900.

Problems of Agricultural Adjustment

The situation was worst in agriculture.[2] In the 1860s the value of agricultural wealth, exclusive of slaves, was halved and the number of livestock fell by a third. Between 1866 and 1880 gross farm income reached the 1859 level only three times, in 1870, 1875, and 1880. The chief problems were not defeat and property destruction, but social disorganization and the much lower productivity of agricultural labor in the postwar period. The old plantation system was gone, but at first no one knew what would replace it. Planters had land but little liquid wealth, while freedmen wanted land and economic independence, and federal policy was ambiguous. Despite the uncertainty, it soon became obvious that the relative position of whites and blacks had not been changed by defeat and emancipation. White planters still had the bulk of agricultural wealth, and black freedmen had little more than the ability to labor. Necessity and tradition drove the two groups together, and after some experimenting with wage labor, a new relationship crystallized. Freedmen refused to work in gangs on plantations, a form of labor they equated with slavery, preferring instead to work individual farms of their own. In any case planters could not pay the cash wages gang labor would entail, and thus planters and freedmen alike turned to sharecropping, an arrangement that had been used on a limited scale with white tenants in the Old South.

Sharecropping was a form of barter that fitted the needs of landowning planters and landless freedmen in a money-scarce society. It entailed the division of large land holdings into small farms to be worked individually by a "cropper" and his family. Planter and cropper entered a contract, usually oral, in which the former agreed to supply the latter with housing to live in, land to farm, and the necessities for making a crop, including implements, livestock, and seed, and sometimes fertilizer. In return the cropper agreed to farm the land as the planter directed, and to divide the crop with him at year's end. The division was usually in halves, but the more the cropper furnished in the way of implements, livestock, and other necessities, the larger his share of the crop might be. If he had a substantial complement of these things, he might be a "share tenant" and receive two-thirds or three-quarters of the crop; if he had a full complement, he could become a cash renter with full control over his crop. Because of the poverty of most croppers, landowners usually not only supplied all the necessities listed above but also "furnished" their croppers, that is, supplied them with food staples and "stood for" their purchases on credit of other necessities from a local merchant. At "settling up" time at the end of the crop year the planter, who handled the business end of these arrangements, deducted from the cropper's share the amount of his "furnish" plus carrying charges. Large landowners soon began operating their own furnish stores, and many merchants began "carrying" croppers of their own. In this manner, the supply merchants became an important force in sharecropping and thus in southern agriculture.

The system was held together by a lien, a contractual claim the landlord or merchant had on the cropper's crop. At the beginning of the year the cropper in effect mortgaged his unplanted crop in return for being carried or furnished until harvest time. In doing so, he surrendered control of his livelihood as well as his crop. He agreed to plant, tend, and harvest the crop as the lienholder directed, and to purchase on credit only what the lienholder allowed and at whatever carrying charges the merchant imposed. (Indeed, no one else would give him credit, for he had no collateral besides his crop.) This arrangement was necessary under the circumstances, and it did provide subsistence for a large mass of almost penniless people. But it was also the source of many ills. "It has crushed out all independence and reduced its victims to a coarse species of servile slavery," wrote Charles H. Otken in *The Ills of the South* (1894). "[It] reduces a large body of people to a state of beggery, fosters a discontented spirit, checks consumption, produces recklessness on the part of the consumer, places a discount on honesty, and converts commerce into a vast pawning shop where farmers pledge their lands for hominy and bacon upon ruinous terms."

It was in fact a pernicious system, pulling everyone it touched in an expanding circle of poverty and insecurity. Its tentacles spread across the section and eventually encompassed most of the agricultural population. Poverty, racism, and greed gave the system an inertia that perpetuated the ills it fed upon, and sharecroppers remained poor and powerless. Most of them were illiterate or nearly so and had little or no experience in the business side of farming and even less in the intricacies of law and contract procedures. Lien laws were weighted against them, and increased the burdens of class and racial discrimination that bore them down. It is not necessary to believe that landowners and merchants were anything but men of ordinary honesty and frailty to see the evils the system involved. They kept all the records, set all the prices and carrying charges, and told the cropper what, if anything, he cleared at the end of the year. The opportunities for error and dishonesty were great.

Yet merchants and landlords were victims too. Their operations were generally small, and they too had to borrow money at sometimes usurious rates. Their margins of profit were usually slim and uncertain. Crop failures, irresponsible croppers, and fluctuating commodity prices were only the most obvious of their problems, any one of which might mean disaster or a lean year. Economic forces explain more of their actions than does greed, including the interest rates of 25 percent or more they charged croppers, and the insistence upon staple production, which fastened one-crop agriculture on the South. Cotton (in some areas tobacco) involved far less risk than any other crop. Handling and storage costs were low and marketability was high, it was not perishable, could not be eaten by croppers or livestock, and was relatively resistant to crop failure until the boll weevil came.

Because of the emphasis on cotton (or tobacco), sharecroppers produced insufficient quantities of food. Growing vegetables, fruit, and poultry and keeping meat animals and milk cows were not encouraged by landowners, were in fact often discouraged. Production of corn and pork, basic items in the croppers' diets, declined from antebellum levels. In 1860 the Confederate South produced thirty-one bushels of corn per capita and 1.74 swine, but in 1900 the comparable figures were twenty-one bushels of corn and .84 swine. Contemporary reports agree that sharecroppers purchased a considerable portion of their basic food, and modern scholars have confirmed the fact that small farms did not produce enough food- or feedstuffs to meet the basic needs of people or livestock. The cropper's diet was inadequate and monotonous, and the result was malnutrition and sometimes pellagra and the physical and social consequences of those things. There is no doubt that the standard of living among the agricultural masses declined in the New South. The rude sufficiency of the slave regime was lost; the same kind of economic forces that once encouraged food production for slaves now discouraged it for croppers.

Croppers could not help themselves out of their condition. An able-bodied farm hand could produce perhaps 2,000 pounds of ginned cotton a year. At 30 cents a pound, a price not unknown just after the war, this was worth $600, but at 10 cents, a good price in the early 1880s, only $200. This total might be supplemented by the earnings of other members of the family, by food and feed production, and in marginal ways by other things. But the sharecropper received only half the income he and his family produced, and 25 percent of that might go for interest on his account at the supply merchant's. Such a scheme allowed for nothing but hard work and continued poverty. "An average family, with one horse, can cultivate about 20 acres of cotton and 10 acres of corn," reported the *Yearbook* of the United States Department of Agriculture in 1908, illustrating the persistence of the pattern. "The average yield of cotton is two-fifths of a bale [per acre], or 200 pounds of lint cotton, worth, say, $20. Twenty acres of this crop would therefore produce an income of $400. On tenant farms, where the tenant furnishes the labor, the custom is for the tenant to take half the crop and to pay half the fertilizer bill, making the income of the family about $175 per annum. This is for average conditions."

Most farms were thus too small to be economic. In 1880 four-fifths of all farms in the cotton belt had less than fifty acres planted in crops. The New South was, as Sidney Lanier and others said, a land of small farms, but it was not an area of small landowners. Unfortunately, census takers at that time counted farms according to operation rather than ownership, lumping owners, renters, and sharecroppers together and obscuring the pattern of ownership and tenancy. A plantation subdivided among ten sharecroppers was counted as ten farms rather than one plantation. On this basis of counting, the number of farms in the section multiplied 2½ times between 1860 and 1880 and the average size fell from 365 to 157 acres. In 1910, when census takers made a special survey of the black belt to correct this distortion, they found that land holdings averaged 724 acres and more than a third of them were plantations divided into five or more tenancies.[3]

The evils of sharecropping were only one of the things that plagued New South agriculture. Another problem was federal and state economic policy. Deflationary monetary policies encouraged a general decline in commodity prices through the last quarter of the century, and national banking policies operated to keep southern agriculture underfinanced. High tariffs raised the price of some manufactured goods while farm prices enjoyed no similar protection. On the state level, tax policy favored manufacturing over agriculture, and government was far more concerned about the problems of businessmen than those of farmers. Farmers themselves often contributed to their own problems. They tried to overcome the effects of falling prices by producing more of the same thing, only to depress prices still further and make it impossible to generate the capital they needed so badly.

The difficulty may be seen in banking, for one of the farmers' great needs was an adequate supply of low-cost credit. The South's banking and credit system was destroyed in the Civil War, and recovery was retarded by poverty, deflation, and a sectional bias in national banking policy. Legislation enacted during the war taxed state bank notes out of circulation and prohibited national banks from making mortgage loans. It also created a new system of national banks, but required each bank to have a minimum capitalization of $50,000 in communities of less than 6,000 people and $100,000 in larger places, sums difficult to raise in the war-ravaged South. The distribution of national bank charters and the circulation of national bank notes were therefore unequal. In 1869 there were only 26 national banks in eight deep South states compared to 829 in New York, Massachusetts, Pennsylvania, and Ohio, and those in the Confederate South had received only $10 million in national bank note circulation compared to $104 million received by New England banks alone. In Rhode Island the authorized circulation amounted to $77.16 per capita compared to 13 cents in Arkansas. By 1880 this situation had improved somewhat, but the South still had only one national bank for each 104,621 inhabitants compared to one for each 7,292 in New England. As late as 1895 the ten cotton states had only 417 national banks, and half of those were in Texas. State banks were unable to fill the void. In South Carolina, for example, state banking capacity did not reach antebellum levels until after 1900, and in Georgia in 1895 there were 123 counties that had no bank at all.

Sharecroppers and Tenants

Sharecropping was a way of life as well as an economic system, and one that encompassed an increasing portion of the agricultural population. The rate of farm tenancy—the portion of farms operated by nonowners—rose from 36 percent in 1880 to nearly 50 percent in 1900, and continued to rise until it passed 60 percent in the Great Depression of the 1930s. At the turn of the century, a third of all white farmers and three-quarters of all black farmers were tenants, though most tenants (55 percent) were whites. Census takers that year counted 678,743 white and 552,401 black tenants in the section, and if each tenant had three or four dependents the size of the tenant population becomes apparent.

The rise of tenancy paralleled the spread of cotton. In 1870 southern farmers tilled 9.2 million acres of the white staple, a figure that increased to 15.9 million acres in 1880 and 24.8 million in 1900, and continued its relentless rise to 34.4 million acres in 1920. Production rose less rapidly. The harvest of 5.7 million bales in 1879 was the first that surpassed the bumper crop of 1859, and that of 1897 was the first to exceed 10 million bales. In 1920 total production was more than 13.4 million bales. Prices fluctuated downward until the end of the century. The average was a good 16.1 cents a pound in 1869, but in the depression year of 1878 it fell to a marginal 8.16 cents and after a modest recovery ranged between 8 and 9 cents in the last half of the 1880s. In the disastrous year of 1894 it dropped below 5 cents, well under the cost of production, and remained below 7 cents until 1900, when a gradual rise took it above 13 cents in 1910 and to 35 cents in 1919 in the boom created by World War I.

Agriculture, indeed the whole economy, revolved around cotton, its production, ginning, marketing, shipping, and manufacture. The boll weevil, which invaded Texas from Mexico in 1892 and spread eastward at a rate of forty or fifty miles a year, was largely a problem of the future. Not until 1908 did the pest cross into Mississippi; but by 1920 it had spread through the Carolinas. Cotton, tenancy, and poverty —these were the trinity of influences that dominated the lives of most New South farmers. Cotton was more than a crop or an industry. It was a dynastic system, as Anne O'Hare McCormick once observed, with its own laws and standards and customs that were peculiarly resistant to change. "It certainly is a burden and a drag upon the life and spirit of the people of the South," Frank Tannenbaum wrote of the "white plague" in 1924. "Cotton is not only king; it is tyrant, and the people of the South, old and young, are its slaves."

There was much truth in this. Cotton was a labor-intensive crop that had to be plowed and hoed several times a year, and picking it was a back-breaking task that required a swollen work force from late summer until well into the fall. Its cultivation was almost a year-round operation that dictated the rhythms of life and bound farmers to what Ellen Glasgow once called "the relentless tyranny of the soil," leaving them little time or energy for anything else. Though *Barren Ground* (1925), in which Miss Glasgow made this remark, is not about cotton farmers, it is a compelling picture of the stifling effects of the hard work and cultural barrenness that afflicted poor farmers throughout the South. "All his life he had been a slave to the land," Miss Glasgow's protagonist, Dorinda Oakley, observed of her father, "harnessed to the elemental forces, struggling inarticulately against the blight of poverty and the barrenness of the soil."

Oakley's example could be multiplied by the hundreds of thousands, and the lives of such folk perpetuated the worst of rural life—isolation, provincialism, and ignorance as well as a peculiar combination of fatalism, inertia, and religious escapism that made for social ineffectuality. For most of the people it encompassed, cotton culture was correlated with social disorganization and the absence of group consciousness; and the resulting inability to combine for political purposes left poor farmers prey to more powerful groups, who found it easy to manipulate their prejudices or play on their credulity. This was one reason for the failure of the farmer protest movements that appeared sporadically in the section—and one reason those movements gave little attention to the problems of sharecroppers and agricultural laborers. Alternately neglected and manipulated by their economic and social superiors, the poorest of the South's agricultural population lived out their lives in quiet desperation amid (as one observer wrote in the 1920s) the "miserable panorama of unpainted shacks, rain gullied fields, straggling fences, rattletop Fords, dirt, poverty, disease, drudgery, and monotony that stretch[ed] for a thousand miles across the Cotton Belt."

Black sharecroppers were worse off than whites, since they had the additional burden of racial discrimination. They were cheated with greater impunity than white croppers, had more difficulty securing credit, and were unable to buy or own land in some areas. In 1880 blacks owned 7.3 percent of all farms in the South, including 6.7 percent of the total farm acreage, and rented an additional 3.4 percent of the acreage for cash, but during the next twenty years they barely held onto these proportions. White landlords, merchants, and bankers generally believed blacks were incapable of farming independently, and their treatment of black sharecroppers often made that belief self-fulfilling.

The Rise of Farmer Protest

The plight of agriculture did give rise to farmer protest. The first protest movement was that of the Patrons of Husbandry, popularly known as the Grange, an organization that originated in the Midwest and spread to the South in the early 1870s. At the peak of its strength in the middle of that decade, it had perhaps 125,000 members in the Confederate South, not including a substantial number in a separate Negro Grange. Like other farmer protest organizations, the Grange appeared first in the trans-Mississippi South and enjoyed its greatest strength in that part of the region. It spread to the Southeast, however, where its greatest appeal was in largely white areas of the piedmont. Its membership included landowners and tenants, though the former apparently predominated. Generally speaking, farmer protest groups seem to have had their chief appeal among small- and medium-sized landowners and mortgagees, a class constantly threatened with falling into tenancy.

The Grange addressed itself to a wide spectrum of farmer problems, especially the scarcity and high cost of credit, the profits of middlemen who handled and processed farm products, and the monopolistic practices of railroads and other big business interests on whom farmers were dependent. The focus of Grange activity was on self-help rather than politics, however, and centered around the sponsorship of business associations and other forms of cooperative activity. Grangers organized cooperative credit plans to provide low-interest loans to farmers, cooperative purchasing arrangements to eliminate middlemen and thus lower prices, and cooperative warehouses and "direct trade unions" to enable farmers and consumers to deal directly with each other. They also encouraged crop diversification, vocational education for farmers, public regulation of railroad rates, and inflationary monetary policies.

Their endeavors were thus directed toward real problems, but Grange cooperatives were often poorly managed and unable to overcome the opposition of established business interests, and in the continued depression of the 1870s farmers had difficulty paying their dues. When many cooperatives failed, confidence in the Grange diminished, and by 1877 the organization was no longer a significant force in the South. It had, however, defined the direction of farmer protest and set the pattern for later farmer movements. Its demise signaled not an end of farmer protest, but a period in which protest was diffused and ineffectual and problems were great. As the downward spiral of commodity prices continued, the burden of debt became greater. An obligation that equaled ten bales of cotton at 10 cents a pound rose the equivalent of more than a bale when the price fell to 9 cents. As the farmer's position seemed to deteriorate, that of the monopolists he dealt with seemed to rise—the merchant who carried his debt, the banker who held his mortgage, the railroad that shipped his cotton, or, more distantly, the fertilizer trust, the cotton seed oil trust, the jute bagging trust (which produced bagging for cotton bales), or the tobacco trust. But not until the late 1880s were farmers able to mount a potentially effective protest against the sources of their difficulties.

Industrial Development

The story of commerce and industry in the New South is notably different from that of agriculture.[4] In these areas recovery from the ravages of the Civil War was less difficult, and growth, in absolute terms, was considerable, especially after 1880. Returns on business investment were often good, and the quality of life among the urban middle class improved, as did the material condition of many workers, though most industrial workers remained powerless and in blighting poverty.

Industrial development in the New South was governed by two things, the section's resources and the nature of its economic dependence. Most industries were small, labor-intensive enterprises that paid low wages for jobs that were mostly unskilled or semiskilled. The principle activities were handling, shipping, and processing agricultural products, including food- and feedstuffs, and extracting timber and mineral resources. Cotton ginning, flour milling, lumbering, mining, railroading, retailing, oil drilling, and naval stores were the most important processing industries, while the production of textiles, that of tobacco products, and that of furniture were the leading manufacturing activities. Around Birmingham, Alabama, the manufacture of iron and steel created the section's largest complex of heavy industry. Most manufacturing enterprises remained small and independent throughout the period, but the consolidation of ownership in railroads, mineral resources, and steel and tobacco production signaled the arrival of big business in the South by the first decade of the twentieth century.

There were many reasons for the pattern of business and industrial growth. The South was rich in natural resources, and since the North had a head start in manufacturing, the extracting and processing of raw materials for northern industries were the readiest roads to economic development. Moreover, southerners had neither the financial resources nor the technical and entrepreneurial skills necessary to compete with northern industry, and this too influenced the pattern of development. Finally, the Conservative regimes encouraged economic growth and created a favorable economic and political climate for that purpose.

Even during the 1860s manufacturing grew notably, in marked contrast to agriculture. The number of manufacturing enterprises in the section increased 80 percent in that decade, the number of workers rose 30 percent, and the value of product was up 28 percent. Capital investment, however, increased only 3 percent and total wages only 8 percent. The early postwar recovery, which these figures reflect, was aided by the fact that the mostly white industrial work force was less disorganized than agricultural labor by the results of the Civil War.

By 1880 the political uncertainties of Reconstruction had receded, and the pace of industrial growth began to accelerate. Advocates of development began to speak of a New South of growth and prosperity. Their figures seemed impressive. Railroad mileage, which had been about 9,000 in 1865, reached 37,181 in 1890 and 54,102 in 1905. By 1890 capital invested in manufacturing had reached $402.5 million, and by 1905 $1,140 million. In that fifteen-year period the value of manufactured goods produced rose from $543.9 million to $1,267 million, and wages paid reached $203.1 million. In that harbinger of the New South, the manufacture of cotton textiles, growth rates were even greater. The number of spindles in operation almost doubled in the 1880s and more than doubled in the 1890s, invested capital rose from $22.8 million in 1880 to $132.4 million in 1900, and the amount of raw cotton consumed increased from 240,284 bales to 1,563,302. In North Carolina, the center of the industry, the number of textile employees exceeded 45,000 in 1902, and in the section as a whole the total was almost 100,000. The amount of bituminous coal mined in the South and border states increased from 6 million tons in 1880 to 26 million in 1890 and doubled again in the 1890s. The quantity of timber cut from southern forests doubled in the 1880s, and that too became a major economic activity.

These figures are more impressive in isolation than in a national context. In 1860 the South (including Kentucky) had had 17.2 percent of the nation's manufacturing establishments and 11.5 percent of the capital invested in manufacturing, but in 1904 the parallel figures were 15.3 percent and 11 percent respectively. In the same period the value of goods manufactured in the section rose from 10.3 percent to 10.5 percent of the national total. In a somewhat different period, 1859 to 1899, the portion of the nation's industrial workers in the southeastern states rose from 9.8 percent to 11.5 percent. In 1910 after all the growth was calculated, only 15 percent of all southerners gainfully employed were engaged in manufacturing.

The New South Movement

For all its growth, then, the New South barely held its own. In no significant category of measurement had the economic gaps between section and nation been closed. This is a basic fact to remember in evaluating both the New South and "the New South movement."[5] That movement consisted of men who envisioned a new South characterized by industrial growth, economic diversity, and other attributes of "progress," especially prosperity, liberal social change, national reconciliation, and racial paternalism.

No sooner had the stillness settled over Appomattox than sprouts of this movement began to appear. J. D. B. De Bow, Benjamin H. Hill, and others began to speak of the necessity for economic and social change. The South, they said, must adapt itself to the realities of a new era, and their message struck a responsive chord. A diverse assortment of ex-Whigs, Conservatives, urban businessmen, sectional moderates, and racial paternalists took up the message, and by 1880 had molded it into a coherent social creed that became a major theme of sectional thought for a generation. The New South as a state of mind if not an economic and social reality was born.

Its most important publicist was Henry W. Grady, editor of the Atlanta *Constitution* from 1880 until his untimely death in 1889. Son of a prominent Athens, Georgia, merchant, Grady rose to become one of the South's best-known and most appealing spokesmen. His address to the New England Society of New York in 1886 was the high-water mark of New South advocacy. Other important publicists included Richard H. Edmonds, who founded the *Manufacturers' Record* in Baltimore in 1882 and made it the foremost advocate of southern industrialization as well as the most complete chronicle of the progress toward that goal. In the lower South, Francis W. Dawson spread the New South creed through his Charleston *News and Courier,* while Henry Watterson did the same thing in the upper South through the Louisville *Courier-Journal.* Daniel A. Tompkins, a textile manufacturer who also owned the Charlotte, North Carolina, *Observer,* was another major advocate. William D. Kelley of Pennsylvania, whose interest in the South derived from investments in railroads, real estate, and minerals, was representative of the considerable number of northern businessmen who joined the movement. Among writers, Philip Alexander Bruce, whose *The Rise of the New South* (1905) was the most important contemporary assessment of the section, was a representative figure, and among liberal reformers, Walter Hines Page was the most important as well as the most exuberant promoter of economic development.

In its original form the New South creed was a straightforward analysis of the southern condition. The section, it held, was poor, its people frustrated, its politics ineffectual, and the basic reason was historical. The South had become entangled in the web of slavery and thus in economic imbalance, states' rights, racial extremism, and the social values those things necessitated. As a result, southerners had resisted progress and the forces of modernism—industrialization, urbanization, nationalism, and such liberalizing social movements as public education and racial paternalism. They had created a brilliant civilization in the Old South only to see it destroyed by the forces of history and modernization. The task in the aftermath was to face the present, not relive the past. Accordingly, the South must diversify its economy, integrate its transportation system, encourage industry. To do this, southerners must give up their agrarian ideals, welcome northern investment, absorb the virtues of the work ethic, and accommodate their society to the demands of the market place. They must also mute their sense of grievance, forgo abrasive sectionalism, and move their section into the mainstream of national development.

On the surface this seemed no more than a southern variation of the nineteenth-century doctrine of progress, but in reality it was much more. The economic and social changes it envisioned were more fundamental than its advocates acknowledged, and the creed therefore contained a contradiction. It promised liberal social change through industrialization but without threatening white supremacy or the economic and political supremacy of established groups. In operation, this contradiction was deepened, for the progress its advocates promised was negated by the kinds of industry they encouraged. Ostensibly a blueprint for overcoming the twin blights of poverty and defeat, the creed became in actuality a rationalization for economic exploitation and privilege. And since many who benefited from it were outsiders, it was also a formula for colonializing the southern economy and inveigling the southern people to accommodate themselves to the needs of the colonializers.

The liberal promise of the creed derived from the mechanistic, even deterministic influence it assigned to industrialism and economic growth. Social progress, it held, was the inevitable consequence of material advancement. "New regions will be lifted from the realm of darkness and opened to the good influence of the civilized world," wrote Philip Alexander Bruce in a striking illustration of this idea. "The growth of the brotherhood of Man that will certainly follow universal material development will be attended in the end by a more reverent sense of the fatherhood of God, and the deeper and keener this sense, the nearer will mankind be to the millenium." Economic development, Bruce wrote on another occasion, will bring the South "a more frequent and more diversified social intercourse, more varied and more refined amusements, a larger number of public schools, and a more thoroughly organized and more efficient system of public education." Infused with "the material spirit," towns and cities would become "centers of wealth and the seats of the highest culture and refinement." Cotton mill villages were already opening new economic and cultural vistas for mill workers, who "very naturally" had become "perhaps the most contented working people to be found in their branch of manufacture in the Union." Even when stated with more restraint, this was a hopeful promise, and one that a poor society uncertain of its future could hardly resist. The South would be saved, in Arthur W. Page's phrase, by "smokestacks and education."

The reality belied the promise. The progress of industry was slow, and poverty remained the reality for most southerners. Racial animosity persisted, farmer protest grew, and social backwardness remained a primary fact of life. The creed, however, served a psychological need as well as an economic function, and its transformation from a blueprint of hope into an ostensible description of actuality went largely unnoticed by contemporaries. But in the transformation the New South it described was no longer presented as an ideal to be striven for but as a reality already achieved.

The change was reflected in the most famous statement of the creed, Henry W. Grady's address to the New England Society of New York.[6] "What is the sum of our work?" Grady asked in a widely quoted passage. "We [in the South] have found ... that ... the free negro counts for more than he did as a slave. We have planted the school house on the hilltop and made it free to white and black. We have sowed towns and cities in the places of theories, and put business above politics. We have challenged your spinners in Massachusetts and your ironmakers in Pennsylvania. We have learned that the $400,000,000 annually received from our cotton crop will make us rich when the supplies that make it are home-raised. We have reduced the commercial rate of interest from 24 to 6 per cent., and are floating 4 per cent.

bonds. We have learned that one northern immigrant is worth fifty foreigners and have smoothed the path Southward, wiped out the place where the Mason and Dixon's line used to be." "We have established thrift in the city and country," he continued. "We have fallen in love with work."

The results, Grady declared, were cathartic. The South had solved the gnawing problems of economic dependence and race relations. "We have achieved ... a fuller independence for the South than that which our fathers sought to win," he said at a time when the section's economy was being colonialized. "No section shows a more prosperous laboring population than the negroes of the South, none in fuller sympathy with the employing and landowning class. [The Negro] shares our school fund, has the fullest protection of our laws and the friendship of our people." Consequently race relations are "close and cordial" and will remain so as long as outsiders keep hands off. In sum, "the new South presents a perfect democracy, the oligarchs leading in the popular movement—a social system compact and closely knitted, less splendid on the surface [than the Old South], but stronger at the core." The future is bright. "The new South is enamored of her new work. Her soul is stirred with the breath of a new life. The light of a grander day is falling fair on her face. She is thrilling with the consciousness of growing power and prosperity."

The New South creed had been transformed by positive thinking. Throughout this and other addresses, Grady's tone was as optimistic as his social analysis was shallow or false. Reflecting the booster's inveterate hopefulness, he and other apologists for the New South seized every sign of economic growth, every hint of racial peace, every instance of social reform as evidence that a new era had arrived. The problem with this was not the optimism displayed, for the South's needs were so great that without optimism its people might have despaired. It was instead the uncritical and often calculating nature of the analysis. Out of it grew what Paul M. Gaston has called the myth of the New South, according to which the section was already a land of progress, prosperity, and social harmony.

The myth was appealing. It enabled the Conservative governments that came to power during Redemption to rationalize problems they would not or could not confront, and thus made the governments as well as the problems more tolerable. It provided a rationale for the Solid South and thereby discouraged political insurgency even as it justified the actions by which the Conservatives quashed insurgency. In terms of public policy it rationalized the politics of laissez faire—assistance to developers, protection for property, hostility to labor unions and social protest. And while making the South safe for Conservatism, it assured northerners and the federal government that all was well in the section, thus encouraging both economic investment and a policy of noninterference in race relations. In all this it served the purposes of established elites, and became, in Gaston's words, "essentially an instrument manipulated by interest groups opposed to change."

In balance, then, the New South creed was a mixed blessing. It encouraged southerners to accept economic diversification, to look to the future instead of the past, and to mute racial and sectional antagonisms. It also helped them reconcile innovation and tradition, and believe that collectively they might do something to influence their own economic future. But it offered them a false analysis of their problems and pointed them toward false solutions. It encouraged them to accept uncritically the values of laissez faire capitalism and the middle-class ethic and to look away from economic and class factors in analyzing their problems. Influenced by social Darwinism, Anglo-Saxonism, and other forms of elitism then current, it fostered undemocratic racial and social values by endorsing a double standard in public policy for white and black, rich and poor, capital and labor, business and agriculture.

The Southernization of Industry

The result was that industry changed the New South less than the New South adapted industry to purposes of its own. Or put another way, the South began to industrialize without experiencing an industrial revolution, without undergoing the kinds of social and intellectual changes that marked the rise of industry and cities in the North. Several factors account for this fact. Most southern industries were small and the jobs they created mostly unskilled or semiskilled, and a disproportionate share of the work force was made up of the most dependent elements of the population—sharecroppers fresh off the farm, white women and children, and a few blacks in menial tasks—all of whom were paid minimal wages for unconscionably long hours of sweated toil in depressing and often hazardous conditions. Such industries perpetuated rather than broke the cycles of poverty and paternalism that beset the section. Much of the industrialization did not grow from changing values in southern society, but was imposed from outside or above, and thus did little to channel social change in progressive directions. It did not even spur urbanization. Though a few cities like Atlanta and Birmingham grew spectacularly, the New South remained overwhelmingly rural. In North Carolina, the state with the largest number of workers in manufacturing, 90.1 percent of the population was rural in

1900. In eleven southern states the proportion of the population residing in urban areas rose from 9.5 percent in 1880 to 13.5 percent in 1900, an annual rate of increase of .2 percent. In contrast, 30.6 percent of midwesterners lived in urban areas in 1900, and 58.6 percent of northeasterners.

The New South remained poor even as industry grew. According to a recent estimate, per capita income, including noncash income, in the Confederate South averaged $86 in 1880 and $100 in 1900.[7] The Census Bureau calculated per capita wealth in the section at $376 in 1880, a little more than one-third that of the rest of the country ($1,086). Twenty years later the figure for the section (including Kentucky) had risen to $509 compared to $1,175 for the nation as a whole, and the figure continued to rise thereafter. But the vagaries of progress were such that the prosperity of the new century widened the absolute gap in these figures. In 1912 the section's per capita wealth stood at $993 compared to $1,950 for the nation as a whole.

The southernization of industry is best seen in the manufacture of cotton textiles. The growth of this industry paralleled the rise of the New South, and no other enterprise absorbed so much of the energy of New Southists or was so often cited by them as the source of economic salvation. Unlike some of the other industries, this one grew out of local enterprise, and during its formative stages was financed almost exclusively by local capital. Not until the turn of the century did the lures of lower labor and transportation costs, special tax incentives, and the absence of unions attract northern textile manufacturers to the South. But once they began to come, the section became the leading textile manufacturing region in the country. By 1904 southern mills were consuming more cotton and producing more yarn than those of New England, and by World War I they were producing half the nation's textile products.

The industry developed according to the pattern pioneered by William Gregg in the factory and mill village he built at Graniteville, South Carolina, before the Civil War. Most factories were located in unincorporated rural areas of the piedmont from western Virginia to central Alabama. Around them were built relatively self-contained mill villages that were also owned and operated by the manufacturing company.[8] These villages contained housing for the workers, who were often hired by the family, and an assortment of social institutions to serve their needs, often including a school, a general store, and a church, and sometimes a lunch room, a medical center, a recreational area, and even garden plots. The villages might therefore have their own minister, school teacher, merchant, social worker, and policeman, all employed by the company.

There were certain advantages in this arrangement. Since most employees were poor whites from rural areas, the villages provided them with better housing and more social intercourse than they had ever had before. But the villages also served to segregate mill workers from the general population and subject them to a paternalism more like that of the plantation than modern industry. Like sharecropping, this system tended to extrude the worst features of paternalism, but it was a paternalism of class rather than race. Owners and managers and workers were all southern whites, and the relationship between them was transient and controlled by economic forces. Like sharecroppers, mill employees were also hired by the family, but unlike sharecropping, mill employment sometimes undermined family roles. Sometimes mothers and children worked while husbands and fathers remained idle, because wage rates for women and children were lower than those for men and the employment of men was therefore held to a minimum. In North Carolina in 1902, the mill work force included 18,177 men, 18,871 women, and 7,996 children under fourteen years of age. Daily wages then averaged around 30 cents for children, 30 to 75 cents for unskilled women, 60 cents to $1 for unskilled men, $1.50 for skilled women, and $2.50 for skilled men. Work weeks averaged sixty-five to seventy hours, though stoppages were common when inventories piled up, and annual earnings were less than the above figures suggest. In all of these things mill workers in the South were worse off than those in New England. Southern mills, however, were often better investments. In 1900 they paid an average return on investment of 15 percent, and some of them paid double and even quadruple that figure.

At first the workers seem not to have questioned mill paternalism, for they had been used to inequities all their lives. Those who flocked to the mills for employment were rural folk squeezed off the land by tenancy or the difficulty of making ends meet as farmers. Perhaps most of them had been sharecroppers, and perhaps most were totally or functionally illiterate. They came to the mills to escape poverty, isolation, and unrewarding toil, and to seek the better life that regular cash wages seemed to promise. To a cropper and his family who year after year saw little or no "cash money," the prospect of earning $5 or $10 a week more than balanced the distastefulness of long hours of monotonous indoor work and the scorn other people had for mill folk.

The reality, they soon found, was far different from the prospect. The work was not physically arduous, but it was far more tedious and dispiriting than farming and was not rationalized by agrarian myths of independence and individualism. It was indoors in sweltering rooms of dank air made leaden with lint, the prolonged breathing of which produced respiratory ailments and susceptibility to consumption (pulmonary tuberculosis). Before long the workers had taken on the sallow coloration and distracted look of the "lint head" stereotype, and their very appearance became a badge of shame. They were a trapped folk, especially those of the first generation, boxed in by fatalism as well as powerlessness. Suspicious by nature of social organization, they found it difficult to see their plight in class terms, and their social energies were directed not at reforming their condition, which they seemed to regard as a natural phenomenon like the weather or crop failure, but at accommodating to it and easing its disappointments.

But that was only at first. They soon concluded that mill paternalism was more grating than that of sharecropping, and they began to develop an objective awareness of their condition. One reason for this seems to have been their segregation into mill villages, which gave them a sense of group identity they never had on the farm. This led them sporadically and uncertainly toward organization, sometimes on their own but often through national union organizers. In the 1880s many of them joined the Knights of Labor, which in 1886 claimed 30,000 members in 487 locals in ten southern states. Later, many of them supported the National Union of Textile Workers, an affiliate of the American Federation of Labor, which between 1898 and 1902 undertook a concerted effort to organize southern textile workers. However, a succession of strikes in Augusta, Georgia, Danville, Virginia, and across the Carolina piedmont ended in complete failure for the union, and textile workers remained almost completely unorganized.

The reason for the failure was not, as New South paternalists insisted, that textile workers were docile and satisfied with their condition. It was instead the ruthlessness of mill management. This fact is documented in Melton A. McLaurin's study of union activity in textile mills in the New South, *Paternalism and Protest* (1971). Mill owners, McLaurin shows, were determined to prevent unionism and willing to do whatever was necessary to accomplish that purpose. They planted spies and *agents provocateurs* in employee organizations, locked strikers out of plants and evicted them from company housing, hired strikebreakers, blacklisted union activists, threatened to close plants permanently or to hire only black workers, tried to discredit unions as unsouthern and organizers as Carpetbaggers, and, where necessary, provoked violence to produce public reaction against union activity. They made skillful use of the surplus of labor in the section and the general hostility to unions. They encouraged the public to equate industry with progress and to believe that industrial development depended upon keeping unions out of the South. Almost invariably, police officials, judges, and political leaders cooperated in these endeavors, as did merchants, bankers, editors, and ministers. The wonder is not that the workers always lost, but that they tried so often to organize. So complete was their failure, however, that in 1903 textile unionism was virtually nonexistent in the section.

Both the South and the mill workers were losers. As communities, the mill villages stagnated. "They give the South no poets, no artists, no politicians, no builders, no engineers, no technicians, no leaders in any field of activity," wrote Frank Tannenbaum in *Darker Phases of the South* (1924). "In the last twenty years," he quoted an unnamed scholar as saying, "out of a population of some three hundred thousand mill people in the state of North Carolina there is not a single person of county importance who has come from the mill village." Perhaps this was exaggeration, but the point was valid. Mill villagers like sharecroppers were casualties of progress in the New South.

The Limits of Economic Development

Forty years after Appomattox the South's economy had still not recovered from the Civil War, and another forty years would pass before general progress was made in overcoming the relative backwardness of the section. Long after the New South era ended, the states of the Confederate South remained at or near the bottom of the nation on all indices of social and economic wellbeing: per capita income and wealth, education and literacy, health care, and others. The absolute progress made in these areas after 1900 helped many people, but it did little to overcome the disparity between section and nation. To use Richard A. Easterlin's calculations again, per capita income in the section rose from 51 percent of the national average in 1880 and 1900 to 62 percent in 1920, but fell back to 55 percent in 1930. The net improvement in fifty years was four percentage points.

Why was this so?[9] The experience of Japan and Germany after World War II suggests that the reason was not simply the destructiveness of war or the total defeat of a popular cause. Nor was it due to a lack of natural resources, for the South had significant deposits of coal, iron ore, and oil, the most essential ingredients of modern industrialization, as well as natural gas, sulfur, phosphates, and other resources that became increasingly important in the twentieth century. It also had an abundance of timber, arable land, rainfall, water power, and transport, as well as a temperate climate, a large supply of willing labor, and an intelligent and resourceful population. Furthermore, state and local governments were sympathetic to development, and investors found the area quite profitable.

The chief problems seem to have been institutional and ideological. These made the South and its people resistant to the social changes necessary for the kind of economic development then occurring in the North. The South emerged from the Civil War economically and socially imbalanced (by northern standards), and some of its institutions and attitudes functioned to perpetuate that condition. The section was too agricultural, its urban middle class too small, its social services too underdeveloped, its hostility to liberal attitudes too pronounced, its poverty too widespread to fall into the northern pattern of development. In addition, federal economic policy, the North's head start, and the growing colonialization of the South's economy operated in the same direction, holding the section in a dependent economic position that helped sustain the pattern of poverty and imbalance. Predictably, the industry that developed was small and low in the value added by manufacturing, and almost as imbalanced as agriculture. So large was the role of textile manufacturing that Douglas F. Dowd has said with pardonable exaggeration that the section "changed from a one-crop agriculture to a virtually one-product industry."

The growth of manufacturing thus had few of the promised results. Agriculture remained stifled by tenancy, landlordism, and racial prejudice. Like the soil they worked, farmers in the New South became and remained depleted. Southern agriculture, unlike that of the Middle West, kept farmers poor and dependent. Urbanization lagged, and southern cities served neither to enlarge markets for agricultural products nor to draw off surplus farm population. Here too the contrast with the Midwest was instructive. The economic development that did occur failed to break the values and institutional arrangements that inhibited social liberalism. Investment in education and other forms of social overhead was limited. The southern mind remained traditional, clinging to its provincialisms—that is, to the things that made it southern —unreceptive to scientific rationalism and social criticism. Much of this was due to the New Southists, who were no more committed to liberal social change than were more straightforward traditionalists. "So far from representing a deliberate break with the past," Wilbur J. Cash wrote, "the turn to Progress clearly flowed straight out of that past and constituted in a real sense an emanation from the will to maintain the South in its essential integrity."

But there was one major change in all this, the spreading economic colonialism. Northern investment was responsible for much of the growth after 1880, but the growth masked the detrimental effects of outside ownership. As major segments of the economy came under northern control, economic decision making was removed from the South and profits were drained away. In 1868, for example, northerners controlled only a negligible proportion of southern railroads. Only 11 of the 280 directors of twenty-five major railroad companies at that time were northerners. By 1900, however, fully 90 percent of the section's mileage was in the hands of northern-owned companies, and it was southern influence that was now almost negligible. Every major line, including the Southern Railway, the Louisville and Nashville, the Atlantic Coast Line, the Seaboard Air Line, and the Illinois Central, was now northern-controlled.

In other areas of the economy a similar, if less complete, pattern of takeover occurred. By the early twentieth century perhaps half the great sugar plantations of Louisiana were northern-owned and a third or more of the large cotton plantations in the lower Mississippi Valley. Large tracts of land and vast stands of timber had been acquired by northerners or Europeans, as had many valuable enterprises in mining and heavy industry. In 1907 the United States Steel Corporation, controlled by J. P. Morgan, took over the giant Tennessee Coal, Iron, and Railroad Company, the principal steel producer in Birmingham, Alabama, whose assets included the vast iron and coal deposits in northern Alabama and southern Tennessee. Except for the oil and gas deposits in Texas and Louisiana, these were the most valuable natural resources of the South, and for them Morgan paid about $35 million, though the mineral deposits alone were estimated to be worth $1 billion.

The Morgan interests, which also acquired control of every major railroad system in the Southeast, made economic decisions not for the purpose of harming or benefiting the South, but for maximizing their own profits. Yet the Morgan holdings were so vast that their decisions became a significant factor in the South's economic development, serving to increase and perpetuate colonialism. A major reason for acquiring the Tennessee Coal, Iron, and Railroad Company was to eliminate competition between Birmingham steel producers and United States Steel's much larger Pittsburgh works. This was accomplished by the "Pittsburgh plus" pricing system, under which steel produced in Birmingham was priced at a level equal to the cost of steel produced in Pittsburgh plus the cost of shipping steel from Pittsburgh to wherever the Birmingham steel was sold. Now, the cost of producing steel in Birmingham was significantly below the cost of producing it in Pittsburgh, yet under this formula Birmingham steel had no competitive advantage even in the markets of Birmingham. In 1909 this system was modified by the "Birmingham differential," a surcharge of $3 a ton added to the "Pittsburgh plus" price, and Birmingham steel was placed at a competitive disadvantage even in Birmingham. Back in 1893 southern mills had produced 22 percent of the nation's pig iron but in 1913 they accounted for only 11 percent. This made sense for Morgan's profit structure but not for the economic wellbeing of the South.

Morgan's domination of southern railroads helped perpetuate a similar disadvantage. Back in the 1870s and 1880s, the nation's major railroad companies had instituted a system of differential freight rates, the purpose of which was to rationalize profit structures while serving the interests of major shippers. One effect of the system was to discriminate against the South by discouraging economic diversification there. This was not a conscious purpose of the arrangement but a result of the fact that it benefited preexisting patterns of traffic. Shipping prices were determined not by weight, volume, and distance, but by the desire to maximize railroad profits. Rates were generally higher in the South than the Northeast, in part because the volume of two-way traffic was lower due to lower population density and less consumer demand. More importantly, the rates were set so that northern manufacturers of finished goods and southern producers of raw materials each had certain advantages. Thus the shipment of southern cotton to New England textile mills was relatively cheaper than the shipment of southern textile products to New England markets. In addition shippers within the South, whether of raw materials or manufactured goods, did not share the advantages of shippers of raw materials into the Northeast. Early in the century, for example, the price of shipping 100 pounds of cotton from Little Rock, Arkansas, to Fall River, Massachusetts, was 47 cents, but to ship the same cotton to Columbia, South Carolina, cost 68 cents.

After 1900 the process of colonialization accelerated. Many of the South's oil, natural gas, and sulfur deposits were acquired by northerners, and after 1910 more and more of the textile industry as well. There were some exceptions. The manufacture of tobacco products, monopolized by James B. Duke's American Tobacco Company, remained in southern hands, but such an exception only proved the general rule. "Like republics below the Rio Grande," C. Vann Woodward has written of these developments, "the South was limited to the role of a producer of raw materials, a tributary of industrial powers, an economy dominated by absentee owners."

The observation is a fitting capsulation of much of the economic development of the New South.

The Conservative Regimes

"Politics is the South's number one problem," V. O. Key wrote, and his observation is especially relevant to the post-Reconstruction era. Between the Compromise of 1877 and the demise of Populist insurgency in 1896, the South was wracked by political turmoil and, in another of Key's phrases, the pathology of democracy. Its politics was dominated by white-hot memories of Reconstruction and Redemption and the myths that already enshrouded those experiences, and by gnawing problems of poverty and social unrest. The period was a watershed in the political history of the section, out of which came the forms and techniques, and most of the issues, that dominated politics for a half century after it ended.[1]

Ostensibly, politics in the period revolved around race and home rule, but in reality matters of class and economics were more important. The issue at stake was not white supremacy—that had been assured by Redemption—but which whites would be supreme and what purposes their supremacy would serve. The coalition that redeemed the South soon broke into two elements. The first and most important element revolved around the loose but effective alliance between businessmen, black belt planters, and urban groups professionally and financially tied to development interests. The second encompassed the mass of white farmers and laborers and an assortment of traditionalists opposed to industrialization and urbanization. Caught in the middle were blacks, whose political role was one of the things that divided whites. Fragmented along racial, occupational, and geographical lines, the mass of southerners were an easy prey to the machinations of the businessman-planter coalition.

The Conservatives

The men of this coalition have been variously called Conservatives, Bourbons, Redeemers, New Departure Democrats, and Confederate

Brigadiers. Following the lead of contemporaries, most historians call them Bourbons, a name that originally suggested, by way of parallel with the royal family returned to the French throne after the defeat of Napoleon, the restoration of an old order, and thus political legitimacy and social reaction. As the Memphis *Appeal* put it, the Bourbons were "a class of old politicians who . . . forgetting nothing and learning nothing, do not recognize any issue as settled by the [civil] war and are ready to inaugurate another rebellion."

The limitations of such a name are obvious. The *Appeal's* definition does not describe the men who controlled southern politics in the aftermath of Redemption; and as historians use it, the term "Bourbon" generally connotes business conservatism and social reaction. C. Vann Woodward, who has studied these men more systematically than anyone else, rejected the name Bourbon altogether in favor of Redeemer, a designation that suggests their common experience and something of their common purpose. However, the men called themselves Conservatives, and that term will be used here, though it too is not entirely satisfactory. They were a diverse group of men, not always in agreement on policies or purpose. Generally speaking they were innovators in economic matters, moderates in race policy once white supremacy was assured, extremists in politics when their own supremacy was threatened, and profoundly conservative in most matters of social policy. What held them together was the common desire for office and a common resolve to reconcile certain forms of innovation with certain elements of tradition.

They were a fascinating, often unattractive lot of men: the troika who ruled Georgia for two decades, Joseph E. Brown, John B. Gordon, and Alfred H. Colquit; the equally durable Mississippi triumvirate, L. Q. C. Lamar, James Z. George, and Edward C. Walthall; Wade Hampton of South Carolina, one of their most commanding figures, and his lieutenant Matthew C. Butler; Governors Francis T. Nicholls of Louisiana, George F. Drew of Florida, and George S. Houston of Alabama, men widely different in background and public purpose; businessman Arthur S. Colyar in Tennessee; and others in and out of politics and business. These men were anything but reactionaries. They did not espouse ancient principles unbendingly or look backward to a golden age in the past. Though some of them were planters, especially in a state like South Carolina, most of them sought not to restore planter hegemony or revive the antebellum social order and its agrarian ideals. On the contrary, their values as well as purposes were bourgeois. They were Whiggish in economic matters, pragmatic in pursuing objectives, united not by common loyalties to a traditional South (though they paid homage to sectional traditions and sometimes used them cynically), but by a common desire for economic advantage and political power.

It is easy to criticize them, for in retrospect their faults loom larger than their virtues. It is also easy to underestimate their significance in southern history. "They left a lasting record of achievement," as Francis B. Simkins once observed. It is doubtful if that record was, as Simkins suggested, "greater than that of any generation of Southerners since the Founding Fathers"; yet their influence on subsequent generations was greater than that of any of their contemporaries, and they are therefore the most important group in the political history of the New South.

Their purpose was, as one of them said, to give the South "white supremacy, peace and prosperity, good government, and low taxation." Redemption had been the first step toward these ends. The next steps, pursued simultaneously, were to contain the blacks, fend off the federal government, mute sectional animosity, and stimulate economic development. In the aftermath of Reconstruction, Conservatives believed, the South was in need of nothing as much as economic development. New factories, railroads, mines, plants, mills, banks, retail stores—these were the crying needs, and to get them it was necessary to encourage investment in commerce and manufacturing and facilitate the exploitation of natural and human resources. These things in turn depended upon securing federal expenditures for internal improvements (as promised in the Compromise of 1877) and attracting northern capital, which could be done only if the South were made politically conservative and economically stable. Toward this end Conservatives involved themselves both as individuals and as a political elite in the South's economic development, and gained politically as well as personally from doing so. They served northern and European interests as corporation counsels, directors, and publicists, securing influence, dispensing privilege, and generally furnishing a southern connection that neutralized every suggestion of Carpetbaggery. Through it all, their motives were civic and disinterested as well as personal and partisan. Like other groups in and out of the South, they tended to equate their own interests with the general welfare, and that fact only partially compromised their purpose.

John B. Gordon was a representative figure. Courtly in manner, dashing in appearance, a hero at Appomattox in the dying hours of the Confederacy, General Gordon was one of the most popular figures in the postwar South, a living embodiment of the Lost Cause whose memory he helped keep alive. His stature in this regard was evidenced by his election in 1889 as the first commander of the United Confederate

Veterans. But that was only one dimension of his postwar career. Gordon was also one of the trio of men who controlled Georgia politics after Redemption, and between 1873 and 1897 he served two terms in the United States Senate and two as governor of the state, and his political influence was felt across the South. In addition, he was a prominent advocate of industry and business and one of the New South's most effective apologists, in which role his political influence and standing as a Confederate hero served him well. For a time he was a well-paid counsel for the Louisville and Nashville railroad, already under northern control, and he invested in manufacturing, mining, and real estate as well as railroads. Across the South Gordon spread the twin gospels of economic development and Confederate tradition, and used his prestige to protect Conservative rule. Political conservatism, economic development, and sectional loyalties sometimes cynically manipulated—these were the basic concerns of General Gordon and the Conservatives.

The Politics of Conservative Rule

To accomplish their purposes, the Conservatives had to hold on to the political dominance they won during Redemption. This was not easy. In the aftermath of Reconstruction the southern people were deeply divided on public issues. The divisions were economic, geographical, and ideological as well as racial and political, and the resulting differences produced a series of insurgencies against Conservative rule in the early 1880s. The immediate objects of controversy were the social and economic policies of the Conservative governments, but the basic issues were deeper: Who would control government and whose interests would government serve? What kinds of property would be taxed and at what rates? At what level would education and welfare services be funded? What would be done to help the embattled farmer? Would a portion of the state debts incurred during Reconstruction be repudiated? Would legislatures be apportioned according to total population (thus enhancing the power of the black belt and the white oligarchies in control there) or according to voter registration or some other basis that would benefit white counties and political insurgents? Would railroads and other monopolies be regulated by public bodies? And what was the best way to protect white supremacy?

On these questions Conservatives often took the unpopular side, and that was the source of their difficulty. Many of the programs they espoused did not have the support of the voting public. Their favoritism toward business was often pronounced, and their tax policies favored business and personality over farmers and realty. Between 1876 and

1880, to illustrate, state revenues in Virginia averaged $2,236,100 annually, of which corporations paid an average of $72,300. Conservative governments made generous tax concessions to attract new factories and railroads—exemptions from all levies for ten years was not uncommon—and the remitted taxes meant limited social services or higher rates for someone else. The tax structure became a patchwork of inequities, and only the startlingly low rates made it acceptable. In 1880 state tax collections in Virginia averaged $1.88 per capita.

Low taxes meant retrenchment in education and social services. During Reconstruction the Radicals had expanded those services and developed tax structures to finance them. With a different order of priorities, Conservatives revamped those tax structures, bringing them in line with the principles of political and economic laissez faire, and the level of government services was reduced. Such problems as poverty, illiteracy, racism, sexism, child labor, and violence were dealt with by neglect, as were the pressing needs of farmers, mill workers, and other dependent groups.

What happened in education was representative.[2] Conservatives were little committed to the values attached to public education in democratic societies. They saw little need for mass education and even less for academic freedom and social criticism, and their administrations were marked by niggardly disregard of the South's educational needs. Those needs were great, too great to be solved in the short run, for poverty made it impossible to finance education and other services at adequate levels. Racial segregation necessitated a dual school system and thus added to the potential cost, though in practice segregation became a device for denying blacks education and thereby economizing at their expense. The high birth rate meant a large school-age population and was another source of potential cost. (In 1880, to illustrate, only 446 of every 1,000 southerners were adults compared to 524 of every 1,000 northeasterners.)

For all these reasons educational progress was modest. As late as 1900, after some progress had been made, the annual expenditure on public education in North Carolina and Alabama averaged only 50 cents for each school-age child, while those in Florida and Texas, the two most generous states, amounted to $1.46 (compared to a national average of $2.84). The typical school was in session less than four and a half months, compared to more than seven months in the rest of the nation, and teachers were paid little more than half the national average. No southern state had a compulsory attendance law, though almost all the other states did, and attendance was far below national norms. Part but not all of this dismal showing was due to the neglect of black education. In South Carolina blacks constituted 61 percent of the school-age population in 1900 but received only 23 percent of the public school fund, and similar though less pronounced disparities existed in the other states.

Under these circumstances the progress made was largely symbolic, though an essential base was being laid for later improvements. The Conservative governments did not abandon the principle of public education or the idea that blacks are entitled to a share of the school fund. Religious and philanthropic groups, largely from the North, established a number of private institutions at all levels, and their endeavors were especially important for the education of blacks. In 1882, for example, northerners donated $1.7 million to southern education, $1.3 million of which went to black institutions. Overall, the most important measure of educational progress was the falling rate of illiteracy, especially among blacks, which reflected the spread of rudimentary education across the section. Still, about one-eighth of all whites and nearly half of all blacks over ten years of age were illiterate at the turn of the century. In the deep South this amounted to nearly a third of the total population. As President John C. Kilgo of Trinity College said in 1903, the public schools of the South could "scarcely be said to stand for education, but only against illiteracy."

The effects of Conservative social policy fell heaviest upon the poor, especially farmers and blacks, and those groups mounted a succession of political insurgencies. The insurgencies were largely futile, but together they had a major impact on the politics of the period. The force behind them was chiefly economic, but that fact was often obscured by crosscurrents of race. Black voting was still widespread, and whites were afraid that divisions among themselves would give blacks the balance of power. Apparently a majority of black men in nine of the ex-Confederate states voted in the presidential election of 1880, and lesser but still large proportions continued to vote throughout the decade. Yet the Conservative governments were so unresponsive to the needs of farmers and other poor whites that those groups turned increasingly to political insurgency and in doing so often sought the support of black voters.

The black electorate thus had conflicting influences. It discouraged political division among white voters but offered white insurgents a potentially large bloc of votes against the Conservatives. The grievances of blacks and poor whites were often the same, yet the racism of poor whites made it difficult for blacks to join with them politically. The latter factor plus the economic dependence of blacks and the persistence of paternalism between them and upper-class whites enabled Conservatives generally to turn the black vote to their own advantage. Conservatives seem to have gotten a considerable share of the black votes actually cast, and in the black belt they often counted an even larger share for themselves than they honestly got. Despite this, the mere existence of a large black electorate exerted a moderating influence on white politicians. Conservatives regularly solicited black votes and made token concessions to get them, while white insurgents tried to keep political attention focused on economic rather than racial issues.

In any event the significance of the black vote was enhanced by the willingness of whites to engage in political protest. In ten ex-Confederate states in the early 1880s, between a third and a half of all votes cast in statewide elections went typically to a party other than the Democrats. According to the estimates in J. Morgan Kousser's *The Shaping of Southern Politics . . . 1880–1910* (1974), between a sixth and a third of this non-Democratic vote was cast by whites, either for Republicans or one of the recurring third parties, variously called Independents, Greenbackers, Readjusters, or Fusionists. In 1879 the Democrats actually lost control of Virginia to a fusion of Readjusters and Republicans.

The Virginia Readjusters may be used to indicate the nature of anti-Conservative insurgency.[3] The Readjusters, who controlled the state government between 1879 and 1883, derived their name from the effort to readjust the state's enormous debt, most of which had been incurred before the Civil War. They believed that since everything else in the antebellum regime had perished in the war, including much of the state's tax base, a large part of the now burdensome debt should be repudiated. (There were parallel movements in all the states to pare down debts incurred during Radical Reconstruction. Those movements, however, were led by Conservatives, and the debts they questioned were often fraudulently incurred. Altogether the Conservative governments repudiated well over $100 million of state obligations, with only a temporary impairment of state credit ratings.)

Debt was only one of the concerns of the Readjusters; their larger purpose was to democratize Virginia politics and make its government more responsive to popular needs. Basically, theirs was an effort to unite blacks and poor whites in the cause of social and political reform; and their victory in 1879, which elevated William E. Cameron to the governorship and William H. Mahone to the United States Senate two years later, was due to popular disappointment with the Conservative administrations of Governors Gilbert C. Walker and James L. Kemper. The Readjusters gave Virginia the most liberal government it had ever had. They repealed the poll tax Conservatives had enacted to curtail voting, raised taxes on railroads and other businesses, increased appropriations for education and public welfare, created a college for blacks, gave state charters and thus special protections to labor unions, and sought to moderate the racial issue. For all this, they were defeated in 1883 in an election contest notable for the widespread use Conservatives made of fraud and racist manipulations.

These tactics demonstrate the effects insurgency had on Conservatives and Conservatism. The retrenchment of social services and disregard for the needs of farmers and other poor people were policies that originated not in callousness but calculation, in the Conservative conviction that the best way to help the South was to encourage economic development. Conservatives in effect revised Jeffersonian political philosophy to suit their own purposes. That government is best, they seemed to say, that governs least, except insofar as it assists developers, protects property and prerogative, and controls economic and political insurgents. The persistence of political protest, however, forced Conservatives to give less and less attention to the program by which they hoped to improve the South and more and more to maintaining their hold on political office. What began as a desire to advance the South through economic growth became in execution a device for controlling the section in the interest of privileged groups. In effect Conservatives sacrificed the ends of their program in the process of securing the means necessary to implement it. To quell insurgency and remain in office, they found it necessary to manipulate racial and sectional prejudices and engage in widespread fraud and violence, and in the process they became more and more dependent on the economic interests that sustained them. As a result the potential good in their program was diminished while the ills were magnified. This more than any other single fact explains and largely justifies their low historical reputation. Their hope for white unity under their own aegis proved illusory, yet they were convinced that only their policies and leadership could save the South. So they turned again to the tactics of Redemption. This time, however, they used the tactics not against blacks or outsiders, but against their fellow southern whites. Violence, ballot box stuffing, vote buying, and certifying fraudulent returns thus became as much a part of the Conservative era as of the Redemption campaigns.

It is another of the sorry chapters in southern history. Election contests became a form of social warfare, and politics the art of fraud and duplicity. Having earlier denounced the Reconstruction regimes as corrupt and unrepresentative of the southern people, Conservatives now presided over governments that were more corrupt and subservient to special interests. Posing as champions of white supremacy and racial solidarity, they used their control of black votes and the election machinery to subvert the will of the majority of whites. While nourishing legends about the Old South and the Lost Cause, they were busy creating a new and quite different South. Waging rhetorical battles against imaginary political Carpetbaggers, they helped economic Carpetbaggers colonialize the section's economy. Proclaiming the sanctity of states' rights in racial matters, they worked long and hard to expand federal activity in internal improvements.

If some of this was pragmatism, much of it was calculation. It is impossible to know the extent of violence, fraud, and chicanery that sustained it, but these were certainly widespread and Conservatives were not entirely responsible. The number of deaths from political violence in Louisiana in 1878 has been variously estimated between thirty and fifty, and the elections there that year showed, in William I. Hair's words, a "general pattern of fraud across the state." Under Conservative rule, Hair reports, "the entire political structure of [Louisiana] came to rest upon a rotten pedestal—the manipulated thousands of Negro voters." Between 1880 and 1888, the Bourbons, as Hair calls them, added 50,000 blacks to the voter registration lists, and in the latter year the number of registrants was larger than the total of adult black males counted in the census of 1890. Virginia, at the other end of the South, was less corrupt than Louisiana, but there too, in Raymond J. Pulley's words, "wholesale bribery and ballot-box stuffing" sometimes occurred. Elections in Virginia were "a farce," wrote a contemporary observer; state and local governments in the Old Dominion rested upon "fraud and chicanery." To turn the Readjusters out of office in 1883, not only did Virginia Conservatives use the electoral tactics Pulley referred to, but some of their supporters staged a murderous race riot at Danville and used the incident as evidence that Readjusters were encouraging a general uprising of blacks.

Mississippi Conservatives were plagued by a black majority as well as a restive minority of poor white farmers, and their use of desperate measures was especially widespread. "It is no secret that there has not been a full vote and a fair count in Mississippi since 1875 [when the state was redeemed]—that we have been preserving the supremacy of white people by revolutionary methods," Judge J. J. Christman told delegates to the state constitutional convention in 1890. "In plain words, we have been stuffing ballot-boxes, committing perjury, and here and there in the state carrying the elections by fraud and violence until the whole machinery of government was about to rot down." Eleven years later former Governor William C. Oates said much the same thing in the Alabama constitutional convention. "White men have gotten to cheating each other," he said, "until we don't have any honest elections."

The Significance of Fraud

The activities Christman and Oates described are greatly in need of study, not only to document their extent but to assess their significance in the history of the South. That Christman and Oates were not exaggerating is apparent from every relevant study of the histories of Mississippi and Alabama. Moreover, similar though sometimes less extreme situations existed elsewhere. No state has been found by its historians to have escaped the fraud, and indications are that this phenomenon was more widespread in the South than elsewhere. Of 183 contested elections to the national House of Representatives between 1875 and 1901, for example, 107 were from twelve southern states, and most of them involved charges of fraud.

The extent of fraud seems to have varied according to the seriousness of the threat to Conservative supremacy. The most pointed threat came during the Populist revolt between 1892 and 1896 and produced the most flagrant instances of fraud. Fifteen blacks and "several" whites were reportedly killed during the 1892 election campaign in Georgia. In that year and again in 1894, Thomas E. Watson of Georgia, the most important leader of southern Populism, was denied reelection to the United States House of Representatives in blatant instances of fraud. In order to prevent Watson's reelection in 1892, the election board of Richmond County (Augusta) certified a vote total from the county almost twice as large as the number of registered voters. In neighboring Alabama Populist leader Reuben F. Kolb was similarly denied the governorship in 1892 and 1894, and in Louisiana the same fate befell Populist candidates in two congressional districts in 1894 and in the gubernatorial election of 1896.

The significance of this phenomenon is less apparent than the extent. It is clear, however, that had politics been open and honest, with every adult male free to register and vote his convictions without pressure or bribery and every vote honestly counted, the political history of the New South would have been vastly different. Redemption might never have come and certainly not as it did, and even if it had come, the Conservative regimes would have been repudiated or so chastened at the polls that their policies would perforce have been greatly modified. If that had happened, social problems might have been addressed more successfully and political divisions might have evolved more normally. The pattern of economic development might therefore have been altered; agriculture might have been made healthier and industry developed in a different context. In a polity accustomed to black voting, the race issue might have been moderated, politics made more realistic, the two-party system preserved, and the Solid South died aborning.

The Potential for Moderation

These might-have-beens suggest that the controlling factor in southern politics between the late '70s and early '90s was not poverty or defeat or the frustrations of poor farmers, or even racial prejudice, but the single-mindedness of Conservatives and the circumstances that enabled them to remain politically dominant. The fraud and irresponsibility that characterized New South politics were not so much expressions of the popular will as denials or manipulations of it. That this was so requires explanation, for it suggests that there existed a moderate impulse among southerners that has not been previously stressed. It should be apparent by now that a potential for political liberalism and racial moderation did exist in the years following Redemption, though its nature and extent are difficult to know. This potential has been widely recognized by historians of farmer protest, political dissent, and the blacks, but its various manifestations have never been studied together. Implicitly if not explicitly most historians have located its source in the popular movements of farmers, blacks, or other exploited groups. In an important variation, set forth in *The Strange Career of Jim Crow* (3rd ed., 1974), C. Vann Woodward located the chief potential for racial moderation among Conservatives, and his view has been widely supported.[4]

This subject is an important one that poses difficult questions. Was the potential for economic, political, and racial moderation great enough to weigh significantly in a general assessment of the New South? If so, what was its source and why was it ultimately ineffectual? And what, if anything, was the relationship between the support for economic and political moderation on one hand and racial moderation on the other?

Consider, for example, the case for the Conservatives as racial moderates. Conservatives did not disfranchise the blacks when they came to power or repeal the civil rights laws enacted during Reconstruction. Nor did they legalize segregation or insist that the color line be rigidly drawn in public transportation. They regularly solicited black votes, appointed token numbers of blacks to minor public offices, and tolerated the election of a few blacks to local offices, state legislatures, and even Congress. Some of them publicly endorsed racial moderation and urged equal treatment of blacks before the law. "I shall be the Governor of the whole people," declared Wade Hampton, the Conservative leader in South Carolina, "knowing no party, making no vindictive discrimination, holding the scales of justice with firm and impartial hand, seeing as far as in me lies, that the laws are enforced in justice tempered with mercy, protecting all classes alike." *"Not one single right enjoyed by the colored people today shall be taken from them,"* Hampton promised when he became governor. *"They shall be equals under the law, of any man in South Carolina."*

This was certainly praiseworthy, but was it merely political rhetoric? It placated the state's black majority, whose political power Hampton and his supporters had just neutralized by violence and intimidation, and it discouraged federal interference in the aftermath of that effort. Those were important considerations, but Hampton and the South Carolina Redeemers had still other reasons for taking a moderate stance. "No harm would be done the South by Negro suffrage," Hampton said on one occasion. "The old owners would cast the votes of their people almost as absolutely and securely as their own.... [Enfranchisement] would only be multiplying the power of the old and natural leaders of Southern politics by giving a vote to every former slave. Heretofore such men had served their masters only in the fields; now they would do no less faithful service at the polls."

The meaning of this is clear. Racial moderation was not an end in itself, but a device for class as well as race control, and with white supremacy assured by the Compromise of 1877, class control became especially important for Conservatives. It was thus paternalism rather than equalitarianism that Hampton and other Conservatives were expressing, a fact that explains but does not destroy their stature as moderates. Hampton's moderation, like that of other Conservatives, was within the framework of white supremacy, and it rested on a demonstrated willingness to use violence to preserve white dominance. Conservatives wanted racial peace and class rule as well as white supremacy, and were willing to make certain concessions to secure those ends. Unlike poor whites, they faced no economic competition from blacks, and it was unnecessary for them to resort to the kinds of extremism practiced by "rednecks." Paternalism and tokenism were much better suited to their purposes. But it should be remembered that much of the moderation this permitted was simply successful intimidation—the threat of violence and a demonstrated willingness to use it often made violence unnecessary, and the resulting quiescence among blacks enabled upper-class paternalists to indulge their moderate impulses.

The moderating effects of this were important, but less so than the racism upon which it rested. Conservatives rose to power by overthrowing the only southern governments that had ever been concerned about the welfare of blacks, and in doing so they effectively neutralized the political power of the race and left blacks prey to white extremists. They contained black voting rather than eliminated it, for the latter was both impossible and impolitic. In office they did nothing to alleviate the economic problems of blacks, nothing to curb the ills of sharecropping or facilitate the acquisition of land. Instead, they enacted lien laws, vagrancy (really peonage) laws, and other measures to keep the race in economic thralldom.

Above all, they exploited the racial prejudices of poor whites in order to maintain their hold on political office. In retrospect this seems their most enduring legacy and the most pointed commentary on their stature as racial moderates. Though there were a few random exceptions to the general pattern, Conservatives encouraged the mass of whites to believe that race mixing (intermarriage), black supremacy, and the reimposition of Carpetbag rule were the only alternatives to white unity under Conservative control. Having reduced black voting to manageable proportions in a process that is discussed in the next chapter, they alternately used it to frighten white dissidents and to cancel out their votes. This set race against race, and thereby did much to destroy the potential not only for racial moderation in the New South but for economic and political liberalism as well.

The potential for liberalism therefore lay chiefly with anti-Conservative dissidents, black and white. Poverty and powerlessness placed these groups in a common predicament and, as in the case of the Virginia Readjusters, they sometimes saw a common need to look to government for help. Had they been able to focus their common effort to achieve reform on economic concerns alone, they might have had considerable success. But the racial division proved too wide to bridge in the face of Conservative manipulation. As a result the sporadic insurgencies of the 1880s were almost invariably unsuccessful, and the mass of whites were thus victimized by a politics in which they themselves had a significant voice.

The Violent South

Another measure of the Conservative era was the persisting problem of violence.[5] Though the subject has never been studied systematically, it is quite possible that criminal violence was more widespread between the Civil War and World War I than at any other time in the South's history. Available statistics are incomplete and not always trustworthy, but all of them point toward that conclusion and also suggest that the South was more violence-prone than any other section of the country. In 1890, 217 persons were charged with murder in Mississippi, the same number as in Ohio, a state with three times as many people. The equivalent figures for Massachusetts and Texas, states of equal population, were 86 and 730 respectively. In the last decade of the century, the number of reported lynchings—murders committed by mobs—averaged 138.4 a year in fourteen southern and border states and 29.1 in the rest of the country. About nine in ten of the southern lynchings involved black victims and white mobs. Half of all prisoners in the nation in 1890 whose crime was homicide were in the greater South, and twenty years later more than half of all convicts serving life sentences (presumably an indication of the seriousness of their crime) were there also. Even if one discounts the apparent tendency of southern courts to impose harsh sentences, especially on blacks convicted of crimes against whites, these figures suggest that serious crime was especially widespread in the South. Throughout the period, newspapers were filled with accounts of murders, shootings, stabbings, lynchings, rioting, and other forms of mayhem.

This condition grew in part from the lingering effects of the frontier and weak institutional development. It also grew out of the Civil War and Reconstruction and Redemption, all of which involved widespread use of violence outside the law. These experiences lessened respect for human life and the processes of law, and under certain conditions encouraged tolerance for mob violence and homicide. The siege mentality that beset the New South combined with traditions of atomistic individualism and direct action to produce group pressures, including vigilantism and mob activity, to insure social conformity and intellectual orthodoxy. "A society or community struggling for its existence," Sheldon Hackney has observed on this point, "tends to define liberty in terms of the freedom of the community as a whole from external threats or restraints." In the New South this meant that liberty was considered in group rather than individual terms. The established social order asserted the right to protect itself from subversion, and in the process law enforcement was necessarily uneven, often in fact capricious, in matters of intense concern. Whites were often, perhaps generally, unpunished for crimes they committed against blacks, or punished less severely than blacks for similar crimes against whites.

Certainly one of the primary functions of law enforcement, including the penal system, was to keep blacks controlled. Thus racial discrimination was the rule rather than the exception. In the deep South in 1880 more than 85 percent of all persons convicted of serious crimes were blacks, and in the Confederate South 71 percent. Only in Texas, where crimes and violence were "western" as well as "southern," were as many whites as blacks convicted. Black convicts seem generally to have received harsher sentences than whites. George Washington Cable found that the average sentence of blacks convicted of burglary in Georgia in 1882 was twice as long as that of whites for the same crime, and those convicted of larceny received sentences five times as long. Prison populations were overwhelmingly black, a fact that added a racial dimension to convict leasing, chain gangs, and other devices for exploiting prison labor.

The extent of crime is unknown. Available data suggest that it was high among both races and (for whatever the data are worth) that both serious and petty crime was higher among blacks. The data, however, do not include participation in organized racial violence—race riots, near riots, lynchings, attempted lynchings, and other forms of vigilantism—for participants were almost never bothered by the law, nor do they include participation in electoral fraud or other political crimes, and for the same reason. The typical homicide in official statistics involved a black killing another black, yet whites were obviously involved in more violent crime than blacks. "Farmers, merchants, bankers, physicians, lawyers, even ministers of the gospel often slay their fellow man in private warfare," wrote B. J. Ramage of the University of the South in 1897, but "after a mock trial are set at liberty not only with no serious detriment to their reputation but in many instances with increased popularity."

The penal system was one of the scandals of the Conservative era. Most prisoners were blacks, and prisons operated on the principle that the purpose of imprisonment was punishment. Treatment of convicts was harsh, and made harsher by the policy that prison systems should support themselves financially so as not to be a burden on the taxpayer. State penitentiaries existed for recalcitrant and disabled felons, but most convicts served their terms in county institutions. For financial reasons, the practice developed of leasing the convicts to private entrepreneurs such as mine owners, railroad construction companies, or large planters, who for a fixed payment to the county or state received the right to work the convicts and in turn the obligation to house, feed, and guard them. The arrangement benefited everyone except the convicts. It made the penal system an economic asset for the states and counties, a means of private enrichment for the lessees, and a source of graft for public officials. Leasing contracts became part of the boodle of political office as well as the source of brutality and scandal. Convicts were not only overworked, poorly fed, and neglected in sickness and injury, but whipped, often maimed, and sometimes killed with impunity. Death rates often exceeded 10 percent annually, and were sometimes twice that figure.

So appalling was the system that it gave rise to the most successful reform movement in the South before the turn of the century. By 1900 several states had abolished convict leasing, and by 1918 all had done so except Alabama. The programs that replaced it, however, were sometimes hardly better. The states and counties began working convicts themselves, on prison farms such as the 15,000-acre Sunflower plantation established by Mississippi in 1895, or in factories built inside penitentiaries, or in chain gangs on county farms and road construction projects.

The Mind of the New South

In the final analysis the Conservatives owed their political success to the conservative nature of southern society in the last quarter of the nineteenth century. Despite all the violence and turmoil and the push for economic development, the New South was basically a conservative society. Among the areas of life that reflected that fact were higher education, social criticism, the status of women, the nature of religion, and the persistence of traditionalism in sectional thought.

In the New South, institutions of higher learning were small, underfinanced, and inferior in quality. In 1881, to illustrate, there were 123 colleges and universities in the section, but their income that year averaged less than $9,000 each. Sixty-nine of them had buildings and grounds valued at less than $50,000, and only five had active endowments of $50,000 or more. In contrast, the sixteen colleges and universities in New England had incomes averaging almost $65,000 each, and only two of them had active endowments of less than $150,000. Twenty years later, in 1901, the income of Harvard University was greater than that of the sixty-six colleges and universities in seven southern states combined.

The quality of higher learning was therefore low. Before the Civil War, southern education had turned inward and become the handmaiden of sectional loyalists. Southern students had withdrawn from northern institutions, and education in the section lost most of its contact with the outside world. The Civil War and Reconstruction increased this isolation. In the last quarter of the nineteenth century few southerners studied outside the section, especially if those who attended Johns Hopkins University in Baltimore be excepted. A survey of the dozen largest northern universities in 1901 found less than a hundred southerners enrolled.

The significance of this finding is enhanced by the fact that southern colleges and universities were provincial, insecure, and conservative. Administrations and boards of regents were controlled by political, religious, or business interests, and had little more independence than the faculties they governed with a firm hand. In 1878 geologist Alexander Winchell was dismissed from Vanderbilt University for his teachings about evolution, and in several other well-known instances professors were dismissed in breaches of academic freedom. These examples, however, were less important than the fact that a system demanding such orthodoxy produced so few dismissals. This suggests that few faculty members held unorthodox views on controversial subjects. "Education reflects far more of the effect of politics, religion, and sectionalism than it appears as a modifying influence upon them," Howard Odum wrote of the 1930s, and his judgment seems even more applicable to the late nineteenth century.

As a result, colleges and universities played no innovative role in cultural and intellectual life. At most they guarded regional pieties and transmitted religious and other orthodoxies to students already conditioned to accept them. (At the turn of the century, half of all college students in the section were enrolled in church-related institutions.) Not even in agricultural education did the Confederate South have a distinguished institution or make a notable contribution. Before the turn of the century apparently no scholar or educator made an issue of racial policy or tried to provoke a serious debate on that subject. This was true of blacks as well as whites, and reflects the conservative influence of northern philanthropy on black education as well as the unity of white thinking on that subject. This was perhaps the most striking instance of the absence of social criticism in the New South, and a measure of the irrelevance of formal education in southern life. "It is only through adequate criticism of themselves that any people can hope to evolve a consistently great literature or a rational system of education, or to make appreciable progress in their manners and morals," wrote William P. Trent of the University of the South in 1897. Yet "few [southerners] have ever been critical enough to gather materials that would be useful to the student of their culture." The reason for this, Trent thought, was "the baleful intolerance, political, religious, and other, which, though weakening, still manifests itself in the press, in the pulpit, on the rostrum, and in the parlor, whenever it becomes necessary to question, even in a tentative way, the importance, or the propriety, or the truth of any idea that has in any way been labeled Southern."

The lot of social critics was even more difficult than that of inquiring scholars. Trent himself, who combined the two roles and was thus doubly suspect, left the South as soon as he got a position in a northern university. George Washington Cable and Walter Hines Page, two other vastly different critics, left in the 1880s, though Page continued to work hard for reform in the section. Lewis H. Blair, whose *A South-*

ern Prophecy (1889) was a cogent analysis of the racial issue, did not leave, but he eventually recanted his liberal views, as did Tom Watson, the Populist reformer. Black critics like T. Thomas Fortune, whose *Black and White: Land, Labor and Politics in the South* (1884) included a call for class solidarity across racial lines, were unheard within the section, and Fortune too left the South for larger opportunities in the North. Critics who were sometimes heard by their fellow southerners, like Charles H. Otken, offered inadequate solutions to the problems they diagnosed. "The remedy for this state of things," Otken wrote after a forceful indictment of crop liens and sharecropping in *The Ills of the South* (1894), "is severe economy, earnest self-denial, and a fixed determination to buy for cash. Two years of self-denial and economy will enable the majority of the Southern white people to buy on a cash basis."

The most incisive social critic in the Conservative era was also the greatest literary figure, George Washington Cable. His reputation as an able fictionist established in *Old Creole Days* (1879) and *The Grandissimes* (1884), Cable became increasingly concerned with social problems, especially problems related to race. In a series of addresses and essays collected in *The Silent South* (1885) and a modern reader, *The Negro Question* (1958) edited by Arlin Turner, Cable set forth a realistic analysis of the race problem and such related issues as convict leasing, black poverty, and the absence of social criticism. He endorsed civil, political, and economic equality for blacks, including integrated schools and public accommodations, and attacked a number of popular orthodoxies. He rejected the idea that races are innately unequal, and disputed the belief that racial prejudice is inborn. He suggested that states' rights was not a constitutional principle, but a rationalization for racial exploitation, and he elevated national above sectional loyalties. He also urged prison reform and federal aid to education, attacked landlordism and the crop lien, and challenged the New South faith in the social efficacy of material growth.

Yet Cable was more liberal than radical, even on racial matters. "We have not proposed to disturb any distinction between the races which nature has made, or molest any private or personal relation in life," he wrote in response to charges that he was encouraging social integration. "The question [of civil rights for blacks] has nothing to do with social relations." Cable believed there was a silent majority of moderates among white southerners—"the silent South"—who would publicly support racial moderation if its members were made aware of the fact that their moderate views were widely shared by other southerners. Cable, however, was never able to reach that majority, if indeed it existed. Instead he aroused bitter criticism from all sides. Historian

Charles Gayarre, a fellow Louisianan, thought Cable suffered from "a diarrhea of words and a constipation of ideas," and Henry W. Grady disputed his views in a widely read article in *Century Magazine.* No one came to his defense, and disheartened he moved to New England. From there he published *John March, Southerner* (1895), an interesting portrait of the boosterism and materialism of the New South, but he largely abandoned social criticism.

The only reformers who had any success before the turn of the century were those who avoided controversial issues relating to race and sectional loyalty. They were thus genteel in nature and often led by indefatigable women like Julia Tutwiler in Alabama and Rebecca L. Felton in Georgia. Temperance, child labor, education, penal reform, and antimonopoly were among their chief concerns, and their modest success applying limited solutions to specific problems illustrated the difficulties of reformers in a conservative society.[6] In such a society even moderate changes might intrude in unforeseen ways into sensitive areas of race or class or politics, and every reform was measured against that possibility.

This concern was illustrated by the issue of federal aid to education. On several occasions in the 1880s that issue was debated in Congress, and thus in the South. The immediate concern was the Blair education bill, which over a ten-year period would have appropriated $105 million to be divided among the states on the basis of their educational needs, a formula that would have given the South a disproportionate share of the money. Indeed, $11 million of the $15 million allocated for the first year would have gone to the southern and border states. Money for education was sorely needed in the South, and the amount authorized by the Blair bill was large enough to have had a major impact. White southerners were thus divided. Many of them, including a number of Conservatives, supported the bill, but many others did not, for reasons that were both racial and philosophical, and their opposition defeated it four times in the United States Senate. Those who opposed the measure feared that federal aid would eventuate in federal control of education and might therefore interfere with racial segregation in the schools. (The separate-but-equal principle had not yet been sanctioned by the Supreme Court.) To allay this fear, the bill specifically prohibited federal interference in educational matters, but not everyone was reassured by such a prohibition. In retrospect there seems to have been little basis for the fear that federal bureaucrats would tamper with school segregation, but in the long run they would surely have exerted some degree of federal control, and from a conservative perspective the fear of federal regulation was therefore justified. Furthermore, the bill would have provided large sums of money for black education and the consequence of that was not predictable.

The Status of Women

The social conservatism of the New South fell heavily upon women, whose status remained subordinate and dependent.[7] The national women's movement, now largely concerned with suffrage, had no real impact in the section before the turn of the century. Women did, however, assume a larger role in public life and thus laid the basis for their later social emancipation.

The public role of women had been enlarged during the Civil War and Reconstruction, and Redemption did nothing to undo the change. The rise of cotton mills brought a new kind of employment for large numbers of working-class white women, who for the first time earned a significant income on their own. The spread of elementary schools and the opening of clerical jobs in business did the same thing for those in the middle class, and as a result many women found themselves in a changing relationship to men. Middle- and upper-class women who did not work for a living expanded their public roles through church-related activities, including missionary societies and the Women's Christian Temperance Union, and then through women's clubs, literary societies, and the United Daughters of the Confederacy. These groups were genteel in character and conservative in purpose, but through them women began to take active roles in civic life, and soon some of them were in the forefront of reform movements and even political causes. Black women, plagued by the additional burden of racial discrimination, made slower progress but along the same lines.

This did not add up to a women's movement. None of the above groups was specifically concerned with women's rights or sexual discrimination, and except in the border South equal rights groups did not appear until after 1900. Indeed, women expended more time and energy on prison reform, education, temperance, and preserving Confederate memories than on advancing their own rights as a group. This was due to their own conservatism as well as the opprobrium men heaped on feminist activity. The antebellum social myth that exalted white women was still repeated, though with less force, and discrimination was still a major fact of life. Divorce was difficult and not socially respectable. In South Carolina it was prohibited altogether, and elsewhere divorce laws were weighted in favor of men. In North Carolina and Texas, for example, the adultery of a spouse was grounds for divorce for a husband but not a wife. Pay differentials were great in all forms of employment, and that fact as well as social pressure encouraged marriage and dependence. Jobs reserved for women were low in prestige as well as pay. Most women still worked as unpaid housewives, mothers, or seasonal agricultural laborers, and their condition in those roles had hardly changed since antebellum days. Traveling across the South at the end of the century, Walter Hines Page found the mass of rural white women "thin and wrinkled in youth from ill prepared food, clad without warmth or grace, living in untidy houses, working from daylight till bedtime at the dull round of weary duties, the slaves of men of equal slovenliness, the mothers of joyless children—all uneducated if not illiterate." If this did not apply to middle- and upper-class women, it was not an inaccurate description of those in the lower half of the economic scale.

The most notable achievement of women was in literature. Excluded from politics, the professions, and other arenas of leadership and creativity, women of talent found writing the most prestigious and intellectually rewarding field open to them. They were well represented among the local colorists of the 1880s and in subsequent literary movements. Mary N. Murphree (who wrote under the pseudonym Charles Egbert Craddock), Kate Chopin, and Grace King were among the important writers of the last two decades of the century, and Augusta Jane Evans Wilson was representative of the large group of popular subliterary writers of the period. By the turn of the century Ellen Glasgow, a major talent, and Mary Johnston, a gifted and enormously popular writer of historical romances, had begun to publish.

Except for Miss Glasgow, these women were mostly sentimentalists, but by the turn of the century the question of women's rights and sexual freedom had begun to intrude into their works. This can be seen in books as different as Kate Chopin's remarkable novel *The Awakening* (1899) and Augusta Jane Evans Wilson's popular *St. Elmo* (1894). *The Awakening* is not only the story of a socially emancipated woman, Edna Pontellier, but an account of her rather sensual sexual life. Mrs. Pontellier's attitude toward sex was presented as amoral, and her sexual desires were pictured as those of a man might be pictured. It was, all in all, a singular work in New South literature, and the criticism it provoked not only obscured its literary merit but discouraged Mrs. Chopin, who died in 1904, from publishing again.

St. Elmo is an altogether different book, unconventional only in the intensity of its endorsement of convention. Mrs. Chopin had been interested in literary realism and individual freedom, but Mrs. Wilson was alarmed by feminism and the prospect of sexual equality. *St. Elmo* therefore exalts "true womanly modesty" and decries the rise of "latitudinarianism in dress and conversation" that was "rapidly reducing the sexes to an equality." Edna, Mrs. Wilson's protagonist, spurned the women's rights movement and worked instead for those rights "which God and nature had decreed" her sex. These included "the right to modify and direct her husband's opinions, if he considered her worthy and competent to guide him," "the right to make her children ornaments to their nation," and "the right to be all that the phrase 'noble Christian woman' means." But they did not include "the right to vote; to harrange from the hustings; [or] to trail her heaven-born purity through the dust and mire of political strife."

It is quite likely that most women in the New South found more to approve in *St. Elmo* than in *The Awakening*. But when, after 1900, a few of them began to take active roles in the women's rights movement, they found support in the works of many women writers, including Ellen Glasgow and Mary Johnston. Miss Glasgow, "a feminist with a vengeance," was never active in organized feminism, but she spread feminist ideas through many of her novels and invariably presented women as morally superior to men. In *Virginia* (1913) she painted a revealing and thoroughly convincing picture of the social restraints on white women of the middle class and the way those restraints tied them to husbands and families and inhibited intellectual development and creativity.

Conservative Religion

The conservative nature of New South society was reinforced by religion.[8] Southerners of both races were religious people who practiced a religion of affirmation. The overwhelming majority were still Baptists or Methodists. Ninety percent of all church members in five deep South states belonged to one branch or another of those denominations, and more than 80 percent of those in Virginia and North Carolina. In the piedmont and Appalachia, Presbyterians were also numerous, as were Catholics in southern Louisiana.

Three major institutional changes occurred in southern religion between the Civil War and 1900. The war completed the eclipse of the Episcopal Church by undermining the tidewater planter class from which its influence derived. Emancipation led to the formation of large all-black denominations. And at the end of the century, holiness sects began to appear among lower-class whites. The rise of black denominations, which had racial as well as religious significance, was the most important of these changes. It institutionalized church segregation and ended racial interaction in religious matters, but gave the black community its most important and successful institution. Blacks, however, remained Baptists or Methodists too, and the primacy of those denominations among both races reflected a religious unity that was far more important for the social historian than the sometimes intense rivalries that divided denominations and congregations. On religious matters of social significance there was a remarkable sameness of belief among southerners.

Among whites, this belief was molded by two important influences. The first was the evangelical tradition of Baptism and Methodism, and the second was the converging community of purpose between those churches and the state, or (to put it differently) between organized religion and political elites. Southerners had always adapted religion to life more than life to religion, and these influences now interacted with the imperatives of the established social order to mold the characteristic religion of the New South. Church government was democratic (though Methodists had imposed a weak episcopacy over the congregation) and the clergy dependent, and the result was a religion that reflected popular social values as well as theological convictions. To clergy and laity alike the purposes of religion were to save souls, to kindle or rekindle faith, to put and keep the individual in a right relationship with God. Success was measured by the number of converts and new church members, and by the degree of emotional catharsis provided the faithful. In both major denominations worship was still an emotional experience inculcating other worldly theology and biblical literalism. Most ministers were uneducated and better at exhortation than exegesis, and in matters of social realism largely innocent. The result was credulous faith and a religion curiously disembodied from the social needs of its adherents.

The churches made little accommodation to modernism. They were hostile to science and skepticism, considered the theory of evolution blasphemous, and had little sympathy for the changes set in motion by the urban and industrial revolutions. They generally opposed labor unions and strikes and tended to blame poverty and its ills on the personal weaknesses of unregenerate people. Urban slum dwellers are "dissipated, vicious, wicked and immoral," declared the Georgia Baptist *Christian Index* in 1900. "Many reformers of the day teach that, if you improve their surroundings and educate them, you can lift them up.... But what these people really need is to be made over again. There is but one power in the world that can do this, and that is the gospel of the Son of God."

In the social milieu of the New South such beliefs widened the gulf between religion and life and encouraged religiosity, the public affectation of religion by people who privately ignored its principles. Religion like politics was co-opted by established elites and subtly corrupted. By the 1880s church groups had become actively concerned with certain kinds of social issues, and like other reformers looked increasingly to the state to accomplish their reforms. The conviction that sin and salvation were matters of individual choice channeled their social concern toward the regulation of personal conduct, and thus toward such things as prohibition (misnamed temperance), sabbath observance, gambling, and divorce, rather than poverty, racism, or government neglect of social and economic problems. They would use government to suppress sinful and undesirable conduct but not to help sharecroppers or mill hands.

This development completed an important transition in southern religious history. For Baptists and Methodists alike, it represented a forsaking of the tradition of religious and social dissent. The transformation had begun much earlier. Antebellum churches had endorsed slavery and puritanical moral codes, and made themselves integral parts of the social system. Now, however, the churches were going further, not only allying themselves with a particular political and economic establishment but making themselves a part of its apparatus of social control. As this occurred, Baptism and Methodism were transformed from dissenting to establishment religions, and the base of their strength shifted from the lower to the middle classes. This explains the rise of holiness sects, new religions which filled the vacuum left among the lower classes as Baptists and Methodists became increasingly "respectable." Both of the latter denominations came to be "more Bourbon than Populist" in their social influence, to borrow a phrase John Lee Eighmy applied to Southern Baptists.

This was one of the ironies of New South history. Church congregations, especially those of the Baptists, were perhaps the most democratic institutions in the section, so democratic that on the denominational level churches had little independent strength. Yet collectively and singly, churches were no more concerned with the socioeconomic problems of their members than was government or business. Only rarely did church leaders question property arrangements or the politics or economics of laissez faire, and even more rarely did they join the efforts of racial moderates, protesting farmers, or social critics. "The minister rarely if ever had anything to say about child labor, sharecropping, illiteracy, or race relations," wrote sociologist Edgar T. Thompson recalling the church services he attended as a child after the turn of the century. "I had known child laborers, sharecroppers, and illiterates, white and black, all my life but I did not know the condition of these people constituted social problems until I was well along in college. We heard much, however, about the evils of dancing, card-playing, and the consumption of alcoholic beverages."

This is hardly surprising. Religion in the New South could not transcend the social milieu in which it existed. If higher education and the urban press lacked intellectual independence and a critical spirit, churches, with congregational control, undereducated clergymen, and dependent hierarchies, could not be otherwise. Both conviction and expediency encouraged church leaders to avoid controversy and offer instead a message of escape or assurance. To the poor and powerless they offered solace and the hope that the next world would be better than this one. To the middle class they provided outlets for the impulse to do good. To the powerful they constituted bulwarks against social disorder. To the guilt-ridden they furnished expiation. To everyone they offered forgiveness for sins and assurances of salvation.

The Traditionalists

The mind of the New South was divided.[9] The New South creed was popular, but it was read and interpreted in many ways and an influential minority rejected it altogether. That minority, the Traditionalists, had an altogether different vision of the section's future. They warned that the headlong rush after New South panaceas was destroying the section's distinctiveness and thus its identity, and surrendering control over the South's destiny to outside forces of innovation and national consolidation. They urged southerners to look to the past and hold on to their sectional distinctiveness, for without that there would be no South. The alternative visions of Traditionalism and New Southism were the polarities that divided the southern mind. Strong forces were pulling the section in conflicting directions. Nationalizing tendencies especially in economics drew the South toward the nation, while others in race and politics pulled it away. The one set of forces encouraged "progress" and nationalism, while the other promoted traditionalism and distinctiveness.

Social thought thus tended to cluster into two sets of ideas that were distinct and in part contradictory but also in important degrees overlapping. The New South creed was Janus-faced. As earlier noted, it looked resolutely forward in important particulars while promising to contain undesirable social change and preserve certain traditional values. New Southists paid homage to sectional loyalties but were prepared to manipulate those loyalties and subordinate them to more immediate concerns. Traditionalists, on the other hand, of whom Thomas Nelson Page, Charles Gayarre, Robert L. Dabney of Virginia, and Charles Colcock Jones of Georgia were representative figures, looked to the past not with cynicism or calculation but with admiration and nostalgia. They therefore nurtured the Confederate tradition and lovingly guarded the section's symbols and myths. To them history and tradition were guiding lights through the wilderness of change, not obstacles to be overcome in a quest for progress. Traditionalists were not sure that the Union victory or even emancipation had been an unmitigated good, nor were they certain that diversification was preferable to an agrarian economy. They valued bourgeois virtues less than those of the antebellum aristocracy, and urged southerners to spurn American ideals in favor of others of their own. They rejected the values implicit in New Southism, especially economic rationalism, the gospel of progress, and what Richard M. Weaver called "the insidious doctrines of relativism and empiricism." They were less pragmatic and compromising than New Southists, more unbending in their devotion to principle, and more alarmed over the decline of hierarchies and orthodoxies.

But they were not boosters or positive thinkers. Instead, they were pessimists in varying stages of dismay over the direction of southern development, viewing with alarm even as New Southists were pointing with pride. They refused to equate progress and economic growth, insisting instead that social improvement was a matter of spiritual elevation. They stressed the depth rather than the superficiality of southern problems, but as pessimists and fatalists they regarded social problems as things to be endured rather than solved. In any case they considered such things as poverty and provincialism less threatening than untried experimentation. Above all, they located the soul of the South in the things that set it apart from the rest of the country and not, as did many New Southists, in the things the section shared with the nation. If Walter Hines Page, one of the most ebullient New Southists, looked forward with equanimity to the end of the South as a recognizable section, Thomas Nelson Page, a dedicated guardian of the past, viewed that prospect as tragic. Traditionalists were thus deeply influenced by the sense of unease and grievance that kept sectional consciousness alive. "We of the *'Old South'* have need, God knows, to stand by each other staunchly," Paul Hamilton Hayne wrote Charles Gayarre in 1885. "The *new generation* hardly comprehends us." "In the *'Young South'* so called," he continued, "I observe a growing tendency towards contempt for the Past, and a truckling spirit, so far as *Yankee* ideas and *Yankee* prejudices are concerned." "You and I are old fogies."

Traditionalists did many things to promote their principles. They were largely responsible for the Confederate tradition that dominated southern historical writing in the last third of the nineteenth century and for other efforts to preserve the memories of the Lost Cause. When Robert E. Lee died in 1870, they organized memorial societies to erect suitable monuments to his memory, and the example proved contagious. Across the South other societies appeared to honor other Confederate heroes and preserve memories of the war and its sacrifices. Organizations of Confederate veterans appeared soon after the war, and in 1889 they coalesced into the United Confederate Veterans. Through local "camps," which numbered more than 1,500 at the turn of the century, and through the pages of *The Confederate Veteran,* that organization played a major role in preserving sectional orthodoxies. In 1895 the United Daughters of the Confederacy joined the effort, by which time the cult of the Lost Cause had acquired the character of a religious endeavor, with its own saints, relics, shrines, rituals, orthodoxies, and holy days, as well as apostates, blasphemers, and theological hair splitters. Lee's and Jefferson Davis's birthdays became holidays, a special Confederate Memorial Day was observed, and courthouse squares from Virginia to Texas were adorned with monuments to the Confederate cause.

Memories of that cause thus remained alive long after northerners had forgotten the war. In her memoirs, *The Making of a Southerner* (1947), Katharine DuPre Lumpkin remembered being "verily baptized" into the Confederate tradition when as a child in 1903 she attended a reunion of Confederate veterans in Columbia, South Carolina. The affair lasted several days, and the 20,000 visitors it attracted nearly doubled the population of that little city. "How thronged were the sidewalks," she wrote recalling the inevitable parade, "thousands of people—and the windows of buildings—people leaned out to cheer and wave Confederate flags." The veterans, old men now almost forty years after the war, paraded only a few blocks, but as they did a throng of school children ran excitedly ahead of them spreading the street with a carpet of flowers. Excitement increased when the surviving signers of the secession ordinance, living relics from a mythic past, rode by. "Bands play[ed] march tunes until one's spine could not stand any more tingles," Miss Lumpkin remembered. And then came "the Stars and Bars, dipping and floating and—Dixie! From end to end along the route, [there was] shouting and cheering, at the Stars and Bars and Dixie. A somber note added to the drama. Behind the marshals, where usually rode the guest of honor, there walked an aged Negro, John Johnson, leading the unmounted horse of General Wade Hampton, the state's most honored hero, recently dead at the age of eighty-four.

The oratory was just as intoxicating. "There is nothing stronger or more splendid on this wide earth than to have borne the sorrow you have borne, than to have endured the pain that you have endured," the veterans were told. "You young men in whose veins beat the blood of heroes," their sons and grandsons were admonished, "uncover your heads, for the land in which you live is holy, hallowed by the blood of your fathers, purified by the tears of your mothers."

Traditionalism in Literature

Traditionalism appeared most systematically in literature. Rooted in the plantation legend that flowered before the Civil War, this literature had no specific beginning. Given the escapist tendencies of southern thought and the felt need of a defeated people to justify their cause, it would have been surprising if legends of assurance and apologia had not appeared. As soon as the war ended, Edward A. Pollard, the Richmond journalist, published a vindication of the South which he titled instructively *The Lost Cause* (1866). In the same year John Esten Cooke published *Surry of Eagle's Nest,* which, with a companion volume, *Mohun* (1869), constituted a pioneering fictional account of the war. Cooke's account has little artistic merit, but in addition to repeating the staples of the antebellum plantation legend it also pointed to the later myths of the Lost Cause and the Old South. Colonel Surry, Cooke's hero, was predictably descended from Cavaliers who had fled to Virginia after the regicide of Charles I, and just as predictably Surry's father "belonged to that old generation of Virginians who have disappeared." Nostalgia and romanticism permeated Cooke's reflections on the antebellum world, and contrasted notably with his treatment of the "prosaic" present. "The flowers bloomed brighter then, and the song of the birds was sweeter," Surry remembered of his childhood. "We will never see those days any more except in dreams." Yet Cooke, a Virginian of moderate sectional views, avoided the issues involved in the war and expressed no regret over its outcome. "Is it wrong to remember the past?" he asked defensively. "I think of it [the war's outcome] without bitterness. God decreed it.... I do not indulge any repinings, or reflect with rancor upon the issue of the struggle. I prefer recalling the stirring adventure, the brave voices, the gallant faces."

This was a formula for escapism and myth, and those qualities became the characteristic elements of Traditionalist—and southern—literature. The most effective application of the formula was in works such as *Uncle Remus* (1881), a collection of black dialect stories by Joel Chandler Harris, who also wrote for Henry W. Grady's *Atlanta Constitution,* and in the short stories and essays Thomas Nelson Page brought together in *In Ole Virginia* (1887) and *The Old South* (1892). Page's dialect story "Marse Chan" (1884), included in the former work, is perhaps the most appealing statement ever made of the myth of the Old South. Other instructive examples include George W. Bagby's popular lecture *The Old Virginia Gentleman* (1884), F. Hopkinson Smith's bemusing account of *Colonel Carter of Cartersville* (1891), James Lane Allen's pleasant tales collected in *Flute and Violin* (1891), and Basil L.

Gildersleeve's uncompromising reaffirmation of "The Creed of the Old South" (1892).

The characteristic mood of these works was nostalgic. The remembrance, in George Cary Eggleston's words, was of "a soft, dreamy, deliciously quiet life ... with all its sharp corners and rough surfaces ... worn round and smooth." "Dem wuz good old times, marster—de bes' Sam ever see," reminisced Thomas Nelson Page's black narrator in "Marse Chan." "Dey wuz, in fac'! Niggers didn' hed nothin' all to do —jes' hed to 'ten' to de feedin' an' cleanin' de hosses, and doin' what de marster tell 'em to do.... Dyar warn' no trouble nor nothin'."

For Traditionalists the attractiveness of the past was a measure of their dismay with the present. As they saw things Swirl was now king, and turmoil and change had forced the South from its accustomed moorings. Class, family, and place were giving way to a bourgeois ethic that measured everything, even a gentleman's word and worth, by standards of materialism and success. The lower classes were restive and, worse, politically active. Social distinctions were crumbling, a new morality was about, and even women were no longer satisfied in their place. To those who were troubled by these things, the Old South seemed in retrospect a land of stability, order, and grace. " 'Lections wuz 'lections dem days," Thomas Nelson Page's black narrator says in "Unc' Edinburg's Drowndin'." "Dee warn' no bait-gode 'lections wid ev' sort o' worms squirmin' up 'gainst one nurr, wid piece of paper d' ain' know what on, drappin' in a chink; didn' nuttin' but gent'mens vote den, an' dee took dee dram, an' vote out loud, like gent'mens." The secret ballot, universal suffrage, decline of aristocratic hegemony—these were marks of the South's decline, as were the threats of "Africanization" and certain "materialistic tendencies" which Page lamented elsewhere.

In matured form the myths of the Old South and the Lost Cause were transposed into a larger myth of southern history. To Page and others the Old South, the real South, had stood for a set of ideals and principles that modern America was greatly in need of. Conservatism, social hierarchy, white supremacy, Christian ethics, limited democracy, conformity to natural law—these were things the South had once represented and, despite the wrongs of Reconstruction and the siren call of progress, things it still clung to. "The South was a barrier against libidinous democracy," in the striking phrase of J. L. M. Curry, a bulwark against political centralization and social fanaticism, a bastion of conservative change and respect for property and law and moral order. And by remaining true to its heritage, it might yet lead the nation out of the wilderness of modernism and materialism and back to traditional virtues. This was the mission of the South, an idea that appeared in works as disparate as Page's novel of Reconstruction *Red Rock* (1898), and Thomas Dixon's mean-spirited tale of Reconstruction and Redemption *The Clansman* (1905).

By the turn of the century, the myths of the Old South and the Lost Cause had begun to undergo an important evolution. The local colorists of the 1880s had passed from the scene, and younger writers of literary merit began to leave the myth to historical romancers. Perhaps the best of the romancers was Mary Johnston, whose enormously popular account of the Civil War in Virginia, *The Long Roll* (1911) and *Cease Firing* (1912), has been called "probably the completest and most authentic embodiment of the Southern myth." But even as the myth was bearing its finest literary fruit, its appeal was ebbing. In a continuing series of novels on the social history of Virginia, Ellen Glasgow, the best of the younger writers, forsook the myth and with the gentle irony that was her trademark began to lay bare its inadequacies, while with the heavier hand of satire James Branch Cabell was making it an object of derision. "I love to serve that legend," remarked Cabell's character, Jack Charteris, also a novelist, in *The Rivet in Grandfather's Neck* (1915). "I love to prattle of 'ole Marster' and 'ole Miss,' and throw in a sprinkling of 'mockin'-buds' and 'hants' and 'horg-killing time,' and of sweeping animadversions as to all 'free niggers'; and to narrate how 'de quality use to cum'—you spell it c-u-m because that looks so convincingly like dialect—'ter de gret house.' Those are the main ingredients." Should his story need a romantic angle, Charteris added, he brought in a wounded Yankee captain and a beautiful southern belle to nurse the captain back to health, and in depicting their inevitable courtship and marriage, Charteris threw in at least one favorable mention of Lincoln, one duel "in de low grouns" just after daybreak, and one scene in which the family silver was hidden from invading Yankees.

The Conservative Era in Retrospect

The fruits of Conservative rule were mixed, and historians have been generally critical of the period. The most positive evaluation of any group of Conservatives is Nash K. Burger and John K. Bettersworth's treatment of the "Confederate Brigadiers" in *South of Appomattox* (1959). "Through their steadying conservatism," these authors wrote, the Conservatives encouraged "peace and reconciliation between North and South" and "effectively silenced" those in both sections who would keep animosities alive. "They beat their swords into ploughshares and led their region back to its proper role in a new and united nation," and despite "the changes and chances of partisan politics and public law" managed to preserve "the ancient social order." They also brought economic development without disturbing "the region's concern for its past and the traditional values" and without destroying "its attachment to the land, its opposition to outside interference, and its insistence upon a caste system." Or, as George B. Tindall put it in *The Persistent Tradition in New South Politics* (1975), they reconciled innovation and tradition. "The Bourbons," Tindall observed, "kept alive the vision of an organic traditional community with its personal relationships, its class distinctions, its habits of deference to the squirearchy."

On the state level, where their diversity is most apparent, the Conservatives have been variously evaluated. In Alabama, according to William D. Rogers, they "gave the state order and a sense of dignity and respectability." But in Louisiana, writes William I. Hair, they made the state "a byword for political corruption and general lawlessness."

Perhaps all of these judgments are correct. The Conservatives were a large and diverse political group who remained in power for a generation, and like all such groups they are not easy to generalize about. The "leavening savor of conservatism" which they brought to the post-Reconstruction South did work to allay sectional animosity and encourage northern investment, and those things were sorely needed in the postbellum South. Moreover, the sectional reconciliation they achieved was largely on their own terms. In addition, many of their shortcomings were shared by other elites in Gilded Age America. Political corruption was widespread in other parts of the country, as were political and economic laissez faire and the subservience of politics to business. Nor were racism and violence unique to Conservatives or the South. The conquest of the plains Indians and expropriation of their lands had a far more devastating impact on weak and dependent people than the Conservatives' treatment of blacks or poor whites; and the subsequent fate of subject peoples in the American empire suggests that white supremacy was a national as well as a southern concern.

Yet Conservatives often carried the faults of the day further than other groups. Their use of electoral fraud was especially widespread, as was their subservience to special interests. Furthermore, their legacy included not only the things they did but many they failed to do, and the example they set for later generations. Their welfare policies were penurious, for example, but more important was the fact that they made penury in such things acceptable. They subverted the democratic process, but more importantly they encouraged southerners to condone such a practice in desperate circumstances. They helped make liberal reform suspicious, illiteracy and poverty tolerable, one-party politics acceptable, one-crop agriculture endurable. And in eliminating Radical Reconstruction and quelling political protest, they helped warp the evolution of liberal democracy in the South and ensnarl reform in the meshes of racism and demagoguery.

Their greatest failure was in vision, not villainy, to borrow Allen W. Moger's phrase. Their political stewardship was harmful in the balance, and their role in national politics was largely confined to protecting interests of their own. Between 1865 and 1912 no southerner was nominated for President or Vice-President by either major party, only two served as speaker of the House of Representatives, and only fourteen were appointed to the President's Cabinet.

Conservatives reflected the narrow perspectives and limited motivations of Gilded Age America. They did little to encourage esthetics and the arts or to foster pride in nonmaterial achievement, and under their leadership the life of the mind and the spirit languished. The section fell further behind the rest of the country in such bellwether things as libraries, museums, art galleries, bookstores, and centers of learning, as well as in diet and health care and perhaps also in standards of housing and public improvements. Of course Conservatives were not directly responsible for all of this, but neither did they do much to counteract it. If, as they seemed to insist, acceptance of such deficiencies was the necessary price of white supremacy, national reconciliation, and economic development, the price was too high. It took generations to overcome the neglect, unwisdom, and abuses of the Conservative era; and because of those things it took much longer than it might otherwise have taken to outlive the devastations of body and spirit produced by the Civil War and Reconstruction.

12

Race and Reform

In 1890 the mounting strength of farmer protest thrust southern politics into a new era. The politics of neglect gave way to a politics of concern, a change that signaled not the triumph of reform, but the fact that protest itself had become the focal point of politics. Many of the older Conservatives were swept from office in that and the next few years by a new political generation, and Conservatism itself was transformed in response to the erupting protest. A new conservatism emerged, one that is more properly written in lower case since it was not so much an organized political group as an agreed-upon body of interests and principles that came to dominate southern politics. In the long run this new conservatism proved far more enduring than the old. By the end of 1896 it had neutralized farmer protest and by the turn of the century had turned the reform impulse to its own advantage. In doing this it accepted an array of political and social changes that made the new brand of conservatism more enlightened and sophisticated than that of the 1880s, but none of the changes did much to alter the interests that controlled southern politics. Less crude in handling dissidents and more flexible in managing public affairs, the new conservatism achieved a degree of public acceptance that the old Conservatives never had. Its finest expression was southern Progressivism, which infused politics after the turn of the century and was the filter through which the principles and policies of the old Conservatism were transmitted to subsequent generations.

This was the age of reform in the South, the long generation that began with the emergence of farmer protest in 1890 and ended with the nation's entry into World War I in 1917. Considered as a whole, the age was one of enlightened, benighted, and disparate change. Its best-known components were Populism and Progressivism, but hardly less important were suffrage restriction and the legalizing of racial segregation, both of which are best understood in the southern context as reform movements. Together with a host of smaller endeavors concerned with social uplift and moral reform, these movements represented a serious effort to solve the South's problems and improve the quality of life among the southern people.

Farmer Protest

Unrest among southern farmers had been chronic since 1870, but until the late 1880s it availed little.[1] The change was due to the emergence of the Farmers' Alliance. Organized in Texas in 1874–75, the Alliance became a sectionwide organization only after 1887, when C. W. Macune became its effective head. Within a year Macune had merged the Texas Alliance with the Louisiana Farmers' Union to form the National Farmers' Alliance and dispatched organizers across the South. Membership mushroomed, and by the summer of 1888 the organization had several thousand state and local affiliates in the section and a reported membership of more than 350,000. At its peak in 1890–91 the Southern Alliance (so called to distinguish it from a parallel Northern Alliance) claimed three million members, and a separate Colored Alliance claimed well over a million more. However inflated these figures were, the Alliance was the largest farmer organization in the history of the South and the most important expression of the reform impulse in the New South. It was the taproot from which the Populist movement derived its ideology and program, and much of its political organization as well.

The program of the Alliance drew heavily upon the Grange movement of the 1870s. To help the farmer, it advocated a variety of cooperative endeavors as well as voluntary acreage restriction and controlled marketing arrangements for important crops, and the political and economic reforms commonly associated with Populism (they are discussed below). Because so much of this program depended upon government action, Alliance leaders decided to take the organization into politics. The decision was momentous, for it transformed the Alliance, the farmer movement, and southern politics. It led to the immediate overthrow of Conservative governments in South Carolina and Texas, and affected politics and government in all the other states to one degree or another. It brought to prominence a new generation of political leadership—Benjamin R. Tillman in South Carolina, Stephen S. Hogg in Texas, Thomas E. Watson in Georgia, and Reuben F. Kolb in Alabama—men who spoke the farmer's language and served the farmer's interest with varying degrees of commitment and effectiveness.

Instead of forming a third party of their own, Alliance leaders decided to work within the Democratic party. The decision was dictated by a desire to avoid the issue of white supremacy and other problems related to political division among whites. The wisdom of the decision seemed to be confirmed when in 1890 Representative Henry Cabot Lodge of Massachusetts introduced a bill in Congress authorizing federal supervision of elections and voter registration in the South. Called the "Force" bill by white southerners, Lodge's measure was prompted by the effort then underway in Mississippi and elsewhere to disfranchise blacks (and thus Republicans), and its approval by the House of Representatives alarmed whites and reinforced their commitment to the Solid South.

The Alliance strategy was spectacularly successful in the elections of 1890. In six states Alliance-backed candidates were elected governor, and in seven they won control of the legislature. In addition, about forty congressmen elected that year were members of the organization or endorsed its principles. In Georgia, where the success was most complete, Alliancemen elected William J. Northen governor and large majorities in both houses of the legislature, and defeated six incumbent congressmen who refused to embrace the Alliance platform. One of the new men they elected to Congress was Thomas E. Watson.

The embattled farmer had spoken. Among his more important successes were those in South Carolina, where Benjamin R. Tillman's election as governor ended the political supremacy of Wade Hampton and his Redeemer regime, and in Texas, where Stephen S. Hogg's elevation to the governorship had a similar impact. When all the results were in, Alliancemen congratulated themselves on having won control of the Democratic party in the South.

The situation, however, was more complex than they realized. It was one thing to win victories at the polls and quite another to translate reform platforms into law, as Alliancemen soon learned. The Democratic party was controlled by men who had little sympathy for Alliance objectives, which meant that Alliancemen had entered the political fold of a mighty and resourceful adversary. The men elected to office with Alliance backing were diverse, inexperienced, and sometimes naive, and proved to be no match for the entrenched Conservatives. Their programs were thus emasculated or rejected altogether, and their hopes turned to disillusionment. It was soon apparent that the Alliance had not taken over the Democratic party as much as the Democratic party had taken over the Alliance, and with it the farmer protest movement. If the party was changed by this process, as it was, farmer protest was changed even more. Farmers who wanted political and economic reform would have to look for it somewhere other than the Democratic party.

But that became clear only later. In December 1890 Alliancemen gathered in Ocala, Florida, to assess their recent victories and discuss the political future. Both the Northern and Southern Alliances were represented, as was the Colored Alliance, whose delegates met in separate sessions. Despite a common desire to wield their organizations into a strong political force, there was little agreement on how this might best be achieved. Northern and Colored Alliancemen tended to favor a third party, because the Democratic party on the national level was controlled by conservatives loyal to Grover Cleveland and thus offered no real alternative to the Republican party. Most Southern Alliancemen, on the other hand, preferred to work within the Democratic party. Memories of the Lodge "Force" bill were still fresh, and the recent elections had convinced them that they now controlled that party in the South.

The disagreement over this question was deep, and a final decision was postponed until a later meeting to be held in St. Louis in early 1892. The major work of the Ocala convention was thus adopting the "Ocala Platform," a statement of programs and principles to be used in evaluating political candidates. This too proved to be a divisive task, though this time the divisions cut across sectional lines. The most controversial item was the subtreasury, a proposal that the federal government operate warehouses for the storage of farm produce and provide low-interest loans to farmers while their produce was stored. This, it was hoped, would provide farmers with money at harvest time but enable them to hold their produce off the market and thus benefit from seasonal price fluctuations. The subtreasury idea was popular among farmers, but commodities dealers and other middlemen opposed it as a socialistic scheme that placed government in competition with private enterprise. In addition to the subtreasury, the Ocala Platform included such familiar demands as monetary inflation, low interest rates, lower tariffs, government ownership of railroads and communications systems, graduated income tax, restrictions on alien land ownership, curbs on speculation in commodities futures, abolition of the national banking system, and direct election of United States senators.

By February 1892, when Alliancemen met in St. Louis to resolve the question of political strategy, the results of their alliance with the Democratic party in the South were clear. In Georgia, where the success had seemed so complete, the Alliance-controlled legislature had extended the powers of the railroad commission and the state fertilizer inspector, created a college for blacks, and enacted a few other meliorative reforms, but had done nothing about the more fundamental problems of credit, crop liens, inequitable taxes, and business monopoly. It had also elected John B. Gordon, one of the old Conservative triumvirate, to the United States Senate.

This was discouraging. The farmers were simply unable to remake the Democratic party in their own image. Where their success in doing so seemed most apparent, as in South Carolina where the Tillman movement was firmly entrenched in power, the concrete achievements were no greater than in Georgia. The position of the Tillmanites was due in large part to their unwavering loyalty to the Democratic party and their effectiveness as racial demagogues. In South Carolina as in Georgia and elsewhere, farmers had the appearance of political power in the Democratic party but could not translate the appearance into substantive reform.

At St. Louis, therefore, the pressure for a third party was irresistible, though Southern Alliancemen were still divided on the issue. Their most important leader, Leonidas L. Polk of North Carolina, endorsed the third-party move, as did most Northern and Colored Alliancemen. The decision was made; the farmers created a party of their own, which they called the People's, or Populist, party. The action split the farmer movement in the South, and by election time in 1892 the Alliance there was only a shadow of its former self. The political promise of 1890 was never realized.

Southern Populism

Southern Populism was a political movement of great potential and little success, and after four years of constant battering by Democrats and white supremacists it disintegrated.[2] Yet its immediate impact was profound, and its long-term consequences lasted for half a century and more. In the South Populism was a social movement as well as a political party. It is best understood as an abortive social upheaval which in spite of its political failures forced the southern people to confront basic questions of economic and social change. What kind of society was the South to become? What place would it have for farmers and agriculture, and thus for industry and cities? What place would it have for blacks, and thus for whites? What groups would dominate its politics, and whose interests would its governments serve? But after forcing these questions to the surface, the Populist movement was not strong enough or enlightened enough to effect positive answers to them.

Before it failed, however, the Populist movement touched the vitals of southern life and aroused intense passions. It challenged established elites by a conscious appeal to the frustrated and dispossessed, and the economic and political changes it proposed were more far-reaching than those put forth by any other reform movement in the New South. Yet Populism was a complex phenomenon that has always meant different things to different people. Some historians have seen it as a radical movement offering realistic solutions to fundamental problems, and some as an episode in the history of Jeffersonian liberalism. Others have described it as a backward-looking effort to retreat from modern realities, while still others have pictured it as an extrusion of the frustrations and darker prejudices of the nation's hinterland. Since it was at once a political party, a social movement, an ideology, and even a state of mind, it no doubt had elements of all of these features. But viewed in a historical context, southern Populism seems chiefly notable for the depth and realism of its social analysis and the genuineness of its commitment to reform. Its leaders, of whom Thomas E. Watson of Georgia was most important, used the rhetoric of Jeffersonian democracy, but their meaning was often deeper. "The Peoples Party says to [the poor white and the poor black]," Watson said on one occasion, " 'You are kept apart that you may be separately fleeced of your earnings. You are made to hate each other because upon that hatred is rested the keystone of the arch of financial despotism which enslaves you both. You are deceived and blinded that you may not see how this race antagonism perpetuates a monetary system which beggars you both.' " "The accident of color," he also said, "can make no difference in the interest of farmers, croppers, and laborers."

Such frank appeals to class interest across racial lines were made by only a minority of Populists. Yet the logic of Populist thought pointed toward such appeals, and if the political process had been free and honest, the movement might have moved further to the left. As it was, the Populists sought, in the words of George B. Tindall, "to organize a party of radical reform based on a coalition of the lower orders, white and black, in conflict with the established powers of the community." They proposed, that is, to shift the economic base of political power. This was what alarmed their conservative critics and made Populism radical in the context of the New South. "Populism collided full tilt with the whole edifice of Southern politics," T. Harry Williams has observed; "with the romantic attachment to images of the past; with the separation of politics and economics; with the entombing one-party system; and with the [white] folk unity forged by Reconstruction. The Populists talked the language of economics and self-interest. They spoke of class consciousness and class legislation, of combining farmers and laborers and sections in one party, of using government to solve economic problems. Most alarming of all, they said that economic self-interest transcended race."

Populist methodology, which pointedly espoused government activism, fitted these purposes. "We believe that the powers of government—in other words of the people—should be expanded . . . to the end that oppression, injustice, and poverty shall eventually cease in the land," read the party's national platform; and southern Populists entered no demurrers on this point. It was in this proposal that Populists made their basic contribution to American and southern reform. Their equation of government with the people and the acceptance of positive government for reformist ends represented a turning point in the history of American liberalism. In a democratic society made interdependent by the industrial revolution, they believed, the Jeffersonian suspicion of government was outmoded.

Yet there were important limitations to Populist radicalism. Populists had no real objections to capitalism and private property or to any of the basic institutions of southern society except Conservative rule and one-party politics. They were not alienated from the southern way of life in any fundamental sense; rather, they were frustrated by their inability to secure a fair share of its material and social rewards. They felt not like strangers in a strange land, but a people victimized in their own land. They regarded themselves as the majority—"the people"—but felt that the people had lost control of their own society to special interests who circumscribed opportunity and robbed them of the fruits of their toil. Thus farmers were driven into tenancy or off the land altogether, and labor was impoverished and made dependent. Accepting a version of the labor theory of value, Populists saw their society as one in which the producers of wealth—farmers, laborers, and small entrepreneurs—were locked in struggle with economic parasites —monopolists, bankers, and other middlemen. In league with corrupt politicans, the latter groups, they said, were using government to favor the rich over the poor through such things as protective tariffs, centralized banking, deflationary monetary policies, and tax concessions.

But after pointing to this link between politics and economics, the main thrust of Populist analysis turned from realism to parochialism. The plight of the farmer and laborer was explained not in terms of economic forces, but as the result of a conspiratorial combination of eastern and European money men who manipulated the economies of two continents for selfish purposes. This undermined the radical implications of Populist analysis, and shifted the analysis in directions that had conservative consequences. For if the plight of poor southerners was due to forces outside the South, there was little reason to pursue basic questions about the organization of southern society. Thus the social realism of advanced Populist thinkers did not permeate the movement, and most of those who joined the movement were only quasi-Populists, men who shared the farmer's grievances but had little understanding of the economic sources of his problems. In politics these quasi-Populists did not push Populist logic to its logical conclusion.

Instead, they viewed reform as a piecemeal process of changes that were basically political instead of economic, and liberal and meliorative instead of fundamental.

The result was that Populism had the same limitations as Radical Reconstruction: it lacked a sufficient economic content. Dominated by landowning farmers and dependent on a constituency that did not grasp its underlying rationale, political Populism never got to the root of the farmers' problems. It had little to offer the poorest farmers—that growing mass of tenants, sharecroppers, and agricultural laborers—and little to help those small landowners imperiled by tenancy. Together these groups were a majority of southern farmers, and in the 1890s they needed land reform as much as the freedmen had in the aftermath of emancipation. Indeed, until the spread of tenancy was halted, little could be done about the general plight of southern agriculture. Nor were Populists prepared to deal with the special problems of black farmers. To have done so would have led them to another issue as untouchable and yet as vital as land reform, the racism of whites. Thomas E. Watson and others like him worked for a political alliance between whites and blacks, but it was a marriage of convenience, not conviction, that they sought, and for limited political purposes. However progressive the efforts of such men were, they rested on expediency rather than a desire to confront the problem of racism, and ended as soon as they came under general assault. Racism like land reform was too deep a problem to deal with.

Yet for all its limitations, Populism offered southern voters something they did not always have, a choice rather than an echo. Populist victory at the polls might well have made a difference in the subsequent course of the section's political history. In office the Populists might have restrained the power of business in meaningful ways and restored some balance to economic and political life. They would surely have made politics more democratic and government less indifferent to popular needs, and they might also have scotched the drift toward racial extremism.

But those things were not to be. As a third party the Populists had little leeway in matters of political strategy. Inside the South they tried to form a coalition of farmers, laborers, blacks, and reformers, and on the national level to forge an alliance between the South and the Midwest. Neither effort was successful. Tillman in South Carolina, Hogg in Texas, and many other farmer-politicians remained in the Democratic party, and in Georgia, Florida, North Carolina, and elsewhere Democrats incorporated much of the Populist program in their own platforms. In addition most blacks saw little future in a party that appealed chiefly to poorer whites, many of whom were racial extremists. The hoped-for coalition never developed.

The party's success in 1892 was disappointing. The sudden death of Leonidas L. Polk of North Carolina, the leading candidate for the presidential nomination, was a major blow to Populist prospects in the South. James B. Weaver of Iowa, who received the nomination, got only about 15 percent of the vote in the Confederate South, and in none of the states was his showing impressive. Candidates for state office fared better, but their actual strength is impossible to determine because of violence and intimidation in the election campaign and fraud in counting the votes. It is clear that in 1892 and again in 1894 several Populists were denied victories they won, in Georgia, Alabama, Louisiana, and elsewhere. Even with Democrats doing the counting, the party's showing, especially in 1894, was impressive in several states. In North Carolina a Populist-Republican fusion won control of the legislature that year, and in Georgia, where fraud was especially widespread, the party received 44.5 percent of the votes counted. In Mississippi the reported total was one-third of the popular vote, and in Virginia in the previous year the party's candidate for governor carried 22 of the state's 100 counties.

The showdown came in 1896. Despite the disappointments of 1894, Populist prospects were still bright. Reaction seemed to be building against the frauds perpetrated by Democrats, and the nationwide depression underscored the necessity for relief and reform. On the national level the conservatism of the Cleveland administration in a period of hard times and popular unrest pointed up the need for a reformist alternative to the Democratic and Republican parties. But as fate would have it, the Populists would be more than disappointed in 1896; both they and their party would in fact be crushed. The cause of their undoing was the Democratic national convention, which turned against President Grover Cleveland and his brand of conservatism and adopted a platform that incorporated the heart of the Populist program. It also nominated a populistic candidate for the presidency, Congressman William Jennings Bryan of Nebraska.

These actions placed Populists in a quandary. If they endorsed Bryan, their party would be destroyed on the national level and their candidates for state and local offices robbed of the rationale behind their candidacy. But it they offered a presidential candidate of their own, the populistic vote would be split and the election of William McKinley, a conservative Republican, assured. Reluctantly, they chose the former course and tried unsuccessfully to get Thomas E. Watson named as Bryan's running mate. The election results fulfilled their worst fears. Bryan carried every southern state only to be overwhelmed by McKinley in the rest of the country, and Populist candidates for lesser offices suffered a similar fate except in North Carolina, where a Fusionist slate of Populists and Republicans was successful. "Our party, as a party, does not exist anymore," lamented Watson after the returns were in. He was right; the party was no longer a significant political force.

What had happened? On the national level the strength of the two-party system had operated to co-opt a major insurgency and pull it into one of the established parties and thus back to the political center. In the South the mechanisms of the one-party system had worked once again to eliminate political divisions among whites and drive a new wedge between blacks and poor whites. Since most blacks had voted—or at least been counted—for the Democrats, populistic whites became in the aftermath more resentful than ever of black voting. Farmer protest had failed, or rather had been contained by the absorptive capacity of the Democratic party and the overriding commitment to white supremacy. Disillusioned, many populistic farmers lost faith in politics and reform, and as their economic situation eased they became politically apathetic. Stripped of its social realism, what remained of the farmer movement was easy prey to racial extremism and political demagoguery. In beating back the Populist threat, Democrats had appealed to the basest prejudices of race and section, and in the aftermath came a new breed of southern politician, demagogues who spoke the language of farmers and the rhetoric of protest but were chiefly concerned with their own political advancement.

The failure of Populism marked the final triumph of the Solid South,[3] a political phenomenon usually dated from 1880. From that year until 1920, when Republican Warren G. Harding carried Tennessee, every electoral vote from the Confederate South was cast for the Democratic candidate for President, and that pattern was repeated again from 1924 until 1948 except in the unusual election of 1928. Outside a handful of counties in Appalachia, this near unanimity also prevailed in local, state, and congressional elections. Through the first half of the twentieth century, for example, every governor except one in the Confederate South and every United States senator except one were Democrats.

The unity these figures suggest was both real and illusory, and the Solid South is a useful as well as a deceptive concept. It is deceptive if it is taken to mean that white southerners were united on all or even most of the political issues they faced between Reconstruction and World War II. But it is useful if it is understood that the divisions among them were within the larger unity demanded by white supremacy. White southerners united politically for one basic reason, to control blacks, for which purpose unity was necessary in dealing with "outside interference" on the race issue. The Solid South was the device which embodied this unity, and the Democratic party was its agency. This made the party in the South not an ordinary political organization, but an instrument of sectional foreign policy as it were, uniting whites behind a bipartisan foreign policy while permitting them to divide on domestic matters unrelated to race. Yet by forcing all whites into one party, this arrangement inhibited political divisions along economic, geographical, or ideological lines, and in that way it served another major function, containing white protest. What seemed on the surface a device for controlling blacks and protecting white supremacy was also an instrument of class control. Its function along this line was perfected between 1890 and 1908 when blacks and poor whites found themselves deprived of the right to vote.

The Declining Status of Blacks

Among the bridges that linked Populism and Progressivism were the movements to disfranchise blacks and poor whites and to legalize racial segregation. To understand those movements, it is necessary to look backward for a moment at the declining status of black southerners after Reconstruction.[4] For blacks the New South was an inhospitable place. Between Redemption and World War I their political power and legal position declined sharply, and their economic and social progress was fitful at best. During this period the race was abandoned by white liberals and thrown back upon its own meager resources, and one by one the guarantees of Reconstruction were lost.

Between 1860 and 1910 the number of blacks in the South more than doubled, and there was relatively little migration from the section. In the latter year four-fifths of all black Americans still lived in the Confederate South, where they constituted 35 percent of the population. In Mississippi and South Carolina they were a majority, as they were in 261 counties across the black belt; and in six deep South states they were almost half (47 percent) the total population. Migration within the South in these years was from the Southeast to the Southwest, and into the cities. Between 1880 and 1910, the net migration of blacks from the Confederate South totaled 689,000, less than half the number of whites (1,547,000) who left the section.

A basic shift in the pattern of population growth occurred, however. The census of 1880 reported that in eight states of the Confederate South the black population was growing at a faster rate than the white population, and in one of the other three states almost as fast. In 1910, on the other hand, the rate of increase of the white population was larger in every state, and that pattern has continued ever since. What this means is that as racial extremism mounted and the status of blacks declined, increasing numbers of the race fled the South. Disfranchisement, the legalizing of segregation, and the rate of racial violence around the turn of the century increased as the proportion of blacks in the southern population crested. White fear that blacks might overwhelm the South by sheer numbers was still widespread at that time, and it was centainly a factor in the triumph of racial extremism. The extremism "worked"; that is, it drove many blacks from the section and "saved" the South for white supremacy. By the 1950s, when the civil rights movement became important, the proportion of blacks in the South's population had dropped far below the level of 1910, and whites accommodated themselves to desegregation with an ease that would have been impossible at the earlier date.

The efforts of white supremacists made black progress difficult after Reconstruction. In 1900, more than a generation after emancipation, blacks owned only about 8 percent of the farms and 6.5 percent of the farmland in five deep South states, and in the section as a whole more than three-quarters of all black farmers were tenants of some kind, mostly sharecroppers. Outside agriculture many of the skilled trades traditionally open to the race began to close after the turn of the century. In the building and machine trades opportunity shrank, and production-line jobs in textiles and other new industries were never open. There remained only menial, dirty, or back-breaking work in such areas as coal mining, turpentining, and logging, and in these black employment was high. But there was another, more positive side of the economic situation that began to open up. The development of segregated communities provided a variety of employment and business opportunities, especially in retailing, the service trades, and some of the professions, and a small but important middle class began to emerge. In 1913, on the fiftieth anniversary of the Emancipation Proclamation, black southerners owned an estimated 550,000 homes, 128,000 farms, 38,000 businesses, and had a total wealth of $700 million. The illiteracy rate, which had exceeded 90 percent in 1863, had dropped to 30 percent.

Despite the progress reflected in these figures, racial discrimination was always the chief determinant of black life in the New South. Violence, fraud, and a variety of socioeconomic pressures combined to keep most blacks poor, dependent, and insecure. The full story of this cannot be told here, but the general pattern may be seen by a brief look at the growing political powerlessness of the race.

It began with the use of illegal and extralegal methods to contain black voting and insure white supremacy in the Redemption campaigns, and continued step by step until the race was completely removed from politics about three decades later. In 1877, to illustrate, the Georgia legislature enacted a cumulative poll tax on the right to vote that produced a notable reduction in voting by blacks (and poor whites). To be eligible to vote after the tax became effective, a Georgian had to pay a poll tax not only for the year in which he registered but for every year since the enactment of the law (or his twenty-first birthday). To miss a payment one year, even when there were no elections, was to double the tax for the following year, and to omit payment for several years made the tax prohibitive for poor men. The effect was striking. In 1888 only 37.3 percent of the potential electorate actually voted in that state (and only 10 percent of the potential black electorate), compared to 65.7 percent of the potential electorate in the rest of the South. South Carolina achieved a similar effect with an "eight ballot box law" in 1882. This law imposed an indirect literacy test on voters by requiring separate ballots and ballot boxes for each office being contested and further requiring the voter to deposit each of his marked ballots in the correct box. A ballot dropped in the wrong box was voided. Election officials were permitted to help illiterate voters, but no penalty was imposed for giving erroneous instructions. Again, the results were remarkable. The Republican vote in South Carolina declined from 58,000 in 1880 to 22,000 in 1884, and the Democratic vote from 112,000 to 70,000. But the Democratic margin rose from less than two to one to more than three to one in a state whose population was three-fifths black.

This piecemeal reduction in black voting was paralleled by the decline in political support for the race. Shortly after he became President in 1877, Republican Rutherford B. Hayes announced that his administration would "require absolute justice and fair play to the negro," but this, he insisted, "could be got best and almost surely by trusting the honorable and influential southern whites." "I believe that your rights and interests would be safer," he told a delegation of blacks, "if [the] great mass of intelligent [southern] white men were let alone by the general government." The paternalism of Conservatives like Wade Hampton thus paid political dividends.

As the federal executive became less concerned with blacks and southern race policy, the Supreme Court began emasculating the guarantees of Radical Reconstruction. In the *Slaughter House Cases* (1873) and *United States v. Cruikshank* (1878), the Court sharply restricted the meaning of the Fourteenth Amendment for blacks. This was done by defining as narrowly as possible the rights of national as distinct from state citizenship, and then ruling that the amendment protected only the rights of national citizenship. The rights of state citizenship would have to be safeguarded by the states, and blacks with complaints against the states must seek redress through state courts or the legislature. This interpretation was broadened in the *Civil Rights Cases* (1883), in which the Civil Rights Act of 1875 was declared unconstitutional. The Court ruled in those cases that the Fourteenth Amendment prohibited the states from practicing racial discrimination in public accommodations but did not prohibit individuals, including proprietors of businesses serving the public, from excluding whomever they pleased from their places of business. Blacks who objected to the exclusion must seek redress through state governments, which could prohibit such acts by law, but not from the federal government, which could not.

Disfranchisement, White and Black

Political redress through state government, which is what the Court was suggesting in these decisions, was a meaningful option for blacks only if they could vote freely. That fact made the movement toward complete disfranchisement all the more significant. That movement began in 1890 in Mississippi and continued until 1908, by which time no blacks at all could vote in most of the South and only token numbers in the rest of the section. This was one of the most important developments in the history of the South.

The demand for complete disfranchisement began in Mississippi and grew in part from the farmer movement and in part from reaction to the Lodge "Force" bill in Congress. Many white farmers had become convinced that elimination of the state's large black electorate was the only way to permit whites to divide politically and thus the one way to foster the kind of political reform movement they supported. Their efforts toward this end had no success, however, until Senator James Z. George, the state's most prominent Conservative, lent his support and joined the farmers' call for a state constitutional convention. An announced purpose of the convention was to devise legal ways to disfranchise blacks and thereby eliminate the fraud that demoralized the state's politics, and to do this in a way that would not invite federal interference. The problem of course was the Fifteenth Amendment, which prohibited racial discrimination in voting rights, and the task was to devise voter qualifications that were ostensibly nonracial but would actually eliminate black voting. However, every possible qualification—literacy, property, payment of taxes, residence, good character, or whatever—would if equitably applied disfranchise large numbers of whites too, especially those who were poor, propertyless, and illiterate.

The latter prospect was a vital consideration. It would mean disfranchising large numbers of sharecroppers, marginal farmers, cotton mill workers, and other whites to whom political protest movements were often appealing. Conservatives in Mississippi and elsewhere recognized the political advantage for themselves in this, but they were skeptical of its acceptability. Would the mass of whites acquiesce in it, especially in a period of social protest? Certainly not if it were done too suddenly and directly. If it were to be done at all, it would have to be done through the process of black disfranchisement and rationalized as a necessary part of the effort to defend white supremacy. The first step would thus be the disfranchisement of blacks, which would be accompanied by laws with loopholes and discretionary authority by which (white) registrars could remove blacks from the voting lists without necessarily removing whites. This plus assurances that the laws would not be used against whites accomplished the first purpose, and laws and loopholes alike were enacted. The most important loopholes were the "understanding clause" and the "grandfather clause." The first of these permitted the registration of any illiterate who gave whatever the registrar thought was a "reasonable" explanation of a section of the state constitution the registrar read to him. Since the basic qualification was typically property ownership or literacy, this gave registrars almost complete discretion in who could and could not register. The effect was to remove the fraud that had long been practiced in the counting of votes by transferring it to the registration of voters. The grandfather clause, pioneered by Louisiana, exempted from the state's new voter qualification laws anyone who would have been eligible to vote under the laws in effect in the state on January 1, 1867. This was the last New Year's Day before Radical Reconstruction, when essentially all adult white males but no blacks had been eligible to vote.

Whether from design or accident, none of the loopholes ever worked very well; that is, few poor or illiterate whites ever used them to qualify for the suffrage. The reason for this seems to have been the fact that the new procedures made registration for such people not only difficult but embarrassing. The poor man was forced to acknowledge his poverty or illiteracy, ask for help in filling out a confusing application form, and otherwise accommodate himself to intricate procedures he did not understand. In any case the loopholes became largely meaningless when poll taxes were imposed, for that made the right to vote cost money.

What began as a racial movement thus became a class movement as well. White farmers had wanted to remove blacks from the electorate to further their own political interests, but it was the Conservatives who gained most from disfranchisement in Mississippi, and the Mississippi example seemed more and more attractive to Conservatives in other states as the Populist threat grew in the mid-1890s. During the height of the threat in 1895, the Tillmanites and Conservatives in South Carolina joined forces in a constitutional convention and accomplished in that state what the Mississippians had already done. The Populist upheaval convinced Conservatives everywhere of the desirability of limiting the franchise as a means of containing political protest, and they now joined the disfranchisement movement. Louisiana (1898), Alabama (1901), and Virginia (1901–02) accomplished disfranchisement by state constitutional conventions. North Carolina (1900), Texas (1902), and Georgia (1908) amended their existing constitutions. Tennessee, Florida, and Arkansas used statutes and poll taxes.

The class as well as the racial nature of this movement was evident in the devices used to accomplish it. The property qualification for voting was quite high, typically requiring ownership of property assessed for tax purposes at $200 or $300. Since tax assessments were far below market value, these figures represented a requirement that in many areas exceeded the average value of property per person. The definition of literacy, typically the ability to read any section of the state constitution, was also much higher than that used by the Census Bureau, which classified anyone as literate who could read or write anything.

The poll tax, however, was the great disfranchiser. A tax on the right to vote, it had no purpose but restricting the size of the electorate. Typically the tax was no more than $1 or $2 a year, but those sums were larger than an average day's pay for a considerable portion of the population. Moreover, the tax was administered in a way that discouraged voting. It was payable months in advance of election day, often at a time of the year when farmers had no cash, and some states required the voter to present his receipt when registering and/or voting. Loss of the receipt meant loss of the right to vote even if the tax had been paid. Under such a system, a poll tax receipt became a ticket to the voting booth, and politicians or employers might buy up a number of receipts to distribute among their supporters for use on election day.

Other devices were also used to discourage voting. The secret ballot, which every state adopted during this period, was itself a literacy test that increased the difficulty and embarrassment of voting for many people. The advent of primary elections for nominating Democratic candidates for public office gave officials of that party control over who could and could not vote in the only meaningful elections in the one-party South. Acting as a private club with control of its own membership, the party excluded blacks from its primaries. This meant that those blacks who managed to register could vote only in general elections in which for state and local offices they had a choice between the winner of the white Democratic primary—and no one.

The impact of these measures on voter registration was impressive. In Mississippi the number of whites registered to vote declined from about 120,000 in 1890 to 68,127 in 1892, and in the latter year there were only 8,615 blacks registered despite the fact that more than half the state's population was black. In Louisiana the number of whites registered to vote declined from 164,088 in 1897 to 91,716 in 1904, a drop of 44 percent, while the figure for blacks fell from 130,344 to 1,342, down 99 percent. In Georgia in 1910 the number of registered white voters was equal to 74 percent of the number of adult white males in the state, but for blacks the ratio was only 4.3 percent.

The effects on voting were even greater. In every presidential election in the Confederate South between 1876 and 1904 the proportion of the potential electorate who actually voted declined. The overall drop was from 65 percent to 29 percent. Between 1892 and 1902 the average number of votes cast for each congressman in Alabama, Mississippi, Louisiana, Florida, Arkansas, and Georgia declined by 60 percent or more, and in Virginia and Tennessee by 50 percent or more. The number of votes cast for the Republican presidential candidate in Mississippi declined from 43,000 in 1884 to 1,500 in 1892. Virginians cast 264,095 votes in the presidential election in 1900 and 129,929 in 1904. Overall, the incidence of voting in Virginia dropped from 147 per 1,000 population in 1900 to 67 in 1904, and continued to drop until it reached 10 in 1940. In a heated senatorial contest in that state in 1911, only 18 percent of the adult males voted, and the winner received the vote of only 12 percent of the potential electorate.

The impact of this sharp decline in voting was felt throughout southern politics. Blacks were left politically helpless, and their disfranchisement was followed by a flood of segregation laws. Racial concerns remained a major political issue, however, for the disfranchised blacks were ideal political scapegoats, and contrary to the hope of populistic whites who had originally supported black disfranchisement, race became more, not less, important as a device for obscuring economic issues. Whites did not divide as farmer dissidents had hoped. Instead, in an electorate confined to white supremacists, commitment to white supremacy became the first test of every candidate for public office. The level of political leadership declined in some respects, and politics at its worst became little more than an outdoor sport, an instrument of amusement and distraction rather than socioeconomic realism. Even at its best it was oligarchic, for the reduced electorate facilitated the dominance of courthouse gangs and personal or statewide machines.

Disfranchisement, then, was not a result of the rise of poor whites to political power, but an incident in the conservative counterrevolution against Populism. It eliminated voters black and white who might disturb conservative interests, and it reinforced the political and economic dominance of business men and black belt planters. It had the distinct advantage for those groups of reducing the need for electoral fraud while guaranteeing acceptable results at the polls. That is, it so restricted the range of choices available to voters that regardless of who won, white supremacy and economic conservatism were secure. The demagogues who soon became familiar fixtures on the political landscape were embarrassing to conservatives but not threatening, for none of them was radical in anything but rhetoric. In fact by focusing the voters' attention on race and personality, they diverted it from economic and social concerns. Reformers too were acceptable, even preferable to demagogues, for they worked only to improve existing structures and thereby enhanced popular support for the established order of things.

That these were among the purposes of disfranchisement was apparent in several ways. Almost all the leaders of the movement were conservative Democrats associated with the political alliance between businessmen and black belt planters, and almost all the opponents were Populists, populistic representatives of the white upcountry, or blacks or Republicans. Only in Mississippi and South Carolina was the influence of farmers notable in the movement, and even there Conservatives played key roles. Everywhere, disfranchisement was accomplished by men espousing elitist attitudes. All of them agreed more or less with the later assessment of a Mississippi congressman who said that the results had been to disfranchise "not only the ignorant and vicious black, but the ignorant and vicious white as well" and to confine the electorate "to those alone, who are qualified by intelligence and character for the proper and patriotic exercise of . . . [the] franchise." "It is not the negro vote which works the harm, for the negroes are generally Republicans," said a delegate to the Virginia constitutional convention of 1901-2, "but it is the depraved and incompetent men of our own race, who have nothing at stake in government, and who are used by designing politicians to accomplish their purposes, irrespective of the welfare of the community."

Opponents of the movement recognized these purposes. The poll tax is a device to rob "the laboring people . . . of their liberties at the ballot box," declared the remnants of the Populist party in Texas in 1902. "Every laboring man who loves liberty, who believes in freedom of suffrage, who prizes his rights of citizenship should vote against the poll tax amendment." That amendment is a "cunning effort of the wealthier classes to defeat the will of the people by disfranchising the poorer classes," added the Texas Federation of Labor.

In an analysis of popular voting on disfranchisement referenda, J. Morgan Kousser found a significant correlation between wealth and voting patterns in five of six states. Whites of middle and higher levels of wealth, he found, were more likely to vote for disfranchisement than those of the lower economic classes. In only one of the five states in which disfranchisement was achieved by a constitutional change was the change submitted to the people for ratification, and in that state, Alabama, it was rejected by a majority of white voters only to be carried by large majorities returned from the black belt.

The disfranchisement movement thus represented a reversal of democratic trends that began in the Age of Andrew Jackson. At the time of the Civil War the general rule in southern politics had been universal white manhood suffrage, and Radical Reconstruction extended that to universal manhood suffrage. The new restrictions on voting were thus reactionary in the classic sense of the term, returning voter qualifications to pre-Jackson formulas. The same was true of other provisions of the new state constitutions, which expanded executive and judicial authority at the expense of the legislature, made more offices appointive, and insulated the judiciary from popular influence.

The Triumph of Segregation

For poor whites, disfranchisement meant political neglect, but for blacks it brought increased repression. Its most immediate consequence was the legalizing of segregation, which was already the general practice in racial contact but had never been written into law. In view of the rigidity and pervasiveness segregation soon attained, this seems surprising. Education had always been segregated except in random instances during Reconstruction and interracial marriage proscribed, but not until the end of the nineteenth century did segregation in public accommodations have the force of law. Between 1887 and 1891 seven states began requiring segregation in public transportation, but the vast majority of segregation laws were passed between 1898 and 1915. Once enacted, however, they constituted a code of racial conduct that was just as extensive as and probably more rigidly enforced than the slave codes of the antebellum era. The new laws touched every point of interracial contact—employment, religion, education, public accommodations, recreation, even sickness and death— and in all of them separate facilities for each race were required. The Supreme Court soon ruled that such facilities were constitutional only if those provided each race were equal, but in actuality that was never insisted upon. For blacks segregation frequently meant no facilities at all.

The meaning of the new racial order was therefore quite different for whites and blacks. For whites segregation provided social insulation from a race of people regarded as inferior and undesirable. For blacks it made life a series of invidious racial tests that inhibited education, economic opportunity, and social mobility and made equal protection of the laws impossible. It also meant poverty, dependence, back-breaking toil, inferior medical care, and shorter life expectancy. It warped social roles and economic activity among blacks, and thus inhibited the development of group pride and the things that constitute community. Among its important results were resentment and frustration among blacks and feelings of arrogance among whites, and thus a further deepening of racial feelings in southern life. At best it encouraged paternalism on the one hand and dependent accommodation on the other.

The belated emergence of legal segregation has been the subject of the best-known debate in New South historiography, and a brief look at that debate will cast additional light on the nature of race relations in the New South. The debate is an outgrowth of C. Vann Woodward's *The Strange Career of Jim Crow,* first published in 1956.[5] Woodward found two things especially strange in the history of segregation. First, "racial segregation in the South in the rigid and universal form it [eventually took] did not appear with the end of slavery, but toward the latter years of the century and later." And second, "before it appeared in this form there transpired an era of experiment and variety in race relations of the South in which segregation was not the invariable rule." This experiment and variety, Woodward suggested, were sufficiently widespread to have constituted a potential alternative to the extremism that triumphed after 1890. The implication was that segregation and racial extremism were not immutable parts of the southern heritage.

Woodward's thesis was a major challenge to previous thinking on this subject, and it has been extensively researched and debated. As modified in the second edition of *The Strange Career of Jim Crow,* which appeared in 1966, it has been generally supported by the weight of evidence. In the 1870s and 1880s public transportation was often unsegregated even in the deep South and the black belt. Moreover, blacks voted in large numbers and were sometimes elected to office, and black voting combined with Conservative paternalism to exercise a moderating influence on race relations. The significance of Woodward's thesis for the general history of the South thus hinges not on the question of whether there were instances of racial moderation and ambiguity in the color line before the late 1890s, but whether those instances were numerous and systematic enough to constitute a potential alternative to the extremism that developed after 1890.

This is a complex issue but one that is central to an understanding of the New South. As Woodward notes, it is "preposterous" to suggest that the '70s and '80s were a golden age of race relations. "On the contrary," he writes, "the evidence of race conflict and violence, brutality and exploitation in this very period is overwhelming." Similar cautions have been sounded by those who endorse his thesis. In an informative study of *Race Relations in Virginia, 1870–1902* (1961), Charles E. Wynes found no "generally accepted code of race mores" in that state. Rather, "inconsistency" was "the most distinguishing factor" in race relations there. Yet Wynes also found that "by the mid-1870s the Conservatives had generally succeeded in putting the Negro in his place," and as a result blacks had ceased to be "a major factor" in Virginia politics. Except on trains, the black Virginian "in nearly all instances met with cold rejection and physical eviction" from public accommodations, Wynes wrote, and "in despair" had "ceased to insist upon being granted many of his rights."

Admittedly, then, the case for racial moderation in the Conservative era is not very strong. In fact in the long range of southern history the moderation that did exist seems better explained by temporary and special circumstances than by a broad commitment to moderation itself. There is little evidence that any significant group of white southerners was committed to racial moderation out of principle rather than expediency. This does not mean that no moderation existed; it suggests instead that the possibility of steering racial policy in a permanently moderate direction depended upon institutionalizing the temporary and special circumstances that made the expediency attractive. Those circumstances included the federal presence during Radical Reconstruction and the possibility until the early 1890s that it might be invoked again. The defeat of the Lodge "Force" bill in 1890 and the repeal of all the Reconstruction election laws in 1894 signaled the end of that possibility. Then, too, the very fact that blacks had the right to vote and exercised it widely after 1877 made their immediate and wholesale disfranchisement impossible. They would have to be disfranchised in stages. As long as blacks could vote, both Conservatives and insurgents had reason to appeal to the race. But as black voting diminished in the 1880s, so did the leverage of the race, and in their growing powerlessness blacks turned perforce from politics to accommodation, and that was another factor that enhanced the freedom of action of whites. By the mid-1890s whites had a free hand in racial matters, and by that time also Conservatives and insurgents agreed that blacks should be disfranchised. As soon as whites had a free hand, they turned toward extremism.

The significance of Woodward's thesis for the general history of the New South is also affected by its restricted definition of segregation. " 'Segregation,' as the word is used here," Woodward wrote, "means physical distance, not social distance—physical separation of people for reasons of race." This is a better definition of the northern form of segregation than the southern. Though the two forms had much in common, they were also meaningfully different. To oversimplify the difference, the purpose of segregation in the North was to maximize the physical distance between the race, while that in the South was intended to enlarge the social distance. Historically, northern whites tended to object to the presence of blacks in their midst and worked to keep the race out of the section. Thus in the antebellum era they supported free soil, one result of which was to keep blacks out of the West, and in some states they passed laws against the in-migration of all blacks. During the Civil War and Reconstruction many of them were concerned to keep the freedmen in the South. Southern whites, on the other hand, have acted differently. "It is not so much the presence of the negro to which the [southern] whites object," Holland Thompson observed in 1914, "but to that presence in other than an inferior capacity."

Whites and blacks in the New South were physically much closer to each other than those in the North. Residential patterns were generally unsegregated; large ghettoes were not typical. In the mid-1870s, for example, 81 percent of the residential blocks in Charleston, South Carolina, were interracial, though the trend was toward increasing segregation, so that by 1920 only 55 percent of the residential blocks in that city were interracial. The persistence of paternalism and deference and economic interdependence kept the races close together even as the social distance between them increased. Often, perhaps typically, whites and blacks worked side by side, even though both understood and acknowledged the distinction between "white" and "nigger" jobs. They also lived side by side in rural as well as urban areas, but everywhere the distinction between "white houses" and "nigger houses" was just as clear. Master and servant, mistress and maid, white children and black nurses traveled together and displayed in public the close relationships that bound them together. Black servants accompanied whites in the white sections of segregated facilities. The aim of the segregation laws was not simply physical separation of the races; the larger purpose was to insure that all interracial contact reflected the supremacy of whites and dependence of blacks.

Despite the weight of tradition, a major evolution occurred in race relations in the New South, and the legalization of segregation around the turn of the century reflected the change. To use Pierre van den Berghe's terminology, the paternalistic pattern of race relations that typifies agricultural, plantation, and preindustrial societies gave way to the competitive pattern characteristic of modern industrial societies. In a paternalistic pattern, the races are separated by slavery or some other institutional arrangement that preserves white supremacy and precludes economic and social competition. This serves to limit racist extremism by removing the necessity for it—whites are not threatened by blacks. It also operates to encourage paternalism and ameliorate the effects of the racism implicit in the inequality of the arrangement. In a competitive pattern, on the other hand, impassable institutional barriers like slavery are eliminated and the masses of the two races are thrown into economic competition with each other. And since nothing now separates the races but race itself, whites become more than ever preoccupied with the racial aspects of their condition, and racist extremism becomes more important as an instrument for asserting and maintaining supremacy.

This schema, as Woodward notes, sheds considerable light on race relations in the New South. The transition from paternalism to competition explains the variations in racial patterns observed by Woodward and others, as well as the turn to rigid segregation around the turn of the century. It underscores the reality of the moderation Woodward described, but suggests that it was a surviving remnant of the past rather than a promise of what might have been in the future.

The Age of Booker T. Washington

For blacks in the New South there was no easy way out of their predicament. At the end of the century the Supreme Court shut them off from the normal avenues of political and judicial redress. In *Plessy v. Ferguson* (1896) the Court ruled in effect that state laws requiring racial segregation did not violate the equal protection clause of the Fourteenth Amendment as long as the laws did not require unequal facilities for the races. This decision formalized the principle that state and local governments could deal with citizens on the basis of their racial identity. Two years later, in *Williams v. Mississippi* (1898), the Court accepted the actions by which blacks had been disfranchised in Mississippi. In both of these decisions the Court refused to look beyond the letter of the law and ask whether the effect was discriminatory, and until it was willing to do that, segregation was safe from judicial interference.

Black leaders were in a dilemma. With political activity and judicial appeal cut off, what could they do? They tried petitions, boycotts, public protests, appeals to northern liberals, accommodationist pleadings, and all of these together, but nothing stemmed the tide of white supremacy. Between 1890 and 1915 one of the major themes in the history of black southerners was the search for answers to basic questions of racial policy. How could the effects of white racism be neutralized? What priorities should be pressed immediately, and in the long run? What place should the race strive for in the South?

Counsel was divided. Isaiah Montgomery, the only black delegate to the Mississippi constitutional convention of 1890 urged acquiescence. A well-off planter, Montgomery voted for the franchise restrictions adopted by the convention and urged blacks to accommodate themselves to the new order of white supremacy. In South Carolina Robert Smalls and Thomas E. Miller offered a different example, and continued the protest tradition of Frederick Douglass. They advised, not acquiescence, but that blacks work for political and civil equality and for federal "interference" to protect their rights. Some blacks despaired of the South, and urged migration to the North or Africa or elsewhere. Benjamin Singleton led an exodus of several thousand to Kansas in the years around 1880, while Bishop Henry M. Turner of the African Methodist Episcopal Church advocated migration to Africa.

Neither colonization nor migration was very attractive. Most blacks supported instead a form of conservative racial nationalism that emphasized accommodation, self-help, and separate community development, while others, a minority at first, supported a more liberal movement aimed at integration and interracialism. This was the era of Booker T. Washington, the foremost advocate of accommodation and self-help and the most significant leader of blacks in the New South era. Born a slave in western Virginia a few years before the Civil War, Washington had little formal education, but that little, under Samuel C. Armstrong at Hampton Institute in Virginia, molded his racial thought in conservative directions. Upon Armstrong's recommendation, Washington was appointed in 1881 to establish a school for blacks at Tuskegee in the heart of Alabama's black belt. With student labor, white philanthropy, and his own untiring effort, he made the school a success, and through its example of vocational education and solicitude for white good will, Washington and his ideas became widely known in the South and the nation.[6]

Washington's prestige rose as the Negro's status declined. The racial policies he endorsed are important not because they were original, but because they were not. To an uncanny degree Washington's thinking embodied the spirit of the times in both the white and black Souths. Moreover, Washington was a resourceful man who spoke with equal facility to northern philanthropists, national political leaders, conservative southern whites, and the mass of southern blacks, and he made himself a go-between for those groups. The immediate need of blacks, he believed, was personal and community improvement, that is, economic betterment, moral uplift, and social progress, including increased group pride and middle-class respectability. The first priority was economic opportunity and the ability to seize it—jobs, skills, land, and training in business enterprise. These would avail the race more than political activity and agitation for civil rights, at least in the short run. "There is but one way out," he wrote in *The Future of the American Negro* (1899), "there is but one hope of solution." Blacks must acquire "property, economy, education and Christian character. To us just now these are the wheat, all else the chaff."

Washington's views were stated most succinctly in his address to the Atlanta Exposition of 1895, which catapulted him into national prominence, and in his remarkable autobiography, *Up from Slavery* (1901). "The masses of us are to live by the production of our hands," he told blacks in an interracial audience at the Atlanta Exposition, and "we shall prosper in proportion as we learn to dignify and glorify common labor and put brains and skills into the common occupations of life." The race must start at the bottom, put first things first, seek progress through work and self-discipline. "It is important and right that all privileges of the law be ours," he said, "but it is vastly more important that we be prepared for the exercise of those privileges." Achievement, especially material achievement, was the key to overcoming prejudice. "No race that has anything to contribute to the markets of the world is long in any degree ostracized," he declared hopefully. "Nor should we permit our grievances to overshadow our opportunities."

The Negro's future was in the South, Washington continued, and progress there depended upon the good will of whites. Only white southerners could eliminate violence and discrimination, and only they could provide the assistance necessary to help blacks through the difficult years of learning and improvement. But to win their help and respect, blacks must accept the realities of southern life. "In all things that are purely social," he said to both races in Atlanta, "we can be as separate as the fingers, yet one as the hand in all things essential to mutual progress." This was the heart of the "Atlanta Compromise," which Washington's address effected between white and black southerners. Whites understood Washington to say that blacks accepted segregation and disfranchisement. Blacks hoped that his accommodationist stance on social and political matters would encourage whites to forswear violence and extremism and assist blacks in the things necessary for economic and social improvement. "The wisest among my race understand that the agitation of questions of social equality is the extremest folly," Washington declared, "and that progress in the enjoyment of all the privileges that will come to us must be the result of severe and constant struggle rather than of artificial forcing." No white supremacist could object to this, or to Washington's promise that with white assistance blacks would become "the most patient, faithful, law-abiding, and unresentful people that the world has seen."

The Atlanta address marked Washington's emergence as the foremost spokesman for southern—and American—blacks. Washington was, however, the leader of an unorganized and dependent people, and his power and influence derived from his ability to satisfy whites and keep blacks in general agreement with views whites found acceptable. His leadership fitted the needs of every significant group of whites in the South and the nation, and they honored him as they honored no other black. His position among blacks, however, was always difficult, and to make it secure he established what one of his critics called the "Tuskegee machine" and spread its tentacles through black America. Through his influence with northern philanthropists, national Republicans, and white southerners he channeled jobs, money, and prestige toward blacks who accepted his views and effectively isolated those who did not. Yet in none of this was Washington a molder; he was instead a conservative whose position and power reflected rather than determined the status of blacks in the South. And he was ultimately unsuccessful. By the time of his death in 1915, his position had eroded as leaders committed to integration and interracial activism had emerged to challenge his views.

Yet Washington left his mark upon his times. To promote his ideas and the welfare of blacks, he sponsored a variety of racial organizations, the most notable of which was the National Negro Business League, which he established in 1900. In this way he sought to inculcate group and community pride and foster the principle of self-help. His example was in part responsible for the multitude of organizations and community endeavors that appeared across black America, from the National Association of Colored Women, organized in 1896, to the National Urban League, established in 1911. Among the organizations were fraternal groups, mutual aid societies, insurance, burial, and benefit societies, Greek letter sororities and fraternities, educational and historical societies. All of them encouraged self-help, racial pride, and group endeavor even when their leaders did not endorse Washington's views on racial policy. The total effect was meaningfully to improve community life in the black South.

Washington was no mere Uncle Tom. He regarded himself as a

realist in difficult times, and many of his policies were realistic adaptations to the nadir in which black southerners found themselves around the turn of the century. Moreover, he led an active secret life that flouted many of the accommodationist principles he supported in public. Covertly he supported court challenges and other actions against white supremacy and used his influence with Theodore Roosevelt and other Republican leaders to encourage the appointment of racial moderates to federal offices in the South. Still, his public opposition to racial protest and his effort to maintain his own position helped compromise the wellbeing of black southerners by playing into the hands of white supremacists. Not Washington but his critics, of whom W. E. B. Du Bois was the most important, would point the way out of the abyss of segregation and disfranchisement.

The Progressive South

The triumph of disfranchisement and segregation coincided with the onset of the Progressive era, the most important period of social and political reform the South had ever experienced.[7] Between the turn of the century and the nation's entry into World War I in 1917, every facet of public life felt the impact of the reform impulse—politics, government, business, agriculture, public welfare, public morals, religion, education, health care, and race relations. The statuses of women, blacks, children, prisoners, unfortunates, inmates of eleemosynary institutions, and many other groups were objects of one sort of concern or another. The Farmers' Union, the National Child Labor Committee, the General Education Board, the National Association for the Advancement of Colored People, the University Commission on Southern Race Questions, the Rockefeller Sanitary Commission, the Anti-Saloon League, the Southern Sociological Congress, the Social Services Commission of the Southern Baptist Convention, and the National Union of Textile Workers were but a sampling of the multitude of groups that sprang up to reform important aspects of southern life.

Southern Progressivism had taproots in both Populism and Conservatism, but its basic nature was chiefly determined by the new conservatism that developed in response to the Populist uprising. It manifested the desire of a growing number of people to do something about the political abuses and social problems that had become endemic in southern life. It was therefore an effort to rationalize politics, streamline government, solve the race problem, restrain business monopoly, and generally improve the quality of life in the South.

But beneath these general aims, southern Progressivism was an amorphous and unorganized phenomenon, less a movement than a series of movements, and more mood and attitude than specific program. The people involved in it often disagreed with or even disapproved of each other. Its coherence derived from their common loyalties to the South and their common conviction that the section had problems that needed reform. It was a major expression of what may for want of a better term be called southern liberalism. Southern Progressivism had important liberal components, which derived from Populism and *Herrenvolk* democracy, but its basic thrust was traditional and conservative. In fact it is best understood as an updating and rationalizing of the Conservatism of the 1880s. The Progressives stripped the Old Conservatism of its political crudeness and economic excesses, infused it with a spirit of efficiency and responsibility, and generally moderated and modernized it. The result was a set of public programs and attitudes that was still racist and elitist and still subservient to the same economic interests. But it was far less crass in serving those interests, and much more effective in reconciling reform and tradition. Progressives taught the old Conservatives the uses of reform, the ways in which "good government" could be used to quiet social protest, enhance public confidence in established institutions, eliminate unwanted kinds of economic competition, and all the while strengthen the political position of those responsible for the changes.

Southern Progressivism thus grew out of southern circumstances. The South had long had desperate problems and many people had long been concerned about them, but not until the end of the 1890s did circumstances make systematic reform possible. The death of Populism ended political insurgency on the left and marked the final emergence of the Solid South. At the same time, the federal government dropped the last vestiges of its interest in racial policy, and reform could thus be undertaken without threatening white supremacy. With white insurgents quiescent, the federal government acquiescent, northern liberals distracted, and southern blacks preoccupied with the accommodationism of Booker T. Washington, white southerners felt free to address the issues of reform.

Those who did so were divided into two groups that will here be called urban Progressives and agrarian Progressives. The basis for the division was the relative influence of Conservatism and Populism. Urban Progressives, those most influenced by Conservatism, were the more numerous and influential of the two groups, and it was they who gave southern Progressivism its basic character. Among their characteristic leaders in politics were governors like Andrew J. Montague of Virginia, Charles B. Aycock and Robert Glenn of North Carolina, Richard I. Manning of South Carolina, Hoke Smith of Georgia, Braxton B. Comer of Alabama, Charles H. Brough of Arkansas, and N. B. Broward of Florida. Outside of politics, urban Progressives included the South's best-known social reformers, among them Walter Hines Page, Professor Edwin Mims of North Carolina and Vanderbilt universities, editor Josephus Daniels of the Raleigh *News and Observer,* editor Clarence Poe of the *Progressive Farmer,* the Reverend Edgar Gardner Murphy of Montgomery, Alabama, Alexander J. McKelway and Charles W. Dabney of North Carolina, historian William Garrott Brown, and Booker T. Washington.

Temperamentally conservative and for the most part members of the rising urban middle class, these men had no sense of alienation from the South, hardly even a feeling of detachment, and the social criticism they produced had little in common with that of the northern muckrakers of the time. Quick to "understand" the section and its problems, they confirmed Richard M. Weaver's observation about southern reformers. "It is very nearly true to say," Weaver wrote, "that if one scratches a Southern liberal, he finds, perhaps not a conservative, but at least one with strong convictions about individualism and local prerogative."

Untainted by agrarian radicalism, urban Progressives directed their social criticism at symptoms rather than fundamental maladies. Thus they worked against such things as racial demagoguery, benighted religion, illiteracy, and the poor health and social apathy of poor whites rather than against white racism, maldistribution of wealth, or the political and economic impotence of the poor. There was a gadfly quality in much of what they wrote, a tendency to insist that any problem of immediate concern, whether hookworm, monopoly, bad roads, one-crop agriculture, one-party politics, or the presence of blacks, was the source of all the South's ills. They never carried their social inquiry very deep, and offered meliorative, even simplistic solutions to the ills that concerned them. In fact they tended to place greater stress on the need for personal improvement than institutional change. "Our institutions [need] to be democratized, our thought to be nationalized, our life to be industrialized," wrote educator E. A. Alderman in 1906, "and the whole process [is] one of education." "There is not an evil at the South for which education—thorough education, more education of the right kind" is not the cure, added Edgar Gardner Murphy in 1907.

Yet urban Progressives and the rising middle classes from which they sprang were committed to good government and the wellbeing of the South, and they were acutely aware of many of the section's problems. If their vision as reformers was limited by their attachment to middle-class values, it was nonetheless a socially responsible vision that derived from an impulse to do good. They were especially concerned to assure white supremacy, to remove the race issue from politics, to prevent the recurrence of agrarian insurgency, and to keep labor organizations away; but they also wanted to eliminate political corruption, regulate railroads and other monopolies, and make government more efficient and more concerned about social problems. These things they believed were necessary to achieve a larger purpose, the preservation of traditional moral values, including the values of economic individualism and the work ethic, which they wanted to imbue with a greater degree of social responsibility. The ultimate objectives were social stability and economic growth and the better life they expected these things to bring.

These objectives, however, were not entirely compatible, nor was the desire for social reform altogether achievable without threatening some of the traditional moral values they wanted to preserve. The accelerating pace of economic change which they applauded was as much a threat to those values as were the political corruption and racial extremism they wanted to eliminate. Upward mobility and commitment to middle-class values led them to advocate the virtues of small property, economic independence, and the gospel of self-help. The only class consciousness they condoned was that of the middle class, which they regarded not as class consciousness at all, but as commitment to a set of objective social precepts. Their distrust of farm protest, labor unions, "uppity" blacks, and political demagogues was in part a distrust of mass democracy, and this plus their Jeffersonian heritage kept them suspicious of government and hesitant to expand its activities in many areas of economic activity. Yet they were also influenced by agrarian factors that made them suspicious of finance capitalism, Wall Street, trusts, high tariffs, and railroads, and sometimes of businesses owned by outsiders. This combined with their desire for social uplift to direct them back toward positive government, and this in the final analysis was their most positive legacy. "The great fundamental residue of the progressive era in Southern government," George B. Tindall has written, "was the firm establishment and general acceptance of the public service concept of the state."

Urban Progressivism was strongest and most conservative in Virginia, where it brought, in the words of Raymond J. Pulley, "triumphant traditionalism" and one of the most conservative, oligarchic political systems in the nation. In other states its strength varied considerably, but in most of them it was the dominant strain of Progressivism. Under its influence, legislatures across the South expanded and streamlined the operations of state government. They created or strengthened public service commissions to curb monopolistic business practices; reduced the political favoritism shown business; passed antilobbying and corrupt practices acts; created statewide tax commissions to equalize assessments and rates; introduced budgeting practices; expanded state responsibilities and expenditures in education, welfare, and health care; created state highway commissions, welfare boards, and other agencies to professionalize state services and rid them of political interference; and sometimes adopted the manager and commission form of government for local areas. The result was improved government and cleaner politics.

In none of these things did urban Progressives differ much from agrarian Progressives. Where they did differ, and greatly, was in style and rhetoric and respectability. The agrarians were sometimes extreme in manner and offensive in their appeals to ignorance and race prejudice, and these facts obscured the programs they stood for. The most Progressive of them—men like James K. Vardaman and Theodore G. Bilbo of Mississippi, whose programs were ultimately more important than their prejudices—represented the left wing of southern Progressivism and the only wing that spoke to the needs of poor white farmers. But even the worst of them—men like Coleman L. Blease of South Carolina, Jeff Davis of Arkansas, and Thomas E. Watson of Georgia in his older days—had popular followings to go with their prejudices because they spoke to a segment of the population ignored by urban-based reformers. Most of them, including such older leaders as Tillman in South Carolina and Hogg in Texas, partook in some degree of both of these tendencies.

Urban Progressives considered these men demagogues rather than reformers, and historians have often accepted that judgment, but the programs they supported fitted readily into the Progressive mold. The best of the agrarians had a clearer understanding of the economic basis of southern politics, even if not the racial basis, and a note of Populist realism often crept into their discussion of issues. The realism, however, was eventually corrupted by racism and shallowness and, for those elected to high office, a tendency to succumb to the blandishments or bribes of business interests. Thus agrarian Progressivism tended to degenerate into showmanship and irresponsibility, just as urban Progressivism tended to dissipate into conservatism or what Sinclair Lewis later called babbitry. In both the movement was toward inconsequence, which meant that Progressivism itself despite the reforms it accomplished represented no turning point in southern history.

The most significant accomplishments of agrarian Progressivism were in Mississippi. As governors of that state, Vardaman (1904–8) and Bilbo (1915–19) were responsible for an impressive list of reforms. The fact that the reforms had only limited results says as much about the nature of Progressivism as it does about the limitations of the demagoguery both men practiced so consummately. In fact the success of both men as reformers was due in large degree to their racial and class demagoguery, which gave each of them a political base broad enough to get elected in the first place and, once elected, to translate his campaign promises into public programs. In an analysis of voting patterns in Mississippi between 1902 and 1911 (and in South Carolina too, where another notable demagogue, Tillman, held political sway), J. Morgan Kousser found no significant correlation between economic class and political support for the demagogues. The political base of men like Vardaman and Tillman was broad, and their success was unaffected by the disfranchisement of so many of the poor whites.

During Vardaman's administration the legislature strengthened the state's Jim Crow laws; passed a stiff vagrancy law to keep black labor controlled; substantially increased appropriations for white schools while carefully restricting money spent on black education; established a school for deaf and dumb whites; provided pensions for Confederate veterans (which in effect constituted a program of old-age assistance); passed antimonopoly legislation; created the office of state agriculture commissioner to oversee farm assistance programs; accomplished a major reform of the prison system; and notably expanded road construction. Vardaman also sought, unsuccessfully, to get the legislature to pass a child labor law, create an elective judiciary, and limit interest rates; he was successful in reorganizing the state government, increasing welfare expenditure, and reforming tax assessments. In the United States Senate, to which he was elected in 1912, Vardaman supported government ownership of public utilities and worked for inflationary monetary policies, low-cost credit to farmers, graduated income taxes, postal savings banks, restrictions on trading in agricultural futures, immigration restriction, women's rights, and the initiative, referendum, and recall. He also opposed American entry into World War I and sought to get the Fifteenth Amendment repealed.

Bilbo, who was one of the most repelling men ever to hold high office in the South, built on Vardaman's accomplishments. His administration was notable for creating a state tax commission and equalizing tax rates, which meant that businessmen and large planters in the Mississippi River delta paid a larger share of the state's tax bill. It was also notable for enacting a statewide prohibition law; for establishing a state highway commission, a pardon board, and a board of bar examiners, thereby reducing political favoritism in important areas of state activity; for building a state-owned limestone-crushing plant which produced fertilizer and sold it at cost to farmers; for establishing a tuberculosis sanitorium and a reform school for white youth; for abolishing the fee system of compensation for many county officials, which had long been a source of venality and abuse of the public trust; for creating a fund to equalize educational opportunities for whites across the state; and for systematizing and expanding adult education programs.

Progress in Education and Welfare

Progressives of all persuasions worked to improve education, health, and social welfare, and in these areas they achieved some impressive results. At the turn of the century, a well-connected group of reformers, among them Charles W. Dabney, John C. Kilgo, Walter Hines Page, E. A. Alderman, and Charles D. McIver, mounted an education crusade that caught the imagination of the entire section. Here was the Progressive reformer at his best, even if a disproportionate share of the improvement went to whites and thus increased the educational gap between the races. In 1901 these men joined with a group of northern philanthropists to organize the General Education Board. Financed by contributions from John D. Rockefeller, Jr., that eventually totaled more than $50 million, this board was the instrument through which the education crusade was conducted; and with the cooperation of a group of "education governors," its accomplishments were notable. By World War I, public expenditures on education in the section had quadrupled, functioning statewide school systems had begun to emerge, at least for whites, and the quality as well as quantity of education available to the mass of southern youth had improved. Teachers' colleges appeared, new and consolidated schools were constructed, attendance rose, illiteracy declined, and most of all, educational progress came to be one of the things by which voters measured political leadership.

In higher education progress was less evident before World War I, but the groundwork was laid for the later emergence of southern universities from their subservience to poverty and orthodoxy. The progress came first to private institutions such as Trinity College (now Duke University), the University of the South, and Vanderbilt. In 1903 Trinity withstood intense public pressure to dismiss historian John Spencer Bassett for an article on the race issue he published in the *South Atlantic Quarterly* (he wrote among other things that Booker T. Washington was "all in all the greatest man, save General Lee, born in the South in a hundred years"), and in 1914 Vanderbilt freed itself from the restrictions imposed by its connection with the Methodist Church. These were harbingers of the future rather than average conditions in the 1910s, but they nevertheless pointed southern universities in a new direction.

The story of progress in health and welfare was also encouraging. All of the states established or strengthened public health departments and gave them responsibilities that went beyond emergency responses to acute problems. The new responsibilities were in preventive medicine and the eradication of endemic diseases, and the change reflected contemporary advances in medical knowledge. In 1898 and 1899 the carriers of yellow fever and malaria were isolated and the stage set for containing and eventually eliminating two plagues that periodically afflicted large parts of the deep South. In 1906 Charles W. Stiles discovered the widespread incidence of hookworm in the South, and that parasite was soon shown to be a major health problem. Walter Hines Page and others interested representatives of the Rockefeller philanthropies in the problem, and in 1909 the Rockefeller Sanitary Commission was established to make a systematic effort to eliminate it. Financed by a grant of $1 million, the Commission had within a few years fulfilled its purpose. Also in 1906 the existence of pellagra was documented, and large numbers of cases of that malady were soon found across the section. Within two years Joseph Goldberger had established the connection between pellagra and inadequate diet, and a remedy was then possible. Both pellagra and hookworm caused lethargy and debility and increased susceptibility to disease, and the progress made in eliminating them greatly improved the health of the southern people.

In combating hookworm and pellagra, the states expanded their public health departments, and these in turn undertook programs against tuberculosis, maternal and infant mortality, and other major health problems. Between 1910 and 1918 expenditures for public health programs increased from $216,195 to $1,316,111 in the Confederate South. State and local governments had committed themselves to public health as well as public education.

These advances grew out of the Progressive impulse to improve the quality of life, an impulse that produced an array of other reforms that can only be mentioned. One such reform was prohibition, the triumph of which made the South legally the driest part of the country if not always the most abstemious. Another was the pioneering efforts of Seaman A. Knapp to improve farming by establishing demonstration farms that gave farmers practical demonstrations in the use of improved techniques and concrete evidence of the advantages of using them. Still another was the organizing of the Southern Sociological Congress, which brought together social workers, social scientists, and welfare officials to study social problems and find practical solutions.

A similar purpose was behind efforts in each of the major religious denominations to bring the social gospel movement to the South. If none of these efforts had much success in practical terms, they were nevertheless important as examples of the larger commitment to reform.

No social problem proved more perplexing to Progressives than child labor. Here was a real problem on which they expended great effort and achieved very little. The difficulty was that child labor existed chiefly in textile factories, and the effort to abolish it brought reformers into conflict with local, as opposed to outside, economic interests. It also ran counter to the traditions of economic paternalism and to the idea that the state should not intrude into matters affecting parental authority. At the turn of the century more than a quarter of all workers in southern cotton mills were under sixteen years of age, and more than half of these were between the ages of ten and thirteen. In North Carolina 18 percent of the mill work force were in the latter age group, and their wages averaged about 30 cents a day.

To combat these conditions, a group of reformers led by Edgar Gardner Murphy established the National Child Labor Committee in 1904. Under the leadership of Murphy and Alexander J. McKelway, who soon became its head, the Committee undertook intensive campaigns in all the textile states to abolish the employment of young children and regulate the hours and working conditions of older youths. The results were limited. Every state soon had restrictive laws, but the minimum age was low, usually twelve, and the maximum hours were long, up to sixty per week, and even these restrictions were poorly enforced. Moreover, these laws recognized the employment of twelve- or thirteen-year-olds and their enactment weakened the movement for further reform.

The Limits of Progressive Reform

The failure of the effort against child labor was one measure of the limitations of Progressive reform: it had little impact on economic privilege or the condition of the very poor. Most reformers had difficulty appreciating the special problems and perspectives of the groups they excluded from the body politic, and these groups included poor whites as well as blacks and women. They therefore rejected the kinds of reforms those groups sought or needed, and those groups benefited less from Progressive reform than did the broad urban white middle class. Progressive reformers were responsible for some important antimonopoly legislation, but its benefits went chiefly to the latter class, as did those of the farm programs they fashioned. The Farmers' Union, the leading farmer organization of the day, was concerned with the problems of landowners rather than tenants. The Progressives did little to benefit sharecroppers or marginal farmers, and the rate of tenancy continued its relentless rise. Similarly, their hostility to labor unions and working-class consciousness excluded cotton mill workers, coal miners, and other nonagricultural laborers from the purview of Progressive reform. Progressive governors often engaged in strikebreaking and other antiunion activities, and unions made few gains during the period. Because they were inclined to see social problems in personal or political terms, Progressives were least effective in areas where basic economic or social changes were needed. They urged the poor not to organize and protest, but to discipline themselves, to work harder and be more frugal and educate their children and strive to live like the middle class.

The women's rights movement, by now absorbed in the suffrage issue, received little support. Though that movement derived from much the same principles as Progressivism itself, male reformers feared it would lead to sexual equality and thus undermine the family and public morality and cast women in unfeminine roles in public. It would also double the potential electorate, black and white, and do so by adding an altogether unpredictable element. Women could vote nowhere in the South until 1917, when Arkansas Democrats permitted white women to vote in the party primaries. When the women's suffrage amendment was added to the Constitution in 1920, only three southern states, Texas, Arkansas, and Tennessee, had ratified it, though the ratification by Tennessee gave the amendment the necessary majority for adoption.

If Progressives dealt with women's rights by inaction, that was not the case with blacks, whom they segregated, disfranchised, and otherwise worked to keep in a subordinate position. The Progressive era coincided with a cresting wave of racism in the South and the nation, and the two movements acted upon each other. It was not that Progressives were more racist than other whites, but that they were not much different. On matters of race they ranged from extremists to moderates, though all but a few of the most benighted encouraged black advancement within segregation. They shared the fears and prejudices common to white southerners, and accepted the new "scientific" racism which used physiological and social science to "prove" that blacks were inferior to whites. They agreed with the findings of contemporary historians, who were then giving scholarly endorsement to what white southerners had always said—that the experience of Radical Reconstruction proved that blacks were incapable of exercising the responsibilities of citizenship.

The social milieu of the early twentieth century reinforced racist thought and drove it toward extremism. Few Progressives accepted the absurdities of Charles Carroll's *The Negro a Beast* (1900), but many of them agreed with the substance if not all the specifics of Thomas Dixon's *The Leopard's Spots* (1902), subtitled *A Romance of the White Man's Burden,* and Robert W. Shufeldt's *The Negro: A Menace to America* (1907). Even Thomas Nelson Page's *The Negro: The Southerner's Problem* (1904) partook, uncharacteristically for Page, of the meanness of spirit then pervading white racial thought. And so gentle a man as Edgar Gardner Murphy penned a body of writings that have been called "the most imposing intellectual apology for white supremacy in southern literature." "This is a white man's country," said Hoke Smith, whose term as governor marked the high tide of Progressive reform in Georgia, "and we are agreed that not only in the state at large, BUT IN EVERY COUNTY AND IN EVERY COMMUNITY the white man must control by some means, or life could not be worth living."

Once segregation and disfranchisement were accomplished, Progressives, like white southerners generally, congratulated themselves on having settled the South's most difficult problem. They were confident the settlement would reduce white extremism and foster the accommodationist spirit among blacks, and in these ways reduce friction and therefore encourage white paternalism and the uplift of blacks. "There is remarkably little friction since negro suffrage has been so much reduced," wrote Holland Thompson in 1914. "One may live long in some parts of the South without realizing that there is a negro problem." "When the (suffrage) fight had been won," declared Charles B. Aycock, the Progressive governor of North Carolina, "I felt that the time had come when the negro should be taught to realize that while he would not be permitted to govern the state, his rights should be held more sacred by reason of his weakness." "I believe in making a negro keep his place," added James K. Vardaman, "but when he does that, he is entitled to the protection of the law."

The anticipated harmony did not materialize. White extremism persisted, and blacks were restive. Booker T. Washington worked secretly against the enveloping discrimination, but much more importantly, a group of blacks outside Washington's influence began pushing boldly for civic equality and social integration. Led by W. E. B. Du Bois, then a sociology professor at Atlanta University, this group joined a number of well-known northern white liberals in 1909 to form the National Association for the Advancement of Colored People.

At last blacks and white liberals had found an alternative to accommodationism. They had also found in Du Bois an articulate spokesman who as early as 1903 had published a telling criticism of Washington in *The Souls of Black Folk,* one of the most moving books in southern literature. Black Americans "should protest emphatically and continually against the curtailment of their political rights," Du Bois declared in 1905. They should insist upon the right to vote and the full enjoyment of civil liberties, and resist all forms of paternalism and segregation. "No man is so good, intelligent or wealthy as to be entrusted wholly with the welfare of his neighbor," Du Bois insisted. "All American citizens have the right to equal treatment in places of public entertainment according to their behavior and deserts." Above all, the South and the nation must recognize and act upon the principle of racial equality. "We refuse to allow the impression to remain," he declared in indirect criticism of Washington, "that the Negro-American assents to inferiority, is submissive under oppression and apologetic before insults."

The NAACP, which committed itself to these principles, had little impact before World War I. Its appearance was nevertheless significant, for it pointed black southerners away from accommodationism and toward liberal integration. The future lay with Du Bois and the NAACP. The Progressives had not solved the race problem as they imagined, but only made its ultimate solution more difficult. They had overwhelmed blacks for the time being, but no sooner was this done than blacks commenced the long and difficult effort to undo the work of the Progressives.

FIVE

THE CHANGING SOUTH 1917-45

The 1910s marked another watershed in southern history. The pace of economic and institutional change accelerated during the Progressive era, and World War I propelled the South into a new age characterized, in Robert Penn Warren's words, by "profound tensions, deep inner divisions of loyalties, new ambitions, new opportunities, new despairs, and new moral problems, or rather old moral problems which had never been articulated and confronted." Suddenly, as George B. Tindall has put it, the section found itself balanced "between two worlds, one dying and the other struggling to be born." Through all the turbulence and growth of the New South era, white southerners had been generally successful in bending the forces of social change to their own imperatives, but after 1917 they were less and less able to do so. Thenceforth, the major theme of southern history was change—the impact of change on the South and the efforts of southerners to resist it, encourage it, or adapt themselves to it.[1]

To comprehend the meaning of this theme, one must remember that the South was a distinctive culture that grew out of and was sustained by a specific combination of forces and circumstances. Those forces and circumstances were described earlier, but are worth recalling here. Among them were a biracial population and a general concern with racial matters; a distinctive economy that interacted with a unique social structure to produce an ideology stressing agrarianism, hierarchy, and tradition; a minority status in the nation that created psychological and political insecurity and feelings of apartness and sometimes of grievance and besiegement. To these the Civil War and Reconstruction added military defeat and occupation, prolonged poverty and cultural backwardness, and a heightened sense of powerlessness. Sectional identity came to be expressed in and perpetuated by not only the general preoccupation with race but a persistent folk culture, an acute defensiveness on matters of sectional concern, and a peculiar pattern of class and race relations that combined paternalism and personalism with deference and a readiness to resort to violence. It was also expressed in a special sense of community that incorporated strong loyalties to place and family, in a social ethic that placed more stress on being than becoming, and in a host of provincialisms and orthodoxies and the pressures that preserved them.

The thrust of social change after 1917 was to undermine all of these things. In place of tradition and unity, change fostered "progress" and pluralism and in myriad ways eroded the South's distinctiveness and pulled the section toward American norms. The proportion of blacks in the population commenced a dramatic decline, the economy began to diversify, the poverty to abate, the sense of grievance and insecurity to dissipate. Race relations and the status of blacks began to improve, and the preoccupation with white supremacy became less acute. The typical southerner moved from the country to the city and from farm to factory or one of the service trades, and in the process lost his physical and some of his intellectual isolation. As this occurred, he began to question his loyalty to the Democratic party and to lose his memories of the Civil War and Reconstruction.

To liberal nationalists all this was progress, and most historians of the modern South are liberal nationalists. Inclined therefore to accent the forces of progressive change, they give little attention to the vitality of traditionalism. The "rise" of the South, the struggle to achieve national standards, and the spread of liberal ideas are the themes of their works. Their message is this: the South at last is overcoming the burden of its benighted past.

To anyone consciously loyal to the traditional South, however, this approach to southern history is destructive of the South itself. From this perspective the social changes mentioned above are a subversive force working to submerge the South into the American mainstream and thereby destroy it as a social and cultural entity. The "rise" of the South thus begins to look curiously like its death. If this is a valid perspective, it points to what might be the final irony of southern history. Sectional loyalists have long boasted that "the South will rise again," and for the three generations since World War I it has been doing just that—if national standards and liberal ways be a proper standard for judgment. Is the result to be extinction—transformation into something that is no longer recognizably southern but only American?

That question will be addressed later, but here it may be said that the possibility now seems a virtual certainty. The South as a self-conscious entity originated around the end of the eighteenth century as a result of the interaction between circumstances within the South and certain economic, political, and ideological changes that had swept the colonies and young nation and the Western world in the preceding half century. It might therefore disappear in the same way, as the result of interaction between a new set of circumstances inside the South and certain forces of consolidation and standardization that have been at work in the nation and the Western world since World War I. Perhaps in Marshall McLuhan's global village there is no room for neighborhood variations, and the South will eventually be remembered as nothing more than a temporary aberration in the relentless march toward national consolidation.

13

The Advancing South

If circumstances have pushed southerners toward traditionalism, history has inured them to change. The discontinuities in their past are more frequent and traumatic than those experienced by most other Americans, and as a distinctive minority in a democratic nation they have always been pulled, often against their will, toward national norms of someone else's choosing. Even in the New South as they busied themselves erecting a new wave of peculiar institutions—segregation, disfranchisement, the Solid South, share-tenant agriculture, the cult of the Lost Cause, and a unique culture of poverty—they had to face counterforces of national integration. The New South movement itself was one such counterforce, and Progressivism was another. Both sought to eliminate important elements of sectional distinctiveness, and both encouraged southerners to adopt American ways in significant areas of public life. Every success of these movements inspired other efforts at reform and progress, or more correctly Americanization, aimed at everything from racial and sexual equality, two-party politics, universal suffrage, labor unions, legislative reapportionment, economic diversification, and public education to franchised food chains, superhighways, and exposure to the national communications media. Whatever one thinks of these things, every success in achieving them marked a step in the standardization of American life and thus in the disappearance of the South as a distinctive culture.

The Return to National Politics

The process of reintegrating the South into national politics may be dated from 1913, when Woodrow Wilson, a southerner by birth and upbringing, became President of the United States and the Democratic party assumed control of both houses of Congress. After half a century in political limbo, southern whites resumed the important role in national politics they had played before the Civil War. Being a southerner was still a liability in seeking the presidency after 1913 and would remain so as long as the South remained distinctive, but it was not a liability for any other office in government. President Wilson's political and social views had been molded by his southern background, and he not only appointed large numbers of southerners to high office in his administration but stood with the white South on vital matters of sectional concern. Three of his initial Cabinet appointments went to southerners and two others to men who were born in the section, and William Jennings Bryan, his first Secretary of State, was especially popular among southern voters. None of the appointees, however, was a sectional chauvinist, and one must be careful not to measure southern influence in the Wilson administration by counting the number of southerners in high executive positions. The men in Wilson's administration owed their loyalties to Wilson, not the South. It was in Congress that sectional constituencies were represented and there that the southern influence was most recognizable. Almost half (47 percent) of the Democrats elected to Congress in 1912 were from the South or the border states, and among them were fifty-two of the fifty-eight most senior members of the party and the chairmen of twenty-three of the twenty-seven most important congressional committees. In addition Oscar W. Underwood of Alabama was majority leader in the House of Representatives, a position Claude Kitchin of North Carolina assumed in 1915, and beginning in 1917 Thomas W. Martin of Virginia held the same post in the Senate.

Not surprisingly the New Freedom, as Wilson's domestic program was called, bore a strong southern imprint.[1] It was not that southerners imposed their views on Wilson, but that northern and southern Democrats shared many interests, and their agreements were more important than their disagreements. Most southerners in Congress were influenced by Progressivism to one degree or another, and were roughly divided along the lines of the urban- and agrarian-based groups discussed in the preceding chapter. Among themselves they differed over the extent to which the federal government should be involved in the economy and the direction its involvement should take. They therefore disagreed over such basic issues as regulation of corporations, public control of money and banking, and federal farm policy. The agrarian-based group was the larger and more influential of the two in Congress, and its influence helped push New Freedom legislation away from the laissez faire Jeffersonianism Wilson had advocated in his election campaign in 1912 and toward government activism of a populistic sort. This was evident in the Federal Reserve Act, which enlarged government control of banking and currency; in the Federal

Trade Commission, which regulated certain kinds of corporate activities; in the Clayton Anti-Trust Act, which strengthened government power in the field of trustbusting; and in a number of measures dealing with agriculture and rural welfare, including low-cost credit and warehouse storage facilities for farmers, and in the agricultural extension services and vocational education.

As an episode in the history of the South, the southerners' support for these measures is important not because of the specifics of the programs, but because the programs significantly expanded the power and function of the federal government. Since Calhoun's day most white southerners had considered the national government actually or potentially hostile to their vital interests, and they had formulated a constitutional and political ideology centering around states' rights to prevent its intrusion upon those interests. But now, as soon as they resumed a primary role in national politics, they were supporting a substantial enlargement of federal activity in important areas of economics and social welfare. In varying but substantial numbers they voted for legislation authorizing the federal government to do such things as educate farmers, build highways, abolish child labor, regulate working conditions for women, and set maximum hours for railroad workers, none of which was justifiable except by a broad interpretation of the Constitution and the Populist principle of positive government. In endorsing these programs, the southerners accepted the public service concept of government on the federal level just as they were already accepting it on the state level.

In subsequent years this concept like everything else associated with the federal government grew enormously, far beyond anything envisioned by those who instituted it. When that occurred, the concept itself was turned against white southerners and used for purposes they considered punitive and even sinister. Using hindsight, one might conclude that their support for expansive federal programs in the Wilson administration was shortsighted. For if the federal government could help farmers or regulate railroads, it could do the same thing for and to other groups when and if the balance of political power shifted. That is, once the principle of federal activism was established, it would be exercised not according to abstract principles, but in response to power relationships in national politics. Having themselves been objects of federal power in the past, southerners might have been expected to be especially wary of extending federal activity in any area.

But they were not, for two apparent reasons. Their participation in the Wilson administration gave them a new sense of political security, and the nature of New Freedom legislation was such that it lulled their sectional sensitivities. Nothing in the New Freedom was inimical to southern interests as defined by the congressmen and the groups they represented. On the contrary, the New Freedom programs served to protect those interests. Except in the regulation of certain aspects of big business, the programs involved little in the way of federal controls. In agriculture the emphasis was on federal assistance, not social engineering or the imposition of federal standards. None of the programs created the kind of vast bureaucracies that characterize federal activities today, and none of them had much potential for generating social change. Instead, all of them, even in the area of business regulation, recognized and worked through established economic and political elites. They were generally administered through state or local offices, and some of them required enabling legislation and matching funds from the states, which gave the states an important degree of control and produced significant regional variations in the operation of some of the programs.

In short, the New Freedom provided federal assistance in areas where southerners wanted it but without federal "meddling." Segregation, disfranchisement, the white primary, the Solid South, sharecropping, the prerogatives of management and landlord—none of these was touched by New Freedom legislation. Not even such democratic reforms as the initiative and referendum or the direct election of United States senators was threatening as long as the disfranchisement of blacks and poor whites continued, and even women's suffrage had no discernible impact on politics or society. In the most important area of all, race relations, the Wilson administration was positively cooperative, extending racial segregation into areas of federal employment where it had never before been practiced, and resisting every effort by blacks to get federal action against segregation and disfranchisement. It was this more than anything else that caused the long-standing fear of the federal government to abate. At last white southerners had the kind of administration they could live with, and they felt more secure than at any time since 1820. At last the threat of outside interference seemed to have subsided to tolerable proportions and the northern majority seemed to have accepted the South's peculiar institutions.

Acceptance of the New Freedom and with it federal activity in certain areas of economic life thus signaled no change in values or purposes, but only a conviction that the South would gain from specific federal programs. This stance was pragmatic and unideological, perhaps surprisingly so, but it must be remembered that neither in nor out of Congress were southern elites opposed to all change. They were not reactionaries nor even conservatives in a strict sense. They were instead eclectics whose attitudes toward social and economic change reflected a varied and sometimes curious mixture of Populism, Conservatism, and *Herrenvolk* democracy. They welcomed change that did not intrude upon the prerogatives of race and class and property, especially economic growth. In fact they encouraged such change even as they acted to harness it to established modes of economic and social control. As they viewed their position in the 1910s, the threat came not from the federal government, which was now in friendly hands, but from the power of giant corporations battened by high tariffs and political favoritism and from the continuing problems of southern agriculture. So they turned to the federal government for help in those areas, confident they could use it for their own purposes without risk to their own interests. And given the tenor of the Wilson administration, that was not an unfounded conclusion.

World War I

No sooner had this pattern of change and response crystallized than World War I came along and accelerated the pace of change to such a degree that many southerners soon feared it was getting out of hand. The war added patriotism and a sense of national urgency to the existing desire for economic development and federal aid, and as the pace of change accelerated, the South's ability to control it diminished. The war was thus a significant event in the section's history, the catalyst or occasion for a series of changes that would eventually transform the South and its people.[2]

Despite the changes of the Progressive era, the South was still a relatively slow-paced society when the war broke out in Europe in 1914. The hostilities, however, brought an immediate increase in demand for American agricultural and manufactured goods and had a pronounced impact in the section. Prices rose rapidly as did production, and employment burgeoned. The largest movement of people since the Civil War was soon underway as thousands of southerners of both races flocked to urban centers and nonfarm employment in and out of the South. The nation was slowly drawn into the vortex of war, and the resulting programs of military and civil preparedness added further to the demand for goods and services and manpower, and thus to the general social ferment. Before the war ended in late 1918, almost a million southerners had served in the military and naval forces, a significant portion of them outside the section. At the same time, vast numbers of northerners had flocked into the South, many of them stationed at the military and naval bases that sprang up all over the section, while many others came to work in the civilian war effort. The effect was to breach the physical isolation that had always been an important part of southern life. Even those who were not themselves involved in the moving about were affected by the general broadening of economic and cultural horizons and made much more aware of the outside world. The sense of distance shrank, and with it the feeling of apartness. The South, as Allen Tate later put it, reentered the world.

The effects of doing so are not easy to gauge. Certainly increased contact with the outside world produced a larger awareness of alternative ways of living, and if this made the outside seem more threatening to some people, it opened new vistas of hope to others and gave everyone new standards of judgment. The results were thus liberalizing for those favorably impressed by other societies, but alarming to those who saw alien ways as a threat to southern traditions. Outside contact pointed up the South's deficiencies as well as its distinctiveness, and not just in matters of race or social mores. The lack of skilled labor, managerial talent, investment capital, and industrial capacity prevented southerners from getting a fair share of war contracts or of new industries created by the war. Poor health and lack of education caused a disproportionately large share of southerners of both races to be rejected by the military and naval services.

The economic impact of the war was more tangible than these things. Between the end of 1914 and the middle of 1920 the South enjoyed a longer period of high prosperity than ever before in its history and poverty was never again as tolerable as it had been. Southerners experienced a revolution of rising expectations that survived the postwar recession of 1920–21 as well as the uneven economic growth of the 1920s. Wartime prosperity meant windfall profits for a few, but more importantly it meant cash income for many who had never really partaken of the money economy. Agricultural prices reached unheard-of levels. Cotton, still the key to the section's economy, fell to 8 cents a pound at the first news of war in 1914 when it appeared that American goods would be cut off from European markets. But it soon recovered and went steadily upward, averaging 35 cents in New Orleans in 1919 and exceeding 40 cents in the first half of 1920. In the banner year of 1919, the cotton crop sold for more than $2 billion, and in tobacco, grains, and other crops a similar pattern occurred. Everyone, even sharecroppers and farm laborers, partook of the good times. Between 1914 and 1919 individual bank deposits in thirteen southern states rose from $2.37 billion to $4.95 billion.

The war was also a landmark in the psychological reunion of the South with the nation. Since 1877 southern loyalties to the Union had ebbed and flowed as the threat of federal interference seemed to rise and fall. The Spanish-American War of 1898 had been accompanied by a wave of national patriotism as large numbers of southerners enlisted in the United States army for the first time since the Civil War. The level of enthusiasm remained high through the Progressive era as northerners and the federal government acquiesced in segregation and disfranchisement. By 1917 memories of the Civil War and Reconstruction had diminished, and the élan generated by wartime urgency produced a positive nationalism that sometimes reached the level of superpatriotism. Commitment to the war effort was as nearly complete as public commitment can be. Southerners volunteered for military service in rates above the national average, subscribed to liberty bonds, harassed "slackers," and in other ways joined in the effort to make the world safe for democracy. A small group in Congress, including Claude Kitchin in the House and James K. Vardaman in the Senate, men whose intellectual roots were in agrarian radicalism, opposed the nation's entry into the war and objected to some of the administration's war policies, but their example only dramatized the commitment of the vast majority of southerners. On eight key measures enacted by Congress during the war—military conscription, the Espionage Act, the Sedition Act, the Lever Food Act, the Railroad Act of 1918, the Overman Act, and two antifilibuster resolutions in the Senate, all of which markedly expanded the powers of the federal government or eroded the South's traditional defenses—senators and representatives from the Confederate South cast a total of only 21 negative votes.

An important transformation occurred. Southerners fused their sectional and national loyalties into a single loyalty, and in a way that bears remarking upon. The white people of the South had always had dual loyalties that were sometimes contradictory, and the contradiction had never been resolved. Nor was it resolved now; instead, wartime patriotism and the new sense of security within the Union made it possible for southerners to merge the two loyalties on terms of their own and in a way that obscured their inherent contradictions. The result was the southerners' own version of the American creed, in which southernism became Americanism writ large. In the new creed the South was said to be the most American part of the country and southerners were being most American when they displayed their distinctively southern qualities. This formulation had great appeal among southerners, for it gave equal range to national and sectional loyalties and thereby enabled them to indulge their patriotic impulses without compromising their sectional interests. In fact it transformed their sectional distinctiveness from a negative to a positive attribute, for it said in effect that in an age of rapid change the South was truer than the rest of the country to the real principles of Americanism.

Thus southerners came to imbue Americanism with the qualities they considered central to their sectional identity. Among those qualities was a version of Anglo-Saxon ethnocentrism that embodied not only white supremacy and all that that implied, but nativism, xenophobia, and the savage ideal as well. Made uneasy by the Bolshevik revolution that occurred in Russia in 1917 and by liberal, labor, and interracial movements that appeared in the South and the nation during and just after World War I, southerners joined other conservative Americans in seeking to merge Americanism with antiradicalism and thus with intellectual conformity, social conservatism, and traditional morality. This effort had its greatest impact after the war, especially in the 1920s, when it influenced every effort to deal with social and intellectual change within the section. Having joined Wilson's effort to save the world for democracy, southerners were prepared when it was over to sign on for another crusade to make the South and the nation safe for orthodoxy.

In the postwar decade the thrust of public policy inside the South would thus have a duality about it. Social and intellectual conservatism coexisted with the continuing commitment to economic growth and "good government." In an age in which interaction with the outside world was increasing, this was a formula for social turmoil. An understanding of that turmoil, which was especially notable in the 1920s, is dependent upon some awareness of the economic, political, and racial history of the years between World Wars I and II.

The Economics of Transition

The postwar decade was a time of economic frustration and change.[3] By conventional measurements the economy grew, but the growth was uneven and not always conducive to social improvement. The fact of growth, however, was unmistakable as was the direction, which was away from agriculture toward industry and the service trades and thus toward diversification and balance. Yet the pace of change was slow, and the section continued to lag behind the rest of the nation. Between 1920 and 1940 the proportion of the population in urban areas rose only eight points, from 24 percent to 32 percent, though the part of the work force in agriculture dropped from one-half to three-eighths of the total. The major areas of growth were still in the processing of agricultural and mineral products, especially oil, chemicals, and forestry products, and in the urban service trades.

Agriculture remained the largest single activity, and cotton was still the basic crop. The white staple accounted for more than half of all cash farm income in the Southeast[4] through the 1920s, and cotton prices remained the best barometer of economic conditions among the largest segment of the southern people. After passing 40 cents a pound in New Orleans in the summer of 1920, the price fell below 14 cents before the end of the year when the demand generated by wartime shortages subsided. Short crops in 1922 and 1923, due in part to the ravages of the boll weevil, pushed the price above 28 cents in the latter year, but that level was not reached again in the decade. The average price was 20 cents in 1927 and 17 in 1929, while production climbed to more than 13 million bales.

Prosperity eluded the farmer, and the story of southern agriculture was once again a tale of low and fluctuating prices as well as uncertain markets, boll weevils, and soil erosion. Fertilizer and pesticide costs combined with low productivity and increased competition from overseas sources to diminish profits and prevent capital accumulation, and the social problems of farm folk remained unattended to. By national standards, southern agriculture was still labor-intensive, fragmented, underfinanced, and undermechanized. The average farm in six deep South states in 1930 was less than seventy acres, too small to provide a decent living.

Continued poverty inhibited social as well as economic improvement. The substantial movement of people out of agriculture was not the result of an enclosure movement or improved productivity, but of rural poverty made worse by the boll weevil, which had become, in Rupert B. Vance's phrase, "the largest consumer of raw cotton in the South." In the 1920s the farm population in Georgia and South Carolina declined more than 15 percent, and there were lesser declines in Virginia, Tennessee, Arkansas, and Florida. Farm acreage also dropped, by 10 percent or more in Alabama, Florida, Georgia, South Carolina, and Virginia and by smaller proportions in all the other states except Texas. By 1930 the scourge of tenancy had enveloped well over half (55.5 percent) of all farms in the greater South.

To the traditional sources of these problems, others were now added. After World War I the South produced an ever smaller proportion of the world's cotton crop. In addition, cotton textiles, the principle usage for the staple, faced new competition from synthetic fibers, and the high tariffs enacted during the Harding administration restricted overseas markets. These problems were partly political, but farmers had no effective political organization, no counterpart of the Farmers' Alliance or the Populist movement or even any agreement on the sources or solutions of their problems. In politics farmer organizations were more than ever dominated by planter interests, and continued to support such proposals as cooperatives, low-cost credit, reduced tariffs, and voluntary acreage restrictions. These things would have helped of course, but much of the political effort of farm leaders now centered around a new proposal, "McNary-Haugenism," which urged the federal government to buy up all farm products that could not otherwise be sold at a fair price and dump them on the world market at whatever price they would bring. This proposal was embodied in the McNary-Haugen Act which passed Congress in 1927 and again in 1928 but which President Calvin Coolidge vetoed on both occasions.

In industry and other nonfarm enterprise there was also substantial growth in the postwar decade, but here too traditional patterns persisted and social progress was limited. During the 1920s the number of factories in the South actually decreased, but this reflected a pattern of consolidation rather than decline, for the manufacturing payroll increased 10 percent (to $1.33 billion), the number of production workers rose 15 percent (to $1.23 million), and the value added by manufacturing was up a substantial 29 percent (to $3.15 billion). Despite this growth the Southeast, which had about one-fifth of the nation's population, had in 1929 less than one-seventh of the manufacturing establishments, about one-eighth of the production workers, and one-twelfth of the manufacturing payroll. Wages were low, typically averaging only 60 or 70 percent of the national level, which was too low to break the cycle of working-class poverty. To use Richard A. Easterlin's calculations once more, per capita income in the Census South, which had risen to 62 percent of the national average in 1920, dropped back to 55 percent in 1930.

Imbalances persisted. Textiles, lumbering, and food processing remained the chief activities, and together accounted for about half the nonagricultural work force. Lumbering, however, was in a state of decline as the section's timber stands had been worked over. The estimated 39 million acres of virgin timber in the section in 1919 dwindled to 12.6 million acres in 1927. The textile industry, in contrast, grew notably, both in absolute and relative terms. By the end of the decade, southern firms accounted for 69 percent of the nation's spindle hours and consumed 76 percent of the cotton used in textile manufacturing. In this and other industries some progress was made in consolidation and diversification, but southern industry like southern agriculture remained backward. Management was unprogressive and labor largely unorganized and powerless despite the waves of strike activity that occurred at the beginning and again at the end of the decade.

The Politics of Traditionalism

In the years between World Wars I and II politics and religion were the chief conservators of traditionalism. Both were controlled by elements of the population that were especially resistant to social change, and since the one brokered power and the other guarded morals, they were together able to insulate the South from many forces of innovation and

Americanization. More than any other groups, politicians and preachers were responsible for limiting the impact of urbanization, education, and increased contact with the outside world.

The basic institution of southern politics was the local oligarchy, the courthouse gang or machine that dominated local government and, indirectly, state politics as well.[5] The power and influence of these organizations constituted the most important and most conservative force in southern politics. The county was the basic unit of government and the one with greatest impact upon the citizenry. It was the county, chiefly, that exercised the police power, built and maintained roads, and administered the school and welfare funds, and thus county governments awarded most of the contracts and franchises, dispensed most of the patronage and influence, heeded or ignored the citizen's complaints. The county was in short the agency through which political power was exercised, and it was the local oligarchy that exercised it.

These oligarchies have never received the study they deserve.[6] Their membership seems to have varied widely from place to place and time to time, for it depended upon the mix of circumstances, personalities, and history in each locality, and thus upon family alliances and other intangibles. As a general rule it was recruited from key elected and appointed officials and certain individuals of local prominence and wealth. Sheriffs, county commissioners, judges, tax officials, and sometimes a mayor or police chief or justice of the peace or foreman of the grand jury were likely members, and perhaps one or more bankers, merchants, planters, and lawyers, and perhaps also the owner or resident manager of one or more of the largest economic enterprises. The group was usually informal and its leadership collective, though one of its members was likely to be *primus inter pares* and occasionally acknowledged as a political boss. In any case the group was likely to function cooperatively, for its members were united by common interest and common commitment to a system in which they were the chief beneficiaries.

Their ideology was understood rather than articulated, and transmitted by a sort of social osmosis. It revolved around a commitment to what the oligarchs regarded as the natural order of things: white supremacy, one-party politics, the Solid South, conservative moral and social values, the prerogatives of property and class, and local control of local matters. It might also include a commitment to the gospel of progress as long as that gospel was defined as new factories, new schools, and economic growth rather than labor unions, academic freedom, and liberal social change. In state, national, and congressional politics, the oligarchs were pragmatic and self-interested, and their relationships with governors, senators, and congressmen usually rested on the principle of reciprocity. They were always anxious to support winners but prepared to come to terms with victorious opponents. Governors and other higher-ups found them ready to "deal" as long as local prerogatives were acknowledged, and since the success of the higher-ups often depended on the assistance or acquiescence of the oligarchs, the mutuality was contagious. For their part, the local organizations were interested in state and national affairs only to the extent that the actions of state or national officials affected local politics. On matters of no local import they were satisfied to give governors and congressmen free rein, which is perhaps one reason many southerners in Congress were internationalists in foreign affairs.

This system of mutually reinforcing interests was buttressed by important structural arrangements. The one-party system of politics prevented the development of institutionalized opposition to elected officials based on issues or ideology, and when opposition did develop, it was likely to revolve around personalities, family alliances, or disputes over the spoils of office. Most political contests were thus spats within the oligarchy or struggles between ins and outs, and victory by the outs brought a change of officeholders but no change in policy. Neither side encouraged the electorate to look to local government for help in solving social or economic problems. Landlordism, racism, poverty, or working conditions in a local factory were thus of little more concern to local government than issues relating to the League of Nations or repayment of European war debts. Groups to whom those problems were important, such as poor whites, sharecroppers, blacks, and mill villagers, were disfranchised or politically apathetic, and those among them who voted were diverted by demagoguery or their own prejudices onto nonissues like white supremacy or the assertion of local rights against outside interests.

The oligarchs' ability to divert, neutralize, or repress potential opposition was thus impressive, and due to several things. The orientation of mass religious denominations discouraged activism in liberal causes, as did the traditions of deference and fatalism among the poor. Wilbur J. Cash's "proto-Dorian convention"—the simultaneous flattery and exploitation of the white masses by their political leaders and economic betters—had a similar effect, as did the ability of established interests to thwart dissent by discrediting or co-opting its leaders. The effectiveness of this co-optation, through retainers, contracts, or bribes, is attested by the fact that one of the stock characters in southern politics was the man who won office by denouncing "politicians" and "interests" only to settle into a comfortable relationship with those groups once he was in office, in effect using his appeal at the polls to force himself into the establishment. So effective was the process of neutralization that opposition to the system itself as opposed to individuals within it was rendered nugatory, a fact that helps explain why so many educated, talented, and liberal-minded individuals of both races left the rural or small-town South. Such people were potentially the most effective opponents of the system, and their loss served not only to drain talent away from areas where it was badly needed but to reduce the potential for effective political protest.

Other factors buttressed the system too. State legislatures were apportioned to favor rural, small-town, and black belt constituencies, and the groups thus benefited were those most committed to the politics of traditionalism. The county unit system in Georgia, which applied a distorted version of the electoral college to Democratic primaries in that state in a way that nullified the political influence of Atlanta and other urban centers, was the best example of this. In some states gerrymandering was used to neutralize political out-groups, as in the "bacon strip" congressional districts that prevented Republicans in western North Carolina from electing one of their number to Congress.

The one-party system was the linchpin of this structure. Senators and congressmen were beholden to the local organizations, and their continued reelection gave them the seniority necessary to protect the organizations and the things they represented. This repeated reelection of officeholders was apparently widespread on all levels of government except for the office of governor, and it produced a generation gap in politics that had profoundly conservative consequences. Ellison D. Smith, who was elected to the Senate from South Carolina in 1908, remained in that body until 1945, to cite one extreme example, and Carl M. Vinson served continuously in the House of Representatives from central Georgia from 1914 to 1965, to cite another.

The growing diversity in the South after 1920 meant that the perpetuation of this system of conservative oligarchy depended upon the continued restriction of the suffrage. Virginia, whose oligarchy was really an efficient statewide machine led by Governor and then Senator Harry F. Byrd, afforded the best example of the relationship between oligarchic government and restricted voting. Between 1925 and 1945 the average number of voters who participated in the Democratic primaries in that state was equal to only 11.5 percent of the voting-age population, and the Byrd organization controlled the state by obtaining a vote equivalent to 6 or 8 percent of the adult population. Elsewhere the situation was less striking, but the total vote in gubernatorial primaries in the Confederate South between 1920 and 1946 averaged less than 30 percent of the voting-age population, and in four states the average was less than 20 percent.

The South in National Politics

Despite the strength of traditionalism within the section in the 1920s and 1930s, important changes occurred in the dynamics of the Solid South and the role of the South in national politics. The changes, however, were more real than apparent until after World War II. In 1945 Republican voting strength was still negligible outside Appalachia, and typically the party could expect to win only two seats in Congress and less than 5 percent of state legislative seats in the Confederate South. But as early as the 1920s the South's relationship with both national parties began to change, and in 1933 the change began to affect the relationship with the federal government. Under the leadership of Herbert Hoover, whose election to the presidency in 1928 was accompanied by the most important break in the Solid South between 1880 and 1960, the Republican party adopted another in its long series of southern strategies aimed at breaking the Democrats' hold on the section. The party abandoned the black-and-tan factions through which blacks had played an important role in Republican affairs in the South, and turned to lily-white groups who supported segregation and white supremacy. The purpose of the change was to build a party base in the white South among groups whose economic and social views were like those of the Republican administration but who had never voted Republican because they questioned the party's reliability on racial issues.

The strategy had much to recommend it. Its objective, simply stated, was to form a political union within the Republican party of economic and racial conservatives. The Democratic party had always been racially conservative in the South, but on economic matters it was often populistic or "radical." This inconsistency was increasingly bothersome to business interests and the urban middle class, and since those were groups of growing political importance, the Republican party stood to gain much from winning their allegiance. The strategy was tested in 1928, and the results were quite encouraging.

The logic of the strategy was enhanced by changes within the Democratic party. As the Republican party dedicated itself to economic growth and social conservatism, it necessarily became the political vehicle of groups to whom those things appealed. Those groups were centered among what were then called "older Americans," that is, groups of north European ancestry whose political strength lay in the nation's "heartlands," especially the Midwest but also the West, and in rural and small-town areas and cities of moderate size. The middle class in the white South seemed a natural ally to such groups, for they too benefited from Republican economic policies and were made uneasy by liberal social change. Partly in response to this movement among

Republicans, the national Democratic party began moving, haltingly, in another direction, seeking to develop its appeal among urban Americans, especially the working classes and white ethnic groups who benefited less from Republican economic policies and were less committed by circumstance and cultural heritage to the social and moral norms espoused by the older American middle class.

Neither party had gone very far in these directions by 1928, but the direction of movement in each was already apparent. Herbert Hoover, the Republican candidate for President that year, was an ideal embodiment of his party's southern strategy, of which he was a major architect. He was also the very symbol of "Republican prosperity" and was a major architect of that too, and he stood for moral and social conservatism, including prohibition and states' rights on racial matters. Alfred E. Smith, the Democratic nominee, seemed in contrast almost a stereotype of everything that made white southerners uneasy. He was an easterner, almost self-consciously urban, a Catholic, a "wet," and relatively liberal in his attitude toward labor, minorities, and social change. The two candidates thus presented southern voters with an unusual dilemma. They both represented change, but of different sorts. Hoover promised economic growth without disruptive social innovation. To vote for him, however, was not an easy matter, for loyalty to the one-party system was the cement that held the South's political structure together, especially in dealings with outsiders. To threaten the one-party mechanism might thus be to threaten what it protected. This forced southerners to choose between ideology and pragmatism. They agreed with Hoover more than with Smith on the issues they considered most important, but few of them had any desire to weaken the South's political defenses or undermine its internal political mechanisms. They chose therefore according to local circumstances. Where those permitted substantive issues to carry the greatest weight, Hoover did well, but where they made party loyalty the primary concern, Smith was more successful.

The results are well known. For the first time since Radical Reconstruction, a Republican candidate made inroads into the Solid South, splitting it in fact into its component parts, the deep South and the peripheral South. Hoover won in the latter by a substantial margin, carrying Virginia, North Carolina, Tennessee, Texas, and Florida, though he lost Arkansas, the home of Democratic vice-presidential nominee Joseph T. Robinson. Smith carried Arkansas and the five states of the deep South. These results showed clearly the potential for political change in the section, but also the strength of political conservatism. Hoover did relatively well in areas where economic and social change was having the greatest impact and where the hold of tradition was loosest. Even in the deep South he carried the cities and suburbs most oriented toward growth, such as Atlanta and Birmingham, but lost those where traditionalism was stronger, such as Charleston, Montgomery, and New Orleans. Smith, on the other hand, did best in areas where blacks were numerous, racial anxieties great, and sectional feelings still intense, and where ruralism, the plantation system, and cotton growing were most important.

Instead of cracking the Solid South, Hoover's performance revealed something of its real nature. Or put another way, Hoover cracked the Solid South if the Solid South is defined as a political institution rather than the things that institution was created to protect. But if it is defined in the latter way, the results of Hoover's showing seem less impressive. Insofar as Smith was the more liberal candidate on social issues, the southerners who voted for him did so in spite of his liberalism. They voted to preserve the institutional structure of the Solid South, for to them that structure was essential to preserve the principles it protected. By the same token, many of those who voted for Hoover did so not because they wanted to destroy the Solid South, but because they believed the principles it encompassed—white supremacy, Protestant control of the nation, puritanism in public morals, conservatism in social policy, and preservation of traditional values—were more important than the form of its politics. The Hoover voters endorsed economic growth, not liberal social change. The differences between them and the Smith voters were important, but the vote for Hoover was not a vote against the principles embodied in the idea of the Solid South any more than Smith's vote was an endorsement of urban liberalism. At most the Hoover vote represented a new flexibility concerning the means of protecting the interests of southern elites; it did not indicate a belief that those interests no longer deserved protection. For "Hoovercrats" the Solid South was a means to more important ends; for loyal Democrats it was an end in itself, for only by preserving its structure could the principles it protected be safeguarded. As an episode in southern history, the Hoover vote was a protest against the national Democratic party for nominating an objectionable presidential candidate, rather than a plea for a two-party South. It was not accompanied by an upsurge of Republican strength in state and local elections, and its impact on subsequent presidential elections was nil.

Politics at Home

State and local politics was little affected by all this. Before 1933, when the New Deal began to have an effect within the region, nothing disturbed the internal political arrangements that had been worked out in the aftermath of the Populist upheaval, and in 1945 those arrangements remained largely intact. "In its grand out-line," wrote V. O. Key of the first half of the twentieth century, "the politics of the South revolves around the position of the Negro." That was certainly true; but it was also true that in the period encompassed by the two world wars white supremacy seemed relatively secure, and for that reason public officials were able to concern themselves with things other than race. Black political activity was at a minimum, race leaders were accommodationist, and disfranchisement and segregation were protected by the federal courts. If politicians in those years talked much about white supremacy and conjured up threats of outside interference in the southern way of life, it was only because those things made it easier to run successfully for office. Once in office, they were able to give attention to the more serious business of expanding state services and making government better serve the public need. As a result the period was one of significant improvement in these areas.

On the state level political leaders were still divided along much the same lines as in the Progressive era. An unorganized grouping of "business Progressives," to use George B. Tindall's term, politically and intellectually linked to the prewar urban Progressives, was now the most important political clustering on the state level and was responsible for the most significant achievements on that level. "The impulse for 'good government' and public services remained strong," Tindall wrote characterizing the group, but "the impulse for reform somehow turned into a drive for moral righteousness and conformity." The latter impulse, however, did not interfere with the former. The commitment to public service was strong, and tied closely to the continuing commitment to economic growth and civic boosterism. A progressive community, Tindall has written, was "one that had good government, great churches, improved schools, industry, business, real estate booms." But it was not one that had strikes or racial unrest or anything else to disturb the image of social stability and economic responsibility.

Typified by the accomplishments of such governors as Harry F. Byrd of Virginia, Austin Peay of Tennessee, Cameron Morrison of North Carolina, Bibb Graves of Alabama, and Richard B. Russell of Georgia, business Progressivism stressed responsibility and service in government and respectability in political conduct. Its spokesmen deplored the style and sometimes the principles of their agrarian-oriented opponents, whom they tried to discredit by equating the worst of them—men such as Eugene Talmadge of Georgia, Theodore G. Bilbo of Mississippi, Thomas J. Heflin of Alabama, and Coleman L. Blease of

South Carolina—with the typical. Their criticism of the agrarians as irresponsible demagogues was seconded by the daily press, the middle-class churches, civic clubs, chambers of commerce, and other representatives of property and respectability, and business Progressives were thus successful in preempting the issue of political respectability. This enabled them to cast their programs in terms of good government and decorum against irresponsibility and unseemliness, thus obscuring in a fog of moralism the class nature of the programs they offered. If their opponents sought political advancement through demagoguery, as they did, business Progressives used homiletics and public decorum for similar purposes, and both groups thereby contributed to the politics of neglect.

Yet business Progressivism had a positive dimension that produced a notable record of accomplishment. Equating good government with efficiency, governors like those named above applied business principles to state administration while expanding public services in education, road building, economic development, and other things. Taxes and indebtedness rose, budgeting practices were instituted, administration was streamlined and centralized. In North Carolina, where the results were more notable than elsewhere, state government expenditures increased about 850 percent between 1915 and 1925, bonded indebtedness rose from $13 million to $178 million during the 1920s, and state and local taxes went up 195 percent. In return, the state's public school system was expanded and improved, the University of North Carolina was made into the best university in the South, and the mileage of paved roads increased from 6,218 in 1925 to 58,703 in 1935. By 1930 education and highways were accounting for perhaps 70 percent of the cost of state government in the South.

With the notable exception of Huey P. Long of Louisiana, who was *sui generis* among southern politicians, agrarian-oriented leaders had no similar record of achievement on the state level. Their most significant service was in Congress, though in neither the Republican-controlled Congresses of the 1920s nor those dominated by Democrats in the 1930s did their accomplishments match the record of the Wilson administration. For reasons that are not altogether clear, political agrarianism was in a state of degeneration, and self-conscious agrarian leaders had become more memorable for style than substance.[7] Among the most colorful of them was Senator Ellison D. Smith of South Carolina, popularly known as "Cotton Ed" because of his championship of cotton farmers and his practice of campaigning from atop a cotton bale on a mule-drawn wagon. There was also Smith's colleague in the Senate, Theodore G. Bilbo of Mississippi, whose consistent support of New Deal legislation was overshadowed by the "Bilbonic plague" he emitted in vitriolic streams of rhetoric. Equally offensive was another senator, Thomas J. Heflin of Alabama, whose stature as the section's most repelling anti-Catholic was reflected in his reference to Pope Pius XI as a "fat old Dago." Among the governors who never reached the Senate one of the most noteworthy was Eugene Talmadge of Georgia, "the wild man from Sugar Creek," a man whose vacuousness on important issues was exceeded only by his success at the polls.

"Proletarian representatives of the proletariat," William A. Percy once called men of this sort, and if that was not the best way to describe them, it did reflect something of the devolution of agrarian radicalism since the days of Populism and the early Tom Watson. The demagogic style of Talmadge and the others was reminiscent of that of Tillman and Vardaman, but it was unredeemed by achievement or realistic advocacy in behalf of poor whites. Agrarian radicalism had begun as a program, but now it was little more than a set of techniques to win office by appealing to prejudice and fear. Its rhetoric was still addressed to lower-class whites, but that only dramatized the shallowness of the commitment to their needs. Eugene Talmadge, who was elected to statewide office in Georgia seven times between 1926 and 1946, including four times as governor, was one of the most successful practitioners of this art, and his failures in office mirrored the degeneration of agrarian protest. Accepting a kind of nostalgic Jeffersonianism that the Populists had long ago rejected, Talmadge was given to advocating panaceas and simplistic solutions to complex problems that he seems not to have understood. Moreover, his opposition to government involvement in economic activity led him to oppose the New Deal and offer himself as a rustic-sounding front man for reactionary business interests working to defeat Franklin D. Roosevelt. Though on the hustings he spoke the language of agrarian protest, in office he developed a mutually rewarding relationship with business conservatives, and the problems of the "rednecks" and "wool hat boys" who voted for him went unattended to.

Insofar as the rhetoric of men like Talmadge had coherence, it rested on the notion that the South was being swept by economic and social changes inimical to the mass of white people, especially small farmers. Economic forces, it held, robbed the small farmer of the fruit of his labor and drove him off the land or into tenancy, while a new morality and other alien influences were threatening him with social displacement. His traditional moorings were thus jeopardized, and one day white supremacy itself might be imperiled.

The fears expressed in these ideas were often quite real, and the appeal of men like Talmadge came from the confidence they inspired as they promised to stem the tide of change. By affirming traditional values, such men gave assurance to people who bore the brunt of changes they did not understand and were inclined to reject. Yet their rhetoric derived from romance, not realism, for it reflected no understanding of social change or of the relationship between economics and politics, nor even the nature of political and economic power. In office, even when they tried, men like Talmadge were ineffective. They simply could not translate their rhetoric into functional programs. In effect they played the role of political lightning rods, drawing off the energies and frustrations of agrarian protest without posing a threat to conservative interests that controlled the South.

A major exception to this pattern was Huey P. Long, who was governor of Louisiana from 1928 to 1932 and then a United States senator until his death by assassination in 1935. Long's intellectual and political roots were in Populism, and he was an accomplished master of rural demagoguery, but he had little else in common with men like Talmadge. Nor did he belong among agrarian Progressives like James K. Vardaman, for Long never used racism as an instrument of political advancement. He most resembles the early Tom Watson, who as a Populist leader sought to transcend the politics of racism and provincialism and mount an effective campaign against what he regarded as predatory economic interests. But unlike the young Watson, Long won high political office, and unlike Talmadge, he used it to highly effective purpose. He never made an accommodation with the economic and political forces he denounced—the New Orleans "ring" of business interests and political placemen, oil and natural gas interests, railroads and other utilities—and if the criterion be constructive reform in the face of entrenched opposition, he was perhaps the most impressive political leader in the history of the South.

Yet his accomplishments were remarkably similar to those of latter-day Progressives. He launched a major program of road and bridge construction, greatly expanded health and welfare services, improved the public school system and provided free textbooks to all pupils, increased taxes on the exploiters of Louisiana's rich natural resources and curbed their inordinate political power, and in a variety of other ways acted to improve the quality of life for the mass of Louisianans. In a state in which the Populist and Progressive movements never had much impact, this program was especially efficacious.

But it had a darker side, too. Long began his public career with a burning desire to help the poor people of Louisiana. This could be done, he felt, only by making the state government more responsive to public needs, which in turn meant that the political and economic power of oil, gas, and other interests would have to be curbed. Because those interests were so powerful, however, Long found it necessary to give more of his time to the means of achieving his ends, that is, to breaking the back of interests that opposed him, than to the ends themselves. This meant he had to gather into his own hands enough power to neutralize theirs. But in the process of doing this, the sheer accumulation of power was somehow transformed in his thinking from a means to an end in itself, and Long became the nearest thing to a dictator any American state ever had. Yet his programs were enormously popular because of the real benefits they provided so many people, and the mass of Louisianans remained fiercely loyal to him at the time of his premature death.

Long is best understood as a product of both the pathologies and possibilities of Southern politics. In an important sense he was, as T. Harry Williams insists in *Huey Long* (1969), a mass leader rather than a demagogue, though he had many of the qualities of both. Like most of the other demagogues who have plagued southern politics since 1890, he addressed himself to real problems, but far more than any of the others he was willing to persevere until he got to the roots of those problems. "Every man of them," observed Gerald W. Johnson of southern demagogues in 1936, "succeeded by promising the underprivileged, not anything radical, but just those things which any government with a keen sense of social responsibility would have provided long ago." What Long "actually gave the Louisiana proletariat," Johnson declared, "is regarded in every section but the South as the merest routine of decent government."

The persistence of demagoguery is thus explained in part by the failure of "respectable" leaders to deal effectively with the real problems of poor whites. Agrarian demagoguery was in fact a logical result of the politics of neglect. If a romantic like Talmadge could exploit that neglect for his own advantage, a realist like Long could use it for a much larger purpose. In office, Talmadge played by the accepted rules despite his celebrated antics, and succumbed to the machinations of entrenched economic powers. Long made his own rules, and through them and his "Share the Wealth" program maneuvered state and national politics leftward toward a confrontation with basic economic and social problems. The tragedy was that Long as well as Talmadge was corrupted by the power of the system both men criticized. That both of them failed suggests that responsible political and social change would have to be imposed from outside or wait upon the processes of economic and demographic change.

Change and Tradition in Race Relations

In race relations as in politics the interwar years were a time of change that made few inroads on traditional ways. In 1941 white supremacy remained intact, blacks were still second-class citizens, and there seemed little prospect of doing much about either of those conditions in the foreseeable future. Yet important forces of change were already at work. Improved education and increased economic opportunity were improving the quality of life in the black South, and political and constitutional changes were preparing blacks for a new assault on segregation and disfranchisement. Moreover, demographic shifts were at work that would ease white fears, and political shifts were occurring that would soon reduce the ability of whites to preserve their absolute supremacy.[8]

Eventually, the most important of these changes would prove to be the outflux of blacks from the South, for without that the others might have been neutralized or prevented altogether. "The race problem cannot be solved," wrote Frank Tannenbaum, a white man of liberal sympathies, in 1924 before the impact of the outflux was generally appreciated. "There is no solution which can be devised that will do all of the things a solution would have to do." This pessimistic view was widely shared at that time in white liberal circles, where the race problem was viewed as something that might be ameliorated by men of good will but not solved as long as whites and blacks lived together in substantial numbers. "Movement of the negro to other sections of the country is the first step in any alteration of the racial situation in the South," Tannenbaum wrote, more in the manner of observation than anticipation. This would alleviate white fear, he explained, thus producing an "inevitable change in the attitude toward the negro" and, as whites came to appreciate the value of the diminishing supply of black labor, better treatment as well. The eventual result would be "a new emotional realignment between the races," one that would enable the South "to escape the vicious cycle of abusing the negro because it fears him, and fearing him because it abuses him." As for the country as a whole, "it will make the negro problem a national problem rather than a sectional one," and thus encourage more realistic thinking in the North.

The out-migration of blacks had begun long before Tannenbaum made these remarks, but only around World War I did it achieve significant proportions. Estimates of the number of blacks who left the greater South range up to a million for the years between 1916 and 1923, a figure that seems too high, though there was considerable moving back and forth between the sections. The net migration from the Confederate South was more than a million and a half between 1910 and 1930 and an additional 2 million between 1930 and 1950. By 1930 more than one in every four blacks born in the Southeast was living elsewhere, and the proportion of blacks in the southern population was dropping steadily, from about 35 percent in 1900 to 25 percent in 1940 in the Confederate South.

The migration was a matter of pull and push. The pull was the prospect of enlarged opportunity in the North, and the push was racial discrimination in the south in the aftermath of disfranchisement and legalized segregation. World War I affected black southerners in much the same way it affected whites, but its total impact on them was probably greater, generating rising expectations as well as increased income, and a social ferment that made the constraints of white supremacy more bridling than ever.

For those who remained in the South, social improvement was difficult and uneven, yet there was important progress, first in education and after 1940 in economics too. Benefits from the social and economic programs fostered by business Progressives were divided unequally between the races, but as the programs grew, their benefits trickled down to blacks as well as poor whites. Improvements in the black school system was steady during the 1920s and despite the retarding effects of the Great Depression continued thereafter. In twelve southern states annual expenditure reached an average of $21.54 for each black pupil in 1940 and rose markedly thereafter. This represented considerable progress even though the comparable figure for whites was $50.14 in 1940 and the absolute gap between the races was greater than ever. Conditions were worst in the deep South—the expenditure for each black pupil in Mississippi averaged only $7.24 in 1940—but schools were being consolidated and upgraded, and most pupils provided with free textbooks, which were often castoffs from white schools. Secondary education became available to ever increasing numbers of blacks, and in every state one or more publicly supported institutions made the transition to college-level instruction. In 1940 the NAACP won a victory in the federal courts establishing the principle of equal pay for black teachers, and since this necessitated a large increase in expenditures, the states became much more concerned about the quality of black education.

Economic progress was less obvious in the interwar years. In fact economic opportunity for black southerners diminished in some respects, thus increasing the push for migration to the North and West. Black employment was least open in the most dynamic areas of the economy, and even where it was easiest, as in lumbering, naval stores, mining, and railroad construction and maintenance, the number of jobs available was static or declining. Between 1910 and 1930 the proportion of black men in the nonagricultural work force in the greater South declined from 26.7 percent to 21.1 percent of the total. In major growth industries such as textiles, furniture manufacturing, chemicals, utilities, paper manufacturing, the urban service trades, and white-collar jobs in business and retailing, blacks were often excluded altogether or restricted to menial jobs or to businesses serving the black community. Professional opportunity was still largely limited to teaching and preaching, the lowest-paid and least prestigious professions, and though not all labor unions excluded blacks, unions generally had the effect of limiting black employment in skilled trades.

At the same time, the boll weevil, mechanization, declining prices, and after 1932 New Deal farm policies were restricting opportunities in agriculture, forcing many blacks as well as whites off the farm or into lower levels of farm work. Between 1910 and 1930 the number of black farm owners in the greater South declined from 220,000 to 182,000, and in the latter year four out of every five blacks in agriculture were still sharecroppers or wage laborers. The problem of black tenancy was never solved; instead, the tenants were forced out of farming and into the towns and cities of the North and the South. In the 1930s alone the number of black tenants and sharecroppers in the Southeast dropped a substantial 27 percent, from 699,000 to 507,000, and the number of black farm owners fell again, to 173,000 in the section as a whole.

The poverty and powerlessness mirrored in these facts placed serious limitations on racial activism. Black southerners would be able to sustain an effective racial movement only when the necessary preconditions had been achieved, and before World War II that had not yet occurred. The middle class in the black South was too small and dependent to mount a frontal assault on white supremacy, and potential allies, whether the federal government, northern blacks, or white liberals, were too indifferent, disorganized, or timid to help much. Efforts at racial reform were necessarily modest, even conservative, and largely the doings of a cautious interracial movement that was dominated by white southerners and dedicated not to integration and equality, but to eliminating the worst abuses of white supremacy and segregation. The movement centered around the Commission on Interracial Cooperation, which had been organized in 1919 to ease inflamed racial tensions in the aftermath of World War I. Led by such high-minded individuals as Will W. Alexander, Willis D. Weatherford, James H. Dillard, Jessie Daniels Ames, Mrs. L. H. Hammond, and others, it became the most constructive force in southern race relations in the interwar years. Under its auspices interracial organizations were established on state and local levels across the South, and special affiliate groups like the Association of Southern Women for the Prevention of Lynching were created to combat specific problems. Because of the stature of its leadership and the moderation of its approach, the

Commission succeeded in making the work of racial reform generally acceptable.

Given the conditions in which it had to work, the Commission's accomplishments were quite positive. Its members worked to reduce lynching and eliminate the tolerant attitude some whites had for that crime, and to counteract the Ku Klux Klan, racist demagogues, and other extremists. They seem to have had much to do with rallying white opinion against both lynching and the Klan—in 1937 a Gallup poll reported that 57 percent of a cross section of white southerners favored a federal antilynching law—and against racial extremism and demagoguery in general. Lynching, which had been declining since the turn of the century, had largely disappeared by World War II, and Klan influence was eclipsed in the middle and late 1920s. The Commission's approach was chary and pragmatic. It worked not to desegregate public schools, for example, but to improve segregated black schools; not to integrate public libraries, but to get branch libraries opened for blacks; not to get blacks appointed to police forces, jury panels, or judicial posts, but to get white policemen, juries, and judges to treat blacks equitably. Among newspaper editors, ministers, civic leaders, and other molders of white opinion, this approach won considerable support, and was an important factor in nudging white opinion and action in moderate directions.

The extent of black support for the Commission is not clear. Race leaders and many middle-class groups and individuals joined it or gave it their public endorsement, but the Commission itself was necessarily controlled by whites. The NAACP was its black-dominated counterpart, an interracial organization whose leadership and membership were predominantly black. It was also more effective outside the South, though many of its national leaders were southerners, among them James Weldon Johnson and Walter White, both of whom served as executive secretary. The NAACP never abandoned its opposition to segregation and other components of white supremacy, but its leaders were pragmatic, and they too worked to improve Jim Crow facilities and expand opportunity for blacks within segregation.

While important, the success of the interracial movement was also limited. In fact its success grew out of the very fact that ultimately compromised it, the easy accommodation with white supremacy. Reformist in nature, the movement had the strength and weakness of moderate movements trying to deal with visceral problems. Each victory it won made segregation more flexible and in the short run at least more endurable. The dilemma of the white racial moderate, which this fact illustrates, was always great. "Unless those forms of separation which are meant to safeguard the purity of the races are present," wrote Thomas J. Woofter, a leader of the interracial movement, "the majority of the white people flatly refuse to cooperate with the Negroes."

That was surely correct; and without the cooperation of whites reform was as yet impossible. "White power" was still the basic element in the racial equation, and the inability or unwillingness of moderates to challenge it meant that basic changes in the equation were still impossible. "Good God, there wasn't but few privileges that we was allowed," Ned Cobb (Nate Shaw), an illiterate sharecropper later recalled of the early 1930s. "If you was flesh and blood and human and tended to want to help and support your friends in the community, and make somethin of yourself—white folks didn't allow you that privilege. But we had the privilege of working for the white man—he who had the chance had better do it; get yourself together and get over yonder in Mr. So-and-so's field or anywhere else he told you and do what he tell you to do. And when pay time come he'd pay you what he wanted to, and in many cases it'd be less than what he'd pay a white man.... Colored man just been a dog for this country for years and years. White man didn't ask you how you felt about what he wanted to do; he'd just go ahead and do it and you had to fall under his rulins. And bein in his home country, he been allowed to do as he please by the capital of the United States."

14

The Benighted South

The ordeal of change conditioned the social history of the interwar years. In matters of popular culture southerners proved especially susceptible to outside influence, perhaps because the resulting changes seemed unrelated to sectional concerns. Urbanized, educated, and affluent groups took readily to consumerism, the new morality, and the new ways those things induced. Signs of Americanization appeared everywhere. "Today the South reads Associated Press dispatches, national advertising, and listens each night to national radio programs," Will W. Alexander observed in the late 1920s. "The heroes of Southern boys today are General Pershing, Ford, Edison, and Lindbergh. The Prince Albert coat and the goatee have entirely disappeared. The Rotarian, true to the national type, is the voice of the community. What the nation thinks the South is largely thinking: that America is God's country and Calvin Coolidge is a great president."

The agency of change was the urban middle class that emerged out of the transformations of the Progressive era and had few class ties to sectional traditions. A product of urbanization and economic growth, the class identified itself with prosperity and modernism, and its example in social matters was contagious. Members of the class tended to be more outward-looking and less upset than other southerners by the effects of outside influence. Among the influences at work upon them were pragmatism, secularism, and science, including Darwinism, Freudianism, and relativity, all of which had subversive implications for the traditional South and its way of life. If this was not entirely clear in 1920, many southerners saw even then that the section was more exposed to outside forces than it had ever been and that the forces were subversive as well as alluring. Gradually and without direction, those forces were intruding into the section, filtering through the curtain of traditionalism even into the nooks and crannies of sectional life and thought. The winds of social change that wafted gently before the war became stronger. Action began to produce reaction, and suddenly, or so it seemed to traditionalists, no one was satisfied in his or her place or content to discharge his or her traditional responsibilities. Established orthodoxies began to be questioned, entrenched authorities challenged, accustomed deferences resented, social conventions resisted as onerous. The widely differing reactions that this produced occasioned social controversies that pitted southerner against southerner, and the cement that had always held southern society together seemed to loosen. The moral authority of the southern way of life itself weakened. Liberals took hope and traditionalists took alarm, and the consequence was a South at war with itself.

The Benighted Image

One facet of the war was expressed in a general image of benightedness that came to characterize popular thinking about the South in the 1920s.[1] This image contradicted another equally important image, that of the progressive South of economic growth and national loyalties, and the fact that two such different images existed together reflected the dual nature of the southern response to change. H. L. Mencken, a Baltimore journalist and social critic, was the individual most responsible for popularizing the image of benightedness, in a landmark essay, "The Sahara of the Bozart [i.e., *Beaux-arts*]," published in 1920. Mencken's target was the South's cultural aridity, which he described in the bleakest language ever applied to the section. The South "is almost as sterile, artistically, intellectually, culturally, as the Sahara Desert," he wrote; it is a "gargantuan paradise of the fourth-rate" that contains "not a single picture gallery worth going into, or a single orchestra capable of playing the nine symphonies of Beethoven, or a single opera-house, or a single theater devoted to decent plays, or a single public monument (built since the [civil] war) that is worth looking at, or a single workshop devoted to the making of beautiful things." The entire section had only one author Mencken thought worthy of mention, James Branch Cabell, and no critics, composers, artists, scholars, or scientists, in all of which it was "an awe-inspiring blank." What caused this sad state of affairs? Mencken blamed it on the Civil War, which had destroyed the Old South, "a civilization of manifold excellences," and the planter aristocracy responsible for those excellences, and in its stead created a South controlled by "poor white trash," whose genius tended toward cultural tastelessness, social bigotry, religious intolerance, and economic boosterism.

Despite its transparent exaggeration, Mencken's indictment was valid enough to provoke a widespread reaction, but the very excesses of his language made his images vivid and enduring. In fact, however, Mencken had described only one of the two major aspects of the benighted image, cultural barrenness, giving scant attention in his essay to the other, social backwardness and bigotry. The latter was of more concern to indigenous liberals than to the Baltimore esthete, though Mencken did much to popularize it too. A good expression of this second aspect was in Howard W. Odum's "A Southern Promise" (1925). In language more restrained than Mencken's, Odum described the South's social benightedness as a consequence of irresponsible politics, widespread poverty, and undereducation. These things, he said, had stifled freedom of inquiry, stunted creativity, and wasted social energies in a blighting defense of orthodoxy. The result was "conflict between races, between classes, between denominations, between visible and invisible government, between dominant demagogues and their following[s]"; and "for years now the dominant note has been negative and the South has been sensitive and 'against' the things that are progressive and the things that are not her own." Another result was fear—of the outside, of truth itself. "The South is still hot-headed, emotional, unthinking in its attitude toward many questions and toward those who do not agree with its opinions or traditions, or those who do not approve its conduct." And "the prevailing forbidden fruit [is not] limited to radical doctrines in politics, economics, education, religion, or sociology, but restrictions encompass the simple, sincere, courageous telling of the truth about the South, its people, its history, its tasks."

A major part of the problem, Odum believed, was the nature of southern religion, which "boasts much, complains continuously, seeks motes in other people's eyes, klans together for persecutions, mobs the weak, has little respect for the truth, is selfishly self-centered, [and] . . . emotionally and lazily inclined toward the easiest way." Thus southerners were "poor in the fruits of social righteousness, justice, and the essence of Christianity." Their religion did not address their problems. "Claiming to be pre-eminently Christian, [southerners are] yet in many instances in danger of breeding a gross spirit of boastful materialism with ecclesiastical dogmatism and of joining political demagoguery in unholy alliance with religious fervor, thus producing a mongrel barrenness, the despair of classification."

Here, then, was the Benighted South: a land of cultural aridity, intellectual conformity, social intolerance, and emotional religion; a people plagued by poverty, ignorance, and insecurity, and by the bigotry, defensiveness, and reactive violence those things induced. This was the South of the Ku Klux Klan, political demagogues, the Scopes trial, and lynching bees. It was far from the whole South; but in the

1920s it was an important part of the whole and the locus of many of the problems that accompanied social change.

The Culture of Poverty

The Benighted South was partly an extrusion of the culture of poverty that encompassed a large portion of the southern people. Just how large that portion was is impossible to say, for poverty is a relative as well as an absolute condition and a state of mind as well as an economic circumstance. But if all the poor could be numbered—the white and black sharecroppers, agricultural laborers, mill villagers, mountaineers, and urban poor—the total would certainly be well over half the population. In twelve southern states, the annual per capita income in 1929 was only 51 percent of that of the Midwest, and for the farm population it amounted to $183. The ensuing decade of depression did nothing to ease this situation, and in the urban South in 1939 more than a third of all families, including two-thirds of all black families, earned less than $1,000, and an additional 18.8 percent were said to earn nothing at all, living totally on welfare or charity.[2]

The cultural effects of such widespread poverty are not easy to know. After World War I, however, scholars began systematically studying poverty and the poor, and many of their studies were sympathetic and discerning. Beginning with the 1920s it is therefore possible to write with some assurance about the interior life of the southern poor. In 1922 Horace Kephart made a pioneering study of *Our Southern Highlanders,* and at the University of North Carolina and elsewhere social scientists began systematic investigations of other groups. Within a few years, poverty was among the most widely studied subjects of southern life, and a number of microstudies revealed the lives of poor people with more wholeness than ever before. The masterpiece of this genre was James Agee's study of three Alabama sharecropper families in the throes of depression, *Let Us Now Praise Famous Men* (1941), which is probably the most compelling evocation of the meaning of poverty in American literature. Theodore Rosengarten's *All God's Dangers* (1974), the reminiscences of an illiterate octogenarian recorded in the 1970s, is almost as compelling an illustration of the life of the black poor in Alabama. A number of novelists explored the life of the poor with considerable success. Dorothy Scarborough produced a deft portrait of tenant farmers in *In the Land of Cotton* (1923), and Erskine Caldwell masterfully delineated the social and psychological ravages of extreme poverty in *Tobacco Road* (1932). In Jeeter Lester, the central character of the latter work, Caldwell produced the most authentic and fully developed portrait of a poor white in American literature.

The works of scholars were not as emotionally satisfying as these works, but they were often more informative. Much about the lives of poor blacks was revealed in Charles S. Johnson's *Shadow of the Plantation* (1934) and Hortense Powdermaker's *After Freedom* (1939), while John Dollard's *Caste and Class in a Southern Town* (1937) told a great deal about the poor of both races. Margaret J. Hagood discerningly studied a group of white tenant farm women in *Mothers of the South* (1939), while Arthur F. Raper's concern was with *Tenants of the Almighty* (1943) and Herbert J. Lahne's with *The Cotton Mill Worker* (1944).

The literature of which these titles are but a tiny sampling described a life that was difficult and often unfulfilling, and but little relieved by creature comforts and wholesome cultural outlets. Life among the poor was largely devoid of esthetics and things that constitute the life of the mind, and among the very poor there was little hope that the future would ever be better. "One house will have only an earthen floor," Horace Kephart wrote of the poorest mountaineers; "another will be so small that 'you cain't cuss a cat in it 'thout gittin' ha'r in yer teeth.' Utensils are limited to a frying-pan, an iron pot, a coffee-pot, a bucket, and some gourds. There is not enough tableware to go around, and children eat out of their parents' plates, or all 'soup-in together' around a bowl of stew or porridge." Such conditions were hardly typical, but across the rural South the poorest people lived in unkempt and dilapidated shacks that afforded little comfort or privacy and nothing of beauty. Their yards were equally unprepossessing, often lacking shrubbery, gardens, fruit trees, and shade trees, and sometimes even outhouses and wells. Such surroundings gave life an air of rootlessness and underscored the lack of economic security that produced the frequent moves of sharecroppers, mill villagers, and other poor.

For most of the poor, life was full of toil. The demands of farm or factory were unceasing dictators of the rhythms of life. Women worked as hard as and sometimes harder than men, for theirs were the cares of housekeeping and childrearing as well as the tasks of farm or factory. And for black women there were often the special demands of housekeeping and cooking for landowning whites. "Last year I travelled from one end of our state to another," wrote a North Carolina woman in 1927. "I saw thousands of women, old and young, mothers and little girls, working in stores and factories ten or eleven or twelve hours a day; or worse working in the factory all night, and taking care of their homes by day.... And I saw working in the fields, hoeing cotton and corn and doing all kinds of hard labor, women and children, white as well as black." Such incessant toil had important social consequences. Leisure time was irregular and leisure activity unplanned; Sunday was literally a day of rest. Overwork discouraged interest in civic life, while physical exhaustion and the sense of powerlessness discouraged cooperative endeavor of every sort.

These remarks apply chiefly to the working poor, by far the largest group of impoverished southerners. They are less true of the minority of classic poor whites still found in sizable numbers in isolated areas of the piney woods and flatlands and on the fringes of the plantation districts. The distinguishing feature of these wretched folk was what it had always been, a lack of commitment to the ethic of the middle class. Yet so strong was the influence of the middle class that the failure to live up to its values, whether moral or material, seems to have induced to one degree or another a sense of guilt or shame even among the most abandoned poor whites. Many of the working poor were related by blood or marriage to members of the middle and lower middle classes, and had hopes of rising in the economic and social scale. The poorest whites, however, had no such hopes. Largely ineffective as workers, they owned little or nothing besides a few personal belongings, and had almost no cash income (the poorest one-fourth of fifty-one white tenant farm families studied in North Carolina in 1923 had average cash incomes of $44 the previous year, well below the average of black sharecroppers in the state).

Outwardly at least, these poorest of southerners conformed to the popular stereotype of poor whites. They were slovenly, uncouth, and sometimes degenerate, as the middle class defined those terms, and thus "sorry folks" to those above them on the social and economic scale. Defeated, unstruggling, and socially apathetic, they seemed not even to aspire to better things. Middle-class observers often described them as contented with their lot, but it is more likely that they were simply resigned to conditions they looked upon with fatalism. They displayed little pride of family and person, and no sense of identification with anything larger than themselves. They were the least churched, least educated, and least political group in the white South. For most of them, sustained periods of deprivation and lifetimes of ignorance had reduced existence to a series of strategies for survival. They furnished a disproportionate share of the white people who got in trouble with the law, not only because of class biases in law enforcement but also because they never internalized respect for the law. The kinds of mayhem and petty crimes they committed against property and person bore striking resemblance to those poor blacks were assumed to commit, and were especially offensive to middle-class interests and sensibilities.

Despite the important differences among them, all the poor of both races tended to share certain social characteristics that may be said to constitute a culture of poverty. Room for self-improvement and psychological autonomy was constricted for all poor people, and thus self-respect and self-justification were universal concerns. This was especially true of the working poor, for whom work itself served important redeeming functions. Work was the readiest source they had for positive self-expression and thus for the sense of self-worth they sorely needed. Producing a good crop, "raising" a large family of "decent" children, or sewing or cooking or housekeeping well were fulfilling experiences for people whose opportunities for achievement were limited. Living respectably served a similar purpose. "There is little expectation of the ladder theory [of economic advancement] working out—materially at least," wrote Margaret J. Hagood of the white tenant women she studied in *Mothers of the South*. "This seems to make it more urgent to attain recognition and respectability in other ways—by bringing up children properly even if the parents are poor; by insisting that 'renters can hold their heads as high as anybody if they live right'; by subscribing to various traditional beliefs as they seek to identify themselves with the economically superior class in their ideology at least."

Concern with self-worth and self-expression helps explain some of the less attractive traits of the white poor, such as sexism and racism. The unwillingness of men to perform household chores even when their wives worked outside the home reflected not only social conditioning but the sometimes desperate need among men in a male-oriented society to assert their social dominance by indulging in social prerogative. The double standard of social and sexual conduct that men insisted upon may have been a manifestation of the same thing. Hunting, loafing, drinking, and casual extramarital sex were activities largely denied women, and partly for that reason especially prized by men. The characteristic expressions of racism among the white poor—direct, unreflective action and mob violence—were perhaps also in part inspired by the felt need to assert male supremacy. Unencumbered by pseudoscientific rationalizations and unrestrained by an ability to achieve their goals indirectly, the white poor practiced a racism that was direct and unpretentious. White supremacy was doubly important to them, for it was one of the few public policies they were given a hand in upholding, and in safeguarding it they found one of the few opportunities they had to assert a man's prerogative of defending his women. The latter seems especially important in view of the fact that poverty made it difficult for poor men to fulfill the role of social and economic providers. In a male-oriented society a man whose wife was obliged to help support the family was seen as not fulfilling his responsibilities as a man, and in his own eyes he was less a man for that fact. Yet among the poor of both races many men were in that position, and the resulting frustration helps explain not only their civic and political apathy but also such social problems as wife beating, child abuse, and alcoholism.

In these and other things the culture of poverty made social change more difficult. Prejudice, provincialism, and social inertia combined to make the poor an obstacle to orderly social evolution. This does not mean the poor were responsible for the social pathologies of the 1920s, for they had no power of any sort. But groups that did have power found the prejudices of the poor useful in their own public dealings with social change. In using and abusing the poor, those groups encouraged the worst rather than the best of their impulses, but they also provided themselves with a scapegoat of unlimited usefulness.

Social Fundamentalism

The Benighted South is best understood as the traditional South resisting social change, and the resistance movement is best described as an exercise in social fundamentalism.[3] The nature of this movement derived from the social values of those who joined it, values that grew chiefly from religious fundamentalism and a broad array of social orthodoxies, especially white supremacy and puritanical morality, and from the defensiveness that often characterized southern responses to outside pressure. Social fundamentalists are remembered today for what they opposed, which is perhaps the way they should be remembered, but many of their concerns were positive. They sought to give voice to the American creed white southerners had developed during World War I, which means that they sought to defend the white South's ethnic and sectional loyalties, its commitment to tradition and religious faith, its acceptance of social hierarchy and deference, its dedication to the tenets of *Herrenvolk* democracy. But in the social milieu of the Benighted South these virtues easily turned into the vices that were their counterparts—xenophobia, racism, intolerance, violence, and defense of special privilege. As a result the effort to preserve the traditional South became chiefly an exercise in prejudice and repression rather than social enlightenment. Perhaps this was inevitable, for social fundamentalists were trying not to adapt modernism and progress to southern ways, but to resist those things (or many aspects of them) altogether. This forced them into the public role, not always uncongenial, of reactionaries and repressers, of trying to impose controls over rising or discontented groups and to force their own standards on everyone suspected of moral permissiveness.

They accepted this role not only because the worst of them were temperamentally authoritarian and ungenerous but because the best of them shared the conservative's insight into the nature of social change. Denizens of the Benighted South, they saw intuitively if vaguely that social change was of one piece and that accepting any part of it advanced the prospects of all of it. As they saw their situation, it was not unlike that of their forefathers in 1860–61—they must fight for their way of life or wait to be overwhelmed. Freedom of thought in the schools, they reasoned, would not simply expose young southerners to outside ideas like Darwin's evolutionary theories; it would sooner or later cause them to question sectional values and eventually produce the kind of social dissidence a hierarchical society could not withstand in a liberal world. Similarly, the women's rights movement would not merely enable women to vote but would alter family roles and institutional structures and thus undermine the family's traditional functions of guarding and transmitting moral values. It was the final steps in these processes, the ultimate transformation of southern life, that concerned thoughtful fundamentalists, who believed, not irrationally, that the best way to avoid basic change was to prevent the things that made it inevitable.

Nor were they wholly incorrect. To social fundamentalists the traditional South was preferable to a South Americanized and liberalized, but in the modern world of change and standardization, the traditional South was a frail creature, especially vulnerable to the siren call of liberalism and too much tinkering would destroy it. It had to be accepted as it was, warts and all—though what reformers saw as warts fundamentalists were likely to see as beauty spots—for in its wholeness lay the soul of the South, the section's essential identity, the sum of things that made it a place apart.

Here too fundamentalists were not incorrect, but the main stream of fundamentalist thought had been compromised before it reached this far. Most fundamentalists wanted to avoid social change rather than adapt it to southern ways, but they also wanted to do that while encouraging economic growth and material improvement without regard to the subversive potential of those things. They also failed to recognize the implications of their own methods of social activism, which included organized and unorganized pressure exerted through politics, law enforcement, public opinion, and economic control, and on occasion mob violence and intimidation. The frenzies of intolerance they sometimes whipped up became symbols of the cause they championed and, because they wrapped themselves in flags of sectional loyalty, symbols of the South itself. Their own actions thus helped discredit the cause of their immediate concern, social conservatism, as well as their larger purpose, preserving the traditional South. The backlash generated against them enlarged the vacuum of responsible leadership on the right side of the political spectrum, and further hastened the disintegration of the traditional South.

Fundamental Religion

Because it mixed extreme methods and conservative ends, social fundamentalism was not a well-integrated social philosophy. It was instead a jumbled mass of social prejudices which acted upon incautious temperament to generate direct action in the interest of regimentation. It nevertheless grew out of a major body of sectional thought and tradition. Its principal taproot was the mass religions of the white South, which gave fundamentalist crusades a decidedly religious character. This is not to say that social fundamentalism was a religious movement, but to call it a social movement that incorporated the religious values of its constituency.

Those values derived from a religion that was little changed since the New South era.[4] The vast majority of southerners, like the vast majority of social fundamentalists, were religious literalists whose churches were still for the most part small and poor, and whose ministers were undereducated, often anti-intellectual, and frequently emotional. In 1921 more than one of every eight Methodist ministers had never finished high school and four in seven had no education beyond high school. At the same time, only about one of every five rural churches in the section had full-time ministers, and well over a third of all rural ministers served four or more churches. As a result the influence of religion was exerted through the forcefulness of individual preachers.

Their message is difficult to translate into social terms. One of the singular facts about southern religion is that it never produced a significant theologian or social philosopher, and the failure is especially evident in the mass churches. This was due in large part to the nature of fundamentalism, which was a religion of personal salvation and emotional catharsis rather than intellectual or philosophical concern, and to the fact that fundamentalism produced no tradition of theological disputation or intellectual dissent. Thus southern religious thought always lacked originality, in social no less than theological matters. It reflected rather than molded secular values."Southern Baptists defended Negro degradation [i.e., racial segregation] in the mid-twentieth century as fervently as they had Negro slavery in the mid-nineteenth,"

Robert M. Miller has written; and his remarks apply equally well to other areas of social policy. Southern churches accepted the established economic order, for example, and their teachings on economic matters were entirely conventional. Few ministers went as far as the South Carolinian who in 1927 described the industrialization of the South as "a spiritual movement" that offered "the largest single opportunity the world has ever had to build a democracy upon the ethics of Christianity." But they seem generally to have preached a social ethic favoring property and management. "The greatest contribution of the churches to the industrial revolution in the South undoubtedly lay in the labor discipline they provided through supervision of the workers," Liston Pope wrote in *Millhands and Preachers* (1942). The churches "mold transplanted farmers into stable, contented, sober citizens and industrial workers," Pope declared, by imbuing them with such qualities as stability, honesty, sobriety, industry, and docility, while providing them an "emotional escape from the difficulties of life in a mill village." As a result, mill managers "agree almost unanimously ... that church members are more stable ... and more dependable workers" and more "reasonable" in matters of labor relations.

Thus organized religion justified and rationalized the southern way of life. In economics as well as race it supported the effort of social fundamentalists to resist social change. Biblical literalism was easily transposed into social and intellectual literalism, into an insistence that the letter of social convention be upheld. Likewise, religious orthodoxy was a prop for secular orthodoxy, especially in matters involving morals and sin. These things, too, pushed religion and social fundamentalism toward common purposes. The repressive nature of the latter combined with puritanism derived from the former to drive both toward bigotry and vigilantism.

The realities of social fundamentalism thus clashed with the tenets of religious fundamentalism that derived from the golden rule, the Sermon on the Mount, and the ideas that God is love and that Christianity is a religion of forgiveness. Christianity is of course an amorphous religion and open to widely differing interpretations, but most southerners accepted it as a religion extolling the individual, to whom it gave equality in the sight of God and the promise of salvation by grace regardless of race or other considerations. However, they also accepted it as a religion emphasizing the doctrine of original sin and human depravity. In their role as social fundamentalists they stressed the latter rather than the former, and this in turn gave greater play to the social puritanism that justified the use of secular instruments to achieve essentially religious purposes.

This sidestepped rather than eliminated the contradiction between social fundamentalism and certain aspects of New Testament Christianity. The contradiction was potentially bothersome, for fundamentalists took social policy as well as religion seriously, but it was resolved by interpreting the social implications of the doctrine of human depravity in a way that transformed the contradiction into a complement. The doctrine of human depravity made sinfulness inevitable, but the promise of salvation by the grace of a forgiving God to anyone who would accept salvation on God's terms gave the individual a choice in the matter. Fundamentalists interpreted this element of personal choice as something that reduced the social dimension of sin and salvation by making those things personal matters between the individual and God. The "saved" individual could thus view social evils as consequences of human depravity rather than extrusions of the social system, and so something for which he, being in a state of grace, had no responsibility. The effect, as Samuel S. Hill has shown in *Religion and the Solid South* (1972), was to assuage the sense of personal guilt that might otherwise have been generated by living in the midst of social evils. The saved individual could relegate potentially troublesome social ills to the periphery of his personal concerns. In effect the ills became things to endure rather than problems to solve, for they were seen as springing from the depravity of men who refused to accept God's grace. In this way, as Hill observed, "many southern whites got relief from the guilt of perpetuating an immoral socioeconomic system by subscribing to the tenets of a guilt oriented theology." The result was to reconcile the southern way of life with New Testament Christianity and thus justify the efforts to protect it from "godless" change.

In this sense, the southern version of Christian fundamentalism was authentically Christian as well as distinctively southern. This fact has not always been appreciated by writers within the Christian tradition, especially those of a liberal Protestant bent who tend to assume that the essence of Christianity is love, tolerance, forgiveness, and the equality of all believers. The implication of this assumption is that "true" Christians must support liberal social policies, or put another way, that racial segregation, class distinctions, and social exclusiveness are un-Christian. Southerners, and not just fundamentalists, rejected this assumption, and did what practicing Christians have always done, molded Christianity to suit their own imperatives. They felt no more compulsion to literalize the brotherhood of man than the fatherhood of God, for to them the kingdom of God was something to be achieved in Heaven. They felt no obligation as Christians to love (in any literal sense) the unregenerate, to say nothing of the degenerate, or to tolerate public violations of moral law. They were also satisfied to accept what they regarded as God-ordained divisions of mankind. Southern Christianity thus accommodated itself to social hierarchy, racial separation, white supremacy, and economic inequality, and as liberal reformers measured such things, it was indifferent to social issues like racialism, poverty, labor disorganization, and certain restrictions on civil liberties. But it was not indifferent to prohibition, divorce, the status of women, the moral content of motion pictures and school books, the religious affiliation of presidential candidates, or the "unnatural" practice of "race mixing." In effect, this set of values accepted the South's way of life as Christian and made only abuses of it sinful.

These things determined the social policies of southern churches. The mass churches were skeptical of the social gospel, which tended to explain sin in social terms, and positively opposed to ecumenism, which necessitated unacceptable doctrinal compromises. Yet they regularly involved themselves in social causes. Their members joined the Ku Klux Klan, the Anti-Saloon League, and a host of lesser organizations dedicated to political or social activism. Perhaps the most conspicuous of these endeavors was the prohibition crusade, led by Methodist Bishop James Cannon of Virginia, who also played a leading role in the effort to defeat the presidential candidacy of Catholic Alfred E. Smith in 1928. Smith's defeat was discussed earlier, but it is worth adding here that in the South Smith faced the organized opposition of conservative Protestants. As Kenneth K. Bailey has observed in *Southern White Protestantism in the Twentieth Century* (1964), ecclesiastical leaders "initiate[d] and direct[ed] a campaign for a specific candidate [Herbert Hoover], in concert with the denominational press, and in conformity with denominational policy pronouncements."

In all of these endeavors, fundamentalists had considerable short-term success. But the tactics they used and the prejudices they cultivated soon began to work against them and eventually contributed to the decline not only of militant fundamentalism but of organized religion itself. Politicians resented the intrusion of the church into partisan politics, and many of them worked actively to end it. Moreover, the intrusion showed organized religion and its leaders in a compromising light, as cultivators of prejudice rather than exhorters of the faith. This invited criticism, not only from professional heretics like H. L. Mencken but from scoffers and liberals and even those fundamentalists who thought the church should stick to saving souls and leave politics to politicians. In addition, many of the things fundamentalists denounced as sinful began gaining social acceptance, whether motion pictures, emancipated women, legalized liquor, or freer discussion of controversial issues.

Thus fundamentalism was in part overtaken by social change, and evidence of its declining influence was unmistakable by the end of the

1920s. The failure to "keep up with the times" alienated a growing segment of the urban middle class, whose influence on popular tastes had become controlling. The Great Depression added to this process by dramatizing the unresponsiveness of churches to economic and social problems and thus their irrelevance in times of social crisis. It was government, not the churches, that confronted the problems of the depression and thus addressed itself to the needs of people. This accelerated a trend that had major implications for southern history, the growing secularization of life. Increasingly, religion was left to preachers and Sunday mornings and treated as a set of abstractions to pay lip service to but not to consult in the real world of everyday living. Church membership continued to rise, but the hold of religion on southern life was loosening, and as it slackened an important feature of sectional distinctiveness diminished. In 1941 the slackening was still far from complete and religion remained a major influence in southern life, but its influence had crested in the fundamentalist crusades of the 1920s and was never again as strong. In the 1950s, when the traditional South was again under attack, this time from the civil rights movement, organized religion played a much smaller role in the section's defense of itself than it played in the 1920s.

Education in the Benighted South

Many of the factors that influenced mass religion in the Benighted South also influenced public education. The story of education in the interwar years was thus one of progress and poverty.[5] Reformers took pride in the notable expansion of educational opportunities, while traditionalists were reassured by the fact that the content of education continued to affirm sectional values. By 1945 the process of creating statewide systems of public schools was generally complete in the white South and well underway in the black. Administration had been centralized, schools consolidated, plants improved, free textbooks and instructional equipment provided, buses furnished rural children, and teacher qualifications upgraded. Between 1927–28 and 1945–46 total funds spent on public education in the greater South nearly doubled, rising from $283 million to $555 million, and the quality and quantity of education at all levels improved markedly for both races.

However, disparities between the South and the nation grew, and education remained under the constrictive influences of the Benighted South. In 1945–46, to illustrate, southerners spent a slightly higher proportion of their income on public education than did people in the rest of the country, but because of poverty, the high birth rate, and a low proportion of students in private schools, this amounted to only

$72.21 per pupil compared to $137.87 in the rest of the country. In 1940, when the Census Bureau began reporting years of schooling instead of literacy rates, a substantial majority of the people in the section still had less than an elementary education. More than 25 percent of all those over the age of twenty-four had less than five years of schooling, and an additional forty percent had only five to eight years.

The social implications of this are important but not entirely clear. It seems likely that there was little in the content of elementary education to encourage critical thinking—certainly that was true of the textbooks used in history and related disciplines—and in the realm of social values the effect of formal schooling was conservative, if indeed it had much effect at all. This was probably also true of secondary and higher education. According to the informed opinion of Howard W. Odum, teacher training programs in the South in the mid-1930s did little more than inculcate prospective teachers with "the mechanics of curricula and methods" and reinforce their "sectional patriotism and loyalties." This was one reason, Odum believed, why "no great strength, liberalism, scholarship, or boldness has emerged from" the education movement in the section, and why schools had never been instruments of social reform.

Odum, however, was judging the schools as vehicles of Americanization. If his comments are turned around and put in traditionalist terms, they mean simply that education in the South was an instrument of socialization, which is to say that it perpetuated traditional values. "Among southerners there is an education that does not educate," Francis B. Simkins wrote after World War II. He meant that formal education did little to change sectional values, and his observation seems generally valid. The student brings to school an "effective indoctrination in local ideals which survives the regimentation of the schools," Simkins declared, and the home far more than the school "determines the cultural outlook of Southerners." Issues raised in the classroom are seldom discussed elsewhere, Simkins noted, and the public pays little more attention to the opinions of teachers than to those of pupils.

The course of higher education was affected by these things too, though a breakthrough was achieved in the interwar years with the emergence of several institutions of genuine quality, notably the state universities of North Carolina, Texas, Virginia, and Louisiana and such private universities as Duke, Tulane, Rice, and Emory. Still, progress was slow and uneven, and the reason was the lack of money and independence that grew out of public indifference and the widespread misunderstanding of what a university should be. In the not unprosperous year of 1927–28, the nation's wealthiest institution, Harvard University, spent more money for library books than the eleven state universities of the Confederate South together, though the Harvard libraries already contained more volumes than the combined libraries of those universities.

That fact reflects the problems of graduate and professional schooling, where southern education was still most deficient. Surveying the twelve southeastern states in 1936, Howard W. Odum could find no university, college of agriculture, or engineering school of the first rank, and "no advanced instruction of the highest order in many of the subjects now demanded in the newer developments in politics, business, agriculture, industry, [and] land utilization." This helps explain why only 3.9 percent of all patents issued by the United States Patent Office in the half century ending in 1943 were awarded to residents of the southern states. No university in the Southeast at the time of Odum's report offered a Ph.D. in civil, chemical, mechanical, electrical, or mining engineering, or in bacteriology, geography, plant pathology, or soil science. Altogether, universities in the greater South and West Virginia awarded only 1.3 percent of the doctoral degrees granted in the United States before 1926 and only 4.8 percent of those granted from 1926 to 1947.

The state of higher education was one example of the limited life of the mind in the Benighted South. The section was the poorest book market in the country and the poorest publishing market too. Of 235 American publishers issuing five or more titles in 1943, only 9 were in the South, and together they published only 121 titles. In 1939, according to W. T. Couch, the *Southern Review,* a quality journal of opinion and criticism published at Louisiana State University, had more subscribers in Tokyo than Alabama and more in New York City than all the South. In 1922 newspaper circulation was 1 for every 13.5 inhabitants in North Carolina compared to 1 for every 1.9 inhabitants in Massachusetts. A dozen years later 1 of every 12.7 rural residents subscribed to a newspaper in nine southern states compared to 1 of every 3.6 rural residents in the nation as a whole (and 1 of every 37.1 residents in rural South Carolina).

These phenomena were not unrelated to another chronic problem, the drain of educated and talented people from the South. Among the estimated 3.5 million persons of both races who left the section between 1900 and 1930 were untold numbers of skilled and talented individuals whose loss impoverished the section. A study of people listed in *Who's Who in America* between 1899 and 1936 found that talented individuals born in the Southeast left the section at a rate almost three times as great as the outmigration of the white population as a whole. Of 6,015 southern-born persons listed in the 1932–33 edition of *Who's*

Who, no less than 2,229 lived elsewhere, including 61.3 percent of all the natural scientists born in the section, 57.8 percent of the architects and engineers, and 49.8 percent of the editors and authors.

The Savage Ideal

The brain drain was part of a vicious cycle that perpetuated the Benighted South. The savage ideal—the phrase Wilbur J. Cash used to describe the compulsion for intellectual conformity[6] inhibited freedom of thought and the development of higher education, and the absence of those things encouraged intellectual and social intolerance. The antievolution crusade, which culminated in the famous trial of a high school biology teacher, John Thomas Scopes, in Dayton, Tennessee, in the summer of 1925, was the most dramatic example of this cycle at work. Southerners had never been receptive to the evolutionary theories of Charles Darwin, which they associated with rationalism and irreligion, and in the effort to resist social change in the 1920s they made those theories a target of fundamentalist wrath. In 1925 the Tennessee legislature forbade public schools in the state to teach "any theory that denies the story of the Divine Creation of man as taught in the Bible and to teach instead that man has descended from a lower order of animals." Similar laws were enacted in Mississippi and Arkansas, as well as Oklahoma, and much the same effect was achieved in other states by school board policy and the force of public opinion.

The aftermath of these laws reveals much about the nature of social fundamentalism and the Benighted South. The laws were not intended to be punitive and never became instruments of oppression. The Tennessee statute provided fines of $100 to $500 for violations, but Scopes was the only violator ever charged in that or any other state, and he was charged only because he and others wanted a confrontation to test the constitutionality of the law. The near unanimity of southern opinion against evolution meant that few teachers "believed in" Darwin's theories or had any desire to "teach" them. Laws against doing so were thus superfluous, and their passage represented no actual curtailment of classroom freedom. Rather, the laws were acts of defiance against liberal change, affirmations of faith in something most southerners accepted uncritically, the Biblical story of creation. The chief effect of the laws and school board policies was in the screening of textbooks, where they did help keep unpopular views out of the classroom. But even so, the laws reflected rather than produced intellectual conformity.

The antievolution crusade was one link in a chain of intolerance that extended from petty acts of self-righteousness to organized campaigns of intellectual and social bigotry and periodic episodes of mass violence. It was the total pattern of events that gave social meaning to the antievolution laws and such things as movie censorship, book banning, and public crusades against conduct deemed immoral or immodest. "A lot of bright-colored bathing suits, decks of cards and novels were missing from Madisonville [Tennessee] homes today," read a news item in H. L. Mencken's *American Mercury* in 1932. "They were burned in front of the Baptist church yesterday following a baptismal service in which thirty-five were baptised. The Reverend W. A. Carroll, who conducted a three-week revival, asked those in attendance to bring their bathing suits, cards, and cheap novels. While 'I'll Never Turn Back' was being sung the Reverend Carroll set fire to them."

By itself such an incident was merely amusing, but in the context of a larger pattern of social conformity it was important. The pattern grew out of fear, and produced the most repelling feature of social fundamentalism, the willingness to resort to wholesale intimidation and violence. The history of the Benighted South is thus sprinkled with incidents of "whitecapping," peonage, labor violence, lynching, and other forms of mob activity.

The pattern of this activity in the interwar years was much like that of earlier periods. Violent crime was widespread. The earliest substantive data on homicide rates in the South are for the years 1920 through 1924, and they reveal an incidence more than two-and-a-half times higher than that in the rest of the country. Evidence for the late 1930s indicates that that incidence persisted through the period.

There was one important evolution in the pattern of social violence, however. Racial violence declined after about 1920 and class violence increased. Of course racial violence did not disappear, but much of that which occurred had a significant economic dimension. An apparently substantial number of blacks remained in virtual (and sometimes actual) peonage in agriculture, turpentining, and sawmilling, and the known episodes of violence that helped keep them there apparently reveal only the tip of a large iceberg. Typically, near peonage resulted from a system in which white planters or employers paid court-imposed fines for blacks who were obliged to work out the fines. If this seems innocent enough on the surface, it was often a device that had sinister results. By a system of easy credit at high interest rates, an employer in league with a cooperative sheriff might keep a laborer perpetually in debt and indefinitely in his employment. In an especially outrageous incident in Jasper County, Georgia, in 1921 a white planter murdered eleven blacks he held in peonage in a vain effort to prevent exposure of his violations of the law, for which he was convicted and sentenced to life imprisonment. In a different kind of incident, in Lake City, South Carolina, in 1920, "white cap" night riders forced blacks to pick cotton for $1 per hundred pounds though the going rate was $1.50. In Warren County, Georgia, in 1937, to cite a similar incident from later in the period, "a mob organized by local planters forced Negro workers at the point of guns to go into the cotton fields and pick cotton for wages below those prevailing in nearby counties." According to Virginius Dabney, who reported this incident, "the same thing happened in a less dramatic and brutal manner in many other cotton belt counties."

The characteristic form of class violence was directed against organized labor. The history of strikes and other labor activity through the interwar years is replete with violence and repression perpetrated not only by management but cooperative police forces and sometimes private mobs as well. Each major wave of strike activity, in 1919–20 and 1929–30 and again in the middle of the 1930s, was accompanied by violence and murder for which management seems largely responsible. In the textile strikes of 1929–30 at least eight people, including one police chief, were killed, and in 1934–35, when labor violence crested in the section, no less than forty-two workers and organizers died violently. Investigations by the United States Civil Liberties Committee revealed that between 1933 and 1937 twenty-seven firms in the South spent $800,000 hiring labor spies, purchasing arms, and breaking strikes. Incomplete records of private detective agencies showed seventy-eight other firms engaged in similar practices. Fearful that unions would inhibit economic growth, local officials often worked with management to keep workers unorganized. "C.I.O. agitators, Communists, and highly paid professional organizers" should stay away from Memphis, warned the mayor of that city in 1937; and his warning was not unique. Nor was the ordinance adopted by the city council of Macon, Georgia, a textile manufacturing center, prohibiting distribution of "any handbill, circular, pamphlet, poster, postcard, or literature of any kind" within the city. The object of the ordinance was labor organizers.

An important aspect of violence was the selective enforcement of sometimes draconic criminal laws. In South Carolina between 1920 and 1926, to illustrate, the rate of conviction of blacks tried for murder or manslaughter was more than twice that of whites tried for those crimes; and 80 percent of the felons executed for crime in that state between 1915 and 1962 were blacks. Prison, penitentiary, and chain gang populations throughout the period were made up disproportionately of blacks and poor whites. Katharine DuPre Lumpkin reported that 41 percent of all persons committed to county and city jails, including chain gangs, in the section during the depression year of 1933 were committed for inability to pay fines, more than two-thirds of which were less than $20. Similar inequities characterized the response of police and courts to labor violence. Strikers and organizers accused of violence tended to receive much harsher treatment than antiunion activists, who were rarely even charged with violating the law. In the Gastonia, North Carolina, textile strike in 1929, seven people supporting the strike were given long prison sentences for the death of a police official; but when police fired tear gas into a line of picketing strikers and then shot into them as they fled, no one was even charged with violating the law, though all of the five people killed and the several others wounded were shot in the back.

If such events were untypical, they were an important part of the milieu that produced the most significant sociopolitical organization in the Benighted South, the Ku Klux Klan. The Klan was the most prominent extrusion of the pathologies of social fundamentalism and the clearest example of the savage ideal at work. Organized in north Georgia in 1915, this revival of a Reconstruction organization presented itself as a reincarnation of the organization that had saved the South in an earlier period of threatening social change, Radical Reconstruction. This view of the original Klan was reinforced by D. W. Griffith's landmark motion picture *The Birth of a Nation,* based on Thomas Dixon's grotesque novel about Reconstruction *The Clansman: An Historical Romance of the Ku Klux Klan* (1905). Released in 1915, Griffith's motion picture presented Reconstruction as a manichaean struggle between prostrate white southerners and vindictive northern Radicals. To accomplish their diabolical designs, so Griffith's story ran, the Radicals had cynically used hapless blacks, manipulating their ignorance and feeding their savage lusts in order to control their votes. The Klan, however, had thwarted this scheme and saved the South for civilization. Griffith's film of this tale was shown continuously in the section for a decade and a half, and seems to have acted as a catalyst for pro-Klan sentiment.

But there were other reasons for the Klan's appeal. Klan spokesmen always presented their organization to the public in positive terms, as an embodiment of Americanism and traditional moral values. They stressed its patriotic and religious character and its commitment to the precepts of social fundamentalism. It is easy to see the appeal of this message to people who had a will to believe it. It was another of the tragedies of southern history. In choosing a vehicle to wage their social wars, the section's most conspicuous defenders selected one whose chief weapons were repression and bigotry. Membership in the Klan was limited to native-born white Protestants, which inevitably meant the cultivation of prejudice against everyone else. Similarly, the emphasis on puritanical virtue in public conduct encouraged repression of those deemed unvirtuous, whether "loose" women, unfaithful husbands, or free thinkers, and the prejudices thus aroused were easily turned against "labor agitators," "race mixers," "bolsheviks," or the merely unknown. When that occurred, the Klan became a ready instrument of personal vengeance, political preference, or economic advantage.

The result was a wide chasm between word and deed in the Klan. The organization attracted not only social reactionaries but large numbers of people who were socially frustrated, culturally or emotionally starved, or apprehensive about matters of social status. These groups joined not only because of the Klan's social principles but because it provided fellowship and a sense of public purpose. Some of them were no doubt lured by the aura of power that attached to the organization, and others by the air of mystery that derived from its secretiveness and religious trappings. Perhaps some of them simply loved violence and mob activity. The Klan was a magnet for the mean-spirited, men whose social prejudices were unredeemed by positive vision, and for the merely ambitious, men like young Hugo Black of Alabama, whose brief affiliation was a stepping stone to political office that eventually carried him to the United States Senate and the Supreme Court.

Though the Klan's appeal was wide during the early and middle '20s, the social composition of its membership is a matter of some dispute. It seems to have attracted people from all walks of life, though the lower middle class and the working poor apparently supplied the bulk of its membership. Its leadership, however, was always in middle-class hands. The "best people" seem to have had little to do with it, while liberals and many conservatives, especially those in the middle and upper classes, worked actively against it. Its appeal varied greatly from place to place, being generally strongest in the deep South and the Southwest. Texas, Alabama, and Georgia were centers of special strength, while South Carolina and Virginia were largely unresponsive to its appeal. In 1922 Klan influence was responsible for electing a United States senator in Texas and a governor in Georgia, and in the next few years a number of state and local officials owed their elections to Klansmen and Klan sympathizers. Membership estimates vary widely, up to several million nationally, but the strength of the organization was much greater than its dues-paying membership. It seems safe to say that the principles avowed in public by Klan spokesmen, though not all the activities of Klan groups, were generally acceptable to the white majority.

Yet the Klan never realized the potential implied in that fact, and the reasons for its failure are instructive. Klan leadership in the persons of William J. Simmons, who resurrected the organization in 1915 and directed its fortunes until 1922, and his successor, Hiram Wesley Evans, was politically untalented and not very credible. As soon as the organization became significant, about 1920, rumors and revelations of peculation, immorality, and illegal activity, sometimes assuming the proportions of major scandal, began to circulate, and the accuracy of many of the charges contributed to the aura of controversy that surrounded the organization. The nature of its leadership as well as its membership drove the Klan toward the worst rather than the best impulses of its constituency, and this plus the secret nature of the organization compromised its potential. Its leaders never developed a meaningful political program or an effective instrument of political activism. In politics, especially above the local level, Klansmen tended to be amateur ideologues who lacked the pragmatism essential to electoral success. Occasionally one of them rode a wave of bigotry into office, but none of them ever compiled a significant record or succeeded in creating an effective political organization. Only in scattered localities did the Klan dominate government, and even then its dominance was often due to the position of a few officeholders, usually in law enforcement, who happened to be Klansmen, rather than the organized strength of the Klan as such.

In the final analysis, the Klan was a victim of its own excesses, and its strength, which seemed so imposing in the early 1920s, faded rapidly after the middle of the decade. As George B. Tindall has observed, it "left a trail of threats, brandings, floggings, emasculations, and murder" across the South, and such acts soon proved to be offensive even to those who formed the bulk of its constituency, the mass of social fundamentalists. Once the will of such people to believe in the Klan had been undermined by repeated revelations of hypocrisy and dastardly activity, the organization melted into inconsequence.

The Klan's prostitution of fundamentalist principles was another blow to social fundamentalism. The Klan seemed to confirm the tendency of fundamentalism to degenerate into excess or irrelevance, which heightened the contrast with moderate reform and made the latter seem much better attuned to the needs of the southern people. The contest between fundamentalists and moderates for control of the South's future thus shifted in the latter's favor, and the shift was consolidated by the advent of the New Deal in 1933, which threw the federal government into the contest on the side of the moderates. The fact that so much of the traditional South still survived in 1941 was due not to the strength of organized fundamentalism, but to the fact that the moderates were themselves traditionalists in important respects.

Depression and a New Deal

In late 1929 the stock market collapsed and in the aftermath the nation was plunged into the longest and deepest depression in its history. The South suffered no more in relative terms than the rest of the country, but its suffering was acute because its people were so poor to begin with.[7] Long after the depression bottomed out, the National Emergency Council published a *Report on Economic Conditions of the South* (1938), which described the section as the nation's number one economic problem and urged special assistance to solve its special difficulties. Whether or not the Council's description of the South was literally correct, its report dramatized what the depression had made manifest, that the South had serious economic problems that could be overcome only with help from the outside.

One measure of those problems could be seen in the immediate impact of the depression, which wiped out the hard-earned gains of the 1920s. Between 1929, the last year of prosperity, and 1932, the worst year of depression, total income payments in the greater South declined 44 percent, cash receipts for farmers were down 61 percent, income from cotton dropped 71 percent, and per capita income fell from $372 to $203. Thereafter the situation eased, but in 1940 most indicators of economic activity were still below 1929 levels. The dislocations caused by the depression affected all segments of the southern people, and the result was an acute crisis of need. "Any thought that there has been no starvation, that no man has starved, and no man will starve, is the rankest nonsense," Representative George Huddleston of Birmingham told a congressional committee in 1932. "Men are actually starving by the thousands to-day, ... in my own district. I do not mean to say that they are sitting down and not getting a bite of food until they actually die, but they are living such a scrambling, precarious existence, with suffering from lack of clothing, fuel, and nourishment, until they are subject to be swept away at any time, and many are now being swept away."

Abject want was only the tip of an iceberg of economic difficulty. Beneath the dark waters of depression lay large and chronic problems suddenly made worse by the general economic downturn. Many southerners were at the point of demoralization. Was the cycle of poverty never to be broken? The answer, it seemed, was no, not if the section was left to its own resources. In 1940 the total banking assets in twelve southern states were only 7.66 percent of the national total, and less than 5 percent of the assets of the nation's insurance companies were in those states. The dependence on outside investors, which these figures revealed, meant growing absentee ownership of resources and business enterprise. "Most, if not all, the large southern plants in such fields as tobacco, rayon, paper and pulp, and petroleum are owned by large national companies which have their headquarters outside the region," reported Calvin B. Hoover and Benjamin U. Ratchford in a survey of *Economic Resources and Policies of the South* (1951), and "the same is true of railroads and often of public utilities."

In researching this subject for a compelling little volume, *Divided We Stand* (1937), Walter Prescott Webb found that only 9 of the 200 largest American corporations that together accounted for nearly a fourth of all the nation's corporate wealth were headquartered in the South. With 20 percent of the nation's land and 27 percent of its population, Webb found, the South had less than 5 percent of the nation's great corporations, less than 10 percent of its wholesale firms, less than 4 percent of its large life insurance companies, and less than 3 percent of the annual income of insurance companies. Its banking institutions had less than $11 of every $100 in demand deposits in the nation's banks, and less than $6 of every $100 in time deposits. Its people paid less than $5 of every $100 of federal income taxes, and the average per capita value of their taxable property was only a third of that of northeasterners ($463 compared to $1,370). Yet the South produced by Webb's calculations more than 45 percent of the nation's oil, nearly 40 percent of the coal, more than 46 percent of the lumber, and nearly 37 percent of sixty-four leading crops.

These were fundamental problems requiring long-range solutions; but in the early 1930s the immediate need was direct relief. In 1933 Franklin D. Roosevelt replaced the ineffectual Herbert Hoover as President and immediately launched a New Deal, a multitude of economic and social programs designed to provide such relief and stimulate a general economic recovery. The New Deal was a national endeavor, but it included the most systematic effort ever made to tackle the special economic problems of the South. In doing this, it pulled the section's economy toward the nation's and fostered a series of major social changes. New Deal programs had a discernible and positive effect at once, and the vast majority of southerners regarded the New Deal as a godsend and Roosevelt as a special benefactor of the South. This eager acceptance of a program that meant a greatly increased dependence on and subservience to the federal government in economic and social life was a signal event in the South's history. Roosevelt's New Deal was different in degree as well as kind from Wilson's New Freedom, and the programs it launched would eventually do much more to draw the South into the national orbit. But before that happened the relationship between the South and the federal government would change markedly. In 1933 that relationship was one in which white southerners sought economic assistance to solve immediate problems; but within a generation it became one in which the federal government used economic assistance to impose "alien" social standards upon the white South.

This outcome was uncalculated by New Dealers and unexpected by southerners, yet the process that produced it was discernible from the outset. Its origins lay in the desperation caused by the depression rather than the nature of the New Deal per se. As the impact of his programs rippled across the section, Roosevelt became the most popular national leader in the South's history. His popularity extended through both races and rested not only upon the relief the New Deal provided but also upon the image Roosevelt projected of a leader who cared about people. In their desperate circumstances, southerners saw the New Deal not as an alien program imposed from the outside, but as a cooperative effort with the federal government to deal with acute problems. Many of them were involved in formulating and implementing its programs, and if their influence was far less than it was in the New Freedom, that fact was obscured by the atmosphere of crisis. In Congress southerners chaired many of the committees that passed upon New Deal legislation, though the basic programs were fashioned in the executive branch where the role of sectionally conscious southerners was never controlling. Under Roosevelt, initiative in the federal government shifted completely to the executive branch, where national influences and loyalty to the President muted sectional considerations. Also under Roosevelt, the South's influence in the presidential wing of the Democratic party waned just as that wing came to dominate the party and the federal government as well.

A consummate politician, Roosevelt went to considerable lengths to work with southern congressional leaders, but the white South was only one element in the political coalition he fashioned and, as it turned out, an element of diminishing influence. Yet a direct confrontation between Roosevelt and the southerners never occurred, for several reasons. Even the most conservative southerners generally supported New Deal legislation during Roosevelt's first term, and as their support lessened that of other southerners did not. Thus most of the southern opposition that developed concerned specific policies rather than the established body of New Deal programs. The support of conservatives for such a program is explained in part by the fact that New Deal legislation was always addressed to specific economic problems in a way that obscured the potential for social change. Like the rest of the country, the South accepted the New Deal on faith in an hour of distress, and only a few of its most conservative spokesmen, men such as Senators Carter Glass and Harry F. Byrd of Virginia and Josiah W.

Bailey of North Carolina, were concerned from the outset about its long-range implications. In fact Populist-minded southerners had long advocated many of the things the New Deal did, especially in agriculture and social welfare, and they were among the most consistent supporters of Roosevelt's policies.

The impact of the New Deal was greatest in economics, where it (together with World War II) commenced an agricultural revolution, stimulated economic diversification, braked the cycle of poverty, and pulled the section's economy into the nation's. In the process (again with the war's help), it undermined the strength of white supremacy, accelerated the process of political centralization at the national level, eroded the power of local oligarchies, and liberalized the Supreme Court. In all of these things, it helped construct the base from which legal and political challenges to the basic institutions of southern life were subsequently launched.

The most important area of immediate change was agriculture. New Deal farm policy was embodied in a number of legislative measures, the most important of which were the Agricultural Adjustment Acts of 1933 and 1938. The chief aim of the policy was to stimulate farm income by raising commodity prices, but a secondary purpose was to improve farming and the quality of farm life by tackling such long-standing problems as tenancy, undercapitalization, low productivity, and overconcentration on one crop. The basic program centered around acreage restrictions and price supports for staple crops. The Department of Agriculture was empowered to decide how many acres of cotton, for example, could be planted in a given year and how the total acreage would be allocated to individual farmers. In return for accepting the acreage allotments, farmers were guaranteed a minimum "parity" price for the cotton they produced. Whatever they could not sell on the open market at or above that price would be purchased by the government. Put into effect in 1933 and altered in detail after the original legislation was declared unconstitutional, this program had the desired immediate effect: crop prices went up. As this occurred, other aspects of the overall policy were implemented. Programs of soil conservation, agricultural education, and low-cost credit were instituted or expanded, new markets were sought for farm products, and modest efforts were made to help tenants become owners. Ancillary programs encouraged rural electrification, marketing cooperatives, and rural resettlement.

Other endeavors not specifically tied to agriculture also had an impact on farmers. The Tennessee Valley Authority, the most important contribution of the New Deal to the Appalachian South, stimulated agricultural reform and economic development in one of the section's poorest areas. Direct relief payments helped many destitute people in rural areas. Make-work programs such as the bridge and road-building projects of the Works Progress Administration provided employment for large numbers of the able-bodied; reclamation and reforestation work in the Civilian Conservation Corps helped many farm youths through the worst years of their lives. Not everyone benefited equally from these programs, and the total effect was to ameliorate rather than eliminate the basic problems of agriculture and rural life, but the relief was welcome and the general impact positive.

Yet the cost was heavy. The programs affected landlord-tenant relationships, and more often than not the landlord benefited at the expense of his tenants. The relevant programs fitted the needs of landowning farmers rather than tenants or agricultural laborers, and were implemented by administrators and advisers more responsive to landowners' concerns than those of other elements of the farm population. Acreage allotments were assigned to landowners rather than tenants, and the benefit payments went largely to the former. A study of the program in the middle of the decade found that owners whose land was divided into tenancies were receiving an annual average of $822 in AAA benefit payments while their tenants together were receiving $108. As Charles S. Johnson and others observed in *The Collapse of Cotton Tenancy* (1935), "the landowner is more and more protected from risk by government activity, while the tenant is left open to risk on every side." In effect, acreage restrictions meant that planters needed fewer tenants, while benefit payments protected planters from the loss of income incurred in reducing their tenancies.

The tenant was the loser, and not even his most desperate efforts at redress such as the Southern Tenant Farmers' Union availed him much. He and especially his sons and daughters were pushed off the land. New Deal programs designed for his benefit, such as the Resettlement Administration and the Farm Security Administration, were steps in the right direction but too small to have much effect. The number of tenant-operated farms in the greater South dropped almost 20 percent in the 1930s and a striking 35 percent between 1929 and 1944, while the number of farm owners increased but by a much smaller proportion. The size of the average farm thus grew, from 106 to 133 acres in the Southeast between 1930 and 1945, reversing a trend that began in the 1860s. At the same time total crop acreage declined, as did the number of mules, horses, and agricultural laborers, while the number of tractors and other types of labor-saving machinery began to increase. Cotton became less and livestock more important in the section's agriculture, and the process of crop diversification proceeded apace. Cotton and cottonseed accounted for 55 percent of cash farm income in ten southeastern states in 1929, but in 1946 they accounted for only 27 percent, and during those years cotton acreage declined more than 50 percent.

Changes in industry and urbanization were less dramatic than those in agriculture during the New Deal years, but they were no less important for the subsequent history of the section. The depression temporarily slowed the movement of people to the city, though World War II revived and accelerated it, and the urban population of the Southeast rose from 30.2 percent in 1930 to 42.6 percent in 1950. The growth of manufacturing was similarly affected. The number of production workers remained static during the depression decade, while the industrial payroll dropped 10 percent. The average wage per worker in manufacturing also dropped, from $883 to $791, and remained less than two-thirds of the national average throughout the depression years. The war, however, reversed these trends and brought unheard-of prosperity, so that by 1947 the number of manufactories had risen an impressive 61.2 percent above 1939 levels, the number of workers was up 50 percent, total wages were up 273.8 percent, and the value added by manufacturing was up 243.9 percent. Significantly, the average annual wage, now $1,968, was almost three-fourths of the national average.

This impressive growth was due to the social reforms of the New Deal as well as the stimulations of World War II. The New Deal was chiefly responsible for eliminating child labor in the section, for shortening the work week to forty hours, for improving working conditions and introducing minimum wages. The minimum wage was low when it was first instituted in 1938, but it benefited a larger proportion of southern than nonsouthern workers in the affected industries, and was thus a meaningful help to southern labor. When the minimum rose from 25 to 30 cents an hour in 1939, more than half (54 percent) of all workers in affected industries in the Southeast received pay raises. The statutory protections extended to labor unions by the New Deal were also important, but union membership grew slowly in the South. State and local governments as well as public opinion remained hostile, and unionization continued to lag far behind the rest of the country. That lag was one factor the states used to attract new industry, and one reason for the success of their effort. In 1936 the government of Mississippi launched a state-funded program to balance agriculture with industry, and soon all the other states had followed suit, using tax incentives, government-constructed plants, and other inducements as bait. Cheap power generated by the Tennessee Valley Authority was an added attraction in a large part of the section.

The New Deal brought a vast increase in federal expenditures in the South, and that too had a decided impact upon the section. In many programs, need was one of the criteria used in allocating funds, and in those programs the South received a disporportionate share of the benefits. Things like the Tennessee Valley Authority had no exact counterpart elsewhere. Welfare payments, whether for direct relief, work relief, old-age assistance, or, later, social security, workman's compensation, or minimum wages, were small in size but they gave many poor people a degree of economic security they never had before, and thus a degree of independence from landlords and local political oligarchs. (In 1935 more than one southerner in six was receiving some form of public assistance.) Low-cost loans and federally sponsored cooperatives undermined the power of local bankers and merchants, and the movement of blacks from sharecropping to the cities loosened the reins of white supremacy.

All of these things meant a growing federal budget, which in turn meant a growing centralization of political authority and economic power in Washington and a revolution in the relationship between the federal government and the states. Many federally funded programs were administered in whole or part through the states, which produced a considerable growth in state and sometimes local governments as well. But overall control remained at the top of the bureaucratic pyramid, and states' rights in the traditional sense declined even as state governments grew enormously as administrative units of federal programs. By 1948 more than one in every six dollars spent by southern state governments came from the federal treasury, and the old meaning of states' rights was dead. At the same time, the state governments were centralizing themselves, and claiming a larger share of the nonfederal tax dollar. In the greater South state governments had received 42 percent of all state and local taxes collected in 1932, but in 1942 the proportion was 60 percent.

Currents of Racial Change

Major changes occurred in the South's role in the Democratic party during the Roosevelt years, changes that weakened traditional sectional defenses. And since parallel forces of racial realignment were also at work, the stage was set for important shifts in the most vital areas of southern life.

The nascent estrangement between the South and the Democratic party that surfaced in 1928 was muted by the depression and the enormous popularity of Roosevelt and the New Deal. Throughout the 1930s economic concerns were more pressing than anything else, and no sooner were these alleviated than World War II came along to again divert attention from sectional concerns. In the extraordinary circumstances produced by these vastly different emergencies, the deteriorating political position of the white South was obscured. Since the days of Andrew Jackson, the presidential wing of the Democratic party had been controlled by an alliance of southerners and westerners. That alliance had engineered the nominations for the presidency of William Jennings Bryan in 1896, 1900, and 1908 and Woodrow Wilson in 1912 and 1916, and prevented Alfred E. Smith's nomination in 1924. Since southerners were usually well organized and sure of their purposes in party councils, they had often dominated this alliance and used it to protect their interests, especially in racial matters. Whenever they felt threatened, they fell back upon the party rule that presidential nominees must receive a two-thirds majority vote, which gave them a virtual veto over unacceptable candidates. At the same time, they used seniority, numbers, and political acumen to make them the most important group in the party's congressional wing.

The nomination of Alfred E. Smith in 1928 over their strenuous opposition indicated that the South's position within the Democratic party had begun to deteriorate even before the New Deal. But the realignments produced by the "Roosevelt Revolution" in national politics accelerated the deterioration. During Roosevelt's first term there occurred a massive shift of voters from the Republican to the Democratic party, and white southerners, who had always been more or less the majority of the minority party, found themselves a minority of the majority. The change was first noticeable in the presidential wing of the party, but even in Congress southerners were no longer the largest group of Democrats and more and more they had to rely on seniority and obstructionism to protect their interests. Even in "the house of their fathers" they were now on the defensive.

One important factor in this change was the evolving role of blacks in the party and thus in national politics. Since the 1890s both national parties had acquiesced in disfranchisement and other policies that preserved white supremacy. Since blacks could not vote anywhere in significant numbers, neither party was concerned about the race. By the 1920s, however, this began to change as a result of population movements. By that decade the number of blacks in the North was quite large, and since they were not disfranchised, their votes were being solicited by Democrats as well as Republicans. The political impact of the black vote was enhanced by the pattern of settlement. Black migrants to the North were funneled into restricted areas of a few large cities, especially New York, Philadelphia, Detroit, Chicago, Cleveland, and Washington, D.C., all but the last of which were in large states of pivotal importance in national elections. In 1924, the same year in which the Democratic national convention was torn apart by issues relating to the Ku Klux Klan, the party established a Negro division in its national headquarters to woo the votes of northern blacks. The immediate effects of doing so were limited, however, for blacks remained loyal to the party of Lincoln and emancipation, and in 1928 when they elected the first of their number to Congress from the North, he was a Chicago Republican, Oscar De Priest.

The New Deal altered the political pattern among blacks as well as among whites. New Deal programs were not racially equalitarian, but they provided badly needed assistance for blacks in the North and the South, and New Dealers showed more concern for the race than any group of federal officials since Radical Reconstruction. Blacks responded by shifting their loyalties to the Democratic party. In 1934 they replaced Congressman De Priest with Arthur W. Mitchell, who thereby became the first black Democrat ever elected to Congress, and since then every black elected to Congress from a majority black constituency has been a Democrat. Perhaps three-fourths of all blacks who voted in 1936 cast their presidential ballots for Roosevelt, who incorporated the race as a junior partner in the political coalition he forged. In that year there had been thirty black delegates or alternates at the Democratic national convention, the largest number ever. More importantly, that convention rescinded the two-thirds rule for nominating presidential candidates, a major blow to the white South. As if to symbolize the changes taking place, Senator Ellison D. Smith of South Carolina walked off the convention floor in protest when a black minister was asked to deliver the invocation, thus beginning the pattern of protest that has characterized the white South's relationship with the Democratic party from then until the election of Jimmy Carter to the presidency in 1976.

The party, however, had not abandoned the southerners or embraced racial equality. What it had done was moderate its commitment to the white South in the process of broadening its electoral base. Two years later, Senator James F. Byrnes of South Carolina, one of Roosevelt's most consistent supporters in Congress, voiced the southerners' concern in debate on an antilynching bill that had widespread support among northern Democrats but not among Republicans. "The white people in the South," he said, had supported the Democratic party because they believed that "when problems affecting the Negro and the very soul of the South arose, they could depend upon the Democrats of the North to rally to their support." But now, he lamented, they found Republicans more understanding.

The influx of blacks into the Democratic party had important implications for the meaning of disfranchisement in the South. Those blacks who were registered to vote, perhaps 150,000 in the Confederate South in 1940, had long been excluded from the Democratic party by white primary rule. They resented the exclusion because it was racially insulting and it prevented them from voting in the only meaningful elections in the one-party South. But its offensiveness had been eased by the fact that most blacks identified with the Republican party and would probably have registered as Republicans even without the white primary rule. As blacks changed their allegiance to the Democratic party, however, the white primary rule became more confining, and their long-standing effort against it took on new urgency. The federal courts had always accepted the white primary on the grounds that primaries conducted under party rules rather than state laws were not part of the election process and thus exempt from the Fifteenth Amendment prohibition against racial discrimination in voting. Back in 1923 the Texas legislature had passed a law requiring the white primary, and when the law was challenged as racially discriminatory the Supreme Court, in *Nixon v. Herndon* (1927), declared it unconstitutional. When the legislature repealed the law, the white primary was restored. Not until 1944, after Roosevelt had liberalized the Supreme Court, was this catch-22 situation overcome. In that year the Court finally agreed, in *Smith v. Allwright,* that primaries were in fact part of the election process. When that occurred, the chief political defense of white supremacy shifted to the various devices that kept blacks from registering in significant numbers.

In the changing circumstances reflected in these developments, southerners faced the question of racial policy during the New Deal years. They did so reluctantly and with indirection. "Segregation is not an argument in the South," John Temple Graves wrote in 1943. "It is a major premise." That was indeed the case among whites, and as a result whites felt no need to examine their racial thinking or even justify their racial policies. There was a growing awareness that the premises behind white supremacy were no longer scientifically or morally respectable, and most educated southerners more or less abandoned them. The accomplishments of blacks in scholarship, the fine arts, the professions, and elsewhere made arguments of innate inferiority difficult to sustain, and after 1933 the racist excesses of Nazi Germany embarrassed the cause of racial supremacy everywhere.

Yet virtually all whites remained convinced that segregation and white supremacy were essential to the wellbeing of the South. By 1940 a sizable body of moderate opinion had developed, based on the position of the interracial movement, but white moderates were reluctant to discuss racial policy lest they arouse extremists and expose the contradictions in their own moderation. However, political changes were forcing them to examine the matter, and the divisions among whites became clearer. The most nearly equalitarian point of view came from the academic community, where a small but influential group of social scientists had been studying racial matters for some time. They centered at the University of North Carolina, where sociologist Howard W. Odum and his colleagues made the race problem one focus of a larger study of the contemporary South. A second important group, which included a number of black scholars and white northerners, undertook a major investigation of the American race problem under auspices of the Carnegie Foundation, and in Gunnar Myrdal's *An American Dilemma* (1944) and a series of supporting monographs eventually produced the most thorough study of the nation's race problem ever made.

The white southerners involved in these studies were individuals of basically equalitarian views who believed that racial change would be a slow and difficult process because of the depth of racial feelings among whites and the impossibility of forcing change upon them. Indeed, they believed, any effort to force the issue would be counterproductive, increasing violence against blacks and wiping out the modest but real gains already made. They expected segregation and white supremacy to continue basically unchanged for the foreseeable future, and since that was the case, they sought to direct racial reform toward moderating white opinion and promoting the kinds of limited goals they considered attainable. Thus Howard W. Odum advocated a "hardboiled, realistic, evolutionary" approach to the race problem in his magnum opus, *Southern Regions* (1936), but continued by cautioning that "it is too big a burden to place upon one or two generations the task of changing the powerful folkways of the centuries at one stroke." Therefore, as one of Odum's associates, sociologist Guy B. Johnson, put it, "the next step in race relations should be to take the inequalities out of the bi-racial system. This step can be taken without destroying the integrity of the races."

Here was the nub of the problem, the fear among whites that reform would lead to social equality and thus to intermarriage and miscegenation. "The reason and the only reason [whites] attempt to deny the Negro his political and sometimes his civic rights," wrote William J. Robertson in *The Changing South* (1927), "is because they are afraid that his next step will be social equality, something which they rightfully consider to be impossible." The success of reform, or so reformers believed, depended upon their ability to allay this fear. "The increasing race pride among Negroes," Guy B. Johnson wrote, "will act as a conserver of racial integrity as far as they are concerned. The old question of social equality is not necessarily involved [in the question of reform], for there is no equality except that which is bestowed willingly in the attitudes and behavior of individuals." In other words, reform within the limits of segregation would not lead to social equality of the races. That would come only when both races wanted it.

This of course avoided rather than faced the issue, but it was consistent with the belief that folkways are changeable only through evolution and with the further belief that racial intermixture is in any case undesirable. To get around the social inertia those beliefs encouraged, reformers divided the race issue into two components, first, civil and political rights for blacks, and second, social equality. The former they would encourage, and the latter they would leave alone. Thus in an essay published in the Agrarian manifesto *I'll Take My Stand* (1930), novelist Robert Penn Warren encouraged "equal rights before the law" for blacks, including the right to vote and to "economic independence," but opposed integration in social relations and public accommodations. "Let the negro sit beneath his own vine and fig tree," Warren urged.

As a program of racial reform, this was cautious indeed. White reformers invariably urged restraint upon blacks. For the logic of their position was that the progress of blacks depends entirely upon the will of whites. "The black man must get on with the white man, no matter what Washington orders or New York wants," wrote John Temple Graves. "Southern whites will not consent to a doing away with segregation [but that] does not preclude a constant improvement in the black man's side of Jim Crow." On matters of race, "it is to [white] Southerners that leadership must be left. Their on-the-spot estimates are the only practical guide."

If this sounds excessively cautious, the reformers just discussed were far more enlightened and realistic than most whites who thought of themselves as moderates. Especially prominent among church spokesmen and civic boosters, the latter groups sought to deal with race problems by silence and positive thinking. Convinced that the issue was too volatile to deal with openly, they urged that it be left alone for the time being and public discussion limited to assurances that conditions were good and getting better. Robert M. Miller found this the prevailing view in religious publications in the interwar years. Such publications "reflected the myth that a peaceful and harmonious relationship existed between the races," Miller wrote, summarizing their editorial opinion. "There was no need to trouble oneself about the 'race problem' for the simple reason that the problem was non-existent. The black and white each had his place in the scheme of things, and it was suggested that this plan was part of God's orderly design for the races. On the one hand, Negroes should be content, law abiding, hard working, peaceful and happy in their subordinate but not onerous status. On the other, it was the white man's duty to be patient, understanding, helpful, kindly but firm in his relations with his child-like, simple, and often mischievous colored wards."

The mass of whites were less prone to rationalization, though their thinking on racial matters was not systematically articulated and has never been studied in depth. "He has nothing against what he calls niggers," William Faulkner wrote of a southern white man in *Intruder in the Dust* (1948). "If you ask him, he will probably tell you he likes them even better than some white folks he knows and he will believe it.... All he requires is that they act like niggers." This was his idea of the natural order of things: "the nigger acting like a nigger and the white folks acting like white folks and no real hard feelings on either side." Perhaps that was the attitude of the mass of whites.

Blacks of course viewed things differently. Because of their dependent position, they were forced to address issues indirectly, for they too saw the necessity of keeping lines of communication open. Accommodationism was the price they paid for the success they had in moderating white supremacy. The support blacks gave their own churches and other organizations and the sacrifices many of them made to support private schools and benevolence societies suggest that integration (defined as physical proximity to whites) was not a primary concern of most of the race. The continuing popularity of Booker T. Washington's ideas and the appeal of Marcus Garvey's brand of racial nationalism suggest the same thing. Desegregation was desirable in the sense that it meant the decline of discrimination, but since interracial social contact was paternal at best, perhaps most blacks found it unappealing to one degree or another. Many whites took this as evidence that blacks preferred segregation to integration, but it seems likely that what they really preferred was personal relationships free of condescension and humiliation.

Accommodation and avoidance were thus policies of necessity for blacks, but policies whose limitations became increasingly apparent. Every victory over discrimination only made the restraints of white supremacy more bridling and the insults of segregation more galling. Inequality, injustice, disfranchisement, poverty, dependence, disrespect, inferior schools, and sometimes psychological emasculation—these were intrinsic parts of white supremacy and would remain basic determinants of black life until white supremacy itself was destroyed. By World War II, conditions permitted this fact to become the basic premise of racial strategy. Accommodation was thus forsworn, and a frontal assault on white supremacy was launched with some prospects of eventual success.

The assault was under overall direction of the NAACP, which even before World War II had had considerable success in establishing important principles in constitutional law, though its efforts had had little impact on the man in the street. The most immediate barrier to black progress was a series of Supreme Court decisions dating back to the nineteenth century that interpreted the Fourteenth and Fifteenth Amendments in ways that protected segregation and disfranchisement. The NAACP challenge to those decisions had begun before World War I, and after early victories over the grandfather clause, zoning restrictions, and other matters of essentially secondary importance, it succeeded in focusing legal attention on the principle of racial discrimination itself. The problem this involved was getting the Supreme Court to judge racial laws not by the letter of their language, but by their effects upon blacks. As a practical matter, for example, trial juries in the southern states were always all white, though in some places an occasional black was empaneled and excused to keep up appearances. In *Norris v. Alabama* (1935), one of the cases growing out of the celebrated trial of nine black youths in Scottsboro, Alabama, for allegedly raping two white women, the Court overturned the conviction of the "Scottsboro boys" on the ground that the absence of blacks from the jury lists deprived the defendants of the constitutional right to trial by a jury of their peers. The absence of blacks from the lists was prima facie evidence of discrimination, the Court ruled, even though the exclusion was not required by law.

This was an important principle even though its intent was sabotaged by tokenism, but it was less important than the success in getting the Court to look behind the letter of the law in cases dealing with segregation itself. In *Plessy v. Ferguson* (1896) the Court had squared segregation with the Fourteenth Amendment guarantee of equal protection of the laws by the legal fiction that separate facilities must be equal facilities, and as late as 1927 the Court affirmed that fiction in *Gum Long v. Rice*. Despite the obvious inequality of Jim Crow facilities, blacks had never been able to get the Court to recognize the inequality and use it to require desegregation as implied in the separate-but-equal principle. Instead, the Court judged segregated institutions by the laws that authorized them, and since none of the laws required inequality, the Court in effect ruled that the institutions were equal. But by the 1930s the political atmosphere was changing, and the absurdity of the Court's stance was increasingly apparent. Therefore attorneys for the NAACP decided to challenge the stance by challenging segregated institutions that were so patently unequal that the Court would no longer be able to accept the old fiction.

They found such institutions in the graduate and professional schools of the southern and border states. Each of the states had an array of such schools for whites, including some of considerable merit, but often they had no facilities at all for blacks. They could not pretend, therefore, that they were honoring the requirements of the separate-but-equal doctrine. The strategy worked. In a series of decisions beginning with *Missouri ex rel., Gaines v. Canada* (1938), the Court ruled in favor of black plaintiffs seeking admission to white professional schools where there were no schools available to blacks. Then the principle was extended to cover black schools that were patently inferior to white graduate and professional schools, and in that way the Court began to insist that the facilities provided blacks be in tangible and intangible ways equal to those provided whites. With that accomplished, the next logical step was to get the Court to see that the largest intangible of all, segregation itself, made separate facilities inherently unequal because of the discrimination and humiliation that inevitably attached to it. If that could be done, the structure of white supremacy would lose its constitutional base, and then black political influence could be used to challenge it through the federal government.

15

The Uncertain South

Out of the social ferment of World War I came not only the conflicting realities of the Benighted South and the Progressive South but a quickening of the life of the mind. Not long after the war the intellectual history of the section entered a new and uniquely creative period. Indeed, the three decades after 1920 are the richest in the history of southern thought. During those years there were basic improvements in public education, notable advances in higher education, a blossoming of scholarship in the social sciences and humanities, and a literary renaissance that resulted in the most significant body of creative writing ever produced by a generation of southerners. The stirrings reached into journalism, criticism, social thought, and history, and a new spirit of skepticism and self-criticism signaled the emergence of southern liberalism as a major body of thought. Significantly, there was much less achievement in technology, theology, the plastic arts, and the physical and natural sciences.

This flowering of the intellect sprang in part from the postwar crisis of sectional identity, which also encouraged boosterism and fundamentalism. Among the intellectuals as well as boosters and fundamentalists, the crisis produced increased concern over the South's identity, and thus over questions of what the South was and had been and what it might become. One result was the most serious and enlightening debate in the section's history over southern character and the future course of southern development.

The Flowering of Southern Studies

That debate, which will be examined presently, was informed by the flowering of southern studies that began around 1920 and continued through the interwar years.[1] Before World War I the most important study of the South had been done by historians and, to a lesser extent, students of literature. During the 1920s, however, the initiative in southern studies shifted to the social sciences, especially sociology, due chiefly to the effort and example of Howard W. Odum, the most important student of the South in the generation. Appointed to the sociology faculty at the University of North Carolina in 1920 as part of the effort by President Harry W. Chase and others to upgrade that institution, Odum soon made Chapel Hill the center of southern studies, attracting a large and capable faculty, including Rupert B. Vance, Guy B. Johnson, and T. W. Couch, and encouraging other scholars at other institutions, among them sociologists Wilson Gee at the University of Virginia and Charles S. Johnson at Fisk University. Through his university's School of Public Welfare and its Institute for Research in Social Science, Odum attracted research grants from national foundations, and through the *Journal of Social Forces,* which he established in 1922, and the University of North Carolina Press he provided publishing outlets for the resulting studies.

His example was contagious. Scholars in the social sciences and humanities organized themselves into regional associations, established scholarly journals devoted to the study of the section, and enormously increased the volume of scholarship about the South. Between 1929 and 1939 the Southern Economics Association, the Southern Political Science Association, the Southern Historical Association, and the Southern Sociological Society were organized, and the *Southern Economics Journal,* the *Journal of Southern History,* and the *Journal of Politics* began publication. At the same time social anthropologists began their first studies of southern life, and black studies matured. Through the Association for the Study of Negro Life and History, the *Journal of Negro History,* and other endeavors, Carter G. Woodson had pioneered the latter field before World War I. Now his efforts were supplemented by those of Charles S. Johnson, who made Fisk University the most important center of black studies during the interwar years, E. Franklin Frazier at Atlanta University, and a growing list of other scholars in several disciplines. The same pattern prevailed in literature and related fields. Two important new journals devoted to criticism and opinion, the *Southwest Review* and the *Virginia Quarterly Review,* were established in 1924 and 1925 respectively, and in 1935 the *Southern Review* first appeared. Together with the *Sewanee Review,* the *South Atlantic Quarterly,* and a number of ephemeral "little magazines," these journals gave southern writers and critics a number of publication outlets of variety and quality.

Perhaps the most important feature of the new scholarship was its tone, which was detached and often skeptical. The effort to be objective, from which the tone derived, set the new generation of scholars apart from the old, and was the source of their most important contributions to sectional self-study. Among historians, the racialism of Ulrich B. Phillip's generation gradually gave way to the equalitarianism of C. Vann Woodward's. Among social scientists, the determinism and racial paternalism that characterized the work of prewar students such as Thomas Pierce Bailey and even infused Howard W. Odum's first book, *Social and Mental Traits of the Negro* (1910), gave way to the critical spirit that informed Odum's later works and those of his colleagues at North Carolina. In literature the apologetics of Thomas Nelson Page had already been replaced by the realism of Ellen Glasgow, to whom critical acclaim finally came with the publication of *Barren Ground* (1925), and this in turn was supplanted by the exposés of T. S. Stribling and then the probing meditations of William Faulkner. The barbed, often impatient social criticism of men like Gerald W. Johnson, Wilbur J. Cash, Virginius Dabney, and George Fort Milton signaled a new era in journalism, in which newspapers became a more effective force for social reform and political responsibility than ever before.

Emergence of Southern Liberalism

For the first time since Jefferson's day a significant body of liberal thought emerged.[2] No longer were southern liberals isolated individuals asea in their own ineffectuality. Instead they were growing in number, in contact with each other, and increasingly influential in academic and journalistic circles. Moreover, they had access to the reading public and sometimes to political leaders as well. If they were not organized, they at least had organizations, for most of them had a veritable compulsion to sponsor "causes" and join reform associations. They were responsible for the proliferation of organizations combating racial discrimination, lynching, the poll tax, and political demagoguery; or encouraging scientific farming, economic development, civil liberties, labor organization, and better education; or working to ameliorate the evils of tenant farming, endemic disease, or social disorganization.

The liberals had a unique relationship with the South. They were reformers whose transparent earnestness grew out of an obvious love for the section and its people. However much they criticized the South, they never renounced it or despaired of its future. Nor did they frontally challenge its most important customs, such as racial segregation, even as they worked to ameliorate them, nor join the Republican party, nor seek to organize the poor and dispossessed of either race. In these and other ways they differed from earlier groups of critics such as the abolitionists and the Reconstruction Radicals. Unlike those groups, indigenous white liberals were able to see the good as well as the bad side of the South, and they refused to judge white southerners by the worst qualities they displayed. This encouraged an optimistic faith that the South could be reformed through the orderly processes of social evolution.

Despite this faith they were less willing than the New Southists or the prewar Progressives, from whom they drew many of their ideas, to gloss over the section's problems. More interested in improving the South than apologizing for it, they dwelt upon its problems rather than its virtues. In and out of academia they viewed the section, in Rupert B. Vance's words, as "a case for analysis and a cause for social action." But since they were moderates by temperament and eager to influence public opinion, they couched their criticisms in constructure and inoffensive language. Few of them made the error of William H. Scaggs, whose largely valid exposé of *The Southern Oligarchy* (1924) was compromised by the intensity of its outrage and the provocations in its language. Frank Tannenbaum's less impassioned detailing of the evils of the Ku Klux Klan, one-crop agriculture, mill villages, and the penal system in *Darker Phases of the South,* also published in 1924, was more typical.

Within a dozen years after these two volumes appeared, liberals of widely differing ideological hues produced an outpouring of social analysis and prescription. From the North Carolina social scientists came such major works as Rupert B. Vance's *Human Geography of the South* (1932), the cooperative survey of *Culture in the South* (1934), edited by W. T. Couch, and, most important of all, Howard W. Odum's monumental *Southern Regions of the United States* (1936). Earlier, Edwin Mims of Vanderbilt University had contributed *The Advancing South* (1926), perhaps the most ebullient statement of the prospects of southern liberalism ever penned, and William J. Robertson had offered *The Changing South* (1927), another encouraging assessment. Virginius Dabney's historical study *Liberalism in the South* (1932) was less optimistic. Gerald W. Johnson's "The Battling South" (1925) and Wilbur J. Cash's first exploration into "The Mind of the South" (1929) typified the iconoclasm of the most outspoken liberals, while Robert W. Winston's autobiography, *It's a Far Cry* (1937) and Broadus and George Mitchell's *The Industrial Revolution in the South* (1930) typified the thinking of those more attuned to business Progressivism.

Despite the diversity reflected in this literature, there were discernible patterns in the body of liberal thought. Southern liberals drew their inspiration from American liberalism as variously expressed in Wilsonian Progressivism, Bryanite Populism, and after 1932 Franklin D. Roosevelt's New Deal, all of which derived from the political and economic ideals of Jeffersonian and Jacksonian democracy. These common sources led to a common analysis of the South's problems and a common prescription of its ills. The chief problem, as the liberals saw it, was that southerners had never fully accepted the precepts and practices of American liberalism, especially liberal industrial capitalism and the things associated with it, especially urbanization, rationalism, and openness to social innovation. Thus what was needed was for southerners to adapt their institutions, social mores, and ways of thinking to the American liberal model. This meant diversifying their economy, eliminating their socioeconomic peculiarities, liberalizing their religion and social policy, forgetting the past, especially the Civil War and Reconstruction, and eliminating sectional consciousness based on defensiveness and feelings of grievance. Almost invariably, however, this prescription for Americanization was accompanied by assurances that the changes would do nothing to destroy the positive attributes of southern life.

As this suggests, most liberals never probed deeply into matters of sectional character. Specifically they failed to explore the relationship between the aspects of southern character they admired and the ills of southern life they wanted to eliminate. Some of the pertinent questions eluded them. To what extent, for example, did the hospitality, personalism, and social graciousness they admired grow out of the social and racial inequality they deprecated? To what extent did the poverty and racism and undereducation they wanted to eliminate help preserve the ethos of rural and small-town society they often praised? Was urbanized society compatible with leisureliness and a strong commitment to locality? The list of such questions is long, and the liberals' failure to deal with them infused their social analysis with a basic contradiction on matters relating to sectional identity, and left them vulnerable to the charges of their conservative critics that they would destroy the South by submerging it in the American mainstream.

A part of the difficulty stemmed from their too uncritical analysis of American liberalism. In fact their entire analysis rested upon their celebration of American society, which they offered as a model for the South to emulate. They too readily assumed that the rest of the country lived according to the liberal ideals it professed, which assumption was strengthened by a prior belief in the efficacy of institutional arrangements. For example, liberals tended to believe that two-party politics produced political divisions along socioeconomic lines, that public education was liberalizing and industrialization progressive, that urbanization destroyed provincialism and exposure to the national media would be intellectually emancipating. They therefore suggested that the South would be liberalized if these changes could be effected.

The suggestion, however, gave scant attention to the demonstrated ability of the traditional South to mold change to its own purposes. It also ignored the problems the suggested changes would generate—urban congestion and alienation, for example, or the social costs of driving rural folk into urban life and factory employment or subordinating southern resources to the demands of industrial capitalism. Buoyed by their own analyses, they tended to measure progress in physical terms—the mileage of newly paved roads, the number of new factory jobs or of days added to the school year, or the value of new farm machinery or new real estate developments. It is not surprising that as the things they wanted were achieved in the generation after World War II, the South remained far different from the liberal society they envisioned.

Yet the liberals made major contributions to sectional thought during the interwar period. They more than any other southerners were prepared to confront the forces of social change, and it was they who first saw that the South could benefit from reform. They did more than any other group to spread new ideas in the section, and their effort had a pronounced effect on social thought. Negatively, it contributed to the image of the Benighted South and to the ideological gap that opened up between liberal thinkers and the mass of southerners. This gap made communication difficult and impeded social discourse and orderly change. While liberals talked of the need for reform and national integration, the mass of southerners flocked to see *The Birth of a Nation* and join the crusade for social fundamentalism.

The Agrarian Alternative

Liberal criticism also had positive results, one of which was the impetus provided for a new round in the recurrent debate on the South and its future. In all of southern history no period contributed so richly to that debate as the few years between the late 1920s and World War II. In addition to the works of the liberals already noted, there appeared in that short span of years Ulrich B. Phillips's essay "The Central Theme of Southern History" (1928), the most influential statement on that subject ever made by a historian; the Agrarian symposium, *I'll Take My Stand* (1930), the most important exposition of conservative thought since the antebellum era; Clarence Cason's pioneering effort to interpret the contemporary South, *90° in the Shade* (1935); Benjamin B. Kendrick and Alex M. Arnett's historical preface to the regionalism of Howard W. Odum, *The South Looks at Its Past* (1935); William Faulkner's prismatic rendering of the southern experience in *Absalom, Absalom!* (1936); and Wilbur J. Cash's impressionistic distillation of liberal thought, *The Mind of the South* (1941).

These works were not always explicitly addressed to questions of sectional character and the future of the South. Not surprisingly, conservative writers dealt more pointedly with those questions than liberals, for their conservative perspective enabled them to see that liberal change was a menace to sectional distinctiveness. "Can the strongly marked character of the South, that deep provincialism buttressed by homogeneity of stock and the stubborn defenses of a group isolated by defeat in war—can it survive the new invasion?" poet Josephine Pinckney asked in 1934. She was not sure, though she found grounds for hope in the southerners' "natural aptitude for taking time" and their strong sense of family and location and religion, in the absence of cities and the presence of blacks, and in the persistence of a "landowning state of mind."

Others were less certain. William W. Ball, the uncompromisingly conservative editor of the Charleston *News and Courier,* lamented, also in 1934, that the "distinguished [i.e., distinctive] South" had already disappeared under the impact of populistic democracy and national centralization. The section, Ball thought, had degenerated into a mere "collection of relatively impoverished divisions, receptive of alms, imitative of and envious of Northern go-getters and their ways." Ellen Glasgow was also apprehensive. "The modern South is in immediate peril less of revolution than of losing its individual soul in the national Babel," she wrote during World War II. "The ambition of the new South is not to be self-supporting, but to be ... more American than the whole of America."

The most pointed statement of conservative concern was made before any of these. It came from a group of literati at Vanderbilt University in the form of a book of essays, *I'll Take My Stand,* published in 1930. Variously called the Vanderbilt, Nashville, or Southern Agrarians because of their unabashed endorsement of agrarian values, the contributors were one of the most important groups in the intellectual history of the South, and the publication of *I'll Take My Stand* was a major event in the story of southern thought.[3]

The Agrarians grew out of a group of writers who had begun gathering at Vanderbilt shortly after World War I. There in 1922 they launched an impressive little magazine of poetry and criticism, *The Fugitive.* The magazine focused upon art rather than politics, and though it survived only three years, the Fugitives, as its contributors came to be known, made major contributions to southern (and American) letters, first in the rather elegant poetry they wrote and later in what one of them, John Crowe Ransom, called the New Criticism. As critics, poets, novelists, and essayists they have an important niche in southern and American literature, but their social thought is more significant for the historian. As social thinkers, the most important of them were Ransom, then a member of the English faculty at Vanderbilt and subsequently editor of the *Kenyon Review;* Donald Davidson, who remained at Vanderbilt through a long career as one of the South's most steadfastly conservative thinkers; and Allen Tate and Robert Penn Warren, both of whom went on to become major literary figures. In literature the Fugitives were innovators, but as social thinkers they were traditionalists espousing conservative humanism.

It was their traditionalism that led them from art to social thought, and from a preoccupation with the form and content of literature to an advocate's concern over the South and its future. The transformation sprang from dismay. They were first dismayed by the waves of Menckenesque criticism heaped upon the South during and after the Scopes trial, but they were also upset by the doings of social fundamentalists and the preachments of economic boosters and liberal reformers who urged southerners to forget the past and follow the American path of development. By the end of the 1920s their concern with social issues overshadowed their interest in art, and they began challenging the section's liberal critics and offering their own vision of the southern past and future. Donald Davidson's "Ode to the Confederate Dead" (1925) was an early indication of their sectional interest, but it was a work of meditation rather than commemoration. However, Allen Tate's *Jefferson Davis: His Rise and Fall* (1929) was frankly defensive of the Old South and its cause, and Ransom's *God without Thunder* (1930) was equally defensive of religious orthodoxy and the South's rejection of rationalism and science. The widespread criticism that greeted *I'll Take My Stand* encouraged the Fugitive-Agrarians to elaborate their ideas. In 1937 Davidson published a collection of essays, *Attack on Levithan,* spelling out his defense of regional particularism. Earlier, Tate and Herbert Agar had put together another symposium, *Who Owns America?* (1936), which attacked the concentration of property in this country; and working independently of the Vanderbilt group economist T. J. Cauley of the Georgia Institute of Technology published *Agrarianism* (1935), the best statement of agrarian economics.

But *I'll Take My Stand,* a collection of twelve essays, was always the major work. In addition to contributions by Davidson, Tate, Warren, and Ransom, it included important essays by historian Frank L. Owsley, whose later studies of *Plain Folk of the Old South* (1950) reflected his Agrarian concerns; novelist Stark Young, whose *So Red the Rose* (1934) was the best fictional distillation of Agrarian views; and author John Donald Wade and historian Herman C. Nixon. As previously suggested, the Agrarian writings by these and lesser figures constituted the most important expression of conservative thought in the South since John C. Calhoun and his contemporaries had formulated the defense of slavery and the Old South a century earlier.

Like the proslavery argument that was its intellectual antecedent, Agrarianism originated in sectional defensiveness. Not long after World War I, as Davidson later explained it, liberals and other apologists for northern economic interests had launched an "abusive and unrelenting" attack upon the South. The purpose of that "campaign of vilification" had been to demoralize the southern people by convincing them of the inferiority of their way of life, all for the purpose of inducing them to adopt northern ways for the benefit of northern economic interests. Advocates of this program talked of "educational uplift, industrialism, and liberalism," Davidson wrote, but they really sought "to destroy much that was valuable in the characteristic life and genius of the southern states," in order "to impose an alien economy and alien systems of thought upon a social structure ill-adapted to them." The message of liberalism and prosperity had been alluring, and those southerners "with a sense of loyalty" had been forced to choose between "the buoyant scalawagism of the progressives and a conservatism that [was] sure to be damned as reactionary."

I'll Take My Stand was an effort to help southerners around this Hobson's choice. The Agrarians boldly advocated "the Southern way of life against what may be called the American or prevailing way." "How far shall the South surrender its moral, social, and economic autonomy to the victorious Union?" they asked. "Of late [southerners have] ... shown signs of wanting to join up behind the common or American industrial ideal," thus deserting their past and the agrarian way of life that made the South distinctive. *I'll Take My Stand* thus argued the merits of agrarian life as opposed to what the Agrarians saw as its opposite, industrial life. In doing this, the Agrarians undertook two tasks, first, to dissect and criticize modern industrial society, and second, to show that the traditional South, specifically the antebellum regime, had had a way of life that offered an attractive and viable alternative. The two tasks were accomplished unevenly. *I'll Take My Stand* contained a powerful indictment of the ills of modern society, one that seems far more pertinent today than it must have seemed in 1930. But as a description of the traditional South the book had serious defects. It was the Agrarians' misfortune and partly their fault that the book was judged almost exclusively by the latter rather than the former. The test applied to it was what it had to say about the South and agrarianism, not how well it exposed the ills of industrial society.

This was probably inevitable. The book invites misreading. Its faults are so glaring that the casual reader can be forgiven for missing its considerable virtues. Moreover, the book was written in the prosperity of the late 1920s but published after the depression began to spread across the country, and the resulting economic dislocations accentuated its faults and made its virtues seem romantic and even inconsequential. But whether read from the perspective of prosperity or that of depression, the Agrarians were urging southerners to stay the growth of industry and cities at a time when most southerners saw such growth as the only way out of the South's economic problems. For that reason, southerners were unimpressed by warnings that industry and cities would bring new social problems or damage the human spirit. To them, the book's argument seemed like a formula for continued poverty, and the Agrarians themselves impractical nostalgics or half-cocked academics tilting at abandoned windmills.

A second problem was of the Agrarians' own making. In discussing the traditional South, they carelessly fused the ideal and the real. They described with some accuracy the social ideals of antebellum planters but compromised the description by writing as if the ideals had been actualities. This distorted both, and obscured the fact that the Agrarians had actually made a compelling statement of southern ideals. That is, they had effectively described what the South as a distinctive society represented to its most solicitous defenders, and thereby had delineated the things its people would have to cultivate if they were to remain distinctive. In this, the Agrarians' discussion was not negated by the wide gap between ideals and actualities in the section, anymore than a discussion of American ideals as embodied in the Declaration of Independence, the Bill of Rights, and elsewhere is negated by the nation's failure to live up to those ideals. That after all is what ideals are, exalted principles to be striven for, and the striving for them gives purpose and direction to public life. If the South of the 1920s and 1930s was to withstand the pressures of Americanization, its people would have to have a set of positive ideals to give coherence to the effort. The Agrarians were endeavoring to delineate such ideals. The problem was that their endeavor was misread by liberals, who preferred American to southern ideals, and unread by social fundamentalists, who could have found in it a rationale for the cause they were compromising by mindlessness and bigotry. The response of both groups was due in part to another of the book's distortions. The Agrarians cast their entire argument in the narrow limits of "Agrarian *versus* Industrial" society when what they really had in mind was traditional as opposed to modern society.

In spite of these weaknesses, the Agrarians' indictment of industrial society deserved a hearing, and had it been heard it might have eased the social pains of industrialization and urbanization in the section. The indictment was of industrialism, not industry per se, for the Agrarians actually advocated a balanced economy in which industry was subordinate to Agrarian pursuits. Industrialism subordinates human concerns to market forces, they charged, uproots people from traditional moorings and throws them into artificial urban settings and unnatural personal relationships. It reduces the individual to an economic integer, they also charged, and makes him subservient to technology. The laborer is thereby brutalized ("His labor is hard, its tempo fierce, and his employment is insecure"), and the organic relationship between labor and life destroyed. This alienates the individual from his means of livelihood and leaves him easy prey to the artificialities of urban life. In large cities people "lose the sense of nature as something mysterious and contingent," the Agrarians wrote, and their attachment to the soil, and with them go the sense of place and family and time that was always the source of individual and community identity. What the individual does or has becomes his source of identity, not who he is or where he lives. Established institutions and hierarchies, especially in religion and social class, are weakened and robbed of their stabilizing effects, and in their place arise socially fragmenting doctrines of equality, individualism, and secularism. The eclipse of institutions of authority and mystery erodes the loyalties and deferences such institutions induce, and weakens the bonds that made traditional societies organic and kept them from atomizing into competing interest groups. When the atomizing of modern societies goes too far, centralized government assumes the integrative functions once performed by social institutions, but in its hands integration becomes consolidation and the result is often totalitarianism.

These things, the Agrarians believed, begin as soon as industrialism intrudes upon traditional societies, for the process undermines the traditional moral bases of human values and relationships and substitutes the cash nexus for them. Personal as well as group relationships become economic relationships, and social harmony is replaced by economic rivalry, or as Stark Young put it in *So Red the Rose,* by "competition without social principles." Everyone is forced to pursue his own interests at the expense of the general welfare. The pursuit of happiness is reduced to an exercise in acquisitiveness, and life itself becomes a "nervous running-around" that lacks "the logic, even, of a dog chasing its tail." The social obligations of property and class give way to triumphant materialism and self-advancement.

The quality of life degenerates. Industrial society, the Agrarians insisted, is inimical to art and religion since those things, like organic human relationships, are possible only where man and nature coexist in harmony. Esthetics and social amenities cannot endure the alienations of modern society, in which there is no room for "manners, conversation, hospitality, sympathy, family life, [or] romantic love," or for "the social exchanges which reveal and develop sensibility in human affairs." Education also suffers, for it too is divorced from life and in mass public schools becomes sterile and artificial and as unsatisfying intellectually as art is made unrewarding emotionally. Life itself becomes "generally dull, mechanical, standardized and mean," and the human spirit is impoverished. "Industrialism," wrote John Crowe Ransom, "is a program under which men, using the latest scientific paraphernalia, sacrifice comfort, leisure, and the enjoyment of life to win Pyrrhic victories over nature at points of no strategic significance." It "is an insidious spirit," he also wrote, "full of false promises and generally fatal to establishments since, when it once gets into them for a little renovation, it proposes never again to leave them in peace."

The Agrarians found the Old South attractive because they found in it the things they believed were lacking in industrial society. Their description of the Old South is thus to be read not as historically accurate, but as a metaphor depicting the ideal society as they saw it. "The dominating structure of a great civilized tradition is certain absolutes—," Allen Tate wrote, "points of moral and intellectual reference by which people live, and by which they must continue to live until in the slow crawl of history new references take their place." The most important of those references were property and property rights, including not only ownership and privilege but moral obligation and social duty. Another was appreciation of "the virtues of establishment," without which social stability is impossible. The good society must be rooted and religious and more rural than urban, its public policies conservative, its government decentralized, its people loyal to family, class, and local community. It must have a positive provincialism, modest prosperity, living memories, and rural virtues. Above all, it must be at peace with itself—its popular ideologies must accept the legitimacy of the established order.

The Old South had had these things. It had been "a gracious civilization" despite its defects, "true and indigenous," "sound and realistic in that it was not at war with its own economic foundations." It struck a fair balance between hierarchy and democracy, and its social order weighed lightly since "people for the most part were in their right place." Even slavery, "a feature monstrous enough in theory," was "more often than not, humane in practice." The economy was balanced, property well distributed, materialism restrained by human concerns and class responsibility, competitiveness contained by an ethic that valued leisureliness as well as work. There was respect for the past and the future and a developed sense of esthetics that expressed itself in the arts of living—"dress, conversation, manners, the table, the hunt, politics, oratory, the pulpit"—rather than the arts of escape such as drama, poetry, painting, and sculpture. Its education had been affirming, its people but little impressed with rationalism and positivist social science. Only its religion had been wrong: the Old South had been Protestant when by everything in the Agrarian prescription it should have been Catholic. Protestantism was the religion of individualism and liberal capitalism, not traditionalism and authority, or as Tate put it, "hardly a religion at all, but a result of secular ambition." The Old South had thus been an anomaly, "a feudal society without a feudal religion," which was one of the reasons its way of life had not survived military defeat.

Despite their literary stature, the Agrarians failed as social advocates. Unlike the liberals they criticized, they were unable to get their ideas treated seriously as a possible basis for social action. One reason for this was the failure to explain how their ideas might be implemented. The most notable attempt at doing that was Frank L. Owsley's "The Pillars of Agrarianism" (1935), which spelled out a government-supported back-to-the-farm program of land redistribution designed to end farm tenancy, reinvigorate the yeoman farmer class, and prevent future concentration of agricultural wealth. The program was fanciful, however, not only because it lacked public support but because it ignored most of the pressing social problems of the rural South. Moreover, other Agrarians seemed to think the ideal society should focus around the planter class rather than the yeomanry. In any case the Agrarians never spelled out the balance they wanted between agriculture and industry or urban and rural life, or explained how an agrarian South could be insulated from forces of nationalization, standardization, and industrialization. They never grappled realistically with the problems of the rural South—not even tenancy, one-crop agriculture, poor health, and poor housing, to say nothing of racial and class prejudice, religious bigotry, illiteracy, violence, and demagoguery, all of which tended to correlate with the degree of ruralism.

Agrarianism was thus an intellectual, not a social movement, and is important chiefly because the Agrarians as conservatives understood better than their liberal critics what was happening to the South in the 1920s and 1930s. "He thinks if the South gets rich again, it will be the South still," Allen Tate said of Stringfellow Barr, who, in criticizing *I'll Take My Stand,* had suggested that the section's only hope lay in industrialization. "But the South is not a section of geography," Tate insisted insightfully; "it is an economy setting forth a certain kind of life." The Agrarians appreciated this fact better than the liberals, and were thus better able to distinguish between the essentials of southernism and the unattractive side of southern life. Just as racialism had enabled Ulrich B. Phillips to see the significance of race in southern identity, so conservatism enabled the Agrarians to see the centrality of conservative values to the distinctive South. And because the Agrarians probed more deeply than liberals into matters of sectional identity, they were better able to see the relationship between the South's socioeconomic system and the essentials of its identity as a distinctive society. The South, they saw, was an ideology and way of life that grew out of circumstance, and to preserve the South it was necessary to preserve the circumstances that fostered its distinctiveness. To destroy that circumstance—the traditional southern society—would be to remake the South into something American and thus unsouthern, which to the Agrarians would amount to an act of parricide.

The Agrarians were correct, of course, even though their analysis of the southern circumstance was too roseate and too little concerned with the pathologies of the Benighted South. They were not mere Cassandras when they warned that the South would be killed by overdoses of liberalism and Americanization, nor merely romantics in suggesting there were positive reasons to preserve the section's distinctiveness. "The benefit which the South can now render to the nation will consist in showing how an American community can really master the spirit of modern industrialism instead of capitulating to it," wrote Ransom in 1929; "that is to say, it will consist in remaining Southern in the pure, traditional, even sectional sense."

As the nation plunged deep into the Great Depression, such a statement seemed irrelevant at best, and Agrarianism was rejected without debate. This was less significant than the fact that conservative thought in general shared the same fate. The sequence of events was important. Just at the time that social fundamentalism was being discredited by its own excesses, the Agrarians published *I'll Take My Stand,* the most important statement of reasoned conservatism in modern southern literature. The Agrarians had no use for social fundamentalists of course, but in spite of that fact they found themselves on the same side of the political spectrum with them, and the excesses of fundamentalists made the limitations of the Agrarians seem all the more disabling. The two expressions of rightist views were lumped together by leftists and jointly discredited, and conservatism itself as a set of systematic ideas about man and society was eclipsed. Even in politics the field was left chiefly to business Progressives and New Dealers, or to demagogues whose appeal derived from factors of personality and emotion largely beyond the realm of formal ideology.

The debate between liberals and conservatives over the South and its future thus ended not because the issues were resolved, but because events produced a default among conservatives and traditionalists. As the New Deal spread its Americanizing influence across the South, economic and political leaders, and most southerners too, came to agree that the South's salvation lay in economic development and Americanization. The South's future thus fell into the hands of groups who regarded sectional traditions and distinctiveness as malignancies to be excised rather than values to be preserved and improved.

Howard W. Odum and Regionalism

The most constructive of the liberal models for southern development was regionalism, a product of the research and imaginativeness of Howard W. Odum.[4] Developed most fully in Odum's major work, *Southern Regions of the United States* (1936), regionalism was at once a device for studying the South, an analysis of its problems, and a program for solving those problems. The product of a 1931 grant from the General Education Board to the Social Science Research Council, *Southern Regions* was the most ambitious effort ever made to assemble data on the contemporary South. It is a veritable gold mine of socioeconomic information, much of it graphically illustrated in scores of charts and maps. Collectively, the data documented the pervasiveness of poverty and thus the South's continued inability to diversify its economy, equalize its income and wealth, solve its health problems, and educate its people. Curiously, Odum presented none of the data in racial breakdowns, and the result was to emphasize the economic nature of southern problems and obscure the racial dimension. The special plight of blacks was hidden in the larger difficulties of farmers and workers.

The omission was a serious one, for it meant that Odum gave too little attention to the role of racism in the cause and cure of the economic problems he detailed. The omission, however, was not unique to Odum. The Agrarians had also neglected racial topics, and so did most other social analysts of the 1920s and 1930s, whatever their political orientation. In the depression of the 1930s as in the prosperity of the 1920s, economics seemed more important than race. Yet the economic problems Odum dissected were to so large an extent the problems of poor blacks victimized by racial discrimination that they could not be solved without also solving the economic consequences of white supremacy. Odum's neglect of racial topics in *Southern Regions* seems especially important in view of the considerable attention he gave those topics elsewhere. The reasons for the neglect are unclear, but the consequences are not: it made the public reception of *Southern Regions* much easier. The book was, after all, a sustained criticism of the South, and southerners did not always honor their critics or read their books. Had Odum added to his candid treatment of economic problems a pointed discussion of racial issues from an equalitarian perspective, he might have reduced his chances for influencing public opinion, and one of his purposes was to move public opinion in the direction of reform.

Odum traced the roots of southern problems to cultural lag. The persistence of frontier attitudes and antebellum traditions, he believed, combined with the kind of conservatism natural to rural folk to produce a series of self-sustaining institutions and folkways—poverty, provincialism, one-party politics, one-crop agriculture, underurbanization, undereducation, and a lack of intellectual skepticism—that perpetuated what he regarded as the chief obstacle to southern progress, the hold of sectionalism over the southern mind. Sectionalism, which to Odum was the negative counterpart of his own regionalism, encouraged "isolation, individualism, ingrowing patriotism, cultural inbreeding, civic immaturity, and social inadequacy." It thus produced like-mindedness and social intolerance as well as too much concern for the past, too much faith in orthodoxies, and the kind of defensiveness that grows out of feelings of inferiority.

To counteract these things and get at the South's problems, Odum offered his concept of regionalism, which he defined as a program of "practical design and planning" directed toward "a continuously more effective reintegration of the southern regions into the national picture." Through regionwide planning he would overcome the drag of sectionalism and raise the South to national levels of social and economic and cultural performance. To accomplish this, it would first be necessary to study the South as a whole by integrating the expertise of history and the social sciences with the pragmatism of social planning and politics. Here was the most important proposal ever made to utilize the knowledge of scholars and planners in the cause of southern reform. Here was also the most important proposal ever made for the Americanization of Dixie; and considering the massive size of *Southern Regions* and the viscid nature of Odum's prose, its reception was phenomenal.

Odum had clearly tapped a popular vein. His evident pragmatism appealed to progressive political and business leaders; his obvious expertise was attractive to scholars, journalists, and social planners; and his liberalism aroused the enthusiasm of reformers and New Dealers. Moreover, his obvious attachment to the South neutralized all but the most chauvinistic of sectional critics. Governor Eugene Talmadge banned *Southern Regions* from the public schools of Georgia for a while in 1941, but across the section the book was widely read by scholars and social reformers, widely used as a textbook in college classes, and went through several printings. Odum had done what the Agrarians had wanted to do and could not, bridge the worlds of scholarship, planning, and politics.

His accomplishment lay in the impetus he gave the scientific study of social problems, however, rather than in his concept of regionalism, which was never implemented in any meaningful sense. In fact, the concept had important practical limitations. Political structures precluded regionwide planning except by federal agencies and made it impossible to give regionalism institutional expression. The Southern Governors' Conference, organized in 1934, was the obvious agency for the latter purpose and the Conference did undertake cooperative efforts on such regionwide problems as freight rate discrimination, but the nature of the Conference prevented its becoming an action agency. Furthermore, social problems varied greatly from state to state, and in some instances, such as the effort to attract industry and investment capital, the states competed with each other. Finally, the sectionalism Odum decried was often the result rather than the cause of the problems he detailed, and there was little promise that his prescription would eliminate it.

Regionalism was never really tested, though, for World War II soon thrust the South and the nation into a new era of economic and social change that made it obsolete. Many of the problems that concerned Odum in *Southern Regions* soon diminished or were transformed. In retrospect, regionalism seems less important than its byproducts, and Odum's significance in southern history rests on other things. Odum did more than anyone else to make southerners aware of their problems and the possibility that something could be done to solve them. He did much to make social criticism acceptable, and to help southerners see that scholarship and expertise, and thus higher education, had practical uses. He also deserves credit—or responsibility—for moving the South along the road to Americanization and thus perhaps to eventual extinction.

The latter was not Odum's doing alone, however. It was also the result of the centrifugal pull of national integration and the eclipse of responsible conservatism within the South. By World War II philosophical conservatism was so little thought of in intellectual and academic circles that William Alexander Percy's uncompromising defense of social hierarchy, *Lanterns on the Levee* (1941), was regarded as an atavism rather than serious social commentary. Without the vibrancy that comes from vigorous advocacy and challenge, southern conservatism shriveled as an intellectual movement and degenerated as a public force into obstructionism modified here or there by boosterism, buffoonery, and racism.

This was unfortunate, for if the winds of change were not altogether resistible by World War II, they were still controllable. No society is ever static; change is a universal rule of life. In the changing South after the war, a vibrant, pragmatic, humanistic conservatism might have channeled change in ways that avoided many of the ills of economic growth and racial adjustment that did in fact occur. By responding responsibly to the forces of change, it might have enabled southerners to retain more control over their own social development rather than allowing control to slip so largely into the hands of outside forces. It might, that is, have enabled southerners to act more constructively in that new era of social change.

Most important of all, a vigorous conservatism might have facilitated the task of keeping interest in sectional identity alive. In the generation after 1945 the very concept of southernness became hazier and hazier, especially among young southerners of both races, who associated it with the racial bigotry and economic reaction of extremists who wrapped themselves and their causes in a mantle of sectional loyalty. The meaning of southernism became confused even in the South with an assortment of bigotries and specious pleadings, and the positive attributes of sectional identity became less and less clear to everyone. Since the postwar South was still more nearly a conservative society than anything else, a responsible conservatism could have spelled out the positive attributes of sectional identity more clearly than could any other social philosophy. Had southerners of that day been better reminded of the positive dimensions of their identity as a people, they might have been more discriminating in choosing leaders and fashioning public policies. But as it was, they lacked a viable conservative ideology to give positive directions to their traditionalist urgings, and so they floundered. And the nation as well as the South was the loser.

Literary Renaissance

One major element in the intellectual flowering after World War I remains to be noted. That was the literary renaissance, which both quantitatively and qualitatively is without parallel in the section's history.[5] It is, indeed, the most important incident in the history of "high" culture in the South, and a major event in the history of American letters. The fact that it began so soon after H. L. Mencken made his dismal assessment of southern culture in 1920 is all the more remarkable. In an informative study, *Renaissance in the South* (1963), John M. Bradbury reported that between 1920 and 1960 southern authors received one Nobel prize for literature (William Faulkner in

1950), eleven Pulitzer prizes for fiction, including one-third of those awarded between 1930 and 1960, four Pulitzer prizes for drama, and five for poetry. In addition, after 1940 they received seventeen New York Drama Critics' awards, and after 1950 three Bollingen prizes for poetry.

These were impressive achievements by any standards, and a reflection of the calibre of the foremost writers of the renaissance. Among the best were William Faulkner, whom many came to consider the nation's greatest novelist; Tennessee Williams, one of the few significant American playwrights; Richard Wright, the foremost novelist of the generation in black America; Ellen Glasgow, one of the nation's premier women novelists; John Crowe Ransom, one of the country's most important literary critics; and Robert Penn Warren, a major literary figure in the generation that began about 1945. Others of major stature included Thomas Wolfe, Erskine Caldwell, and Eudora Welty, and in the generation after World War II, William Styron. There were also James Branch Cabell, T. S. Stribling, Elizabeth Maddox Roberts, DuBose Heyward, Julia Peterkin, Jean Toomer, Dorothy Scarborough, Paul Green, Lillian Hellman, Donald Davidson, Allen Tate, Stark Young, and Josephine Pinckney, and then Katharine Anne Porter, Carson McCullers, and Caroline Gordon, and still later Flannery O'Connor, James Agee, Randall Jarrell, Ralph Ellison, and Truman Capote.

The renaissance had no beginning or ending and has never been satisfactorily explained. In 1924 one student estimated that in all the South there were no more than five authors whose works would endure for a decade, and a year later Gerald W. Johnson was still wondering in Menckenesque fashion if the South should not be "dismissed as a possible field of American culture." By that time, however, unmistakable signs of change were appearing. Between 1922 and 1926, William Faulkner, T. S. Stribling, and Julia Peterkin published their first works, and in the same years there appeared Ellen Glasgow's *Barren Ground* (1925), Dorothy Scarborough's *In the Land of Cotton* (1923), DuBose Heyward's *Porgy* (1925), Jean Toomer's *Cane* (1923), and Elizabeth Maddox Robert's *The Time of Man* (1926). If there was still any doubt about what was happening, it evaporated in 1929 when Faulkner published both *The Sound and the Fury* and *Sartoris* and Thomas Wolfe's first novel *Look Homeward, Angel,* appeared. By then critics were describing the South as the nation's "literary land of promise"; and the promise was amply fulfilled in the next two decades.

How is such a remarkable change to be explained? The things that contributed to the general intellectual awakening after World War I were important of course, as was the genius of the writers themselves;

but given the unique nature of creative writing and the high level achieved by so many southern writers between 1925 and 1950, those things hardly constitute a full explanation. It is easier to account for the nature of renaissance writing and the relationship between the writers and the South. Both of these things seem to have grown out of the sudden acceleration of social change after World War I and the exaggerated sense of sectional self-consciousness that induced. Among sensitive and cerebral individuals this engendered an intense self-awareness, and for southerners generally, a period of acute introspection. Many of them began to think more systematically about the South than ever before, what it was, what it had been, what it might become. "With the war of 1914–18," wrote Allen Tate in a widely quoted passage, "the South re-entered the world—but gave a backward glance as it stepped over the border; that backward glance gave us the Southern renascence, a literature conscious of the past in the present."

Donald Davidson offered a similar but less poetic explanation. Social change after World War I, he wrote, pushed the South, "a traditional society," into "a moment of self-consciousness favorable to the production of great literary work." In a traditional society, he explained, "if modernism enters to the point where the society is thrown a little out of balance but not yet completely off balance, the moment of self-consciousness arrives. Then a process begins that at first is enormously stimulating." The stimulation comes from the unevenness of change, which exposes the innermost realities of the society and thereby dramatizes its contradictions and tensions. Southerners came to see, as they had never seen before, the difference between myth and reality in their past and present—between gentility and violence, hospitality and prejudice, wealth and poverty, white and black. Where the social and intellectual chemistry is favorable, as it was in the South at that time, this process can, as Louis D. Rubin has suggested of Mississippi, "dislodge the potential writer from his community, send him away from it and then back to it, cause him to examine his life with the artistic detachment that is born of spiritual estrangement and yet with the compassion that comes of friendship."

If these things do not explain the southern renaissance, they make its nature more comprehensible. As an episode in the intellectual history of the South, the renaissance is important not because of the quality of the literature it produced, but because of what the literature had to say about the South. The writers were a diverse group personally as well as artistically, and their treatment of the South ranged from the biting exposés of T. S. Stribling and Erskine Caldwell to the quiescent reportage of Eudora Welty. Some of them, like James Branch Cabell, wrote little about the South or southern themes, but most of them wrote little about anything else. All of them seem to have had in one degree or another a love-hate relationship with the section, which led them to seek things of enduring value in southern life even as they wrote of its shortcomings. Better than any other group, they illustrate the alienation that came to exist between the South and its intellectuals. If none of them was fundamentally antisouthern, many of them were accused of being, and much of what they wrote was not appreciated by the mass of southern readers. In fact, some of them, like Faulkner, Caldwell, and Stribling, were popularly regarded as little better than apostate purveyors of prurience. When Faulkner was awarded the Nobel prize, the most prestigious of all literary awards, the editor of the largest newspaper in his home state of Mississippi could think of no better way to describe him than as "a propagandist of degradation" who "belongs in the privy school of literature."

Whatever the relationship of individual writers to the South, the body of renaissance literature is distinctively southern, and that fact locates the renaissance in the history of southern thought. There is in the literature an exaggerated concern with time and place, and with history, history not in the conventional sense but in the sense of the presentness of the past. Occasionally the division between past and present is blurred altogether, but more often the heavy weight of history is made all-pervading, not only in the lives of leading characters but in the life of the South as well. Typically history appears as just that—a heavy weight, an obstruction to overcome, an obstacle to justice and truth and liberation. This view of the past encourages the brooding sense of evil that characterizes so much of the literature, and the preoccupation with the tragic dimension of human experience. The characteristic tone is one of pessimism about man's fate and potential, a pessimism that sometimes plunges to the depths of melancholia but more often dwells on the ambiguity of the human condition. Happy endings—the progressive view of history—are rare indeed; even in *Gone With the Wind* the hero does not get the heroine, and neither of them, apparently, lived happily ever after. Art, however, is never subordinate to message; concern for the artistic dimension of expression is always uppermost. Form as well as substance is thus important, and there is great stress upon characterization and motivation. There is, overall, less explicit concern with some subjects than one might expect, especially religion, blacks, and racism, though there are of course notable exceptions. The number of well-developed black characters in the works of white authors is surprisingly small, though again the exceptions are notable. Race is dealt with chiefly through race relations; the race problem typically appears not at the center of the story but as part of a background of history, tragedy, or ambiguity.

Though the renaissance grew in part from a general concern for the South, most writers dealt with southern identity only indirectly, and their interpretations of southern history are implicit rather than explicit. In renaissance literature the South appears less as a place than a culture, a mood, a set of traditions, sometimes an almost mythic locale where faults and virtues are both larger than life, and life itself is full of muddying paradox. The South is a people tied down by the sins of their fathers—slavery, defeat, poverty, despair, prejudice—as well as their own limitations, a land of violence and bigotry, pretense and poverty, and sometimes decay, but also of hope and heroism and the steely virtues that come from incessant struggle.

These themes are best revealed in the works of William Faulkner. In trying to understand Faulkner, however, it is important to remember that he was rarely concerned with the South as such. Rather, as Robert Penn Warren has put it, Faulkner took the southern "world, with its powerful sense of history, its tangled loyalties, its pains and tensions of tradition, its pieties and violence, and elevated it to the level of a great moral drama on the tragic scale." The South and his fictionalized locale, Yoknapatawpha County, were thus vehicles for a larger message; but acknowledging that, one can still find in Faulkner's work a good bit of the most insightful writing about the South and its history ever penned.

Faulkner's treatment of the South is spread throughout his Yoknapatawpha stories, but appears most explicitly in *Absalom, Absalom!* (1936), perhaps his best novel; "The Bear" (1942), perhaps his best short story; *Sartoris* (1929), the earliest of his Yoknapatawpha tales; and the trilogy chronicling the rise of the Snopes family, *The Hamlet* (1940), *The Town* (1957), and *The Mansion* (1959). Together, these works record the building of a social order in the Old South and its piecemeal destruction in the Civil War and Reconstruction and the subsequent triumph of northern capitalism. The old order had many redeeming qualities—dignity, courage, honor, and a commitment to social justice —but was itself founded on sin and injustice—the dispossession of the Indians and the enslavement of the blacks or, as one of the characters in *Absalom, Absalom!* expressed it, "not on the rock of stern morality but on the shifting sands of opportunity and moral brigandage." This infused the social order with guilt, and put a great curse on the section and its people. The plagues of Civil War and Reconstruction had been necessary to excise the guilt, but in part because southerners fought so well and in part because the enemy was also corrupt, the excision was incomplete. After Reconstruction, the old order tried to reassert itself, but northern capitalism and materialism proved a more difficult enemy than northern arms had been, and the effort ultimately failed.

The order and its values gave way to a new order dominated by a new class of men that sprang from the landless whites of the prewar era. Wedded to northern capitalism and its social values, this new class, personified by the ubiquitous family of Snopes, rose to economic and social supremacy in the New South.

In the struggle that preceded this transformation, representatives of the old order—the Sartorises, Compsons, Sutpens, and DeSpains—lost out because the values they cherished prevented them from competing in the amoral, even unscrupulous world of the Snopeses. But in vanquishing the Sartorises and their kind, the Snopeses had corrupted themselves and the South, killing off the virtues but not the vices of the old order and replacing them with the vices but none of the virtues of capitalist materialism. The New South thus inherited the worst of both worlds. The problems of the Old South, especially racism and guilt, survived in the New, and to them were added poverty, defeat, and the corruptions of materialism. In Faulkner's writings, the modern era is one of moral confusion and decay, and the heavy weight of the past is not lightened by the qualities that pay in the present—materialism, cleverness, greed. "It is as if Faulkner were saying that honor, courage, pride, pity, love were outmoded attributes in the twentieth-century South," Louis D. Rubin has written, "and that animal shrewdness and avarice were all that mattered now."

This picture of the modern South as a place of economic transformation and moral retrogression was common in the works of Faulkner's contemporaries, as was its corollary, the idea that in spite of its defects the Old South had had redeeming virtues. Faulkner's significance lay not in the uniqueness of his vision of the South, but in the artistic genius with which he expressed it and, perhaps, also in his success in infusing the South's story with pathos and tragedy. No other writer approached his effectiveness in these respects. T. S. Stribling, for example, stereotyped both the section and its history in a trilogy of novels, *The Forge* (1931), *The Store* (1932), and *Unfinished Cathedral* (1934), that traced the triumph of the material spirit in a society infused with racism, hypocrisy, and provincialism. Ellen Glasgow's novels of life in modern Virginia told a similar story of transformation, but with more attention to nuance and complexity. Hers too was an account of the triumph of commercial civilization, the middle class, and populistic democracy, and the decline of an aristocracy unable to adapt to changing times. She too was dissatisfied with the new order. "Pride of name and place has long since yielded to pride of pocket," she wrote of the modern South in 1943, "and even pride of pocket is slowly giving way before the bleak democracy ensured by financial chaos."

The novels of Erskine Caldwell were concerned with poor whites rather than aristocrats or the bourgeoisie. They told an altogether different kind of story from those of Miss Glasgow, Stribling, or Faulkner, but they reflected similar themes of moral degeneration amid economic change. Caldwell's best work, *Tobacco Road* (1932), is the classic tale of poor whites, and despite a surface concern with sensuality and ribaldry is told with sympathy and insight. Jeeter Lester, the central figure, is the grandson of the man who, before the Civil War, had opened up and claimed as his own all the land in the neighborhood where Jeeter lived in the early years of the Great Depression. But Jeeter's father had lost much of the land, and when Jeeter lost the rest he became a sharecropper on land he and his family had owned for three generations. Within a few years, however, even that was lost, when his landlord ceased "carrying" his croppers, cutting off their credit at the local store and leaving them to their own devices.

For several years before the beginning of the novel in the early 1930s, Jeeter had not farmed, and long periods of malnutrition, family disintegration, and psychological debasement had taken their toll on him. He became a defeated, unstruggling man, preoccupied with his physical wants, drained of all humanity. But occasionally his old hopes revived, his old love of the soil and rural life rose to the surface of his consciousness. "I think more of the land than I do about staying in a durn cotton mill," he said, explaining his refusal to move to town and seek work in the despised factories. "You can't smell no sedge fire up there, and when it comes time to break the land for planting you feel sick inside but you don't know what's ailing you. . . . But when a man stays on the land, he don't get to feeling like that. . . . Out here on the land a man feels better than he ever did. . . . God made the land, but you don't see Him building durn cotton mills."

Thomas Wolfe, another major renaissance writer, seems more embittered in his criticisms of the South than most of his contemporaries, but his sporadic references to the section revealed similar themes of spiritual decline and moral confusion in the midst of economic growth. In *The Web and the Rock* (1939), he wrote of the South's "inability to meet or to adjust itself to the conditions, strifes, and ardors of a modern life; its old, rich, appomattoxlike retreat into the shades of folly and delusion, of prejudice and bigotry, of florid legend and defensive casuistry." "There was something wounded in the South," he said in *You Can't Go Home Again* (1940), "something twisted, dark and full of pain which Southerners have lived with all their lives—something rooted in their souls beyond all contradiction, about which no one has dared to write, of which no one has ever spoken." Just what this was Wolfe never explained, though he suggested that it might have come from the "old war, and from the ruin of their great defeat and its degraded aftermath," or "from the evil of man's slavery, and the hurt and shame of human conscience in its struggle with the fierce desire to own."

As these examples suggest, the South and its most talented writers were ill at ease with each other by the 1930s, but the uneasiness had positive as well as negative results. Certainly the South was no longer a Sahara of the *beaux-arts,* as Mencken had charged in 1920. Perhaps it had never been; but by the 1930s its writers were producing a large share of the nation's best literature, and Mencken withdrew his charge. "There is now in the South a minority of opinion that is quite as enlightening as that to be discovered in any part of the country," he wrote in 1935. Southerners, he conceded in a change of metaphors, no longer isolated themselves in "cultural Tibets" amid Himalayas of ignorance and prejudice. On the contrary, "there is a new spirit all over the South and it begins to come to grips with reality." He might have added that the new spirit was propelling the section away from the kind of civilization he once found appealing in the Old South and toward an altogether different world of Americanization.

The Limits of Change

In the period between the two world wars, the South and its people had faced a sustained period of change. The resulting problems were difficult and often handled poorly, but the cumulative impact was great. Yet the traditional South was a vital organism, and its capacity for resisting change or bending it to its own devices was also great. Thus in 1941 the South was still a distinctive section and its folk a people apart. The changing South was also the enduring South. As important as the economic and institutional changes of the preceding generation had been, they had not produced equivalent changes in attitudes and values. When the new world war commenced a new era in the section's history, the South was still the South.

SIX

THE PRESENT SOUTH, SINCE 1945

World War II again accelerated the pace of social change. Building onto the New Deal, it pushed the South through another historical evolution, and when it was over, traditionalists were losing control of things. One after another the South's peculiar institutions began falling to the onslaughts of Americanization, and presently the South itself was threatened.[1]

The three decades after 1945 thus witnessed more fundamental change than any period in the section's history except the 1860s and 1870s, and the changes in these two periods bear an interesting relationship to each other. Events in the Civil War and Reconstruction set the contours of southern history for several succeeding generations, and those since 1945 promise to do likewise. The long phase of southern history that began in 1860–61 was dominated by sectional influences, influences that since 1945 have been diminished or eliminated altogether. That phase of the section's history has thus ended, or is in the process of ending, and in its stead is emerging a new phase in which national forces are controlling. The "sectional South" has given way to an "American South" in which traditional sources of grievance and distinctiveness have abated or disappeared. By

1977 white racial fear had subsided to the point that it was a less controlling factor in southern life than it had been at any time since the South became a conscious section. Public life was desegregated, the legal structure of white supremacy had been dismantled, and on the surface at least the pattern of race relations was moving toward national norms. The typical southerner now lived in a sizable metropolitan area, his living standard and the opportunities available to his children were better than ever in the section's history, and he lived more like his American counterpart than any of his ancestors ever did. Industrialization had triumphed, the hold of ruralism was broken, and southern agriculture had been transformed. Socioeconomic conditions were moving toward national patterns, and cultural as well as physical isolation was a thing of the past. The Solid South had gone with the wind and with it one-party politics, disfranchisement, the political supremacy of the black belt, and the isolation in national politics.

These structural changes gave new urgency to old questions of sectional identity and the South's future. By 1977 they had not yet produced changes of equivalent proportions in sectional attitudes and values; but whether that was evidence sectional identity would survive or a passing example of cultural lag had become a pressing question for everyone interested in the South. For those who hoped the South would endure, the cause for concern was—and is—great.

16

The American South

The 1940s was another pivotal decade. The coming of World War II ended the long depression, and the prosperity it brought continued after the return of peace. Per capita income tripled during the decade, and the proportion of the work force in agriculture declined to 22 percent. Wartime employment drew hundreds of thousands of people from farm to city, and between 1940 and 1950 no less than 1.8 million southerners, four-fifths of them blacks, moved to other parts of the country. In Alabama, Arkansas, Georgia, and Mississippi the black population actually declined, and in those states plus Louisiana and Texas the rural population did likewise. Southerners were moving around as never before, and the movement further reduced provincial barriers and encouraged the idea that change is a normal condition of life.

The war had other important results. The growth of federal spending increased the dependence on the national government, while outside investment in new industry intermeshed the South's and the nation's economy. Federal job training programs, including those of the military services, raised the level of marketable skills, and the postwar GI Bill of Rights provided educational opportunities on a scale never before available. Unparalleled numbers of women entered the work force during the war, and many of them remained when it was over, adding not only to family income but to the social transformation as well. Sustained prosperity brought added creature comforts. Electricity, hard-surfaced roads, and indoor plumbing spread even into remote areas; labor-saving devices and other consumer goods became more accessible; education continued to improve, and adequate health care became available to more people. The quality of life improved remarkably.

The war, and the Cold War that followed, turned southern interests outward. Whites supported the war effort avidly despite the seeming conflict between the nation's announced war aims and their own way of life.[1] To them this was another crusade to save democracy, now threatened by the militarism of Germany and Japan. In the years before Pearl Harbor, public opinion polls invariably found southerners more committed than other Americans to preparedness and a strong American stance in world affairs. More than other Americans, they considered helping Britain more important than avoiding war, and thought the general policy of isolationism unwise. Their attitudes, however, were more those of unilateralists in world affairs than cooperationists. Thus during the Cold War southerners were more sympathetic than other Americans to a large American military establishment and to forceful policies against the Soviet Union and China, and less sympathetic to third world revolutionary movements or the relaxation of Cold War tensions.

These views are readily explained by ethnocentrism and the penchant for direct action, but they were also affected by the continued preoccupation with the race issue. Despite repeated insistence that the two things were unrelated, the nation's professed commitment to democracy and self-government during and after the war was in fact contradicted by the South's racial system, and the contradiction was a source of irritation and concern. Black southerners responded to the second world war with more sophistication than to the first, and many of them saw the new emergency as an opportunity to exact better treatment for themselves. The result was a growing restiveness among the race and increased apprehensiveness among whites. The South escaped the kind of race rioting that occurred in New York and Detroit in 1943, but racial tensions rose perceptibly. In 1943 sociologist Charles S. Johnson counted 111 racial incidents in the section of sufficient importance to attract attention in the national press, the largest being disturbances in Mobile, Alabama, and Beaumont, Texas. Together, these incidents reflected the full range of the racial problem—employment, housing, voting, law enforcement, segregated accommodations, and tensions between local whites and blacks from other parts of the country—and each of them added to the rise of racial consciousness. The problem, as Johnson observed, was that "the great majority of southern Negroes are becoming increasingly dissatisfied with the present pattern of race relations and want a change," while "the great majority of southern whites ... seem unable to contemplate the possibility of change in any fundamental sense."

The changing black attitudes were spelled out in a symposium, *What the Negro Wants* (1944), edited for the University of North Carolina Press by Rayford W. Logan in the middle of the war. Among the contributors were Roy Wilkins of the NAACP, A. Philip Randolph of the Brotherhood of Sleeping Car Porters and the March on Washington Movement, W. E. B. Du Bois, Mary McLeod Bethune, Langston Hughes, Sterling A. Brown, Charles H. Wesley, Doxey A. Wilkerson, and others. The consensus of their views was that blacks wanted "eventually to enjoy the same rights, opportunities and privileges that are vouchsafed to all other Americans and to fulfill all the obligations that are required of all other Americans." This meant "eventual first class citizenship and eventual full integration into the public life of the American people," which in turn meant "equality of opportunity," "equal pay for equal work," "equal recognition of the dignity of the human being," and "abolition of public segregation." "There can be no equality *with* segregation," insisted Roy Wilkins. "Complete equality, therefore, envisions the abolition of the segregated schools."

Whites were perplexed by such statements, and the threatening impasse forced the federal government to take a larger role in racial policy. Black activism had increased even before the nation entered the war, and the rigidities of white supremacy threatened the preparedness effort. That effort, for example, opened up large numbers of jobs in defense industries, and when blacks found themselves excluded from most of the jobs they began pressuring the federal government. In the spring of 1941, A. Philip Randolph and others organized a mass march on Washington to protest the discrimination, and their action had an immediate effect. In return for Randolph's promise to cancel the march, President Roosevelt issued an executive order in June 1941 forbidding racial discrimination in defense industries and creating a Fair Employment Practices Committee (FEPC) to oversee the effort to achieve that objective.

The order had only limited effect in the South, though black employment rose markedly during the wartime labor shortage. Roosevelt's action was a pioneering step in a controversial area, and as limited as he and the Committee could make it. The Committee had no enforcement authority—that was left to the courts—and its members interpreted their mandate narrowly, for they had no inclination to challenge southern race policies. "There is no power in the world—not even in all the mechanized armies of the earth, Allied and Axis—," said Chairman Mark Ethridge, a Kentuckian, "which could now force the Southern white people to the abandonment of the principle of social segregation." Yet the symbolic importance of Roosevelt's order was great, for it marked a milestone in the slow shift of the federal government away from its traditional acquiescence in racial discrimination. The order as well as the principle it embodied was anathema to white southerners, who succeeded in destroying the Committee in 1946 by withholding funds from it in Congress, but for several years thereafter fair employment was a major object of sectional controversy.

Postwar Alternatives

When the war ended in 1945, the South was at a crossroads. Its people faced several alternative paths to the future, any one of which they could knowingly choose, or they could leave the choice to impersonal forces of social change. The progress toward Americanization was well advanced, and controllable only if its meaning were grasped and its processes consciously directed toward "southern" ends. In this sense southerners of the postwar years faced their own rendezvous with destiny, to borrow one of Roosevelt's phrases, their one last chance to save the South from assimilation into the national mainstream. Options concerning the course of southern development were not yet closed; the initiative in southern life had not yet passed to those who would destroy its distinctiveness. The choices, however, were narrow and closing. The vast majority of southerners welcomed economic growth and social improvement, and only a small minority showed any concern over the subversive potential of "progress." On the other hand, whites were anxious to preserve white supremacy and the institutional arrangements surrounding it, while blacks were already at work trying to destroy those things.

Thus whites and blacks faced the prospects of change with differing expectations; yet change itself had curiously similar implications for both. Just as Americanization promised eventually to strip whites of their identity as southerners, so racial integration promised ultimately to deprive blacks of the traditional sources of their own identity as a group. That is, carried to its logical conclusion, integration would eliminate race as a source of social identity and eventually destroy black institutions and communities by absorbing them into those of the white majority.

It is often remarked that southern whites and southern blacks have no group identity apart from each other, that the one is a meaningful social category only in apposition to the other, and this is one sense in which that is true. The identity and ethos of both groups sprang from the same kinds of things—from a sense of fear and grievance and feelings of apartness, and from the perceived need for unity which those things induced. Over the years both groups had developed a degree of protonationalism, and became a kind of nation within a nation. To that extent both had resisted the American melting pot and opted instead for cultural pluralism, and with each the resistance had been born in part of perceived necessity. Thus black institutions and communities had originated at least in part as defense mechanisms against racial discrimination, and were maintained in part for the same reason. Whites had come to regard those institutions and communities with contempt, and used the distinctive features they exhibited as added justification for treating blacks invidiously. Yet for blacks segregated institutions and communities had served positive functions, not only as havens against humiliation and persecution but sources of pride and spurs to achievement. Without pressing the point too far, the same thing might be said of the peculiar institutions of the white South. These too had originated as defensive reactions against fear, and were perpetuated not only for protective purposes but as marks of distinctiveness and sources of pride as well. Moreover, they were regarded with varying degrees of disdain by other Americans, and the fierce pride southerners took in them was partly a defensive reaction against the outsiders' disdain. Claims about the superiority of the southern way of life did for whites what shouts of "Black is beautiful" did for blacks.

The parallels go further still. Since group consciousness in each race was partly a mark of oppression, the challenge for both in 1945 was to eliminate the oppressive aspects of those things that encouraged group consciousness without destroying the positive elements. For whites this meant eliminating the evils perpetuated by their own institutions—racism, poverty, provincialism, and intolerance—while preserving the good—such things as personalism, leisureliness, and attachment to locality and family and tradition. For blacks it meant removing the racist stigmas attached to their own institutions and communities while overcoming the disabilities produced by discrimination and at the same time achieving a pattern of integration and separatism that would permit full equality without destroying black communities and institutions.

These tasks are innately difficult, and by 1945 they might have been impossible. The white South and its way of life were so closely identified with racial oppression and assorted forms of backwardness and depravity that black and white reformers alike were convinced that Americanization—a second Reconstruction—was the only way to remove those ills. It was, it seemed, necessary to destroy the South in order to save its people. By the same token, black institutions and communities were so entwined with racial discrimination that reformers and equalitarians, including the emerging generation of black leaders, had come to the conclusion that integrating them out of existence was the only way to do away with discrimination. Here too, the destruction of a people's institutions seemed necessary to save the people themselves.

The result was that white and black southerners worked at cross purposes at a time when each could have benefited from the understanding and assistance of the other. Blacks strove to destroy the white South's distinctive institutions in order to eliminate racial discrimination, while whites labored to repress blacks in order to preserve their own dominance and the sense of security it gave them. In the resulting struggle, the underlying questions were obscured: How did southerners of each race envision the future of the South in the nation? What place did blacks envision for themselves in the South and the nation? How could tradition and social change be balanced so as to secure the benefits of both without suffering the drawbacks of either?

Of course neither race perceived the issues in these terms, in part because neither thought through its situation or developed a social philosophy to define it. The preoccupation with immediate concerns led to a neglect of ultimate goals on all sides. Frustrated by the barriers of segregation, blacks and equalitarian whites turned to integration without much thought about its long-range implications. "Separate educational facilities are inherently unequal," the Supreme Court decreed in *Brown v. Board of Education of Topeka* (1954), accepting the integrationist ideal. Total integration was of course one way to attack the very real problem of racial discrimination, but it allowed no room for black institutions. Would there be no black institutions in the equalized and standardized future?

Apparently not; but the larger failure of social thought was not that of racial integrationists. It was that of white conservatives. The white South was still more conservative than anything else, and in this new era of social transformation only a humane and conservative social philosophy could adequately express its best ideals, point up its basic problems, and call forth the better impulses of its people. The absence of such a philosophy, or rather the lack of systematic social thinking of any kind, among opinion molders and public leaders, a result in part of the eclipse of conservatism in the interwar years, had fateful consequences. It left those groups who were sure of their purposes, especially economic boosters and racial extremists, with a political advantage, and the result was to encourage undirected economic growth and social change on the one hand and blind efforts to prevent racial or political reform on the other. The larger result was to reinforce the idea that the distinctively southern aspects of southern life consisted of its worst rather than its best features.

As these things developed, their racial aspects loomed larger and larger, and conservative defenders of sectional causes turned increasingly to racism, obstructionism, and discredited political devices. Reading such disparate works as Charles W. Collins's *Whither Solid South?*

(1947), James J. Kilpatrick's *The Sovereign States* (1957), and William D. Workman's *The Case for the South* (1960), one is struck today by the outdatedness, even unreality, of their arguments. It is as if the authors had become disembodied from the time in which they lived. Their defense of the traditional South had none of the cogency and tightness (once certain initial premises were accepted) that characterized the best of proslavery thought in the old South. It was instead legalistic, derivative, and sometimes mean-spirited. It served chiefly to affirm popular prejudices, though its aridness also enhanced by way of contrast the appeal of moderates like Georgia Governor Ellis G. Arnall and Mississippi editor Hodding Carter. For all their limitations, works like Arnall's *The Shore Dimly Seen* (1946) and *What the People Want* (1948) and Carter's *Southern Legacy* (1950) were remarkably better. Not only did these authors appeal to the generous impulses of whites, but their faith in the efficacy of time and economic growth and the good will of most whites enabled them to write more pointedly of long-range solutions to racial as well as other problems.

The difficulty with most moderates in the postwar years was not one of spirit or of blindness to the necessity for reform. It was instead a shallowness of social analysis, a failure to probe deeply enough to see the roots of southern problems and the limitations of the liberal premises upon which their analysis rested. Arnall, for example, whose thinking was sometimes decidedly populistic, believed that the South's problems were largely economic. "Fundamentally, the problem of the Negro in the South is a problem of economics," he wrote. "In general, the basic civil liberties of Negro citizens are respected thoroughly in Georgia." White southerners, he believed, were generally committed to "man's basic and inherent right of self government" and to man's "capacity, both mentally and morally, to exercise that right." The race problem was therefore not so deep that it could not be solved "by mutual understanding, by adherence to the basic laws of the land, by democratic processes, by solutions of the underlying economic problems that aggravate the plight of the various minorities, [and] by an appeal to the inherent good sense and good heart of all men of good will."

If this seems more piety than realism, it did point to a human factor that would eventually help southerners through the trauma of desegregation. It was also more useful than the prescriptions of racial liberals like Lillian Smith of Georgia, many of whom were too overcome with guilt to be effective public activists, or of other moderates like Hodding Carter, who were neutralized by their own views of white racism. "Neither mockery nor protest nor legislation can, in the ascertainable future, change the white South's conviction that racial separateness at the mass levels of personal contact is the only acceptable way by which large segments of two dissimilar peoples can live side by side in peace," Carter wrote in *Southern Legacy.* "Any abrupt Federal effort to end segregation as it is practiced in the South today would not only be foredoomed to failure but would also dangerously impair the present progressive adjustment between the races."

The Economic Miracle

The process of racial change had already begun when Carter wrote this, and it was made easier by the economic miracle that occurred during the quarter century after 1950.[2] Indeed, the 1960s was the decade of greatest economic growth in the section's history, and when it ended, the long generations of poverty and economic frustration were over for most southerners. If the section was still behind the rest of the country in most economic indicators in 1970, poverty and its assorted ills were no longer the molding forces they had once been in southern life. "Analysis of [the most recent] standard economic indicators," wrote economist M. I. Foster in 1972, "does not label the South as backward —still behind national levels on the average, but not backward."

Foster's assessment seems justified, for it reflects the considerable growth of the '50s and '60s as well as the continuing problems of the '70s. By anyone's standards, the growth was impressive. In twelve southeastern states, not including Texas, the gross product of goods and services in constant dollars increased at an average annual rate of 4.6 percent between 1950 and 1970, significantly above the 3.4 percent for the rest of the country, and rose in absolute figures from $52.4 billion to $129.9 billion. Moreover, the growth was broadly based, affecting every major area of economic activity, and its effect was to bring the section's economic profile in line with the nation's. Thus in 1970 only 4.3 percent of the section's total product was in agriculture, while manufacturing accounted for 30.9 percent (compared to 3.5 percent and 29.9 percent in the rest of the country). The effort to attract industry had succeeded; even in Mississippi, the section's most rural state, manufacturing had become far more important than agriculture. Altogether, the gross manufacturing product in twelve southeastern states rose from $11.3 billion in 1950 to more than $40 billion in 1970, and per capita income, which nearly tripled in those years, reached almost 80 percent of the national figure.

The changes in agriculture were especially dramatic. In the Confederate South, the number of farms decreased 63 percent between 1940 and 1969 and farm population fell 83 percent, while the size of the average farm more than doubled and the value of products sold multiplied 10.7 times. The acreage in cropland dropped significantly, and that in pasturage rose dramatically. By the early 1970s, income from beef cattle was more than three times that of cotton, which now accounted for only 7 percent of the value of farm products and was less significant economically and socially than at any time since 1800. Mechanization markedly increased productivity after 1950, while displacing an estimated 115,000 farm workers annually. Most of those displaced were blacks, sharecroppers, and/or casual laborers, and it was those groups that bore the social brunt of agricultural change. By 1970 there were only 98,000 black-operated farms in the section, and sharecropping and farm tenancy were no longer significant problems. Less than one farmer in eight was still a tenant of any sort, and the typical tenant was now a cash renter.

The transformation was visible as well as fundamental. Gone from the countryside in the 1970s were those legions of human cotton pickers and casual agricultural laborers who once symbolized southern farming—only a negligible portion of the cotton crop was now picked by hand. In their stead were wage workers skilled in operating the increasingly sophisticated machines that rendered obsolete traditional kinds of farm labor. Both diversification and specialization had come to characterize southern agriculture, the growth areas of which had become livestock, egg and broiler production, dairying, cereal grains, and beans. Farming had become a business rather than a way of life, and as that occurred the family farm began to disappear and the plantation became an agribusiness unit rather than a social patriarchy.

Certain economic problems persisted. Though every segment of the population partook of the new prosperity and enjoyed a notable rise in living standards, economic growth was uneven and left significant pockets of poverty. Growth was greater in states like Florida, Georgia, and North Carolina than Mississippi and Arkansas, and in urban than rural areas. It benefited upper- and middle-class people more than the poor, whites more than blacks, and the educated and skilled more than the uneducated and unskilled. Welfare, social security, and other income transfer programs helped unemployed, elderly, and other dependent groups, as did the general rise in minimum wages. But income and wealth remained more unevenly distributed than in the rest of the country, so that in 1970 the poorest fifth of southern families received only 4.8 percent of all regional income while the wealthiest fifth received 43.3 percent. Using an index based on low income, high postnatal mortality, and low participation in food stamp and commodity distribution programs, a 1968 study of malnutrition located 256 "hunger counties" in the nation, 220 of which were in the Confederate South.

The continuing poverty was concentrated among blacks and rural folk. On the basis of federal guidelines, 23 percent of all rural white families in the greater South were poor in 1970, as were 54 percent of rural blacks. In the same year, the median income of black families in the section was $4,000 below that of white families ($5,226 to $9,240). For all the prosperity, median black income, which had been 46 percent of that of whites in 1959, had improved to only 57 percent in 1970. Black southerners remained three times as likely as whites to be poor and far more likely to live in substandard housing and receive inferior education; and southerners generally stood in a similar relationship to other Americans. In 1970 almost half (46 percent) of the poor people in the nation lived in the Census South, and the drag of their poverty caused the absolute gap in per capita income between the South and the rest of the country to increase even in the prosperous 1960s. In 1970 no southern state had a per capita income as high as the national average.

These things reflected continuing economic imbalances. The section remained an area of considerable poverty and great natural wealth. At the end of the '60s the greater South accounted for 53 percent of all the mineral resources produced in the United States, 100 percent of the sulfur and bauxite, 29 percent of the coal, 69 percent of the crude oil, 81 percent of the natural gas, 31 percent of the lumber, and 32 percent of the electric energy produced. Moreover, it contained 70 percent of the crude oil reserves, 80 percent of the natural gas reserves, and 42 percent of the commercial forest lands, and its ports handled 35 percent of the nation's export tonnage. Yet much of its industry was still extractive and "soft." In 1970, 38 percent of all manufacturing jobs in the section were in textiles, food, and apparel, all relatively low in wages and value added by manufacturing. Textile manufacturing was still a major enterprise, and still reflected the problems of southern industry: wages were relatively low, union membership was small, racial discrimination widespread, and management slow to accept responsibility for the special health problems of employees. In 1974 hourly wages in the industry averaged $3.17 compared to $5.92 in automobile manufacturing and assembly and $6.44 in steel production, and fringe benefits averaged about 30 cents an hour compared to more than $1 in those other two industries. The disparities are explained in part by the fact that only 15.6 percent of all nonagricultural workers in the section were organized at the end of the '60s compared to 28.4 percent for the country as a whole, which in turn reflected the fact that ten of the eleven states in the Confederate South had right-to-work laws. Conservative business and political leadership kept state and local taxes low in the section, and levels of support for education and welfare services remained substantially below national averages.

After 1970 the problems that stemmed from these imbalances began to loom larger. The economic recession and the energy crisis, and the consequent slowing of economic activity, strained the weakest links in the section's economic chain. Almost overnight, the lack of planning in past growth, including inattention to the proper mix of economic activity, became apparent, while the ecological crisis revealed the fact that much of southern industry, especially chemicals, petrochemicals, pulp and paper, and strip mining, was polluting the environment. The slackening of growth rates in the mid-1970s completed an economic cycle, and the problems and possibilities of the near future promised to be different from those of the immediate past.

Racial Transformation

The economic miracle occurred during a period of momentous racial transformation, and sustained prosperity made the transformation easier than it might otherwise have been. Certainly the transformation was less painful than one could have expected in 1945. Looking back upon it, the relative ease of its accomplishment seems far more striking than the difficulties it involved.[3] Twice before in their history, white southerners had been forced to confront the whole question of racial policy, once in Radical Reconstruction and again in the aftermath of the Populist uprising, and on each occasion they had succumbed to their worst impulses. This time, however, was quite otherwise.

The reasons for the difference seem fairly obvious. The earlier extremism grew out of the circumstances of the 1870s and 1890s as whites saw them, circumstances that no longer existed in the 1950s and 1960s. By the latter decades, blacks and white moderates were strong enough to influence events, and white extremists were no longer in complete control of things. Interracial movements were better organized and more influential than ever before, blacks were stronger and more assertive, and the federal government, including the courts, more sympathetic to blacks. These things enabled reformers to generate countervailing pressures against white southerners, but the most basic reason for their success seems to have been the demographic changes that relieved the racial fears of white southerners and enabled them to accept moderation in racial policy. In the five deep South states, to repeat figures already cited, the black population declined from 52.6 percent of the total in 1890 to 29.1 percent in 1970, and in the rest of the Confederate South from 29.4 percent to 16.2 percent. The number of majority black counties, which stood at 261 in 1910, was down to 102 in 1970 and still falling. The massive outmigration of blacks reflected in these figures not only eased the fears of southern whites, but the vast growth of black population in northern states increased the influence of the race in national politics and provided one of the bases of strength for the civil rights movement.

Within the South there were other important population shifts. Urbanization drew people of both races from rural and black belt counties to metropolitan centers and thus from areas especially resistant to racial change to those more tolerant of it. The effects of this shift were increased by a series of Supreme Court decisions, including *Baker v. Carr* (1962) and *Reynolds v. Sims* (1964), that mandated equal representation by population in all elective political bodies (except the United States Senate). As a result, large numbers of state legislative seats were transferred from rural and black belt counties to urban and suburban areas, and with them went the locus of political power within the states. In the new centers of power, black influence was often great by the 1960s because of numbers as well as organization and the ease of political participation. Thus in Atlanta, where blacks were quite active politically, the population was 51 percent black in 1970, while in Georgia as a whole, in some parts of which black activism was low, the proportion was only 27 percent. In Richmond (42 percent black), Birmingham (42 percent), New Orleans (45 percent), and other large cities a similar pattern prevailed. Moreover, most urban centers now contained large numbers of whites who had moved into the South from other parts of the country since 1945 and whose racial awareness was not conditioned by the section's historical experience.

There were still other factors encouraging moderation and flexibility. The Cold War and the rise of the nonwhite world created a situation in which the Soviet Union could exploit racial discrimination in the United States for international political purposes. This embarrassed southerners as well as the federal government, and was one factor in the government's increasing support of the civil rights movement. Still another factor was the moderation of that movement. Only in the narrow perspective of absolute white supremacy did the movement seem radical, for its methods and purposes were squarely in line with those professed, if not always practiced, by the nation. This not only made possible its legal and political successes but enabled charismatic leaders like Martin Luther King to win a hearing in the national media and in so doing arouse the nation's conscience and educate whites on the real meaning of white supremacy.

By the 1950s the countervailing relationship between black protest and white supremacy was sufficiently balanced to accelerate the slowly building process of pressure and counterpressure. When desegregation began in the middle of the decade, it did so in isolated, token instances in the border South and spread haltingly into the upper South before making its first spasmodic intrusions into the deep South. At first it involved only public schools, but it was gradually extended to public accommodations, voting rights, and other areas of public life. The growing role of the federal government followed the same gradualist pattern, as did, in reverse, the declining effectiveness of white resistance. The result was a classic example of steady but gradual social change, rapid enough to sustain the determination of blacks but sufficiently slow to give white supremacists time to accommodate to each new acceleration even as they shouted "never."

Since the pressures for change were unrelenting, the delaying tactics ultimately had a positive effect, not only serving as a catharsis for white supremacists, a safety valve that channeled their frustrations into what they regarded as constructive activity even as they succumbed to desegregation, but also, when the process was over and they had lost, providing a rationalization for accepting the new racial order. Having waged a determined fight and lost, white supremacists were able to console themselves that they had done all they could honorably do, only to be overwhelmed by the might of the federal government. What prevented their defeat from being turned into a new Lost Cause was the absence of the kind of acute racial fears that had existed after the Civil War. The demographic changes since 1890 enabled them to see, after desegregation began to spread across the section, that the change did not threaten the substance but only the form of white supremacy. They also saw, and soon, that the most objectionable features of desegregation could be neutralized by resegregation. The process of desegregation was far uglier than this might suggest, was in fact often punctuated by violence, intimidation, and displays of meanness and bigotry, and was sustained not by white moderation so much as black determination and federal power. But granting that, it was still less painful and more successful than any other movement for racial reform in the section's history. If racial discrimination was still an important fact of southern life in 1977, as it was, the improvements since 1945 were nevertheless phenomenal, and if white southerners deserved much of the blame for the continued discrimination, they merited some of the credit for the progress that had been made.

Civil Rights: Action and Reaction

The civil rights movement grew out of the political and legal advances of the New Deal era. By 1947 those advances were sufficient to encourage President Harry S. Truman to appoint a Committee on Civil Rights to study the problem of racial discrimination and recommend measures for improving the status of blacks. Among the Committee's fifteen members were two southerners, both whites, Frank P. Graham, then president of the University of North Carolina, and Mrs. M. E. Tilly, an Atlanta civic leader. Both Graham and Mrs. Tilly endorsed the Committee's landmark report, *To Secure These Rights* (1948), which offered a bold challenge to segregation and disfranchisement. "A law which forbids a group of American citizens to associate with other citizens in the ordinary course of daily living," it read, "creates inequality by imposing a caste status on the minority group." In line with this view, the Committee made a long list of recommendations that became the platform of the civil rights movement for the next decade and a half. The Committee recommended that federal laws be enacted to abolish segregation in the armed services, public schools, and public accommodations, including housing, that poll taxes and racial discrimination in voting be outlawed, that lynching be made a federal crime, that federal funds be denied any public or private agency practicing racial discrimination, and that the Fair Employment Practices Committee be reestablished on a permanent basis.

Despite the political risk involved, Truman made these recommendations the basis of his own civil rights program. In 1948 he issued an executive order abolishing segregation in the armed forces and other federal agencies, and asked Congress to reestablish the FEPC, abolish poll taxes, make lynching a federal crime, and prohibit segregation in interstate transportation. White southerners denounced these proposals, and some of them staged an abortive political revolt against Truman's election that year. Despite the failure of this "Dixiecrat" movement, which is discussed below, Truman's recommendations had little impact outside the military services. Congress refused to enact any of his program, and even desegregation of the armed forces took several years to complete. Beginning with the Korean War (1950–53), however, military service introduced large numbers of southerners of both races to desegregated living, and the experience was thus an important step toward breaking down racial barriers in the larger society.

Stymied in Congress, civil rights advocates turned to the courts. Appointments by Roosevelt and Truman had given the Supreme Court a liberal majority for the first time in its history, and the prospects for desegregation cases were thus brighter than ever before. By 1948 black leaders had come to agree that Jim Crow public education was the keystone in the arch of segregation, and if challenged successfully might collapse the entire structure of legalized white supremacy. In *Gaines v. Canada* (1938) and a series of subsequent decisions involving higher education, the Supreme Court had begun looking beyond the letter of the law and into the actual condition of segregated facilities, and as a result was admitting black students to white graduate and professional schools wherever the schools provided the race were demonstrably inferior (or sometimes nonexistent). To prevent this principle from being extended to public schools, white officials in every state had undertaken a belated but substantial effort to improve black schools and make them more nearly equal to those provided whites. Between 1940 and 1952 annual per pupil expenditures for blacks in the greater South increased from $21.54 to $115.08 and from 43 percent of that spent on each white pupil to 70 percent and continued to rise thereafter.

The effort was too late, however. Once, blacks might have accepted separate but equal schools, but now they had become convinced that public school desegregation was the first step toward racial equality. The improvement of black schools thus only encouraged blacks to insist upon desegregation. Under NAACP auspices a number of cases were filed in the federal courts before 1950 challenging the assignment of black pupils to segregated schools on grounds not only that the schools were physically inferior to those of whites but that segregation itself deprived black pupils of equal educational opportunity. The Supreme Court agreed to hear five of the cases, and thus to review the constitutional issue of state-imposed segregation. Its decision was finally announced on May 17, 1954, though implementation was delayed another year as the justices heard arguments on how best to accomplish the difficult task of desegregation.

The decision is known, ironically, by the name of a case from Kansas, where school segregation was permitted by local option; but *Brown v. Board of Education of Topeka* had its chief impact in the South. It was, in fact, the most important judicial ruling in the South's history. Unlike such other landmark decisions as *Plessy v. Ferguson* (1896) and *Dred Scott v. Sandford* (1857), the *Brown* ruling did not affirm prevailing attitudes or practices, but dictated a revolutionary change in social relationships that were at the heart of southern life. "Does segregation of children in public schools solely on the basis of race, even though the physical facilities and other 'tangible' factors may be equal, deprive the children of the minority group of equal educational opportunities?" the Court asked. The answer was forthright: "We believe that it does." To segregate black pupils "from others of similar age and qualifications solely because of their race generates a feeling of inferiority as to their status in the community that may affect their hearts and minds in a way unlikely ever to be undone." Thus "separate educational facilities are inherently unequal" and a violation of Fourteenth Amendment guarantees of equal protection of the laws.

The implications of this for all forms of legalized segregation were obvious and far-reaching. The Court had set aside *Plessy v. Ferguson* and the long list of subsequent rulings buttressing the separate-but-equal principle, and thus removed the constitutional authority for *de jure* separation of the races in all areas of public life. The changes this mandated were too sweeping to be achieved at once; so in 1955 the Court ruled that school desegregation could be accomplished "with all deliberate speed" over what amounted to an indefinite period of time. The latter ruling was unprecedented, for it provided in effect that certain constitutional rights could be denied blacks while whites wrestled with the problem of social change. But the transition period this permitted eventually proved to be a key to the relative orderliness of the desegregation process.

The immediate response to the *Brown* decision was relatively restrained. Apparently whites expected it to have no more practical impact than earlier equalitarian pronouncements from Washington, such as Franklin D. Roosevelt's executive order prohibiting discrimination in defense industries in 1941. As its meaning sank in, however, a pronounced turn toward adamancy became evident. As early as the fall of 1956 a pattern of black action and white reaction emerged, and it continued until white resistance was broken. Blacks in a given locale would organize a "movement" and petition for desegregation of schools and sometimes for the end of discrimination in other areas of public life, and for creation of an interracial committee to handle local problems. Whites invariably rejected these overtures, and used their political and economic power to neutralize the black effort that lay behind them. They also organized counter movements of their own. As early as 1955 white Citizens Councils and other groups began appearing, especially in the deep South, and here and there the Ku Klux Klan was revived. Through intimidation, economic pressure, and sometimes violence these groups counteracted the immediate threat to white supremacy and effectively cut blacks off from the usual avenues of political redress. Only occasionally did blacks have any success in the first years of the movement. Their first important breakthrough came in Montgomery, Alabama, where in 1955–56 a boycott of the city bus system demonstrated the effectiveness—as well as the difficulties—of united direct action. It also raised to prominence the most important leader the civil rights movement produced, Martin Luther King. A man of extraordinary charisma and eloquence, King better than anyone else articulated the hopes of black southerners and touched the conscience of whites. From then until his untimely death by assassination in 1968, he and his organization, the Southern Christian Leadership Conference, were catalysts for many of the most important breakthroughs in the movement toward desegregation and black equality.

As white resistance stiffened, racial tensions rose. When the federal courts ordered token school desegregation at scattered points in the border states and upper South in the fall of 1956, segregationists protested the orders and sometimes staged confrontations to prevent their implementation. The result was violence in Clinton and Nashville, Tennessee, Sturgis, Kentucky, and other places. A year later Governor Orval E. Faubus of Arkansas precipitated a major crisis when he used the state's police power to prevent token desegregation at Central High School in Little Rock. His action forced a reluctant federal government to use the national guard to enforce the orders of a federal court, and the aftermath was a long period of turmoil and heightened racial tension.

Faubus's failure to prevent desegregation at Central High School did not deter other segregationists, however, and similar though usually less serious incidents occurred elsewhere during the next several years. Violence flared sporadically, though it was never the principle instrument of segregationsits. Between 1955 and 1960, according to figures compiled by the Southern Regional Council, six people, all blacks, were killed in race-related violence in the South, a figure that contrasts notably with the ninety-seven killed in the riotous years from 1963 to 1968. Overt violence was always less important than political and economic power and the use of law enforcement agencies as weapons of intimidation. Thus confronted with the full resources of the white South and without meaningful assistance from the federal government, blacks found themselves unable to realize the promise of the *Brown* decision. In 1955 in Orangeburg, South Carolina, to illustrate, fifty-seven black parents petitioned the school board to assign their children to desegregated schools. White Orangeburgers were "stunned" by the action, which they declared to be a breach of the community's long-standing interracial harmony, and used economic and other pressures to force most of the signers to withdraw from the petition. So successful were they that the schools in Orangeburg were not desegregated for almost a decade.

Meanwhile, segregationists were also active in Congress, using their seniority and influence to neutralize the threat of federal action in behalf of blacks. In March 1956, 101 of the 128 members of Congress from the Confederate South signed a "Southern Manifesto" denouncing the *Brown* decision on constitutional grounds and urging the states to "resist forced integration by any lawful means." The idea for the Manifesto originated with J. Strom Thurmond, who as governor of

South Carolina led the Dixiecrat political revolt in 1948 and was now a senator from the palmetto state. The Manifesto was without legal standing, but it served to encourage resistance within the South. Even in Congress, however, the influence of extreme segregationists was eroding, and in 1957 and 1960 federal civil rights laws were enacted for the first time since Radical Reconstruction. The laws were too weak to have any immediate effect on the pace of desegregation, but they established a civil rights division in the Department of Justice, enlarged federal jurisdiction in the area of civil rights, and created a federal Civil Rights Commission to investigate racial discrimination and make recommendations for corrective legislation to Congress.

Such modest gains on the national level were no match for the vigorous actions by white supremacists in state and local governments. According to one count, state legislatures in the Confederate South enacted 450 prosegregation measures in the years immediately following the *Brown* decision. In general, those measures made desegregation (and most of the devices blacks were using to attain it) illegal, and erected elaborate new defenses for segregation. For a time every state in the section committed itself more or less to what Virginia Senator Harry F. Byrd called "massive resistance," total opposition to desegregation in any form, especially in the public schools. The maintenance of segregation was elevated above all other public policies, including education itself. Following Byrd's advice the Virginia legislature abolished the state's compulsory school attendance law, enacted a pupil assignment plan, voted to withhold funds from any school ordered to desegregate, and authorized tuition grants to students whose schools were closed as a result of a desegregation order. In line with these policies, the public schools of Prince Edward County, one of the five systems specifically involved in the *Brown* cases, were closed for five years, and reopened only when the state was ordered to do so by the federal courts.

In justifying their actions, segregationists reached back to the constitutional theories of John C. Calhoun and Thomas Jefferson. Editor James J. Kilpatrick of the Richmond *News Leader* revived the antebellum theory of interposition, according to which each state had a right to protect its citizens by interposing its sovereignty between them and the federal government whenever the federal government acted unconstitutionally. The legislatures of Virginia and the five deep South states passed resolutions asserting that right. "The Constitution ... was formed by the sanction of the several states, given by each in its sovereign capacity," resolved Alabama legislators, who also resolved that "the decisions and orders of the Supreme Court of the United States relating to separation of the races in the public schools are as a matter of right, null, void, and of no effect" and that "as a matter of right this State is not bound to abide thereby."

Civil Rights: Black Liberation

Interposition was a legal frivolity, but the political power behind it had blunted the civil rights movement. In the fall of 1960, less than two-tenths of 1 percent of all black pupils in public school in the Confederate South were enrolled in schools with whites, and other areas of life were hardly more desegregated. At such a pace it would take several hundred years to complete the process of desegregation.

With conventional avenues of reform thus rendered ineffectual, blacks turned to direct action and civil disobedience. The first incident occurred in February 1960 when four students from North Carolina Agricultural and Technical College staged a "sit-in" at a segregated lunch counter in a Greensboro department store and remained after being refused service and ordered to leave. Their arrest made them heroes as well as examples, and sit-ins were soon occurring all across the South, often involving large numbers of demonstrators protesting segregation not only at department store lunch counters but at public parks, beaches, and hospitals, on public transportation, in hotels, restaurants, and even churches and cemeteries. This represented a significant escalation of black activism. Its object was to desegregate entire communities rather than specific institutions and eliminate discrimination in employment, voting, and law enforcement and public accommodations, and to do so by direct, insistent action. The initial response of whites was adamant opposition and escalations of their own. Large numbers of blacks were arrested, convicted, and fined, and some of them imprisoned, and many of those in and out of jail were subjected to varying degrees of brutality. The cost to individuals was sometimes great, but persistence and numbers, plus growing federal involvement and the economic cost to recalcitrant businesses and communities, soon produced widespread desegregation.

The process was sobering for both races. Tensions rose again in the short run and violence increased, but the campaigns revealed the vulnerability of segregation to concerted black activism. The effort produced a new unity and sense of purpose among blacks, and showed the race to whites in a new and uncompromising light. The results were educational in the most fundamental sense of the term. White leaders —political, business, religious, civic—were forced to deal with blacks for the first time as something other than supplicants, and in the process they came to see the real meaning of segregation and the inequities it forced upon blacks. In countless local communities this lesson was learned, and its larger meaning was reinforced by massive demonstrations in selected cities, many of them organized and led by Martin Luther King. In one such incident in the spring of 1963, police in Birmingham, Alabama, used dogs, high-powered fire hoses, and other brutal devices against massed demonstrators, many of them school children. Films of this shown on national television generated widespread revulsion against segregationists, as did the arrest of King, the apostle of nonviolence. King's eloquent yet impassioned "Letter from a Birmingham Jail" turned the revulsion into sympathy for the black cause. In the summer of the same year, every major element of the black movement joined in a march on Washington, and staged there perhaps the largest demonstration in the nation's history, the highlight of which was King's most compelling address, "I Have a Dream." Two years later, in the spring of 1965, the movement crested in another march organized by King and the Southern Christian Leadership Conference from Selma to Montgomery, Alabama.

The results of the new activism were by this time apparent. The pace of school desegregation quickened, and in the fall of 1965, 6.1 percent of all black pupils in the South were in school with whites. More importantly, the demonstrations had forced the federal government to take a positive role in the struggle for racial equality. President Lyndon B. Johnson (1963–69), ironically the first southerner in the White House in a century, committed the government at last to the kind of affirmative policies necessary to end overt discrimination and help blacks overcome the heritage of discrimination. Once this occurred, the government's enormous power and economic resources were used to promote equality rather than tolerate inequality, and the segregationists' control of racial policy was soon broken.

Two key weapons in the effort were the Civil Rights Acts of 1964 and 1965, both of which Congress passed over strenuous objections from southerners. In fact the 1964 act was passed after the Senate for the first time in its history voted cloture against a southern filibuster, an action that signaled the loss of what had been one of the section's most effective defenses. The 1964 act was a public accommodations law that declared segregation in public places to be illegal, and vigorous enforcement soon eliminated *de jure* and most *de facto* segregation. The law also prohibited discrimination in employment, and gave the government several important devices for promoting equality by affirmative action. It empowered officials to withhold federal funds from any agency, business, or institution practicing racial discrimination, and to file suit in federal court against anyone (individual or organization) engaging in segregation or discrimination. It also created a federal agency to assist local communities in solving the problems of desegregating themselves.

The 1965 Civil Rights Act dealt chiefly with voting rights, and eliminated the considerable obstacles that still remained to black registration and political participation. It authorized the appointment of federal registrars and election observers wherever less than half the voting-age population was registered, and prohibited the use of extraneous qualifications and complicated registration procedures. All or parts of seven states were affected by the law—Virginia, North Carolina, South Carolina, Georgia, Alabama, Mississippi, and Louisiana—and its vigorous implementation brought an end to the long history of disfranchisement. This was a major achievement. The number of blacks registered to vote in the Confederate South had been increasing for a long time, but only slowly. From 150,000 in 1940 the total rose to 1,400,000 in 1960, but the latter figure still represented only 28 percent of those of voting age. Registration remained difficult in rural and black belt areas in the deep South, and elimination of the poll tax between 1962 and 1966 had had only limited effect. In Mississippi, for example, a prospective voter in 1965 had to meet the longest residency requirement in the nation, pay the highest poll tax, and survive the most complicated registration procedure. He could pay his poll tax only between December 1 and February 1 and only to the county sheriff, an official the black Mississippian generally preferred to avoid. After bringing himself to the sheriff's attention by paying his poll tax, the prospective voter had to seek out the registrar of voters who was also clerk of the county court and an elected official who often ran for office by boasting of his effectiveness in keeping blacks off the voting lists. After proving to the clerk he had paid the poll tax (the sheriff did not notify the clerk), he had then to pass a literacy test, demonstrate "a reasonable understanding of the duties and obligations of citizenship," and establish his "good character" by having his name published for two consecutive weeks in a local newspaper. During that two-week period other registered voters could challenge his fitness to vote by filing an affadavit with the registrar. If he survived all these requirements, he had to return to the registrar's office to ask whether his application was approved, for he was not otherwise notified of its disposition.

The impact of the voting act was soon apparent. By 1970 the number of blacks registered to vote had reached 3.3 million, a figure equal to two-thirds of those of voting age and 17 percent of all registered voters in the section. White registration had risen even more rapidly, however, as whites acted to counteract the rise of black political influence. Altogether in the 1960s, about 6 million names were added to voting lists in the section, 70 percent of them whites. Most of the new white registrants were of relatively low economic status, and their return to politics was also a notable event.

Civil Rights: Ambiguous Outcome

With the dramatic rise in their voting strength, blacks began to play an expanding role in elective politics. In 1967 only 72 members of the race held elective office in the Confederate South, but by 1971 the number had risen to 711, and by 1974 to 1,179. The latter figure was still less than 2 percent of all elective offices in the section, but it reflected a rapidly changing situation that promised to continue to improve. Every election year saw significant increases in the numbers of black candidates and winners, and in the importance of the offices they held. In 1972 Andrew Young and Barbara C. Jordan were elected to Congress from Atlanta and Houston respectively, and the following year Maynard Jackson was elected mayor of Atlanta. Victories at such levels were still rare, but altogether in 1974 there were forty-six black mayors and a few dozen black legislators in the South, and the governments of five black belt counties were more or less completely controlled by the race.

More important than this was the moderating influence the large black electorate had on white officeholders and politics generally. By 1970 the black vote was a significant element in the politics of every state, and its importance continued to grow as the Republican party's strength rose and in effect split the white vote. A lengthening list of white officeholders owed their election to black voters. In 1970, to illustrate, blacks supplied the margin of victory for Governor John C. West of South Carolina, Senators Lawton Chiles of Florida and Lloyd M. Bentzen of Texas, and Mayor Moon Landrieu of New Orleans, and their votes had become crucial for Democratic presidential candidates.

These changes were paralleled by the final triumph of desegregation. In the fall of 1971 the last dual school districts were abolished, and technically the educational system was completely desegregated. That year 90.8 percent of all black pupils were enrolled in interracial schools. Yet here as elsewhere the result was curiously ambiguous. Even as blacks made significant gains in politics and socioeconomic conditions, the consequence of desegregation in public schools and many other areas of public life proved to be not integration but growing resegregation without benefit of law. Wherever the proportion of black pupils in desegregated schools surpassed one in four or one in three, white parents began withdrawing their children and organizing private schools, or moving to largely white suburban areas whose public schools had few black students because of residential segregation.

This trend appeared in large cities as well as the black belt. When desegregation began in Atlanta in 1961, for example, the public school population was 62 percent white, but by 1975 it was only 12.9 percent white. In New Orleans, Memphis, and Dallas a similar though less drastic shift occurred, and in those cities in 1975 more than three-quarters of all black pupils were in schools with student bodies more than 90 percent black. In the section as a whole after desegregation was completed, in 1972–73, only 46.3 percent of all black students were attending majority white schools, a figure that seems impressive only when compared with that for the rest of the country, which was 28.3 percent. But even that figure was deceiving, for the "tracking" of students according to scores on achievement tests often produced considerable resegregation within ostensibly desegregated schools.

Desegregation thus had little impact on what now emerged as the section's most obvious educational problem, racial differences in school achievement. Whether in or out of desegregated schools, black pupils tended to perform less well than whites, and the lag in their performance tended to increase with grade level. This racial disparity had always existed, as sociologist James S. Coleman documented in his massive study *Equality of Educational Opportunity* (1965), but desegregation made it a more pressing concern for both races but especially whites. Only when it was eliminated would it be possible to speak of equal educational opportunity. Its persistence was a signal failure of the educational system, and the failure of educators to solve the problem encouraged others to try. One such effort was "busing," the transportation of pupils across neighborhood or school district lines for the purpose of achieving racial (and also, hopefully, achievement) balance. The researches of Coleman and other social scientists suggested that the integration of students by achievement levels tends to raise the performance of low achievers. Aside from family background, they found, the most important environmental influence on the student's performance was his or her fellow students.

Thus placing low achievers in the midst of high achievers would hopefully have positive results. After desegregation was completed in 1971–72, busing became the most impassioned racial issue in the section. Wherever it was imposed, always by a federal court order, it aroused heated and often organized opposition among most whites and some blacks. Though racial factors were clearly the chief reason for the opposition, busing could be and often was opposed on the grounds that it violated the concept of neighborhood schools and thus of local self-government. It was therefore a convenient target for covert segregationists, whose attacks were aided by its dubious educational results. Its future use was therefore problematical. The controversies it generated were symptomatic of a larger fact: in 1977 the South's most important educational problem was the same as it had been in 1954, unequal opportunities for blacks. The desegregation struggle had changed the form but not the substance of the basic problem.

Much the same could be said of race relations in general. The legal and institutional props of discrimination had been removed by 1977, and insofar as the law could require it, the South was an equalitarian society. Yet racial inequities remained, and though some of them promised to diminish with time, others defied apparent solution. Desegregation had been achieved; genuine integration remained elusive.

Yet there were grounds for hope. The progress of blacks was continuing and promised to have accumulating effects, while white racial attitudes had changed remarkably. It was too much to say in 1977 that white southerners had become committed to racial equality or even reconciled to desegregation, but they no longer thought as they had in 1945. If public opinion polls are to be trusted, whites had come to tolerate desegregation, at least in public places and relationships not intimately social. In 1942 a Gallup poll had found them virtually unanimous (98 percent) in their endorsement of segregated schools, but in 1973 only 16 percent said they would object to their children attending school with "a few" blacks. However, if the school were half black, 36 percent of them objected, and if majority black, 69 percent. Significantly, these percentages were not much different from those of whites in the rest of the country—6 percent, 27 percent, and 63 percent respectively. Another measure of regional distinctiveness was disappearing.

The process by which this moderation occurred has not been studied systematically, and its dynamics are unclear. Part of the change was due to desegregation itself and the grudging respect blacks won for themselves in the long struggle for equality. Part of it was also due to the moderate goals of the black struggle, goals whites themselves had always admired. In 1945, to illustrate, 61 percent of white southerners had answered affirmatively when asked in a public opinion poll, "Are all men created equal?" But when asked later in the same interview, "Are Negroes equal to whites?" only 4 percent answered yes. Both responses would seem to be important. If the one reflected the depth of racist feelings, the other evinced a potential for tolerance and equality that might be put to positive use. This potential was encouraged after 1954 by opinion molders—religious spokesmen, the daily press, political and business leaders—the vast majority of whom eventually became voices of moderation. The growing appeal of liberal ideas was also important, for during the desegregation campaign southern liberals became generally committed to racial equality. At the same time, traditionalists quit talking of segregation and white supremacy, at least in public discourse, and spoke instead of such things as local rights, law and order, and "welfare chiselers."

But there were other less positive factors that were also important in moderating white opinion. The most important of these was the discovery that desegregation did not mean the end of white supremacy. Blacks were, after all, a minority of the population, and politics and the economy were firmly controlled by whites. Realization of this fact was perhaps the essential step in the acceptance of desegregation, for it signaled the muting of white racial fears. Whites discovered that they could give up the form of absolute segregation because the substance of white supremacy was unthreatened. They could, in effect, do what white northerners had always done. The result was a new flexibility that included much talk about the achievement of racial equality and of the South being better able to solve its racial problems than the rest of the country. "We have integrated our state, and we are proud of it, not because it is the law but because it is the American way," boasted Governor John J. McKeithen of Louisiana in the early 1970s. "The time for racial discrimination is over," echoed Georgia Governor Jimmy Carter.

Blacks too were affected by the undeniable progress toward moderation. "The South holds greater promise than any other region," declared state Senator Julian Bond of Georgia, a rising leader who urged northern blacks to return to the South. "Black Southerners can see, for the first time since the 1870s, some darkness at the end of the long white tunnel," added author Lerone Bennet, a Mississippian who had migrated to Illinois and who was no pollyanna on racial conditions in the South. The success of the racial movement rekindled the feelings blacks had always had for the South, enabling them better to see its positive attributes, and since the change came just as the urban crisis emerged in the North, it caused some of them to question the preferability of other parts of the country. The South was always "down home" to many of those who had left it, and now it seemed to improve as the rest of the country grew worse. When this occurred, out-migration slackened, and the movement away from the section showed signs of reversing itself. Between 1970 and 1974, the Census Bureau reported recently, the number of blacks who left the Census South was smaller than the number who entered. The figures are not large, 241,000 to 276,000, and the change is too brief to be considered permanent, but it is a fitting commentary on the "Second Reconstruction" and the changes it produced in the South.

It is also a development pregnant with implications for the future of the South.

Political Transition

In the years after World War II, southern politics was preoccupied with economic growth, social improvement, and race relations, three issues that had curiously contradictory tendencies.[4] The effort to attract industry, federal spending, and other sources of development pulled the section toward the nation, as did the effort to promote social progress; but growing racial anxieties intensified sectional consciousness. In the 1940s and 1950s, politicians outdid each other with promises of new schools, more jobs, and improved social services, as well as pledges to preserve segregation and resist outside interference in the southern way of life. Their programs constituted a kind of latter-day business Progressivism entwined with absolute white supremacy—the old promise of economic growth without undesirable social change. The voice of the section became alternately that of the economic booster and the diehard segregationist, the one confident and eager for certain kinds of change, the other fearful and insistent upon certain kinds of continuity.

Southern politics was controlled by individuals and groups committed in varying degrees to these conflicting purposes, and the increasing importance of government gave politicians a new significance. The effort to achieve conflicting purposes tended to pull politics and business together while pushing politicians toward racial extremism. Both tendencies had fateful consequences, though the latter was by far the more obvious development. "The basic fact about the new southern politics," wrote Donald R. Matthews and James W. Prothro in 1966, "is that most southern Negroes desperately want something that most southern whites are adamantly unwilling to give—equality." That was especially true of the generation before 1966, and the result had been to make politicians more rigid than other white southerners on matters of racial policy. In election contests in which everyone was a white supremacist, victory often went to the candidate who promised the most literal commitment to white supremacy. Perhaps the most spectacular result of this was Governor George C. Wallace's famous stand in the schoolhouse door in a vain attempt to prevent desegregation at the University of Alabama, but more important was the fact that it made elected officials major obstacles to orderly racial change. It encouraged them to cultivate the racial fears of their constituents, pander to their prejudices, and lead them to believe that sheer determination would neutralize every threat to segregation. Not surprisingly, every important development in southern politics between 1945 and 1977 grew directly or indirectly from the politics of race—the growing alienation between whites and the national Democratic party, the rise of the Republican party, the disintegration of the Solid South, the emergence of the blacks, and many of the chronic controversies with the federal government, and most recently the transition to moderation.

As this list suggests, the white South fought a losing, rear-guard action. By 1970 every one of its traditional political defenses had been breached. The white primary and the poll tax had been eliminated, the disfranchisement of blacks ended, the unity in dealing with outsiders lost. Southern influence in the Democratic party had been eclipsed and the hold over Congress broken. Within the South, the dominance by the black belt had been ended, and the power of local oligarchies diminished. In short, southern politics had undergone a revolution in form as well as substance. The electorate had become larger and more active, politics more representative of all the people, and government more responsive to social needs. Even demagoguery had become more like that in the rest of the country. The patterns molded in Reconstruction were thus broken, and in politics as other things the South moved toward the nation.

The Politics of White Supremacy

President Truman's message to Congress on civil rights in 1948 placed white southerners in a political dilemma. In preparation for the presidential election of that year, Truman was tilting the Democratic party toward racial and economic liberalism, and thus toward its liberal and northern wings at the expense of southern conservatives. Yet in 1948 as in 1928, solidarity within the Democratic party and the seniority this produced in Congress were still the most effective weapons in dealing with outsiders, and since no alternative weapons suggested themselves, Truman's action was doubly threatening. If the Democratic party could disregard the white South on this most vital of all issues, the future would be difficult indeed. Theoretically at least, defection to the Republican party was the most logical alternative. Southern conservatives, especially those in Congress, had been generally pleased with the record of the Republican-controlled Eightieth Congress (1947-49), had in fact formed a voting coalition with conservative Republicans to defeat Truman's social and economic programs as well as his civil rights proposals. Inherited antipathies to the Republican party were still great, however, and the party's presidential candidate that year,

Governor Thomas E. Dewey of New York, seemed too much an "eastern liberal."

A second alternative was withdrawal into a third party. This had several potential advantages. It might insure Truman's defeat and thereby demonstrate to Truman and party liberals that the South was essential to Democratic victory. Barring that, it might deny an electoral majority to both Truman and Dewey and thus throw the election into the House of Representatives, where a united South might be in a position to determine the winner and thus to exact concessions from him. To most southerners, however, still loyal Democrats, this seemed farfetched, and they decided to voice their protest from within the party of their fathers.

The result was divided counsel and hesitation and, ultimately, ineffectuality. When the Democratic national convention adopted a relatively liberal civil rights platform incorporating the proposals Truman had made to Congress, all the Mississippi and part of the Alabama delegation walked out in protest. The other southerners remained, however, and registered their protest by supporting Senator Richard B. Russell of Georgia as the party's presidential nominee. Truman easily won the nomination, and when that occurred, a third party movement developed in the deep South. Shortly after the national convention ended, those who most resented its actions held a convention of their own in Birmingham, Alabama, where they formed the States Rights party, familiarly known as the Dixiecrats, and nominated Governors J. Strom Thurmond of South Carolina and Fielding J. Wright of Mississippi for the presidency and vice-presidency.

This effort too was unsuccessful. Thurmond carried only four states—South Carolina, Alabama, Mississippi, and Louisiana—and in those states he rather than Truman was listed on the ballot as the official Democratic candidate. His 39 electoral votes were not enough to influence the outcome of the election. Truman's gamble had paid off; he had flouted the South on the racial issue and won. His victory and Thurmond's poor showing had dramatized the disunity among the southerners. To be sure, the disunity was due in part to the fact that Truman's civil rights program had had no real impact in the section, had in fact presented southerners with a theory rather than a condition. But the failure of the Dixiecrats signaled the inability of the deep South and the peripheral South to pull together in national politics. Even during the height of the desegregation controversies after 1954, southerners never united behind a single political strategy. Even Governor Wallace of Alabama, a much more effective campaigner than Thurmond, carried only five states as the presidential candidate of the American Independent party in the election of 1968.

The disunity revealed in 1948 suggested that white southerners needed to rethink their political strategies and regroup around a generally acceptable (and therefore moderate) consensus. But that of course was the very thing disunity made impossible. The growing economic and social pluralism in the section, plus the relaxing of racial fears in the wake of population shifts, was fragmenting the white South in ways that precluded the traditional kind of unity, even on racial matters. If whites still agreed that white supremacy was desirable and even necessary and local control of race policy was essential, they were divided by the varying intensity of their convictions and could not agree on how best to accomplish their purposes. There were major differences not only between the deep South and the peripheral South but between areas of high and low concentrations of blacks, between dynamic metropolitan centers and the relatively stagnant black belt, and between affluent whites insulated from the effects of desegregation and the relatively poor who bore the brunt of racial change. And after black voting became important, there was an additional division between those whites who would make at least a minimal accommodation to the interests of black voters and those who made no accommodation at all. Out of these several divisions emerged three groupings: those who remained in the Democratic party, those who turned to the Republicans, and those who from time to time sought a third party of their own.

These groupings were less apparent or important before 1960 than afterwards, and for a while in the 1950s the reaction against the *Brown* decision almost obscured them completely. For several years following that decision, the political pendulum swung toward extremism and unity. Hardline opponents of desegregation emerged across the section, especially in the deep South—men like Orval E. Faubus, who served six terms as governor of Arkansas between 1954 and 1966; John Patterson, the man who "out-niggered" George C. Wallace to win the Alabama governorship in 1958; Governors Marvin Griffin of Georgia and George Bell Timmerman of South Carolina, both of whom served between 1954 and 1958; and the political organization of Senator Harry F. Byrd in Virginia. Yet there was always a countercurrent of moderation, which carried Leroy Collins into the governorship of Florida in 1954 and 1956 and made Earl K. Long governor of Louisiana in 1956. If Collins and Long were not equalitarians by today's standards, they did seek to keep the response to desegregation flexible and within the bounds of the law, and their elections were evidence that the political response to the racial crisis was always mixed.

After 1960 the division among whites led increasing numbers of them to vote Republican, thus deepening the division and eventually spreading the two-party system across the section. The Republican vote first became important on the presidential level and from there trickled down to state and congressional levels. The Dixiecrat movement expired after Thurmond's defeat in 1948, but dissatisfaction with the national Democratic party continued as the party came increasingly under the influence of northern liberals. Inherited antipathy to the Republican party was still strong in the deep South, where the perceived need for white unity was greatest, and for this reason Republicanism made its initial breakthrough in the peripheral South. There, voters were less preoccupied with race and more concerned about economic and social policy, and many of them found the conservative Republicanism of Dwight D. Eisenhower attractive. In the presidential elections of 1952 and 1956, they voted in impressive numbers for Eisenhower, and in 1960 when Eisenhower's Vice-President, Richard M. Nixon, was the Republican nominee, they voted for him too. In each of those elections, the Republicans carried Virginia, Florida, and Tennessee, and in addition Eisenhower won twice in Texas and once in Louisiana (1956). In the entire Confederate South, Eisenhower received 48 percent of the popular vote in 1952 and 49 percent four years later, while Nixon won 46 percent in 1960.

Meanwhile, voters in the deep South remained generally loyal to the Democratic party despite the fact that the party's presidential candidates in those years, Adlai E. Stevenson and John F. Kennedy, were more liberal on racial and other matters than Eisenhower and Nixon. This anomalous situation was due chiefly to political inertia and the desire to maintain white solidarity, but it was encouraged by the fact that the growing resentment against federal race policies had shifted from the Democrats to the Republicans when Eisenhower became President. Chief Justice Earl Warren, the man most responsible for the *Brown* decision, was after all a Republican and an Eisenhower appointee, and it was Eisenhower who used the national guard in Little Rock in 1957 to desegregate Central High School.

John F. Kennedy's victory in the presidential election of 1960 shifted the resentment back to the Democrats. Kennedy and especially his successor Lyndon B. Johnson increased the federal commitment to desegregation and racial equality, and as that occurred, Republican voting strength increased dramatically in the deep South and spread into state and congressional politics. In 1961 John G. Tower became the first Republican elected to the Senate from the Confederate South since Reconstruction, when he won a special election in Texas. After the 1962 elections, however, Republicans still held only one of twenty-two seats in the Senate from the Confederate South, 7 of 103 seats in the House of Representatives, and 75 of 1,789 seats in the state legislatures. In the decade since Eisenhower's impressive showing in 1952, the party had gained only one seat in the Senate, five seats in the House, and twenty-four in the state legislatures.

In the peripheral South, however, the inherited resistance to Republicanism was clearly dissolving, and with the presidential candidacy of Barry M. Goldwater in 1964 the process spread through the deep South as well. Senator Goldwater, from Arizona, voted against the Civil Rights of 1964 and was an outspoken critic of federal activism in social and economic matters as well as racial policy. To segregationists, he was clearly the white man's candidate in the contest against President Johnson. Among white southerners generally, in fact, Goldwater was the most attractive presidential nominee since Franklin D. Roosevelt, and a majority of them voted for the Arizonan in every state except Texas. However, blacks voted almost unanimously for Johnson, and this enabled him to carry the peripheral South. Thus Goldwater won only the five states of the deep South (plus his native Arizona).

Despite the temporary reverses experienced in the peripheral South under Goldwater, Republican strength grew rapidly throughout the section after 1964. Richard M. Nixon, who led the party to presidential victories in 1968 and 1972, developed a southern strategy that included the white South in a coalition of elements he hoped to merge into a new national majority. This new majority was to be conservative and Republican and would, Nixon hoped, displace the liberal Democratic coalition which Franklin D. Roosevelt had put together in the 1930s and which was breaking apart in the 1960s.

Nixon's strategy was more successful in the South than elsewhere. In 1964 the mercurial senator from South Carolina, J. Strom Thurmond, had changed his party affiliation from Democratic to Republican, and thereafter played a major role in pointing southern Republicanism in conservative, Nixonian directions. Two years later Claude R. Kirk was elected governor of Florida, Winthrop Rockefeller became governor of Arkansas, and Howard Baker won a seat in the Senate from Tennessee. The party's strength crested in 1972, when President Nixon carried every state in the section, the first candidate to do so since Franklin D. Roosevelt in 1944. After Nixon's sweep, Republicans held 34 of the section's 108 seats in the House of Representatives and seven of the twenty-two seats in the Senate. All in all, between 1961 and 1975 the party elected at least one governor in six of the eleven states, at least one senator in six of the states, and congressmen from all of them. By the latter year Virginia and Tennessee had become effectively two-party states, and Florida and North Carolina largely so. There were now Republican movements of varying strength in all the states, at least on the state and congressional levels though not always on the local level. As far as presidential politics was concerned, the South was no longer Democratic. In the seven presidential elections between 1948 and 1972, Democrats won only 24.5 of the possible 77 state votes, and no state in the deep South cast an electoral vote for the Democrats in 1964, 1968, or 1972. In 1969 the proportion of southerners who identified themselves as Democrats fell below 50 percent for the first time, and it continued to drop thereafter, though most of the non-Democrats identified themselves as independents. The shift reflected in these figures seems fundamental and therefore likely to endure. In 1976, however, Republican strength in the section ebbed most notably when Jimmy Carter of Georgia was the Democratic presidential candidate. Carter won impressively in the section, carrying every state in the Confederate South except Virginia. In several states, however, his margin of victory was supplied by blacks, and the impact of Carter's presidency on southern politics is not yet clear.

Democrats responded to the Republican challenge after 1959 in a variety of ways. Some of them in the deep South turned to demagoguery and extremism in an ultimately vain attempt to avoid both desegregation and Republicanism. Thus voters in Mississippi elected a succession of extreme governors, all Democrats—Ross Barnett in 1959, Paul Johnson in 1963, and John Bell Williams in 1967—while those in Alabama elected George C. Wallace in 1962 and after his dramatic stand in the schoolhouse door elected his wife Lurleen B. Wallace to succeed him in 1966 because the state constitution prevented his serving two successive terms. In neither of these states did Republicans make much headway on the gubernatorial level in these years. In Georgia, however, they made a serious bid for the governorship in 1966, running conservative businessman Howard H. Calloway against the axe-handle-wielding Democrat, Lester G. Maddox, only to lose when the election was thrown into the Democratic state legislature after neither man won a majority of the popular vote.

The appeal of such men as Maddox, Wallace, and Ross Barnett was especially strong among whites of lower and moderate economic status, whose political role expanded as the voter registration lists grew longer in the 1960s. These voters were often populistic or liberal on economic issues they thought would benefit "the little man," but conservative or reactionary on racial matters and resentful of federal policy toward blacks and welfare recipients. Often outraged by the actions of black militants, student radicals, and activists against the Vietnam War, they wanted more "law and order," less "coddling" of social activists, and less spending on welfare. They also wanted less federal intrusion in local control of racial and social policy and more vigorous assertion of American prerogatives in international affairs. They were, in short, alienated from the liberal consensus that dominated national politics, and their alienation was part of a larger dissatisfaction that reached into all parts of the country and was far broader than the racial concerns that first gave it political coherence in the South. Governor Wallace, elected again in 1970 and 1974, best articulated the fears and hopes of this group, and his considerable appeal in other parts of the country was another evidence of the decline of southern distinctiveness in politics.

The Wallace constituency was one of three major political clusterings that emerged out of the transformations of the 1960s. A second clustering consisted of latter-day business Progressives and other relatively affluent and development-oriented groups, and centered in the peripheral South and suburbia. These groups were more concerned with economic growth and social improvement than race, and to them Wallace's stand on the latter was too rigid just as his stance on economic policy was too populistic. Nor did they share Wallace's concern over federal bureaucrats or the high level of federal spending, which they regarded as essential to continued economic progress. Among the effective spokesmen for this group were such governors as John Connally of Texas, Albertis S. Harrison of Virginia, and Donald S. Russell of South Carolina. The appeal of Nixon Republicanism was strong among this group, though for a variety of reasons most of them remained Democrats while often voting Republican.

The third political clustering that emerged out of the 1960s consisted of groups more attuned to racial and economic liberalism and more at home in the national Democratic party. Among these were blacks and white racial moderates, organized labor, which had some strength in states like Virginia and Texas, and whites of populistic persuasion who were more concerned about economic opportunity than racial separation. In scattered localities other groups were a part of this coalition—Mexican-Americans in southern and western Texas, Jews in Miami, academic liberals in a few university centers.

The existence of these three large but disparate clusterings gave southern politics a new unpredictability by the late 1960s. The clearest evidence of the clusterings came in the presidential election of 1968, when each grouping was represented by a candidate rather closely associated with its views. That year Governor Wallace was the nominee of his own American Independent party, Vice-President Hubert H. Humphrey represented the liberal Democrats, and Republican Richard M. Nixon appealed to economic and social conservatives. The division of the popular vote between these men revealed just how fragmented the southern people had become: Wallace received 34.7 percent of the vote in the Confederate South, Humphrey 31 percent, and Nixon 34.3 percent.

These results were evidence that the South had entered a period of political transition, the outcome of which is not yet apparent. By the mid-1970s, however, certain things were clear. Southern politics had become less concerned with race and more with a broad spectrum of national issues. The two-party system seemed likely to remain, and the section to become better integrated into national politics. The level of political rhetoric was lower than it had been for generations and the quality of government higher. Racial extremism had been renounced, even by veteran officeholders who had once been notable for their rigidities. In his inaugural address in 1962, Governor Wallace had promised "segregation forever" but had subsequently presided over the desegregation of Alabama and did so with unexpectedly good grace. Senators Herman E. Talmadge of Georgia and J. Strom Thurmond of South Carolina had made a similar transition as had other prominent leaders.

Perhaps the most remarkable change was the altered nature of the southern Democratic party. The Dixiecrat mentality largely disappeared, and the party moved toward the political center even in states like Mississippi, where Governors William Winter (elected in 1971) and Cliff Finch (elected in 1975) nudged the party and the state government toward moderation on a broad spectrum of issues, including race. In all the states blacks were brought into the party's organizational activities at all levels, not only because national leaders demanded it but because blacks insisted on it and it was necessary to ward off the Republican challenge. In 1977 state and local governments were still more concerned with neutralizing the hopes than fulfilling the needs of blacks, but they had changed notably in this respect since 1945, and continued to change. Moderates such as Jimmy Carter in Georgia, Dale Bumpers in Arkansas, John C. West in South Carolina, and Reuben Askew in Florida, each of whom served a term as governor in the 1970s, had become more representative of party leadership in the section than old-line white supremacists or economic reactionaries.

The depth as well as the breadth of these changes offered grounds for hope that the advent of racial moderation and responsible government constituted a permanent change in the course of sectional politics. The old extremism had grown out of the unity made possible by fear; the new moderation expressed the disunity and need for compromise made possible by racial and economic confidence. Yet the change is not complete. The fear among whites of black domination has largely disappeared, but its lingering effects have not. White racial feelings are still important and when combined with other resentments and anxieties still offer fertile ground for demagoguery and reaction. The widespread opposition to busing, the impressive showing of Governor

Wallace in the 1972 presidential primaries in Florida, North Carolina, and elsewhere, and the adroit use of "law and order" and other issues with racial overtones all evidence the tenuousness of the new moderation. Major political differences still remain between whites and blacks, and political contests still have racial dimensions. But by 1975 southern politics was a far cry from what it had been in 1948, as the election of Jimmy Carter to the presidency dramatized. The fears of the Dixiecrats expressed a generation ago had come to pass, and the South seemed a better place for that fact.

17

The Enduring South?

By the 1950s the accumulating effects of social change had generated a new—and final?—crisis of sectional identity. The *Brown* decision of 1954 mandated fundamental changes in racial policy, and thus dramatized the precarious position of all the South's distinctive institutions. By then it was clear that economic growth, social improvement, and other consequences of "progress" and Americanization were destroying the South by making it indistinguishable from the rest of the country. Questions the Vanderbilt Agrarians had raised a generation earlier were raised again, and the section's future became the subject of a new round of public discussion. This time, however, the question was not whether the South should welcome "progress," but whether "progress" was destroying the South and, if so, whether that was cause for concern.

    The pluralism previously noted in politics was even more evident in intellectual circles, and there was wide disagreement over these questions. Liberal nationalists were generally pleased with the course of events, for they welcomed Americanization. Conservatives, much more concerned with sectional matters, were alternately alarmed and dismayed. Other groups less easily categorized leaned in one or the other of these directions, and the result was a confusion of voices. Events were rendering discussion irrelevant. The relevant literature recorded the transformation, but no group of latter-day Agrarians appeared to try to stay the course of events. *This Changing South, The Changing South, Change in the Contemporary South, The South in Continuity and Change,* and *The Deep South in Transformation* were illustrative titles published in the two decades after 1954, as were *The Emerging South, The Uncertain South, The Changing Politics of the South, The Disruption of the Solid South,* and *The Americanization of Dixie.*

Some observers were more concerned than others about what was happening to sectional distinctiveness. In 1957 Louis D. Rubin and James J. Kilpatrick brought together a group of conservatives to restate the principles of *The Lasting South,* but even as they did so John T. Westbrook announced the "Twilight of Southern Regionalism" and a year later Harry S. Ashmore published an *Epitaph for Dixie.* "Except for the weather and the scenery there is nothing regional about the Louisiana of present reality. The people of the Baton Rouge vicinity do not differ in any essential way from the natives of Gary, Indiana, or Richmond, California," Westbrook wrote. "The happy truth is that the South has lost its 'regional integrity' " and been transformed into a new land, "growing lustily, a rich South, urban, industrialized, and no longer 'Southern,' but rather northernized, Europeanized, cosmopolitan." Rubin saw much the same thing but found in it less cause for elation. The South is undergoing a "gradual absorption into the mainstream of American history," he wrote in 1964. "Most of the factual data is already in; the larger meaning is and has long since been apparent; the result is foregone. There is nothing that can change it now."

Others were less certain on this point, though few agreed with the irrepressible Francis B. Simkins when he insisted in *The Everlasting South* (1963) that "despite many changes, [the South] is as much different from the rest of the United States today as it was in 1860." Most observers were more apt to agree with the uncertain estimate C. Vann Woodward made in "The Search for Southern Identity" (1958). Change and Americanization have "already leveled many of the old monuments of regional distinctiveness," Woodward noted, "and may end eventually by erasing the very consciousness of a distinctive tradition along with the will to maintain it." This process might be scotched, he hoped, if southerners could keep alive a consciousness of their distinctive historical experience. This, he thought, offered the best hope for preserving the section's identity.

But this was the problem. The consciousness Woodward spoke of could be sustained only by the distinctiveness and sense of grievance that it expressed, and those too were disappearing. The historical experience of southerners was becoming less and less exceptional, and as that occurred, southerners like other Americans became less and less conscious of their past. Who in 1960 or 1970 still read John C. Calhoun or William Gilmore Simms or Thomas Nelson Page? Who any longer knew the resentments of Reconstruction or the legends of the Lost Cause as vital, personal realities? Who was still gripped by the racial and political fears that induced secession, or felt the sense of apartness that nourished the cultural nationalism of the Old South? Who indeed?

And without those things, what would keep the South alive? "Why not plan and act on the principle that what is needed is not a New South but a South that is inextricably and indefinably a part of the entire United States?" asked former Congressman Frank E. Smith of Mississippi, urging southerners to *Look Away from Dixie* (1965). "What purpose is there in the future South's being anything but a large and populous part of the United States?"

What indeed?—except that the nation would lose an important element of pluralism and particularism and southerners a way of life whose best qualities had much to offer in an age of standardization and alienation. The southerner's traditional attachment to locality and family and his sense of history might have helped him and other Americans mitigate the rootlessness and anxieties of mass urban society, just as his conservatism might have braked the headlong rush toward undirected "progress." His traditional sense of community, of class responsibility, and the social obligations of property might have slowed the mindless surrender of all public responsibility to government by reminding his fellow Americans of the dangers of political centralization as well as the limitations of mass institutions, whether public schools or impersonal welfare bureaucracies or others. His respect for tradition and institutions and constitutionalism might have helped limit the growth of government power or at least reduced the likelihood of its abuse. His sense of the tragic might have blunted the excessive optimism of liberals and their exaggerated faith in social reform and the periodic disillusionments this produced. As it was, his personalism and mannerliness did help the South ease aspects of the racial problem that baffled more liberal northern communities. One need not make these redeeming qualities the central features of southern life to appreciate the cost to the nation of its envelopment of the South.

But these things were of little concern. The discussion of Americanization hinged not on them, but on the simpler question of whether the South was or was not disappearing. Those who foresaw the imminent demise of the section based their assessment on the structural changes that had occurred since World War II. They did this because they tended to locate the taproot of southernness in the section's distinctive institutions and to see the destruction of those institutions as a death warrant for the South. Those who were less pessimistic, on the other hand, found the essential expression of southernness not in institutions, but in the sectional mind, that collection of attitudes, values, traditions, hopes, and fears that differentiated southerners from other Americans. While the former group was lamenting or applauding the South's impending disappearance, the latter group was pronouncing the section alive and well and its future only partly clouded. In *The Southerner and World Affairs* (1965), Alfred O. Hero demonstrated the persistence of a distinctive sectional mind despite all the changes of the preceding generation, and John S. Reed reaffirmed the point in *The Enduring South* (1972). Both authors drew heavily upon public opinion polls to support their conclusion, and their works showed conclusively that the kinds of attitudes and values that had traditionally distinguished southerners from nonsoutherners still existed, even if in diminished degree. In the mid-1970s southerners remained not only more concerned than other Americans about racial matters but more committed to fundamental religious beliefs and authoritarian social values, more tolerant of force and violence, more attached to locality, more concerned with personalism and mannerliness. They were also more conscious of a distinctive identity and more defensive about their distinctiveness, somewhat less committed to the values of the work ethic, and less liberal in their voting patterns.

The question, then, was not whether southerners were still distinctive, but what to make of the continued distinctiveness. "There is still a South, a self-conscious and publicly identifiable culture," wrote Samuel S. Hill in 1972, and one would have to agree with him—at least for the time being."The South persists as a coherent collection of assumptions, values, traditions, and commitments." Borrowing sociologist Clifford Geertz's definition of a culture—"an historically transmitted pattern of meanings embodied in symbols, a system of inherited conceptions expressed in symbolic form by means of which men communicate, perpetuate, and develop their knowledge about and attitudes toward life"—Hill concluded that the South was still a recognizable culture, though one whose distinctiveness was increasingly limited to things that defied quantification. Along the same lines, Lewis M. Killian used the sociologists' concept of minority groups to study *White Southerners* (1970), and pronounced them to be a recognizable minority. Other Americans still perceived southerners as a group apart, Killian noted, and singled them out for differential treatment, while southerners in turn regarded themselves as objects of collective discrimination and displayed a minority psychology.

Is the persistence of these differences evidence that the South will endure after all? Or is it merely the kind of lag one expects to find in an interim period between fundamental institutional changes and consequent attitudinal changes? The elemental nature of these questions is best illustrated by rephrasing them. Did the essence of the South consist of its peculiar institutions—such things as white supremacy, racial segregation, one-crop agriculture, plantation economy, one-party politics, cotton mill villages, poverty, illiteracy, isolation, ruralism, and sharecropping? Or did it inhere in the kinds of attitudes Hero and Reed found still existing? Or both? And if both, what was the relationship between the two components and between them together and the specific set of circumstances—demographic, economic, geographical, and otherwise—that gave rise to them? If the South consisted chiefly of the institutions that once distinguished it from the rest of the country, it has already disappeared; but if it was primarily a distinctive set of attitudes, it is still alive, for the institutional changes since 1945 have not yet been paralleled by attitudinal changes of equivalent magnitude.

But clearly both of these things were integral parts of the South, and it is therefore important to understand their relationship to each other and to the basal circumstances out of which they grew. It has been argued implicitly throughout this study that southernness was an ideology extruded by a distinctive way of life which grew in turn from a specific set of circumstances. If that argument is valid, southernness and thus the South cannot long survive the destruction of the way of life—the peculiar institutions—that expressed it and the set of circumstances that produced it. If this is indeed the case, the disappearance of the South as a distinctive cultural entity has already been ordained, and writers who speak hopefully of an enduring South are basing their hope not on fundamental features but on vestigial remains. One does not have to wait for identicalness in the results of public opinion polls in the South and the rest of the nation before acknowledging the section's demise. On the contrary, one would expect regional variations of the sort that distinguish midwesterners or New Englanders from other Americans to endure.

Historians have not yet treated this aspect of southern history in depth. Only one of them, Charles P. Roland, has surveyed the history of the section since 1945, and Roland's informative survey, *The Improbable Era* (1975), documents the process of Americanization while stressing "the paradox of southern continuity in the midst of immense regional change." Much of the continuity it depicts consists of "subtle inner distinctions"—though it was not Roland's purpose to assess systematically the basic question of continuity and Americanization. Any such assessment is likely to be pessimistic, at least for those who hope the South will endure.

The South is and was a sectional rather than a national culture, and is as it has always been especially vulnerable to forces of national standardization. It has no epicenter of its own, no metropolis to define the tastes and values of its people, not even control of its own economy. It has no political instrument to articulate and guard its interests, nor does it have the ethnic or religious unity necessary to sustain a sense of apartness. Its nationalism was never as pronounced as that of French Canadians, Irishmen, Poles, or other peoples who endured long experiences as nations within other nations. The South sprang not from national or cultural or religious oppression and not from a national identity demanding positive expression, but from racial and other fears and the circumstances that generated those fears, and its most characteristic expression was in a sense of grievance. It is not likely to outlast for very long the things that created and sustained its self-consciousness. "The South is just about over as a separate and distinct place," John Egerton wrote in 1975; it is rapidly becoming a history without a country. "The South is going to die," Egerton quotes a Ku Klux Klansman as saying. "That's right: The South isn't going to be anymore. We're going the way of the rest of the country."

Reluctantly, one must agree. What is left of southern history is likely to be largely epilogue. The worst fears of the South's greatest champions have come to pass. Will the best hopes of its most constructive critics soon be realized?

Notes

CHAPTER 1

1 The works quoted in this introductory section, all of them major items in the interpretive literature of the South, are David Smiley, "Quest for the Central Theme of Southern History," *South Atlantic Quarterly,* LXXI (Summer 1972), 307–25; David M. Potter, "The Enigma of the South," *Yale Review,* LI (Autumn 1961), 142–51; Potter, "On Understanding the South," *Journal of Southern History,* XXX (November 1964), 451–62; George B. Tindall, "The Benighted South: Origins of a Modern Image," *Virginia Quarterly Review,* XL (Spring 1964), 281–94 (quoting H. L. Mencken); Louis D. Rubin and James J. Kilpatrick, eds., *The Lasting South* (Chicago, 1957), which includes the quotation by Richard Weaver; Francis B. Simkins, *A History of the South* (New York, 1965); Lerone Bennett, "Old Illusions and the New South," *Ebony,* XXVI (August 1971); and Edgar T. Thompson, ed., *Perspectives on the South* (Durham, 1967).
2 The literature on the problems of writing southern history is large. For insightful discussions see Charles Sydnor, "The Southern Experiment in Writing Social History," *Journal of Southern History,* XI (November 1945), 455–68; David M. Potter, "Depletion and Renewal in Southern History," in Potter, *The South and the Sectional Conflict* (Baton Rouge, 1968), 177–98; George B. Tindall, "Commentary," in Thompson, ed., *Perspectives on the South,* 89–93; Avery O. Craven, "The South in American History," *Historical Outlook,* XXI (March 1930), 105–9; and several of the presidential addresses to the Southern Historical Association, which are reprinted in George B. Tindall, ed., *The Pursuit of Southern History* (Baton Rouge, 1964). On the problem of defining the South as a section see Francis B. Simkins, "The South," in Merrill Jensen, ed., *Regionalism in America* (Madison, 1951), 147–72; and Frederick Jackson Turner, "The Significance of the Section in American

509

History," *Wisconsin Magazine of History,* VIII (March 1925), 255–80. On the subject of blacks as southerners see L. D. Reddick, "The Negro as Southerner and American," in Charles G. Sellers, ed., *The Southerner as American* (Chapel Hill, 1960), 130–47; and C. Vann Woodward, *American Counterpoint* (Boston, 1971).

3 *American Historical Review,* XXXIV (October 1928), 30–43.

4 Among the important statements of the idea are [William Gilmore Simms], "Is Southern Civilization Worth Preserving?" *Southern Quarterly Review,* n.s., III (January 1851), 189–225; William P. Trent, "Dominant Forces in Southern Life," *Atlantic Monthly,* LXXIX (January 1897), 42–53; and William Garrott Brown, "The South in National Politics," reprinted in William B. Hamilton, ed., *Fifty Years of the South Atlantic Quarterly* (Durham, 1952), 101–13.

5 The ensuing quotations are from Frederick Jackson Turner, *The United States, 1830–1850* (New York, 1935), 209; Craven, "The South in American History," 105–9; H. C. Nixon, "Southern Regionalism Limited," *Virginia Quarterly Review,* XXVI (Spring 1950), 168; Francis B. Simkins, "Unchanging White Supremacy," *Current History,* XXV (November 1958), 282–86; Howard W. Odum, *The Way of the South* (New York, 1947), 66; William Styron, "This Quiet Dust," *Harper's Magazine,* CCXXX (April 1965), 136; Bruce L. Clayton, *The Savage Ideal* (Baltimore, 1972), 182; and Samuel S. Hill, *Religion and the Solid South* (Nashville, 1972), 24.

6 For informative discussions of Phillips's scholarship generally see Eugene D. Genovese, "Race and Class in Southern History: An Appraisal of the Work of Ulrich Bonnell Phillips," *Agricultural History,* XLI (October 1967), 345–58, and the commentaries by David M. Potter, Kenneth M. Stampp, and Stanley M. Elkins which accompany it. See also Genovese's introduction to the reprint of Phillips, *American Negro Slavery* (Baton Rouge, 1966). For important evaluations of Phillips's central theme see James M. McPherson, "Slavery and Race," *Perspectives in American History,* III (1969), 460–73; and George B. Tindall, "The Central Theme Revisited," in Sellers, ed., *The Southerner as American,* 104–29.

7 In addition to Phillips's central theme, the most important efforts to interpret the South's history include Wilbur J. Cash, *The Mind of the South* (New York, 1941); and C. Vann Woodward, "The Search for Southern Identity," reprinted in Woodward, *The Burden of Southern History* (Baton Rouge, 1968), 3–25. These works are discussed below. Other major interpretations include David M.

Potter, "The Enigma of the South"; George B. Tindall, "Mythology: A New Frontier in Southern History," in Frank E. Vandiver, ed., *The Idea of the South* (Chicago, 1964), 1–15; Louis D. Rubin, "An Image of the South," in Rubin and Kilpatrick, eds., *The Lasting South*, 1–15; James McBride Dabbs, *Who Speaks for the South?* (New York, 1964); Howard W. Odum, *The Way of the South;* Henry Savage, *Seeds of Time* (New York, 1957); Charles W. Ramsdell, "The Southern Heritage," in W. T. Couch, ed., *Culture in the South* (Chapel Hill, 1934), 1–23; T. Harry Williams, "The Distinctive South," in Williams, *Romance and Realism in Southern Politics* (Athens, 1961), 1–16; Earl E. Thorpe, *Eros and Freedom in Southern Life and Thought* (Durham, 1967). A useful reader is Monroe L. Billington, *The South: A Central Theme?* (New York, 1969). Among textbooks, Francis B. Simkins and Charles P. Roland, *A History of the South* (4th ed., New York, 1972) is most concerned with interpretation. The earlier editions of this work, by Simkins alone, are in fact the best general presentation of the conservative view of southern history.

8 C. Vann Woodward, "White Man, White Mind," *New Republic*, December 9, 1967, 28–30. For a more extended critique see Woodward, "The Elusive Mind of the South," in Woodward, *American Counterpoint*, 261–83. For responses to Woodward's evaluations see Joseph L. Morrison, "W. J. Cash: The Summing Up," *South Atlantic Quarterly*, LXX (Autumn 1971), 477–86; and Richard King, "The Mind of the South: Narcissus Grown Analytic," *New South*, XXVII (Winter 1972), 15–27. For other commentaries on Cash's work see Donald Davidson, *Still Rebels, Still Yankees* (Baton Rouge, 1957), 191–212, and Louis D. Rubin, "The Mind of the South," *Sewanee Review*, LXII (Autumn 1954), 683–95, both of which are critical; and Joseph K. Davis, "The South as History and Metahistory: The Mind of W. J. Cash," in Lewis P. Simpson, ed., *The Poetry of Community* (Atlanta, 1972), 11–24. Cash's first effort to interpret the section was "The Mind of the South," *American Mercury*, XVIII (October 1929), 185–92. The quotations below from Dewey W. Grantham and Sheldon Hackney are from Grantham, "Interpreters of the Modern South," *South Atlantic Quarterly*, LXIII (Autumn 1964), 525; and Hackney, "*Origins of the New South* in Retrospect," *Journal of Southern History*, XXXVIII (May 1972), 201.

9 William A. Foran, "Southern Legend: Climate or Climate of Opinion," South Carolina Historical Association *Proceedings, 1956*, 6–22. See also Edgar T. Thompson, "The Climatic Theory of the Plantation," *Agricultural History*, XV (January 1941), 49–60.

512 *Notes*

10 The essay is reprinted in Woodward, *The Burden of Southern History*, 3–25.
11 Sheldon Hackney, "Southern Violence," *American Historical Review*, LXXIV (February 1969), 906–25.

PART ONE INTRODUCTION

1 On historians and the colonial South see Clarence L. Ver Steeg, "Historians and the Southern Colonies," in Ray A. Billington, ed., *The Reinterpretation of Early American History* (San Marino, 1966), 81–99; Hugh F. Rankin, "The Colonial South," in Arthur S. Link and Rembert W. Patrick, eds., *Writing Southern History* (Baton Rouge, 1967) 3–37; and Lester J. Cappon, "The Need for Renewed Interest in Early Southern History," *Journal of Southern History*, XIV (February 1948), 108–18. The best general histories of the colonial South are Wesley F. Craven, *The Southern Colonies in the Seventeenth Century* (Baton Rouge, 1949); and Thomas J. Wertenbaker, *The Old South: The Founding of American Civilization* (New York, 1942). The most extended textbook treatment of the colonial South is in Clement Eaton, *A History of the Old South* (3rd ed., New York, 1975), 1–113; and Francis B. Simkins and Charles P. Roland, *A History of the South* (New York, 1972), 13–74. Interpretive studies that treat the colonial South most systematically are James McBride Dabbs, *Who Speaks for the South?* (New York, 1964); and Henry Savage, *Seeds of Time* (New York, 1959).

CHAPTER 2

1 It is of course anachronistic to use the term "southerner" before the development of sectional consciousness, but since no better term suggests itself, it will be used here.
2 Important works on the subject include David Bertelson, *The Lazy South* (New York, 1967); Perry Miller, "Religion and Society in the Early Literature of Virginia," *William and Mary Quarterly*, 3rd ser., V (October 1948), 492–552; *ibid.*, VI (January 1949), 24–41; Edmund S. Morgan, "The Puritan Ethic and the American Revolution," *ibid.*, XXIV (January 1967), 3–43; Babette M. Levy, "Early

Puritanism in the Southern and Island Colonies," American Antiquarian Society *Proceedings,* LXX (1960), pt. 1, 60–348; and C. Vann Woodward, "The Southern Ethic in a Puritan World," in Woodward, *American Counterpoint* (Boston, 1971), 13–46.

3 Louis B. Wright, *The First Gentlemen of Virginia* (San Marino, 1940), is perhaps the best of the admiring portraits of the planters. For an instructive contrast in social analysis of the planter class see Wilbur J. Cash, *The Mind of the South* (New York, 1941), chap. I; and the biting critique of Cash in Eugene D. Genovese, *The World the Slaveholders Made* (New York, 1969), 137–50.

4 Jack P. Greene, "Foundations of Political Power in the Virginia House of Burgesses, 1720–1776," *William and Mary Quarterly,* 3rd ser., XVI (October 1959), 485–506; and Greene, *The Quest for Power* (Chapel Hill, 1963). An alternative view of Virginia politics, which suggests that Virginia on the eve of the Revolution was a middle-class democracy, is presented in Robert E. and Katherine Brown, *Virginia, 1705–1786: Democracy or Aristocracy?* (East Lansing, 1964). The Browns' view rests upon a willingness to equate democracy with the rights and opportunities available to adult white males. "Naturally it was undemocratic to exclude slaves, servants, women, and children [from the suffrage]," they write, "but since such exclusions were made in all colonies, the problem is reduced to the extent to which *free adult white men* were excluded from political action." The Browns' work is an instructive example of traditional scholarship that is uninformed by the recent attention to race and class. The student will get a clear illustration of how the new scholarship has altered the picture of the colonial South by comparing the Browns' work with a work like Edmund S. Morgan, *American Slavery, American Freedom: The Ordeal of Colonial Virginia* (New York, 1975).

5 The most important of these studies which have implications for the evolution of southern identity are Winthrop D. Jordan, *White over Black* (Chapel Hill, 1968); Morgan, *American Slavery, American Freedom: The Ordeal of Colonial Virginia;* Stanley M. Elkins, *Slavery: A Problem in American Institutional and Intellectual Life* (Chicago, 1959); David Brion Davis, *The Problem of Slavery in Western Culture* (Ithaca, 1966); Carl N. Degler, "Slavery and the Genesis of American Race Prejudice," *Comparative Studies in Society and History,* II (October 1959), 49–66; Degler, *Neither Black nor White* (New York, 1971); Marvin Harris, *Patterns of Race in the Americas* (New York, 1964); Louis Ruchames, "The Sources of Racial Thought in Colonial America," *Journal of Negro History,* LII (October 1967), 251–72; Alden T. Vaughan, "Blacks in Virginia:

A Note on the First Decade," *William and Mary Quarterly,* 3rd ser., XXIX (July 1972), 469–78; Peter H. Wood, *Black Majority: Negroes in Colonial South Carolina from 1670 through the Stono Rebellion* (New York, 1973); and Genovese, *The World the Slaveholders Made.*

6 See Wesley F. Craven, *White, Red, and Black: The Seventeenth Century Virginian* (Charlottesville, 1971), 84.

7 See, however, Gerald W. Mullin's pathbreaking study of slavery in eighteenth-century Virginia, *Flight and Rebellion* (New York, 1972); and Peter H. Wood's equally insightful study of early South Carolina, *Black Majority.*

8 Robert S. Cotterill, *The Southern Indians* (Norman, 1954) is a standard survey of the subject. There is also much general information in Verner W. Crane, *The Southern Frontier, 1670–1732* (Durham, 1929); Craven, *White, Red, and Black,* 39–72; and Gary B. Nash, *Red, White, and Black: The Peoples of Early America* (Englewood Cliffs, 1974). See also Nash, "The Image of the Indian in the Southern Colonial Mind," *William and Mary Quarterly,* 3rd ser., XXIX (April 1972), 197–230; Wilcomb E. Washburn, "The Moral and Legal Justifications for Dispossessing the Indians," in James M. Smith, ed., *Seventeenth Century America* (Chapel Hill, 1959), 15–32; and William S. Willis, "Divide and Rule: Red, White, and Black in the Southeast," *Journal of Negro History,* XLVIII (July 1963), 157–76. The most satisfactory introduction to the problem of perspective in studying the Indians is Francis Jennings, *The Invasion of America: Indians, Colonialism, and the Cant of Conquest* (Chapel Hill, 1975). Bernard W. Sheehan, *Seeds of Extinction: Jeffersonian Philanthropy and the American Indian* (Chapel Hill, 1973) is also a perceptive discussion.

CHAPTER 3

1 The most important items in the recent literature, none of which deals explicitly with the question of southern consciousness or identity, include Winthrop D. Jordan, *White over Black* (Chapel Hill, 1968); Donald L. Robinson, *Slavery in the Structure of American Politics, 1765–1820* (New York, 1971); David Brion Davis, *The Problem of Slavery in the Age of Revolution, 1770–1823* (Ithaca, 1975); Robert McColley, *Slavery and Jeffersonian Virginia* (2nd ed., Urbana, 1973); and Duncan J. McLeod, *Slavery, Race and the*

American Revolution (London, 1974). Other important works on aspects of the influence of slavery and race are noted in subsequent notes in this chapter.

2 Leland J. Bellot, "Evangelicals and the Defense of Slavery in Britain's Old Colonial Empire," *Journal of Southern History*, XXXVII (February 1971), 19–40.

3 See, for example, the original edition of the textbook by Clement Eaton, *A History of the Old South* (New York, 1949); Eaton, *The Freedom of Thought Struggle in the Old South* (New York, 1964); Eaton, *The Growth of Southern Civilization, 1790–1860* (New York, 1961); and Richard Beale Davis, *Intellectual Life in Jefferson's Virginia, 1790–1830* (Chapel Hill, 1964). Davis's work devotes only 11 of 434 pages of text to the subject of slavery.

4 This has been done in a series of significant studies, among them the works by Robert McColley, Donald L. Robinson, Winthrop D. Jordan, and David Brion Davis cited in note 1 of this chapter. Other informative studies include William Cohen, "Thomas Jefferson and the Problem of Slavery," *Journal of American History*, LVI (December 1969), 503–26; Donald G. Matthews, *Slavery and Methodism* (Princeton, 1965); H. Shelton Smith, *In His Image, But ...* (Durham, 1972); Gordon E. Finnie, "The Antislavery Movement in the Upper South before 1840," *Journal of Southern History*, XXV (August 1969), 319–42; and Don K. Bates, "Abolition, Deportation, Integration: Attitudes toward Slavery in the Early Republic," *Journal of Negro History*, LIII (January 1969), 33–47.

5 See Staughton Lynd, "The Compromise of 1787," *Political Science Quarterly*, LXXI (June 1966), 225–50. For a discussion of slavery in the Constitutional Convention see Howard A. Ohline, "Republicanism and Slavery: Origins of the Three-Fifths Clause in the United States Constitution," *William and Mary Quarterly*, 3rd ser., XXVIII (October 1971), 563–84. For an in-depth computer analysis of sectional voting patterns in Congress between 1774 and 1781 see H. James Henderson, *Party Politics in the Continental Congress* (New York, 1976). For a more general discussion see Joseph L. Davis, *Sectionalism in America, 1774–1787* (New York, 1976).

6 Since there was little distinctively southern about land speculation in the Southwest, a discussion of that subject is omitted here. Thomas P. Abernethy, *The South in the New Nation, 1789–1819* (Baton Rouge, 1961), contains a superb account.

7 See especially Jackson Turner Main, *The Social Structure of Revolutionary America* (Princeton, 1965); Main, "The One Hundred,"

William and Mary Quarterly, 3rd ser., XI (July 1954), 354–84; and Main, "The Distribution of Property in Post-revolutionary Virginia," *Mississippi Valley Historical Review,* XLI (September 1954), 241–58. For a work stressing the democratic nature of the Virginia social structure see Robert E. Brown and Katherine Brown, *Virginia, 1705–1786: Democracy or Aristocracy?* (East Lansing, 1964).

CHAPTER 4

1 James H. Johnston, *Race Relations in Virginia and Miscegenation in the South, 1776–1860* (Amherst, 1970).
2 The literature on Calhoun is quite large. The most complete biography is Charles M. Wiltse, *John C. Calhoun* (3 vols., Indianapolis, 1944–1951); the most readable biography is Margaret Coit, *John C. Calhoun* (Boston, 1950). The best introduction to Calhoun's thought is Richard N. Current, *John C. Calhoun* (New York, 1963). See also Richard Hofstadter, "John C. Calhoun, the Marx of the Master Class," in Hofstadter, *The American Political Tradition* (New York, 1948), 67–91; Gerald Capers, *John C. Calhoun* (Gainesville, 1960); and August O. Spain, *The Political Theory of John C. Calhoun* (New York, 1951). On states' rights see Arthur M. Schlesinger, Sr., "The States Rights Fetish," in Schlesinger, *New Viewpoints in American History* (New York, 1922), 220–44; and Robert J. Harris, "States Rights and Vested Interests," *Journal of Politics,* XV (November 1953), 457–71.

CHAPTER 5

1 See William N. Parker, ed., *The Structure of the Cotton Economy of the Antebellum South* (Washington, 1970), especially the articles by Robert Gallman and Diane Lindstrom; Sam Bowers Hilliard, *Hog Meat and Hoecake: Food Supply in the Old South, 1840–1860* (Carbondale, 1972); and the discussion of this topic by Robert W. Fogel and Albert Fishlow in Ralph L. Andreano, ed., *New Views on American Economic History* (Cambridge, 1965), 187–224.

2 This subject is developed in Douglass C. North, *The Economic Growth of the United States, 1790–1860* (Englewood Cliffs, 1961). For a critique of North's emphasis on the role of cotton in national economic development see Morton Rothstein, "The Cotton Frontier of the Antebellum United States: A Methodological Battleground," *Agricultural History*, XLIV (January 1970), 149–65.
3 Phillips developed this view most systematically in "The Economic Cost of Slaveholding in the Cotton Belt," *Political Science Quarterly*, XX (June 1905), 257–75; and in *American Negro Slavery* (New York, 1918). An important refinement of Phillips's view is in Charles W. Ramsdell, "The Natural Limits of Slavery Expansion," *Mississippi Valley Historical Review*, XVI (September 1929), 151–71.
4 See Lewis C. Gray, *History of Agriculture in the Southern United States to 1860* (2 vols., Washington, 1933); Robert R. Russel, "The General Effects of Slavery upon Southern Economic Progress," *Journal of Southern History*, IV (February 1938), 34–54; and Kenneth M. Stampp, *The Peculiar Institution* (New York, 1956).
5 This was done by Alfred H. Conrad and John R. Meyer, "The Economics of Slavery in the Antebellum South," *Journal of Political Economy*, LXVI (April 1958), 95–130, an article that proved to be something of a historiographical watershed. A good selection of the resulting literature is reprinted in Hugh G. J. Aitken, ed., *Did Slavery Pay?* (New York, 1971). Perhaps the most formidable criticism of Conrad and Meyer's findings is Edward Saraydar, "A Note on the Profitability of Ante Bellum Slavery," *Southern Economic Journal*, XXX (April 1964), 325–32. The best criticism of their conception of the problem of profitability is Douglas F. Dowd, "The Economics of Slavery in the Ante Bellum South: A Comment," *Journal of Political Economy*, LXVI (October 1958), 440–42. Eugene D. Genovese incorporates some important criticisms in *The Political Economy of Slavery* (New York, 1966). The most systematic effort to integrate the finding that slavery was profitable into the broader economic history of the Old South is Robert W. Fogel and Stanley L. Engerman, *Time on the Cross* (Boston, 1974). Their work has, however, been effectively criticized. See especially Paul A. David, et al., *Reckoning with Slavery: A Critical Study in the Quantitative History of American Negro Slavery* (New York, 1976). The historiography of profitability is reviewed in Harold D. Woodman, "The Profitability of Slavery: A Historical Perennial," *Journal of Southern History*, XXIX (August 1963), 303–25.
6 The basic studies include Richard A. Easterlin, "Interregional Differences in Per Capita Income, Population and Total Income,"

in *Trends in the American Economy in the Nineteenth Century* (Princeton, 1960), 73–140; Easterlin, "Regional Income Trends, 1840–1950," in Seymour E. Harris, ed., *American Economic History* (New York, 1961), 525–47; Robert E. Gallman, "Commodity Output, 1839–1899," in *Trends in the American Economy in the Nineteenth Century* 13–67; Gallman, "Gross National Product in the United States, 1834–1909," Conference on Research in Income and Wealth, vol. XXX: *Output, Employment, and Productivity in the United States after 1800* (New York, 1966), 3–76; Stanley L. Engerman, "Some Economic Factors in Southern Backwardness in the Nineteenth Century," in John F. Kain and John R. Meyer, eds., *Essays in Regional Economics* (Cambridge, 1971), 279–306; Engerman, "The Effects of Slavery upon the Southern Economy: A Review of the Recent Debate," *Explorations in Entrepreneurial History*, 2nd ser., IV (Winter 1967), 71–97; Robert W. Fogel and Engerman, "The Economics of Slavery," in Fogel and Engerman, *The Reinterpretation of American Economic History* (New York, 1971), 311–41; Fogel and Engerman "The Relative Efficiency of Slavery: A Comparison of Northern and Southern Agriculture in 1860," *Explorations in Economic History*, VIII (Spring 1971), 353–67.

7 From Easterlin, "Regional Income Trends, 1840–1950," 528.
8 From Engerman, "The Effects of Slavery upon the Southern Economy: A Review of the Recent Debate," 84. Engerman revised Easterlin's figures to include Texas in 1840, which at that time was not a part of the United States. The chief effect of the revision was to change the South's ratio of national income from 76 percent to 77 percent in 1840 and from 72 percent to 80 percent in 1860.
9 See Marvin Fischbaum and Julius Rubin, "Slavery and the Economic Development of the American South," *Explorations in Entrepreneurial History*, 2nd ser., V (Fall 1968), 116–27.
10 See Gavin Wright, "Slavery and the Cotton South," *Explorations in Economic History*, XII (October 1975), 439–51.
11 On this point see the discussion by Conrad, Meyer, Dowd, Engerman, and others in *Journal of Economic History*, XXVII (December 1967), 518–60; and Douglas F. Dowd, "A Comparative Analysis of Economic Development in the American West and South," *ibid.*, XVI (December 1956), 558–74.
12 Gavin Wright, "'Economic Democracy' and the Concentration of Agricultural Wealth in the Cotton South, 1850–1860," *Agricultural History*, XLIV (January 1970), 63–93; and Robert E. Gallman, "Trends in the Size Distribution of Wealth in the Nineteenth

Century: Some Speculations," Conference on Research in Income and Wealth, vol. XXXIII: *Six Papers on the Size Distribution of Wealth and Income* (New York, 1969), 1–25. For the effects of this on growth and diversification see Morton Rothstein, "The Antebellum South as a Dual Economy: A Tentative Hypothesis," *Agricultural History,* XLI (October 1967), 373–82.

13 The literature on slavery is voluminous. The modern restudy of the institution began with Kenneth M. Stampp, *The Peculiar Institution* (New York, 1956), and has continued in such major works as Stanley M. Elkins, *Slavery* (Chicago, 1959; 2nd ed., New York, 1963); John W. Blassingame, *The Slave Community* (New York, 1972); George P. Rawick, *From Sundown to Sunup* (Bridgeport, 1972); Fogel and Engerman, *Time on the Cross;* and Eugene D. Genovese, *Roll, Jordan, Roll* (New York, 1974). The old standard work, Phillips, *American Negro Slavery,* has been completely superseded in its treatment of the slaves but is still useful in its discussion of some facets of the economic and institutional history of the institution. Lawrence W. Levine, *Black Culture and Black Consciousness: Afro-American Folk Thought from Slavery to Freedom* (New York, 1976) is an exemplary study of aspects of the interior history of the slave community. Ira Berlin, *Slaves Without Masters: The Free Negro in the Antebellum South* (New York, 1974) is a superior study of a related subject.

14 On the usefulness of this collection for historians see C. Vann Woodward, "History from Slave Sources," *American Historical Review,* LXXIX (April 1972), 470–81; and John W. Blassingame, "Using the Testimony of Ex-Slaves: Approaches and Problems," *Journal of Southern History,* XLI (November 1975), 473–92.

15 The best study is Herbert G. Gutman, *The Black Family in Slavery and Freedom, 1750–1925* (New York, 1976).

CHAPTER 6

1 The literature on the question of guilt is large. The best recent statement of the guilt hypothesis is Charles G. Sellers, "The Travail of Slavery," in Sellers, ed., *The Southerner as American* (Chapel Hill, 1960), 40–71. William W. Freehling, *Prelude to Civil War* (New York, 1966), contains another good statement. The hypothesis has never been systematically tested, but criticisms of it are contained in Eugene D. Genovese, *The World the Slaveholders*

Made (New York, 1969); and David Donald, "The Proslavery Argument Reconsidered," *Journal of Southern History,* XXXVII (February 1971), 3–18. The historiography of the subject is briefly treated in James M. McPherson, "Slavery and Race," *Perspectives in American History,* III (1969), 460–73.

2 Important works of the Owsley school include Frank L. Owsley and Harriet C. Owsley, "The Economic Basis of Society in the Late Antebellum South," *Journal of Southern History,* VI (February 1940), 24–45; Owsley and Owsley, "The Economic Structure of Rural Tennessee, 1850–1860," *ibid.,* VIII (May 1942), 161–82; Harry L. Coles, "Some Notes on Slave Ownership and Land Ownership in Louisiana, 1850–1860," *ibid.,* XI (August 1943), 381–94; Herbert Weaver, *Mississippi Farmers* (Nashville, 1945); Blanche Henry Clark, *The Tennessee Yeomen, 1840–1860* (Nashville, 1942); and Owsley, *The Plain Folk of the Old South* (Baton Rouge, 1949).

3 See James C. Bonner, "Profile of a Late Ante-Bellum Community," *American Historical Review,* XLIX (July 1944), 663–80.

4 These figures are from Fabian Linden, "Economic Democracy in the Slave South: An Appraisal of Some Recent Views," *Journal of Negro History,* XXXI (April 1946), 140–89; and Gavin Wright, " 'Economic Democracy' and the Concentration of Agricultural Wealth in the Cotton South, 1850–1860," *Agricultural History,* XLIV (January 1970), 63–93. See also Randolph B. Campbell, "Planters and Plain Folk: Harrison County, Texas, as a Test Case, 1850–1860," *Journal of Southern History,* XL (August 1974), 369–98.

5 George M. Fredrickson, *The Black Image in the White Mind* (New York, 1971), contains the most systematic discussion of the *Herrenvolk* idea in the Old South. The term "egalitarian racism" is from William L. Barney, *The Road to Secession* (Princeton, 1972).

6 On the question of industrial workers in the Old South see Robert S. Starobin, *Industrial Slavery in the Old South* (New York, 1970); Broadus Mitchell, *William Gregg, Factory Master of the Old South* (Chapel Hill, 1928); Thomas P. Martin, "The Advent of William Gregg and the Graniteville Company," *Journal of Southern History,* XI (August 1945), 389–423; Richard B. Morris, "The Measure of Bondage in the Slave States," *Mississippi Valley Historical Review,* XLI (September 1954), 219–40; and Norris W. Preyer, "The Historian, the Slave, and the Antebellum Textile Industry," *Journal of Negro History,* XLVI (April 1961), 67–82.

7 Two especially instructive examples of Simms's social thought are "The Morals of Slavery," in *The Pro-Slavery Argument* (New York,

1968), which is a reprint of "Miss Martineau on Slavery," *Southern Literary Messenger,* III (November 1837), 641–57; and "Is Southern Civilization Worth Preserving?" *Southern Quarterly Review,* n.s., III (January 1851), 189–225. Among Simms's novels, *Woodcraft* (Chicago, 1890, orig. ed., 1854) is perhaps the best statement of his social views. On Simms's place in southern thought see Jon L. Wakelyn, *The Politics of a Literary Man* (Westport, 1973); Clement Eaton, *The Mind of the Old South* (Baton Rouge, 1964), 181–201; and William R. Taylor, *Cavalier and Yankee* (New York, 1961), 261–97.

8 On the influence of Scott see Grace Warren Landrum, "Sir Walter Scott and His Literary Rivals in the Old South," *American Literature,* II (November 1930), 256–76; and Jay B. Hubbell, *The South in American Literature, 1607–1900* (Durham, 1954), 188–93. Mark Twain's comments on Scott are in his *Life on the Mississippi* (New York, 1911), 332ff.

9 The major studies of the legend are Francis P. Gaines, *The Southern Plantation* (New York, 1925); and Taylor, *Cavalier and Yankee.*

10 Literature on the Old South and the frontier is extensive. On the historiography of the subject see Todd M. Lieber, "The Significance of the Frontier in the Writing of Antebellum Southern History," *Mississippi Quarterly,* XXII (Fall 1969), 337–54. See also Avery O. Craven, "The 'Turner Theories' and the South," *Journal of Southern History,* V (August 1939), 291–314; and Stanley M. Elkins and Eric L. McKitrick, "A Meaning for Turner's Frontier, Part II: The Southwest Frontier and New England," *Political Science Quarterly,* LXIX (December 1954), 565–602. On southern Indians see Charles M. Hudson, ed., *Red, White, and Black: Symposium on Indians in the Old South* (Athens, 1971). On the removal of the Indians from the South see Dale Van Every, *Disinherited* (New York, 1966).

11 The standard history is William S. Jenkins, *Pro-Slavery Thought in the Old South* (Chapel Hill, 1935). On scientific racism see William Stanton, *The Leopard's Spots* (Chicago, 1960). The best modern anthology is Eric L. McKitrick, ed., *Slavery Defended* (Englewood Cliffs, 1963). On racial aspects of southern thought see Fredrickson, *The Black Image in the White Mind.*

12 Among the most widely cited Biblical passages were several from the Pentateuch and from the writings of Paul. Among these were Genesis 9:25; Leviticus 25:44–46; the Tenth Commandment; I Peter 2:18–20; I Timothy 6:1–2; Romans 13:1; I Corinthians 7:20–21.

CHAPTER 7

1 The basic study of the historiography of Civil War causation is Thomas J. Pressly, *Americans Interpret Their Civil War* (rev. ed., New York, 1962). A more recent assessment and the best introduction to the subject is David M. Potter, "The Literature on the Background of the Civil War," in Potter, *The South and the Sectional Conflict* (Baton Rouge, 1968), 87–150. Other recent discussions of the literature include Eric Foner, "The Causes of the American Civil War: Recent Interpretations and New Directions," *Civil War History*, XX (September 1974), 197–214; Robert W. Johannsen, "Background to Conflict: Slavery, Abolition, and Politics," in William H. Cartwright and Richard L. Watson, Jr., eds., *The Reinterpretation of American History and Culture* (Washington, 1973), 327–56; C. E. Cauthen and Lewis P. Jones, "The Coming of the Civil War," in Arthur S. Link and Rembert W. Patrick, *Writing Southern History* (Baton Rouge, 1965), 224–48. Recent discussions of historiographical issues include David Donald, "American Historians and the Causes of the Civil War," *South Atlantic Quarterly*, LXIX (Summer 1960), 351–55; James M. McPherson, "Slavery and Race," *Perspectives in American History*, III (1969), 460–73; and Robert E. Shalhope, "Race, Class, Slavery, and the Antebellum Southern Mind," *Journal of Southern History*, XXXVII (November 1971), 557–74. An informative anthology of basic statements of the causes of the war is Edwin C. Rozwenc, ed., *The Causes of the American Civil War* (Boston, 1961). The most systematic recent study of the coming of the war is David M. Potter, *The Impending Crisis, 1848–1861* (New York, 1976).

2 The most systematic statement of this view is Alexander H. Stephens, *A Constitutional View of the Late War between the States* (2 vols., Philadelphia, 1868–1870). The classic Confederate apologia is Alfred T. Bledsoe, *Is Davis a Traitor, or Was Secession a Right Previous to 1861?* (Richmond, 1866).

3 Statements of this view are in Henry Wilson, *History of the Rise and Fall of the Slave Power in America* (3 vols., Boston, 1872–1877); and Herman E. von Holst, *Constitutional and Political History of the United States* (8 vols., Chicago, 1876–1892). A more moderate version is in James Ford Rhodes, *History of the United States from the Compromise of 1850* (8 vols., reprint, New York, 1902–1920).

4 Among the most important of these works on the South are Steven A. Channing, *Crisis of Fear: Secession in South Carolina* (New

York, 1970); William W. Freehling, *Prelude to Civil War* (New York, 1966); George M. Fredrickson, *The Black Image in the White Mind* (New York, 1971); and William L. Barney, *The Secessionist Impulse* (Princeton, 1974). See also James A. Rawley, *Race and Politics: 'Bleeding Kansas' and the Coming of the Civil War* (New York, 1969).

5 On the historical literature concerning this subject see William J. Donnelly, "Conspiracy or Popular Movement: The Historiography of Southern Support for Secession," *North Carolina Historical Review*, XLII (January 1965), 70–84. The fullest discussion of the election results is in Ollinger Crenshaw, *The Slave States in the Presidential Election of 1860* (Baltimore, 1945).

CHAPTER 8

1 On the general subject of Confederate historiography see Frank E. Vandiver, "Some Problems Involved in Writing Confederate History," *Journal of Southern History,* XXXVI (August 1970), 400–10; Charles W. Ramsdell, "Some Problems Involved in Writing the History of the Confederacy," *ibid.,* II (May 1936), 133–47; and Douglas Southall Freeman, *The South to Posterity: An Introduction to the Writing of Confederate History* (New York, 1939). Useful historiographical and bibliographical essays are Mary Elizabeth Massey, "The Confederate States of America: The Homefront," in Arthur S. Link and Rembert W. Patrick, eds., *Writing Southern History* (Baton Rouge, 1965), 249–72; John G. Barrett, "The Confederate States of America at War on Land and Sea," *ibid.,* 273–94; and Robert F. Durden, "Civil War and Reconstruction, 1861–1877," in William H. Cartwright and Richard L. Watson, eds., *The Reinterpretation of American History and Culture* (Washington, 1973), 357–76. See also Allan Nevins, James I. Robertson, and Bell I. Wiley, *Civil War Books: A Critical Bibliography* (2 vols., Baton Rouge, 1967–1969). Among the most informative discussions of the South in Civil War fiction are Robert A. Lively, *Fiction Fights the Civil War* (Chapel Hill, 1957); Louis D. Rubin, "The Image of an Army: The Civil War in Southern Fiction," in R. C. Simonini, ed., *Southern Writers: Appraisals in Our Time* (Charlottesville, 1964), 50–70; and Edmund Wilson, *Patriotic Gore* (New York, 1962). On the role of blacks see Clarence L. Mohr, "Southern Blacks in the Civil War: A Century of Historiography," *Journal of Negro History* (April 1974), 177–95.

524   Notes

2 See Clifford Dowdey, "The Case for the Confederacy," in Louis D. Rubin and James J. Kilpatrick, eds., *The Lasting South* (Chicago, 1957), 28–45; and Frank E. Vandiver, "The Confederacy and the American Tradition," *Journal of Southern History,* XXVIII (August 1962), 277–86.

3 Among the general histories of the Confederacy the most important are Frank E. Vandiver, *Their Tattered Flags* (New York, 1970), which is the best evocation of the Confederate experience by a historian; E. Merton Coulter, *The Confederate States of America, 1861–1865* (Baton Rouge, 1950), the best social history; Clement Eaton, *A History of the Southern Confederacy* (New York, 1954), the best factual survey; and Charles P. Roland's *The Confederacy* (Chicago, 1960), a perceptive synthesis of historical scholarship. Clifford Dowdey's *The Land They Fought For* (Garden City, 1955) is a notable popular history. Among the store of novels on the Confederate experience, Stark Young's *So Red the Rose* (New York, 1934) is a good statement of the Confederate case. Among the best histories of the war are Bruce Catton's *Centennial History of the Civil War* (3 vols., 1961–1965); and Allan Nevins, *The War for the Union* (4 vols., 1959–1971).

4 Confederate strategy has been the subject of much historiographical debate. Among the best general discussions of the subject are Thomas L. Connelly and Archer Jones, *The Politics of Command* (Baton Rouge, 1973); Russell F. Weigley, *The American Way of War* (New York, 1973), 92–127; T. Harry Williams, "The Military Leadership of North and South," in David Donald, ed., *Why the North Won the Civil War* (Baton Rouge, 1960), 23–48; Williams, *Americans at War* (rev. ed., New York, 1962), 55–91; Frank E. Vandiver, *Rebel Brass* (Baton Rouge, 1956); Thomas L. Connelly, *Army of the Heartland* (Baton Rouge, 1967); and Connelly, *Autumn of Glory* (Baton Rouge, 1971). Robert L. Kerby, "Why the Confederacy Lost," *Review of Politics,* XXXV (July 1973), 326–45, is an interesting discussion of Confederate strategy in light of modern wars of national liberation. Ludwell H. Johnson, "Civil War Military History: A Few Revisions in Need of Revising," *Civil War History,* XVII (June 1971), 115–30, is an informative historiographical discussion.

5 Lee's generalship has been the subject of much study, most of it quite sympathetic. The best case for Lee was made in Douglas Southall Freeman, *Robert E. Lee: A Biography* (4 vols., New York, 1934–35), which is also the best biography. T. Harry Williams, "Freeman, Historian of the Civil War: An Appraisal," *Journal of Southern History,* XXI (February 1955), 91–100, is an informative

critique. Charles P. Roland, "The Generalship of Robert E. Lee," in Grady McWhiney, ed., *Grant, Lee, Lincoln and the Radicals* (Evanston, 1964), 31–71, is a cogent defense of Lee and Confederate strategy. Among the best criticisms of Lee's generalship are J. F. C. Fuller, *Grant and Lee* (London, 1929), and the works by Thomas L. Connelly cited in the preceding note. For summary statements of Connelly's criticisms see Connelly, *The Marble Man: Robert E. Lee and His Image in American Society* (New York, 1976). For a rejoinder to Connelly's earlier criticisms see Albert Castel, "The Historian and the General: Thomas L. Connelly versus Robert E. Lee," *ibid.,* XVI (March 1970), 50–63.

6 There is no completely satisfactory biography of Davis. The best is Hudson Strode, *Jefferson Davis* (3 vols., New York, 1955–1964), which is too uncritical. The most convincing defense of Davis as a Confederate strategist and leader is Frank E. Vandiver, "Jefferson Davis and Confederate Strategy," in Avery O. Craven and Frank E. Vandiver, eds., *The American Tragedy* (Hampden-Sydney, 1959), 19–32; Vandiver, *Their Tattered Flags,* is also sympathetic. The most convincing criticism of Davis is David M. Potter, "Jefferson Davis and the Political Factors in Confederate Defeat," in David Donald, ed., *Why the North Won the Civil War,* 91–114, which is reprinted in Potter, ed., *The South and the Sectional Conflict* (Baton Rouge, 1968), 263–86. See also Grady McWhiney, "Jefferson Davis and His Generals," in McWhiney, ed., *Southerners and Other Americans* (New York, 1973), 83–104; and William J. Cooper, Jr., "A Reassessment of Jefferson Davis as War Leader: The Case from Atlanta to Nashville," *Journal of Southern History,* XXXVI (May 1970), 189–204.

7 The literature on why the Confederacy lost the war is voluminous. Virtually every major and many minor works on the Confederacy treat the subject at some length. On the historiography of the subject see Robert D. Little, "Southern Historians and the Defeat of the Confederacy, Part I," *Alabama Review,* III (October 1950), 243–62; and Little, "Southern Historians and the Defeat of the Confederacy, Part II," *ibid.,* (January 1951), 38–54. See also Grady McWhiney, "Who Whipped Whom? Confederate Defeat Re-examined," *Civil War History,* XI (March 1965), 5–26.

8 David M. Potter, "The Historian's Use of Nationalism and Vice Versa," *American Historical Review,* LXVII (July 1962), 924–50.

9 One major aspect of Confederate racial thought is studied in Robert F. Durden, *The Gray and the Black: The Confederate Debate on Emancipation* (Baton Rouge, 1972).

10 The best brief discussion of northern racism and of its role in the

northern war effort, as well as the best survey of major items in the recent historiography of this subject, is C. Vann Woodward, *American Counterpoint* (Boston, 1971), 140–83. The principal study is V. Jacques Voegeli, *Free but Not Equal: The Midwest and the Negro during the Civil War* (Chicago, 1967).

CHAPTER 9

1 Secretary of State William H. Seward, who was shot in the same conspiracy that killed Lincoln.
2 This subject has many facets, including the transition from war to peace, the impact of the war and the changes it produced, and the response of white southerners to military defeat. The general histories of Reconstruction, noted below, all treat these topics in varying depth, as do the general histories of the South noted elsewhere. Among the interpretive histories of the section, Wilbur J. Cash, *The Mind of the South* (New York, 1941), and James McBride Dabbs, *Who Speaks for the South?* (New York, 1964), give special emphasis to the impact of the war. C. Vann Woodward, "The Search for Southern Identity" and "The Irony of Southern History," both reprinted in Woodward, *The Burden of Southern History* (rev. ed., Baton Rouge, 1968), are the best inquiries into the meaning of defeat. See also Robert Penn Warren, *The Legacy of the Civil War* (New York, 1961). The impact of the war on the planter class is detailed in James L. Roark, *Masters without Slaves: Southern Planters in the Civil War and Reconstruction* (New York, 1977). The most systematic study of white attitudes toward postwar policy in the immediate aftermath of defeat is Michael Perman, *Reunion without Compromise* (New York, 1973), especially valuable because of its use of newspapers. The cultural change produced by the war is the focus of Clement Eaton, *The Waning of the Old South Civilization, 1860–1880s* (Athens, 1968). The war's impact on southern thought is treated in Richard M. Weaver, *The Southern Tradition at Bay* (New Rochelle, 1968); and Jay B. Hubbell, *The South in American Literature* (Durham, 1954). The economic impact of the war is the focus of Ralph Andreano, ed., *The Economic Impact of the American Civil War* (Cambridge, 1967); and James L. Sellers, "The Economic Incidence of the Civil War in the South," *Mississippi Valley Historical Review,* XIV (September 1927), 179–91. See also Paul W. Gates, *Agriculture and the Civil*

War (New York, 1965). Among the many informative accounts of travelers who toured the South in the aftermath of the war are Whitelaw Reid, *After the War: A Tour of the Southern States, 1865–1866* (New York, 1965; orig. ed., 1866); and John Richard Dennett, *The South as It Is: 1865–1866* (New York, 1967; orig. ed., 1866).

3 The following discussion of Reconstruction concentrates on the political aspects of postwar readjustment, treating the racial and economic factors as they relate to politics. Parallel economic, racial, and intellectual developments in the postwar South are treated in later chapters.

4 The historiography of Reconstruction has undergone a major revision in recent years. The old view, systematized by a school of historians inspired by William A. Dunning at Columbia University in the late nineteenth and early twentieth centuries, is illustrated in such works as Walter L. Fleming's readable *The Sequel of Appomattox* (New Haven, 1921); Claude A. Bowers's popular and influential *The Tragic Era* (Boston, 1929); and E. Merton Coulter, *The South during Reconstruction, 1865–1877* (Baton Rouge, 1947). This view was marred by a strong bias in favor of conservative white southerners and against other groups involved in Reconstruction. It was not unlike the interpretation offered by conservative whites themselves in Hilary A. Herbert, ed., *Why the Solid South?* (Baltimore, 1890). Recent revisionist studies have eliminated this bias, which rested on social conservatism and, for many, racism as well. Especially perceptive discussions of these issues are found in Kenneth M. Stampp, *The Era of Reconstruction, 1865–1877* (New York, 1966), 3–23; Howard K. Beale, "On Rewriting Reconstruction History," *American Historical Review,* XLV (July 1940), 807–27; Bernard A. Weisberger, "The Dark and Bloody Ground of Reconstruction Historiography," *Journal of Southern History,* XXV (November 1959), 427–47; and Vernon L. Wharton, "Reconstruction," in Arthur S. Link and Rembert W. Patrick, eds., *Writing Southern History* (Baton Rouge, 1965), 295–315. A more recent discussion is Gerald N. Grob, "Reconstruction: An American Morality Play," in George A. Billias and Gerald N. Grob, eds., *American History: Retrospect and Prospect* (New York, 1971). The views of the revisionists have come to dominate the study of Reconstruction, and are reflected in recent general surveys of the subject. The best survey is Rembert W. Patrick, *The Reconstruction of the Nation* (New York, 1967).

5 The socioeconomic makeup of the antebellum Whigs is discussed in Charles G. Sellers, "Who Were the Southern Whigs?" *American*

Historical Review, LIX (January 1954), 335–46; Grady McWhiney, "Were the Whigs a Class Party in Alabama?" *Journal of Southern History,* XXIII (November 1957), 510–22; and Richard P. McCormick, "Suffrage Classes and Party Alignments: A Study of Voter Behavior," *Mississippi Valley Historical Review,* XLVI (December 1959), 397–410. On the persistence of Whiggish influences after the death of the Whig party see Thomas B. Alexander, "Persistent Whiggery in the Confederate South, 1860–1877," *Journal of Southern History,* XXVII (August 1961), 305–19. The influence of persistent Whiggery is stressed in C. Vann Woodward, *Reunion and Reaction: The Compromise of 1877 and the End of Reconstruction* (rev. ed., New York, 1956). For a criticism of the idea and an informative resume of the relevant literature see John V. Mering, "Persistent Whiggery in the Confederate South: A Reconsideration," *South Atlantic Quarterly,* LXIX (Winter 1970), 124–43.

6 Many historians have recently stressed the significance of racist forces in Reconstruction, among them W. R. Brock, *An American Crisis: Congress and Reconstruction, 1865–1867* (London, 1963); and LaWanda and John H. Cox, *Politics, Principle, and Prejudice, 1865–1866* (Chicago, 1963).

7 A good brief survey of the role of blacks in Reconstruction is Robert Cruden, *The Negro in Reconstruction* (Englewood Cliffs, 1969). The recent revolution in black historical studies has produced a number of important works on Reconstruction, among them Willie Lee Rose, *Rehearsal for Reconstruction* (Indianapolis, 1964); Joel Williamson, *After Slavery: The Negro in South Carolina during Reconstruction, 1861–1877* (Chapel Hill, 1965); Peter Kolchin, *First Freedom: The Response of Alabama's Blacks to Emancipation and Reconstruction* (Westport, 1972); John W. Blassingame, *Black New Orleans, 1860–1880* (Chicago, 1973). Vernon Lane Wharton, *The Negro in Mississippi, 1865–1890* (Chapel Hill, 1947), is an important older work. The best work on black southerners in the Civil War is Bell I. Wiley, *Southern Negroes, 1861–1865* (rev. ed., New Haven, 1965).

8 August Meier, "Negroes in the First and Second Reconstruction of the South," *Civil War History,* XIII (June 1967), 114–30. On Reconstruction policy toward blacks see also Louis S. Gerteis, *From Contraband to Freedman: Federal Policy toward Southern Blacks, 1861–1865* (Westport, 1973).

9 The pervasiveness of northern racialism is stressed in many recent works, among them C. Vann Woodward, "Seeds of Failure in Radical Race Policy," in Woodward, *American Counterpoint* (Boston, 1971), 163–83; and V. Jacques Voegeli, *Free but Not Equal*

(Chicago, 1967). The equalitarian impulses of Radicals and other reformers are emphasized in James M. McPherson, *The Struggle for Equality* (Princeton, 1964); LaWanda and John H. Cox, "Negro Suffrage and Republican Politics: The Problem of Motivation in Reconstruction Historiography," *Journal of Southern History,* XXXIII (August 1967), 303–31; and Hans L. Trefousse, *The Radical Republicans* (New York, 1969).

10 George M. Fredrickson, *The Black Image in the White Mind* (New York, 1971), 166. On the same subject see also Voegeli, *Free but Not Equal,* 105–12.

11 The best discussions of Johnson and his relationship with southerners are Eric L. McKitrick, *Andrew Johnson and Reconstruction* (Chicago, 1960); and Cox and Cox, *Politics, Principle, and Prejudice.* On Johnson's commitment to white supremacy see Hans L. Trefousse, *Impeachment of a President: Andrew Johnson, the Blacks, and Reconstruction* (Knoxville, 1975).

12 The following discussion draws on David M. Potter, *Division and the Stresses of Reunion* (Glenview, 1973), 152–230.

13 This "tragic legend of Reconstruction" is best described in Stampp, *The Era of Reconstruction,* 3–23.

14 For a discussion of the extent of white disfranchisement see Forrest G. Wood, "On Revising Reconstruction History: Negro Suffrage, White Disfranchisement, and Common Sense," *Journal of Negro History,* LI (April 1966), 98–113.

15 Richard L. Hume, "The 'Black and Tan' Constitutional Conventions of 1867–1869 in Ten Former Confederate States: A Study of Their Membership" (unpublished Ph.D. dissertation, University of Washington, 1969).

16 See LaWanda Cox, "The Promise of Land for the Freedmen," *Mississippi Valley Historical Review,* XLV (December 1958), 413–40. On the land program in South Carolina see Carol Blesser, *The Promised Land* (Columbia, 1969).

17 The revisionist literature on these groups is large and growing. The restudy of Scalawags began with David Donald, "The Scalawag in Mississippi Reconstruction," *Journal of Southern History,* X (November 1944), 447–60; and has been continued in Allen W. Trelease, "Who Were the Scalawags?" *ibid.,* XXIX (November 1963), 445–68; Warren A. Ellem, "Who Were the Mississippi Scalawags?" *ibid.,* XXXVIII (May 1972), 217–40; Otto H. Olsen, "Reconsidering the Scalawags," *Civil War History,* XII (December 1966), 304–20; and William C. Harris, "A Reconsideration of the Mississippi Scalawags," *Journal of Mississippi History,* XXXII (February 1970), 3–42. On Carpetbaggers see Richard N. Current, "Carpet-

baggers Reconsidered," in D. H. Pinkney and Theodore Ropp, eds., *A Festschrift for Frederick B. Artz* (Durham, 1964); Current, *Three Carpetbag Governors* (Baton Rouge, 1967); Jack B. Scroggs, "Carpetbagger Constitutional Reform in the South Atlantic States, 1867–68," *Journal of Southern History,* XXVII (November 1961), 475–93; William C. Harris, "The Creed of the Carpetbaggers: The Case of Mississippi," *ibid.,* XL (May 1974), 199–224; and Otto H. Olsen, *Carpetbagger's Crusade: The Life of Albion W. Tourgee* (Baltimore, 1965).

18 While the historical reputations of Carpetbaggers, Scalawags, and blacks have risen in the hands of revisionist historians, that of the Conservatives has fallen sharply. A balanced assessment of them is in Patrick, *The Reconstruction of the Nation.* An excellent study of one group is Jack P. Maddex, *The Virginia Conservatives, 1867–1879* (Chapel Hill, 1970). The best general treatment of the Conservatives as Redeemers is in C. Vann Woodward, *Origins of the New South, 1877–1913* (Baton Rouge, 1951), 1–74.

PART FOUR INTRODUCTION

1 The best historiographical resume is Paul M. Gaston, "The 'New South,'" in Arthur S. Link and Rembert W. Patrick, eds., *Writing Southern History* (Baton Rouge, 1965), 316–36. The most complete bibliography is Charles B. Dew, "Critical Essay on Recent Works," which is appended to the 1971 reprint of C. Vann Woodward, *Origins of the New South, 1877–1913* (Baton Rouge, 1951), 517–628. The recent notable progress in studying the New South began with the scholarship of Woodward, the foremost historian of the era. On Woodward see David M. Potter, "C. Vann Woodward," in Marcus Cunliffe and Robin M. Winks, eds., *Pastmasters* (New York, 1970), 375–407. For an insightful appraisal of his most important work see Sheldon Hackney, "*Origins of the New South* in Retrospect," *Journal of Southern History,* XXXVIII (May 1972), 191–216. Woodward's other works include *Reunion and Reaction: The Compromise of 1877 and the End of Reconstruction* (rev. ed., New York, 1956); *The Strange Career of Jim Crow* (3rd ed., rev., New York, 1974); and *Tom Watson, Agrarian Rebel* (New York, 1938).

CHAPTER 10

1 The literature on the economic history of the postbellum South is considerable, though it has never been synthesized into a general work. Study of the impact of the Civil War should begin with Ralph Andreano, ed., *The Economic Impact of the American Civil War* (Cambridge, 1967), especially Eugene M. Lerner, "Southern Output and Agricultural Income, 1860–1880," 109–22; and Stanley L. Engerman, "The Economic Impact of the Civil War," *Explorations in Entrepreneurial History,* 2nd ser., III (Spring-Summer 1966), 176–99. Aspects of problems created by the war are treated in Engerman, "Some Economic Factors in Southern Backwardness in the Nineteenth Century," in John F. Kain and John R. Meyer, eds., *Essays in Regional Economics* (Cambridge, 1971), 279–306; Roger L. Ransom and Richard Sutch, "Debt Peonage in the Cotton South after the Civil War," *Journal of Economic History,* XXXII (September 1972), 641–669; Ransom and Sutch, "The Ex-Slave in the Post-Bellum South: A Study of the Economic Impact of Racism in a Market Environment," *Journal of Economic History,* XXXIII (March 1973), 131–48; Joseph D. Reid, "Sharecropping as an Understandable Market Response: The Post-Bellum South," *ibid.,* 106–30; William E. Laird and James R. Rinehart, "Deflation, Agriculture, and Southern Development," *Agricultural History,* XLII (April 1968), 115–24; and Theodore Saloutos, "Southern Agriculture and the Problems of Readjustment, 1865–1877," *ibid.,* XXX (January 1956), 58–76.

2 New South historians have been more interested in farmer protest than agricultural economics, and the literature on the latter is less voluminous than on the former. But see Stephen DeCanio, *Agriculture in the Postbellum South* (Cambridge, 1974), an econometric study. Other important works include Anthony M. Tang, *Economic Development in the Southern Piedmont, 1860–1950: Its Impact on Agriculture* (Chapel Hill, 1958); and Harold D. Woodman, *King Cotton and His Retainers: Financing and Marketing the Cotton Crop of the South, 1800–1925* (Lexington, 1968). Fred A. Shannon, *The Farmer's Last Frontier: Agriculture, 1860–1897* (New York, 1945), a study of American agriculture, gives some attention to the South. The best work on cotton, Rupert B. Vance, *Human Factors in the Cotton Culture* (Chapel Hill, 1929), concentrates on the twentieth century. Matthew B. Hammond, *The Cotton Industry* (New York, 1897), is informative on the New South era; while

James H. Street, *The New Revolution in the Cotton Economy* (Chapel Hill, 1957), focuses on a later generation. J. Carlyle Sitterson, *Sugar Country: The Cane Sugar Industry in the South, 1753–1950* (Lexington, 1953), is an exemplary study. Economic as well as social factors are treated in Thomas D. Clark, "The Furnishing and Supply System in Southern Agriculture since 1865," *Journal of Southern History,* XII (February 1946), 24–44; Clark, *Pills, Petticoats, and Plows: The Southern Country Store* (Indianapolis, 1944); and Jacqueline P. Bull, "The General Merchant in the Economic History of the New South," *Journal of Southern History,* XVIII (February 1952), 37–59.

3 On the survival of the plantation after the Civil War see Merle Prunty, Jr., "The Renaissance of the Southern Plantation," *Geographical Review,* XLV (October 1955), 459–91; Prunty, "The Census on Multiple-Units and Plantations in the South," *Professional Geographer,* VIII (September 1956), 2–5; and Roger W. Shugg, "Survival of the Plantation System in Louisiana," *Journal of Southern History,* III (August 1937), 311–25.

4 The literature on business and industry in the New South is quite large, though there is no general synthesis. Broadus Mitchell and George S. Mitchell, *The Industrial Revolution in the South* (Baltimore, 1930); and Broadus Mitchell, *The Rise of the Cotton Mills in the South* (Baltimore, 1921), are informative older works. Jack Blicksilver, *Cotton Manufacturing in the Southeast: An Historical Analysis* (Atlanta, 1959), is the best study of that subject. Robert S. Smith, *Mill on the Dan: A History of Dan River Mills, 1882–1950* (Durham, 1960), is an informative company history, as is Patrick G. Porter, "Origins of the American Tobacco Company," *Business History Review,* XLIII (Spring 1969), 59–76. John F. Stover, *The Railroads of the South, 1865–1900* (Chapel Hill, 1955), is an important work that shows the penetration of northern interests. On industrial labor, the basic study is F. Ray Marshall, *Labor in the South* (Cambridge, 1967), which focuses on union activity. Melton A. McLaurin, *Paternalism and Protest: Southern Cotton Mill Workers and Organized Labor, 1875–1905* (Westport, 1971); and Glen Gilman, *Human Relations in the Industrial Southeast: A Study of the Textile Industry* (Chapel Hill, 1955), treat the most important industry.

5 The best work on this subject is Paul M. Gaston, *The New South Creed: A Study in Southern Mythmaking* (New York, 1970).

6 The address is printed in Henry W. Grady, *The New South and Other Addresses* (New York, 1904). Other important examples of the New South creed are Walter Hines Page, "The Rebuilding of

Old Commonwealths," *Atlantic Monthly*, LXXXIX (May 1902), 651–61; and the June 1907 issue of *World's Work*.
7 See J. Morgan Kousser, *The Shaping of Southern Politics* (New Haven, 1974), 64–65; and Everett S. Lee et al., *Population Redistribution and Economic Growth, United States, 1870–1950* (Philadelphia, 1957), 349, 753.
8 Most of the scholarship on mill villages and mill workers focuses on the period after 1900. Among the best works are Liston Pope, *Millhands and Preachers* (New Haven, 1942), a study of the strike in the mills at Gastonia, North Carolina, in 1929.
9 For answers see Douglas F. Dowd, "A Comparative Analysis of Economic Development in the American West and South," *Journal of Economic History*, XVI (December 1956), 558–74; and William H. Nicholls, *Southern Tradition and Regional Progress* (Chapel Hill, 1960).

CHAPTER 11

1 The best general treatment of politics during the period of Conservative supremacy is C. Vann Woodward, *Origins of the New South, 1877–1913* (Baton Rouge, 1951). J. Morgan Kousser, *The Shaping of Southern Politics* (New Haven, 1974), which focuses on disfranchisement, is also quite informative. There are general discussions in T. Harry Williams, *Romance and Realism in Southern Politics* (Athens, 1961); Dewey W. Grantham, *The Democratic South* (Athens, 1963); and George B. Tindall, *The Persistent Tradition in New South Politics* (Baton Rouge, 1975). A number of important works focus on the political history of individual states. Among them are William I. Hair, *Bourbonism and Agrarian Protest, Louisiana Politics, 1877–1900* (Baton Rouge, 1969); William W. Rogers, *The One Gallused Rebellion: Agrarianism in Alabama, 1865–1896* (Baton Rouge, 1970); Albert D. Kirwan, *Revolt of the Rednecks, Mississippi Politics: 1876–1925* (Lexington, 1951); Allen W. Moger, *Virginia: Bourbonism to Byrd, 1870–1925* (Charlottesville, 1968); William J. Cooper, *The Conservative Regime, South Carolina, 1877–1890* (Baltimore, 1968); Allen J. Going, *Bourbon Democracy in Alabama, 1874–1890* (University, 1951); Jack P. Maddex, *The Virginia Conservatives, 1867–1879: A Study in Reconstruction Politics* (Chapel Hill, 1970); Roger L. Hart, *Redeemers, Bourbons, and Populists: Tennessee, 1870–1896* (Baton Rouge, 1975); Chester A. Barr, *Reconstruction to Reform: Texas Politics, 1876–1906* (Austin,

1971); and Judson C. Ward, "The New Departure Democrats of Georgia: An Interpretation," *Georgia Historical Quarterly,* LXI (September 1957), 227–36. On the evolution of historiographical thought on the Conservatives see Dewey W. Grantham, "The Southern Bourbons Revisited," *South Atlantic Quarterly,* LX (Summer 1961), 286–95.

2 The basic information on education in the New South is in the annual *Report of the Commissioner of Education.* Charles W. Dabney, *Universal Education in the South* (2 vols., Chapel Hill, 1936), and R. C. Simonini, ed., *Education in the South* (Farmville, 1969) are also useful, as are Allan M. Cartter, "The Role of Higher Education in the Changing South," in John C. McKinney and Edgar T. Thompson, eds., *The South in Continuity and Change* (Durham, 1965), 277–97; Allan J. Going, "The South and the Blair Education Bill," *Mississippi Valley Historical Review,* XLIV (September 1957), 267–90; and Charles F. Smith, "Southern Colleges and Schools," *Atlantic Monthly,* LIV (October 1884), 542–57.

3 The most informative accounts of insurgent movements are Charles C. Pearson, *The Readjuster Movement in Virginia* (New Haven, 1917), and Helen G. Edmonds, *The Negro and Fusion Politics in North Carolina, 1894–1901* (Chapel Hill, 1951).

4 The relative moderation of Conservatives on racial matters is also discussed in Woodward, *Origins of the New South,* Paul M. Gaston, *The New South Creed* (New York, 1970), and George M. Fredrickson, *The Black Image in the White Mind* (New York, 1971), all of which focus their discussion on the ideas of paternalistic Conservatives. Woodward's thesis on the evolution of segregation, which is the major focus of *The Strange Career of Jim Crow,* is discussed in the following chapter.

5 On violence, crime, and the penal system see Horace V. Redfield, *Homicide, North and South* (Philadelphia, 1880); B. J. Ramage, "Homicide in the Southern States," *Sewanee Review,* IV (February 1896), 212–32; H. C. Brearley, *Homicide in the United States* (Chapel Hill, 1932); Blake McKelvey, "A Half Century of Southern Penal Exploitation," *Social Forces,* XIII (October 1934), 112–23; Fletcher M. Green, "Some Aspects of the Southern Convict Lease System in the Southern States," in Green, ed., *Essays in Southern History* (Chapel Hill, 1949); Jane Zimmerman, "The Penal Reform Movement in the South during the Progressive Era, 1890–1917," *Journal of Southern History,* XVII (November 1951), 462–92; Frank Tannenbaum, *Darker Phases of the South* (New York, 1924), 74–115; *Report of the United States Commissioner of Labor, 1886, Convict Labor* (Washington, 1887); U.S. Census Office, *Report on Crime, Pauperism, and Benevolence in the United States ...*

1890 (Washington, 1896); and U.S. Commissioner of Labor, *Convict Labor* (Washington, 1905).

6 Populism and other reform movements growing out of farmer protest are discussed in the following chapter.

7 On women and the women's rights movement in the New South see Anne F. Scott, *The Southern Lady* (Chicago, 1970); Scott, "The 'New Woman' in the New South," *South Atlantic Quarterly,* LXI (Autumn 1962), 473–83; Clement Eaton, "Breaking a Path for the Liberation of Women in the South," *Georgia Review,* XXVIII (Summer 1974), 187–99; Aileen S. Kraditor, *The Ideas of the Woman Suffrage Movement* (New York, 1967); Kraditor, "Tactical Problems of the Woman Suffrage Movement in the South," *Louisiana Studies,* V (1966), 289–306; and Guion Griffis Johnson, "The Changing Status of Women," in McKinney and Thompson, eds., *The South in Continuity and Change,* 418–36.

8 There are several excellent studies of New South religion, among them Rufus B. Spain, *At Ease in Zion: Social History of the Southern Baptists, 1865–1900* (Nashville, 1967); Hunter D. Farish, *The Circuit Rider Dismounts: A Social History of Southern Methodism, 1865–1900* (Richmond, 1938); John Lee Eighmy, *Churches in Cultural Captivity: A History of the Social Attitudes of Southern Baptists* (Knoxville, 1972); and H. Shelton Smith, *In His Image But... Racism in Southern Religion, 1780–1910* (Durham, 1972). See also Joseph H. Fichter and George L. Maddox, "Religion in the South, Old and New," in McKinney and Thompson, eds., *The South in Continuity and Change,* 359–83; and Samuel S. Hill, ed., *Religion and the Solid South* (Nashville, 1972).

9 Major aspects of the intellectual history of the New South are treated discerningly in Gaston, *The New South Creed;* and Richard M. Weaver, *The Southern Tradition at Bay* (New Rochelle, 1968). Francis P. Gaines, *The Southern Plantation* (New York, 1925), discusses the plantation legend. For a good collection of short stories illustrating the myth of the Old South see Gene Baro, *After Appomattox: The Image of the South in Its Fiction, 1865–1900* (New York, 1963). Paul H. Buck, *The Road to Reunion, 1865–1890* (Boston, 1937), traces the rise of sectional reconciliation.

CHAPTER 12

1 The best survey of farmer protest is Theodore Saloutos, *Farmer Movements in the South, 1865–1933* (Berkeley, 1960); and the best historiographical resume of the subject is Allen J. Going, "The

Agrarian Revolt," in Arthur S. Link and Rembert W. Patrick, eds., *Writing Southern History* (Baton Rouge, 1965), 362–82. Other useful works include Robert C. McMath, *Populist Vanguard: A History of the Southern Farmers Alliance* (Chapel Hill, 1976); Francis B. Simkins, *The Tillman Movement in South Carolina* (Durham, 1926); Simkins, *Pitchfork Ben Tillman, South Carolinian* (Baton Rouge, 1944); and C. Vann Woodward, *Tom Watson, Agrarian Rebel* (New York, 1938). There is also considerable information on farmer protest in the studies of state politics cited in note 1 of Chapter XI.

2 The literature on southern Populism is extensive. The best treatment is in Lawrence Goodwyn, *Democratic Promise: The Populist Movement in America* (New York, 1976), and in two works by C. Vann Woodward in *Origins of the New South, 1877–1913* (Baton Rouge, 1951), 235–63, and *Tom Watson, Agrarian Rebel.* There are informative general discussions in George B. Tindall, *The Persistent Tradition in New South Politics* (Baton Rouge, 1975); T. Harry Williams, *Romance and Realism in Southern Politics* (Athens, 1961); and Dewey W. Grantham, *The Democratic South* (Athens, 1963). A significant older study is Alex M. Arnett, *The Populist Movement in Georgia* (New York, 1922). Older studies of Populism on the national level, such as John D. Hicks, *The Populist Revolt* (Minneapolis, 1931), and Richard Hofstadter, *The Age of Reform* (New York, 1955), concentrate on the Midwest.

3 On the origins of the Solid South see Dewey W. Grantham, "The Forging of the Solid South," in Grantham, *The Democratic South,* 15–41. On its demise see George B. Tindall, *The Disruption of the Solid South* (Athens, 1972). On its political usefulness on the national level see David M. Potter, *The South and the Concurrent Majority* (Baton Rouge, 1972). For a contemporary explanation of its existence see Hilary A. Herbert, ed., *Why the Solid South?* (Baltimore, 1890).

4 The best general account of blacks in the period is in John Hope Franklin, *From Slavery to Freedom* (4th ed., New York, 1974). August Meier, *Negro Thought in America, 1880–1915* (Ann Arbor, 1963), is a distinguished work. The declining status of Negroes is traced in C. Vann Woodward, *The Strange Career of Jim Crow* (3rd ed., New York, 1974), and in Rayford W. Logan, *The Negro in American Life and Thought: The Nadir* (New York, 1954). The decline of Negro voting is traced in J. Morgan Kousser, *The Shaping of Southern Politics* (New Haven, 1974). There are several important studies of blacks in individual states, among them Vernon Lane Wharton, *The Negro in Mississippi, 1865–1890* (Chapel

Hill, 1947); George B. Tindall, *South Carolina Negroes, 1877–1900* (Columbia, 1952); Charles E. Wynes, *Race Relations in Virginia, 1870–1902* (Charlottesville, 1961); Frenise A. Logan, *The Negro in North Carolina, 1876–1894* (Chapel Hill, 1964); Helen G. Edmonds, *The Negro and Fusion Politics in North Carolina, 1894–1901* (Chapel Hill, 1951); and Andrew Buni, *The Negro in Virginia Politics, 1902–1965* (Charlottesville, 1967).

5 Woodward has reviewed this debate in "The Strange Career of a Historical Controversy," in Woodward, *American Counterpoint* (Boston, 1971), 234–60. Joel Williamson, whose *After Slavery: The Negro in South Carolina during Reconstruction, 1861–1877* (Chapel Hill, 1965) is a major challenge to Woodward's thesis, has put together an informative collection of relevant readings in *The Origins of Segregation* (Boston, 1968).

6 Louis R. Harlan, *Booker T. Washington: The Making of a Black Leader, 1856–1901* (New York, 1972), the first volume of a projected two-volume work, is a distinguished biography. The best brief interpretation of Washington's purposes and historical significance is in Meier, *Negro Thought in America, 1880–1915*.

7 The most systematic and extensive treatment of southern Progressivism is in Woodward, *Origins of the New South, 1877–1913;* and George B. Tindall, *The Emergence of the New South, 1913–1945* (Baton Rouge, 1967). Other enlightening studies include Hugh C. Bailey, *Liberalism in the New South: Southern Social Reformers and the Progressive Movement* (Coral Gables, 1969); Bruce Clayton, *The Savage Ideal: Intolerance and Intellectual Leadership in the South, 1890–1914* (Baltimore, 1972); Virginius Dabney, *Liberalism in the South* (Chapel Hill, 1932); Herbert J. Doherty, Jr., "Voices of Protest from the New South, 1875–1910," *Mississippi Valley Historical Review,* XLII (June 1955), 45–66; Dewey W. Grantham, Jr., *Hoke Smith and the Politics of the New South* (Baton Rouge, 1958); William F. Holmes, *The White Chief: James Kimble Vardaman* (Baton Rouge, 1970); Jack T. Kirby, *Darkness at the Dawning: Race and Reform in the Progressive South* (Philadelphia, 1972); and Arthur S. Link, "The Progressive Movement in the South, 1870–1914," *North Carolina Historical Review,* XXIII (April 1946), 172–95. There are also informative commentaries in Grantham, *The Democratic South;* Williams, *Romance and Realism in Southern Politics;* and Tindall, *The Persistent Tradition in New South Politics*. On the state level see especially Sheldon Hackney, *Populism to Progressivism in Alabama* (Princeton, 1969); and Raymond H. Pulley, *Old Virginia Restored: An Interpretation of the Progressive Impulse, 1870–1934* (Charlottesville, 1968).

PART FIVE INTRODUCTION

1 Easily the most significant general work on the South since World War I is George B. Tindall, *The Emergence of the New South, 1913–1945* (Baton Rouge, 1967), a work that focuses on the theme of change in the period encompassed by the two world wars and on the growing standardization of the South according to national norms. It gives less attention to the other side of the theme, the persistence of sectional distinctiveness. Thomas D. Clark, *The Emerging South* (2nd ed., New York, 1968), has a wealth of information on economic and social history between 1920 and the 1960s; and V. O. Key, *Southern Politics in State and Nation* (New York, 1949), is the most systematic treatment of politics. Monroe L. Billington, *The Political South in the Twentieth Century* (New York, 1975), is a useful survey.

CHAPTER 13

1 Arthur S. Link, "The South and the 'New Freedom': An Interpretation," *American Scholar,* XX (Summer 1951), 314–24, emphasizes the southern contribution to Wilson's program, while Richard M. Abrams, "Woodrow Wilson and the Southern Congressmen, 1913–1916," *Journal of Southern History,* XXII (November 1956), 417–37 downplays the southern influence. Howard W. Allen, "Geography and Politics: Voting on Reform Issues in the United States Senate, 1911–1916," *ibid.,* XXVII (May 1961), 216–28, emphasizes the conservatism of southern congressmen during the Wilson years.
2 The only general account of the impact of the war on the South is Tindall, *The Emergence of the New South,* 33–69.
3 The literature on the southern economy during the 1920s is large, but there is no general synthesis. The best survey is in Tindall, *The Emergence of the New South,* chaps. III, IV, and X. Calvin B. Hoover and Benjamin U. Ratchford, *Economic Resources and Policies of the South* (New York, 1951), contains a wealth of information for the period beginning with 1929. Emory Q. Hawk, *Economic History of the South* (New York, 1934), is an informative textbook; and A. E. Parkins, *The South: Its Economic-Geographic Development* (New York, 1938), is an informative economic geography. Other

important general works include John L. Fulmer, *Agricultural Progress in the Cotton Belt since 1920* (Chapel Hill, 1950); Clarence Poe, "The Farmer and His Future," in W. T. Couch, ed., *Culture in the South* (Chapel Hill, 1935); Jack Blicksilver, *Cotton Manufacturing in the Southeast* (Atlanta, 1959); Harriet L. Herring, *Southern Industry and Regional Development* (Chapel Hill, 1940); Robert P. Brooks, *The Industrialization of the South* (Athens, 1929); F. Ray Marshall, *Labor in the South* (Cambridge, 1967); and Sterling D. Spero and Abram L. Harris, *The Black Worker* (New York, 1931). The social dimensions of economic problems are stressed in Rupert B. Vance, *Human Factors in Cotton Culture* (Chapel Hill, 1929); Vance, *Human Geography of the South* (Chapel Hill, 1932); and Liston Pope, *Millhands and Preachers* (New Haven, 1942).

4 In the age of statistics, the lack of geographical uniformity in the area designated "the South" is a potential source of confusion. Here, unless otherwise indicated, "the South" is used to mean the eleven states of the Confederacy. "The Southeast" is the area so designated by Howard W. Odum in *Southern Regions* (Chapel Hill, 1936)—the Confederate South less Texas but including Kentucky. "The greater South" is the area covered in the LSU *History of the South*—the Confederacy plus Kentucky and Oklahoma.

5 The best studies of the political history of the interwar years are the works by Key, Tindall, and Billington cited in note 1 of the Introduction to Part 5 of this study. There are also insightful discussions in George E. Mowry, *Another Look at the Twentieth Century South* (Baton Rouge, 1972); George B. Tindall, *The Disruption of the Solid South* (New York, 1972); and David M. Potter, *The South and the Concurrent Majority* (Baton Rouge, 1972).

6 But see Jasper B. Shannon, *Toward a New Politics in the South* (Knoxville, 1949), 38–53; and the brief discussion in Ralph McGill, *The South and the Southerner* (Boston, 1963), 161–65.

7 On the agrarian demagogues see Reinhard A. Luthin, *American Demagogues* (Boston, 1954); A. A. Michie and Frank Rhylick, *Dixie Demagogues* (New York, 1947); and Gerald W. Johnson, "Live Demagogues and Dead Gentlemen," *Virginia Quarterly Review,* XII (January 1936), 1–14. The best work on Huey P. Long is T. Harry Williams, *Huey Long* (New York, 1969); the best on Eugene Talmadge is William Anderson, *The Wild Man from Sugar Creek: The Political Career of Eugene Talmadge* (Baton Rouge, 1975).

8 The most important general studies of the racial issue in this period are Gunnar Myrdal, *An American Dilemma* (New York, 1944); and C. Vann Woodward, *The Strange Career of Jim Crow*

(3rd ed., New York, 1974). C. S. Mangum, *The Legal Status of the Negro* (Chapel Hill, 1940), and Bertram W. Doyle, *The Etiquette of Race Relations in the South* (Chicago, 1937), also treat important subjects. Dan T. Carter, *Scottsboro: A Tragedy of the American South* (Baton Rouge, 1969) is a deft account of the most important racial incident of the interwar years; and Arthur I. Waskow, *From Race Riot to Sit-in* (Garden City, 1966) is the best account of the post-World War I upsurge of racial violence. Of the many general works dealing with blacks in this period, E. Franklin Frazier, *The Negro in the United States* (New York, 1949), is perhaps the most informative. For examples of black thinking on racial policy see Rayford W. Logan, ed., *What the Negro Wants* (Chapel Hill, 1944); James Weldon Johnson, *Negro Americans, What Now?* (New York, 1934); and Robert R. Moton, *What the Negro Thinks* (Garden City, 1929). On the interracial movement see Wilma Dykeman and James Stokeley, *Seeds of Southern Change: The Life of Will Alexander* (Chicago, 1962); and Willis D. Weatherford and Charles S. Johnson, *Race Relations: Adjustment of Whites and Negroes in the United States* (Boston, 1934). On black migration see T. Lynn Smith, "The Redistribution of the Negro Population in the United States, 1910–1960," *Journal of Negro History,* LI (July 1966), 155–73; C. Horace Hamilton, "Continuity and Change in Southern Migration," in John C. McKinney and Edgar T. Thompson, eds., *The South in Continuity and Change* (Durham, 1965), 53–78; and Henderson H. Donald, "The Effects of the Migration on the South," *Journal of Negro History,* VI (October 1921), 421–34. There is much information on economic conditions in Raymond Wolters, *Negroes and the Great Depression* (Westport, 1970), and F. Ray Marshall, *The Negro and Organized Labor* (New York, 1965).

CHAPTER 14

1 On development of this image see George B. Tindall, "The Benighted South: Origins of a Modern Image," *Virginia Quarterly Review,* XL (Spring 1964), 281–94. For expositions of the image see H. L. Mencken, "The Sahara of the Bozart," in Mencken, *Prejudices, Second Series* (New York, 1920); Howard W. Odum, "A Southern Promise," *Social Forces,* III (May 1925), 739–46; and William H. Skaggs, *The Southern Oligarchy* (New York, 1924). For an account of the circumstances surrounding the publication of

Odum's article see Willard B. Gatewood, "Embattled Scholar: Howard W. Odum and the Fundamentalists, 1925–1927," *Journal of Southern History,* XXXI (November 1965), 375–92.

2 In addition to the works noted in the following discussion, see F. N. Boney, "The Redneck," *Georgia Review,* XXV (Fall 1971), 333–42, for an interesting discussion of the problem of understanding and appreciating the white poor. Shields McIlwaine, *The Poor-White from Lubberland to Tobacco Road* (Norman, 1939) is a study of literary images. For representative examples of the studies of poor whites in the interwar years see E. C. Branson, "Farm Tenancy in the South," *Social Forces,* I (May 1923), 450–57; John Walker McCain, "Some Small-Town Folk Beliefs of the Carolina Piedmont," *ibid.,* XII (March 1933), 418–20; and Ervilla A. Masters, "Some Findings of a Standard of Living Study Made of White Farm Families on Sand Mountain, Alabama," *ibid.,* XVI (March 1938), 366–69.

3 I use this term to encompass a set of ideas generally accepted by a loose and varied grouping of people who did not always agree on specific social policies. Generally, social fundamentalists included those who sought through various forms of direct action to resist liberal social change. More specifically, they included those people who joined or sympathized with the Ku Klux Klan and other similar organizations or belonged to churches which practiced the most literal-minded theology; and those whose social activism was chiefly determined by social and racial prejudices or whose social policies were characterized by repressiveness and regimentation. No one has yet studied the general fundamentalist movement in the South in all its ramifications, and there is no work that synthesizes its history. There are, however, a number of works on many of its basic components that illustrate its nature. See for example Norman F. Furniss, *The Fundamentalist Controversy* (New Haven, 1954); Maynard Shipley, *The War on Modern Science* (New York, 1927); Ray Ginger, *Six Days or Forever? Tennessee v. John Thomas Scopes* (Boston, 1958); L. Sprague de Camp, *The Great Monkey Trial* (Garden City, 1968); Edmund A. Moore, *A Catholic Runs for President: The Campaign of 1928* (New York, 1956); Virginius Dabney, *Dry Messiah: The Life of Bishop Cannon* (New York, 1949); Lawrence W. Levine, *Defender of the Faith William Jennings Bryan: The Last Decade, 1915–1925* (New York, 1965).

4 There are a number of enlightening works on the history of religion in this period, among them Kenneth K. Bailey, *Southern White Protestantism in the Twentieth Century* (New York, 1964); Samuel S. Hill, Jr., *Religion and the Solid South* (Nashville, 1972);

John Lee Eighmy, *Churches in Cultural Captivity: A History of the Social Attitudes of Southern Baptists* (Knoxville, 1972); Robert M. Miller, "The Protestant Churches and Lynching," *Journal of Negro History,* XLII (April 1957), 118–31; Miller, "The Attitudes of American Protestantism toward the Negro, 1919–1939," *ibid.,* XLI (July 1956), 215–40; Edmund deS. Brunner, *Church Life in the Rural South* (New York, 1923); Joseph H. Fichter and George L. Maddox, "Religion in the South, Old and New," in John C. McKinney and Edgar T. Thompson, eds., *The South in Continuity and Change* (Durham, 1965), 359–83; and Edwin M. Poteat, "Religion in the South," in W. T. Couch, ed., *'Culture in the South* (Chapel Hill, 1934). On black religion see E. Franklin Frazier, *The Negro Church in America* (New York, 1963).

5 There is no general history of education during this period, but there are informative discussions in Edgar W. Knight, "Recent Progress and Problems in Education," in Couch, ed., *Culture in the South,* 211–28; H. Clarence Nixon, "Colleges and Universities," *ibid.,* 229–47; John Gould Fletcher, "Education, Past and Present," in Twelve Southerners, *I'll Take My Stand* (New York, 1930); Allan M. Cartter, "The Role of Higher Education in the Changing South," in McKinney and Thompson, eds., *The South in Continuity and Change,* 277–97; and Cartter, "Qualitative Aspects of Southern University Education," *Southern Economic Journal,* XXXIII (July 1965), 39–69. On related subjects see Harold L. Geisert, "The Trend of the Interregional Migration of Talent: The Southeast, 1899–1936," *Social Forces,* XVIII (October 1939), 41–47; Wilson Gee, "The 'Drag' of Talent out of the South," *ibid.,* XV (March 1937), 343–46; and W. T. Couch, "Southern Publishing," *Sewanee Review,* LIII (Winter 1945), 167–71. On black education see Horace Mann Bond, *Negro Education in the South* (Washington, 1939).

6 The savage ideal thrived in the milieu described in the works cited in note 3 above. The best general discussion of violence is Sheldon Hackney, "Southern Violence," *American Historical Review,* LXXIV (February 1969), 906–25. See also H. C. Brearley, "The Pattern of Violence" in Couch, ed., *Culture in the South,* 678–92; Stuart Lottier, "Distribution of Criminal Offenses in Sectional Regions," *Journal of Criminal Law and Criminology,* XXIX (September-October 1938), 329–44; and Lyle Shannon, "The Spatial Distribution of Criminal Offenses by States," *ibid.,* XLV (September-October 1954), 264–73. On related topics see Pete Daniels, *The Shadow of Slavery: Peonage in the South, 1901–1969* (Urbana, 1972); Virginius Dabney, "Civil Liberties in the South," *Virginia*

Quarterly Review, XVI (Winter 1940), 81–91. On the Ku Klux Klan see Charles C. Alexander, *The Ku Klux Klan in the Southwest* (Houston, 1962); Kenneth T. Jackson, *The Ku Klux Klan in the City, 1915–1930* (New York, 1967); and Arnold S. Rice, *The Ku Klux Klan in American Politics* (Washington, 1962).

7 The literature on the South during the depression and New Deal years is large and growing. The best survey is Tindall, *The Emergence of the New South,* chaps. XI–XIX. Howard W. Odum, *Southern Regions* (Chapel Hill, 1936), and Calvin B. Hoover and Benjamin U. Ratchford, *Economic Resources and Policies of the South* (New York, 1951), both contain a wealth of information. Katharine DuPre Lumpkin, *The South in Progress* (New York, 1940), and Walter P. Webb, *Divided We Stand* (New York, 1937), are also informative. On the plight of sharecroppers and the agricultural poor see Howard Kester, *Revolt of the Sharecroppers* (New York, 1936); James Agee and Walker Evans, *Let Us Now Praise Famous Men* (Boston, 1941); Donald H. Grubbs, *Cry from the Cotton: The Southern Tenant Farmers Union and the New Deal* (Chapel Hill, 1971); and David E. Conrad, *The Forgotten Farmers: The Story of Sharecroppers in the New Deal* (Urbana, 1965). On other topics see "Labor in the South," *Monthly Labor Review,* LXIII (October 1946), 481–586; Howard B. Myers, "Relief in the Rural South," *Southern Economic Journal,* III (January 1937), 281–91; Charles T. Taylor, "Some Economic Consequences of Federal Aid to Southern Agriculture," *Southern Economic Journal,* XIV (July 1947), 62–72; Rupert B. Vance and Nadia Danilevsky, "Population and the Patterns of Unemployment in the Southeast, 1930–1937," *ibid.,* VIII (October 1940), 187–203; William C. Holley et al., *The Plantation South, 1934–1937* (Washington, 1940); and Charles S. Johnson et al., *The Collapse of Cotton Tenancy* (Chapel Hill, 1935). On politics see Frank Freidel, *F.D.R. and the South* (Baton Rouge, 1965); and James T. Patterson, *Congressional Conservatism and the New Deal* (Lexington, 1967).

CHAPTER 15

1 On the development of southern studies see Dewey W. Grantham, "The Regional Imagination: Social Scientists and the American South," *Journal of Southern History,* XXXIV (February 1968), 3–32; J. Kenneth Morland, "Anthropology and the Study of Culture,

Society, and Community in the South," in Edgar T. Thompson, ed., *Perspectives on the South: Agenda for Research* (Durham, 1967), 125–45; and Dewey W. Grantham, "The Twentieth Century South," in Arthur S. Link and Rembert W. Patrick, eds., *Writing Southern History* (Baton Rouge, 1965), 410–44. Works on Howard W. Odum are cited in note 4 below.

2 The problems involved in the use of such terms as "liberal" and "conservative" are obvious. The terms have never been defined to everyone's satisfaction, and I have used them only because no better terms suggest themselves. They are meant to designate loose, unorganized, and sometimes overlapping groupings according to their stands on political, economic, and social issues of sectional significance. "Liberals" were those individuals and groups favoring social changes that would move the South toward American norms, including racial reform within white supremacy, economic diversification, two-party politics, the muting of sectional consciousness, and other reforms noted in the following discussion. They therefore included individuals who joined or sympathized with organizations ranging from the cautious Commission on Interracial Cooperation and its more "liberal" successor, the Southern Regional Council, to activists in the labor movement and the more explicitly "liberal" Southern Conference for Human Welfare. "Conservatives" were more resistant to American norms, especially outside the realm of economic growth, and were traditionalists in matters relating to public morals. "Social fundamentalists" were thus "extreme" conservatives, those whose conservative social values derived from prejudices that were unredeemed by a positive social vision, and who sometimes condoned illegal or extralegal pressures to achieve their goals. For representative accounts of liberals at work see Wilma Dykeman and James Stokeley, *Seeds of Southern Change: The Life of Will Alexander* (Chicago, 1962); Thomas A. Krueger, *And Promises to Keep: The Southern Conference for Human Welfare, 1938–48* (Nashville, 1967); and Donald H. Grubbs, *Cry from the Cotton: The Southern Tenant Farmers Union and the New Deal* (Chapel Hill, 1971). For representative statements of conservative thought see, in addition to Twelve Southerners, *I'll Take My Stand* (New York, 1930), which is discussed below, Josephine Pinckney, "Bulwarks against Change," in W. T. Couch, *The Culture of the South* (Chapel Hill, 1934), 40–51; William Alexander Percy, *Lanterns on the Levee* (New York, 1941); Francis B. Simkins, "The Everlasting South," *Journal of Southern History,* XIII (August 1947), 307–22; and Richard M. Weaver, *The Southern Tradition at Bay* (New Rochelle, 1968).

3 There are a number of informative works on the Agrarians, among them John L. Stewart, *The Burden of Time: The Fugitives and the Agrarians* (Baton Rouge, 1965); Alexander Karanikas, *Tillers of a Myth: Southern Agrarians as Social and Literary Critics* (Madison, 1966); and Richard Gray, *The Literature of Memory: Modern Writers of the American South* (Baltimore, 1976). Donald Davidson, *Southern Writers in the Modern World* (Athens, 1958), contains the assessment of one of the major Agrarians. See also Davidson, *Still Rebels, Still Yankees* (Baton Rouge, 1967). John T. Westbrook, "Twilight of Regionalism," *Southwest Review*, XLII (Summer 1957), 231–34, is critical; Richard M. Weaver, "Agrarianism in Exile," *Sewanee Review*, LVIII (Autumn 1950), 586–606, is the appreciation of an admirer; Thomas J. Pressly, "Agrarianism: An Autopsy," *Sewanee Review*, XLIX (April-June 1941), 145–63, is a balanced assessment. See also Edward S. Shapiro, "The Southern Agrarians, H. L. Mencken, and the Quest for Southern Identity," *American Studies*, I (Fall 1972), 75–92. Among the many informative statements by Agrarians not noted in the text are Frank L. Owsley, "The Pillars of Agrarianism," *American Review*, IV (March 1935), 529–47; Owsley, "A Key to Southern Liberalism," *Southern Review*, III (1937–38), 28–38; John Crowe Ransom, "The South Defends Its Heritage," *Harper's Magazine*, CLIX (June 1929), 108–18; and Ransom, "The South—Old or New?" *Sewanee Review*, XXXVI (January 1928), 139–47.

4 On Odum see George B. Tindall, "The Significance of Howard W. Odum to Southern History: A Preliminary Estimate," *Journal of Southern History*, XXIV (August 1958), 285–307; George L. Simpson, "Howard W. Odum and American Regionalism," *Social Forces*, XXXIV (December 1955), 101–6; and Rupert B. Vance and Katharine Jocher, "Howard W. Odum," *Social Forces*, XXXIII (March 1955), 203–17. For Odum's assessment of *Southern Regions* a decade after its appearance see Odum, "Social Change in the South," *Journal of Politics*, X (May 1948), 242–58.

5 The literature on the literary renaissance is quite large. John M. Bradbury, *Renaissance in the South: A Critical History of the Literature, 1920–1960* (Chapel Hill, 1963), is the best survey. Louis D. Rubin and Robert D. Jacobs, eds., *Southern Renascence: The Literature of the Modern South* (Baltimore, 1953), and Rubin and Jacobs, eds., *South: Modern Southern Literature in Its Cultural Setting* (Garden City, 1961) contain informative articles. Louis D. Rubin, *Writers of the Modern South* (Seattle, 1963), and C. Hugh Holman, *Three Modes of Southern Fiction* (Athens, 1966), treat discerningly some of the major writers. C. Vann Woodward, "The Historical Dimension," in Woodward, *The Burden of Southern His-*

tory (Baton Rouge, 1968), 27–39, is the best assessment of the value of the literature for historians.

PART SIX INTRODUCTION

1 Historians have only begun to write the history of the South since 1945. The only survey of the period is Charles P. Roland, *The Improbable Era: The South since World War II* (Lexington, 1975), which includes a good brief bibliographical essay. There is some historical background in Neal R. Pierce's surveys of *The Deep South States of America: People, Politics, and Power in the Seven States of the Deep South* (New York, 1974) and *The Border States: People, Politics, and Power in the Five Border South States* (New York, 1975); and in Pat Watters's insightful *The South and the Nation* (New York, 1969). Alfred O. Hero, *The Southerner and World Affairs* (Baton Rouge, 1965), a major study of southern attitudes, is much broader than the title implies. A number of the many works published during this period on sectional character are noted in Chapters 1 and 17. But see also William Peters, *The Southern Temper* (New York, 1954); Stetson Kennedy, *Southern Exposure* (New York, 1946); Frank E. Vandiver, ed., *The Idea of the South* (Chicago, 1964); and Charles G. Sellers, ed., *The Southerner as American* (Chapel Hill, 1960). There is a great deal of information in such cooperative works as John C. McKinney and Edgar T. Thompson, eds., *The South in Continuity and Change* (Durham, 1965); Allen P. Shindler, ed., *Change in the Contemporary South* (Durham, 1963); Robert B. Highshaw, ed., *The Deep South in Transformation* (University, 1964); and H. Brandt Ayers and Thomas H. Naylor, eds., *You Can't Eat Magnolias* (New York, 1972).

CHAPTER 16

1 The history of the South during World War II is still largely unwritten, and there is as yet no systematic assessment of the full impact of the war. The best survey is in George B. Tindall, *The Emergence of the New South, 1913–1945* (Baton Rouge, 1967), 687–

731, but Tindall's treatment of the war years is far more summary than his detailed discussions of the 1920s and 1930s. The most extensive contemporary commentary is John Temple Graves, *The Fighting South* (New York, 1943); but see also Dillard B. Lasseter, "The Impact of the War on the South and Implications for Postwar Development," *Social Forces,* XXIII (October 1944), 20–26; and Charles S. Johnson, "The Present Status of Race Relations in the South," *ibid.,* 27–32. On the South and foreign policy see Wayne S. Cole, "America First and the South, 1940–41," *Journal of Southern History,* XXII (February 1956), 36–47; Alexander DeConde, "The South and Isolationism," *ibid.,* XXIV (August 1958), 332–46; Charles O. Lerche, *The Uncertain South: Its Changing Patterns of Politics in Foreign Policy* (Chicago, 1964); Alfred O. Hero, *The Southerner and World Affairs* (Baton Rouge, 1965); and Hero, "Changing Southern Attitudes toward United States Foreign Policy," *Southern Humanities Review,* VIII (Summer 1974), 275–95.

2 There is a wealth of information on economic development since 1945. Among the major works are Calvin B. Hoover and Benjamin U. Ratchford, *Economic Resources and Policies of the South* (New York, 1951); Thomas H. Naylor and James Clotfelter, *Strategies for Change in the South* (Chapel Hill, 1975); Marshall R. Colberg, *Human Capital in Southern Development, 1939–1963* (Chapel Hill, 1965); Albert W. Niemi, *Gross State Product and Productivity in the Southeast* (Chapel Hill, 1975); and M. I. Foster, "Is the South Still a Backward Region, and Why?" *American Economic Review,* LXII (May 1972), 195–203. See also the articles on economic subjects in John C. McKinney and Edgar T. Thompson, eds., *The South in Continuity and Change* (Durham, 1965).

3 Race and politics are the two most widely studied areas of southern life since World War II. The best bibliographical essay on the civil rights movement is James M. McPherson et al., *Blacks in America: Bibliographical Essays* (Garden City, 1971), 301–404. The history of that movement is surveyed in Benjamin Muse, *Ten Years of Prelude: The Story of Integration since the Supreme Court's 1954 Decision* (New York, 1964); and Muse, *The American Negro Revolution: From Non-Violence to Black Power, 1963–1967* (Bloomington, 1968). The progress of school desegregation is best traced in the monthly *Southern School News* (1954–1965). The best accounts of white resistance include Numan V. Bartley, *The Rise of Massive Resistance: Race and Politics in the South during the 1950s* (Baton Rouge, 1969); Neil R. McMillen, *The Citizens' Council: Organized Resistance to the Second Reconstruction* (Urbana, 1971); and Robert C. Smith, *They Closed Their Schools: Prince Edward County,*

Virginia, 1951–1964 (Chapel Hill, 1965). See also James W. Silver, *Mississippi: The Closed Society* (New York, 1964); James G. Cook, *The Segregationists* (New York, 1962); and Len Holt, *The Summer That Didn't End* (New York, 1965). Wilma Dykeman and James Stokeley, *Neither Black nor White* (New York, 1957) is a good statement of early reactions to the *Brown* decision. On Martin Luther King see King, *Stride toward Freedom: The Montgomery Story* (New York, 1958); and David L. Lewis, *King: A Critical Biography* (New York, 1970). Donald R. Matthews and James W. Prothro, *Negroes and the New Southern Politics* (New York, 1966), is the best treatment of its subject. Sar A. Levitan, William B. Johnston, and Robert Taggart, *Still a Dream: The Changing Status of Blacks since 1960* (Cambridge, 1975), is a recent assessment of the progress and continuing problems of blacks.

4 The literature on politics since 1945 is extensive, though there is no systematic study that matches V. O. Key's work on the preceding half century, *Southern Politics in State and Nation* (New York, 1949). William C. Havard, ed., *The Changing Politics of the South* (Baton Rouge, 1972), is the most thorough analysis. However, Numan V. Bartley and Hugh D. Graham, *Southern Politics and the Second Reconstruction* (Baltimore, 1975), and Jack Bass and Walter DeVries, *The Transformation of Southern Politics: Social Change and Political Consequence since 1945* (New York, 1976) are better-integrated studies and the best introduction to the study of the period. Alexander Heard, *A Two-Party South?* (Chapel Hill, 1952), was written when the two-party system was still largely a dream; but only twenty years later George B. Tindall published a small volume announcing *The Disruption of the Solid South* (Athens, 1972). The ideas behind the strategy to increase Republican strength in the section are discussed in Kevin P. Phillips, *The Emerging Republican Majority* (New Rochelle, 1969); and Richard M. Scammond and Ben J. Wattenberg, *The Real Majority* (New York, 1970). An outstanding study of one state is Numan V. Bartley, *From Thurmond to Wallace: Political Tendencies in Georgia, 1948–1968* (Baltimore, 1970). The voting of southerners in Congress is traced in H. Wayne Shannon, *Party, Constituency and Congressional Voting* (Baton Rouge, 1968); and Hubert R. Fowler, *The Unsolid South: Voting Behavior of Southern Senators, 1947–1960* (University, 1968). See also Marshall Frady, *Wallace* (New York, 1968); and the enlightening essay by Dewey W. Grantham, "The South and the Reconstruction of American Politics," *Journal of American History,* LIII (September 1966), 227–46.

Index

Abolition, 131
　proliferation of, 112–113
　and sectionalism, 111
Adams, John, 116
Agrarian demagoguery, 392–395
Agrarians, 445–453
Agriculture (*see* Cotton; Farms and farming; Plantation regime; Sharecropping)
Alien and Sedition Laws, 116–117
American Colonization Society, 112
American Revolution:
　military strategy in, 218
　and Southern consciousness, 72–76
Antietam, Battle of, 227
Armed forces, desegregation of, 480
Arnall, Ellis G., 473
Awakening, The (Chopin), 321, 322

Baker v. Carr, 478
Banking, in New South, 283–284
Baptism, 323, 324
　and slavery, 78
Bell, John, 201, 202, 203
Benezet, Anthony, 81
Bilbo, Theodore G., 392–393
Birmingham, Ala., 299, 486
Black codes, 255–256
Blacks:
　and Black studies, 440
　and Booker T. Washington, 356–359
　during Civil War, 248–252
　and Conservative rule, 305–307, 311–315
　declining status of (New South), 344–346
　and Democratic party, 430–431
　and disenfranchisement, 346–351
　and economic boom, 476
　and education, 319–320, 397
　and Indians, 64–65
　interior history of, 58–60
　out-migration of, 396, 491
　and penal system, 419–420
　population of, 20, 44, 57, 77, 88, 89, 91, 109, 262, 343–344, 467
　and Populism, 340–341
　and Progressivism, 368–370
　and Reconstruction, 255–260, 261–263
　　Conservative policies on, 267–269
　　Radical policies on, 263–265
　　and Redemption period, 274–275
　　significance of, 272–276
　　Reconstruction strategies of, 246–247
　and religion, 322–323
　and sharecropping, 286
　as Southerners, 9–11
　See also Civil rights movement; Race and race relations; Slavery
Blair education bill, 319–320
Bond, Julian, 491
Border states, compared to Confederate states, 109
Bragg, Braxton, 227
Breckenridge, John C., 201, 202

549

Britain, and Civil War, 214–215, 217, 229–230
Brown v. Board of Education of Topeka, 472, 481–482
Bruce, Blanche K., 263
Buchanan, James, 196, 197–198
Bull Run, Battles of, 225, 227, 231
Butler, Pierce, 85
Byrd, Harry F., 387

Cable, George Washington, 317, 318–319
Caldwell, Erskine, 461–462
Calhoun, John C., 90, 172
 career and philosophy of, 118–123
 and nullification crisis, 114–115, 118
 pro-slavery arguments of, 179
California, 193
Carolina Indians, 63–64
Carpetbaggers, 260, 265–267
Carter, Hodding, 473–474
Carter, Jimmy, 491, 498, 500, 501
Cash, Wilbur J., 66
 on southern character, 20–25
Charleston, S.C., distribution of wealth in, 95
Child labor, 367, 428
Chopin, Kate, 321, 322
Civil Rights Act of 1866, 258–259
Civil Rights Acts of 1964 and 1965, 486–487
Civil rights movement:
 birth of, 479–480
 Black-activist period of, 485–487
 conservative attitudes toward, 472–473
 and moderate whites, 473–474
 and national politics, 493–501
 outcome assessed, 488–492
 and school desegregation, 481–485, 486, 488–489
 and busing, 489–490
 and voting rights, 487–488
 See also Blacks, Race and race relations; Slavery

Civil War:
 casualties in, 230–232, 235
 causes of, 185–204
 and Compromise of 1850, 192–196
 differing viewpoints of, 185–188
 economic factors in, 196–198
 and election of 1860, 201–202
 and secession, 202–203
 slavery-expansionism issues as, 188–196
 underlying issues of, 198–200
 Confederate homefront in, 222–225
 Confederate preparedness for, 212–215
 Confederate strategic failures in, 215–218
 destructive impact of, 235–237
 military overview of, 225–229
 Confederate defeat analyzed, 229–232
 and Missouri controversy, 106–107
 racial policies during, 248–252
 social impact of, 237–240
 start of, 207–208
 Union preparedness for, 212–213
Clay, Henry, 115
 and Compromise of 1850, 192–193
Cleburne, Patrick R., 250
Climate, historical impact of, 25–27
Cobb, Thomas R. R., 159
Collins, Leroy, 495
Colonial South:
 development of slavery in, 56–58
 and Indians, 61–65
 motives for settlement of, 37–39
 and plantation system, 42–46
 racial patterns in, 53–56
 religion in, 39–40
 social ethic in, 40–42
 social structure of, 46–53
 upcountry in, 65–67

Index

Commission on Interracial
  Cooperation, 398–399
Committee on Civil Rights,
  480–481
Commodity output, in Old South,
  134
Compromise of 1850:
  failure of, 192–196
  tenets of, 192–193
Compromise of 1877, 272–274
Concurrent majority:
  and John C. Calhoun, 119–123
  political use of, 123–124
Confederacy:
  assessment and overview of,
    208–212
  birth of, 204–206
  civilian efforts in, 222–225
  failure of, 232–233
  financing of, 223–224
  leadership of, 220–222
  preparedness for war of, 212–215
  strategic failures of, 215–218
Congress, 110
  and Missouri controversy,
    104–105
  and Reconstruction, 253,
    256–263
Connally, John, 499
Conservatives and conservatism:
  vs. regionalism, 455–456
  era evaluated, 330–332
  identified and characterized,
    301–304
  vs. moderate potential, 311–313
  politics of, 304–309
  and violence, 313–316
Constitution (*see* Unionization)
Constitutional Convention, 83–86
Cotton:
  boom in, 90, 91–92
  decreasing importance of, 475
  economic importance of,
    127–138, 130
  and sharecropping, 282, 284
  and World War I, 380
Cotton gin, impact of, 90, 91

County governments, 385
Crittenden, John L., 207

Davidson, Donald, 446, 447, 458
Davis, Jefferson, 203, 236, 250–251,
  260
  on Civil War causes, 186
  ineffectiveness of, 220–222
  military strategy of, 216,
    217–218
Democracy, in Old South, 158–161
Democratic party, 124, 195–196,
  197, 198, 201
  and Blacks, 430–431
  and civil rights movement,
    493–501
  and Farmer's Alliance, 334–337
  and Franklin Roosevelt, 429–430
  post-Civil War, 241–242
  and Southern unity, 342–343
  waning influence of (1920's),
    388–390
Disenfranchisement, 346–351
Dixiecrats, 480, 494, 496
Douglas, Stephen A., 193, 194, 196,
  201, 202
Douglass, Frederick, 10–11, 165
Drayton, William Henry, 73–74
Dred Scott decision, 86, 196
DuBois, W. E. B., 369–370

Early, Peter, 88
Education:
  and civil rights movement,
    481–485, 486, 488–489
  and Blacks, 397
  in colonial South, 45–46
  and Conservative rule, 305–306
  inadequacy of (1917–1945),
    414–417
  in New South, 316–317, 319–320
  in Old South, 161–163
  and Progressivism, 365–366
  See also Civil rights movement
Eisenhower, Dwight D., 496
Emancipation Proclamation, 233,
  249, 250

Enforcement Acts, 271, 272
Equality of the Sexes and the Condition of Women, The (Grimke), 171
Erikson, Erik H., 7
Evangelicalism:
  in Jeffersonian South, 96–98
  in New South, 323
  and slavery, 78–79
Expansionism, as Civil War cause, 188–196

Fair Employment Practices Committee, 469–470, 480
Farmer's Alliance, 334–337
Farms and farming:
  changes in (post-1940's), 474–475
  and Civil War, 224
  economic significance of, 126–127
  and National Farmer's Alliance, 334–337
  and New Deal, 426–428
  and Populism, 340
  See also Sharecropping
Faubus, Orval E., 483, 495
Faulkner, William, 456–457, 459, 460–461
Federal government:
  assistance from, 274
  and New Deal, 428–429
  and Wilson administration, 377–379
First Continental Congress, 72, 73
Force Act, 115
Fort Sumter, 207–208
Fourteenth Amendment, 258, 260
Freedman's Bureau, 246, 252, 254, 256, 257, 264–265
Fremont, John C., 196
Free soil movement:
  and Civil War, 190–192
  economic implications of, 139
Fugitives, 445–446
Fugitive slave laws, 194
Fundamentalism (religious):
  basic tenets of, 410–412
  decline of, 413–414

  and Southern hypocrisy, 412–413
  tenets of, 97–98

Gabriel Prosser's slave conspiracy, 72, 87
Garrison, William Lloyd, 112
Geography, diversity of, 7–8
Gettysburg, Battle of, 228, 231
Glasgow, Ellen, 322, 441, 457, 461
Goldwater, Barry M., 497
Gordon, John B., 303–304
Gorgas, Josiah, 222–223
Government and politics:
  and civil rights movement, 492–501
  in colonial South, 48
  and *Herrenvolk* democracy, 161
  during Jeffersonian era, 93–95
  and local oligarchies, 385–387
Grange, 286–287
Grant, Ulysses S., 228
  election of, 269–270
Great Revival of 1801–1805, 96–98
Gregg, William, 164
Grimke, Angelina, 170–171
Grimke, Sarah, 170–171
Guilt, of pro-slavery planters, 154–156

Hammond, James M., 164–165
Harper, William, 113–114
Hayes, Rutherford B., 273–274, 345
Helper, Hinton Rowan, 166
Henry, Patrick, 72, 75, 84
Herrenvolk democracy, 159–161
Hoover, Herbert, 389–390
Hill, Samuel S., 506
Humphrey, Hubert H., 499

I'll Take My Stand, 446–448, 452
Income:
  during Great Depression, 423
  in New South, 279, 294
  in 1940's, 467
  in 1970, 475, 476
  post-World War I, 384
  by region, 134–136

Indians:
　in colonial South, 61–65
　in Jeffersonian South, 89
Industrialization:
　Agrarians vs., 448–450
　lag in, 130
　of New South, 287–289
　　working conditions in, 293–297
　Old South attitudes toward, 178
　post-World War I, 384
　and social class, 163–166
Inflation, and Confederacy, 224

Jack, Gullah, 107
Jackson, Andrew, 114, 115
　and *Herrenvolk* democracy, 159–160
Jay, John, 85
Jay-Gardoqui treaty, 84–85
Jefferson, Thomas, 88, 100, 107, 117–118
　and slavery, 82–83
Jeffersonian South (1775–1809):
　distribution of wealth in, 95
　growth and change during, 89–93
　religion in, 96–98
　and slavery, 79–83
　social structure of, 93–95
John Brown's raid, 189
Johnson, Andrew:
　and impeachment, 269
　Reconstruction policy of, 253–263
Johnson, Lyndon B., 486, 496, 497

Kansas, and slavery, 194–195
Kansas-Nebraska Act, 194–195
Kennedy, John F., 496
Kennedy, John Pendleton, 174–175
Kentucky Resolutions, 117
Killian, Lewis M., 506
Kilpatrick, James J., 504
King, Martin L., 482–483, 486
Ku Klux Klan, 261, 270, 271, 399, 482
　overview of, 420–422

Land speculation, during Jeffersonian era, 90
Lanier, Sidney, 205–206
Lee, Arthur, 74–75
Lee, R. E., 236, 260
　characterized, 219
　military strategy of, 216–217, 218, 219–220, 226–227, 228
Liberalism, emergence of, 441–444
Lincoln, Abraham:
　assassination of, 253
　election of, 189, 201
　and Fort Sumter, 207
　on new Confederacy, 206
　racial policies of, 248, 249–250
　Reconstruction policies of, 251–253
Literature:
　of New South, 321, 328–330
　of Old South, 173–175
　and poverty, 404–405
　renaissance in, 456–463
Little Rock, Ark., 483
Local politics, oligarchies of, 385–387
Long, Earl K., 495
Long, Huey P., career of, 394

McClellan, George B., 225, 226–227
McNary-Haugen Act, 383–384
Madison, James, 85
Manufacturing (*see* Industrialization)
Memminger, Christopher C., 164
Mencken, H. L., 402–403
Methodism, 323, 324
　and slavery, 78
Mexican War, as Civil War cause, 189–190
Middle class, in colonial South, 49–50
Mind of the South, The (Cash), 20–25
Mississippi:
　agrarian Progressivism in, 363–365
　Scalawags of, 266–267

Mississippi plan, 272
Missouri, and slavery controversy, 104–107
Missouri Compromise, 106, 190
Morgan, J. P., 299–300

Nashville Convention, 193
National Association for the Advancement of Colored People, 369, 370, 399, 436
National Farmers' Alliance, 334–337
Nationalism:
  and Confederacy failure, 232
  vs. sectionalism, 109–110
  and World War I, 380–381
Nat Turner rebellion, 111
Nebraska, and slavery, 194–195
New Deal, 423–429
  and agriculture, 426–428
  attitudes toward, 424–426
  and industry, 428
New England Anti-Slavery Society, 112–113
New Englanders, compared to Southern colonists, 39–40, 41
New Freedom programs, impact of, 376–379
New Mexico, 193
New South (1870–1917):
  banking system in, 283–284
  Conservatives of, 301–304
  Conservative politics of, 304–316
  and disenfranchisement, 346–351
  economic limitations of, 297–300
  farmer protest in, 286–287, 334–337
  government economic policy in, 283
  industry in, 287–289
    working conditions in, 293–297
  mind of, 316–320
  overview and evaluation of, 330–332
  and Progressivism, 359–370
  religion in, 322–325
  and segregation, 351–355
  sharecropping in, 279–283, 284–285
  and traditionalism, 325–327
  in literature, 328
  voting fraud in, 308–311
  women in, 320–322
New South movement, overview and appraisal of, 289–293
Nixon, Richard M., 496, 497, 499
North:
  and liberal change, 107–108
  military strategy of, 217
  preparedness for war of, 212–213
  race in, 14
  slavery in, 79
North Carolina, and business Progressives, 392
Northwest Ordinance, 86
Nullification crisis, 114–115, 119–120

Ocala Platform, 336
Odum, Howard W., 403, 440, 441, 442
  and Regionalism, 453–456
Old South (1800–1861):
  basic economics of, 126–130
  and slavery, 130–134
  compared to North, 125–126
  democracy in, 158–161
  education in, 161–163
  and federal assistance, 109
  income in, 134–136
  and industrialization, 163–165
  mind and philosophies of, 171–179
  and Missouri controversy, 104–107
  overview of, 101–102
  "Plain folk" of, 156–158
  population of, 108–109
  pro-slavery arguments in, 179–182
  women in, 166–171
  See also Plantation regime

Openchancanough, 63
Orangeburg, S.C., 483
Owsley, Frank L., 156

Paine, Thomas, 81
Panic of 1819, 104
Penal system, in New South, 315–316
Phillips, Ulrich B.:
  thesis of, 11–20
    evaluation of, 17–20
    historians on, 15–17
    impact of, 14–15
    tenets of, 11–13
Pinckney, Charles Cotesworth, 86
"Plain folk," of Old South, 156–158
Plantation regime:
  basic economics of, 126–130
  Civil War impact on, 239–240
  economic health of, 136–141
  emergence of, 42–46
  planter hegemony in, 151–153
  See also Old South
Planter class:
  Civil War impact on, 239–240
  in colonial South, 46–49
  hegemony of, 151–153
  and industrialization, 163–165
  during Jeffersonian era, 89–90
Polk, James K., 190
Poll tax, 345, 348, 350–351
Poor white class, 406–407
  in colonial South, 50–53
Populism, 310
  failure of, 340–343
  tenets and methodology of, 337–339
Potter, David, 1, 4
Poverty:
  culture of (interwar years), 404–408
  historical role of, 28–29
Powhatans, 62–63
Presbyterians, and slavery, 78
Presidential elections:
  of 1860, 201–202
  of 1876, 273
  of 1896, 341–342
  of 1928, 389–390
  1952 through 1976, 496–498, 499, 501
Primary elections, 431–432
Progressivism:
  agrarian, 363–365
  basic tenets of, 359–360
  and education, 365–366
  and health, 366–367
  and race, 368–370
  urban, 360–363
  and welfare, 366–367
Publishing, 416

Quakers, and antislavery, 77

Race and race relations:
  as central theme, 12–20, 30–31
  and Compromise of 1877, 272–274
  and Conservative Reconstruction policy, 268
  defined, 13
  and fear, 87–88
  during interwar years, 395–397
  in literature, 459
  post-World War II conditions in, 470–472
  and poverty, 407
  as Reconstruction issue, 242–245, 246–247
  and reform (New Deal years), 430–437
  roots of, 53–56
  transformations in (post-1940's), 477–479
  during World War II, 468–470
  See also Blacks; Civil rights movement; Slavery
Racism:
  defined, 13
  See also Race and race relations
Radical Reconstruction, 259–265
Railroads, 129, 288, 298–299, 300

Ransom, John Crowe, 445, 446
Readjusters, 307
Reconstruction:
  during Civil War, 248–252
  conservative race policy in, 267–269
  and Johnson administration, 253–263
  key issues of, 240–242
  and Lincoln administration, 251–253
  racial aspects of, 242–245
  Blacks' strategies in, 246–247
  radical approaches to, 259–263
  race policies of, 263–265
  and redemption period, 270–275
  significance of, 272–276
  and southern character, 22
  southern expectations concerning, 245
Reconstruction Acts, 259
Redemption campaign, 270
Regionalism, Odum on, 453–456
Regional south, compared to sectional south, 3–5
Religion:
  in colonies, 39–40
  fundamentalist, 410–414
  in New South, 322–325
  in Jeffersonian South, 96–98
  in pro-slavery arguments, 181–182
  of slaves, 147
  in upcountry, 66–67
  See also specific denominations
Republican party, 195, 196, 197, 198
  and civil rights movement, 493–494, 495–498
  increased popularity of (1920's), 388–390
  post-Civil War, 241–242
Revels, Hiram, 263
Revivalism, 96
Revolutionary War (See American Revolution)
Reynolds v. Sims, 478

Richmond, Va., 218
  in Civil War, 224, 226–227, 228
Rights:
  Old South attitudes toward, 177
  See also Civil rights movement
Roland, Charles P., 507
Roosevelt, Franklin D., and New Deal, 424–426
Rubin, Louis D., 504
Rutledge, Edward, 75

"Sahara of the Bozart, The," 1, 402–403
St. Elmo (Wilson), 321–322
Scalawags, 260, 265–267
Scopes trial, 417
Scott, Sir Walter, 173–174
"Search for Southern Identity, The," 27–28
Secession, 202–205
  See also Civil War
Sectionalism:
  disappearance vs. endurance of, 503–508
  and economic change, 88–93
  and liberal change, 107–108
  and Missouri controversy, 104
  vs. nationalism, 109–110
  overview of, 99–100
  racial dimension of, 111–113
  and religious revival, 97
Sectional south, compared to regional south, 3–5
Segregation:
  legalization and spread of, 351–355
  See also Blacks; Civil rights movement; Race and race relations
Seniority system, Congressional, 124
Seven Days, battle of, 227
Seward, William H., 206
Sharecropping:
  basic principles of, 280–281
  inefficiency of, 282–283
  during interwar years, 398

lifestyle under, 284–286
negative effects of, 281–282
Sherman, William T., 264
Simms, William Gillmore, 172, 176–177, 178, 205
Slavery:
    and American Revolution, 73, 74–76
    and antislavery movements, 112–113
    arguments for, 179–182
    as Civil War cause, 188–196
    and colonial middle class, 50
    and Confederate defeat, 233–234
    emergence of, 56–58
    and slave insurrection, 60, 87–88, 107
    and Indians, 62
    and industry, 136, 164–166
    and Jeffersonian South, 79–83
    and Missouri controversy, 104–107
    in North, 79
    opposition to, 76–79, 82
    and plantation system, 43–44
    planter class attitudes toward, 153–155
    profitability of, 131–134
    rationalizations for, 81–82
    slaves' life under, 141–149
        community life of, 146–147
        family life of, 147–148
        and master-slave relationship, 145–146
    and Unionization, 85–86
Smiley, David, 1, 2
Smith, Alfred E., 389–390, 413
Smith, Ellison D., 392
Smith, Frank E., 505
Social class:
    in colonial South, 46–53
    and disenfranchisement, 347–348, 350–351
    industrialization and, 163–166
    and southern character, 23
    and violence, 418–420

Social fundamentalism, 408–410
    and intellectual conformity, 417–418
South:
    benighted image of, 402–404
    defining of, 1–2
    economic boom in (post-1940's), 474–477
    economic transition of (post-World War I), 382–384
    endurance assessed, 503–508
    and Great Depression, 423–429
    intellectual conformity of, 417–422
    and Ku Klux Klan, 420–422
    and New Freedom programs, 376–379
    outlook for, 508
    Phillips thesis on, 11–20
    problems studying, 3–11
    See also Colonial South; Jeffersonian South; New South; Old South
South Carolina:
    and nullification crisis, 114–115
    during Reconstruction, 263
    slave unrest in, 60
Southern character and southerners, 2–3, 29–30
    and Cash thesis, 20–25
    and Confederate soldiers, 213–214
    in 1970's, 506
    vs. outsiders, 31
    See also Southern consciousness
Southern Christian Leadership Conference, 483
Southern Commercial Conventions, 197
Southern consciousness:
    and American Revolution, 72–76
    and antislavery movement, 76–79
    See also Sectionalism; Southern character and identity
Southern Homestead Act, 265
Southern Manifesto, 483–484

Southern Regions of the United States (Odum), 453–456
Southern studies, in interwar years, 439–441
Soviet Union, and U.S. racial problems, 478
State politics:
  in interwar years, 391–395
  See also Government and politics
States rights:
  and John C. Calhoun, 121–122
  rise of, 115–118
Stephens, Alexander H., 188, 203, 256
Stowe, Harriet Beecher, 194
Strikes, 165
Suffrage:
  for Blacks, 345–346
    and civil rights movement, 487
    and disenfranchisement, 346–351
    during Reconstruction, 258, 259, 261–262
  during Jeffersonian era, 93–94
  for women, 170
Sugar, impact of, 90, 91, 92
Sumner, Charles, 195
Supreme Court, 110
  and Blacks, 345–346, 355, 480–482
Swallow Barn (Kennedy), 174–175

Tallmadge, James, 104
Talmadge, Eugene, 393–394
Taney, Roger B., 86
Tate, Allen, 458
Taxes, and Conservative rule, 304–305
Taylor, Zachary, 191
Tenant farming:
  and New Deal, 427
  See also Sharecropping
Tennessee Valley Authority, 426
Textile industry, 288, 294–297
  in 1970's, 476
Three-fifths clause, 85, 88

Thurmond, J. Strom, 483–484, 494, 496, 497, 500
Tilden, Samuel J., 273–274
Tobacco Road (Caldwell), 462
Traditionalism:
  and New South, 325–327
  in literature, 328–330
Truman, Harry S., 479, 480, 493, 494

Uncle Tom's Cabin (Stowe), 194
Union (*see* North)
Unionization, sectional issues and, 83–86
United Confederate Veterans, 327
Upcountry, in colonial period, 65–67
Urbanization, and New South industrialization, 293–294
Utah, 193

Vesey, Denmark, 107
Violence:
  and social class, 418–420
  See also Redemption period
Virginia:
  and Byrd machine, 387
  in Civil War strategy, 217, 218
  in Confederacy, 208
  education in, 163
  and Readjusters, 307–308
  wealth distribution in, 95
  See also Virginia settlers
Virginia settlers:
  motives and roots of, 38–39
  and religion, 39–40

Wade-Davis Act, 251–252
Wallace, George C., 492, 494, 496–499, 500–501
War of 1812, 103
Washington, Booker T., career of, 356–359
Washington, George, 75
Watson, Thomas E., 338, 341
Wesley, John, 78
Westbrook, John T., 504

West Virginia, 208
White supremacy (see Blacks; Civil rights movement; Race and race relations; Slavery)
Whitman, Walt, 210
Whitney, Eli, 91
Wilkins, Roy, 468, 469
William and Mary College, 45
Wilmot Proviso, 190
Wilson, Jane Evans, 321–322
Wilson, Woodrow, New Freedom of, 376–379
Wolfe, Thomas, 462–463

Women:
in colonial South, 42, 49
in New South, 320–322
in Old South, 166–171
and poverty, 405–406
and Progressivism, 368
Woodward, C. Vann, 27–29, 504
Work ethic, in colonial South, 41–42
World War I, impact of, 379–382
World War II:
attitudes toward, 468
impact of, 467